Contents

List of Figures	iv
List of Tables	vii
Glossary of Symbols	x
Introduction	xi
Stage one What is Economics?	1
1 Choice	3
2 The Economic Problem	16
3 Systems	33
4 Characteristics of the System	46
Stage two Economics in Action	65
5 Consumption	67
6 Production	85
7 Demand and Supply	98
8 Business Behaviour	118
9 Human Resources and Unemployment	148
10 Wages and Unemployment	165
11 The Financial System	184
12 International Trade	208
13 The Balance of Payments	231
14 Government in the UK	241
15 Aggregate Economic Activity	260
Stage three Economic Problems	277
16 Inflation	279
17 Balance of Payments Policy	304
18 Protecting the Consumer	328
19 The United Kingdom and the European Economic Community	338
20 Government Policy	356
21 Economic Growth	368
22 Cost Benefit Analysis	382
23 Other Economic Systems	393
24 Economic Development	410
Index	427

List of Figures

Figures

a	The structure of *Investigating Economics*	xii
b	The level of economic activity – topics and chapter references	xiii
1.1	Marginal utility and disutility	6
3.1	A biological system	34
3.2	Rabbits – a grassland system	35
3.3	Economic systems	42
3.4	Measurements of economic systems	43
4.1	Exchange in a simple peasant society	49
4.2	Exchange in a modern society	50
4.3	Modern economic system with overseas sector	52
4.4	Stock and flows	53
4.5	Simplified money flows between four parts of a modern economic system	59
4.6	Market economy	62
4.7	Command (centrally planned) economy	62
5.1	Components of total domestic expenditure, UK, 1978	70
5.2	Consumers' expenditure in the UK at current prices and at 1975 prices, 1970–80	72
5.3.	The household's short-run consumption/income relationship	76
5.4	Effect of an increase in savings on the consumption/income relationship	78
6.1	Value added and value of output	86
6.2	Value of production at market prices and at factor cost, before and after the imposition of an indirect tax on sales	89
6.3	UK gross domestic product at market prices and at 1975 market prices, 1970–80	93
6.4	Annual growth rate of GDP at market prices and at 1975 prices, 1968–80	94
7.1	An individual consumer's demand curve for tomatoes	100
7.2	Probable effect on demand of an increase in income	102
7.3	Market supply curve for tomatoes	106
7.4	Likely effect on supply of a fall in the price of raw materials used in production	107
7.5	Demand, supply and equilibrium market price for tomatoes	108
7.6	Effects of an increase in supply	109
7.7	Price determination with a downward sloping supply curve	113
7.8	Effects of a fixed price (1)	115
7.9	Effects of a fixed price (2)	116
7.10	The Australian beef market	117

Figures

8.1	Production plans of a large enterprise	123
8.2	Diminishing marginal productivity	124
8.3	Relationship between average and marginal product curves	125
8.4	(a) Resource requirements (b) Costs of production	127
8.5	Costs of production	128
8.6	Long-run costs	129
8.7	Profit maximising for the price-taker	133
8.8	Profit maximising under monopoly conditions	136
8.9	The pessimistic 'do-nothing' oligopolist	140
8.10	Business behaviour and market forms	141
8.11	Demand curve for sugar	144
9.1	Determinants of the size of the labour force	151
9.2	Age structure of population in England and Wales, 1976	155
9.3	Activity rates, 1971	157
9.4	Unemployment by age, 1979	160
10.1	Index of average earnings and retail prices index, 1973–80	167
10.2	Possible effects of an increase in wages	167
10.3	Marginal costs and revenue of labour	169
10.4	Effects of wage increase on employment	170
10.5	Effects of an increase in product prices or labour productivity on the demand for labour	170
10.6	Supply curves of a particular type of labour to a specific industry in differing bargaining positions	177
11.1	Principal financial institutions	185
11.2	The UK banking sector	204
11.3	Interest rates	205
11.4	The financial system – principal flows and operators	206
12.1	Three-way trade	210
12.2	Trade possibilities between high and low demand countries	211
12.3	United Kingdom external trade by commodity, 1978	215
12.4	UK merchandise trade by area, 1955–73	219
12.5	Share of UK trade with the EEC and Western Europe	221
12.6	Shares of world trade, 1978	222
13.1	UK balance of payments, 1978	233
13.2	UK balance for official financing, 1967–80	234
14.1	UK general government expenditure by function, 1978	243
14.2	Proportional taxation	249
14.3	Progressive taxation	250
14.4	(a) The UK personal income tax schedule (b) UK average and marginal rates of tax	252
14.5	Regressive taxation	253
14.6	Lorenz curve	255
15.1	Gross domestic product and total domestic expenditure in the two sector economy	261
15.2	Relationship between GDP and total domestic expenditure in the UK, 1978	261
15.3	Aggregate consumption and aggregate production	266
15.4	Production, consumption, investment and aggregate demand	268

Figures

15.5	Effects of an increase in investment spending on total spending and income	271
15.6	Circular flow of income	274
16.1	Index of retail prices: (a) 1966–74 (b) 1974–80	281
16.2	Annual percentage increase in retail price index 1967–80	282
16.3	A relationship between inflation and unemployment	294
16.4	Shift of the inflation – unemployment curve following increase in aggregate demand	296
17.1	External balance	309
17.2	Unemployment, inflation, cost competitiveness and expenditure	310
17.3	External equilibrium and internal objectives	311
17.4	Floating exchange rates	316
17.5	Effects of foreign competition in a free-trade situation	320
17.6	Effects of imposing a tariff	320
18.1	Market-sharing agreement between dairies	332
18.2	Solo marketing of petrol	333
19.1	Effect of an increase in supply when demand is price inelastic	342
19.2	Effects of a fall in demand	343
19.3	Employment in agriculture and agricultural output, 1968–79	348
19.4	EEC agricultural prices, volume of production and real income per head, 1973–79	349
19.5	European Social Fund	352
20.1	Tax and government spending burdens	357
20.2	Enterprise Zones	359
20.3	Main features of Enterprise Zones	360
20.4	Public payroll	364
21.1	External diseconomies	376
21.2	An environment tax	379
21.3	A subsidy	380
22.1	Consumer surplus	386
23.1	Institutions in the Soviet Command system	395
23.2	Gosbank's role in the economy	398
23.3	Structure of the Yugoslav economy	405
24.1	Tunisia	417

List of Tables

Tables

2.1	Different forms of the economic problem	19
2.2	A relationship and a plausible explanation	31
3.1	Organisational features of primitive and modern economic systems	45
5.1	Consumers' expenditure at current prices, UK, 1978	69
5.2	Availability in households of certain durable goods, UK, 1969–79	73
5.3	Consumption expenditure at current prices, at constant prices and at constant prices per head, UK, 1974–78	74
5.4	Actual and real disposable income	75
5.5	Consumption expenditure and disposable income, UK, 1968–80 (£m at 1975 prices)	80
5.6	Income elasticities for foodstuffs in the UK, 1969	81
5.7	Patterns of expenditure: variation with household income, 1978	82
5.8	UK gross domestic product at market prices, 1978	83
5.9	UK gross domestic product 1978 at 1975 market prices (£ million)	84
6.1	Value added of a firm in successive years	87
6.2	Aggregated value of production in a two industry economy	87
6.3	Gross domestic product UK, at factor cost by industry, 1978 (£ million)	90
7.1	An individual consumer's demand schedule for tomatoes	99
7.2	Market demand schedule for tomatoes	99
7.3	Typical effects of changes in the determinants of demand	103
8.1	Relationship between total fixed cost and average fixed cost	126
8.2	Relationship between average product per worker and average worker requirement per unit of output	126
8.3	The effects on Firm B's profits of different policies of Firm B and reactions by Firm A	142
8.4	Effect on Firm A's profits of the different policies of Firm B and reactions by Firm A	142
8.5	Demand schedule for sugar	145
8.6	Price elasticity of demand and total revenue	147
9.1	UK labour force 1978 (mid year estimates)	149
9.2	Components of UK population growth, actual and projected, 1951–91	150
9.3	Benefits and costs of immigration	152
9.4	Activity rates, UK 1971, by age and sex	156
9.5	Distribution of employment in the UK	158

Tables

9.6	Employees in employment in manufacturing and services in the UK	159
9.7	Duration of unemployment, April 1980, GB	160
9.8	Unemployment by region, UK, December 1979 and October 1982	161
9.9	Relative unemployment rates, GB, 1970–78	162
9.10	Rates of unemployment in various countries	163
10.1	Real earnings as a business cost, UK, 1973–80	172
10.2	Wages share as a percentage of GDP at factor cost, UK, 1970–78	175
10.3	Industrial disputes, UK, 1970–80	179
11.1	London clearing banks: sterling assets and liabilities as at 16 January 1980 (£ million)	191
11.2	Bank of England: Issue Department	195
11.3	Bank of England: Banking Department	196
12.1	Opportunity costs: a two country example	209
12.2	Opportunity costs: a three country example	209
12.3	Money costs: a two country example	212
12.4	UK imports, percentage share of total by value, 1960–82	216
12.5	UK import volume index numbers, 1968–80 (1975 = 100)	217
12.6	UK exports, percentage share of total by value, 1960–82	217
12.7	UK export volume index numbers, 1968–80 (1975 = 100)	218
12.8	UK imports, analysis by source; percentage share of total value	220
12.9	UK exports, analysis by destination; percentage share of total value	220
12.10	UK principal import suppliers	220
12.11	UK top export markets	222
12.12	Export and import price indices and terms of trade (1970 = 100)	227
13.1	UK balance of payments, 1977–80 (£ million)	231
13.2	Relationships in the balance of payments	232
13.3	Principal invisible credits and debits in UK balance of payments current account 1978 (£ million)	235
13.4	Official Financing, UK 1975–78	237
14.1	Public expenditure, 1978–79	244
14.2	General government receipts, 1980/81, UK	247
14.3	Taxation and miscellaneous receipts, UK, 1979–80	248
14.4	Distribution of incomes in the UK before and after income tax, 1976/77	254
15.1	Business responses to stock changes	264
15.2	Production, consumption, investment and aggregate demand	267
15.3	Effects of a change in investment spending	270
16.1	Implicit price deflator of gross domestic product, UK	283
16.2	Possible causes of inflation	284
16.3	Increase in consumer price index: various countries, 1975–78	286

Tables

16.4	Policy instruments that may influence the rate of inflation	287
16.5	Effects of changes in tax receipts and welfare payments on the level of aggregate demand	291
16.6	UK incomes policy, 1972–79	302
17.1	Foreign exchange reserves as a percentage of world trade, 1960–70	313
18.1	Principal types of restrictive trade practice and agreement	330
19.1	Degrees of self-sufficiency of the Community for various basic food stuffs (average 1976–79)	347
19.2	Share of the EEC in world food trade (1977)	347
19.3	Distribution of EEC budget spending on agriculture (millions units of account)	349
19.4	Estimated supply in days of intervention-type stocks held in the EEC, August 1981	350
19.5	EEC Social Fund, UK allocations, 1973–78 (£ million)	351
19.6	European Economic Community population and GDP, 1979	354
19.7	The EEC in the world economy in 1979	355
20.1	Taxation and GDP, UK 1970–81	357
20.2	Taxes as percentage of total taxation, UK	358
20.3	Government revenue from North Sea oil and gas	366
21.1	Index number of GDP, 1968–80	368
22.1	Suggested areas for cost benefit analysis	383
22.2	Cambrian Coast railway – costs of retention	389
23.1	Ownership of consumer durables in the Soviet Union, 1965–75 (number per 100 households)	402
23.2	Principal differences between Soviet and Yugoslav economic systems	404
23.3	Yugoslav growth rates, per annum 1947–68	406
23.4	Rate of inflation in Yugoslavia, Italy and Greece, 1972–73 to 1977–78	407
23.5	Rate of increase of industrial production in Yugoslavia, Greece and Italy, 1972–78	407
24.1	GDP, population, GDP per head for selected countries, 1976	411
24.2	Growth in real GDP, Australia and Tunisia, 1972–77	413
24.3	Real GDP and population of selected countries 1972 and 1977	414
24.4	Estimated levels of real consumption in 1960 (UK = 100)	415
24.5	Capital formation in Tunisia	420

Glossary of Symbols

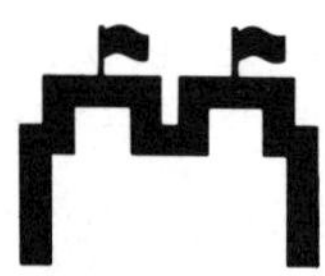

Government sector

State budget

Government business

Business sector

State financial institutions

Financial sector

Peasant household

Household sector

Peasant market

Market sector

Overseas sector

Introduction

Investigating Economics was originally published as a textbook of economics for final school courses in Australia. This edition is an adaptation and revision of the Australian second edition made suitable for the UK economy and students of economics in the UK. The title *Investigating Economics* was chosen to emphasise that there is much economics that the student can discover by his or her own enquiries.

An important feature of the approach adopted in *Investigating Economics* is problem solving. This seems particularly appropriate in economics. The economic problem is at the heart of the discipline. In addition, many of the issues economists are confronted with lend themselves to a problem solving approach. By stressing problem solving, the essence of economics is also given the prominence it deserves.

The economic problem is commonly described as the need to make decisions under conditions of scarcity. The problems approach is one of developing methods of 'solving' the economic problem in any particular form it may take. The approach aims to:

1 identify the problem;
2 develop the necessary skills to investigate the problem; and
3 recognise that decision-making means conflict between competing ends, and that there is often a need for trade-off between such ends.

In contrast, some economics texts place prime emphasis on description and explanation of the existing British economic system. They relate economics solely to the economic system of the materialist society and thus concentrate on the subject-matter of traditional economics rather than on the methodology. A danger of this approach is that the economist becomes identified with a particular set of values and objectives, and consequently may be called upon to bear the blame for any failures of the system – maybe for its 'undue' emphasis on economic growth, its failure to safeguard the environment, its inability to control inflation, or its failure to remove social misery. In educating young economists to believe that economics relates solely to the existing type of economic system we limit their opportunities to participate in decision-making, in a society in which the economist's methodology, above all others, relates to decision-making.

This does not mean that problem-orientated economists will ignore the economic system. Study of problems within the system and those presented by the system as a whole provide the main area in which this training is to be gained. However, the economists come to the study of the economic system as critics, in the sense that they ask whether the system is operating efficiently; if it is satisfying society's objectives; if it can be improved! The economists therefore become involved in controversial issues and recognise that there is a fundamental distinction between positive and normative aspects of questions. They use their skills to investigate relationships and to settle those questions that can be settled by an appeal to the facts, thereby bringing to light the issues that reduce to matters of opinion.

The objective of the problems approach at school or college level should not be construed as an attempt to turn the student into a skilled professional economist, well-versed in mathematical techniques, full of advanced economic theories. Instead, it is designed to develop an attitude of mind and a logical way of thinking about economic problems which, coupled with a basic knowledge of concepts and relationships, will take the student a long way in distinguishing between true and false reasoning. There has been discussion in recent years about the desirability of allowing students freedom to research topics of their own choice, to seek out their own resource materials and to depart from the practice of slaving over prescribed economics texts. Such a trend is to be welcomed, but for it to be successful it is essential that the student first obtains the necessary skills for research. But given the skills, the newspaper provides a fruitful source of problems, controversy and muddled logic that seldom can be provided in even the most carefully written textbook.

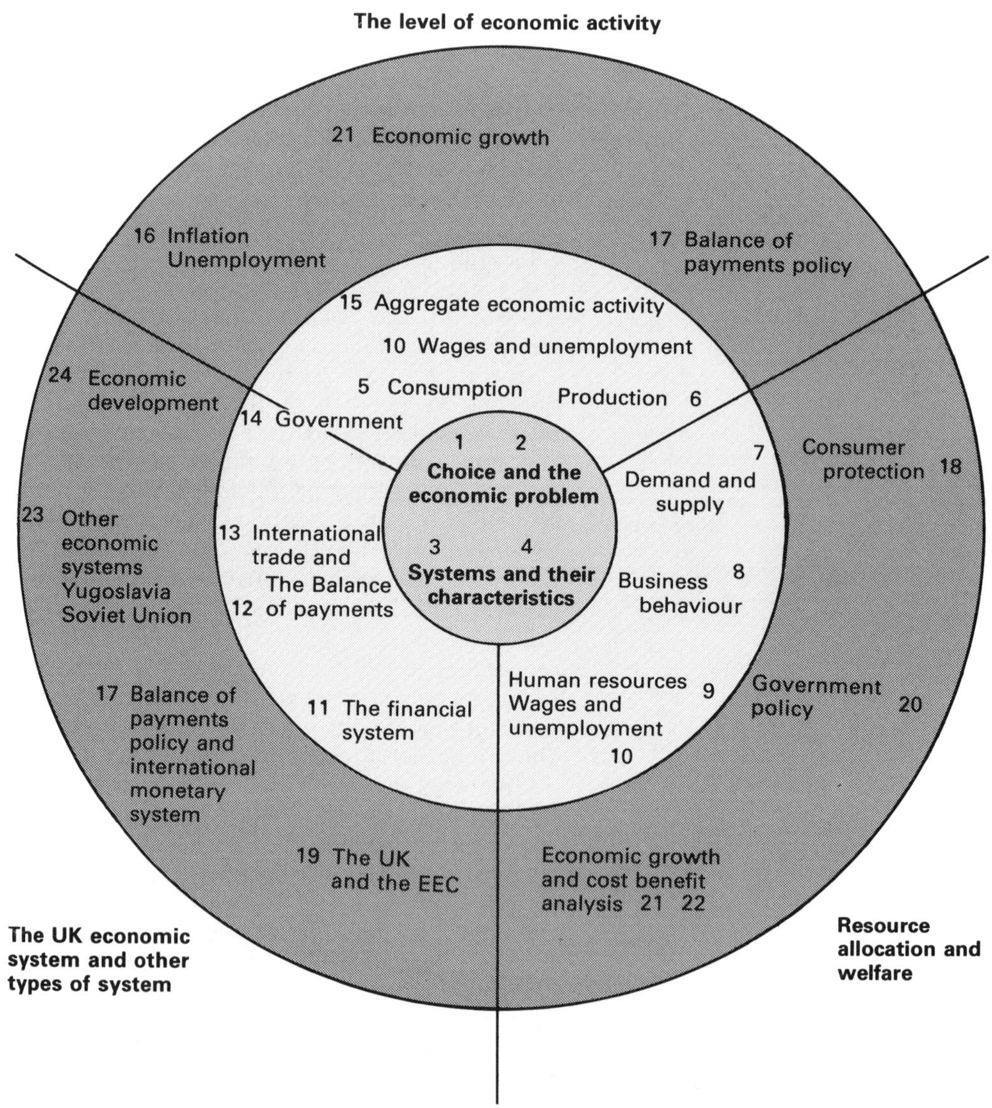

Figure a The structure of Investigating Economics

Investigating Economics is designed to provide the student with the opportunity to develop these skills. The problems it sets are scattered throughout the text. At times they complement the exposition of a particular aspect of an economic system or some issue in economics. On other occasions the topic is introduced through the problem itself. Attention is given to particular economic problems. Since the early 1970s soaring inflation, rising unemployment, falling growth rates and worsening international monetary problems have caused western governments great concern. The confident assertions of success made by economists in the 1950s and 1960s have a hollow ring when faced with the dismal performance of the 1970s and 1980s. These problems and the more recent responses by economists are emphasised in this edition. Possible links between expectations and inflation and real wages and unemployment are given particular attention.

During the 1970s increasing attention has been paid to social welfare problems and the microeconomic tools of the economist have been brought to bear on these issues, for example, on the environment and consumer protection, distribution of income and social policy.

In terms of content and organisation a spiral principle is observed in the book with simple early treatment of problems being followed by more detailed work, as additional tools and institutional equipment are added. The structure of the book is set out in Figure a.

The diagram is composed of three rings that relate to three stages in the development of the economics.

Stage one (the inner ring) presents the economic problem and the general characteristics of economic systems.
Stage two (the middle ring) provides fundamental tools and concepts

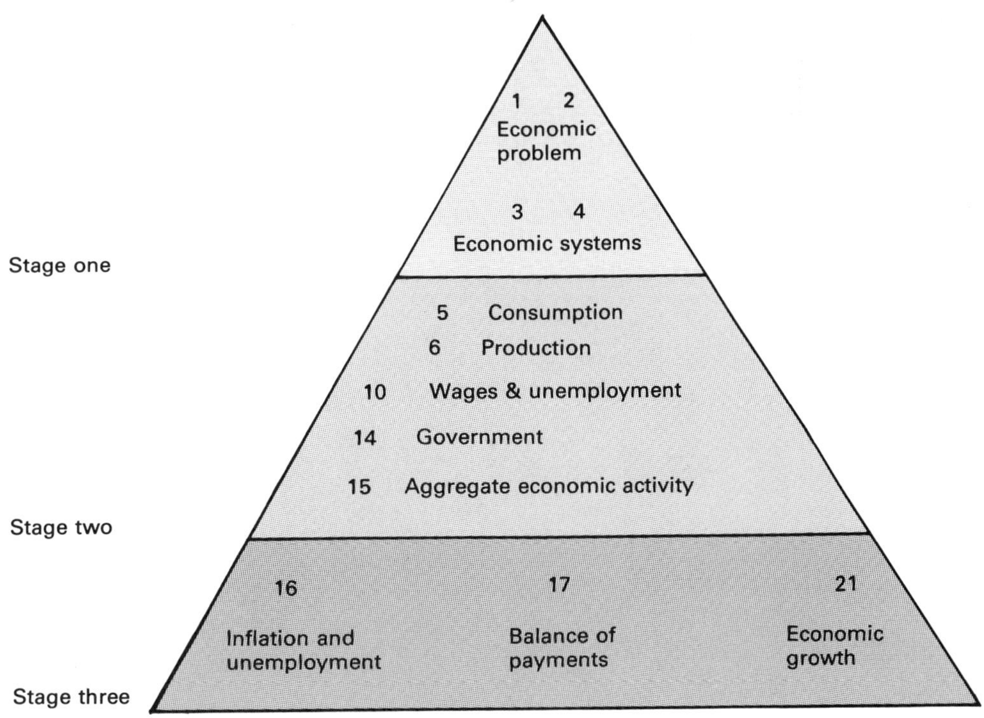

Figure b The level of economic activity – topics and chapter references

needed to study economics and also a framework of economic institutions in the UK.
Stage three (the outer ring) builds on this knowledge to consider contemporary economic problems in the UK and overseas.

In addition to this 'layered' approach the diagram has arranged the contents in three principal vectors spreading from the centre. These vectors deal with three aspects of economics:
1 the level of economic activity,
2 resource allocation and social welfare,
3 economic systems and their institutions.

Figure b shows the relationship between the topics included in one of these vectors; the level of economic activity.

Although *Investigating Economics* has not been tailored to any single syllabus the contents have been selected to meet the needs of a wide range of students studying various economics courses throughout the UK. Inevitably, however, the scope of the book is wider than any particular syllabus. It should be apparent that it is neither practicable nor desirable to study the entire content material in a single year's study unless it is a part of a preliminary principles or political economy course at a tertiary institution. Choice of what to include is left to the discretion of teachers and student enquirers, or more pragmatically to the dictates of the syllabus.

Stage one

What is Economics?

Chapter 1 Choice

Satisfaction depends on the achievement of desires

How would you answer the question, 'What do I want from life?' Our success (or failure), our satisfaction (or frustration), depends on the extent to which our desires are accommodated and our expectations are fulfilled.

Some of the things people commonly say they desire are:

to make friends and win the respect of others,
to be healthy,
to have sufficient wealth to be able to buy all they want,
to have a satisfying job – or maybe to have sufficient income not to work at all,
to live peacefully, protected from war, crime, riots and exploitation,
to live in a pleasant and unpolluted environment,
to make personal decisions free from the restrictions of the rules and regulations imposed by governments or private individuals,
to have the security of knowing that the future will not bring misery.

Other common desires relate to promoting the well-being of other people, and to living in accordance with a moral or religious code. Each individual will be able to list a number of specific objectives that he or she would like to achieve, such as owning a hi-fi set, going on an overseas tour, qualifying as a doctor and owning a weekend country cottage. These specific objectives are particular means to attainment of one or other of the general aims listed above.

Ranking desires is difficult

The members of a group, such as your economics class, are likely to express broadly similar desires, but individual specific differences would quickly become apparent. If the members of a group were asked to rank the desires in the list above by assigning them numbers 1, 2, 3, . . . in order of their importance, they would probably find it extremely difficult – and some might say that the task is impossible. It is likely that there would be considerable disagreement between the members of the class on how to rank the various desires. Most people want to be wealthy *and* healthy, but many would find it almost impossible to say whether or not they would rather be healthy than wealthy. The choice would be more manageable if we had precise definitions of what is meant by 'healthy' and 'wealthy', and if the alternatives to being healthy or wealthy were stated in concrete terms. Would you prefer an income of £20 000 per year but with terminal cancer, to the grinding poverty of an income of £2000 a year paired with an occasional cold? Such information about the exact alternatives open to us would doubtless have an important influence on our ranking of health against wealth.

Decision-making affects well-being

Fortunately, in real life, we seldom have to make this blunt choice between health and wealth. In fact, you may wonder whether it is worthwhile even attempting to specify our desires and to consider their relative importance to us. Although we seldom have to make decisions on the grand scale of 'health or wealth', we often make decisions which reflect the importance we attach to our broad general objectives. For example, two school leavers may be faced with the opportunity to take either a dangerous, exhilarating and well-paid job as a deep sea diver, or a dull, but safe job in the local supermarket. If one opted for the diving job and the other for the retailing job this would indirectly give us clues about the relative importance each places on wealth, job satisfaction, and security. Most people face up to the question, 'Should I take up smoking?' or 'Should I stop smoking?' This calls for assessment of whether the additional satisfaction and sense of well-being gained from smoking outweighs the health hazard, the loss of physical fitness and the financial cost. Do you think that some of your desires would be (or are) promoted by smoking? Would some of your desires be adversely affected?

Opportunity cost

Decision-making invariably means choosing between alternatives. The essence of rational choices is the balancing of favourable consequences of an action against the unavoidable associated unfavourable consequences. The selection of one attractive alternative requires the rejection of others. Buying one particular long-playing record with your weekly allowance means going without something else that could have been bought with the money. The true cost of the decision to buy the record does not lie in handing over the money itself. Rather, the true cost arises from our unavoidable closing off of the possibility of enjoying some alternative – a book, seeing a film or a new hair style – when we buy the record. The alternative most desirable possibility that has to be foregone is called, by economists, the *opportunity cost*. In economics and in decision-making in general, the idea of opportunity cost is very important and crops up continually. If a decision is to be a sensible one it must be made after calculating not only the direct benefits from the decision (satisfaction gained from owning the record) but also the benefits that are being forfeited (from not going to a football match, or buying a book). The question, 'What am I missing by doing this?' is every bit as important as the question 'What will I get out of this?'

1.1

Suppose that you are given £5 for your birthday by an aunt who expects you to buy a record with it, and accompanies you to the record shop while you make your choice. Should it turn out that there is only one record in the shop which is to your taste, what is the opportunity cost of the purchase? If the shop also sells books and you believe your aunt would not be offended if you suggested using her gift for either a record or a book, how does this influence the opportunity cost of buying the record?

What is the opportunity cost of the extra sleep?

In practice the satisfaction derived from living comes from the partial attainment of the various desires, for we rarely completely fulfil any one of our desires and certainly never fulfil them all. Most of us are reasonably healthy, fairly well off, much liked by some people and only a little – or not at all – by others. We find our school, or our job, partly interesting, partly mere routine and partly dull or distasteful, and so on. . . Our overall well-being depends in part on the situation in which we find ourselves, and in part also on the decisions we make as we go through life. Changes in our well-being depend critically upon the big, maybe once-for-all, choices such as 'Should I leave school now and try for a job, or proceed further with my education?' But it depends also on the outcome of the multitude of day-to-day decisions about what to buy, what to wear, what to eat, where to go, and what time to go to bed. Our overall satisfaction from such decision-making is increased when such a decision brings us additional satisfaction. Economists call the extra satisfaction anticipated to follow from a decision such as buying a new book, or a new record, the *marginal* satisfaction. Sometimes they use the term *marginal utility* but 'utility' means much the same thing as 'satisfaction'. The term 'marginal' is used widely by economists in their discussions of decision-making. It refers to a change in something (satisfaction, or production, or revenue, or costs, or profits) that results from a change in some other quantity (or 'variable'). Thus, the marginal satisfaction from buying a long-playing record is the increment to our total satisfaction that comes from owning *one* more record. The marginal revenue for the record shop is the increment to its total sales revenue that comes from the sale of the *one* more unit of product. The marginal product of an additional salesperson hired by the record shop is the increment to the product (volume of records sold) consequent upon hiring the extra employee. The usefulness of both the idea of opportunity cost and the idea of marginal utility in decision-making are illustrated in the following example.

Marginal satisfaction and marginal utility defined

Consider the problem faced by an advanced student who faces an important music examination in a week's time. Her career in music depends on it. Life is made difficult for her because during the week a series of jazz concerts by a famous visiting American group are going to be held in the city. If she is to be sure of doing well in the exams it will be necessary to spend each evening practising. But she also knows it may be years before she has another chance to hear this jazz group, for this series is their farewell appearance in the UK. Her problem resolves itself into a decision on how many evenings she can afford to go to the jazz concerts and how many she should devote to practice. The logical approach is to compare the satisfaction obtained from spending the time in alternative ways; of measuring the opportunity cost of going to the concerts. Two questions have to be answered, therefore.

Choice between alternatives when time is the limiting factor

1 How much extra satisfaction will she gain by going to a jazz concert?
2 How much satisfaction will she lose if she does not practise on that particular evening?

The additional satisfaction the student derives from an evening at the concert is likely to depend on the number of concerts she goes to during the week. A single visit may bring great satisfaction, and a second considerable satisfaction. The extra satisfaction from going to the third and fourth evenings may be much less. The marginal satisfaction from successive outings diminishes. This is what the economist calls *diminishing marginal utility*. Similarly, the opportunity cost changes too. The loss of one evening of practice may not cause much concern to the

Diminishing marginal utility

young student since it is unlikely to make a critical difference to her examination result. The loss of satisfaction is not great, or put another way, the dissatisfaction felt – or *marginal disutility* – is small. But the source of unease is likely to grow as more and more practices are missed.

Graphs as an aid to understanding the problem

The part played in decision-making by the benefits of additional satisfaction from going out and the costs of dissatisfaction from not practising can be illustrated with a diagram. Figure 1.1 graphs the marginal satisfaction or utility from each additional evening at the concerts, and the marginal dissatisfaction or disutility from each missed practice. (For the purposes of the illustration we pretend that we can actually measure the marginal satisfaction and dissatisfaction – perhaps by attaching some form of 'psycho-meter' to her. Of course in some situations the extra advantages and disadvantages of a decision can be measured in observable units, for example, if her choice was between devoting her time to working as a hired baby sitter or to giving piano lessons for a fee.)

Utility is maximised where marginal utility = marginal disutility

The graph needs careful study. Points on the downward sloping line indicate the *extra* utility gained from each additional evening at the concerts. Thus point 'a' shows that an extra 6 units of utility are gained by going out for two nights rather than one. The *total utility* obtained from going out is the sum of the marginal utilities obtained from each individual night. Thus if the student went out every night of the week the total satisfaction is 28 units (7 + 6 + 5 + 4 + 3 + 2 + 1). Similarly the 'b' point on the upward sloping line, indicates that an extra 3 units dissatisfaction will be experienced as a result of not practising for a second evening. The total dissatisfaction from not practising at all is 49 units (1 + 3 + 5 + 7 + 9 + 11 + 13). If the student went to every concert the total satisfaction would be outweighed by the dissatisfaction. It is clear that if her choice were the all-or-nothing one of spending the entire week at the jazz series or at practice, she would forgo the entire jazz series. But, as in so many of our choices, she can choose between

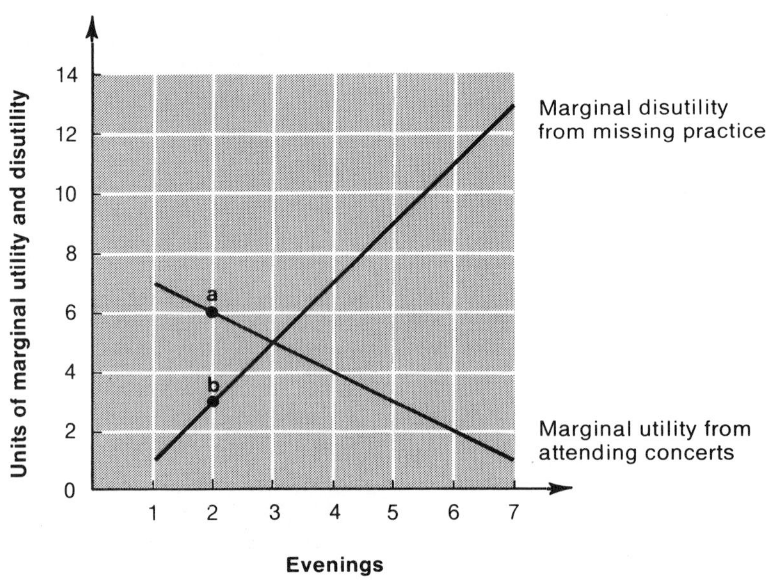

Figure 1.1 Marginal utility and disutility

some concerts and some evenings at practice. She will produce the most desirable outcome by going to concerts until the marginal utility from attending one more night just balances the marginal disutility from not practising on that night. The *net* gain from going out on the first evening is 6 units (7 – 1), the net gain from the second evening 3 units (6 – 3), there is no net gain from the third evening out (5 – 5) and by the fourth evening there is a net *loss* of 3 units (4 – 7). The third evening at the concert is the critical one. The first two are worthwhile and the fourth not worthwhile. Whether or not the student goes on the third evening is a toss up. Of course it may be impossible to think of satisfaction in terms of such measurable units. Nevertheless, it is often helpful to ask whether the extra benefits from proceeding further with a particular course of action are greater than, equal to, or less than the extra costs. In fact, you adopt this approach unconsciously. Whether or not you now go on to read the next paragraphs will be decided by your anticipation of the extra benefit from pressing on (and possibly increased understanding) set against the marginal disadvantage (heightened fatigue or increased boredom).

The same approach can be used to explain why consumers decide to buy certain quantities of a particular good. For example, some people buy meat pies during football on a Saturday afternoon, and it is possible to think in terms of the extra satisfaction they derive from eating each additional pie. For most people the marginal utility from eating the second and third pies is much less than the initial satisfaction gained from the first. There is a distinct possibility that a fourth pie will actually *reduce* the total utility (marginal utility is negative) in which case it would not be consumed even if it were offered as a gift. But because each pie costs around 40 pence, it is likely that the average football supporter will have decided that he can make better use of his money than to buy the third or perhaps even the second pie. That is, although the marginal utility of a third pie is positive, it is less than the marginal utility to be had from buying 40 pence worth of another good.

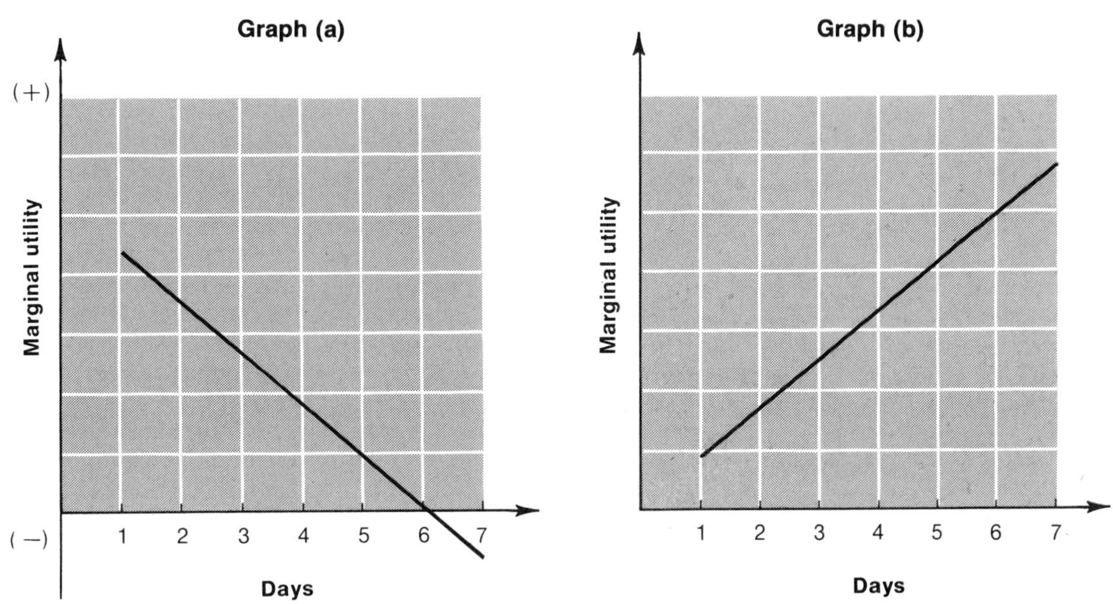

1.2

The graphs on page 7 show the marginal satisfaction two individuals A and B derive from going surfing on the successive days of a week's holiday. Suggest reasons why the shape of the curve differs for the two people. Would you expect the curve for B to continue to rise if the holiday were extended by another week?

1.3

Draw a graph that conveys the following information:
1 A student always derives the same marginal satisfaction each time he spends an evening at a discotheque.
2 The marginal dissatisfaction from the loss of each evening spent in study grows slowly for the first few evenings, but thereafter grows rapidly.
3 The maximisation of total satisfaction occurs if the student goes to the discotheque four times during the week and studies on the other three evenings.

1.4

It was said that sometimes we can measure the advantages and disadvantages of a decision in observable units. Suppose that an executive takes time off from work to play golf. We might measure:
1 her estimate of the relationship between the profits of her business and the number of afternoons she spends on the golf course,
2 the amount she expects to save on doctors' bills by being healthier as a result of taking time out for her golfing.

Draw a graph showing the anticipated effects on business profits and doctors' bills of additional afternoons at golf. Mark in the maximising position on your graph. What led you to draw the two curves with the particular shape you have given them? If it actually turned out that the firm makes more profit, the more afternoons the woman devotes to golf, what does this tell us about the marginal product of the time she spends at work?

Profits maximised where marginal revenue equals marginal cost

This principle of maximising satisfaction by equating marginal benefits with marginal costs followed by the pianist and the pie-eater has many applications in the business world. Businesses are keen to maximise their monetary profits and make production plans accordingly. Sales bring in revenue, but production incurs money costs. To maximise profits it is necessary to determine the level of output at which the difference between total revenue and total costs is as great as possible. This use of the marginal principle can be very useful in determining the output level. The business may be able to estimate the *marginal revenue* (additional revenue) that comes from the sale of each extra unit of output. It may also be able to calculate the *marginal cost* (the additional cost incurred in producing each additional unit). If it then equates the marginal revenue with the marginal cost, this will indicate the level of output at which profits are at their greatest, using the same general approach that the pie-eater unconsciously used in making the decision to maximise his total satisfaction. (A qualification to this rule is discussed in Chapter 8.) The difference is that, in the business decision, money is the measure of advantages and disadvantages rather than utility.

1.5

Imagine that you own an engineering workshop that is capable of assembling high performance sports cars on a small scale and that you want to maximise profits from such an operation. You estimate that your production costs will vary with the number of cars you produce in a given period; the more cars you produce the cheaper the cost of producing each car up to a maximum of six cars a month. You also estimate that to sell the additional cars it will be necessary to successively lower the price. Your estimates of total production costs and total sales revenue are as follows:

Number of cars produced each month	Total production costs (£)	Total sales revenue (£)
1	14 000	18 000
2	26 500	33 500
3	37 500	46 500
4	47 000	58 000
5	55 000	66 000
6	61 500	71 500

1 Calculate the marginal production costs you will incur by producing each additional sports car, that is, 1st, 2nd, 3rd, 4th and so on.
2 Calculate the marginal sales revenue the business will derive from successively larger monthly production levels.
3 On a graph, plot the marginal costs and marginal revenue of producing (and selling) your cars. Now use this graph to determine how many cars the business should produce if it is to maximise profits. What is the maximum profit your business can make?
4 Suppose you have a business partner who has not got a very good head for figures. Explain simply to him why comparing marginal costs with marginal revenue can be used as a safe guide to determine the most profitable quantity to produce.
5 Total sales revenue is the product of the number of cars produced and the price set for that volume of production. Can you add a fourth column showing the price set for each volume of production? (Later in Chapter 7, you will see that the relationship between the level of production and sales and the price at which sales can be made is what economists term 'the demand schedule'.)

Cost benefit analysis

The small workshop that assembles motor vehicles is able to make its production decisions by comparing the estimated marginal production cost and marginal sales revenue from each extra car made and sold. However, some activities of governments, public corporations, nationalised industries and private businesses require decisions about whether to proceed with large and complex projects that may involve a money outlay of millions of pounds. For example, in 1968 the government established a commission to investigate the siting of a third international airport for London. To make a decision about whether or not to proceed with such a project, the government will need to estimate the costs of constructing the airport, acquiring the land and providing facilities. It will also calculate the revenue it expects to obtain from the airport. However, in addition to these direct costs and benefits, there are indirect costs and benefits it should consider. A new airport may bring other benefits; for example a new road network to the airport would also improve access in the area for people living in the vicinity of the new airport. On the other hand, local residents may lose the advantage of pleasant country surroundings and have to put up with a great increase in noise.

Cost benefit analysis is a technique that assesses the indirect effects as well

Cost benefit analysis is an approach to decision-making that attempts to assess both the direct and indirect costs and benefits of a project. When undertaken by public authorities, the purpose of such studies is to assist the decision-maker in determining whether the project is worthwhile from the viewpoint of society as a whole. To use this technique, it is necessary to convert the social benefits and costs into money terms. This requires finding some way of measuring the intangibles, such as the benefits from improved access to the city and the costs of the added noise pollution. The determination of such money values is sometimes extremely difficult, though analysts have adopted ingenious ways of measuring these effects. In Chapter 22 some important cost benefit studies made in recent years are examined in detail, together with some of the more difficult problems investigators have had to face.

1.6

Sullom Voe – Shetland Isles

The photographs on page 11 show Calback Ness in the Shetland Isles before and after the construction of the Sullom Voe oil terminal. Development such as this not only provides benefits to society but imposes costs as well. From the evidence of the photographs what costs do you think the development has imposed? Draw up a list of what you think are the principal benefits and costs to the community of the oil terminal. It might help to think in terms of the impact on different groups in the community, for example the residents of the Shetland Isles, tourists to the area, the landowners and so on. If you were in the position of making the decision whether such a project as the oil terminal should take place, how would you assess the overall balance of social advantage or disadvantage? How difficult do you think it would be to assess levels of compensation for those who bear the various costs of developments such as this one? Are all of the costs quantifiable in financial terms?

1.7

In the 1970s the mining company Rio Tinto Zinc was refused planning permission to drill exploratory test-bores for copper in parts of the Snowdonia National Park in North Wales. Considerable agitation by local residents, environmentalists and other pressure groups led to active public debate over the issue. At the same time, the National Coal Board was conducting a series of test drillings for coal in rural parts of Yorkshire, principally around the market town of Selby. Subsequent discoveries of coal have led to the development of the area with considerable investment in new mines, handling terminals and so on.

Sullom Voe, Shetland Isles, before and after the construction of the oil terminal

1 What reasons can you think of for the National Coal Board being allowed to conduct mineral exploration surveys and the Rio Tinto Zinc Company being refused permission?
2 Are the environmentalist arguments against such forms of development in rural areas justified in your opinion?
3 If you were responsible for presenting a case against the Rio

Tinto Zinc Company's proposals, what arguments would you use to prevent the Company proceeding with its plans?
4 What arguments for and against such proposed activities would the Government be prepared to accept before making a final decision on giving the go-ahead or not? (Think in terms of wider effects of development on the local community, on the nation as a whole in terms of mineral supplies, and on prices and employment, for example.)

Decision-making and uncertainty

Uncertainty results in expectations not being realised

A careful consideration of the benefits and costs of a particular course of action does not guarantee that the decision-maker will be satisfied with the outcome, which may be quite different from what he expected. The pianist's estimation of the effects of not practising may be quite false; the automobile firm may find that no one wants to buy its cars; the executive may have a heart attack whilst playing golf; and the airport noise may be less annoying than people had anticipated.

Many of the consequences of decisions cannot be foreseen with certainty. The recognition of this uncertainty makes decision-making more difficult, and sometimes more exciting. Farmers face the problem of planning their business knowing that they have no control over the weather and often little influence on the prices they receive for their products. An oil exploration firm can never be sure of the pay-off to its efforts until the drill-holes have actually been sunk. Other businesses have to anticipate the decisions of their competitors, and the likely effects of these decisions on their own profits.

Distinction between risk and uncertainty

The apparent existence of so much uncertainty might suggest that there must be continual frustration of decision-makers. But there are some methods for reducing the problem of uncertainty. First, a distinction can be made between *risk* and *uncertainty*. The difference is that in a risk situation it is possible to calculate the probability of events occurring, whilst in an uncertain situation such a calculation of probability is impossible. Careful record-keeping of past events, such as weather information and the frequency of discovery of oil deposits in rock strata of specific types, helps specialists to calculate the probability of a desired outcome. This then assists the decision-makers to plan with more confidence. To the insurance companies, the calculation of the risk factor and the sale of insurance against such events occurring is a business in itself. Paradoxically, where risks can be calculated precisely, uncertainty disappears. Thus, if a fire insurance company can know for certain the probability of an insured person suffering loss by fire, it can then quote premiums which ensure that its income from premiums will cover its payments to claimants.

Second, although it often appears that individuals continually alter their purchases, apparently creating an impossible situation for the individual business, observers skilled in market research techniques have been able to predict what the consumer response to new products is likely to be. This eliminates much of the uncertainty. Economists continuously monitor the behaviour of the economy and usually are able to make reasonably reliable forecasts of important economic quantities, such as our export income and the probable rate of inflation over the next year.

Scarcity, decision-making and the economic problem

Most of us recognise that we will never achieve all the things we want. Even if it were possible to fulfil all of our *immediate* wants – perhaps a motor cycle, a transistor radio, a holiday in Cornwall – we should soon become conscious of new and equally pressing wants. These new wants would be stimulated by the advertisements for small sports cars, hi-fi sets and holidays in Bermuda, and also by our observation of the consumption patterns of others. Even should these wants be fulfilled, new horizons would open before us, and always there are those 'pie in the sky' wishes that we have no real prospect of fulfilling – a Ferrari sports car or our own tropical island for example. If we are honest with ourselves, we must recognise that our wants are capable of expanding indefinitely and that we will never satisfy them all.

Scarcity

Two obstacles make it inconceivable that we will ever achieve complete satisfaction: on the one hand, our ability to keep coming up with new wants, and on the other, the hard fact that we lack the *means* of satisfying all our wants. Our means are scarce. In the realm of our personal decision-making our time is scarce. There is not enough time in a day to do all the things we would like to do. Economists use the term *scarcity* to refer to any situation in which resources are inadequate to meet desires. Commonly, they distinguish three categories of resources:

1 Natural resources – naturally occurring solids, liquids and gases, natural vegetation and native animals.
2 Human resources – human skills and labour power.
3 Man-made resources – tools, machines, vehicles, factories and processed materials that have been made as aids for further production.

Limited supplies do not necessarily mean scarcity

These resources are always limited in supply. The physical constraints of Planet Earth, the size and skills of its population and the sum total of its past discoveries, knowledge, and productive efforts limit the resources available at any time. However, it is possible for resources to be limited in supply, but not be scarce. This occurs when a particular resource is in such abundance as to meet all requirements for it. In the past, fresh air and open space for recreation were given as examples of resources that were limited but not scarce so that, without effort, each of us could consume as much as we desired. In some parts of the world, this is no longer true because of air pollution and urban overcrowding.

And scarcity does not imply rarity

Some naturally occurring minerals are only found in small quantities but, as yet, there is no use to which they can be put. Thus they are not scarce resources to the economist.

The economic problem involves more than scarcity; it means conflict between alternatives

The need for decision-making only arises where there is *scarcity* requiring the *allocation* of resources between *competing ends*. A resource is scarce, and there will be an allocation problem, if it is not possible to meet all the desired competing uses of the resource simultaneously. If a person is dedicated to a single goal in life but lacks sufficient resources to completely achieve that goal, his resources are scarce.

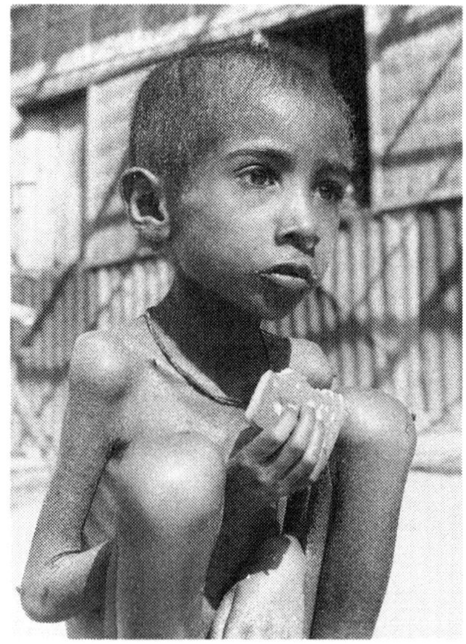

Is wheat scarce?

However there is no economic problem to be solved, for no decision is required about how to allocate the limited resources. Our pianist faced an economic problem because there was a conflict between her exams and the jazz concerts. If the concert were to be cancelled, but she still felt that she needed more time to improve her examination prospects, she would be aware of scarcity, but she would not have had an allocation (or choice) problem.

Suppose that there exists somewhere in the Amazon rainforests a tribe whose members have no desire for clothing or shelter and who depend on fish for their livelihood. Suppose also that they are unable to catch all the fish they desire. Scarcity exists because their food supplies are inadequate, but there is not an economic problem – there is no decision to be made. The tribe continues to catch as many fish as possible. Of course, in the real world it is difficult to find examples of societies which have a single objective although, in time of war, the objectives of society (and hence allocation decisions) are much simplified. The purpose of these examples is to make the distinction between situations where decision-making is involved, and situations of scarcity. Scarcity is one of the elements that makes decision-making necessary, but scarcity without alternative objectives does not give rise to an allocation problem.

1.8

During a staff-room discussion one of the historians present claimed that the people of today were not nearly as happy as those who lived in 18th Century Europe. His argument was that the effects of centuries of decision-making designed to increase people's well-being had not produced a happier or more contented community. Discuss in class the validity of his claims. Do you think that there was anything in them? You may wish to centre the discussion on the following issues.

1 To what extent is it possible to compare the happiness, satisfaction or utility experienced by the peoples of different generations?
2 Can you visualise situations in which the majority of people make decisions designed to increase their individual satisfaction, but where the end result is a loss of satisfaction for all? (A decision to have a quiet picnic at a secluded beach is one such example.)
3 In such a situation what steps, if any, might society consider taking to deal with the problem?

Chapter 2 The Economic Problem

Materialism

In the United Kingdom there is great emphasis on the acquisition of material possessions and the use of services. This materialism pervades both the affluent societies of Western Europe, North America and Australasia and the impoverished countries of Asia, Africa and Latin America; it is so universal that we regard it as a reflection of the human character. We have basic wants – food, clothing and shelter – but people typically strive for much more than the provision of these bare essentials.

As a society becomes more affluent, the notion of what constitutes basic wants is likely to change. The terms 'necessities', 'comforts' and 'luxuries' are applied to goods and services to which we attach successively less importance. These same terms are used in other societies, but there are wide differences between the specific goods which are classified as being in the three categories.

Some people make a distinction between our material well-being (or material welfare) and our general well-being. *Material well-being* refers to the satisfaction derived directly from goods and services. *General well-being* is a broader concept which refers to the total satisfaction derived from all dimensions of life, both material and non-material. It encompasses such aspects of life as our health, sense of purpose and our friendships. Economists have tended to assume that increases in the quantities of goods and services available to people increase their material welfare and that this is likely to promote their general welfare. But a number of economists have raised the issue of whether or not the pursuit of material well-being may be at the expense of other dimensions of well-being. They point, for example, to the loss of the satisfaction from work which accompanies the highly productive modern manufacturing processes.

Standard of living

A term encountered frequently in discussions about material welfare is the *standard of living*. An individual who enjoys a permanent increase in the resources at his or her disposal is able to substitute more interesting goods for the mundane cheaper foods, acquire a more recent model car, go to the theatre more often, buy more clothes, and so on. It is this greater command over goods and services which constitutes the improvement in that person's standard of living. If the quantities of goods and services consumed by two families in the same society differ significantly, we say that the family with more at its disposal has the higher living standard. Comparisons of the living standards of people living in different countries (or in the same country at different times) is much more difficult because the environments in which they live may differ greatly (Australia and Norway for example) and the people may have different priorities (the Australians and Chinese, for example). We can compare the physical goods available to the inhabitants of two countries, but this does not permit us to make precise judgements about the relative standards of living. Swedish people have more cut glass, fur coats and better heating, less beer, surfboards and fewer adequate cooling devices than Australians. Both countries obviously have relatively high standards of living, but we cannot be dogmatic and assert that the standard in one is clearly better than that of the other. By contrast, the standard of living of the populations of the Indian subcontinent is clearly far inferior to that of affluent countries such as Sweden and Australia. And most people would agree that living standards in Pakistan are superior to those in Bangladesh. But the ranking of living standards in, say, Pakistan, China and Papua New Guinea is likely to be more controversial, although all three countries would be classified as 'poor', and certainly much poorer than, say, Malaysia, which many observers would not classify as 'poor'. The unsatisfactory nature of international indicators of poverty is discussed in detail in Chapter 24.

The materialistic society's economic problem

The economic problem was defined in the previous chapter as arising from the inevitable allocation of scarce resources between competing objectives. In a society where improvement in the standard of living is keenly desired, the economic problem calls for marshalling of the available human, natural and man-made resources and organising them to produce the maximum possible desired goods and services. The existence of scarcity of resources is reflected by the importance that individuals and groups in society attach to the ownership of these resources. If all resources were freely available and adequate to meet all requirements, there would be no advantage to any individual from claiming ownership of some resource. The practice of paying a price for the transfer of ownership is evidence that the resource is scarce. In the United Kingdom, the existence of wage and salary payments to workers, and prices for materials, fuels, machines, metals, farm products and consumer goods and services is evidence that human, natural and man-made resources are all scarce. As we shall see in Chapter 7, these prices act as a social device, rationing access to the limited resources.

> Transfer of ownership at a price is evidence of scarcity

There are some goods and services that are provided to users without payment by them, even though they are scarce. For example, we can all become borrowers at a 'free library', even though books (and librarians) are scarce. There are no charges to cyclists for the use of the roads or to pedestrians for strolling in public parks and gardens. Although no money changes hands directly, these goods and services are not costless to provide. The resources used in providing them all have alternative uses and the owners of them have to be compensated for providing them. The goods and services are only 'free' to the user. A third party – a ratepayer or taxpayer – inevitably is required to bear the cost.

Another situation where, at first sight, it may be thought that scarcity has been overcome is when farmers cannot find buyers for their products at acceptable prices. There have been occasions when farmers have deliberately 'ploughed in' fields of potatoes, cabbages and other root and vegetable crops when prices have been too low to make harvesting the crop for market profitable. Similarly, tomato growers have dumped their fruit during gluts rather than run to the expense of packaging and transporting the produce to the market. The situation when it is less

> Occasional over-production does not mean that the resources used were not scarce

unprofitable to destroy or throw away the crop can be seen as a purely temporary one. It certainly does not mean that the produce was a 'free good', for the resources used in growing those crops (land, labour, machinery, fertilisers, etc.) still had to be competed away from their alternative uses.

The economic problem of the materialistic society has to be faced at both an individual and a group level. It is seen in its simplest form where the individual household would like to be able to buy far more than it can afford. Either consciously or unconsciously, it must assign priorities to the desirable purchases to match its actual expenditures to its limited means.

The household's economic problem

In our society, the household's lifetime income is largely determined by the market prices for the quantities of productive resources possessed by its members. The scarcer and more highly sought after are these resources, the higher the family's income is likely to be and therefore the higher its living standards. For example, doctors, accountants, lawyers, university teachers, owners of large properties and bookmakers receive relatively high incomes. Their families enjoy a high standard of living because their particular skills are relatively scarce. By contrast, clergymen, agricultural workers and railway porters receive relatively low incomes, and their families rank among those who experience lower standards of living.

At the group level, each government – whether local or national – faces the economic problem when it decides how to allocate its revenues to the alternative expenditures in the most effective manner. Local government, for example, has to resolve the competing claims on funds for education, housing, transport, law and order and so on. If it wishes to expand its total expenditure it may either seek larger transfer payments from central government or it may increase its own revenue raisings. Over time, growth of the nation's productive capacity permits governments to increase their expenditures without a commensurate curtailment of private expenditures. Nevertheless, any increased command over the nation's scarce resources by a government reduces the resources available either to another level of government or to the private sector.

2.1

1 Consider the following list of articles and allocate them between the three categories: 'necessities', 'comforts' and 'luxuries'.

beef steak	milk
beer	surfboard
oranges	air conditioner
daily newspaper	radio
bread	coffee
butter	tea
car	automatic toaster
television set	bicycle

2 Compare your classification with other class members.
Why are there differences between your groupings?
Would you expect any difference in the grouping of the items by (a) your parents, (b) your grandparents, and (c) a newly arrived Indian migrant family?

2.2

1 Can you suggest examples of situations in which:
(a) An increase in the availability of a good at your disposal might lead to a decrease in your material welfare?

(b) An increase in the use of a good might lead to an increase in your material welfare, but to a loss in your general welfare?
2 If you suggest cases where more of a good leads to a loss of welfare, can you suggest why people do not refuse such goods?

2.3

In the summer of 1976 the United Kingdom experienced a severe drought. As a consequence, water conservation measures were introduced, such as a ban on the use of hose-pipes. In more usual climatic conditions such restrictions do not apply. Does this mean that water is a 'free good'? Research has shown that a significant proportion of domestic water supplies are wasted through indiscriminate use. How would pricing domestic water supplies prevent this occurring so readily?

2.4

In what sense do we have a 'free' health service in the United Kingdom?

Spiritual communities' economic problem

Allocation of time and human resources

In many societies there are groups who reject the importance generally given to pursuit of material possessions. For example, most religious communities have been formed to proclaim religious beliefs and ideals. But, even these communities have to face up to a form of the economic problem. They have a number of objectives which they seek to promote but they are subject to certain restraints, including, of course, limited time. In the Middle Ages the Benedictine monasteries (named after St Benedict), were committed to the worship of God, to teaching and to maintaining the material self-sufficiency of the monastic community. The monks had to allocate their limited time and productive resources between worship, study, food production, eating and sleeping. They adopted a way of allocating their time between these competing ends by accepting the Rule of St Benedict. Essentially, the monks' response

	Materialistic society	Monastic community
Ends	Material well-being Food, clothing, shelter, durables, etc.	Spiritual well-being Worship of God Teaching instructions Sufficient material benefits for survival
Scarce means	Human and non-human resources: land, labour, capital	Resources of monks (time) communal resources of the monastery
Allocation	Individual and business decisions: the market system and/or government planning	1 Rule of St Benedict 2 Decisions by Abbot

Table 2.1 Different forms of the economic problem

to the scarcity situation was to divide the 24 hours between eight hours of prayer, eight hours of learning, teaching and labour, and eight hours of eating and sleeping, according to the prescription of the Rule. Table 2.1 shows the essential similarity between the economic problem of a materialistic community and that of a monastic community. In fact, the method of allocating resources in the monasteries was not so different from that used now in some of the modern planned materialistic economic systems such as the Soviet Union.[1]

2.5

1 Does India's economic problem differ from that of the United Kingdom?
2 Can it be said that the United Kingdom has been more successful than India in solving the economic problem?

2.6

'Drop-out' is a term sometimes applied to individuals, such as hippies, hermits, and tramps who fail to conform to the pattern of behaviour expected of people living in a society. Can an individual avoid the economic problem by becoming a drop-out?

2.7

The lotus-eaters were a group of people whose way of life was described by Homer in the Greek legends (*The Odyssey*, Book 9) and also by Tennyson in his poem 'The Lotus-Eaters' (A. Tennyson, *Collected Poems*). Read either of these accounts. Can it be argued that the lotus-eaters did not have an economic problem?

2.8

'Economics' has been defined in many different ways, and the differences may be confusing. A good definition of economics is one that gets at the essence of the economic problem, and also indicates the subject matter of economics. From the following definitions of economics proposed by various famous economists, select the one you prefer and give reasons for your choice.

1 Economics is a study of mankind in the ordinary business of life; it examines that part of individual and social action which is most closely connected with the attainment and with the use of the material requisites of well-being. (Alfred Marshall[2])
2 'Economics is the science which studies human behaviour as a relationship between ends and scarce means which have alternative uses.' (Lionel Robbins[3])
3 'Economics is what economists do.' (Jacob Viner[4])

What economists do

What was your reaction to the third definition of economics in question 2.8: 'Economics is what economists do'? It is a neat way of avoiding the issue for it does not tell us what economics is, nor what economists do. Further, although most economists spend their time 'doing economics' – studying economic problems – their work often overlaps with that done by other social scientists: geographers, historians, political scientists and sociologists. There are specific branches of study called 'economic history', 'economic geography', and 'mathematical economics'.

Economics itself had its origins in a subject called 'political economy'. In their efforts to understand human behaviour some economists have made considerable use of psychology. It is not very helpful to be told that economics is what economists do when they make these excursions into other disciplines.

Economics is more than a study of material welfare

A second objection to Viner's definition of economics is that it limits economics to the areas of interest currently developed by economists. If it is conceded that economics is really the study of the economic problem in whatever form it may appear, then the Viner definition is unduly restrictive. There are many problems for which the tools used by economists and the logic and reasoning of economic science may be seen as relevant, even though the great majority of economists are concerned rather narrowly with the economic problems of the materialistic society. The overriding concern of economists with material well-being is not surprising, for our society gives a high priority to material objectives. This explains why economists talk mainly about output, national income, economic growth, inflation, and the balance of foreign payments. In the past they have had relatively little to say on issues of conservation, pollution, the quality of life and similar matters. But as society has become more concerned with these subjects and given relatively less weight to the achievement of material objectives, the attention of economists has shifted.

The basic questions what, how much and for whom?

All economists are interested in the question: How does a society (or an individual or group within the society) organise itself to meet its material objectives? The question is more manageable if it is extended and we ask what is it that determines:

What kinds of goods and services will be produced with the available resources?

What quantities of each of these goods and services will be produced?

How will the goods and services be shared (or distributed) between the members of society?

In considering how a society is organised to deal with the economic problem, economists raise three closely related questions:

Is the society allocating its resources in a rational way?

Are the society's scarce resources being utilised as fully as possible?

What is the rational use of the available resources when account is taken of the interests of future generations as well as the present one?

Allocation of resources

To ask whether society is allocating its resources in a rational way is another way of asking: Are we producing that particular output of goods and services that we most want to produce? Clearly, if there is over-production of some goods with stocks piling up, but a chronic shortage of other keenly-desired goods, resources have been misallocated and the composition of output should be adjusted.

It is also possible that by a reallocation of resources it would be possible to continue producing all the goods we presently produce *and* some additional ones. For example, if by convention women are prevented from undertaking some forms of work or if the period of training for certain types of work is unnecessarily prolonged to discourage people from entering those trades, then our present output will fall below the maximum potential. Such misallocations of resources occur in all societies. One of the economist's tasks is to identify such situations and to advise on appropriate reallocations. As we shall see in later chapters, misallocations may be much more subtle than these illustrations. For example, the economic arguments involved in the cases for and against the protection of the domestic textile industry from the influx of cheap foreign imports are quite complex. The economist is interested in questions such as the following. Is the United Kingdom sensible to devote resources to a textile industry which is finding it difficult to survive without special protective measures? Is it in our society's best interests to reallocate the resources from the textile industry and allow more imports into the country?

Other questions arise in the choices made in the economy between the relative importance of, and balance between, the private and public sectors of production. Should more resources be diverted to public sector activities such as road building, education, and hospital construction? If so, from what activities should the resources be withdrawn?

2.9

Mexican peasants have a simple diet of corn (maize) and beans. Corn by itself is not adequate, but the beans provide the proteins and vitamins needed in a balanced diet. Imagine a small Mexican community in which twenty peasants cultivate 20 hectares of arable land. Suppose that each peasant is capable of cultivating one hectare of land and growing on it either 100 kilos of beans or 125 kilos of corn in a season.

1 Calculate the following alternative combinations of corn and beans that the village could produce in a single season:

Some of the possibilities	Corn production (kilos)	Bean production (kilos)
20 peasants produce corn, 0 produce beans	. . .	. . .
16 peasants produce corn, 4 produce beans	. . .	. . .
12 peasants produce corn, 8 produce beans	. . .	. . .
8 peasants produce corn, 12 produce beans	. . .	. . .
4 peasants produce corn, 16 produce beans	. . .	. . .
0 peasants produce corn, 20 produce beans	. . .	. . .

The full list of possibilities has not been given, but from the above six possibilities you can see the general pattern.

2 Calculate the opportunity cost to the community of producing
(a) an extra 250 kilos of corn,
(b) an extra 50 kilos of beans.

3 Draw a graph showing kilos of beans on the vertical axis and kilos of corn on the horizontal axis. Plot all the alternative combinations of the two crops on the graph by drawing a line through the points corresponding to the six specific possibilities given in the table. Such a line is called a *production possibility curve or production frontier*. It shows the entire range of possible outputs from which the particular actual output may be selected.

4 Suppose that the best diet (from a nutritional viewpoint) is 75 kilos of corn and 40 kilos of beans per person. If the actual production per person includes 80 kilos of beans has there been a misallocation of resources? If so, how should the available productive resources be redistributed to achieve a better outcome?

Logically, the problem of ensuring the full utilisation of the available productive resources must necessarily be resolved if resources are to be properly allocated. Unless all the available resources are used, the actual output of goods and services must be less than the potential maximum. Of course, human resources can never be fully employed in the sense that there is no person seeking work. Even at the most favourable times there are people seeking their first jobs and people who are voluntarily changing their jobs or whose employers have decided are not contributing sufficient to cover their wages.

Full employment of resources

Economists have been more concerned, however, with those situations where many people are unemployed and machines and factories are idle. During the Great Depression of the 1930s, unemployment never fell below 10 per cent of the insured population; the average for the decade was 16 per cent. At that time, many people eager to work remained unemployed for years. Workers who had jobs that they disliked dared not give notice because their chances of finding another job were slim. Thousands who wanted to continue with their current jobs were told that their employers could no longer profitably employ them. That was a situation where a vast pool of unused resources, both human and man-made, existed in a community where many people were struggling to have their most basic wants satisfied.

The reasons why the economic system of the day broke down in the Depression have been studied intensively by economists, and we are hopeful that the consequent increase in knowledge will enable us to prevent such a situation from occurring again. But even if massive unemployment can be prevented, the problems of business recessions with unemployment on a smaller scale will remain. Further, the decline of particular industries may have serious effects on the living standards of local communities; for example, the run-down of the fishing industry has brought unemployment and stagnation to the ports of Humberside, and steel plant closures have severely hit the towns of Consett and Corby.

Present versus future use of resources

The allocation of resources between the output of goods to serve our present needs and the output to serve future needs is another important element of the economic problem. Modern societies seek a high standard of living now, but another objective is to have a continuously rising standard of living. This latter desire is known as the *economic growth* objective. Modern governments strive to promote target rates of growth such as that the value of the goods and services produced by, or available to, the residents of the country should increase in successive periods by some specified percentage – say, by 3 per cent per year. Economists investigate what growth rates are feasible and advise on how they can be obtained.

There is a conflict between higher living standards now and a higher rate of economic growth. The production of goods and services for our current use and enjoyment depends both upon the quantities of available resources and also upon the uses to which they are put. Natural and human resources can be used to produce goods and services directly, but alternatively they can be put to work in the creation of

Investment

more (man-made) resources, which, in turn, make it possible to produce more goods and services available for use at a future time. This action of using resources to expand our productive capacity is called *investment*.

Decisions to invest require that the current use of some goods and services is foregone in order that the capacity to produce goods in the future is increased. Investment is warranted where the benefits (in the form of the increased flow of goods and services) in the future are assessed as outweighing the disadvantages of currently going without the additional goods and services that could have been produced and consumed now had the investment not been undertaken.

Even if a society chooses not to make the current sacrifices necessary to increase its future living standards, it must still divert some of its resources from current consumption to sustain its existing productive capacity. Unless, as machines wear out (depreciate), they are replaced, productive capacity will decline.

A second problem involving choice between the present and the future is posed by the case of exhaustible resources. In the case of potentially renewable resources such as fisheries, too rapid exploitation now may deplete the resource and hence today's consumption will be at the expense of future consumption. By their very nature, non-renewable resources such as gas fields eventually will be exhausted by exploitation. At present rates of use, the known stocks of the common forms of fossil fuel, except for coal, will last for only a comparatively short time. Some people urge that use of these energy forms should be rationed to provide supplies for future generations. An alternative view is that our generation should not impose public controls upon use of these fuels. Proponents of this view (which is at present the prevailing one) argue that substitute energy forms and technologies are likely to be discovered before shortages of fossil fuels cause serious problems for subsequent generations. Further, it is argued, later generations will enjoy the benefits of new scientific discoveries and new technologies which will permit continuous improvements in living standards despite their having less favourable sources of fuel than are available to us.

Conflict between short-term and long-term benefits

Nevertheless, we cannot dismiss the possibility that today's high living standards may be bought at the expense of those of future generations. Too rapid a rate of usage and depletion of North Sea oil and natural gas supplies may offer immediate profits for the companies concerned and well-paid employment for their workers, but later generations may come to condemn us for the consequences. Society is paying more attention to the consequences for the future of decisions about how to use resources. But the future discoveries of resources, the future improvements in technology and the future patterns of wants are unknown; consequently, the decisions about allocation of resources involving trade-offs between the interests of present and future generations are exceedingly difficult.

Effect on current living standards

Attitudes to this problem will be influenced by current living standards in the society concerned. The residents of a poor country with a high rate of infant mortality and widespread malnutrition will be reluctant to constrain the use of the country's fishing resources in the interests of the unborn. The people of Papua New Guinea may appreciate that the copper reserves of Bougainville represent a significant part of the world's known supplies of copper ore, but their desire for economic improvement puts great pressure upon them to mine the ore body at a rapid rate. The British people are aware that if they delay the rate of depletion of their North Sea oil reserves more sales can be made later at higher prices (as world oil supplies taper off) but it has been decided that their pressing current economic problems justify a high rate of current production.

Countryside affected by industry. Must use of resources always produce such results?

2.10

1 Failure by the United Kingdom to conserve its productive resources could lead to a fall in the material welfare of its residents in the future.
2 Failure by the United Kingdom to conserve its productive resources now could increase the material welfare of its residents in the future.

These statements appear to be contradictory, but taken within appropriate contexts each statement is sensible! Can you see how this can be?

2.11

Imagine that you are a politician standing for election in a marginal constituency. You know that the election is going to be very close. How would you present your views on the subject of 'open-cast mining of coal supplies' if your constituency:
1 included a large farming community;
2 was in an area of outstanding natural beauty;
3 covered an area of heavy industrial development?

2.12

Value judgements
1 Read the following ten statements.
(a) Seat belts save lives.
(b) Solar not nuclear.
(c) Smoking is a health hazard.
(d) You should stop smoking.
(e) An increase in income tax will lead to people buying less beer.
(f) If the demands by trade unions for higher wages are granted this will quicken the pace of inflation.
(g) Trade union demands for higher wages must be resisted.

(h) The government should spend more money on education.
(i) Failure to study explains most examinations failures.
(j) Men and women should receive equal pay for equal work.

2 Tick those statements with which you agree.
You may have noticed that the statements are of two types. In one category are statements, such as 'Seat belts save lives', the validity of which can be tested by applying a process of reasoning to the discoverable facts. An examination of accident statistics and a comparison of injuries and fatalities arising from accidents in which seat belts were worn, or not worn, assists us to deduce whether the wearing of seat belts reduces the number of road deaths. We would have to check that other factors were not responsible for differences in death rates. For example, if seat belts are an optional extra generally provided in expensive, well-built cars but not in cheaper, less sturdy cars, the different death rates of users and non-users of belts would not in itself prove the efficacy of the belts. However, we can visualise controlled tests, the results of which would be generally acceptable to logical minds as a proper test of the validity of the statement. Such testable statements are called *positive* statements.

The second category in the list are the *normative* statements. These cannot be tested in the same way, because whether you agree with them depends upon your assessment of what ought to happen – about what is desirable behaviour or a desirable state of the world. Statements such as 'Solar not nuclear' represent a mixture of positive and normative propositions. A person who proclaims 'Solar not nuclear' is implicitly asserting that, as a matter of fact, the use of nuclear fuels involves serious risks of accident and pollution. Given sufficient time and tests it may be that we could get agreement as to precisely what those risks are. But even if agreement on that aspect is reached, people will remain divided on the issue of 'Solar not nuclear', because some will say that we ought not to take those known risks, whereas others will argue that the benefits of cheap nuclear energy outweigh the adverse consequences of accepting the risks. Because this dispute arises from, and reflects, differences in individuals' valuations of various immeasurable ends, such as the value of human life – that is, differences in value judgements – there is unlikely to be unaminity on this issue. Similarly, if we took the statement 'Belt up and live', we could isolate a testable aspect – does the wearing of seat belts save lives? – and normative aspects such as – is it desirable to give the government the power to coerce people, even if only by propaganda, to wear seat belts? Some people who accept that seat belts do save lives nevertheless oppose public campaigns to influence people to wear belts because they consider the extension of the State's intervention in private decisions to be even more harmful than the additional fatalities. In the UK, it was decided in 1983 to make the wearing of seat belts in vehicles compulsory. This was despite some opposition to the law as a limit on individual freedom of action.

3 Divide the remaining eight statements into the two groups 'positive' and 'normative'. Include in the normative group all statements with a normative aspect. Discuss your answers with other members of the class.

4 Compose three statements, one which is positive, one which is normative and one which has both a positive and a normative component. Exchange your statements for those of another class member and discuss each other's statements.

Economists make positive statements when they investigate the effects or analyse the causes of an event. A textbook discussion of the causes of economic growth will be concerned with positive analysis. But economists make value judgements deliberately and openly because they seek to influence economic policies towards a state of the world they regard as desirable. For example, an economist may criticise the objectives of society, perhaps arguing that excessive concern with rapid economic growth is imposing undue sacrifices upon future generations. When this happens economists are likely to disagree among themselves about the appropriate economic policies to be followed. Thus E.J. Mishan[5] argues that resource conservation and anti-pollution measures are essential if the human race is to avoid its 'doomsday', and that these policies should replace economic growth as a central objective.[6]

Value judgements produce disagreements among economists

However, many economists disagree with Mishan and claim that economic growth is necessary, not only to remove poverty and raise living standards, but also to pay for anti-pollution measures. One of Mishan's critics has said that the primary concern should be to provide decent living conditions for English industrial workers now and if that means slum conditions for the fish in English rivers so be it. Who is advocating the 'right' policy? Clearly, the 'growth versus conservation' argument cannot be solved by scientific enquiry, for much of the dispute arises from differences about values. Of course, the protagonists can reach agreement on common positive statements, such as the rate at which certain resources will be depleted under certain policies. Persons of goodwill will strive to reach agreement on the factual questions – to determine what are the facts of the case. But if they have different sets of values, agreement on the facts will not necessarily lead them to advocate common policies. To some people, a whale has at least an equal right to life as has a person; to others the killing of a whale to supply cheap pet food is acceptable.

Economists hold differing views about how a country's production of goods and services should be shared between its residents and these in part reflect different value judgements. To some, income shares should be based on the principle that those who work hard, or are skilful, should receive the largest share of the national wealth. Others believe that the government has a responsibility to see that incomes should be redistributed to provide all with a basic standard of living, regardless of their capacity or willingness to contribute to production. These differing opinions lead economists to advocate different policies.

Arguments for and against economists making value judgements

There is even disagreement among economists about whether they should be making value judgements. Some argue that the economist should content himself with positive statements – with examining existing relationships between means and ends and of measuring these relationships where possible. On that view, the economist's role of adviser is confined to explaining to governments, businesses, banks, trade unions and so on the effects or implications of alternative policies, and assessing whether their objectives can be realised and if so the costs of achieving such goals. For example, the UK government may seek to reduce the level of unemployment by a number equal to 1 per cent of the labour force. The economist's task will be to investigate the various ways in which this can be accomplished and to specify the costs of the alternative policies. These policy options are then presented to the government as a menu from which they may choose.

Other economists argue that the economist has a wider role than that of simply acting as an adviser, and that the economist should make clear his own opinions about what is the best policy alternative. Sometimes economists are forced to make value judgements because there is no clear expression about what society really wants. They have to interpret the expressed objectives of society such as 'full employment' before they can explore the relationship between means and ends. Although they have no more 'right' than anyone else to say what is best for society, economists usually have readier access to relevant data on which to base practicable judgements. To say that they have no superior right to determine objectives does not mean that they have no right whatsoever. Refusal by an adviser to make any sort of value judgement means taking a neutral attitude to what goes on around us, and most economists are not prepared to act in this detached way, any more than a physicist is prepared to conceal his own view of the desirability of alternative nuclear policies. In practice, economists who advise governments seldom act in a completely unbiased way. Their personal opinions about what is best for society inevitably intrude. Few people who have studied a problem carefully can fail to favour one policy action rather than another, and in presenting advice to the policy-makers, understandably, they are likely to present the option they believe to be best in a particularly favourable manner.

Today there is some criticism of those economists who claim that economics is a value-free science, and that they are able to give impartial advice to whoever seeks it. Critics of this view argue that the great majority of economists in western industrial societies (or indeed in the planned economies) never raise the really important questions about how their economic society is organised. They are so conditioned by the society in which they live and by the training they have received, it is said, that they do not question (indeed, may never have given any thought to) critical matters such as the power structure of the society, and the mechanisms for the distribution of income. Hence, it is argued, their advice tends to perpetuate the existing social structure.

In this book controversial issues are discussed frequently, particularly in Chapters 12 to 24. The merits of different types of economic systems are explored in Chapters 23 and 24. Armed with your knowledge of the distinction between positive and normative values, and the warning that it is extremely difficult for an author to refrain from presenting his favoured policy options, you will better be able to assess the material presented. When the authors are conscious that important value judgements are being made, these will be pointed out, but the reader should be continuously aware of the importance of the positive–normative distinction.

2.13

1 Do you agree with the view that economists should not hesitate to make value judgements when analysing a problem? If you believe that they should not, explain why, and then try to think of any situations in which they should express an opinion. If you believe that economists should make value judgements, explain why, and then try to think of any situations in which they should not express an opinion.

2 Imagine that you are a professional economist instructed to prepare a report on the consequences of two alternative methods of raising additional tax revenue. One method is to increase a particular tax on a good which is consumed mainly by the wealthy and whose well-being you consider is damaged by its consumption. The other alternative method is to increase a tax on a good consumed by many people on low incomes. However, this change would greatly advantage a few existing wealthy people who make a substitute product to the one proposed for the higher tax. Can you envisage how your own value judgements could influence and enter into the report you prepare?

The economist's approach to problems

Economists share, with other social scientists, a common approach to problem solving. In general the first stage involves identifying a problem or a question to solve. Collecting information and sorting out relevant data on the particular issue then follows. However, obtaining the right answers depends on the art of asking the right questions.

Insatiable curiosity

The first requirement is that the good economist must be interested in the problem. He will want to find out the answer and be prepared to spend time and trouble in doing so.

Seeing for yourself A colleague of mine used to say the first thing an economist needs is a stout pair of boots. What he meant was that getting out, looking at the world about us, and observing the ways in which people behave is an essential part of the economist's job.

Asking others Interviews, discussions, sample surveys and censuses provide much of the basic information about the way in which people behave.

Reading the records Often the economist makes use of work done by other people. Facts and figures that have been collected previously provide a mine of information. Some of the basic data needed to examine a relationship may already have been gathered, sorted and published. The economist's task then will be to track down such information and investigate whether it is suitable for solving the problem.

An important collector and publisher of statistics is the Central Statistical Office. One publication, particularly useful is the *Annual Abstract of Statistics*, which contains a great deal of information on subjects such as population, labour, social conditions, trade and payments and so on. Another very useful publication is the yearly guide called *Britain: An Official Handbook*. The Government publishes these through HMSO together with many other useful sources such as the *Monthly Digest of Statistics*, the *United Kingdom Balance of Payments*, and *Social Trends*. There are also many other sources of information published which draw upon official and other statistics.

2.14

You are now prepared to begin an investigation of an economic relationship. Your local newspaper will provide an appropriate starting point for the study of the relationship that exists between the age and the price of secondhand cars. Knowledge of this relationship might well be useful to the potential used or new car buyer.

1 Investigate the relationship between the age and the price of either British Leyland Minis manufactured during the last ten years, or Ford Cortina Saloons manufactured during the last ten years.

You will be able to obtain much of this information by looking at the newspaper advertisements (reading the records). You may also want to get additional information by visiting secondhand car dealers (see for yourself) and by asking others. Use the statistical information you collect to plot, on a graph, the price of each car against its year of manufacture. Put the year of manufacture of the car on the horizontal axis of the graph and the price of the car on the vertical axis. Use a bold dot to represent each observation you make. If there appears to be a clear relationship between price and year of manufacture, draw that line (either a straight line or a smooth curve) on the graph which best fits the points you have plotted.

2 Use the information you have gathered to describe the relationship. Can you suggest explanations for the pattern of the relationship?

3 If you have no information about models of a particular year, would you be reasonably confident that you could estimate or predict their price by considering the prices you have obtained for earlier and later models?

4 From your study, including your interviews and personal observations, what other factors, apart from the make and the age of the car, have important effects upon its price?

5 You may be able to find publications which circulate in the motor trade and give the going prices for secondhand cars. Check your observations against the published lists.

When economists investigate a relationship their inquiry may be performed in three stages:

1 collection of the data and identification and measurement of the relationship;
2 explanation of the relationship in a plausible manner; and
3 testing the suggested explanation of the relationship.

Identification

For many practical purposes, all the economist is concerned with is to establish that a relationship exists and can be measured. In your investigation about cars and their prices, it was necessary only to measure how much cheaper cars become as the model dated, for that is what is of interest to the would-be purchaser.

But we might want to push the study further and go on to the second stage: explaining the relationship. This requires thinking up a plausible explanation, constructing what we call a theory or a model. For example, the economist might suggest the following theory of why older cars were cheaper than new cars.

Relationship to be explained	Elements in a possible explanation
The price of cars and their age are inversely related.	1 Cars deteriorate as they get older; they become more expensive to run. 2 People are not prepared to pay as much to buy cars that are more expensive to maintain. 3 Car dealers charge prices people are prepared to pay.

Table 2.2 A relationship and a plausible explanation

Explanation

These three elements can be put together to provide a plausible explanation of the relationship. If cars deteriorate with age and become more expensive to maintain, and if people are not prepared to pay as much for cars that are expensive to maintain, and if car dealers set prices people are prepared to pay in order to keep their stocks turning over, then the price of cars and their ages will be inversely related.

The three elements are called assumptions, and the adequacy of the model depends on whether these are good assumptions. The three if's need to be tested and confirmed. If the testing shows that the assumptions are invalid or that the process of reasoning was faulty, then it will be necessary to look round for another theory, with another set of assumptions. If it were found that there is no evidence to support the contention that cars deteriorate with age, then a basic element of the theory breaks down.

One alternative which might be tried would be to replace assumptions 1 and 2 with:

1 Newer cars are preferred to old because of the different styling.
2 People are prepared to pay more for styles which are in vogue.

These can be combined with the original assumption 3 to give a new theory that is ready to be tested.

2.15 How can the prices in the sketch be explained?

2.16 Another set of relationships can be tested with the help of the classified advertisements in the Saturday morning paper. Newspapers carry a large number of estate agents' advertisements that provide information about the size of the house, its location, condition, special features, and the price the owners hope to sell it for.

By studying this information carefully you should be able to get some idea about why there are price differences between the various houses. This problem is more difficult than 2.14. There you looked only at the relationship between age and price of a particular make of car. Here a number of relationships are involved simultaneously. Once you have collected the data from the newspaper it will help to ask such questions as these. What evidence is there to suggest that:

1 the price of the house is influenced by its location;
2 the price of the house is influenced by its size;
3 the price of the house is influenced by the construction materials used;
4 the price of the house is influenced by its condition.

How can you obtain answers to each of these questions? That is, how can you separate the effect, say, of location on the price of a house from the influence of the number of bedrooms?

What theory or theories could you put forward to explain these relationships?

Notes

1 See Chapter 23 for an account of the organisation of two planned economic systems: the Soviet Union and Yugoslavia.
2 A Marshall 1920 *Principles of Economics* 8th edn. Macmillan, p 1.
3 L Robbins 1935 *An Essay on the Nature and Significance of Economic Science*. London, repr. 1952, p 16.
4 Cited by K E Boulding 1966 *Economic Analysis* 4th edn. Harper & Row, New York, and John Weatherhill Inc., Tokyo, p 3.
5 E J Mishan 1969 *The Costs of Economic Growth*. Penguin.
6 Economic growth is discussed in more detail in Chapter 21.

Chapter 3

Systems

There are many kinds of systems; for example, the solar system, the nervous system, weapons systems and economic systems. A system may also contain subsystems. An economic system includes a banking system, a transport system and many production control systems. For the particular problems we are considering, at times we may even think of a major system as part of an even larger system: for example, the solar system as part of the universe, and the economic system as part of the larger social system embracing the entire set of interrelationships and institutions which make up a coherent society. Although there are great differences between the various physical and social systems, they have a number of common features.

Any system is a network of parts that interlock to form an overall pattern. Some thinkers emphasise the orderly relationship between the various parts of a system. Certainly, the word 'systematic' conveys this idea of order and organisation: we think of orderliness in the movement of sun and planets in the solar system.

In an ecological system, it is the behaviour of the parts of the system that is important. Groups of animals and plants react one to another and to their environment, and, from the interaction between the various groups, the patterns of the system emerge and evolve. Such a biological system is shown in Figure 3.1.

Equilibrium

Many types of systems attain a position of equilibrium. *Equilibrium* is a state of balance. A system is said to be in equilibrium if the forces at work in the system interact in such a way as to maintain the relationship between the various parts of the system. In later chapters the significance of equilibrium to economic systems will be investigated. For the moment, the nature of an equilibrium can be understood more easily by thinking about a highly simplified biological system of only two parts: rabbits and grasslands. Such a system makes a good starting point because it has similarities with a simple economic system. Both the rabbits and the grasslands behave in a certain predictable, or characteristic, way. Rabbits, given half a chance, reproduce rapidly. In our simple system the only natural check on their numbers is the amount of food available – grassland. Similarly, given suitable climatic conditions, grass will grow rapidly unless checked by rabbits.

The system will attain equilibrium if the available grassland is sufficient to sustain the existing rabbit population and if this population, in turn, is such as to maintain the grass at its current quantity. It will not be in equilibrium if the rabbits are multiplying and the grassland is shrinking, nor if the rabbit population is shrinking so that the grassland is growing rapidly.

It can be seen from these examples that maintenance of equilibrium requires particular relationships between one part of a system and the size of the other parts. Look again at Figure 3.2. Without the grassland the rabbits would starve; without the rabbits and other 'first order consumers', the 'second order consumers' could not exist. Conversely,

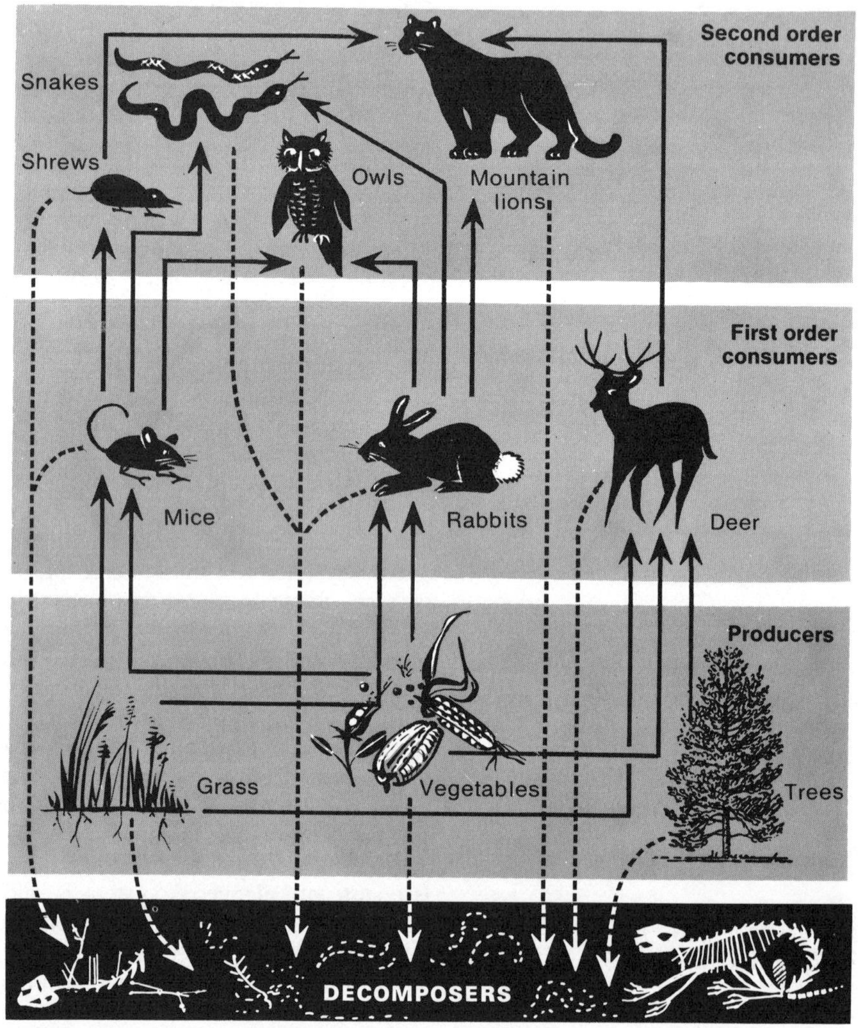

Figure 3.1 A biological system

Source: Biological Science: The Web of Life, Australian Academy of Science, Canberra, 1st edn. 1967, p 10

if grass, vegetables and trees – the 'producers' in the diagram – were not disposed of by some means, their environment would choke with greenery and the entire system would collapse. Such an interdependence of one part of a system on the others is an important factor in the equilibrium of an economic system. As you find out about each subsystem in the economic network, you will see just how precarious the balance is – how much each component part can influence and affect the others.

An equilibrium is said to be *stable* if the relationship between the parts of a system is restored after being temporarily disturbed. For example, if farmers lay poison regularly for a year, this will check the rabbit population and permit the growth of grassland. Once they stop laying poison, however, the flourishing grassland may encourage breeding of the rabbits and the original balance will tend to be restored.

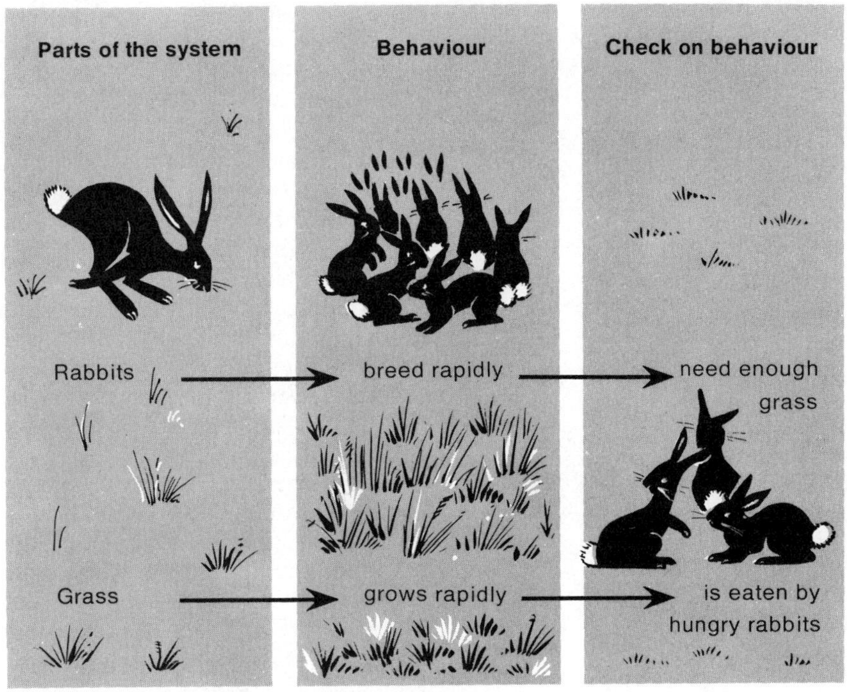

Figure 3.2 Rabbits – a grassland system

3.1

You could demonstrate that the rabbit grassland system is likely to have a stable equilibrium by considering the effects of the following temporary disturbances:

1 the laying of rabbit poison for a single season.
2 unusually good rains for a few seasons.
3 a drought for a few seasons.

In each case ask yourself what the immediate effect will be on the part disturbed; how the other part of the system will be affected; and how this in turn will affect the part first disturbed. Remember that each of these disturbances is only a temporary jolt to the system. Could such a temporary jolt cause a permanent change to the system?

3.2

An unstable equilibrium is one where a temporary jolt to a system is not followed by a restoration of the original relationship. Using your general knowledge of the physical and natural systems, can you suggest some examples of unstable equilibrium and the sorts of disturbances that could change or destroy these systems? What about a fire in natural bushland – or in an urban area?

Economic systems

As a society responds to its economic problem – by converting scarce resources into goods and services to satisfy its most pressing wants – a pattern of organisation emerges. The most important elements of any economic system are, of course, the people who make up that society. Individuals and groups have come to fulfil particular roles in the modern economies that have evolved through the actions of other groups and individuals in the past. These roles may be thought of as parts of the system. The various roles are filled by households, businesses, financial institutions (such as banks and life assurance companies), trade unions and governments. The behaviour of individuals in households, businesses and the other institutions is directed towards the objectives they consider important. The actions of people in an economic system reflect their sense of values, their personal interests, their opportunities, their understanding of the system and of others in it. Individuals come into contact with one another, mix, impose checks upon one another, agree, disagree, form interest groups, co-operate and compete. From this interaction and interdependence emerges the pattern of organisation which we call an *economic system* or an *economy*.

Economics is about people; a social system

One of the key features of an economic system, then, is that it is a component of the social system; it concerns people, their needs, wants and values. Economics cannot be simply a technical exercise of utilising resources in the most efficient manner to obtain high levels of production. Decisions about the economy are inevitably made within a framework of social, political and legal rules (both formal and informal) in ways that reflect the interests and ethics of particular groups in that society.

The work of the economist and the policy-maker is closely related but there is more than a subtle distinction between the world of economics and politics. The economist is in a position to give his advice on matters of purely technical opinion; it is not for him to formulate policy. The politician is open to many other sources of influence and circumstances and policies will always reflect expediency, ideology, personal values and in a democratic community a wide range of other than purely economic considerations. The politician is always at liberty to disregard the economist's advice. The economist is there to put before the politician the different options available and their expected consequences as he sees them. (This brings to mind the amusing idea of the often sought 'one-handed economist', the economist who when faced with a problem to solve does not respond, 'Well on the one hand this, but on the other hand . . . ')

An observation from Keynes, however, adds a salutary note to the above discussion '. . . . . the ideas of economists and political philosophers, both when they are right and when they are wrong, are more powerful than is commonly understood. Indeed the whole world is ruled by little else. Practical men, who believe themselves to be quite exempt from any intellectual influences, are usually the slaves of some defunct economist.'[1]

The individual has little influence on the system

Seldom can an individual household have a significant effect upon the operations of the system. Businesses will not change production plans to cater for one consumer, but if many households change their purchasing pattern they are likely to influence what is produced. For example, one person may switch from red to white wine without any impact upon the industry but when, as has happened in this decade, there is a general shift of preferences, readjustments by the winemakers follow promptly. In some cases, however, consumers as a whole may not be powerful enough to influence production. For example, in the past the automobile industry was able to ignore consumer demand for a better warranty system because there was little that the unorganised individual consumer could do about it. The emergence of a consumer movement has persuaded government of the need for legislation to protect consumers, and this has gone some way to removing the imbalance of power in situations where there are a few cohesive producers.

The individual member of society often finds his freedom of action limited by some properties of the system. Then he must choose between conformity or accepting a lower material living standard. Conforming may mean working a set numbers of hours, taking holidays at the same time each year, retiring at a certain age, joining a trade union, studying to obtain a particular credential, investing money in particular ways, living in a given area, and even refraining from wearing certain clothes. Failure to conform may lead to the disapproval of others with associated economic repercussions.

Pressure groups

One of the features of the economic system of the UK is the influence that pressure groups can exercise. Developers and conservationists, employers' federations and trade unions, retailers and consumers, manufacturers' organisations, farmers' groups, pensioners' representatives, women's liberationists, student unions and many other groups are continually using the strength of their combined numbers to persuade local and central government to adopt economic policies in their favour. The government accepts pressures from these sorts of groups as a matter of course, though not all governments will favour the same groups. Fundamental economic questions are often resolved in ways that reflect the extent to which these pressure groups have won the attention of the decision-makers.

3.3

The textile industry in the United Kingdom has experienced severe competition from foreign producers in recent years. The share of imported textiles in the domestic market has increased and the domestic industry has been run down, mills have closed, jobs have been lost. This has lead to demands from textiles manufacturers and textile unions for protection for the industry against imports of cheap foreign products.

1 What arguments would you present to the Government asking for such assistance if you were a textile workers' union leader?
2 From the Government's point of view, examine situations where they should resist the claims of a group using pressure tactics. Are there any rules or criteria a government might adopt as a guide to deciding which groups in the community to listen to and which claims to reject?

Types of economic system

There are considerable differences between the economies of various nations; they are organised in different ways to deal with the economic problem. The intelligent enquirer will want to know why the different economic systems have evolved and what the results have been. He will want to know whether one type of system can be rated as 'the best' and whether his own country's economic system can be improved in any way. A study of comparative economic systems focuses on the different ways that various societies have gone about achieving their economic objectives from the resources at their disposal and within the historical, social and political frameworks from which their particular systems have developed.

Reasons for classifying economic systems

The task of describing economic systems is a difficult one. For convenience it is usual to classify economic systems into three or four groups, the members in each group having common characteristics. Such a classification should not give the impression that all the countries within a group have identical systems; in fact, no two economies are organised in exactly the same way. Nor should it be thought that differences between countries classified into different categories are quite clear-cut; in fact, it is often difficult to decide whether a particular country should go into one category rather than another. Nevertheless, the classification has considerable value because it forces us to think about the essential features of the organisation of different societies.

Bases for classification

We could separate the 'rich' countries from the 'poor' countries. Assuming that 'rich' means having a high material standard of living, such a division can be made by comparing the average income per head of peoples in various countries, as is done in Chapter 24, 'Economic Development'. Another way of ranking countries is by comparing on a per capita basis their production of important basic goods and services such as coal, iron, steel, electricity and cement, and their provision of certain goods and services such as housing space, food, motor cars, telephones, hospital beds and tertiary education.

Using this general method of classification, the UK is ranked as one of the group of rich countries, alongside the United States, Canada, Sweden, West Germany and New Zealand. But this classification is based on results. It does not distinguish the type of economic system used. To understand economic systems fully we must investigate the methods employed by a country to solve its economic problem rather than focus upon the results of those efforts. We want to know what the differences are in the method of organisation, in the behaviour of the parts of the system, and in the effective power of economic pressure groups. In short, in investigating an economy, we want to find out why and how the system evolved, what the system will produce, how much will be produced, and how production and its rewards will be distributed.

The rejection of the 'results' classification of countries in favour of 'methods employed' does not mean that the former is not useful. We cannot investigate the reason why a country is rich or poor unless we first determine whether it is rich or poor in relation to other countries. But our concern here is with the organisation of a system, and systems with quite different forms of organisation may achieve similar outcomes in terms of material living standards.

A common way of classifying economic systems on the basis of their organisation is into the following three groups:

command (or planned) economies,
market economies,
traditional primitive economies.

Command (or planned) economies

A command economy is one in which the decisions about what to produce and how to distribute it among members of society are made by a bureaucratic system. It is the government departments and planning agencies who determine or asses the needs of the community and organise production accordingly. This may involve fixing production targets at national, district and factory levels and allocating the materials needed to fulfil these targets. It may require that the government assigns workers to their jobs, and to plan the education and vocational training of individuals so that they are able to fit into production plans.

Communist countries are commonly cited as examples of command economies, and later, in Chapter 23, the economic systems of two communist countries – the Soviet Union and Yugoslavia – will be discussed. In theory, it is possible to think of a command system in which buying and selling are not allowed to affect prices or to determine what is to be produced. In practice, we shall see, the Eastern European communist countries are all distinguished by the small role for private enterprise, but they have approached the economic problem in quite different ways. For example, in Yugoslavia prices and markets play a critical part in determining what shall be produced. It is more accurate to describe the Yugoslav system as 'market socialism' than as a 'command' or consciously 'planned' system.

Market economies

Prices and profits as signals in market economies

A market economy is one in which the important economic decisions are the outcome of an interaction of buyers and sellers in the marketplace. Here the priorities of consumers can be assessed by seeing what *prices* they are prepared to pay for goods and services and in what quantities they are prepared to buy them. The prices and profits received by suppliers act as signals that indicate to businesses whether they are producing things people want in the quantities they want. Low prices or unsold goods mean lower profits or outright losses. Businesses react to lower profits by trying harder to convince consumers of the merits of their products, by changing production, or maybe by going out of business.

In much the same way, workers sell their productive services – their labour – for wages and salaries. Businessmen and women use their initiative to organise production and earn profits. The more highly sought-after a productive skill, the greater its price in the market, other things being equal. In a market system, the goods and services produced by the society are distributed to the individual members on the basis of the market valuation of their contributions to that production. The scarcer the product or productive service, relative to demand, the greater the potential reward to the person who is able to supply it.

The term *price system* is sometimes used instead of market system, because it emphasises the role that prices play in a market economy. It is possible to imagine an economy organised entirely by a price system, without the deliberate interference of governments or planning agencies. More detailed investigation of the way a market economy operates is given in Chapters 7 and 8.

Traditional primitive economies

Custom subsistence barter in primitive economies

A traditional primitive economy is one where the customs of the people – their social, cultural and religious traditions – determine their way of life and their way of reacting to the economic problem. The most primitive economies have little of the kind of order found in modern economies. Each household, clan, village or other group strives to fulfil its own immediate needs – to *subsist*. This might be achieved by cultivation, hunting, making things, and by *barter* (the direct swapping of goods with one another).

Economists concerned with the determinants of the pace of economic development argue that sticking to old ways and customs is one reason why economic development[2] is so slow in many poor countries. Some traditions may present obstacles to the drive for higher material living standards. An American economist, Albert Hirschman, distinguished two quite different traditional attitudes among the peoples of undeveloped countries, and both, he claimed inhibited economic development. The first was among peoples who formed close tribal groups.

> The individual members of such a society usually have a definite place and the possibility of change and improvement in their economic fortunes hardly enters their horizon. The total product having long been stationary, individual improvement could only take place at the expense of other members and of the cohesiveness of the group. Exceptional performance is therefore discouraged and penalised by a variety of social mechanisms of which the accusation of practising witchcraft is the best known.[3]

In the second kind of society, often found in Latin America, the individual member of the society is strongly motivated by desires for personal advancement, but the method of achieving this advancement is seen 'not as a result of the systematic application of effort and creative energy . . . but as due either to sheer luck or to the outwitting of others through careful scheming . . . These attempts to reach success through short-cuts obviously diminish the flow of energies into activities that will stimulate economic development'.[4]

Hirschman referred to the *ladino* and *mestizo* societies of Latin America as examples of societies in which the intensely individualistic behaviour of the members acted as a check on economic development.

The problem of classification

Although three types of economic system have been distinguished – command, market and traditional – the problem remains in trying to put countries neatly into one or other of the categories. By-and-large, communist countries are command economies; western countries have placed great reliance on the price mechanism; and many primitive societies are dominated by traditional attitudes and customs. But no modern economy today conforms entirely to one of the three systems, and in those systems where inflexible attitudes are taken to the use of both command and price methods the economy shows strains.

Markets in command economies and planning in market economies

In command systems, planning is most important, but some of the eastern European countries, notably Yugoslavia and Rumania, are increasingly using a modified price system to provide incentives for effort and tests of efficiency.

In modern market economies, there is considerable government intervention, regulation and control, modifying the working of the price mechanism. The society accepts that some provision should be made for those of its members who have a weak economic position in the market economy. This provision involves a whole range of subsidies and welfare services covering health, education, unemployment benefits and cash social security benefits. In many countries where extensive use is made of the market, there is also planning for long-term economic development. Such plans and regulations provide for control of the use of natural resources such as minerals and forests, zoning of industry, location of towns, the integrated provision of basic energy supplies, planning of transport systems, the control of pollution, and many other aspects of the lives of their citizens and future citizens.

Traditional economies in a pure form are not commonly found except in extremely remote areas. The primitive societies have gradually discarded their conservative attitudes as they try to develop along the lines of the advanced economies. The market system's prices and profits provide incentives and planning accelerates the development process. Thus many developing countries exhibit characteristics of all three types of systems.

'Mixed economy' an unsatisfactory term

One response to the problem of classifying economic systems has been to introduce into discussions a fourth term – *mixed* or *semi-planned* economy. This is intended to cover those societies that make use of prices and incentives based on the profit motive, but also use government or planning authorities to modify the working of the price system. Commonly the UK is referred to as a mixed economy. At first this appears to resolve the problems of classifying economic systems; any economy that does not conform exactly to traditional, market or command types can be called 'a mixed economy'. But on reflection, this solution can be seen to be illusory. We have seen that the first three systems are really theoretical types, and real world economies do not conform exactly to any one of them. All economies are fixed. The extent to which any one of the three is relied upon in any country's system varies considerably, and the assignment of particular economies to one or other of the categories is most satisfactory where one particular type clearly predominates. Where, as in the case of Yugoslavia, the mix of price and command methods of organisation comes close to that in some Western European countries, the classification problem is difficult.

All economic systems are a mixture of three types

Figure 3.3 presents one solution to the classification problem – it sets out a framework allowing for many combinations of the different types. The three points of the triangle represent the three model types of economic system. The areas within the triangle represent the whole range of real world economies which exhibit, to varying degrees, some characteristics of each of the three systems. In this area, points representing the relative position of fifteen countries have been marked as a rough guide of how important tradition, the market and planning are in each economy. The nearer a country lies to any corner of the diagram, the closer its economic system resembles that particular model system. The Soviet Union is close to the bottom-left corner, indicating that many of the features of its economy are based on command or planning. Papua New Guinea is near the top of the diagram – tradition still dominates large areas of economic life in that country – although it is now rapidly developing. The UK is placed close to the bottom-right corner of the diagram: the market continues to play an important part in decision-making here.

But the fact that *no* country lies at a corner reflects that no country conforms exactly to any of the models. Yugoslavia lies well out from the command corner and Sweden lies well out from the market corner. China and Mexico lie nearer to the top of the diagram though their economic systems are quite different. Mexico shows the effects of tradition beneath its market system, whereas China's traditions underlie its distinctive attempt to establish a command economy. It should be

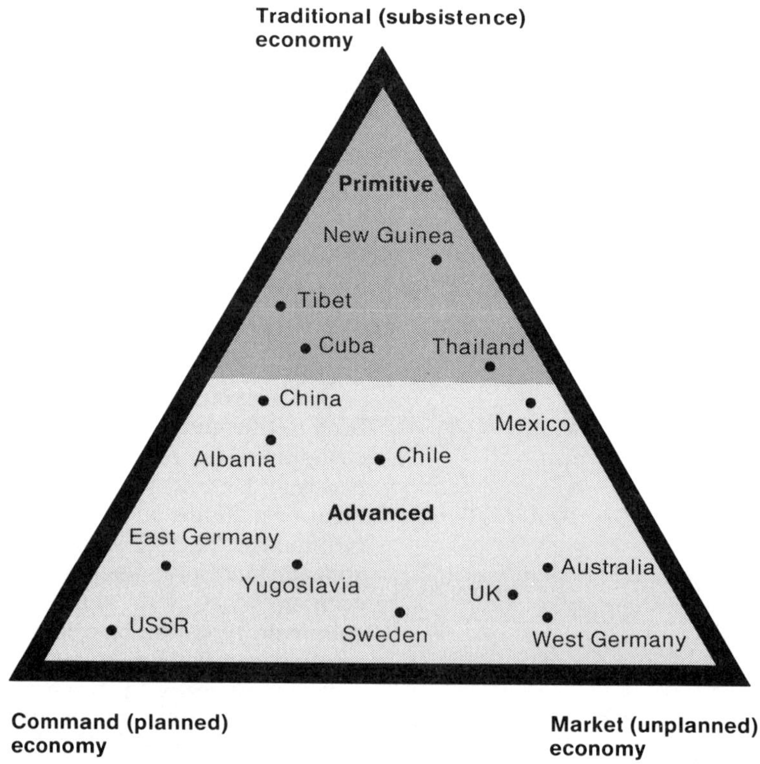

Figure 3.3 Economic systems

appreciated that each country's position on the diagram reflects the author's judgement and you may consider the position of one or more of the countries to be inappropriate.

3.4

1 Would you have positioned Australia, the United Kingdom and the Soviet Union as they are in the diagram, or do you think that in relation to each other the Soviet Union and the United Kingdom should be nearer the corners? Discuss your ideas with others in the class.
2 Where on the diagram would you put the following countries: the United States, Italy, India, Nigeria, South Africa, Chile and Indonesia.

Features of an economy which are indicators of its classification

In using the diagram, you may have had difficulty in deciding just how far from a corner each country should be put. Is there some way we could measure those features of a country's economy that indicate how highly planned it is, or how important the market is? Although we cannot do it very accurately, it is possible to measure some features of a country's economy that will give us a rough guide: for example, a study of the working population can tell us a lot about a country's economic system. One of the features of command systems is that a large proportion of the workers are employed in enterprises and activities conducted by the government. On the other hand, in a market system, most workers are employed by private enterprise. In a primitive traditional system (where subsistence agriculture is common) many

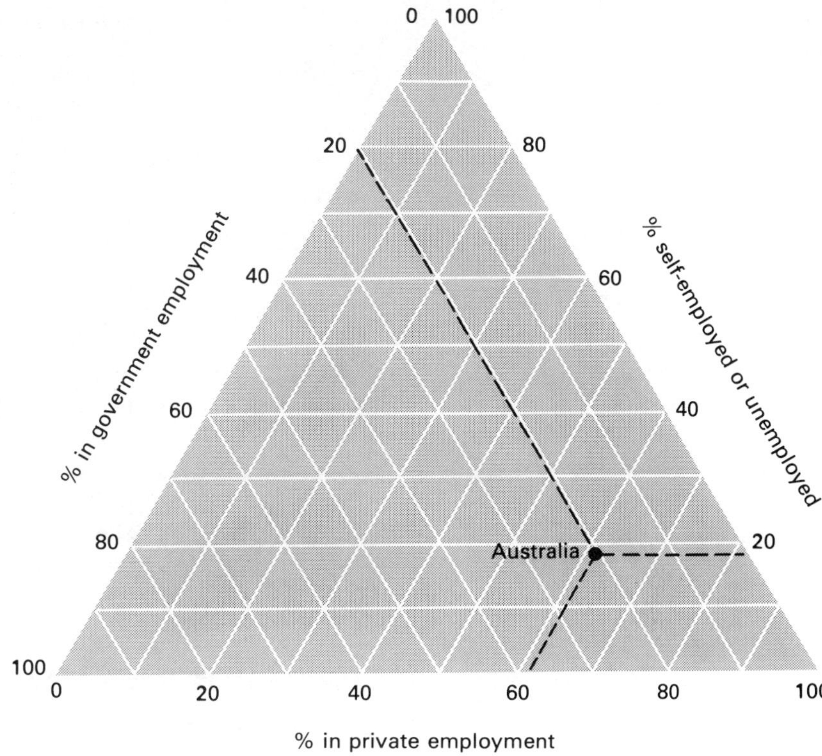

Figure 3.4 Measurements of economic systems

people are self-employed and are not involved in the market exchanges; both the government and private business sectors are relatively minor employers of labour. A study of a country's workers being:

self-employed or unemployed,
working for the government, and
working for private employers,

helps us to fix countries on the diagram.

Figure 3.4 has been marked with an isometric grid (instead of squares it uses triangles with 60° angles). Any point on the diagram has three co-ordinates instead of the conventional two. The values relevant to the point are then read off on the three axes. These axes have been graded so that any point on the diagram measures the *relative* importance of the three variables.

The horizontal axis measures the percentage of the population privately employed (measured from left to right). The right diagonal axis measures the percentage of the population unemployed or self-employed (measured from bottom to top). The left diagonal axis measures the population employed by government (measured from top to bottom). In the figure, 62 per cent of Australia's working population is privately employed, 20 per cent works for the government and 18 per cent is self-employed or unemployed. Note that because of the construction the three components must add up to 100 per cent.

3.5 The following information will make it possible for you to mark the countries on a diagram such as 3.4.

Country	Percentage of working population: Self-employed or unemployed (%)	Private employment (%)	Government employment (%)
Taiwan	54	35	11
Kenya	68	22	10
Nigeria	92	4	4
Soviet Union	12	3	85
United States	12	74	14

Research the most recent figures available for the United Kingdom and mark the position of the UK on your diagram.

3.6 Imagine that drought produces major crop failures simultaneously in India and China. How would you expect each system to deal with the situation (1) as an emergency, and (2) in a longer period of time? Similarly, what would be the response of a primitive society?

Primitive and modern economic systems

Besides the classification of command, market, traditional and mixed economies, another distinction that can be made is between primitive and modern economic systems. Figure 3.3 is again helpful here. A horizontal line runs through the middle of the figure separating the apex from the base. It separates the traditional subsistence economies from the command and market economies. This is useful because most primitive systems are essentially traditional, whereas modern economic systems – those of the advanced industrial nations – are some mixture of market and command. Earlier we rejected the idea of classifying countries simply as rich or poor because we wanted to know the methods a society uses to organise production. But whether a country is rich or poor largely depends upon two considerations:

the resources at the country's disposal, and

the economic system it adopts to utilise these resources.

The type of system is very important. A country with a primitive economic system will probably be poor even if well endowed with resources and if it does begin to develop its resources it is likely to do so by using modern methods of organisation. It is also true that a country without adequate resources will remain poor, even if it adopts a modern economic system.

The differences between the organisational characteristics of primitive and modern economic systems are striking.

Again, though we may draw a line in the diagram, there is no clear division between primitive and modern economic systems. The development of specialisation and exchange, the use of man-made resources and the emergence of a monetary system is a gradual process. When we compare the economies of different countries, rather than distinguishing between those that specialise, mechanise, or use money and those that do not, we find distinctions in the degree of these activities.

Primitive	Modern
Lack of specialisation, self-sufficiency	Specialisation, competition, co-operation and exchange between the members of a community and between communities
Little use of capital investment	Widespread use of capital investment
Barter or primitive monetary systems	Existence of a sophisticated monetary system and financial institutions

Table 3.1 Organisational features of primitive and modern economic systems

In the next chapter, we investigate in more detail the significance of each of these features of modern economic systems to find out just why they are so essential if a country's residents are to achieve high material living standards.

3.7

Once a clear pattern in a society's economic system becomes so established as to be readily identifiable, how flexible is the system? How stable is it likely to prove?

1 Do you think there were any major changes in the United Kingdom's economic system during the years of the Wilson and Callaghan Labour Governments of 1974 to 1979? Was there, for example, an identifiable trend away from the market type of system towards more public ownership and elements of a command economy during those years? If you believe that this was the case, what evidence do you have to support these views?
2 With the coming of the Conservative Government to power in 1979 and its re-election in 1983, have there been any changes in the economic system towards or away from a market economy? Support your answer with evidence.
3 Do you know of any countries whose systems have changed either gradually or abruptly? What could be the reasons for such changes?

Notes

1 J M Keynes 1936 *The General Theory of Employment, Interest and Money* Macmillan. Professor J Robinson states as an insight into the relationship of the economist and economics with society that, 'the purpose of studying economics is not to acquire a set of ready-made answers to economic questions, but to learn how to avoid being deceived by economists'.
2 The distinction between the terms economic 'development' and economic 'growth' is discussed in Chapter 24.
3 A O Hirschman 1958 *The Strategy of Economic Development*, Yale University Press, New Haven, pp 11–12.
4 Hirschman, p 16.

Chapter 4

Characteristics of the System

Specialisation and exchange

When you take a job you will probably become a specialist, concentrating your skills on performing a single task or a related group of tasks. This may mean operating a lathe or a typewriter, or becoming a teacher, or a bank cashier. Most people specialise because financially it is the most rewarding opportunity. The specialist is able to earn a money income that will permit him to use and enjoy more goods and services than he could if he attempted directly to provide them all for himself. The extreme alternative to specialisation is complete self-sufficiency – you could grow your own food, keep animals, make your clothing, build your shelter, and provide your own power and transport. A moment's reflection is enough to convince most people that this alternative is unacceptable. At best, it offers lower living standards and at worst, starvation. It is not a coincidence that in many poor countries specialisation is not well-developed whereas there is a high degree of specialisation in the advanced industrial countries.

Benefits of specialisation

The economist wants to know how specialisation is capable of raising living standards, and whether there are any situations in which specialisation is not beneficial. Specialisation can lead to an increase in living standards if it increases the quantity of goods and the supply of services that can be produced from available resources. It can do this in two ways:

Specialisation permits productive skills and other resources to be used in the most efficient way.

Continued practice leads to the development of skills and the improvement of the production techniques.

Activity 4.1 is designed to help you discover the conditions under which specialisation can increase production and living standards by the more efficient use of productive skills. It makes use of a very simple economic model, which may appear unrealistic. However, unrealistic models are used by economists quite deliberately whenever an important idea can be expressed more clearly that way than by a complicated example. Of course, such simple models would be useless if they did not tell us something important about the real world. Fortunately, this model does.

Economic models

4.1

Two bachelors, Paddy and Mick, live in a boggy area. Both are independent and self-sufficient. They each grow potatoes as a basic foodstuff and dig peat for their fuel supplies. In a normal season they each devote half their working time to growing potatoes and half to peat digging. Their production of peat and potatoes is as follows.

	Potatoes (bags)	Peat (loads)
Paddy	150	75
Mick	100	100

Paddy is better fed but Mick is warmer.
It occurs to Paddy that, if he devoted his time solely to digging potatoes, he could produce 300 bags in a season; alternatively, if he concentrated on digging peat; he could product 150 loads. By observing Mick's work habits he comes to the conclusion that Mick is not as good at growing potatoes; but is better at digging peat. He calculates that if Mick specialised in potato-growing he would produce 200 bags, or alternatively if he dug peat he would produce 200 loads. This, then, is the position:

	Potatoes (bags)		Peat (loads)
Paddy	300	or	150
Mick	200	or	200

Paddy reasons that since he can produce more potatoes than Mick, and Mick can dig more peat than him, they will both benefit if he grows all the potatoes and leaves the peat-digging to Mick.

1 Imagine that you are Paddy. Prove to Mick that you can both be better off if you grow the potatoes and he digs the peat and the surpluses are exchanged. To convince Mick that he is better off than before, you will have to demonstrate that he will be getting at least as many potatoes and as much peat as before, and more of at least one of them. Similarly, you will have to satisfy yourself that the deal leaves you better off too.
2 Suppose that Mick counters your argument by saying that he ought to grow the potatoes and that you should dig the peat. Demonstrate to him that specialisation of this type cannot possibly benefit both of you.
3 Calculate the opportunity costs to Paddy of producing:
(a) 1 bag of potatoes,
(b) 1 load of peat.
4 Calculate the opportunity costs to Mick of producing:
(a) 1 bag of potatoes,
(b) 1 load of peat.
5 From the example of Paddy and Mick, work out which one of the following statements is true.
(a) Two individuals can benefit from specialisation and exchange only if each produces the good in which he has a *higher* opportunity cost than the other person.
(b) Two individuals can benefit from specialisation and exchange only if each produces the good for which he has a *lower* opportunity cost than the other person.
Explain your answer as fully as possible.

It has now been established that there are certain conditions under which specialisation can bring an increase in production and gains to both producers. But whether both benefit and, if so, the extent of the benefit is determined by the terms on which they agree to exchange their surpluses. A specialist will not benefit from specialisation if he strikes such a poor bargain that he finishes up with fewer goods than if he had aimed at self-sufficiency.

4.2

1 Imagine you are Paddy. What is the highest price (in terms of potatoes) that you are prepared to pay to obtain each load of peat from Mick? Then explain what it was that led you to decide on such a price.
2 Now put yourself in Mick's place and decide on the lowest price (least number of bags of potatoes) you are prepared to accept for each load of peat. Similarly, explain what it was that led you to decide on your minimum price.
3 Discuss your answers to (1) and (2) in class and speculate on what price level might be acceptable to *both* producers. How might they reach agreement on such a price?

In Activity 4.1, Mick was better at digging peat and Paddy was better at growing potatoes. Mick used less resources than Paddy to produce a given amount of peat, whereas Paddy used less resources to produce a given amount of potatoes. Mick, therefore, had an *absolute advantage* in peat production and Paddy had an absolute advantage in potato production. When each recognised this, they appreciated that subject to agreeing with one another on an appropriate rate of exchange, they could both gain by specialisation and exchange of their products.

Comparative advantage

Surprisingly, perhaps, it is possible to show that specialization can still be beneficial even if one of the producers loses his absolute advantage. The benefit is still there provided the more productive man specialises in that activity in which his superiority and efficiency is most marked. This will be the activity in which his opportunity cost is lower. Economists say that he holds a *comparative advantage* in such an activity.

4.3

You can work out the comparative advantage for yourself, by modifying the Paddy and Mick example in the following way. Suppose the principal alternatives facing Paddy and Mick now are:

	No specialisation	Complete specialisation	
	Alternative 1	Alternative 2	Alternative 3
Paddy	150 bags potatoes 125 loads peat	300 bags potatoes	250 loads peat
Mick	100 bags potatoes 100 loads peat	200 loads peat	200 bags potatoes

Now Paddy can produce more potatoes *and* more peat than Mick if he were to specialise in either. Show that both can gain if Mick devotes all his time to digging the peat and Paddy grows all the potatoes and devotes some time to digging peat. You can do this *either* by comparing total production resulting from each of the three alternatives, *or* by calculating the opportunity cost of a bag of potatoes, or load of peat, for each man. As Mick has a lower opportunity cost in peat digging he is said to have a *comparative advantage* in that activity.

Dynamic benefits of specialisation

The second reason why specialisation may be beneficial is that it permits the continuous practice of a limited range of skills and, over time, this leads to tasks being performed more rapidly and more accurately. It can result in workers becoming aware of flaws in production techniques, and in being able to suggest ways in which the product can be improved. Thus even if, initially, no advantage will be gained from specialising, benefits may emerge with time.

Specialisation depends on co-operation

The gains from specialisation can only be realized if there is co-operation between the specialists. Mass production has been made possible through assembly-line techniques, in which the individual attends to a single activity: perhaps a very simple one. These techniques require that the individual worker surrenders his independence. The high degree of organisation, co-operation and supervision involved means that workers have to work together in a single place – a factory or maybe a packing depot. Some individuals must fulfil the role of employers, others become managers, and the majority become non-managerial employees. The difference between the very simple form of economic system in which each household is also a separate productive unit, and a modern economic system in which households and the productive units are separated, is shown in Figures 4.1 and 4.2. The complexity of the modern system is said to be justified because it permits the production of more goods and services than would otherwise be possible.

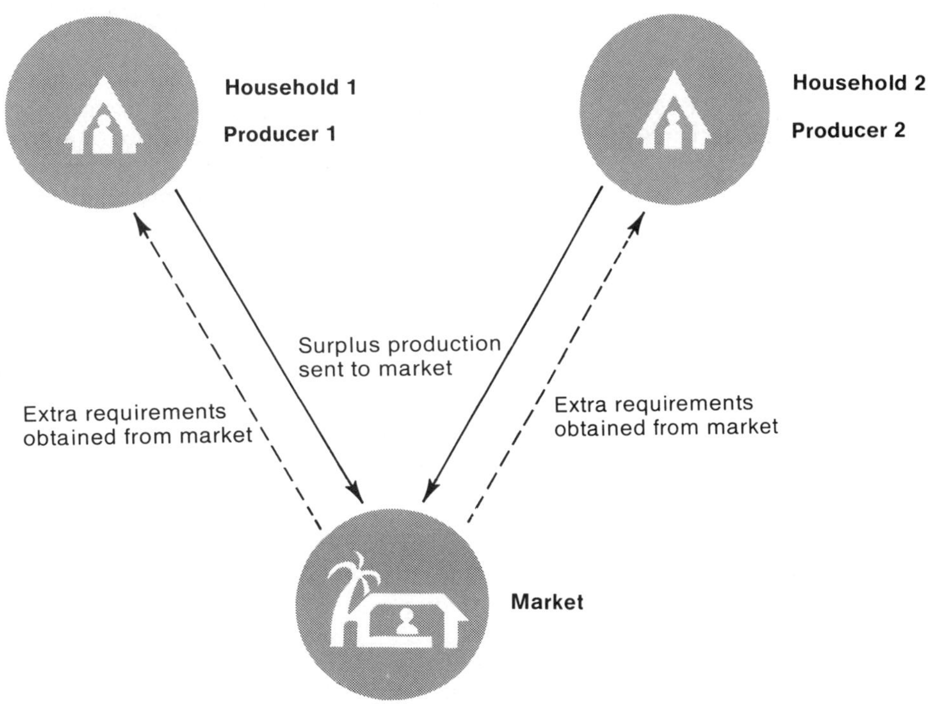

Figure 4.1 Exchange in a simple peasant society

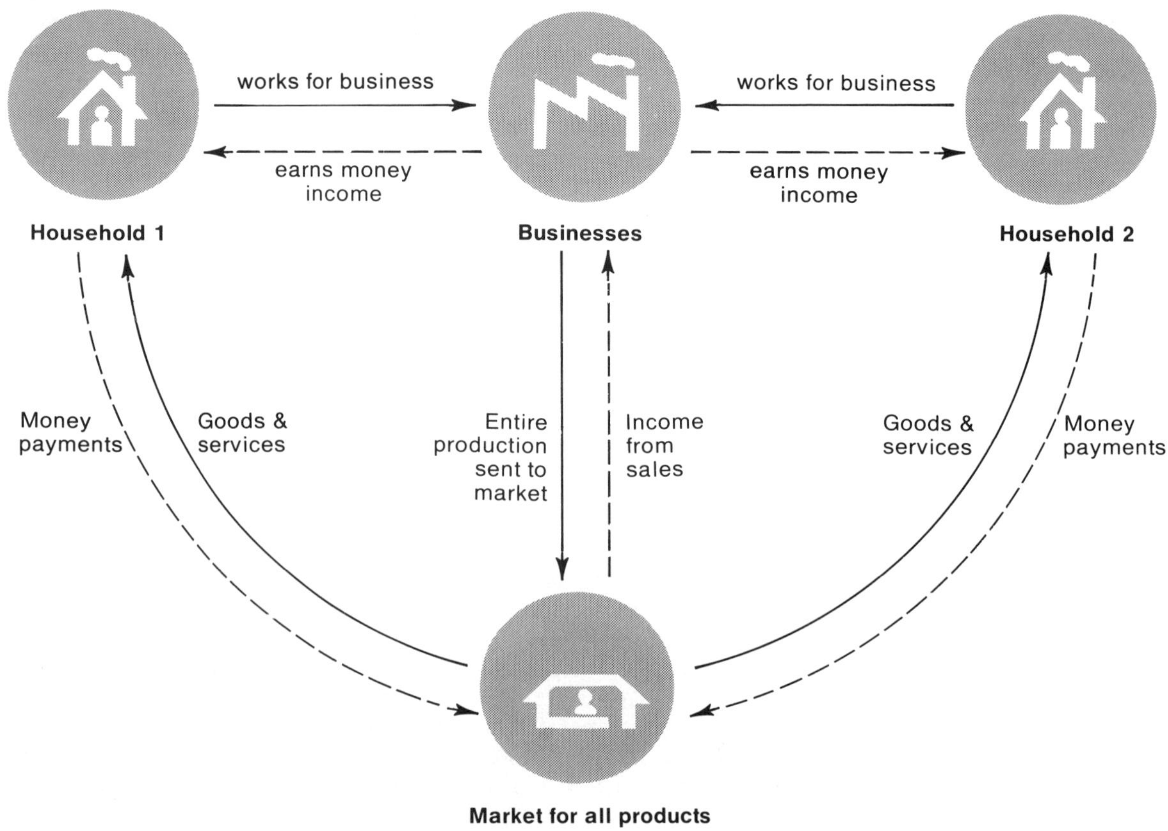

Figure 4.2 Exchange in a modern society

Gains from specialisation depend upon exchange

It is important to realise that successful specialisation depends on the development of an appropriate exchange system, for without exchange the specialist will almost certainly be worse off than if he had aimed at self-sufficiency. In Figure 4.1 a simple market-place exists for the selling of surpluses and the buying of requirements. In Figure 4.2 two types of market exist. First, there is the market in which businesses sell their goods and services to the households. Second, there is the market in which the households sell their productive services to the businesses. Without suitable institutions to facilitate the sale of goods and the hiring and employment of labour and other resources, the modern economic system could not exist. Moreover, the failure of such institutions to operate effectively will influence the efficient operation of the system and deprive individual parts of the benefits it would otherwise bring. For example, a failure of employers' representatives and trade unions to agree on appropriate wage rates may result in men and women being stood down, production of some goods being suspended, the flow of those goods to markets halted, and a fall in the consumption of such goods. It will also result in a reduction in incomes, and a loss in ability to buy goods and services. In a command economic system, mistakes by the central planning agency can lead to a misallocation of productive resources – to the over-production of some goods and to the inadequate production of others, with the result that the well-being of the people suffers.

4.4 Successful specialisation depends upon the existence of a suitable exchange system. Specialist workers can be put out of work if there is no market for the product they help to make. It cannot be sold for one reason or another.

A second problem is that technological change may lead to machines replacing the specialist worker. Automation in the printing industry, in telecommunications and in data processing have all lead to the loss of workers' jobs. In many cases the displaced worker has been a skilled specialist with no alternative occupation to fall back on.

A third, and rather different, problem is that some types of specialisation require the worker to repeat a simple manual operation over and over again. The benefits come, as we have seen, from the speed achieved by concentration on a single task. The task may require little intelligence. Indeed in some industries applicants are given a test and those considered too intelligent are not given a job. In such industries those who do obtain jobs face the prospect of boredom, of being treated as cheap machines and they do not expect to gain any job satisfaction.

What means could we in the UK use to overcome these problems, or do they raise such serious social questions that we should consider discouraging excessive specialisation?

4.5 Sometimes the natural resources of an area – its climate, the skills of its people and its transport services – lead to its residents specialising in particular types of activities. To what extent have industries in your region, or locality, been established to take advantage of local conditions? What influences work against the concentration of particular industries in different parts of the UK?

Overseas trade

The benefits of specialisation also apply to international trade. Just as the individuals within a community, and the community as a whole can benefit from the division of labour, so a community can benefit from concentrating its productive activities and trading with the rest of the world. In fact, for a long time the gains from international trade were demonstrated by using simple models of the peat/potatoes type.[1]

Figure 4.3 extends the diagrammatic representation of a modern economic system (given in Figure 4.2) by adding an overseas sector. The diagram shows that there is a flow of goods and services to overseas countries (exports) and a flow of money from overseas countries (export receipts). Similarly, there is a flow of goods and services from overseas countries (imports) and a flow of money to overseas countries (import payments). In the diagram, these flows pass between the business sector and the overseas countries sector and not between the households and overseas countries. This is done partly to simplify the diagram as much as possible. and partly because the great majority of the exports and imports of a modern country such as the UK pass through businesses, even if their origin or their final destination is the household.

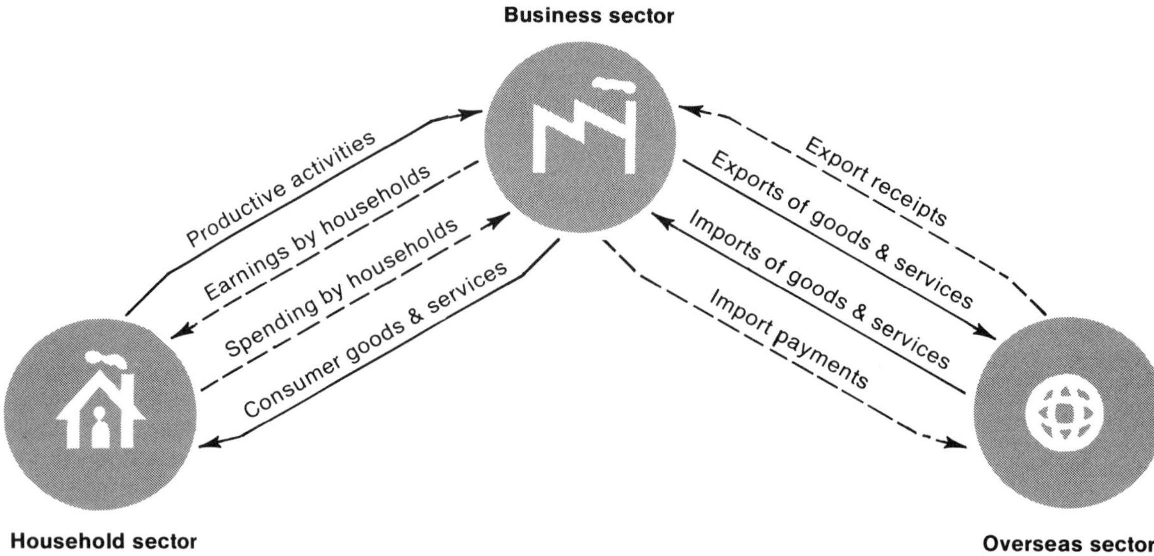

Figure 4.3 Modern economic system with overseas sector

4.6

From a recent copy of the *Annual Abstract of Statistics*, find the following information:
1 The annual value of exports in a recent year.
2 The annual value of imports in the same year.
3 Exports and imports are classified for statistical purposes into a large number of divisions. Determine from these more detailed tables the five most valuable export divisions and the five most valuable import divisions in that year.

4.7

The problems that specialisation can bring to the individual were considered in Activity 4.4. This discussion can be extended to include the possible economic problems that the residents of a country may face if it specialises and becomes highly dependent on its trade. Are the problems different if the specialisation takes the form of concentration upon a limited range of products, or takes the form of trading several commodities with a limited number of foreign countries?

Countries that have been, or are, highly dependent on a few products include New Zealand and Australia (rural products), Malaysia (rubber and tin) and Saudi Arabia (petroleum). What has been done to overcome the problem by each of them and what more could be done?

Some important technical terms – flows and stocks

In Figures 4.2 and 4.3 the solid lines indicate the movement of goods and services between households and businesses and the dotted lines indicate the movement of money between them. Frequently, economists talk about the flow of goods and services or the flow of money. The measurement of a *flow* is one that relates the amount of a variable to a period of time (perhaps an hour, a day or a year). Thus, whenever we talk about the quantity of an article produced in a year, or the amount of wages an employee receives in a week, we are referring to a flow. The time element is of critical importance. A salary payment of £200 has no meaning unless the time period for which it applies is stipulated.

Stocks are quite different because they do not require reference to a period of time for them to have meaning. They exist at any moment and they can be measured at any moment of time. For example, the amount of money in a person's savings bank account is measured at a point of time. We say that she has £250 on a certain day. This is a stock. Similarly, we can measure (count) the number of people , or cars, or houses in the UK on a specified date by a census.

The difference between a stock and a flow is illustrated in Figure 4.4. The diagram shows a river which is running into a lake and running out again at the other (lower) end. The quantity of water that passes a given point on the banks of the river in a specified time (say a second) is a flow measurement. The volume of water in the lake can be measured at any given moment without any reference to a period of time.

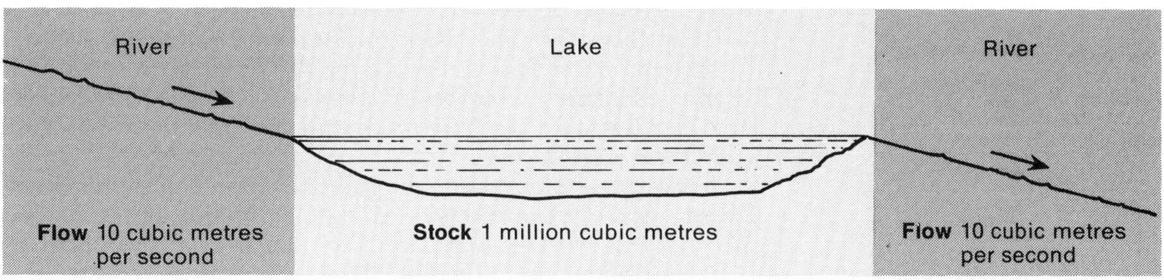

Figure 4.4 Stock and flows

Often the study of a subject involves the economist in using both flow and stock measurements. For example, a study of population necessitates not only the consideration of the size of the population at a specific moment of time (stock) but also the number of births and the number of deaths during that period (flows). Together, the two flows affect the size of the stock. The analogy between the population, and the lake and the two rivers in Figure 4.4 should be obvious.

Capital stock

Similarly, economists talk about the national stock of capital when they refer to the aggregate of all man-made resources in a country. Investment, the creation of additional man-made resources in a specified period, is a flow that increases the capital stock. Depreciation, the using up or wearing out of man-made resources in a specified period, is a flow that decreases the capital stock. Once again, the analogy with the lake and rivers is apparent and there are parallels with the population case, with investment being analogous to birth and depreciation to death.

4.8

Study each of the following six statements.
An executive's income was £35 000 per year.

The UK Official reserves of gold and foreign currency totalled \$16 977 m at the end of 1982.

There were 454 trade unions in the UK at the end of 1979.

Registered unemployment totalled 2 969 000 at the end of May 1983.

Notes and coins in circulation in the UK at the end of 1980 amounted to £10 425 m.

In 1979 steel production in the UK was 21.4 million tonnes.

1 In each case identify whether a stock or a flow measurement is being made.

2 Now identify a stock measurement or flow measurement that might be related to the one given in each case. For example, we have seen that capital is a stock measurement and investment is a related flow measurement. Like wise, the number of births per year is a flow measurement and population is a related stock.

Consumption and production

The terms *consumption* and *production* have been used on a number of occasions in this chapter. Although widely used in everyday language, they have special meanings in economics and it is important to grasp these at this stage. The essential feature of consumption is that it is the utilisation of goods and services for the direct satisfaction of personal wants. Similarly, *consumption expenditure* is the expenditure on goods and services that are purchased with the intention of increasing the purchaser's satisfaction.

This meaning of consumption differs from the common use of the word, which refers to acts of eating or drinking. It also differs from a second sense in which the word is used in everyday language, when consume simply means 'to use'. Thus, you may read that 'an aluminium industry consumes large quantities of electric power'. You should be clear that the economist is not using the term in either of these common usages. To him, consumers are people who purchase goods or services for satisfaction rather than profit; they are thus often equated with households. There are a number of technical problems that economists and statisticians have encountered in trying to determine which particular purchases constitute consumption expenditure. The economist's formal definition of consumption, and its interpretation will be discussed in the next chapter.

The terms *production* and *productive activities* also have different meanings for the economist from the ones employed in everyday usage. Production is not limited to making and growing things; nor are growing and making things necessarily production to the economist. By production, economists mean providing something that is capable of satisfying the wants of consumers directly, or providing something that can be used in the production of something else. The manufacture of useless articles is not production to the economist; it is unproductive activity – a waste of time and of scarce resources. In practice the usual test of whether an activity is productive or not is whether the end product can be bought or sold, or alternatively, whether the maker of the product intends it for his own direct use and thinks that it will increase his standard of living.

Productive activities involve the manufacture of an article and the growing of a crop: but also include activities which have no tangible end-product. The provision of services such as entertainment, repair work, transport, warehousing and retailing are examples. Each of these activities is productive because the end-product or the intangible service can be bought and sold – it has value to the person who uses it.

Widespread use of capital equipment

The second of the important organisational features of all modern economic systems is their intensive and widespread use of man-made resources, to which we give the name *capital*. The benefits of diverting resources from the production of consumer goods to the production of capital goods have already been referred to in Chapter 2, where two features of the use of capital were emphasized:

The use of capital usually increases the quantity of a good which can be produced and reduces the time in which it can be made.

The use of capital is an indirect way of producing a good. It involves some initial sacrifice in consumption because resources have to be diverted from the production of consumer goods to the production of capital goods.

A decision to use more capital in the production process requires that the long-term benefits of the consequent increase in production have to be balanced against the sacrifice of current production that must be accepted if the additional capital is to be created. Often the long-term gains far outweigh the short-term sacrifices.

Some of the newly-created capital may be required to replace capital equipment which has worn out, become obsolescent, or been used up in other ways. But most of it consists of extra equipment to further increase production. Without buildings, roads, trucks, ports, ships, tools, plant and equipment, we should be reduced to a primitive existence notwithstanding our willingness to engage in specialisation and exchange.

There is a clear link between the productive capacity of different countries and the proportion of production that is devoted to capital formation. Those countries with a high annual production value per head are the ones that devote a relatively high proportion of their output to creating more capital for future production.

Capital formation and affluence

One comparison of capital formation in various countries was carried out in the mid-1960s using 1958 data by Professor Kuznets,[2] the 1976 Nobel Prize winner in economics. The study showed that those countries that had an annual value of production of over US$1000 per head (United States, Canada, Australia, New Zealand and some western European countries) devoted between 22 and 24 per cent of the value of production to capital formation. In contrast, the countries of Africa and Asia (excluding Japan) that had an annual value of production of less than US$200 per head devoted only about 14 per cent to capital formation.

There is a tendency to look at the comparative figures for rich and poor countries and to say that if only the latter were to divert more of their resources into the production of capital goods, their development problems would be overcome, and that the gap between rich and poor would soon be closed. Such a view is a gross over-simplification of both the link between the capital stock and prosperity and also of the whole problem of international poverty.

First, there may be problems in finding projects that use capital profitably. Putting complex equipment in the hands of unskilled operators may be an expensive mistake. Similarly, building factories to be run by untrained managers may result in production failures.

Second, the sacrifices required in deferring consumption are likely to be more painful to the inhabitants of a poor country than a rich country. A poor country will have serious difficulties in committing more than, say, 10 to 15 per cent of production to capital formation because the short-term costs of going without basic consumer goods are great.

Third, the government of a developing country that attempts to find ways of increasing the capital stock more rapidly may make itself unpopular and runs the risk of being overthrown, possibly by force.

4.9

In June 1973 a magazine article described some aspects of life in a Chinese commune.

> It had one tractor station with 16 tractors. Half the cultivated land was ploughed by machinery and the balance by 2800 water buffaloes.[3]

Try to imagine the situation in the commune and suggest possible reasons why the members continued to use buffaloes rather than tractors for the remainder of the ploughing.

Existence of a sophisticated monetary system

The third feature of a modern economic system is the use of money and the development of a variety of financial institutions. Money helps an economic system to function efficiently in two ways:

- it is a means of exchange, making buying and selling easier,
- it makes borrowing and lending easier.

Money as a means of exchange

The processes of exchange would be seriously inhibited without the use of some form of money. Specialisation would not be fully developed, and breakdowns in the exchange system would be more likely.

The alternative to the use of money is a barter 'system'. Barter (direct exchange) only works satisfactorily if two conditions are fulfilled:

- only two persons are involved in the transaction,
- each wants what the other has to offer and they can agree that the items to be exchanged are of equal value.

When these conditions are removed the task of securing a satisfactory exchange is made more difficult.

4.10

Study the following situations:

Situation 1	Wants	Surplus for exchange
Consumer A	a sweater	6 kg bacon
Consumer B	6 kg bacon	a sweater

Situation 2	Wants	Surplus for exchange
Consumer A	a sweater	6 kg bacon
Consumer B	6 kg bacon	4 saucepans
Consumer C	4 saucepans	a sweater

1 How many individual exchange transactions are required in each situation before all consumers are satisfied?
2 What would be the outcome in Situation 2 if Consumer A only had 3 kg of bacon to exchange, although it was generally accepted that a saucepan was worth 2 kilos of bacon?
3 How many individual transactions might be necessary to satisfy everyone if there were five consumers with wants that could not be satisfied directly by concluding an agreement with one of the other consumers? Try drawing up a (Situation 3) table to assist you.

Money as a measure of value

Of course, the great advantage of money is that each consumer/producer can sell his surpluses for the all-purpose asset, money, and then use it to purchase his specific wants. The maximum number of the transactions in which he is involved will be two. In Activity 4.10 (2) the members of the community were satisfied (we will suppose) when a sweater was exchanged or 6 kg bacon, which was exchanged in turn for 4 saucepans. If this set of exchange rates is agreed upon by all consumers, then their prices can be expressed in terms of any one of them. Thus, we can say that the price of a sweater is 6 kg bacon, and likewise that the price of a saucepan is 1.5 kg bacon.

We can even imagine a situation in which bacon came to be used by the community as a form of money. For this to happen it would be necessary for all members of the community to be prepared to accept bacon in exchange for their surpluses even though they had no direct use for it. Clearly, the use of bacon as money is not entirely satisfactory. In the first place, it is not a convenient article to pass round (sweaters or saucepans also have disadvantages). Secondly, the quality of such goods deteriorates with use and age and consequently their intrinsic value deteriorates too.

Money as a measure of value

Communities have developed the use of bank notes, coins and other tokens to overcome the problems associated with the use of consumption goods as money. These modern forms of money provide a simple, convenient and easily recognisable way of exchanging goods and services. Nowadays, the value of materials used in notes and most coins is only a fraction of their face value and this means that there needs to be general acceptance of, and confidence in, the form of money being used. A loss of confidence in the currency will result in people refusing to accept it in payment of debts and in them refusing to hold their wealth in the form of money.

Money as an aid to borrowing and lending

Financial institutions

Accompanying the use of money, has been the development of financial institutions. In a modern society such as the UK, these institutions fulfil a number of diverse roles. The banks – both commercial and the central bank – are responsible for the issuing of notes and coins, the control of the supply of money, and the provision of the day-to-day requirements of the community for exchange, borrowing and lending.

Other financial institutions such as the short-term money market, the life assurance offices, building societies, finance companies, branches of foreign banks and credit unions provide a variety of specialised financial services. These financial institutions make it easier for households and businesses, governments and overseas enterprises, to borrow and lend money to one another.

Households are often able to raise their future living standards if opportunities for saving (deferring consumption) are available. Individuals, by saving, are able to provide for such things as retirement (through life assurance), to finance their children's education and to finance a long holiday. Opportunities for them to advance their present consumption and their current living standards are provided by access to borrowing against the security of future income.

Businesses depend very heavily on funds that the financial institutions make available. The establishment of a business, or its subsequent expansion, may be conditional upon obtaining access to funds because of the considerable time that may be involved before there is a cash flow into the business from the sale of its output. Businesses also add to their profits by lending their surplus funds to financial institutions until they are required.

Capital does not mean money to an economist

The funds provided by financial institutions are often the means whereby a business is able to increase its physical stock of capital. Unfortunately, to the everlasting confusion of students, the term 'capital' is used in several different ways in everyday commercial language. Sometimes it is used to mean a stock of money. Sometimes it refers to the shareholders' funds in a business enterprise. However, as we have seen, an economist reserves the term capital for either:

the physical stock of man-made aids to production, or

the associated monetary measure of that stock.

It is important that you should understand that these are the meanings which are given to the term in this book, unless specifically mentioned otherwise.

The whole set of financial institutions constitutes the money market. Often it is called the capital market, but this latter term is a misnomer because it uses capital in the loose commercial sense of 'money'. The role of the money market is wider than that of providing funds that are used to increase the community's physical stock of man-made resources – its capital. For example, part of the business of finance companies consists of making funds available for the purchase of consumer goods on instalment credit (hire purchase).

Figure 4.5 is a very simple picture of a modern economy and the place of the financial institutions in that economy. In the economy of

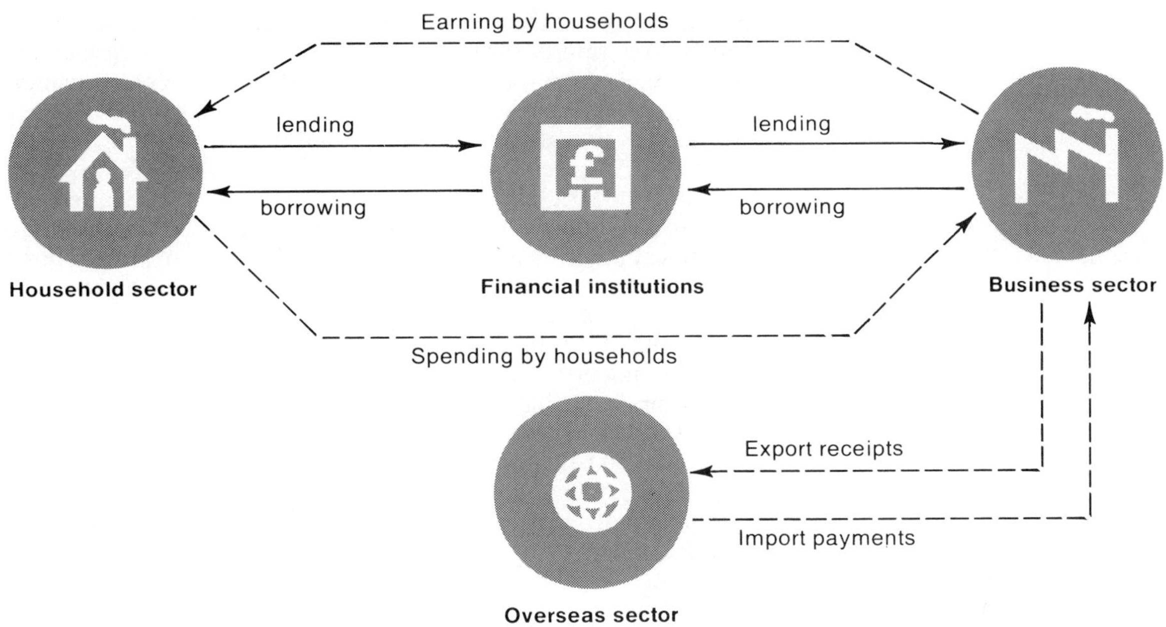

Figure 4.5 Simplified money flows between four parts of a modern economic system

the UK, most of these financial institutions are businesses, which aim to make profits in the same way as other business enterprises. They are thus only distinguished from the 'business' sector of the diagram by the specialised functions they perform. The diagram only shows money flows between the sectors; for simplicity it excludes the reverse flows of goods and services, which balance these money flows. In reality, the relationship between the four sectors is more complicated. Foreign financial institutions have played an important part in the UK's economic development and there are important money flows between them and the UK money market. The links in a poor country between the business sector and foreign businesses and financial institutions are often of critical importance because such countries are unable to finance a sufficiently rapid rate of capital formation from domestic saving and thus have to rely heavily on foreign funds.

The role of government

It has been emphasised that the three principal organisational features of a modern economic system are specialisation, the use of capital and the use of money. Modern economic systems range from a market type with a minimum of government regulation to the command type, the implication being that it is possible for the residents of a country to enjoy high living standards under economic systems in which the role of government differs markedly. If this proposition is accepted then it gives rise, naturally, to the question: Why is it that people become so concerned about the amount of government control and ownership if different systems are capable of yielding equally satisfactory results?

The answer is that it is not true that different systems give equally satisfactory results. They are likely to give quite different results in some important respects. Each system has its particular advantages and disadvantages and whether one is preferred to another will depend upon the objectives that the society is trying to achieve.

Arguments for an uncontrolled market economy

There is a general agreement that there is a part for government to play in a modern economic system. Institutions are required to enforce laws and administer justice. Stable government is recognised as one of the preconditions for the economic development of primitive societies; it is therefore a prerequisite for a modern economic system.

The case for an economic system of the market–system type, operating with a minimum of government intervention, is based on two main arguments:

The price mechanism is said to be very responsive both to changes in wants, and also to conditions under which goods and services are supplied. It therefore allocates resources in an efficient manner.

Market systems tend to reward most generously the powerful economic groups in a community – those who through initiative and enterprise or through past events find themselves in a strong bargaining position when buying or selling.

Arguments against an uncontrolled market economy

To some people these arguments are not persuasive reasons for maintaining an unregulated market system. First, many critics point to the weaknesses of an unregulated price system, arguing that it is more likely to experience fluctuations in the level of business activity, mass unemployment, rapidly rising prices and difficulties in balancing payments and receipts for overseas transactions.

Second, critics of the market system argue that an economic system should distribute goods and services in such a way that individuals from groups other than the economically powerful also share in high living standards. The market system will not generate satisfactory incomes for the aged, the unemployed, families with one parent, the sick and children from poor homes, because they have no marketable resources. Increasingly, it has been accepted that these disadvantaged people should be helped by government and provided with incomes in the form of social services payments financed by tax levies on those able to earn reasonable incomes through the market.

Third, the decisions of private businesses tend to be made on the basis of whether a particular activity will be profitable. Without government planning and control there is no assurance that these decisions will necessarily benefit society as a whole. In an economy without government controls on pollution, or other safeguards on the conservation of resources and the environment, businesses may derive short-term private benefits and also immediate benefits for consumers, but these activities may harm the quality of life of the community at some later period.

If profit is the sole determinant of whether a business is to provide a service, there is the possibility either that the service will not be provided at all or that it may be of poor quality. In the UK, governments have been conscious of this danger and have taken control of certain essential services such as electricity supply, telecommunications, railways and broadcasting.

Command economies – pros and cons

In contrast, the principal advantage of a command, or centrally planned economy is that such a system is well suited to determine and to achieve objectives and priorities. In most command economies where the notion of public profit replaces that of private profit, the central planning staff are able to establish planning targets and to issue the directives they believe necessary to achieve these objectives. Particular industries can be fostered directly through priority grants and the direction and training of the required skilled manpower.

The command economy is in a much better position than an unregulated market economy to deal with problems such as pollution, the building of transport systems and town development. The superiority of command systems in achieving priority targets is confirmed by the practice of converting market economies to much more highly planned economies in times of war and national emergency, and the use made of direct planning by developing countries.

The disadvantages of command systems are precisely those characteristics that are the principal advantages of a market system. Command systems are not nearly as good at adjusting to changing conditions. A command economy has no equivalent to the price signals that consumers and producers note, and respond to, in a market economy. Instead, formal planning decisions are required to change production, and delays and wastage may result from these processes. Often stressed, too, is the loss of individual freedom of action which goes with government planning and control.

Figures 4.6 and 4.7 show the principal monetary flows in a market economy in which there is some government regulation and the principal money flows in a command economy. The market economy, Figure 4.6, differs from Figure 4.5 only by the inclusion of a government sector and the inclusion of such money flows as taxes raised by the government, and subsidies and other payments made by the government.

The illustration of a command, or centrally planned, economy emphasises not so much the planning aspect of government but the ownership by the government (the state) of the means of production and the financial institutions. The government sector is shown as including the business sector and the financial institutions. Figure 4.6 can be considered to be a simple representation of the main money flows in the economic system of the UK, whereas Figure 4.7 is more representative of the economic system of the Soviet Union or Romania. Notice that in Figure 4.7 the profits of the state businesses flow to the state. In a market system, profits are the traditional rewards for enterprise and risk-taking.

In Chapter 3 it was emphasised that it is difficult to make a clear distinction between market and command economic systems. It was said, on the one hand, that there is a greater or lesser degree of government intervention, regulation, ownership and control in all market economies. In some, such as Sweden, there is a very great degree of government planning and control.

On the other hand, in many of the planned economies, the market forces are allowed to play a part in the organisation of production. In Russia, agricultural production (particularly horticulture) is carried out by a private enterprise sector as well as the public sector.

The extreme example of the use of market forces by a socialist economy is that of Yugoslavia, where attempts to encourage individual initiative and to reward effort have led to the establishment of worker-controlled factories that have considerable individual autonomy. Instead of central planning, these factories are intended to organise their production plans in response to market forces. Unfortunately, to date, the Yugoslav experiment has not been an unqualified success. Rapidly rising prices and a high rate of unemployment suggest that perhaps the

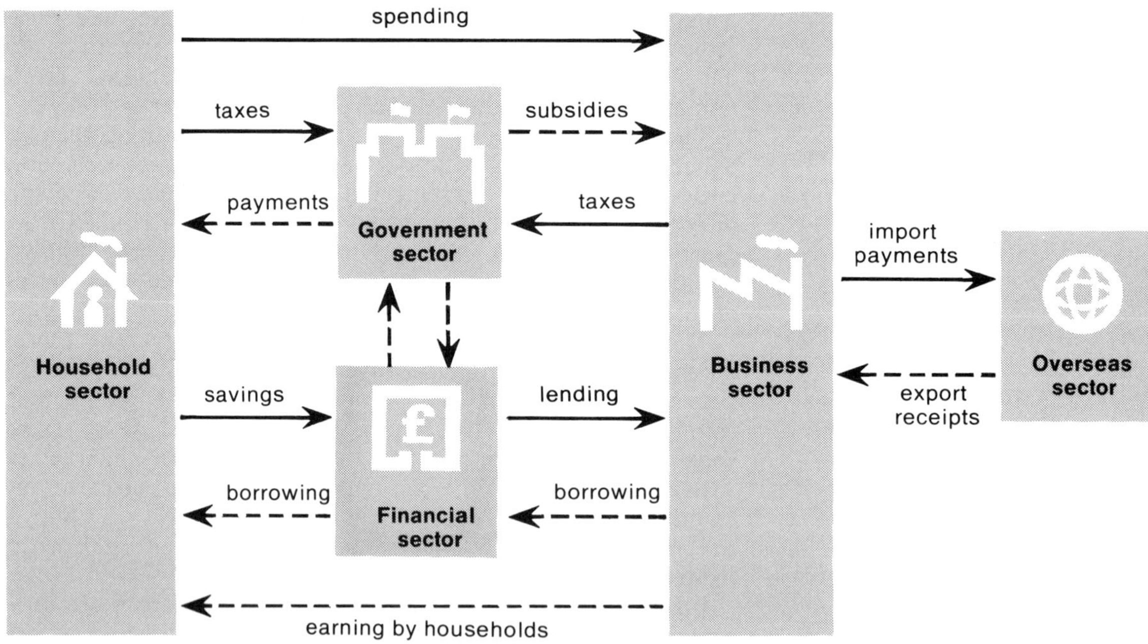

Figure 4.6 Market economy

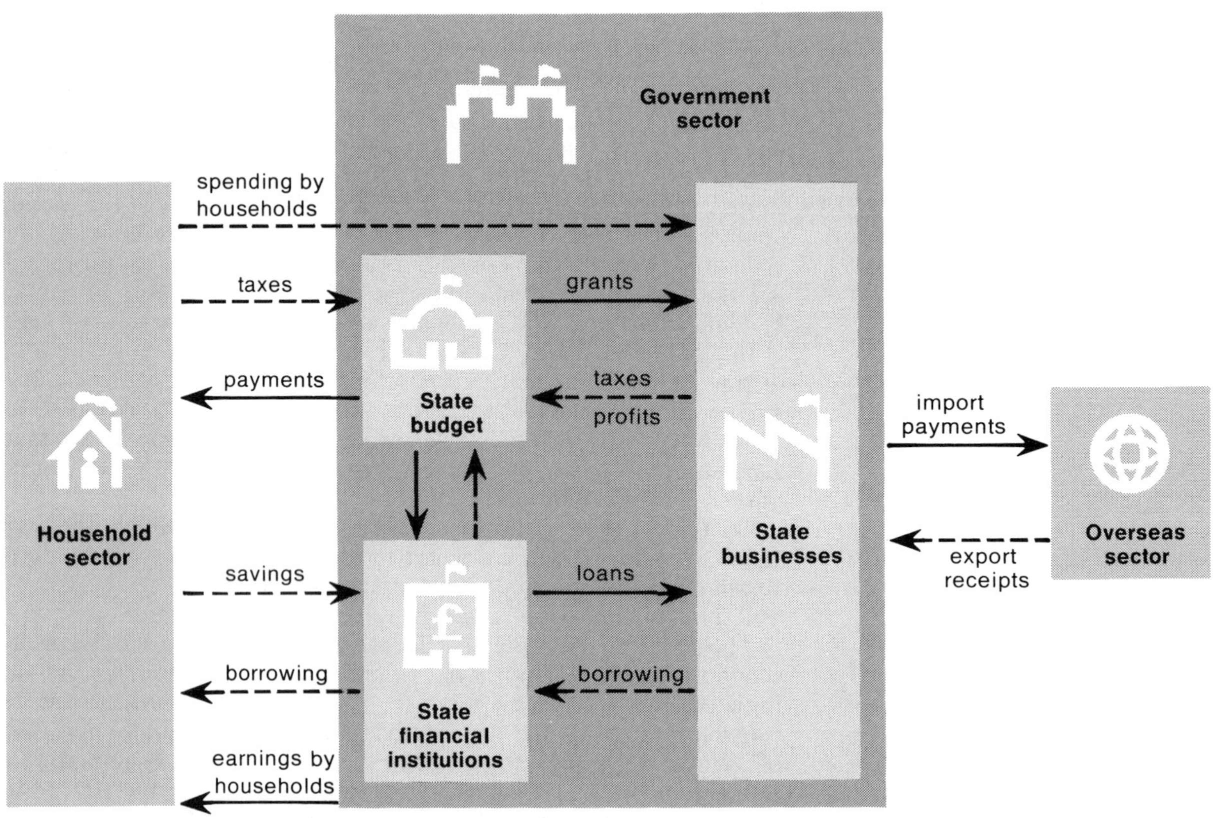

Figure 4.7 Command (centrally planned) economy

Yugoslavs have not yet managed to achieve the perfect balance between a market and a command system.

4.11

Imagine a situation in which the services of the Post Office, British Rail and British Gas were provided by private enterprise and that the business or businesses concerned were determined to maximise their profits. How might the prices and quality of these differ from those provided at present? Is there anything to suggest that UK citizens would be disadvantaged if these services were provided by private businesses?

4.12

Attempt to draw a diagram of a centrally planned economy, similar to Figure 4.7 but with some of the business enterprises outside the control or ownership of the government sector.

4.13

The economic system of the UK has been described as a modern, government-regulated market system. It has been called modern because it has a high degree of specialisation, makes intensive use of capital and has developed a sophisticated monetary system. Market forces play an important part in solving the economic problems in the UK, but this mechanism's workings are also influenced to a considerable extent by government regulation and control at all levels. Of particular importance is the government's role in working to achieve the economic objectives of full employment, price stability, economic growth, a satisfactory overseas payments position and a more equitable distribution of income between groups in the community. As a result there is now much more government regulation and control in the UK, and in most other western industrial countries than there was fifty years ago. Can it be inferred from this that the command system is superior to the market system? Explain your conclusions as fully as possible.

Notes

1 The nineteenth-century economist David Ricardo used a model comprising two countries, England and Portugal, and two products, cloth and wine. He then demonstrated that England could benefit by specialising in exporting cloth if it held a comparative advantage in that product. D Ricardo 1951 *On the Principles of Political Economy and Taxation* ed. P Sraffa. Cambridge University Press, ch 7.

2 S Kuznets 1966 *Modern Economic Growth Rate, Structure and Spread.* Yale University Press, New Haven, pp 426–7.

3 Ralph Wragg 1973 'China Today'. *Woman's Day*, Melbourne, 4 June, p 7.

Stage two

Economics in Action

Chapter 5

Consumption

Consumption was defined in Chapter 4 as the utilising of goods and services for the satisfaction of wants rather than for the purpose of making profits. *Consumption expenditure* is then expenditure on goods and services incurred to satisfy wants. The distinction between expenditure incurred to satisfy wants and that incurred to increase profits provides a benchmark for separating consumption and investment expenditure. We saw in Chapter 4 that investment expenditure leads to an increase in the stock of capital, and so enhances productive capacity. An increasing level of consumption expenditure is evidence that more goods and services are being purchased by a country's residents. We have already (in Chapter 2) pointed to the need for caution in equating increased material living standards with greater general welfare, and in Chapter 24 we will make some further qualifications. But in broad terms, increased consumption expenditure is prima facie evidence of increased welfare.

Problems of measurement

Before consumption can be measured, a country's economists and statisticians need to adopt a usable definition of consumption expenditure. The national income and expenditure accounts published in the form of the *National Income Blue Book* (*NIBB*) contain a measure of consumption by households called 'consumers' expenditure'. The inclusion of various expenditures in this aggregate is made on the basis of a number of principles:

1 An expenditure on 'newly produced' final goods or services is considered to be consumption if it satisfies personal wants. If the expenditure is of a capital nature (that is, produces a continuing stream of productive services), it is classified as investment. The critical question asked about any purchase is not 'What is the good that has been purchased?' but 'Who has bought it and what was their purpose in buying it?' If a family buys an estate car for personal transport, the statistician treats this as consumption expenditure, but if a company purchases an identical vehicle for a sales representative to use on the job the purchase is classed as investment expenditure.

2 Consumption is sometimes defined as 'the purchase of goods for immediate use'. This definition has the weakness that many of the goods purchased are used, and satisfy wants, over a longer period than the immediate period. Consumer durables such as television sets, washing machines and furniture are utilised over a number of years, as are motor vehicles, but because the services they yield satisfy personal wants, they are included as consumption in the National Income Accounts.

3 An important exception to the list of new goods and services treated as consumption is purchases of new houses and flats. Expenditure on them is classed as investment on the grounds that they constitute an

increase in the country's capital stock. The existing stock of houses provides a continuous flow of shelter, which is one of man's most basic needs. The value of this shelter is included as current consumption. The statistican calculates the total rents paid by tenants to landlords, and then adds an 'imputed rent' to take account of all the owner-occupied houses. The imputation is a calculation of what the rent would have been if the owner were really a tenant paying rent to a landlord. By this device, all houses are treated as if they were part of the capital stock producing a flow of services – shelter – for those who wanted it. Imputed values are also calculated for food produced and consumed on farms (but not for food grown in suburban gardens).

5.1

Which of the following items can be classed as consumption expenditure?
purchase of meat by a housewife,
purchase of a copying machine by a business,
purchase of animal feed by a circus,
taking a 'go now, pay later' holiday,
purchase of feed for cows on a farm,
use of home-grown feed by a farmer to fatten his own cows,
purchase of a washing-machine by a household on instalment credit,
taking out fire insurance on a private house.

5.2

Imagine you were the statistician who had the responsibility for deciding whether either (1) life insurance, or (2) purchases of old (as distinct from new) houses should be treated as consumption expenditure. What decision would you make about each item, and why?

Aggregate private consumption expenditure in the UK in 1978 is shown in Table 5.1.

The largest items of consumer spending are food (over 18 per cent) and housing (14 per cent). Of the 9 per cent spent on durable goods, a significant proportion of this is spending on motor vehicles. Together with running costs of motor vehicles, shown as a separate item of 5 per cent, this amounts to an important element of private spending.

Consumers' expenditure is the largest component in the total value of goods and services purchased by UK residents in a given period. The other forms of expenditure are:

1 government final consumption (such as on the provision of education and defence) including spending by local authorities as well as central government;

2 gross fixed investment (such as the construction of factories, plant, machines, roads and so on) by private firms, nationalised industries or by the government;

3 value of increase in stocks (covering changes in the value of stocks and work in progress held by firms).

The total of those forms of expenditure upon final goods and services by UK households, government and businesses is called the total domestic expenditure. In 1978 total domestic expenditure was £159 billion. Details of the main types and percentage composition of total domestic expenditure are shown in Figure 5.1.

Item	Total £ million	Total per cent
Food	17 952	18.7
Alcoholic drinks	7 471	7.8
Tobacco	3 933	4.1
Housing	13 855	14.4
Fuel and light	4 650	4.8
Clothing	7 366	7.7
Durable goods	8 823	9.2
Other household goods	2 435	2.5
Books, newspapers and magazines	1 388	1.4
Chemists' goods	1 478	1.5
Miscellaneous goods	4 608	4.8
Running costs of motor vehicles	5 227	5.4
Travel	3 207	3.3
Communications	1 410	1.5
Entertainment and recreational services	1 952	2.0
Catering (meals and accommodation)	4 233	4.4
Insurance	1 387	1.4
Other services etc	6 091	6.3
Expenditure overseas, less expenditure by foreign tourists in the UK	−1 380	−1.4
	96 086	

Note: Components do not add precisely because of rounding.

Table 5.1 Consumers' expenditure at current prices, UK 1978

Source: *Annual Abstract of Statistics 1980*, HMSO

Dangers of double-counting

Figure 5.1 shows the purchases of households, private businesses and the government sector on *final* goods and services. This term 'final' is important. Its use indicates that amounts paid for raw materials, or semi-finished products, or for wages are excluded. This is essential if double counting of these expenditure items is to be avoided. Consider an enterprise assembling washing machines. When it sells the final product, it charges the consumer a price that covers the cost of all materials including time switches made by a components manufacturer. If both the final sale of the machine to the consumer and the original purchase of the switches by the assembler are counted, the cost of the switch will have been counted twice – once as the product of the manufacturer and again as if it were also the product of the assembler.

Changes in stocks

One exception to this general rule about excluding purchases of semi-finished products is that net increases in stocks during the accounting period are included. This is quite consistent because such stocks are not used in final products *in the period* and hence are not counted more than once.

The term 'government final consumption expenditure' is somewhat misleading because the government current expenditure is rather different from expenditures by persons seeking to satisfy wants. Economists therefore restrict the term 'consumption' to 'private final consumption' and place all government expenditure in a separate

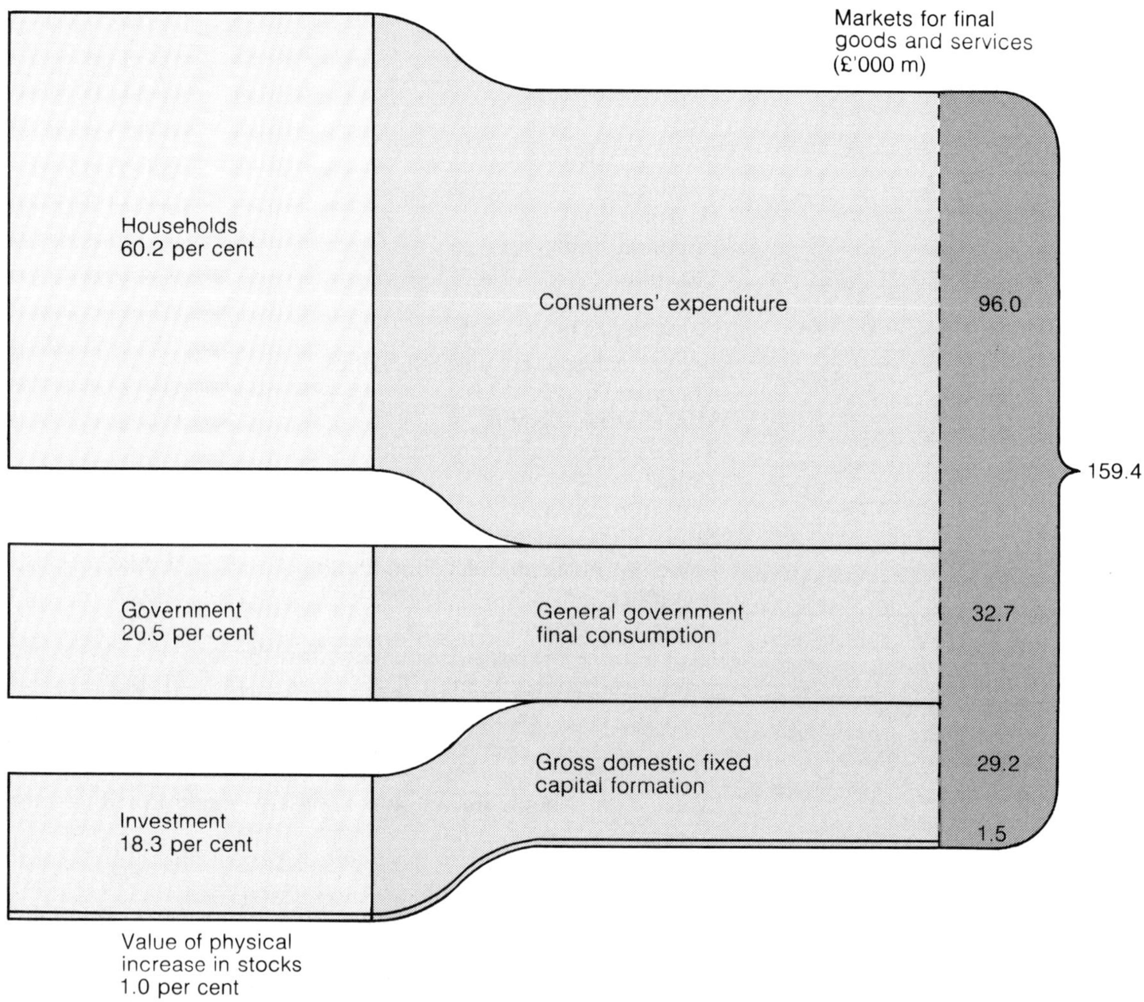

Figure 5.1 Components of total domestic expenditure, UK, 1978

Government expenditure is excluded from consumption

category. They then investigate the relationships between the level of economic activity and the various aggregates, consumption, government expenditure and private investment. Later, we shall examine the relationship between consumption and the level of economic activity and to do this it is essential that consumption by households is not confused with government expenditure.

On some occasions it may be necessary to distinguish between government current expenditure and government capital formation. In Figure 5.1 gross domestic fixed capital formation amounted to 18.3 per cent of total domestic expenditure in 1978. This included expenditure on all final products of a capital nature: the purchase of machines, factories, offices, vehicles and equipment by businesses. It also included the capital expenditure by government and public enterprises on such things as equipment, roads, hospitals and other buildings. When considering the additions to the nation's capital stock, we are able to distinguish between that following from government capital expenditure and that from private gross capital formation.

Definition of 'gross'

The word 'gross' in the terms 'gross national product' and 'gross capital formation' calls for an explanation. It indicates that the aggregate makes no allowance for the depreciation of capital equipment during the period. (We discussed this earlier on page 53). Existing capital equipment is constantly wearing out and being replaced. The actual net increase in a country's stock of capital could be determined by calculating both the increases in the capital stock and the reductions caused by the wearing out of old capital. An alternative approach would be to estimate the amount of capital formation required to maintain the capital stock and to deduct this amount from the gross capital formation.

Depreciation

Depreciation allowances can only be estimates of the amounts required to maintain capital intact. They are based on the assumption that a particular piece of capital will decline in value each year, by a given percentage of its original cost (or sometimes in relation to its replacement cost). If these depreciation estimates were accurate measures of the amounts needed to maintain capital intact, they would enable statisticians to calculate the actual fixed capital formation occurring in any year. In practice, the accurate measurement of depreciation would pose enormous problems and for this reason no great accuracy can be assumed for the aggregate 'net national product' where:

Net national product = gross national product – depreciation

A further reason for devoting more attention to gross national product than to net national product is that changes in the former aggregate are more directly linked to changes in the level of employment and production. (These relationships are discussed in Chapter 15.)

Economists are interested in what has happened to the level of aggregate consumption expenditure in the UK in recent years. It is by far the largest component of expenditure, and significant changes in consumption must have important influences on the operation of the economy as well as having an important bearing on the issue of whether citizens are becoming better off.

Figure 5.2 shows how final consumers' expenditure has increased from 1970 to 1980, from about £31 000 m to £133 000 m. During the period, the share of consumers' expenditure of total domestic expenditure was around 59 to 63 per cent. The figure also shows that at current prices consumption expenditure increased rapidly during the 1970s. The annual rate of increase was on average between 14 and 16 per cent, but the greater part of this increase in expenditure was the result of the rapid rise in prices at that time.

Real consumption

To measure *real* consumption, that is, the quantity of goods and services consumed, consumption is also measured at average (or constant) prices. The quantities purchased in any year are valued at the prices ruling in a selected year. Such a device helps to eliminate the effects of inflation.

Figure 5.2 shows consumers' expenditure at average prices, in addition to the information relating to market prices. The selected year is 1975. Aggregate consumption for each of the years 1970 to 1980 is then calculated on the basis that 1975 prices prevailed for the entire period. Figure 5.2 shows that consumption at constant prices did not rise steadily over the period nor at the same rate as expenditure at market prices. From 1973 to 1977 expenditure at 1975 prices actually declined to the 1972 level before starting to rise again. It is not apparent from the graph of current market prices that this had occurred. The

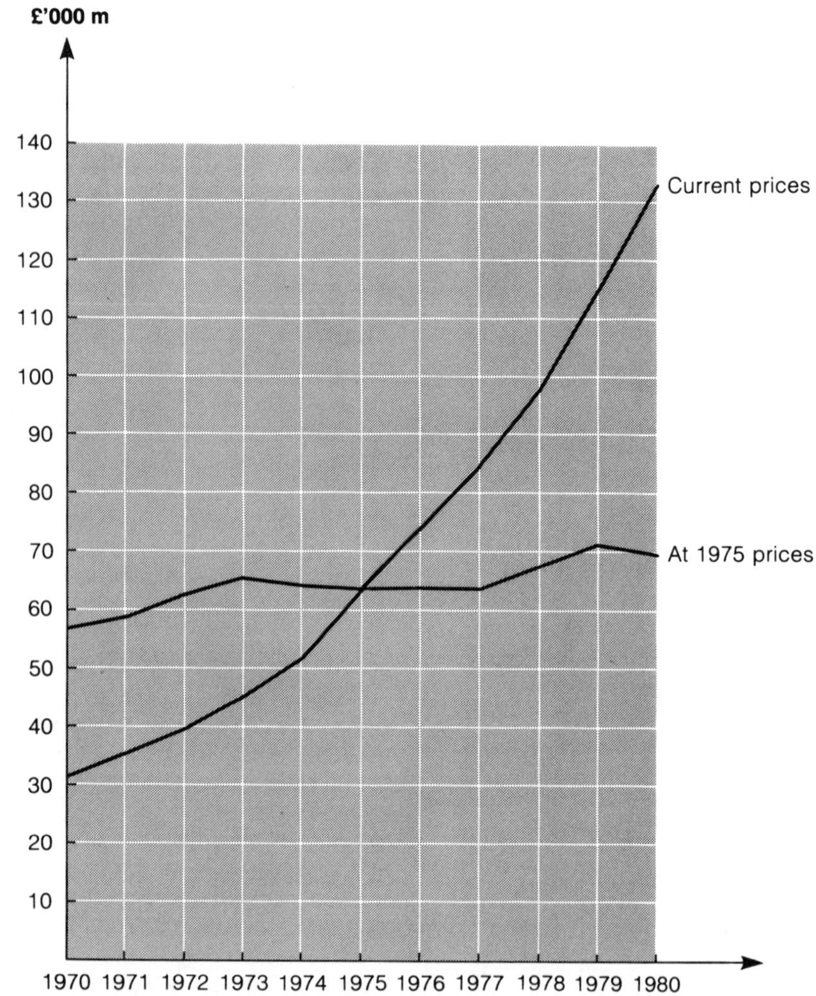

Figure 5.2 Consumers' expenditure in the UK at current prices and at 1975 prices, 1970–80

Source: Annual Abstract of Statistics 1982, Tables 14.12, 14.14, HMSO

annual rate of increase in consumption therefore is much exaggerated in money terms compared with the actual change in real terms. Note that the selection of 1975 as the base year for constant prices means that total consumption for that year is the same whether expressed in market or constant prices.

Consumption expenditure at average or constant prices indicates whether consumption of the total physical quantity of goods and services is increasing. It has several shortcomings as a measure of whether the living standards are increasing. Firstly, it does not take into account changes in the size of population. The more who share a given quantity, the smaller is the amount available for each individual.

Consumption per head as an indicator of changes in consumption

Secondly, it does not allow for changes in the distribution of income. Consumption expenditure per head may be rising, but some groups may be experiencing falling living standards whilst others are enjoying much greater than average increases.

5.3

Suppose that you read the following correspondence in your daily newspaper. How would you write to the Editor in an attempt to resolve the issue?

> Sir,
> I was amazed to read a report in your paper that consumer spending has risen by 20 per cent in the last year. As a retired pensioner I can tell you that it's just not true. I have a real struggle these days with the prices going up all the time. I'm certainly no better off than I was last year, or even five years ago.
>
> *Worried Pensioner*
>
> (The following day)
> Sir,
> I am sure that we all sympathize with the worried pensioner. It is misleading to say consumption is rising, despite the figures quoted in your initial report. My investigations show that in the last ten years the proportion of our national income that is spent by consumers has fallen. The official statistics also show that there has been a big increase in spending by government and private businesses. And that in my opinion is the trouble. We need to reduce private and government capital formation so that consumption can increase again. After all consumption is the purpose of economic activity.
>
> *Budding Economist*

5.4

What conclusions might reasonably be drawn about economic conditions in countries where:
(a) consumption expenditure at market prices is rising at a slower rate than consumption expenditure at constant prices;
(b) consumption expenditure at market and constant prices is falling but consumption expenditure per head is rising;
(c) consumption expenditure is falling both absolutely and relative to gross national expenditure;
(d) gross national expenditure at market prices is rising more slowly than the general level of prices.

	1969	1970	1971	1972	1973	1974	1975	1976	1977	1978	1979
Number of households supplying data	7008	6393	7239	7017	7126	6695	7203	7203	7198	7001	6777
	Percentage										
Car	51.2	51.6	51.2	53.3	53.9	55.7	57.0	55.2	57.2	57.6	57.9
One	45.1	44.6	44.3	45.3	45.1	45.3	46.4	44.5	46.2	45.2	44.3
Two	5.7	6.2	6.2	7.4	8.0	9.3	9.6	9.6	9.7	10.9	11.7
Three or more	0.4	0.8	0.7	0.6	0.8	1.1	1.0	1.1	1.3	1.5	1.9
Central heating, full or partial	25.1	29.6	32.2	37.4	38.5	43.0	46.7	47.1	50.8	53.8	55.0
Washing machine	62.7	64.9	64.3	65.5	66.6	68.9	71.9	72.3	74.6	75.0	76.6
Refrigerator	60.3	65.6	68.8	74.2	77.6	81.8	85.3	88.1	89.9	91.6	92.9
Television	91.2	91.4	91.4	93.2	93.4	94.0	94.8	95.6	96.0	95.6	95.8
Telephone	32.1	35.0	37.8	42.1	43.4	49.5	51.9	52.6	56.8	62.0	67.2

Information derived from Family Expenditure Survey.

Table 5.2 Availability in households of certain durable goods, UK 1969–79

Source: *Annual Abstract of Statistics 1982*, HMSO

5.5

From the data in Table 5.2:
1 Comment on the changing standards of living implied by the statistics.
2 How consistent are these conclusions with the information presented in Figure 5.2 and in Table 5.2?
3 Is it possible to draw conclusions about the level of consumption expenditure, standards of living and general economic conditions, from information on the ownership of consumer durables? What other forms of data would you require to make firmer conclusions on these matters?

	Consumption expenditure at current prices (£ million)	% increase on previous year	Consumption expenditure at (1975) constant prices (£ million)	% increase on previous year	Consumption expenditure at constant (1975) prices per head (£)	% increase on previous year
1974	52 088	14.5	64 418	−2.3	1 151	−2.2
1975	63 704	22.3	63 704	−1.1	1 139	−1.0
1976	73 765	15.8	63 852	+0.2	1 142	+0.3
1977	84 132	14.1	63 313	−0.8	1 133	−0.8
1978	96 086	14.2	66 728	+5.4	1 195	+5.5

Table 5.3. Consumption expenditure at current prices, at constant prices and at constant prices per head, UK 1974–78.

Source: Annual Abstract of Statistics 1980, Table 14, HMSO

5.6

1 From the figures shown in Table 5.3 what conclusions can reasonably be drawn about economic conditions in the UK during the period 1974 to 1978?
2 Obtain similar information for more recent years. What changes in the situation can you infer from these figures?

The level of aggregate consumption

The total amount that a country's residents will be prepared to spend on consumption during any given period depends on a number of influences. Of these the most important appear to be:

the level of real disposable income,
the level of savings relative to expected future needs.

Consumption and the level of real disposable income

The relationship between aggregate consumption and aggregate real disposable income can be understood more easily by considering the link between the income and consumption of a single household. The term *real disposable income* needs an explanation. Disposable income is simply the amount left at a household's disposal to spend or to save after providing for income tax and other direct taxes.[1]

Gross income – direct taxes = disposable income

The amount that the household spends is likely to be more closely related to its disposable income than to its gross income, for an increase in gross income may be offset by an increase in tax payments. The emphasis on *real* disposable *income* is also important because an increase in a household's actual disposable income may bring a much smaller increase in the household's purchasing power if prices are rising. Such a situation is illustrated in Table 5.4. In the second year the household's disposable income was 25 per cent greater than in Year 1. However, prices of goods and services rose during that period by 10 per cent. As a result, the real disposable income, which measures the household's capacity to purchase quantities of goods and services, increased to only £2273. The increase in income effectively allowed it to increase its purchases by a maximum of about 13.5 per cent.

Year	Actual disposable income (£)	Price index	Method		Real disposable income (£)
Year 1	2000	100	2000 × 100/100	=	2000
Year 2	2500	110	2500 × 100/100	=	2273

Table 5.4 Actual and real disposable income

The economist is interested in the relationship between the household's capacity to purchase quantities of goods and services (its real disposable income) and its willingness to do so (its real consumption expenditure). Figure 5.3 depicts the likely relationship between the two over a short time period. The vertical axis measures real consumption expenditure and the horizontal axis measures the household's real disposable income. The 45° line is often used in diagrams showing the relationship between income and expenditure. Its significance lies in the fact that when both axes are measured on the same scale then all points along the 45° line have the same value on both axes. The 'propensity to consume' line indicates the amount being spent on consumption at each level of real disposable income. At point F, £1800, out of a real disposable income of £2000, is devoted to consumption expenditure. At G, £2200 out of £2500 goes on consumption. The line joining these points is called the propensity to consume line and the term 'propensity' simply refers to the proportion of disposable income that the household is prepared to spend. The *average propensity to consume* is calculated by dividing real consumption expenditure at any point on the line by real disposable income. Thus, at point F, average propensity to consume is 1800/2000 = 0.9. Likewise at G, average propensity to consume is 2200/2500 = 0.88.

Propensity to consume

Another important notion, from the economist's standpoint, is the *marginal propensity to consume*, which measures that proportion of each *extra* pound of disposable income going on consumption. The marginal propensity to consume is measured by the slope of the propensity to consume line in Figure 5.3. The increase in real disposable income, between F and G, is £500 (from £2000 to £2500) and this leads to an

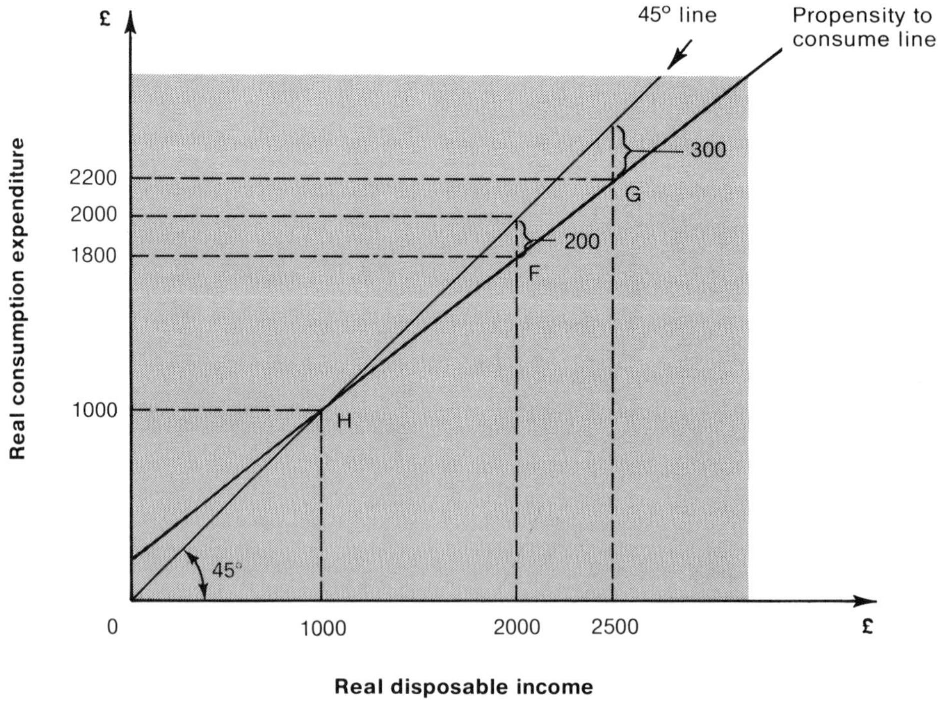

Figure 5.3 The household's short-run consumption/income relationship

increase in consumption of £400 (from £1800 to £2200). The marginal propensity to consume is calculated as:

$$\frac{\text{Increase in consumption}}{\text{Increase in disposable income}} = \frac{2200 - 1800}{2500 - 2000} = \frac{400}{500} = 0.8$$

This figure indicates that there is a positive relationship between consumption and real disposable income. As the latter increases, so real consumption increases. In fact, 80 per cent of each additional pound goes on consumption. Point H on the propensity to consume line, and the section of the line to the left of that point, call for some comment. At H both income and consumption are £1000, whilst to the left of H consumption appears to exceed income. The explanation of this lies in recalling that the diagram relates to the household's activities over a short period of time. If the household's income fell below a certain level, then in the short term it might very well be prepared to maintain a level of consumption expenditure over and above the income it received. This could be done by drawing on savings, but clearly such a practice could not go on indefinitely; consumption plans would have to be adjusted ultimately.

Propensity to save

The relationship between the 45° line and the propensity to consume line gives, therefore, an indication of what proportion of disposable income the household is saving. Since all disposable income is either spent or saved, it follows that the vertical distance between the 45° line and the propensity to consume line measures the amount of saving occurring at any level of disposable income. The term *marginal propensity to save* refers to the proportion saved of each extra pound of disposable income. Between F and G saving increases from £200 to £300; £100 of the extra £500 is saved,[2] so the marginal propensity to save is 100/500 = 0.2.

Although this discussion of the relationship between disposable income and consumption expenditure has been based on the likely actions and attitudes of a single household, statistical studies show that the relationship between aggregate real disposable income and aggregate real consumption expenditure takes a similar form. This should hardly come as a surprise because if the great majority of households behave in a similar way to the individual household in Figure 5.3 then we should expect to find aggregate consumption rising when aggregate disposable income increases. Indeed, we should expect the aggregate propensity to consume line to look like Figure 5.3.

Consumption and the level of savings

The household's consumption expenditure may also be influenced by reconsideration of whether its accumulated savings are adequate. Many households keep part of their wealth in the form of money or liquid assets. They do so to ensure that they are able to pay their way even if their income declines, so that they can meet unexpected expenses (such as a major car repair) and so that they can take the opportunity of securing bargains.

The amount that a particular household keeps in these liquid reserves, for such purposes, will be influenced in part by the size of its disposable income. The larger the income, the larger the amount that a household is likely to save in any given period. But the amount it saves, and hence the amount it consumes, will also be influenced by its assessment of the future. If it believes that in the future there is a greater chance of its income ceasing, or if it believes it likely that it will face heavier expenses, then it may decide that accumulated savings are inadequate and that it should save a higher proportion of its income. For example, the household may revise its expectations during a period of worsening unemployment and decide to save more in case members of the household become unemployed in the future.

During the 1970s, the savings ratio in the UK increased from less than 10 per cent to 15 per cent by 1978. Over the same time period, both the rate of inflation and the level of unemployment were rising.

Savings ratio is that proportion of disposable income which is saved. There is a strong suggestion here that the savings plans of householders were being revised. This was possibly due to the fear of unemployment and to the fact that, with inflation eroding the real value of savings, households were increasing their savings to try and maintain their real value.

Figure 5.4 illustrates this by depicting the effect of a radical revision of consumption following a change in expectations. Suppose, in the first instance, that propensity to consume line 1 operates. Aggregate real disposable income is £20 000 million. Aggregate consumption is shown by F and savings by S_1. Suppose now, that *uncertainty* about the future leads to a decision to increase savings by FG. This can only take place at the expense of consumption and the propensity to consume line is shifted downwards. Consumption is now shown by G and savings by S_2. The relationship between consumption and disposable income is then shown by propensity to consume line 2. Consumption is reduced for *all* levels of real disposable income. Clearly, when talking about changes in consumption expenditure it is important to distinguish between movements along the propensity to consume line caused by changes in aggregate disposable income and changes in the

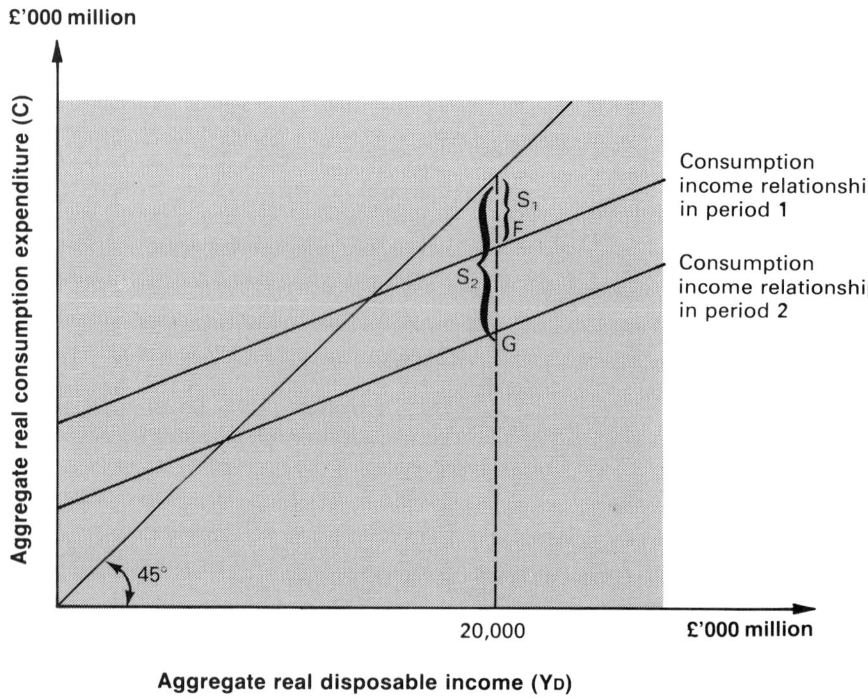

Figure 5.4 Effect of an increase in savings on the consumption/income relationship

position of the whole curve brought about by other influences such as a revised assessment of the adequacy of existing accumulated savings. In the second half of the 1970s consumers have been urged to spend more in an endeavour to produce an upwards shift in the propensity to consume line. The consequences of spending a high proportion of real disposable income on the level of economic activity are discussed in detail in Chapter 15, but it can be easily seen that it would stimulate production to meet the greater spending.

Many other influences affect the level of consumption. One of these is inflation. Another is the distribution of income. The effects of these on aggregate consumption are considered in exercises 5.8 and 5.9.

5.7 The following data relates to a single household:

Personal consumption per year (£)	Disposable income per year (£)
6150	6000
6375	6300
6600	6600
6825	6900
7050	7200
7275	7500
7500	7800
7725	8100
7950	8400
8175	8700
8400	9000

1 Draw a graph showing the consumption/disposable income relationship (the propensity to consume line) and mark in the 45° line.
2 Calculate the average and the marginal propensity to consume at income £7500.
3 How does the relationship between the average propensity to consume and the marginal propensity to consume vary between different levels of disposable income?

5.8

Consumption spending and inflation
It is very difficult to assess the likely effect of inflation on real aggregate consumption; that is, we are not really sure how the propensity to consume line will be shifted.
Among the suggestions that have been made are:
1 If households expect prices to rise rapidly they will buy goods now rather than later when they are more expensive.
2 During inflationary periods the value of savings is reduced. Consequently householders may decide they want to save more to protect themselves.
3 Rapid inflation may be accompanied by fears that there will be a serious reduction in business activity. This fear for the future will accelerate the rate of saving.
4 The income consumption relationship is expressed in real terms already. Therefore the rate of inflation will have no effect on the level of consumption.

Which, if any, of these propositions about inflation do you think is plausible? What effect do you think will expectations about the future rate of inflation have on the level of aggregate consumption?

5.9

Another influence which is said to affect the level of consumption is the distribution of income in a society. It is known that households on low incomes spend a higher proportion of their incomes than the more wealthy households. Hence a transfer of income from rich to poor, so that there is a more equal distribution of income, will lead to an increase in the proportion of aggregate income that is spent.

The following information relates to an imaginary under-developed country. Until 1979 the country, which based its economy on the export of petroleum, was ruled by its traditional monarch with the income from exports going to a small privileged class. In 1979 a popular uprising occurred and a government dedicated to improving the lot of the masses came to power. The population of the country was 1 000 000 before and after the bloodless coup. Other information relating to the distribution of income and the propensity of residents to consume is as follows:

Percentage of population earning	Before coup	After coup	Average propensity to consume
\$100	80	25	1.0
\$1000	19	75	0.8
\$50 000	1	nil	0.3

1 Calculate the percentage of aggregate income earned by each group before and after the coup.
2 Calculate aggregate consumption and the average propensity to consume in the country before and after the coup.
3 What effect did the revolution have on the level of saving within the country?
4 Draw a diagram showing the old and the new relationships between aggregate consumption and aggregate real disposable income.

5.10

	Consumption (constant prices)	Personal disposable income (constant prices)
1968	55 880	60 419
1969	56 169	61 005
1970	57 676	63 352
1971	59 557	64 585
1972	62 999	69 597
1973	65 911	74 069
1974	64 418	75 051
1975	63 704	74 707
1976	63 852	74 773
1977	63 313	73 560
1978	66 728	78 682
1979	70 088	83 728
1980	69 778	84 867

Table 5.5. Consumption expenditure and disposable income in the United Kingdom 1968 to 1980 (£m at 1975 prices)

Source: adapted from *Annual Abstract of Statistics, 1980 and 1982*, HMSO

1 Plot the information from Table 5.5 on a graph.
2 Calculate the average propensity to consume for 1968, 1973 and 1978. What trend if any can you identify?
3 Extend the table to incorporate the most recent data and calculate the average propensity to consume for the latest year.

Income elasticity of demand

Businesses planning future production find it useful to have indicators of the quantities of various products consumers are likely to purchase as incomes increase. Economists have attempted to provide such information by measuring the way in which households change their consumption of particular goods in response to income changes. This measure is called the *income elasticity of demand*.

Income elasticity of demand can be expressed in two ways:

1 $$\text{Income elasticity of demand} = \frac{\text{percentage change in quantity purchased}}{\text{percentage change in income}}$$

2 $$\text{Income elasticity of demand} = \frac{\text{change in quantity purchased}}{\text{original quantity purchased}} \div \frac{\text{change in income}}{\text{original income}}$$

The two formulations amount to the same thing. Using method 1, if the consumer's income rises from £80 per week to £100 (an increase of 25 per cent) and his purchases of milk rise from 10 litres to 11 litres (an increase of 10 per cent) the income elasticity of demand for milk will be

10/25 = 0.4. Alternatively, using formulation 2, income elasticity

$$= \frac{1 \text{ litre}}{10 \text{ litres}} \div \frac{£20}{£80} = 0.4.$$

For many food products and other basic items, the income elasticity of demand is less than one. This means that a given percentage increase in income will result in a smaller percentage increase in the quantity of the good purchased. The demand for such goods with respect to income is said to be *inelastic*. If, on the other hand, an increase in income leads to a larger percentage increase in the quantity purchased, the demand for the good with respect to income is said to be *elastic*. If the consumer's income and the quantity of a good purchased increase by the same percentage, the result is an income elasticity of 1 or unity; demand is then neither elastic nor inelastic.

The terms 'elastic' or 'inelastic' can also be used when comparing the income elasticity of demand for different goods. Thus, if the income elasticity for cabbages is 0.4 and for tomatoes 0.7, we can say that demand for tomatoes is *relatively elastic* even though it is inelastic in *absolute* terms.

It is also conceivable that an increase in income might lead to an absolute decline in purchases of a certain good, or for a fall in income to lead to an increase in purchases. Such goods are said to have a *negative income elasticity*. For example, suppose a 5 per cent increase in income led to a 20 per cent fall in purchases of a good. Then:

$$\left(\frac{\text{change in purchases}}{\text{original purchase}}\right) \frac{-2 \text{ kg}}{10 \text{ kg}} \div \frac{£5}{£100} \left(\frac{\text{change in income}}{\text{original income}}\right)$$

$$= \frac{-2}{10} \times \frac{100}{5} = -4$$

Such goods are called *inferior* goods, though the term does not imply that they are necessarily sub-standard or defective in any way. Usually the reason for the decline in purchases is that the increase in income permits the consumer to switch to goods that he prefers but previously was unable to afford. Table 5.6 shows that, in the UK the income elasticity of most foods is less than 1 and that a number of the common, basic foods are inferior foods; potatoes, margarine, bread, and even tea.

Milk	0.2	Beans	1.1
Cream	0.9	Oranges	0.5
Cheese	0.2	Fruit juice	1.2
Beef	0.3	Bread	−0.2
Corned meat	−0.2	Tea	−0.1
Poultry	1.0	Coffee beans	1.7
Butter	0.1	Salt	0.1
Margarine	−0.3	All foods	0.2
Potatoes	−0.2		

Table 5.6 Income elasticities for foodstuffs in the United Kingdom, 1969

Source: *Household Food Consumption and Expenditure*, 1969, Annual Report of the National Food Survey Committee, Ministry of Agriculture, Fisheries and Food, HMSO, 1971.

The overall elasticity for goods was only 0.2 per cent. In the period since 1939 the proportion of consumption expenditure going on food in the UK had fallen from over 30 per cent to about 19 per cent in 1978.

In practice, there are two methods of measuring income elasticity of demand for a product. First, households can be surveyed from time to time, changes in their incomes recorded and changes in the quantities of the goods they purchase noted. The main problem in using this method is that consumers also change their purchases in response to price changes and it is difficult to separate the two effects.

Cross-section analysis

The alternative is called cross-section analysis because it consists of surveying a cross-section of the population on a single occasion. Families of a given size but with different incomes are interviewed and their purchases of goods recorded. The differences between the purchases of richer and poorer families are then treated as if they represented the different purchases typical households would make as their incomes increased. This method largely overcomes the price problem and also has the advantage that speedy results can be obtained. There is no need to wait for incomes to rise.

5.11

Calculate the income elasticity of demand for tomatoes by a family. When its weekly income is £75 it buys 3 kg. When its weekly income rises to £90 it buys 3.5 kg. Assume no change in price occurs in the meantime.

Proportion of expenditure allocated to:

	(i) Housing	(ii) Fuel, light and power	(iii) Food	(iv) Alcoholic drink and tobacco	(v) Clothing and footwear	(vi) Household and other goods	(vii) Transport and vehicles	(viii) Services and miscell-aneous	Sub-total of groups (i), (ii) and (iii)
Households with income:									
in the lowest 20%	22	11	30	6	6	11	6	8	63
in the second 20%	17	8	27	8	8	13	10	9	52
in the third 20%	15	6	26	9	8	14	13	9	47
in the fourth 20%	15	5	24	9	9	14	14	10	44
in the highest 20% of the income distribution	13	4	21	8	10	16	16	12	38

Table 5.7 Patterns of expenditure: variation with household income 1978

Source: *Economic Progress Report* No. 117 Jan 1980

5.12

Table 5.7 presents information about the way households in the UK on different income levels spent their income in 1978.

By studying the table it is possible to see in broad terms which commodities, or groups of commodities, increase as a proportion of expenditure as income of households' rises. Housing, fuel, light and power, and food, make up the essential items of households' expenditure, and the proportion spent on these items can be seen to vary from 63 per cent of the lowest 20 per cent of incomes to

38 per cent in the highest 20 per cent of the income distribution. From this information it is possible to see in a very rough and ready way the income elasticity of demand for the different commodity and service groupings. As each 20 per cent step in the income distribution is taken into account the proportion of expenditure on each item varies, but not by the same proportionate amount of increase or decrease. For each of the levels of income it is possible to judge which goods or services are more income elastic, or inelastic, relative to other groups.

From the table, work out the percentage increase or decrease in expenditure as household income increases. What do you conclude about consumer response to a higher income in terms of the results you have obtained for spending on food, alcohol and tobacco, transport and vehicles, and services?

Total domestic expenditure represents the aggregate of all consumption, government and investment expenditures in the economy. To this aggregate, exports of goods and services are added to give total final expenditure at market prices. Exports represent expenditures by foreigners on goods and services produced within the UK and these therefore contribute to the level of production and the level of incomes earned in the economy. Imports, and expenditures by UK residents on foreign goods and services, then must be subtracted from total final expenditure to produce an aggregate measure of the total flow of goods and services produced by the economy. This measure is known as the gross domestic product at market prices. Thus, for the economy as a whole, aggregate expenditure equals aggregate production or output. In Chapter 6 the measurement of gross domestic product from aggregating output is discussed more fully.

Consumers' expenditure	96 086
General government final consumption	32 693
Gross domestic fixed capital formation plus changes in stock	30 746
Total domestic expenditure at market prices	159 525
Exports of goods and services	47 636
Total final expenditure at market prices	207 161
Less imports of goods and services	–45 522
Gross domestic product at market prices	161 639

Table 5.8 UK gross domestic product at market prices 1978 (£ million)

Source: *Annual Abstract of Statistics, 1980*, HMSO

Consumers' expenditure	66 728
General government final consumption	23 623
Gross domestic fixed capital formation plus changes in stocks	21 614
Total domestic expenditure at market prices	111 965
Exports of goods and services	32 343
Total final expenditure at market prices	144 308
Less imports of goods and services	–31 626
Gross domestic product at market prices	112 682

Table 5.9 UK gross domestic product 1978 at 1975 market prices (*£ million*)

Source: *Annual Abstract of Statistics 1980*, HMSO

Notes

1 Direct taxes, such as income tax and death duties, are taxes which are borne by the person on whom they are levied, as distinct from indirect taxes, such as value added tax and import duties, which are paid by one person but may be passed on to another. For example, the breweries hand over the money raised from excise but the price of beer to drinkers is increased by the excise.

2 With all income either spent or saved the marginal propensity to consume and the marginal propensity to save must add to 1. In this case 80p of each extra pound goes on consumption and the 20p balance is saved. Similarly, the average propensity to consume and the average propensity to save also sum to 1.

Chapter 6

Production

Living standards in the UK depend upon the current production of goods and the supply of services. From the discussion of Chapter 5 we have seen that both the past performance of the economy and the likely level of production in the future also have some significance for welfare. Some of these relationships between the past, the present and future, and between production, consumption and investment are complex, but at this stage the following relationships are clear:

1 Living standards in the current period are affected by production and consumption in past periods. For example, a television set produced and purchased three years ago continues to contribute to a household's sense of well-being, as do its stocks of furniture and clothing acquired in the past.

2 There are clear links between current production and current consumption. The more goods and services produced with a country's resources, the more is available for consumption and the higher the standard of living that can be supported.[1]

3 Current production is, in turn, affected by the production of capital goods in past periods.

4 The propensity to consume in the current period may be affected by expectations of the future. The possibility of shortages in the future may influence decisions about whether to spend more and save less.

These relationships need to be investigated thoroughly if the operation of the economy of the UK is to be understood. But first, we need a satisfactory method of measuring production. Accordingly, this chapter is concerned with aggregate production and its connections with aggregate consumption and expenditure, discussed in Chapter 5.

The measurement of production

The monetary value of the goods and services produced during a specified period is called the *gross domestic product* (GDP). It is the aggregate of the values of production of each individual enterprise in the economy. However – and this is critical – the value of production of the individual firm is *not* measured by the value of the receipts it obtains from the sale of its product in the market-place. The term *value of output* refers to these sales receipts. For each product, the sales receipts are the price of the product multiplied by the quantity sold. *Value added* is the value of output less the cost of intermediate goods purchased from other firms and used up in production. The reason for the exclusion of these intermediate goods from the calculation of the value of production was given in Chapter 5. Expenditure on 'final goods' (but not of the inputs purchased by enterprises) was included in the aggregate 'total domestic expenditure'. The end products of some industries are the

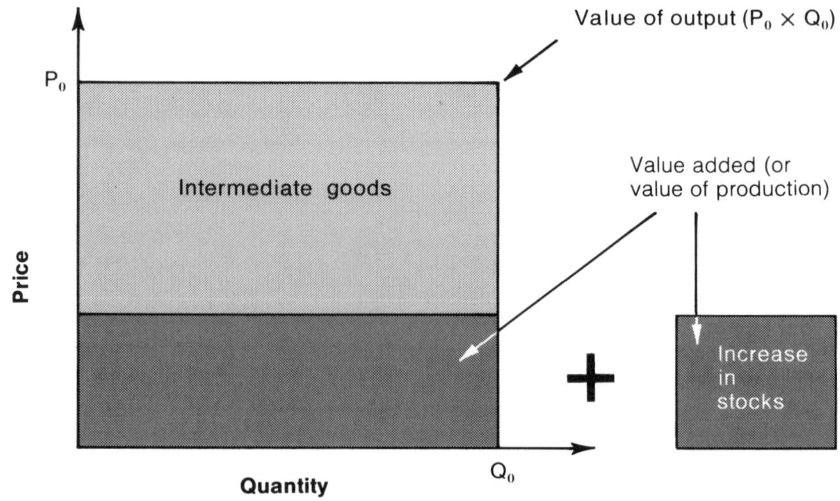

Figure 6.1 Value added and value of output

basic intermediate goods of others. The motor vehicle assembly industry uses the products of many industries: steel, electronics, petrochemicals, engineering. If we were to add together the amounts the assembly industry pays to the supplying industries for components, and the receipts it receives when it sells the assembled product, the result would involve double counting. If for each industry we included the full value of its sales as the value of production, the final aggregate we obtained would depend upon whether or not the various stages in production were integrated within one firm or were carried out successively by separate firms who sold their output to other firms. Retailers and wholesalers would then appear as the most important industries, because the value of their sales are greater than that of the manufacturers.

One solution to this measurement problem is to add together only the market prices of all final goods and services. A deficiency of this approach is that it does not indicate the relative contribution made to production by each particular industry. That is, the value of the productive activity of those enterprises selling intermediate products to other industries and of industries that sell to wholesalers is not distinguished. The distinction between the value of output and the value added of a firm is illustrated in Figure 6.1.

Value of output (or value of sales receipts) is the large box – price P_0 × quantity Q_0. Value added is value of output less intermediate goods plus the other small box, 'increase in stocks'. The addition of 'increase in stocks' is necessary because there are intermediate goods produced during the period but not yet used in the production of final goods. By incorporating the increase in stocks into value of production, the latter effectively becomes value of sales less the equivalent of the intermediate goods used in their production. Table 6.1 illustrates these relationships.

Changes in stocks

Suppose that in 1978, heavy purchases of intermediate goods occurred; sales of final goods realised £100 000 and stocks increased by £10 000. By identifying separately the net increase in stocks, it can be

	1978	1979
Sales during years	100 000	100 000
less purchases of intermediate goods during the year	40 000	20 000
	60 000	80 000
plus net increase in stocks during the year	10 000	–10 000
Value added	70 000	70 000

Table 6.1 Value added of a firm in successive years

seen that the equivalent of only £30 000 of intermediate goods was used in production. In 1979, when £100 000 sales were again recorded, purchases of intermediate goods amounted to only £20 000. However, there was a net reduction in stocks during the year of £10 000, so that again the equivalent of £30 000 of intermediate goods was used to produce final sales of £100 000 and, once more, the value of production was £70 000.

Components of value of production

The value of production, or 'value added' by an industry, is made up of two principal components which correspond to the rewards paid to major groups involved in the productive process:

1 wages and salaries of the employees and the management, which account for a large part of the difference between value and cost of the intermediate goods;

2 *gross operating surplus*, the term given to the residual sum from which the owners of the enterprise receive their rewards and from which taxation is paid.[2]

Table 6.2 shows how, in a simple two-industry economy, the value of production of the two industries, which purchase intermediate goods from one another, is aggregated to obtain the gross domestic product. Industry B purchases £20 million of intermediate products from industry A, which is the entire output of A. Industry A buys £10 million of intermediate products from B which also sells £26 million to consumers. Gross domestic product for the economy, £26 million, is simply the sum of the value of production, £10 million for A and £16 million for B.

	Industry A (£ million)	Industry B (£ million)	Aggregate GDP (£ million)
Value of output	20	36[2]	
less intermediate goods	10	20	
Value added	10	16	26
(of which) wages & salaries	6	8	
Gross operating surplus	4	8	

Note:
(1) There is no increase in stocks.
(2) The balance (£26 million) of B's sales is sold to consumers.

Table 6.2 Aggregated value of production in a two-industry economy

Difficulties in measuring production

Statisticians encounter problems when measuring value of production

Although the general idea behind the calculation of value of production for an industry and resultant GDP is clear enough, the statistician faces considerable problems when he actually attempts to measure the value of production. Some of these problems are similar to those faced when measuring consumption.

Not all goods enter the market

First, not all goods produced are sold. Farmers produce food that they and their families eat, and some home owners live in their own houses whereas others let them to tenants. A value is imputed to each of these types of production. This tallies with the value imputed for the consumption of such goods. They are treated as if they were produced, bought and sold.

Some goods and services are sold below cost of production

Second, many goods and services are provided by government at no cost, or at a cost that bears no relation to market prices. Clearly, such activities are productive and must be measured in some way. The method used is by assessing the wages and salaries paid to those engaged in the provision of these goods and services.

Some production is ignored by the statistician

There are many productive services (productive because they yield utility or satisfaction to someone) that the statistician makes no attempt to measure. Home maintenance and repairs by the house-owner are an alternative to spending money on services. The housewife substitutes for a paid housekeeper, but only the latter is deemed to contribute to national production. The problems in attempting to measure the value of such personal non-market productive services would be immense.

Understanding the principle is more important than memorising the statistician's decisions

Inevitably, some of the decisions of statisticians about how to measure particular items, or how to value certain activities, must be arbitrary. From the student's viewpoint, it is sufficient to understand the general principles behind the calculation of value of production. It is not necessary to become absorbed with the details of the accounts, and it certainly is futile to memorise how the National Income Accounts treat specific items (as some students have done in the past).

Gross domestic product at factor cost

Nevertheless, there are two technical terms that call for explanation and distinction. These are *gross domestic product at market prices* and *gross domestic product at factor cost*. The former corresponds to the value of production measure discussed above, namely, the market value of all goods and services produced in the UK less the cost of intermediate products. The second term, GDP at factor cost, measures the value added to production corresponding to the payments to the factors of production: to labour and management through wages and salaries and to the owners of capital through profits in the gross operating surplus.

Adjustment to factor cost

The aggregate GDP at market prices differs from GDP at factor cost because, in many industries, the value of production is distorted by indirect taxes levied upon, or subsidies paid to, the industry by the government, thereby affecting market prices. Accordingly, GDP at factor cost is defined as:

Gross domestic product at market prices
less indirect taxes
plus subsidies

= Gross domestic product at factor cost

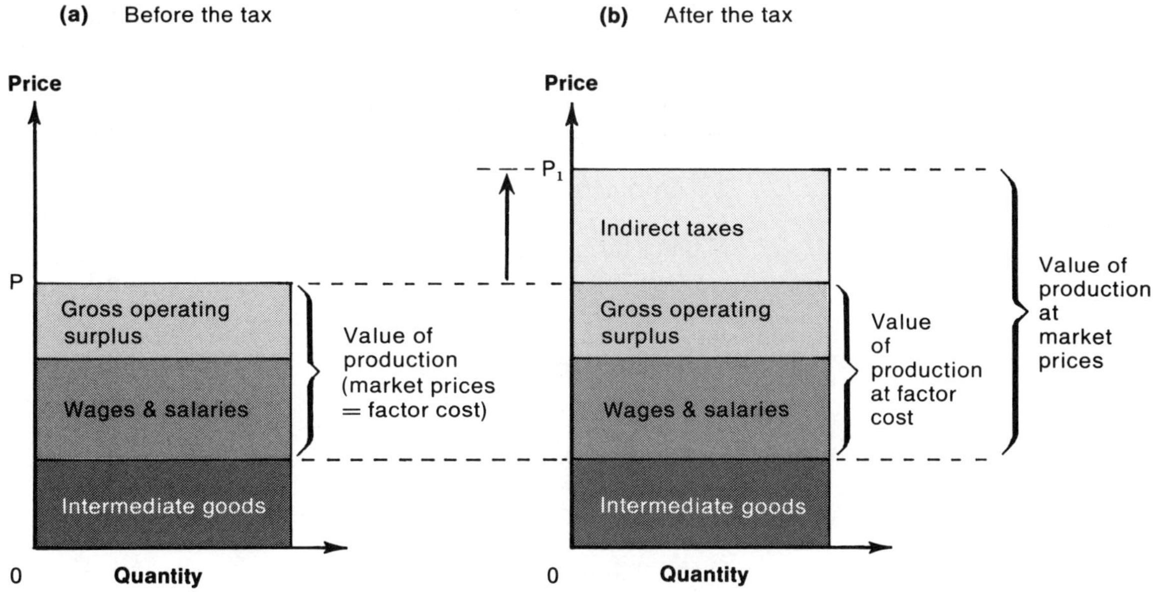

Figure 6.2 Value of production at market prices and at factor cost, before and after the imposition of an indirect tax on sales

Figure 6.2 demonstrates the effect of the imposition of an indirect tax on an industry's product. In Figure 6.2(a), when no tax operates, the value of production at market prices is equal to the value of production at factor cost; the value of production is then divided between the factors of production or resources. Figure 6.2(b) shows that, when the tax is added, the price to the purchaser is increased, the market value of output increases, and the value of production at market prices also increases: however there has been no increase in the earnings received and in the value added by the factors of production. Consequently, the method of calculating value of production, which deducts indirect taxes, is a better indicator of the value added to production by resources employed by the industry.

Effects of a subsidy on GDP at market prices

It is somewhat more difficult to depict the effects of a subsidy on an industry. But essentially a subsidy has the opposite effect of a tax. It may, for example, result in customers paying a lower price, in a lower market value of output and a lower value of production at market prices. No change occurs in the productive process but in the rewards paid to the factors of production. Accordingly there is a change in the value of production measured at factor cost.

Some industries are subject to indirect taxes while others are receiving subsidies. GDP at factor cost aggregates the value of production of each industry on this factor payment basis.

Table 6.3 provides detailed information about the gross domestic product of the UK by industry group. The table shows that in the UK, primary and secondary industry contributed less than half of the total value of production in 1978. Primary industry, which includes mining and quarrying as well as agriculture, forestry and fishing, contributed less than 6 per cent to the total value of production. Manufacturing industry accounted for only 28.7 per cent. Together with other secondary industry groups, the secondary sector produced 38.2 per cent

Industry	£ million	Percentage of GDP
Agriculture, forestry and fishing	3 715	2.6
Mining and quarrying	4 467	3.1
Total primary industry	8 182	5.7
Manufacturing	40 690	28.7
Construction	8 610	6.1
Gas, electricity & water	4 772	3.4
Total secondary industry	54 072	38.2
Transport	7 677	5.4
Communication	4 011	2.8
Distributive trades	14 687	10.3
Insurance, banking, finance and business services	11 268	7.9
Ownership of dwellings	8 578	6.0
Public administration and defence	10 197	7.2
Public health and educational services	9 674	6.8
Other services	18 680	13.2
Adjustment for financial services	–6 098	–4.3
Residual error	1 071	0.8
Gross domestic product at factor cost	141 999	100.0

Table 6.3. Gross Domestic Product at factor cost, UK, by industry, 1978 (£ million).

Source: *Annual Abstract of Statistics, 1980*, HMSO

of total output. It is clear that, in the UK, production amounts to much more than growing, mining, making and constructing goods for our own use and for export.

Tertiary sector

The service industries, or the *tertiary sector*, accounted for over 55 per cent of the value of production. Of particular importance are the distributive trades (over 10 per cent), public administration and defence, public health and educational services (approx 7 per cent each). The adjustment for financial services is necessary to avoid double-counting of the output of the insurance, banking, finance and business services in the GDP total. Some lay persons consider that the tertiary sector is 'unproductive' or that its contribution is less important than that of the primary and secondary sectors. But without an efficient distribution system and adequate financial services those goods most wanted may not be produced, or may be produced in the wrong quantities, or may be unavailable at the time and in the place that they are needed. Services of a personal nature such as education and travel make obvious direct contributions to our living standards.

6.1

Study Table 6.3 on page 90. Compare the share of GDP at factor cost generated in particular industries in 1978 with the respective shares in 1971 and the shares for the latest year for which figures are available. Can you identify any trends that indicate the decline in importance of any group? Which industry groups would you expect to experience the greatest increase in relative size during the 1980s?

6.2

In 1776, Adam Smith, the Scottish author of *The Wealth of Nations*, expressed firm views on what constituted 'production' and what did not.

> There is one sort of labour which adds to the value of the subject on which it is bestowed: there is another which has no such effect. The former, as it produces a value, may be called productive; the latter, unproductive labour . . . The labour of some of the most respectable orders of society is . . . unproductive of any value, and does not fix or realise in itself any permanent subject or vendible commodity, which endures after that labour is past . . . the whole army and navy are unproductive labourers. They are the servants of the public and are maintained by a part of the annual produce of the industry of other people . . . In the same class must be ranked some of the gravest and most important, and some of the most frivolous professions: churchmen, lawyers, physicians, men-of-letters of all kinds; players, buffoons, musicians, opera singers, etc.[3]

There is not much doubt that Adam Smith would not have considered boxing as a productive activity. What arguments could you put forward to counter the view advanced by Smith? Is there any justification for believing that it might be better not to include such activities when measuring the GDP?

Production or destruction?

6.3

In an imaginary economy, the industry groups are: primary industry, secondary industry and tertiary industry, the last being divided into wholesaling, retailing and government services. The table below presents the aggregate costs of materials, wages and salaries, gross operating surplus, any indirect taxes or subsidies and value of sales of each of these five industry groups.

(£ million)

Industry group	Cost of materials	Wages & salaries	Gross operating surplus	Taxes (+) & subsidies (–)	Sales
Primary	800	900	600	–200	2100
Secondary	2100	1500	1200	0	4800
Wholesaling	4000	600	1000	+700	6300
Retailing	5500	700	900	0	7100
Government services	500	500	0	0	0

1 Can you explain why the value of the sales of the retailing industry is greater than that of secondary industry, despite the fact that the value of production is smaller?
2 What is meant by 'gross domestic product at market prices'? Try to calculate it for this economy.
3 What is meant by gross domestic product at factor cost? Calculate it for this economy and explain your method.

6.4

Figure 6.2(a) showed the value of production of an industry at market prices and at factor cost before and after the imposition of an indirect tax on sales. Using a similar pair of diagrams, illustrate or indicate the value of sales and the value of production at market prices and at factor cost, before and after the government granted a subsidy to the industry. (Assume that the industry did not have to pay an indirect tax.) Discuss your result with other members of the class.

Growth of production

For many years the attainment of a high and continuing rate of economic growth has been said to be one of the principal objectives of the UK governments of both main parties. It is only in the last ten years or so that there has been any widespread questioning about whether a rapid rate of economic growth will necessarily lead to improvements in general welfare. That debate is summarised in Chapter 21. Another matter that has caused some disagreement is whether the growth in the value of production is the most appropriate method of measuring economic growth, particularly if there is a desire to make international comparisons. That problem is considered in Chapter 24.

Measures of the growth rate

Usually economists express the economic growth rate in terms of the percentage rate of increase in real gross domestic product or, alternatively, in the per capita rate of increase of real gross domestic product. Increases in real gross domestic product is commonly selected because ultimately the country's production of goods and services determines the ability of its residents to consume. Other things being equal, the greater the aggregate production the larger the quantities available for consumption. The emphasis is again on 'real' gross domestic product because for many purposes the important question is 'is the quantity of goods and services being produced, increasing?' As noted in Chapter 5, it is necessary to exclude the effect of price changes to determine this. This is done by measuring aggregate production at constant prices. In Chapter 5 consumption expenditure and total domestic expenditure were measured in real terms by expressing them in average 1975 prices. The same has been done for gross domestic product in Figure 6.3.

Figure 6.3 compares the gross domestic product at current market prices with the gross domestic product at average 1975 prices, for the period 1970 to 1980. The need to express GDP in real terms comes out clearly in the figure. It can be seen that, whilst there was a great increase in GDP at market prices during that period, particularly after 1974, GDP measured at 1975 prices did not increase steadily over the period and actually declined from 1973 to 1975. After 1975, GDP measured at constant prices once again increased. If GDP at market prices had been used to measure the economic growth rate in the UK then the

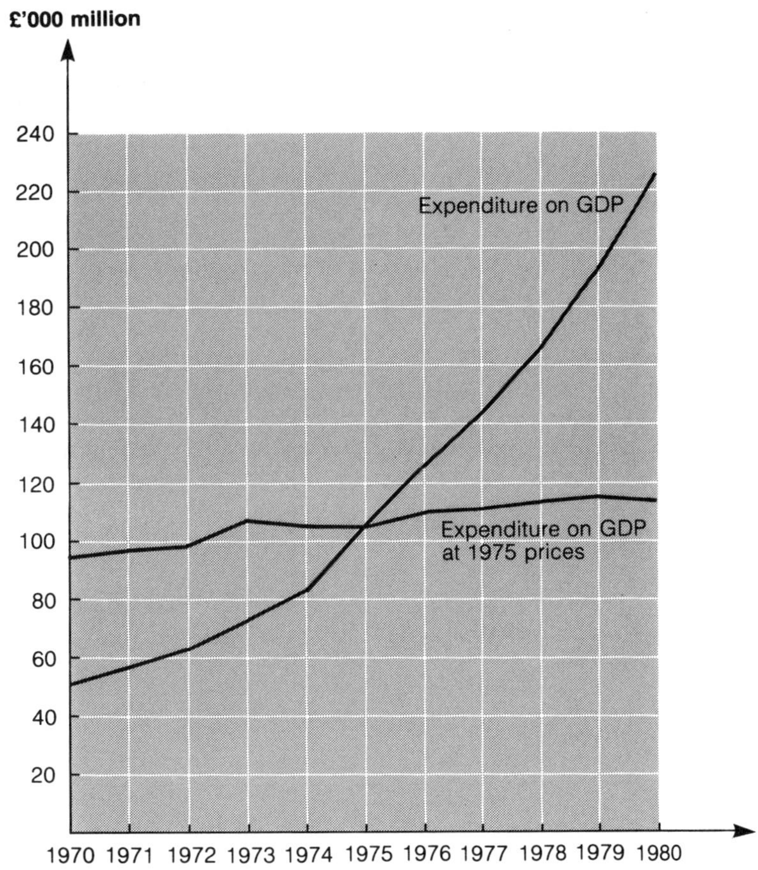

Figure 6.3 UK gross domestic product at market prices and at 1975 market prices, 1970–80

Source: Annual Abstract of Statistics 1982, Table 14, HMSO results for this period would have been very misleading. From 1979 to 1980 GDP again declined and in 1980 stood at the 1978 level.

The difference between market prices and constant prices is brought out equally clearly in Figure 6.4. This shows the annual rate of increase of UK gross domestic product at market and at 1975 prices. At market prices the growth rate was rising for most of the period, reaching a peak of almost 26 per cent in 1974. It is clear that much of this increase was the effect of rising prices. The more useful measure – the change in gross domestic product at constant prices – shows a much altered picture. Over the period, the growth rate varied between 8 per cent and –1.5 per cent. For much of the time 1968 to 1978 the growth rate has been about 2 or 3 per cent. Note that, in 1973 and 1974 and again in 1980, the level of GDP declined in real terms and a negative change is seen in the growth rate. The second measure that economists find useful is the percentage increase in real gross domestic product per head of population. The aggregate real GDP is invaluable when economists are

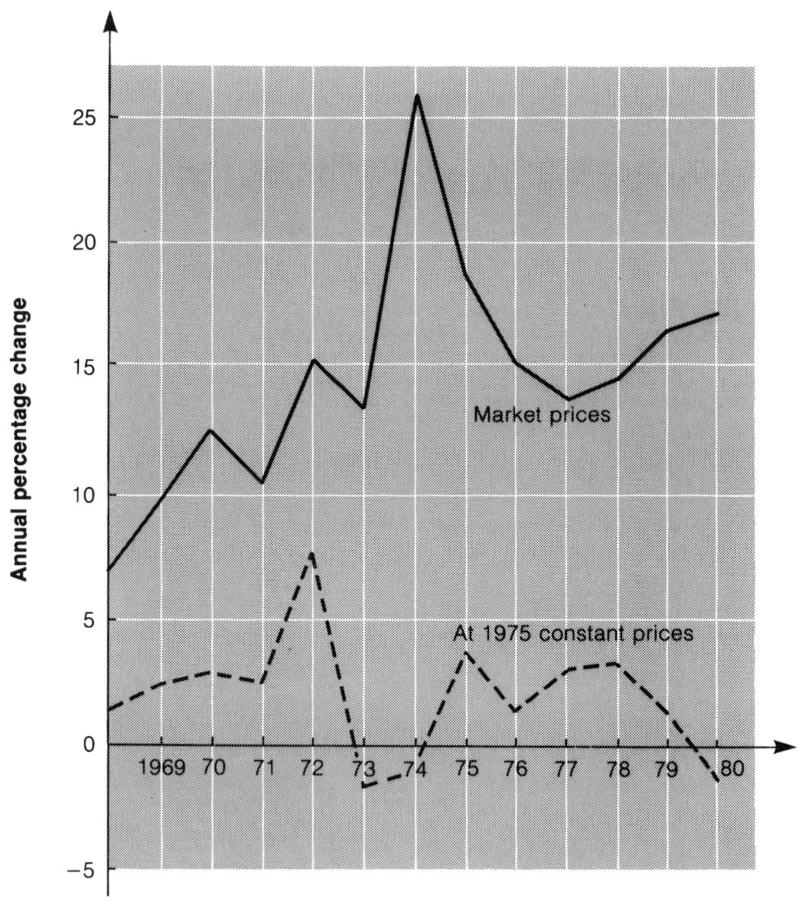

Figure 6.4 Annual growth rate of GDP at market prices and at 1975 prices, 1968–80

Source: Annual Abstract of Statistics 1982, Table 14, HMSO measuring a country's economic performance. Real GDP per head is often more appropriate for consideration of changes in living standards. If a country's population is increasing, real GDP per head will be increasing at a lesser rate than aggregate real GDP. However, during the 1970s in the UK population did not grow at the same rate experienced in the 1960s. After 1974 the population overall declined slightly in absolute numbers as a consequence of a falling birth rate. Thus, the actual rate of increase in GDP per head was very little different to the rate of increase in aggregate real GDP. To illustrate the effect of population growth on GDP consider the following example: if real GDP increased by 3 per cent per year and the population increased by 1 per cent per year then the actual rate of increase in real GDP per head is almost 2 per cent. The rate of increase of real GDP per head is calculated as follows:

$$\text{Rate of increase of real GDP} \div \text{Rate of increase of population} \times 100 = \text{Rate of increase of real GDP per capita}$$

$$\frac{103}{100} \times \frac{100}{101} \times 100 = 101.98 = \text{approx. } 102$$

The relationship between the size of a country's population and the rate of growth of its gross domestic product is a complex one. It is examined in Chapter 9 where population and human resources are considered. The calculation above makes clear that an increasing population must necessarily have the effect of making the rate of increase of real gross domestic product per head lower than the rate of increase of aggregate real GDP, but this does not mean that an increasing population will retard economic growth. Much depends upon the nature of the population increase. Additions to the labour force have a direct effect upon a country's productive capacity, and so a population increase due primarily to the immigration of persons of working age, will give the greatest stimulus to growth.

The evidence of Figure 6.4 is that production of goods and services in the UK increased only very slowly overall during the 1970s. In terms of real gross domestic output per head, the economy declined or stagnated for much of the period. One feature of the period has already been noted, the rapid rise in prices in the 1970s. Some people regard inflation as the cause of the decline in the growth rate. Government policies to counter inflation, and the reaction of businessmen to those policies, together with the economic situation, accentuated the problem. International influences, such as increasing oil prices and the decline and recession in the world economy, have also played their part and it is argued that the government could do little to offset these. The study of these important problems, unemployment, inflation, low levels of growth, and the explanations and solutions proposed by economists and politicians, form a major part of our investigations in Stage 3 of this book. Aggregate gross domestic product at constant prices is the most informative measure of economic growth, but aggregate gross domestic product at current market prices is useful for many purposes. For example, if we wish to measure the growth rates and relative importance of different sectors of an economy, the current price measure is more suitable.

6.5

What immediate effects would you expect each of the following events to have on the value of a firm's production? (By 'immediate' it is meant that the business does not have sufficient time to react to the event by changing its operations or its selling policies in any way.)

1 a reduction in the physical quantities of products purchased from the firm over the last quarter,
2 a direction by a prices tribunal that it reduce its prices by 5 per cent,
3 an increase in the price of the intermediate goods it purchases,
4 a fall in the sales tax levied upon its products,
5 an increase in the rate of taxation levied upon its profits
6 a reduction in the volume of output of the firm,
7 an increase in the wage rates paid to its employees
8 a rise in the depreciation allowances made by the firm,
9 a decision to purchase new machinery for the firm,
10 an increase in orders for the firm's products.

6.6

The following table gives some information about an imaginary economy. There are five separate industry groups identified in the table reflecting the sectors of economic activity. However, the tertiary sector has been divided into wholesaling, retailing and government services.

£ million

Industry	Cost of materials	Wages and salaries	Gross operating surplus	Taxes(+) & subsidies(–)	Sales
Primary	2 400	2 700	1 800	$x1$	6 300
Secondary	6 300	4 500	$x2$	0	14 400
Wholesaling	$x3$	1 800	3 000	2 100	18 900
Retailing	16 500	$x4$	2 700	0	21 300
Government services	1 500	1 500	0	0	0

1 Calculate the values of $x1$, $x2$, $x3$ and $x4$ which are missing from the table.
2 Calculate the value added for each industry.
3 Calculate the gross domestic product at factor cost for the economy.
4 Examine the reasoning for treating government services as production, even though in this example the services are not sold. On what basis are government services valued as production?

6.7

Explain how, in the UK economy, government services such as education and health are included as production in national accounts. Does the inclusion of such output measured at cost adequately reflect its contribution to national output?

Notes

1 A qualification to this point is that often economists assume that there is a lag between production and consumption – that the consumption in a particular time period is influenced by the level of production and income in the previous period. Here, however, the terms 'past', 'present' and 'future' are being used in a very general way.

2 As on past occasions, the word 'gross' refers to the fact that no allowance for the depreciation of capital equipment is made. This applies to both gross domestic product and gross operating surplus.

3 Adam Smith 1776 *An Enquiry into the Nature and Causes of the Wealth of Nations*, Book II, ch 3. Reprinted by University Paperbacks, Methuen, 1960, vol 1 pp 351–2.

Chapter 7

Demand and Supply

Demand

The individual's consumption pattern is determined by the interplay between his anticipated satisfaction from the various goods and services and the terms (or prices) on which those goods and services are available. The term *demand* needs careful explanation to distinguish it from similar words, such as 'desire' or 'want'. There is a demand for a product if consumers want to purchase the good and have the necessary financial ability to do so. Thus, the desire for an article may be great or it may be needed urgently, but there is only an effective market demand for it if the would-be consumer is able to offer to purchase it at the going price.

Determinants of demand

The quantity of a good demanded by a consumer at any particular time will depend upon a number of determinants of demand. These are:

1 The consumer's tastes or preferences	affect willingness to buy
2 The price of the good 3 The income at the consumer's disposal 4 Prices of all other goods and services	affect consumer's ability to purchase

Notice that determinant 1 (tastes) refers to the consumer's desires, whilst determinants 2, 3 and 4 are influences affecting the consumer's financial ability to purchase the good.

As the word 'determinant' suggests, each of the four plays a part in determining the quantity of any particular good purchased by a consumer. It cannot be said that any one determinant is more important than the others, because any sensible decision by a consumer will take into account all four determinants. Tastes are a basic determinant, of course, because unless there is a desire for a good it will not be purchased even if the price is zero. But, equally, the other determinants are relevant. A sufficiently high price, a low income or the availability of a cheap substitute good will produce the same end result as lack of desire – that is, zero demand.

Although it cannot be said that any one of the determinants of demand is more important than the others, it has been possible to learn a great deal about the ways in which each of them affects consumer demand.

Inverse relationship between price and quantity demanded

One of the earliest discoveries was that there is often an inverse relationship between the price of a good and the quantity demanded: that is, if the price goes up the quantity demanded goes down, or if the price goes down then the quantity demanded goes up. Before we can be absolutely certain that such a relationship exists, it is necessary to be sure that the other determinants are not changing when we are measuring the effects of the price change. If the consumer's disposable income is falling whilst at the same time the price of the good is increasing, it would be invalid to say that the price increase is producing the observed fall in the quantity demanded.

The inverse relationship between the price of a good and the quantity demanded in a given period can be shown in two ways: either in a table as a *demand schedule*, or on a graph as a *demand curve*.

Price of tomatoes (pence per kilo)	Quantity of tomatoes demanded (kilos per week)
10	1.75
20	1.50
30	1.25
40	1.00
50	0.75
60	0.50
70	0.25
80	nil

Table 7.1 An individual consumer's demand schedule for tomatoes

Table 7.1 shows the different quantities of tomatoes that a consumer is prepared to buy at various prices. For the demand schedule to have any meaning the units in which price and quantity are measured must be stated. So, too, must the period of time to which the measurement relates. If the time period was a month, rather than a week, the quantities shown in the schedule would be proportionately greater.

If the demand schedules of all consumers are added together, it is possible to show their combined total demand for tomatoes at various prices. The final schedule produced in this way is called a *market demand schedule*.

Price of tomatoes (pence per kilo)	Quantity of tomatoes demanded (tonnes per week)
10	80
20	40
30	35
40	30
50	25
60	20
70	17
80	15

Table 7.2 Market demand schedule for tomatoes

The market demand schedule also shows an inverse relationship between price and quantity. Notice that the left-hand column showing price is the same in Table 7.2 as in Table 7.1, but that the quantities demanded and units of measurement (in the right-hand column) are quite different. Obviously the larger the population covered by the particular market, the larger the quantities in this column.

Demand curves

The second way to show the relationship between the price of an article and the quantity demanded is by a *demand curve*. The two variables, price and quantity demanded, are measured on the two axes of the graph. It has come to be accepted that price should be measured on the vertical axis and quantity demanded per unit of time on the horizontal axis. The quantity demanded at any price is then marked as

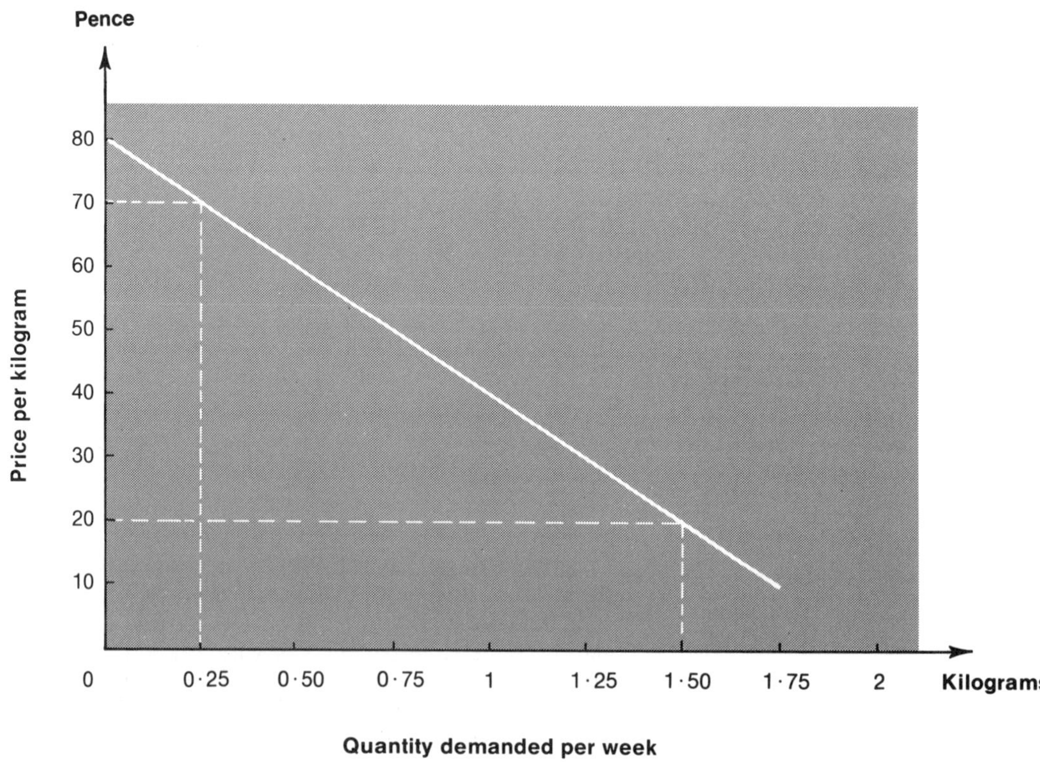

Figure 7.1 An individual consumer's demand curve for tomatoes

a point on the graph and the points joined together to form the line known as the demand curve. The information contained in Table 7.1 has been used in Figure 7.1 to draw the demand curve for tomatoes of an individual consumer. In the graph, the inverse relationship is shown by a line sloping downwards from left to right.

The demand curve is a pictorial representation of what the consumer is willing and able to buy. It indicates the maximum quantity he or she is prepared to buy at any given price, or the maximum price the consumer is prepared to pay for any given quantity.

7.1

1 Using the data given in the market demand schedule (Table 7.2), draw a market demand curve for tomatoes.
2 Now compare Figure 7.1 with the graph you have drawn. At the price of 80p per kilo the individual consumer was not prepared to purchase any tomatoes, but there was an aggregate quantity of 15 tonnes demanded. Does this mean that the market demand curve is incorrect?

The measurement of a demand curve is an extremely difficult task for the economist, partly because of the problem of ensuring that the effects of changes in determinants other than price have been excluded, and partly because of the difficulty of gathering information over a sufficiently wide range of prices. When economists are able to measure demand curves in practice they frequently find that they are neither straight lines nor smooth curves. Instead they may contain kinks or wobbles that reflect the ways in which people react to price changes. But, for convenience, most of the curves drawn in this chapter are smooth lines.

Reasons why the demand curve slopes downwards from left to right

Despite the difficulties experienced in measuring real demand curves the evidence indicates that demand curves nearly always slope downwards from left to right. Why is this so? First, typically the consumer values extra units of an article less highly than earlier units, and is not prepared to give up (pay) as much per unit for a large quantity as he will for a smaller quantity. The economist describes this as the existence of diminishing marginal utility. Second, as the price of a good falls, so the financial ability of the consumer to purchase it increases: the purchasing power of his income becomes greater. Furthermore, the fall in price makes *other* goods *relatively more expensive*, and it may become worthwhile to substitute the good which has become cheaper. The amount by which the quantity demanded increases as the price falls will depend on how strongly the consumer desires the good. The stronger the desire, the greater the sense of gain from owning additional units and hence the larger the increase in the quantity demanded after a particular price fall.

Changes in the conditions of demand

A demand curve shows the relationship between the price of a good and the quantity demanded when all the other determinants of demand are constant. But if one or more of the other determinants changes then it is said that there has been a change in the conditions of demand. Thus, an increase or decrease in income, an increase or decrease in the price of another product or a change in the consumer's likes and dislikes are all changes in the conditions of demand. Such changes usually destroy the existing price–quantity demanded relationship and result in it being replaced by a new one. In graphical form, this means that a new demand curve replaces the old one and a shift of the demand curve has taken place.

Changes in the consumer's disposable income

The likely result of an increase in the consumer's income is to shift his demand curve to the right, because his ability to purchase goods and services has been increased. Such a movement in the demand curve is shown in Figure 7.2. D_1D_1 represents the original demand curve and D_2D_2 is the demand curve that exists after the increase in income. The arrow indicates the direction in which the demand curve has been shifted. The effect of the shift of the demand curve is that the consumer is now prepared to purchase greater quantities than before at each and every price. Instead of buying 1 kg of tomatoes per week when the price is 40p per kg, he is prepared to buy 1.5 kg.

In aggregate, the effect will be similar. An increase in consumers' incomes is likely to produce a rightwards shift in the market demand curve. A fall in incomes will have the opposite effect. The ability of consumers to purchase goods is reduced and the demand curve moves to the left.

Changes in the prices of other goods

The effects on demand of changes in the prices of other goods are a little more complicated. Such goods may be substitutes – effective alterna-

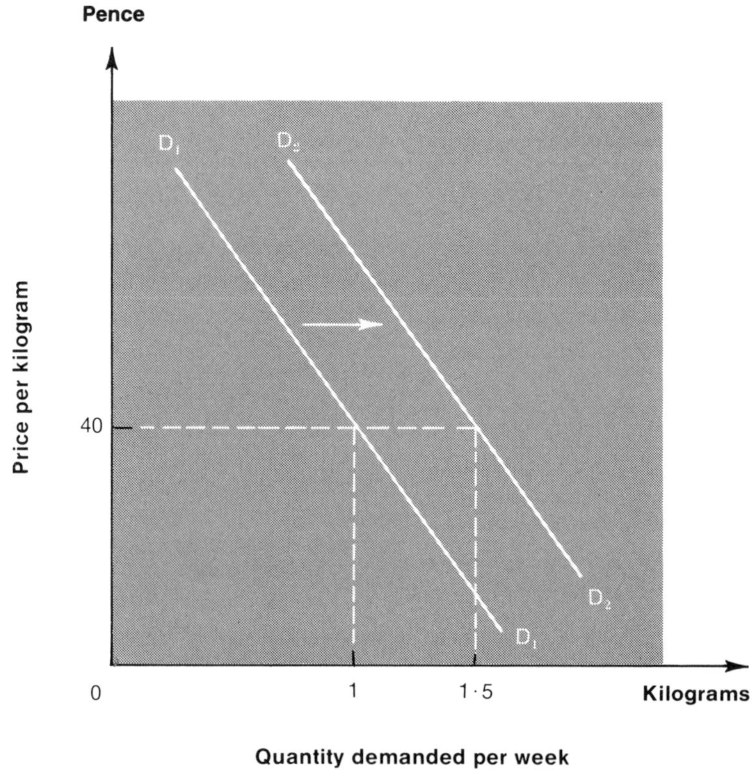

Figure 7.2 Probable effect on demand of an increase in income

tives for the good in question. Or they may be complementary goods – goods which are normally used with the first good. Or alternatively the consumption of the other good may have very little effect upon the demand for the article we are considering.

Substitutes

The effect of an increase in the price of a substitute product is likely to be an increased demand for the original product. For example, a rise in the price of canned tomatoes is likely to lead to consumers buying more fresh tomatoes; the demand curve for fresh tomatoes is shifted to the right. A change in the price of a complementary good will have the opposite effect to the change in price of a substitute. For example, lettuce and fresh tomatoes are considered by many people to be complementary goods in salads. A rise in the price of lettuce may deter consumers from buying lettuce, and also lead them to reduce their purchases of tomatoes. The rise in lettuce prices moves the demand curve for tomatoes to the left.

Complementary goods

Changes in tastes

Changes in consumers' tastes and preferences occur for reasons that are quite unrelated to price and income changes that have been considered so far. Implicit in the idea of a change in tastes is the notion that the consumer increases or decreases his purchases of a good for some other reason than a change in its price or a change in disposable income. Some common causes of changes in tastes are:

seasonal changes (weather conditions);

advertising (creates or strengthens desires, though poor advertising may have the opposite effect);
affluence of neighbours ('keeping up with the Joneses' syndrome), or dictates of fashion;
desires changing as one gets older.

You will probably be able to think of other factors that produce changes in tastes and thus cause demand curves for goods to move to the left or right.

Confusion between movements of and movements along the demand curve to be avoided

Changes in the quantity that consumers are prepared to buy may be caused either by changes in the price of a good or by changes in the conditions of demand. The distinction between the two causes is clear if a demand curve diagram is used. A change in the price of the good results in a movement *along* the existing demand curve, but a change in the conditions of demand results in a *shift* in the demand curve to left or right.[1] It is important to be able to distinguish clearly between movements along the demand curve, and movements of the demand curve itself when talking, writing or thinking about the solution of a problem. The best way to do this is by using different terms. Economists use the term increase (or decrease) in demand to refer only to those situations in which there has been a rightwards (or leftwards) shift of the demand curve, caused by a change in the conditions of demand.

Determinant of demand	Change	Effect on graph	Technical description of the effect
1 *Price*	increase	movement upwards along existing demand curve	fall in the quantity demanded
	decrease	movement downwards along existing demand curve	increase in quantity demanded
2 *Income*	increase	rightwards shift of the demand curve	increase in demand
	decrease	leftwards shift of the demand curve	fall in demand
3 *Prices of other goods*			
(a) substitutes	increase	rightwards shift of the demand curve	increase in demand
	decrease	leftwards shift of the demand curve	fall in demand
(b) complementary goods	increase	leftwards shift of the demand curve	fall in demand
	decrease	rightwards shift of the demand curve	increase in demand
4 *Tastes*	increase in desire to buy	rightwards shift of the demand curve	increase in demand
	decrease in desire to buy	leftwards shift of the demand curve	fall in demand

Table 7.3 Typical effects of changes in the determinants of demand

The term increase (or decrease) in quantity demanded can then be reserved for movements along the existing demand curve, caused by changes in the price of the good. The use of either of these terms indiscriminately to mean both movements along a curve and shifts of the curve is a continual cause of mistakes. Similarly, it is desirable that terms such as the expansion or contraction of demand be avoided for, even if the person using the term is clear about the meaning he has given to the term, it is still likely to give rise to misunderstandings if not in general use. Table 7.3 summarises the effects of the principal changes in demand and the appropriate technical term used to describe the effect.

7.2

Economists tell us that there is an inverse relationship between the price of a good and the quantity that consumers are prepared to purchase. But recently a study of the wine industry showed that the price of wine *and* the quantity consumed had increased. How might this paradox be explained?

7.3

Imagine that the principal airlines operating international flights to and from Australia hire you to estimate the demand for flights from Australia to London. You have already calculated a demand schedule for these flights which is as follows:

Single tourist class air fare, Australia – London (A$)	200	400	600	800	1000	1200	1400	1600
Number of tourist class seats demanded each week ('000)	100	80	60	40	30	20	15	10

Prepare a series of graphs to show the airline managers the probable effects on the demand for air tickets of the following events or occurrences:

- a reduction in the single air fare from $1200 to $600;
- an increase of $100 in the departure tax;
- a reduction in the price of suitcases;
- an aggressive advertising campaign by the airlines;
- the introduction of Concorde on the London to Australia route;
- the introduction of cheaper stand-by tickets by a rival charter airline;
- an increase in the cost of accommodation in London.

Supply

The quantity of a good that is consumed depends not only on demand but also on the supplies of it that producers make available to the market at each given price. Just as demand requires willingness and financial ability to purchase a good, so the term 'supply' indicates a willingness and financial ability on the part of producers to sell the good.

The quantity they are prepared to supply depends upon the determinants of supply. These are:

1 The price received for the good	affects revenue	affect profitability of the enterprise
2 Productivity of inputs used 3 Prices of inputs used 4 Taxes or subsidies imposed on production 5 Prices of alternative products	affect costs of production of the good	

Underlying the notion of supply and its determinants is the knowledge that the willingness and financial ability of producers to supply a product depends on their being able to make profits (or at least to avoid making sustained losses). To do this a producer must be able to secure a price for the product of the business which will cover the costs of production. Further, the greater is the price, the larger will be the volume of production it will be profitable to produce. Determinant 1 relates to the price received for the product. Determinants 2, 3 and 4 all are influences on the cost of production.

Determinant 2 concerns the relationship between the quantity of a good and the quantities of inputs which the producer must acquire to produce it. The more productive these resources, the smaller the quantity of resources required to produce a given output. If the producer finds some way – a reorganisation of production for example – whereby a smaller quantity of resources is used to produce a given output, then the cost of production will be reduced.

Determinant 3, the price paid for resources, includes wages to employees, prices of materials, semi-finished goods, plant, machinery and power purchased from other producers. The higher these prices, the greater will be the production costs.

Many businesses are affected directly or indirectly by government taxes or subsidies. A tax on the sale of a product has the effect of raising a business's cost of supplying the article; it is another payment that the firm must make over and above the production costs before the article is available to sell. Subsidies are negative taxes. They are sums of money paid by government to business, and from the producer's viewpoint they amount to a reduction in the effective production costs.

Finally, determinant 5, the prices of alternative products, has a bearing on supply. A sheep farmer may decide to switch from wool to mutton and fat lamb production if the price of the latter products offers him greater profits.

The relationship between the price of a good and the quantity supplied in a given period can be shown as a *supply schedule*, or by a *supply curve*. As with the demand counterparts, it is necessary to hold all the other determinants constant to isolate the direct influence of price. Figure 7.3 represents a market supply curve for tomatoes.

Supply curves

It is common practice to draw the producer's supply curve and the market supply curve so that they slope upwards from left to right. This indicates that producers are prepared to supply greater quantities of the good as the price increases. At a price of 10p per kg, even the most efficient producers do not find it worthwhile to grow tomatoes, but when the price increases to 20p they are prepared to supply 10 tonnes. At 30p, supply is greater still for two reasons: first the most efficient producers will produce more (perhaps reducing their lettuce production because tomato production is now more profitable) and second, because at 30p other producers can cover their costs.

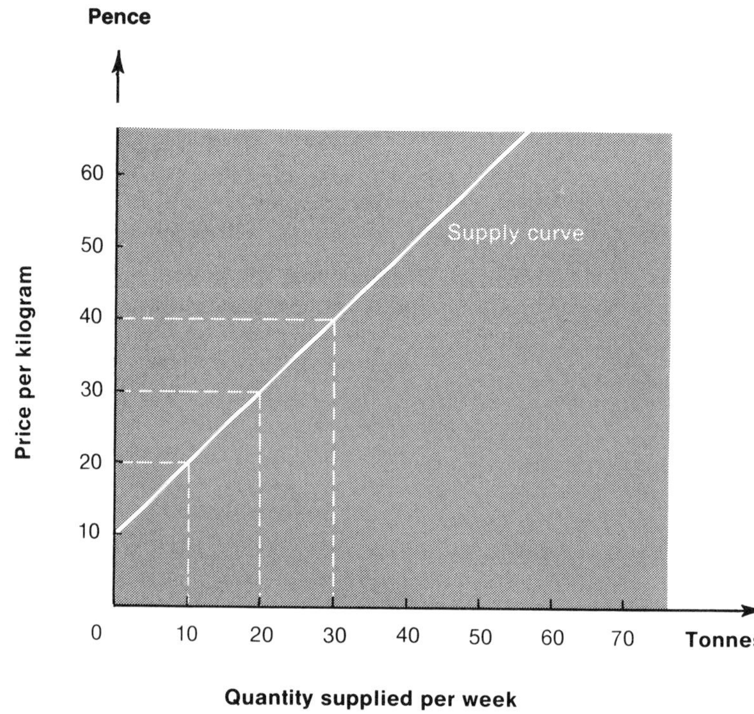

Figure 7.3 Market supply curve for tomatoes

Supply curves for many products slope upwards from left to right because the production costs of the individual firms increase as output is increased. This occurs particularly in farming and other rural industries where the farmer can get greater output from his land if he is prepared to work it more and more intensely, and apply greater and greater quantities of fertiliser. However, there is also a great deal of evidence to show that in other types of industries, such as manufacturing, it is common for the individual business's supply curve to be horizontal (or even for it to slope downwards). In that situation the individual business, and maybe the industry as a whole, is able to reduce production costs per unit as it increases output. This situation is explained more fully in Chapter 8.

Changes in the conditions of supply

The supply curve shows the relationship between price and the quantity supplied per unit of time, other things being equal. Changes in the conditions of supply cause the supply curve to shift to the right or to the left, just as changes in the conditions of demand cause the demand curve to shift. Once more, extreme care is needed to distinguish between movements along the curve and shifts of the curve itself. A shift in the supply curve to the right is an 'increase in supply', and to the left, 'decrease in supply'. A movement upwards along the supply curve is an 'increase in the quantity supplied' and a movement downwards along the supply curve is a 'decrease in the quantity supplied'.

Figure 7.4 shows the effect on the supply curve of a fall in the price of materials to producers. A change in the conditions of supply has

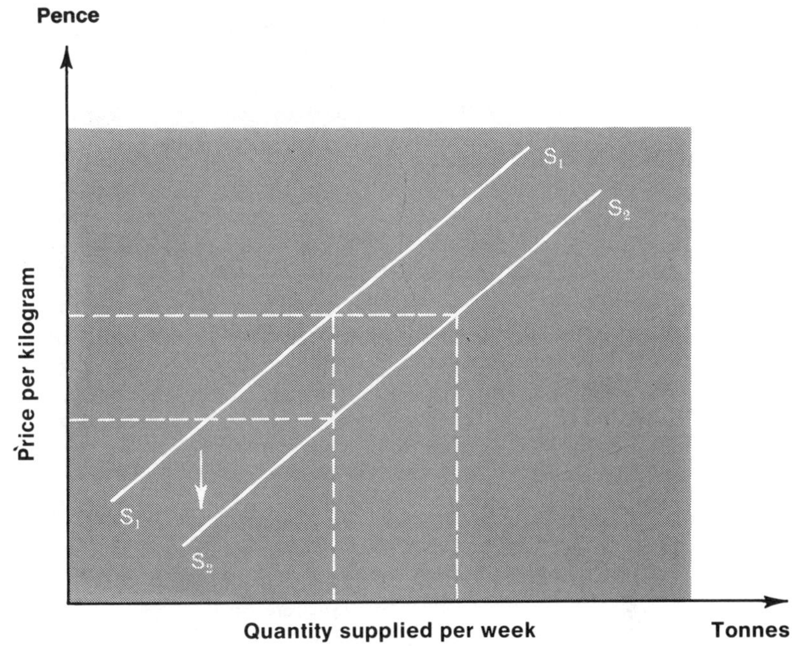

Figure 7.4 Likely effect on supply of a fall in the price of raw materials used in production

Identify the determinants of supply

occurred since determinant 3 is affected. The lower price of materials means lower production costs, and this means that it is possible to produce *any* given quantity of the good more cheaply. The supply curve has moved down or, looked at another way, has shifted to the right; there has been an increase in supply. An increase in the productivity of resources (determinant 2) or a government subsidy (determinant 4) would have a similar effect.

7.4 Explain why it is that something which causes a *fall* in the production costs of a given output can also lead to an *increase* in supply at a given price.

7.5 The photograph on page 107 shows lamb carcases on the hook at an abattoir. Identify the determinants of supply for dressed lamb. Then construct a table for the determinants of supply, similar to the one for the determinants of demand (Table 7.3). On this occasion give specific examples of determinants of the supply for carcase lamb and show the likely effects of changes in these determinants.

Price determination

The price at which a good is sold may be determined by the interaction of demand and supply. Figure 7.5 shows the market demand curve (Figure 7.2) and the market supply curve (Figure 7.3) for tomatoes on the same graph. The curves intersect at a point on the graph that represents a price of 40p per kg and a quantity of 30 tonnes per week. This price is unique because it is the only price at which there is equality between the quantity demanded and the quantity supplied.

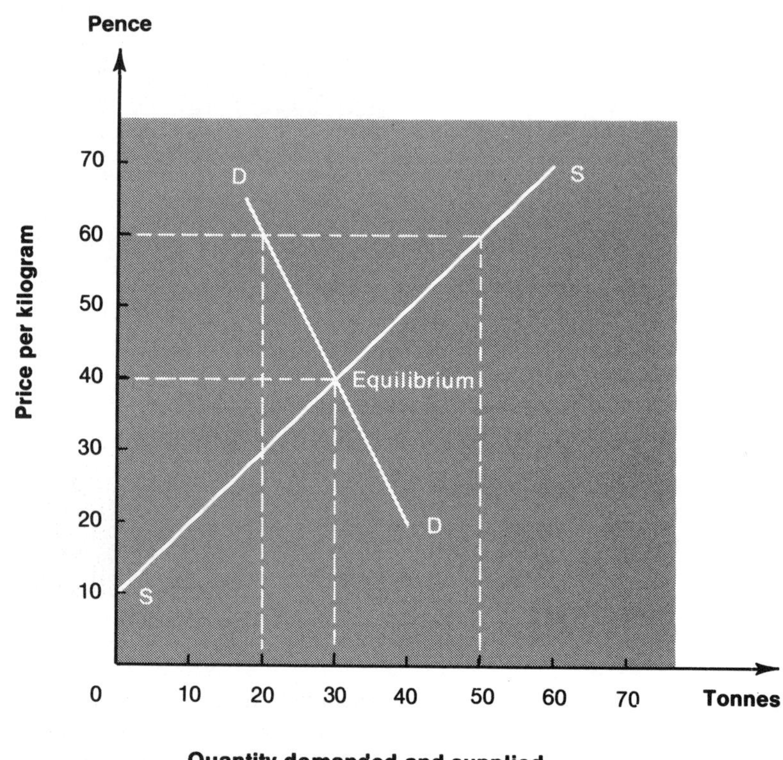

Figure 7.5 Demand, supply and equilibrium market price for tomatoes

Equilibrium

The market will be cleared at that price; all supplies will be purchased and all would-be buyers will be able to make their desired purchases. Such a position is one of equilibrium.

This equilibrium is stable if, in the event of the price changing, the behaviour of producers and consumers results in the price returning to its former level. For example, suppose suppliers initially set the price at 60p per kg; the quantity supplied would exceed the quantity demanded by 30 tonnes. The market would not be cleared and stocks would accumulate. But if suppliers reacted to the stock build-up by lowering their prices and consumers responded to the lower prices by buying more, the price would fall towards the equilibrium price.

7.6 Suppose that in the situation depicted in Figure 7.5 the price of tomatoes was initially set at 30p per kg. Describe the course of events that might follow, and demonstrate how reasonable behaviour by consumers and suppliers will lead to the price rising to 40p per kg.

Price changes

The probable cause of a permanent change in the equilibrium price of a good, or the quantity of it that is sold, is a change in one of the conditions of demand or one of the conditions of supply. For example, a fall in the price of materials to producers is likely to cause an increase in supply. Such an increase in supply will result in a fall in price and an increase in the quantity of the good that is purchased. This result is demonstrated in Figure 7.6. The supply curve has shifted to the right and intersects the demand curve at the new equilibrium position. Notice that buyers' behaviour is represented by a movement along the market

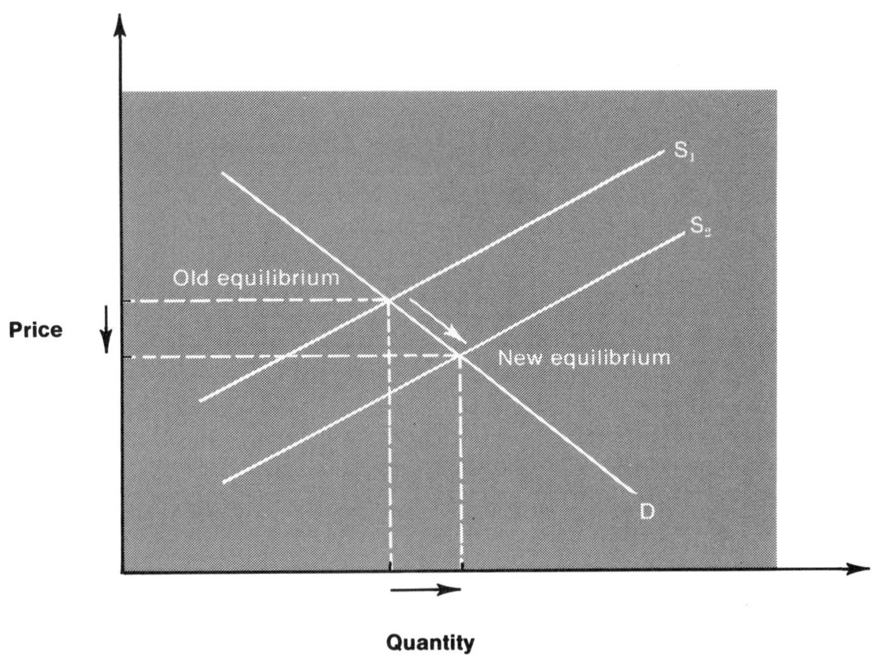

Figure 7.6 Effects of an increase in supply

Changes in supply do not cause changes in demand

demand curve; there has been no shift in this demand curve. Buyers have reacted to a price change by purchasing a greater quantity. It is essential to realise that a change in the conditions of supply does not produce a change in the conditions of demand. The two sets of conditions are completely independent. The demand curve would shift if consumers' incomes, their tastes or the prices of other goods had changed. None of these things has happened. Similarly, a change in the demand conditions will not cause a change in the conditions of supply. A shift in the demand curve will not produce a shift in the supply curve.

7.7

1 Using the following information, draw curves of the demand and supply for apples on a graph. Show, for the equilibrium position, the price and the quantity purchased.

Market demand schedule		Market supply schedule	
Price (pence per kilo)	Quantity demanded (tonnes per weeks)	Price (pence per kilo)	Quantity supplied (tonnes per week)
10	36	10	6
20	32	20	12
30	28	30	18
40	24	40	24
50	20	50	30
60	16	60	36

2 Suppose that the pear season begins and there is a fall in the demand for apples, such that at each price supply of apples is 10 tonnes per week less. Draw the new demand curve on the diagram and show for the new equilibrium position, the price and the quantity purchased.

7.8

Producers of perishable products sometimes find themselves in the unfortunate situation that, having produced a certain quantity and brought it to the market they have no option but to take the market price, no matter how low that market price might be. In such circumstances the demand and supply schedule for peaches might be:

Price (pence per kilo)	Quantity supplied per week (tonnes)	Quantity demanded per week (tonnes)
10	20	36
20	20	32
30	20	28
40	20	24
50	20	20
60	20	16

1 Using this demand and supply schedule, draw a graph to determine the price and quantity purchased.

2 What would be the effect of a fall in the demand for peaches such that, at each price, the quantity demanded is 12 tonnes less per week?

7.9

A businessman once reasoned in the following manner:

If there is an increase in the demand for my product it will not benefit me at all, because the price will rise and this will cause an increase in supply which will bring the price back down to its original level.

Examine his reasoning critically using your knowledge of the demand and supply mechanism. Use a diagram to reveal the fallacy in his argument.

7.10

Complete the following sentences by choosing the best alternatives from the list.

1 A change in consumers' incomes is likely to lead to:
a fall in demand for transistor radios,
a change in the conditions of demand for transistor radios,
a change in the conditions of supply for transistor radios,
a fall in the quantity of transistor radios demanded.

2 An increase in the price of transistor radios occurs as a result of a government tax being levied on them. This increase in price results in:
an increase in the quantity of radios supplied,
an increase in the quantity of radios demanded,
a fall in demand for transistor radios,
a fall in the quantity of transistor radios demanded.

3 The increase in the price of transistor radios is likely to lead to:
a fall in the demand for batteries,
a fall in the quantity of batteries demanded,
an increase in the demand for batteries,
a fall in the supply of batteries.

4 The increase in the price of transistor radios is likely to lead to:
no change in the quantity of cassette recorders demanded
a fall in the supply of cassette recorders,
an increase in the demand for cassette recorders,
a fall in the demand for cassette recorders.

7.11

In the diagrams on page 112, DD and SS are the demand and supply curves for a product. The subscripts 1 and 2 indicate respectively the original curve (time 1) and the curve (time 2) that has replaced it at a later time.
Look at each of the diagrams carefully. In each case:
1 say what change has occurred in the price of the good and the quantity sold,
2 explain what event or events might have led to the change.

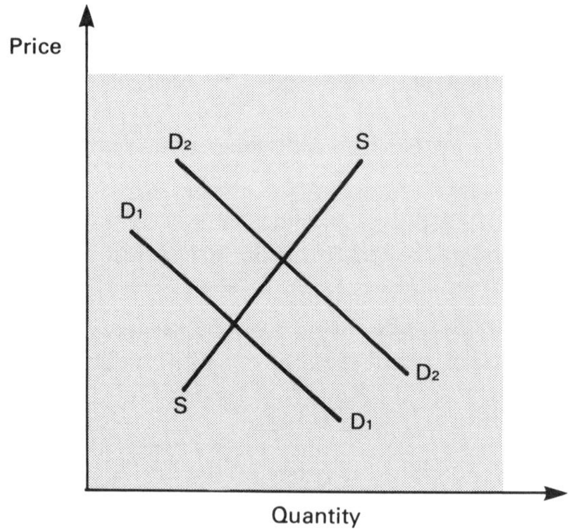

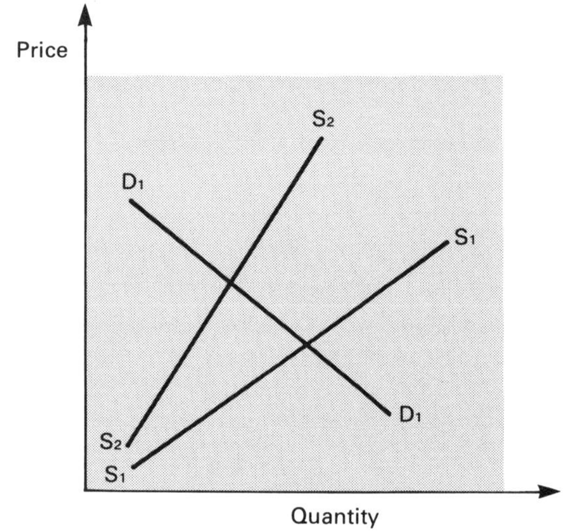

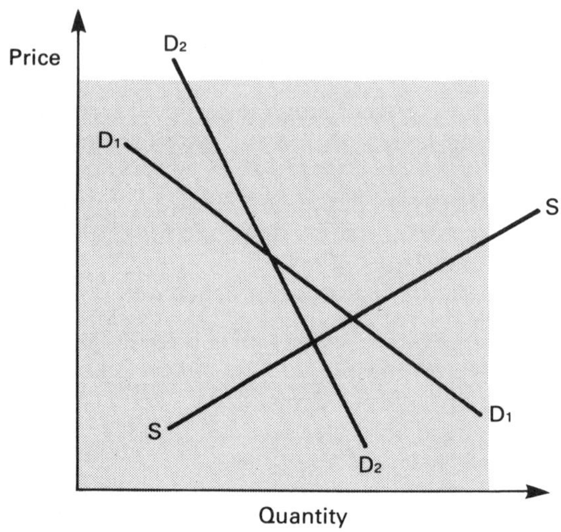

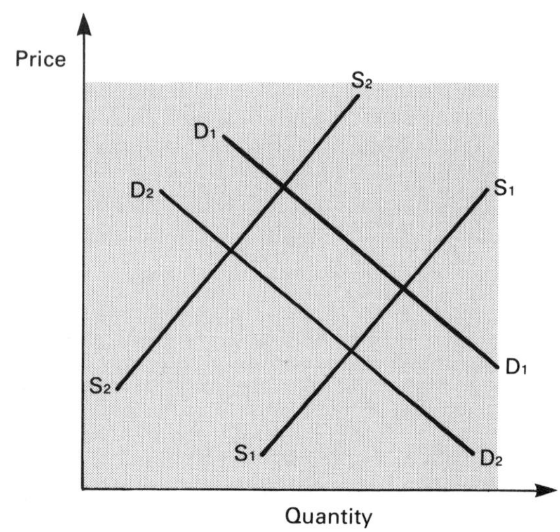

7.12

The demand for hotel accommodation in Cornwall is much greater in the summer than in the winter months.

1 Draw a demand and supply diagram showing the difference between the winter and summer situations and comment upon the implications for the charges set by hotel operators.

2 Analyse the possible effects on room charges of each of the following events:

(a) the introduction of cheap railway fares for families booking in advance to travel to the West Country,
(b) an increase in wage rates paid to hotel staff,
(c) a rise in unemployment,
(d) a fall in the price of package tour holidays to Spain,
(e) a successful comprehensive advertising campaign by the English Tourist Board encouraging tourists to take holidays in the UK.

Limitations of the demand and supply mechanism

There are a number of very important limitations in the explanantion of the way in which demand and supply help to determine prices. Consequently appreciation of the nature of these limitations is essential if the value of this type of analysis is to be understood.

Supply curves do not always slope upwards from left to right

Earlier it was said that upward sloping supply curves are common in agriculture. In the manufacturing and the service industries horizontal and downward sloping supply curves are common. In those industries, the costs of the firms may fall as their output is increased. For example, a large retail store may be able to increase its sales by 10 per cent without employing any additional workers; consequently the cost per unit of output will fall with the increase in sales. However, the fact that a supply curve does not slope upwards is in itself not a limitation to the analysis. In Figure 7.7 the supply curve slopes downwards. At a price of P_2 the quantity supplied exceeds the quantity demanded. The effect of this is that stocks will build up. This is then likely to induce suppliers to cut down production. But as they do so the costs of production rise and the tendency is for the price to rise to P_1 with the quantity being sold falling to Q_1.

Unexpected business reactions

In Figure 7.7 we would expect businesses to react to the build-up in stocks when price is below the equilibrium by cutting production. But they might decide to carry the larger stocks, at least for a period, rather than cut production, and in that case the price will not move up to

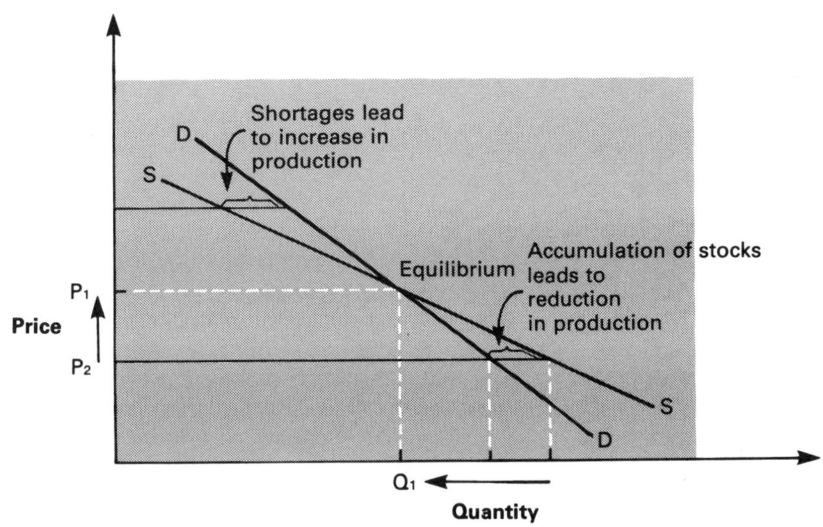

Figure 7.7 Price determination with a downward sloping supply curve

P_1 but will be held at P_2. Can you suggest reasons why businesses may accept the stock build-up, at least for some period?

Price-takers and price-makers

In Figure 7.5 the market price of tomatoes was determined by the relative positions of the demand and supply curves. Neither the buyers nor sellers were able to dictate to the other what the price should be. Both buyers and sellers were *price-takers*. Market situations in which the buyers and sellers are price-takers, where demand and supply jointly determine price, most commonly occur where there are many suppliers of the product and many buyers. This situation is discussed more fully in Chapter 8. No supplier is able to set a price without reference to the prevailing market price, for if he charges more than this price, he will make no sales and will soon be out of business. Rural industries, such as tomato-growing, provide us with some of the best examples of price-takers and demand and supply in action.

However, there are many situations in which a business has effective control of the price for its product. Such a business is known as a *price-maker*. In general, the fewer the number of businesses in an industry the greater the degree of freedom that any one of them will have to determine the price for its product. In many of the UK's manufacturing industries this is the case, and the simple demand and supply analysis we have developed fails to explain satisfactorily how price and quantity sold are determined. The model needs modifying to deal with the situation in which a firm appears to set the price. This price-maker situation is considered in the next chapter. For the present, it is worth noting that even when the business is a price–maker, the demand for its product is of critical importance and will always be taken into consideration when the price is set. Important, too, are the determinants of supply. A fall in the cost of raw materials is likely to lead to a price reduction. In other words, most of the determinants that affect the price of a good when the businesses are price-takers are also relevant when the business is a price-maker.

Government intervention

Price and quantity controls

The demand and supply mechanism is useful for studying agricultural industries. But in the UK, as in many other countries, governments and market authorities have intervened in the market to fix prices or to influence the quantity of farm products produced. In the EEC, the agricultural industries are subject to the Common Agricultural Policy (CAP) which sets target prices for many foodstuffs. In order to ensure target prices are obtained, the authorities actively intervene in the market to buy stocks at intervention prices if target prices are not achieved. This is examined in more detail in Chapter 19. Such intervention disturbs the normal price–quantity relationship by preventing the free determination of an equilibrium position. At first it may seem that, because this intervention is so common, it makes our study of demand and supply worthless. Fortunately, this is not true – in fact the reverse holds. It is very difficult to understand how modern marketing schemes work unless one first appreciates the working of demand and supply. The effects of government intervention can normally be shown by simple modifications to the demand and supply diagram.

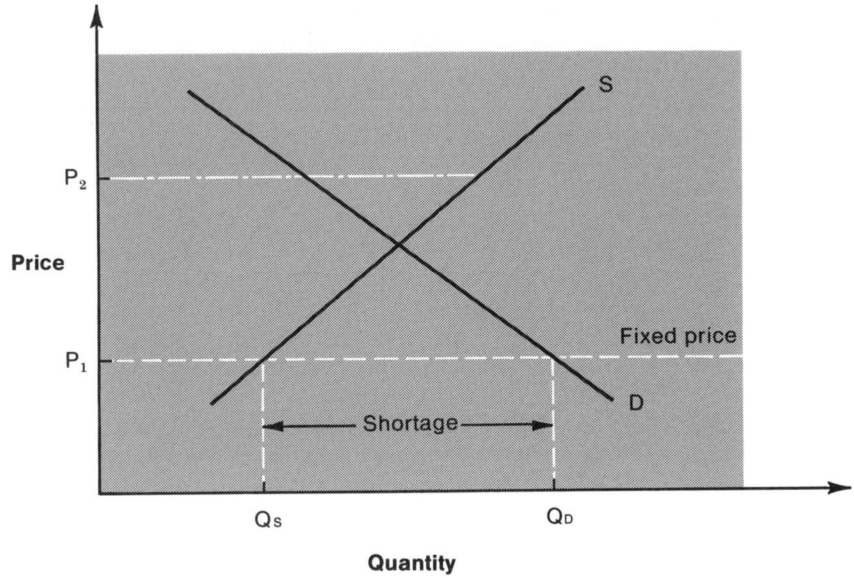

Figure 7.8 Effects of a fixed price (1)

Effects of a fixed price

In Figure 7.8, the government has fixed the price of wheat at P_1. The effect of fixing the price at P_1 is that purchasers can be sure that the official price will be no higher than P_1 and suppliers that P_1 will be the maximum official market price. However, at a price of P_1 per unit, the quantity demanded is greater that the quantity supplied ($Q_d - Q_s$). The demand and supply schedules are still relevant. The imposition of the fixed price, P_1, does not induce sellers to supply more than Q_s, as shown by the supply curve. This is the quantity they would be prepared to supply if that price prevailed in a free market. Likewise, the demand price still shows the quantity, Q_d, that the consumers desire to take at the fixed price, P_1. One effect of setting the price at P_1 is the emergence of a shortage, $Q_d - Q_s$, and this is likely to lead to the development of a *black market*. A black market is an illegal market in which unsatisfied purchasers offer a higher price than the official price.

7.13 The analysis based on Figure 7.8 suggests that there may well be some undesired effects if a government intervenes in a market by introducing a marketing scheme based on a fixed price. Can you think of any advantages of marketing schemes with fixed prices that might justify their use despite the drawbacks outlined above?

Fig 7.9 shows the effect on the market if a fixed price of P_2 is set by the government. In the UK, the effect of the Common Agricultural Policy (CAP) of the EEC for many agricultural products, has this result in the market. The aims of the CAP in setting a fixed price above the market equilibrium price are two-fold: to ensure a higher income to farmers through higher prices and to encourage increased production and self sufficiency. However, at a price of P_2 per unit, the quantity supplied is greater than the quantity demanded ($Q_s - Q_d$). Suppliers make available Q_s to the market, but since consumers take only Q_d at

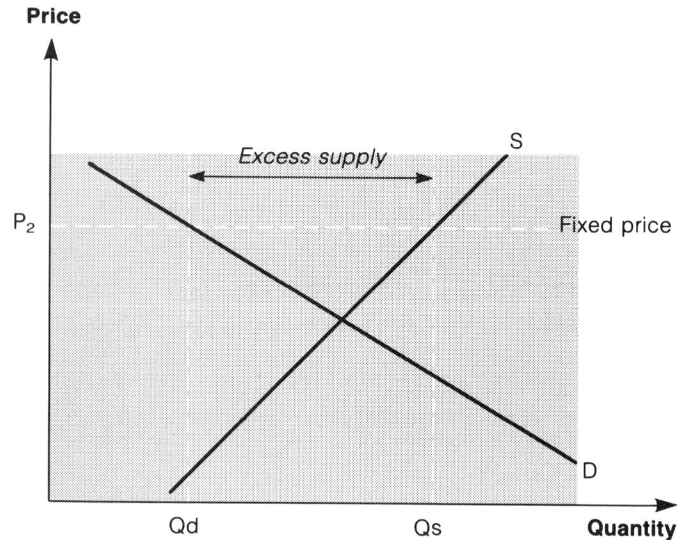

Figure 7.9 Effects of a fixed price (2)

the fixed price, the excess supply is bought up by the government in order to maintain the price. These stocks, bought by the authorities through their intervention in the market, form the surpluses held in government warehouses. This simple analysis helps to explain the existence of the 'butter mountains' and 'wine lakes' that have resulted from the operation of the CAP in those products.

7.14

Analyse the following situations using demand and supply diagrams, suitably modified.
1 In the housing market the government decides that market rents should not rise above a certain level (a maximum rent), but that they may be lower depending on market conditions. Show how the effects of this decision can be analysed with a diagram.
2 If the government wished to ease the housing problem by encouraging more private rented accommodation in the market is the policy of a maximum rent likely to achieve this? What would be the effect of a government imposed minimum rent above the market equilibrium level?

7.15

On one particular day in September 1979 the price of gold increased by 28 dollars to 380 dollars an ounce on the gold markets. In spite of the rise in price, the demand for gold was increasing as more buyers entered the market. *The Guardian*, Wednesday 19th September, 1979 said that 'Normal economic laws are being turned upside down as higher prices seem to attract more buyers.' Show by a demand and supply diagram how 'normal' economic analysis can explain this behaviour and the 'normal laws' of demand and supply still hold.

7.16

Figure 7.10 is a very simple representation of the market for Australian beef. Part is sold at home. The curve AD shows the domestic demand for beef. Part of production is sold overseas at

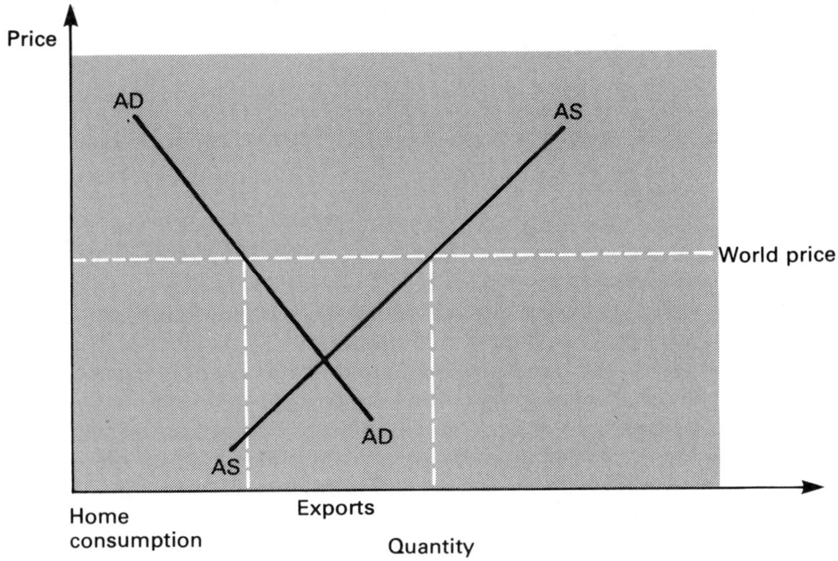

Figure 7.10 *The Australian beef market*

the world price. The quantity sold at home and the quantity exported are both marked on the diagram. The line AS is the Australian supply curve.

1 Explain why the line marked world price is drawn as a horizontal line.

2 Analyse the effects on price and quantity sold if overseas markets are closed to Australian beef.

3 Analyse the effects on price and quantity sold at home and overseas if the Australian Government agreed to pay beef producers a subsidy of x cents per kg.

4 How does a fall in the world price of beef affect the well-being of beef producers and Australian consumers?

Notes

1 A change in the conditions of demand (say, a change in tastes) may result in a demand curve moving both to right and left at the same time – rotating on a point. This would mean that consumers were more (or less) willing to purchase at higher prices, and less (or more) willing to purchase at lower prices. Perhaps an appeal to snobbery?

Chapter 8 Business Behaviour

Profit maximisation

An economic system comprises the activities of different groups and individuals in the society. In the UK, approximately 70 per cent of production is organised by privately-owned enterprises. That is, private businessmen make the decisions as to what is to be produced, and how much should be produced. An explanation of how the system works must involve understanding the motives behind their decisions.

Profits as an incentive to producers

The traditional explanation has been that businessmen engage in production to further their own interests to make profits – and as much profit as possible. This was Adam Smith's view of business motives. The prospect of profit greater than the income obtained as an employee is the incentive to enter business. The prospect of these greater rewards encourages some people to run the inevitable risks of loss involved in organising production and estimating consumers' future requirements. Adam Smith regarded the desire to maximise profits as a powerful force making businessmen receptive to consumers' demands; opportunities for making profits come from producing those goods and services that consumers want, and are prepared to pay for.

Criticism of the profit maximisation assumption

In recent years, business activity has become much more complex. It is no longer clear that production decisions can be entirely explained in terms of a desire to maximise profits.

Many of Britain's important industries are dominated by large companies. By the end of 1976 there were 16 716 public companies registered in Great Britain. In mid-1977 the number of companies quoted on the Stock Exchange was 3437.[1]

Separation of ownership and control in companies

The owners of these companies, the shareholders, are seldom the people who decide how production is to be organised. The shareholders derive the profits, but the decision-makers are directors and executives who earn fees or salaries, supplemented possibly by tax-free expense allowances and payments in kind, such as a company car or company housing. This division between the ownership and management of business has led to suggestions that the decision-makers may sacrifice some profits for shareholders to promote their own personal satisfaction. For example, the manager may be interested in acquiring as much power as possible, through the growth of the firm, through the establishment of new departments or the introduction of new products, although some of these activities may not be profitable. Alternatively, the decision-maker may seek satisfaction by arranging an easy life for himself instead of submitting to long hours of work and the pressures that the search for new markets, new ideas and new techniques may demand. So long as he can make enough profit to keep shareholders content, he need not exert himself in an effort to achieve maximum potential profit.

Management's interest

Profits as a constraining influence on the businessman

Even when the management is seeking the success of the business rather than personal satisfaction, business objectives may still differ from the idea of profit maximisation. The objective may be to maximise sales turnover, or to create conditions for the growth or survival of the firm, which conflict with immediate plans for quick profits. Management may place a high priority on keeping shareholders happy and do this through their dividend policy, which will necessitate maintaining a certain degree of profitability.

There is widespread agreement that these motives operate and affect UK business decisions to some degree, but there is also general recognition that the profit motive is still very important. Many of the motives or objectives of UK businessmen can be linked directly with profit maximisation. Where other goals seem more important than profits, the latter still acts as a constraint on the businessman. For example, an executive may be determined to increase his own importance in the firm, or he may be looking for an easy life, but either way he will need to ensure that the profit performance of the division under his control is satisfactory, or he may find himself out of a job. In the last resort, shareholders may replace the directors of the company, though this would be a remarkable event. A more common result is for share prices of the company to fall because the managers have failed to live up to potential. Such a company becomes a potential take-over target. This helps to explain why many managers think in terms of keeping shareholders happy. They do this by making profits and paying dividends, which help to maintain share prices.

Parent companies demand profits from their subsidiaries

Managers of subsidiary companies are usually under pressure from the parent company to produce high profits and this lends further weight to the assumption that firms maximise profits.

Long-run profit maximisation results in different policies from short-run maximisation

A most important distinction is that between short-term profits and long-term profits. A business may decide not to charge high prices, even though it may forgo immediate profits by doing so. It may reason that to do so would jeopardise its position in the long run. High prices may attract competitors, or prompt government intervention to prevent exploitation of consumers. Businesses that appear to bypass opportunities for quick profits may be acting quite rationally. In the long run their profits may be greater.

Profit maximisation for sole proprietorships and partnerships

Many primary producers and producers in the retail trades are sole proprietorships or partnerships. In the UK, about 85 per cent of all businesses are sole traders or partnerships. The problem posed by the separation of ownership and control does not exist and the profit motive remains as the principal objective for most of these producers. For many farmers and small shopkeepers the difference between maximising profits and avoiding making losses is a slim one. To survive, they must maximise profits.

Overall, profit maximisation remains the major underlying objective of private business and serves well in explaining private business activities.

How a business aims to maximise profits

If a business is to maximise its profits it must give consideration to three separate policy areas:

1 It must minimise the cost of producing any given output. It must therefore seek the cheapest and most efficient means of producing goods of the required quality, select the appropriate production techniques and eliminate waste.

2 It must ensure that any given output is sold for the highest possible price, consistent with maintaining the long-term position of the business. Its marketing and sales divisions, aided by advertising campaigns where appropriate, will endeavour to see that consumer demand for the firm's products is maintained.

3 It must decide on the level of production that it believes will bring the greatest profits, after considering the alternative cost and revenue patterns that arise from producing different quantities of its products. Having decided, it may then go on to set a price for its product.

In practice, a business cannot set a price for its product and ensure that consumers buy a predetermined output at that price. Consumers determine how much they buy at any given price. But the business usually plans production on its estimate of how much consumers will buy at a particular price. If it misjudges the market then it may incur severe losses. Normally, businesses have some flexibility in their production plans which allows them to vary output. The alternatives are to let stocks of their products increase or run down, or to make an appropriate price adjustment.

State ownership and control

Particularly important in the UK is the government owned business undertaking, more commonly referred to as the nationalised industry or public corporation. This form of ownership and state control is of considerable importance in basic areas of industry such as energy supply, transport, communications and public utilities. Together with the services provided by, and trading activities of, local authorities and central government, the nationalised industries and public corporations make up the public sector of the economy and account for over a fifth of total consumption of goods and services.

Governments operate businesses for a variety of reasons, some of which were mentioned in Chapter 4. It may be that private enterprise is unable to operate a service profitably, but government judges that the need for the service is sufficient to justify a government-run service, perhaps at a loss. Secondly, it may consider that a privately operated service would not be in the public interest. Often these two arguments are related. For example, the costs of providing public transport or public utilities in rural areas may be too expensive for a private business undertaking to provide. Since such services would prove uneconomic for the private sector to provide, the state has decided that the public sector should be responsible and that some consumers should be subsidised.

In fact the requirements imposed by governments on nationalised industries vary, but generally a specified target, such as a rate of return on capital, is set for each industry. The extent of state ownership in other instances may be determined by the acquisition of shares in companies (often as a result of state investment as a rescue operation). The features in common with all the public sector undertakings are that it is the government that provides the funds to operate them (augmented in some cases by public borrowing) and the government that bears the risk of losses and takes any profits.

This means that nationalised industries and public corporations frequently do not operate with the intention of maximising profits. They may also be required by government to consider the welfare of consumers and this may lead to a pricing policy quite different from that adopted by privately owned companies. Some possible approaches to government pricing policies are examined later in this chapter. However, it is important to appreciate that even when a government business undertaking does not attempt to maximise profits in the same way as a private undertaking, it will usually be required to operate as efficiently as possible. This may involve rigorous cost controls, an approved pricing policy and often a requirement that it aim at showing a specified return on funds employed.

8.1

Most accounts of how a market economy determines what shall be produced explain business behaviour in terms of the desire to maximise profits. But suppose some major businesses (perhaps the major chains of retail stores) were more concerned with achieving a 5 per cent increase in their sales turnover (that is, revenue from sales) than with profit maximisation. What effects might this have on the operation of a market economy? For example, would the market be more, or less responsive to changes in consumer demand? Would firms employ more people? Would they advertise more? Would they charge the same prices for their products as when trying to maximise?

8.2

Consider one type of government or public sector undertaking that commonly makes losses on part or all of its activities, such as transport services. To what extent do you consider the situation to be unsatisfactory? Why does it make losses? If you believe that its existing policies that lead to losses can be justified, then provide such a justification. If, on the other hand, you are unhappy about management policies, what changes would you advocate?

8.3

Imagine that there are only two businesses in an industry that produces a range of sporting goods. One firm is the subsidiary of a foreign company, it adopts aggressive marketing policies with the intention of achieving high profits. Its competitor is an old established family business that prides itself on the standards of service set and conducts its business in a rather leisurely fashion without using pressure tactics to achieve sales. Discuss the sorts of policies the two firms might follow. In what ways might they differ? Is it possible that both are seeking to maximise profits? Suppose the owners of the second firm plan to sell up and retire in five years time. What difference, if any, might this make to their policies?

Production costs

Costs and supply

In Chapter 7 we saw that the quantity of a product a business is prepared to supply at any given price will be determined in part by its costs of production. If it is to maximise profits, production and distribution costs must be minimised. The cost of producing any level of output will depend upon the productivity of the physical resources used and the prices the business has to pay for the use of these resources.

An important set of decisions concern how production is to be carried out; what materials are to be used, types of machines, factory layout, composition of the labour force. Occasionally, the business may find itself with no important decisions to make about how it produces an article, or what resources it uses. Then it simply hires the resources it requires for the production process. A taxi-driver needs only his cab and licence. More often there are alternative ways of producing – alternative materials and alternative configurations of plant and equipment are available. An example is the production of textiles involving a choice between an automated plant using few workers and much capital and, at the other extreme, a factory with a large workforce using the

Alternative production technologies

simplest machines. Between these extremes lie a whole range of intermediate possibilities.

Selection of production methods cannot be divorced from the prices the firm has to pay for resources. Cost minimisation depends on choosing those techniques that yield the lowest cost per unit of output. Thus, the use of large numbers of unskilled workers may appear to be a technically unsophisticated method of production. It may even be labelled 'technically inefficient' when contrasted with methods using labour-saving machinery. But it may still be cheaper in many situations.

Choice of production methods will depend upon the scale of the business's operations. Large expensive machines that operate most cheaply when operated continuously may be quite inappropriate for the firm producing small quantities of a product in a given period.

The time element, too, is of critical importance to a firm as it plans production. Naturally, it estimates what the expected market demand for its product will be and the cheapest way of producing that output. But it also has to consider that demand may vary as time goes by, and it needs to consider the implications of changes in demand. It therefore needs to calculate the costs of changing its level of production and how quickly and easily it can change its production methods to cater for changes in market conditions.

Short and long run

Economists have found it convenient to distinguish between short-run and long-run adjustments to business conditions. The *short run* is usually thought of as a period in which the business finds that *opportunities to vary its operations* are restricted by technical or financial considerations. Either there are physical limits to changing the quantities of productive resources it employs, or many of its costs are fixed; it is committed, by contracts, to hiring certain human and non-human resources for a specified period. By contrast, the *long run* is thought of as a period in which the business has maximum flexibility to *change the scale of its operations*. It can build new factories, hire or fire its workforce, or reorganise its production methods completely.

Figure 8.1 is a diagrammatic representation of the planning and development of the Dunlin oil field in the North Sea from 1973 to 1978. Crude oil production from the field began in August 1978, more than five years after the discovery and initial appraisal drilling. During those five years, over £330 million had been invested before a penny in revenue was received. For large projects such as this, large amounts are invested in evaluation and project planning, all of which would be lost if the decision had been not to proceed.

When the terms are used in this sense, it should be clear that they do not refer to specific periods of time. The short run may vary from a few weeks in one industry to several years in another. A manufacturing concern facing a substantial increase in demand for its products may deal with the emergency by getting existing staff to work overtime and by running machines when they should be shut down for servicing. Given additional time, it may be able to improve its supply position by taking on more labour and fitting a few extra machines into its existing factories. But the final solution (the long-period answer) may be to scrap the existing factory completely and to build another with double the capacity.

The time horizon for a mining company wishing to increase production may be many years. In the short run it may be able to expand production from existing operational mines. But the commissioning of new mines will occur only after feasibility studies and

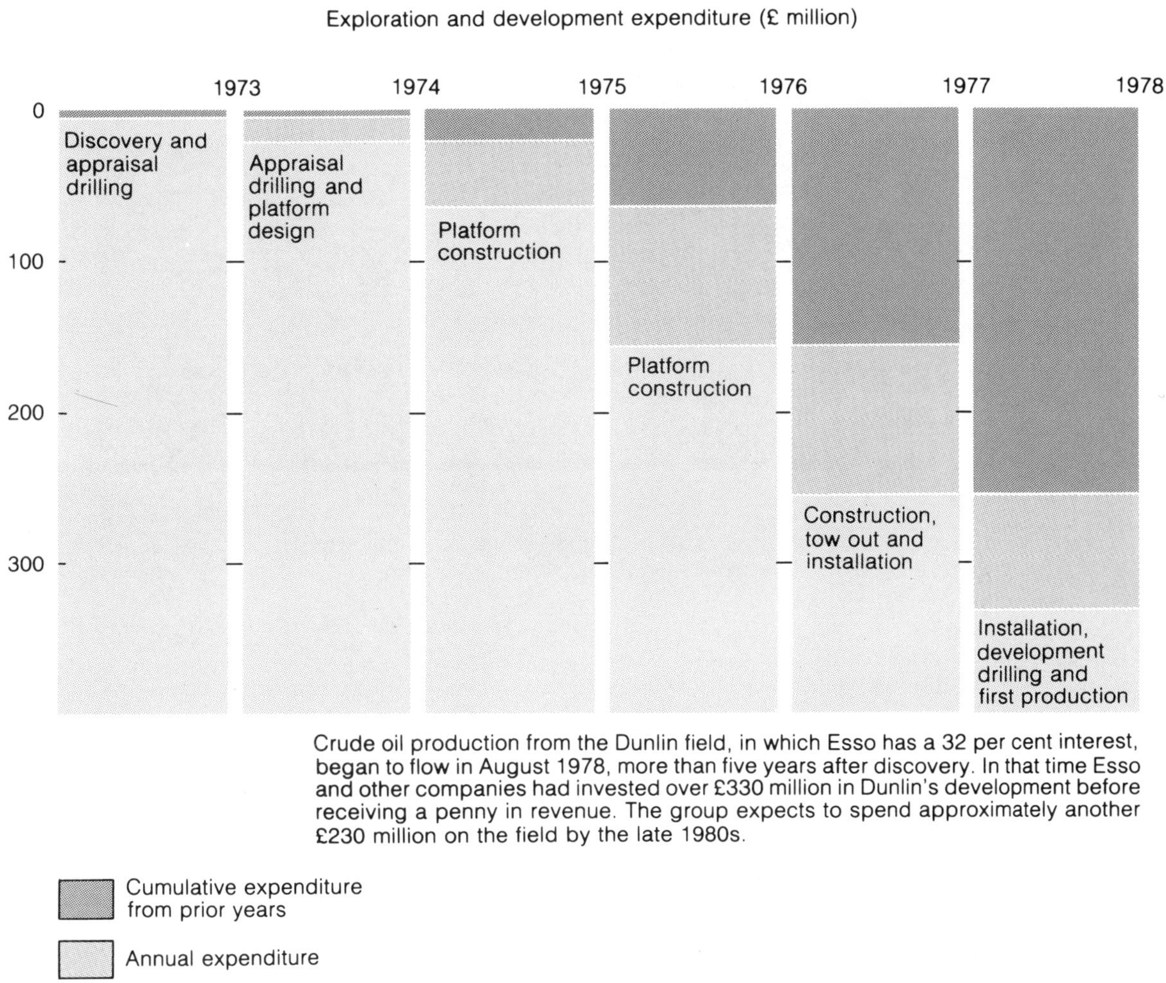

Figure 8.1 Production plans of a large enterprise

Based on *Esso Petroleum Company Ltd Accounts and Annual Report 1978* on Exploration and development expenditure on the Dunlin oil field in the North Sea 1973–1978, page 13

the necessary preparatory engineering and constructional work have been completed.

The length of time from the decision to produce to actual production presents its own hazards. By the time the scale of operation has been altered, a reversal in the market conditions that appeared to justify it may also have occurred.

Economic significance of short period

The economic significance of the short period is that the lack of flexibility in production may compel the enterprise to use relatively expensive production methods to vary production levels. If floor space cannot be increased, workers will have to be crowded into the existing area and output per worker may be reduced even if total production rises. This is so because sooner or later the productivity of these resources declines.

Marginal productivity

The term *diminishing returns* is used to describe the relationship between additions to output, the marginal product and additional incre-

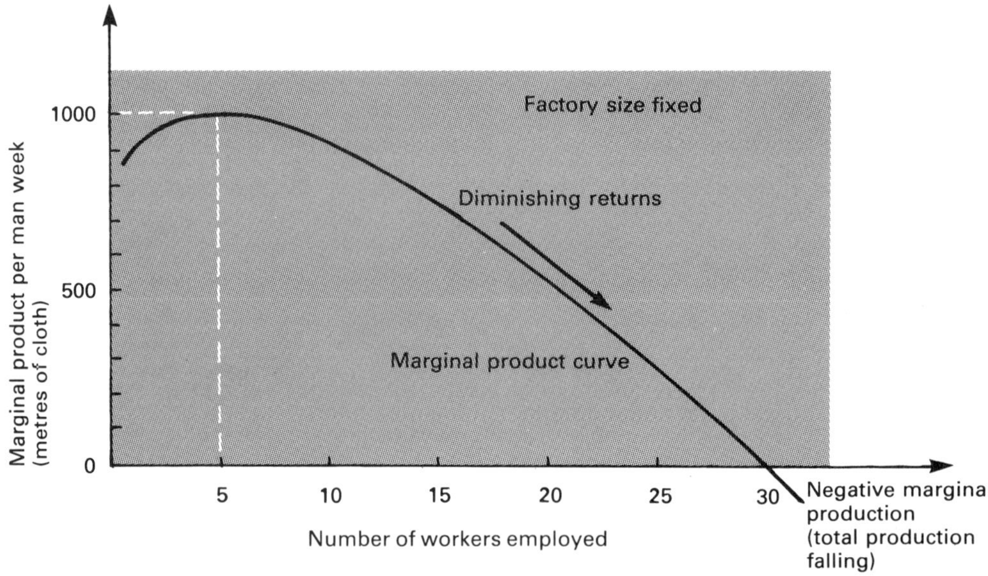

Figure 8.2 Diminishing marginal productivity

ments of variable resources. Figure 8.2 illustrates this relationship. The size of the factory (the fixed resource) is constant. Workers, measured on the horizontal axis, are the variable resource. The vertical axis measures the marginal product; the additional metres of cloth produced as a result of employing each additional worker. The diagram shows that the effect of employing the fifth worker is to increase total output by 1000 metres per week. Thereafter the employment of additional workers continues to raise total output but their marginal product diminishes. The thirtieth worker has a marginal product of zero because the net effect of employing him is that total production is unchanged. If further additions were made to the firm's labour force, it appears likely that total production would actually be reduced. The marginal product would be negative.

Average productivity

Another way of showing the relationship between production and the employment of resources is to record average product per person as the labour force increases. This involves dividiing total production by the number of workers employed. Figure 8.3 shows the relationship between the average product curve and the marginal product curve. Average product increases at first and then declines. Notice that the marginal and average product curves have a similar shape and that the marginal product curve cuts the average product curve at its highest point.

There is a clear link between the average of a series of numbers and the next additional number, as every cricketer knows. A number, or score, higher than the ruling average will increase the average, whereas a score below the average will pull it down. If we look on the marginal product curve as recording the series of additional scores, then it will pull up the average as long as it is above the average and pull it down as long as it is below. Hence it must cut the average product curve at the latter's highest point or maximum.

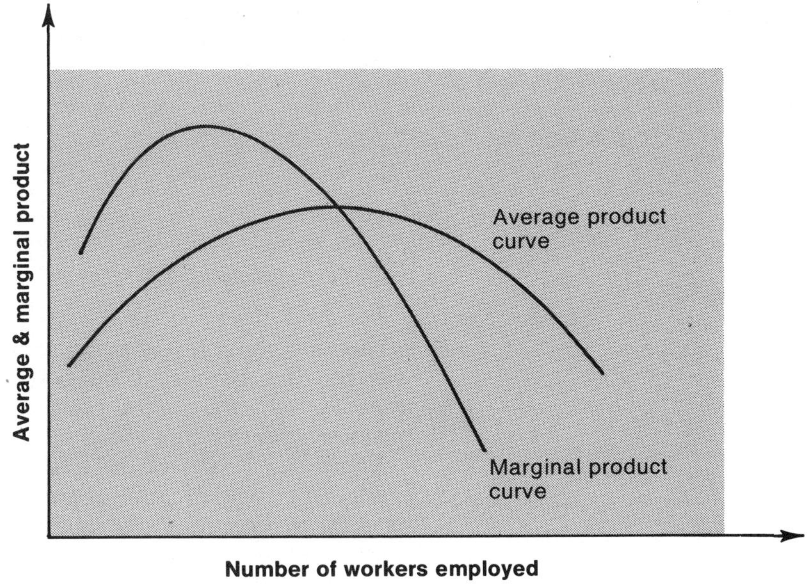

Figure 8.3 Relationship between average and marginal product curves

8.4

Figure 8.3 shows the relationship between a marginal product curve and an average product curve for a firm in a textile industry. Consider a farmer with a fixed amount of land on which to grow crops. Do you think that the average and marginal product curves showing the relationship between output of wheat and successive applications of superphosphate would be similar to those in Figure 8.3? Explain your reasoning. Figure 8.3 shows the average product curve to be positive at all levels of input, but is it possible that average product, too, might become negative at any stage?

Prices of resources as a determinant of production costs

The second element which determines the cost of producing any given output is the price the business has to pay for productive resources. Suppose that the prices the business has to pay for the materials used are fixed and that wage rates are fixed too. The cost of producing any level of output will be determined by multiplying the number of units of each resource used by the price of that resource. These costs can be broken down into two, in the short period: fixed costs and variable costs.

Fixed costs are contractual obligations the business must meet. Normally they are associated with the use of those fixed resources that have to be used if the business is to produce anything at all in the short period. The greater the business's production the smaller the average fixed cost. This may sound strange, but it is the simple and inescapable result of spreading a fixed expenditure over a large number of units. Average fixed cost must be lower, while to talk about marginal fixed cost is to talk of something which must be zero by definition.

Variable costs are costs that the business can avoid in the short run. The wages of workers and the costs of materials are usually regarded as variable costs, because in the short run the business may hire more or fewer workers, buy more or less materials, and in so doing vary

Total fixed cost (£) (1)	Output (metres of cloth) (2)	Average fixed cost per metre (£) (1) ÷ (2) = (3)	Marginal fixed cost (4)
1000	50	20.00	0
1000	120	8.33	0
1000	200	5.00	0
1000	300	3.33	0

Table 8.1 Relationship between total fixed cost and average fixed cost

production costs. If we assume that the price of these variable resources is fixed, then changes in the cost of producing the good will be determined by changes in the productivity of the variable resource as the business attempts to vary its output level.

Figure 8.3 expresses the relationship between average and marginal product per worker (unit of variable resource), but the same data can be used to determine the number of workers required to produce a single unit of output in a given period such as a week. Instead of dividing total output by the number of workers to derive average output, the number of workers is divided by total output to determine the average variable resource usage. This procedure is shown in Table 8.2. Thus if 5 men are needed to produce 400 metres of cloth per week, the manpower requirement for 1 metre of cloth is $\frac{5}{400} = 0.0125$ man weeks. In addition, it is possible to calculate the *marginal resource requirement*: the extra unit of the variable resource needed for the production of an extra unit of output. These average and marginal resource requirements can then be plotted on a graph, as in Figure 8.4(a).

No. of workers employed (1)	Total ouput (metres of cloth) (2)	Average product (2) ÷ (1)	Average number of workers per metre of cloth (1) ÷ (2)
5	400	80	0.0125
10	600	60	0.0167
15	750	50	0.02
20	800	40	0.025

Table 8.2 Relationship between average product per worker and average worker requirement per unit of output

The second step in calculating production costs is to multiply the number of units of variable resource required to produce a unit of output by the price of that resource. The resulting information can then be graphed as in Figure 8.4.

The first feature of Figure 8.4(a) is that the curves are 'U'-shaped – the other way up to the curves in Figure 8.3. As we have said, they contain the same information as Figure 8.3, but expressed in a different way. Figure 8.3 shows the average output per worker, whereas Figure 8.4(a) shows the average number of workers used per unit of output.

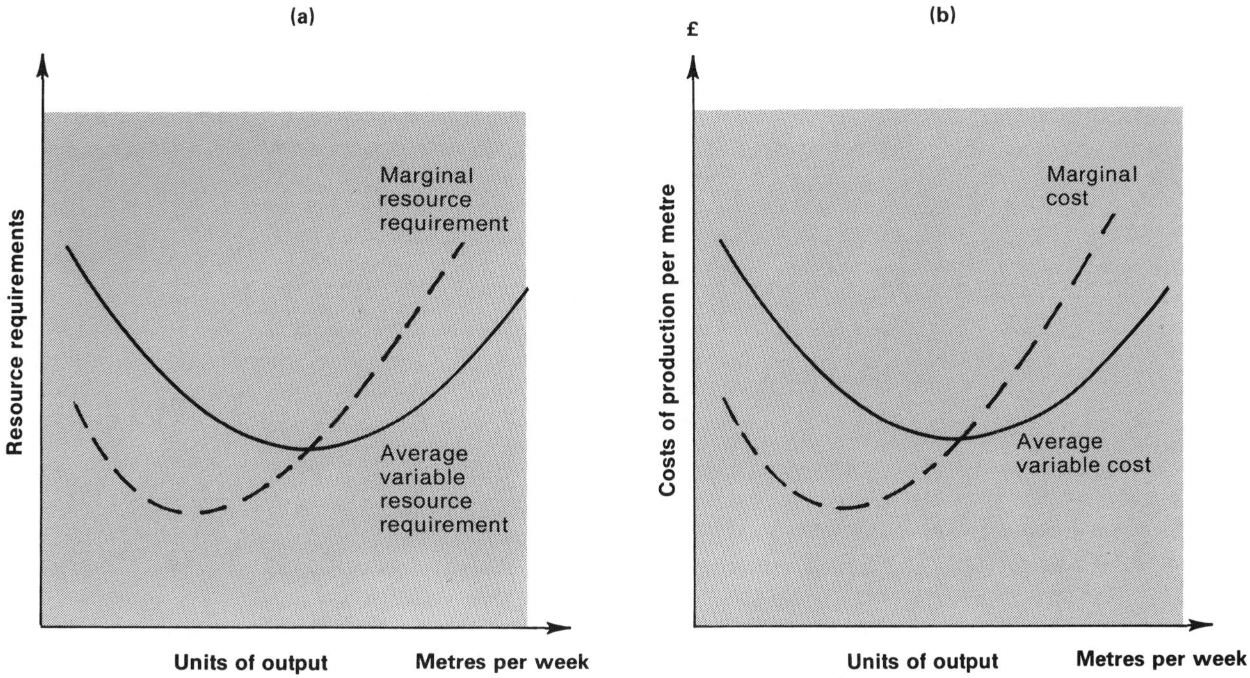

Figure 8.4(a) Resource requirements
(b) Costs of production

Figure 8.4(b) appears similar to Figure 8.4(a). But it is expressed in money terms. It is assumed that the money wage is the same for each worker. When production is 400 metres of cloth, each metre requires 0.0125 man weeks as we have seen. If the weekly wage is £100, the cost will be £1.25 per metre. That is £100 × 0.0125. A higher production figure of 800 metres per week requires proportionately more labour and the cost will then rise to £2.50 per metre.

In addition to the average resource use curve and the average variable cost curve, the diagrams show the respective marginal resource use and marginal cost curves. Each bears the same relation to its average curve that we have come to expect from Figure 8.3. The marginal cost curve is of considerable importance to economists in the study of business behaviour and profit maximisation.

The two categories of costs, fixed and variable, must be combined to give a complete picture of what a business's average costs of production will be in the short period. This has been done in Figure 8.5.

The highest of the three average cost curves is obtained by adding together the points on the average fixed cost curve and the average variable cost curve. For example, consider the average cost of producing 400 metres of cloth. The average fixed cost (a) is £2.50 per metre (£1000 ÷ 400) and the average variable cost is £1.25 per metre (£500 ÷ 400) giving an aggregated average cost of £3.75 per metre. As the average fixed cost curve has no marginal cost curve, there is only one marginal cost curve: that relating to the average variable cost curve.

In the long period, the business will be able to select the most suitable production technology. The likely effects of this flexibility are shown

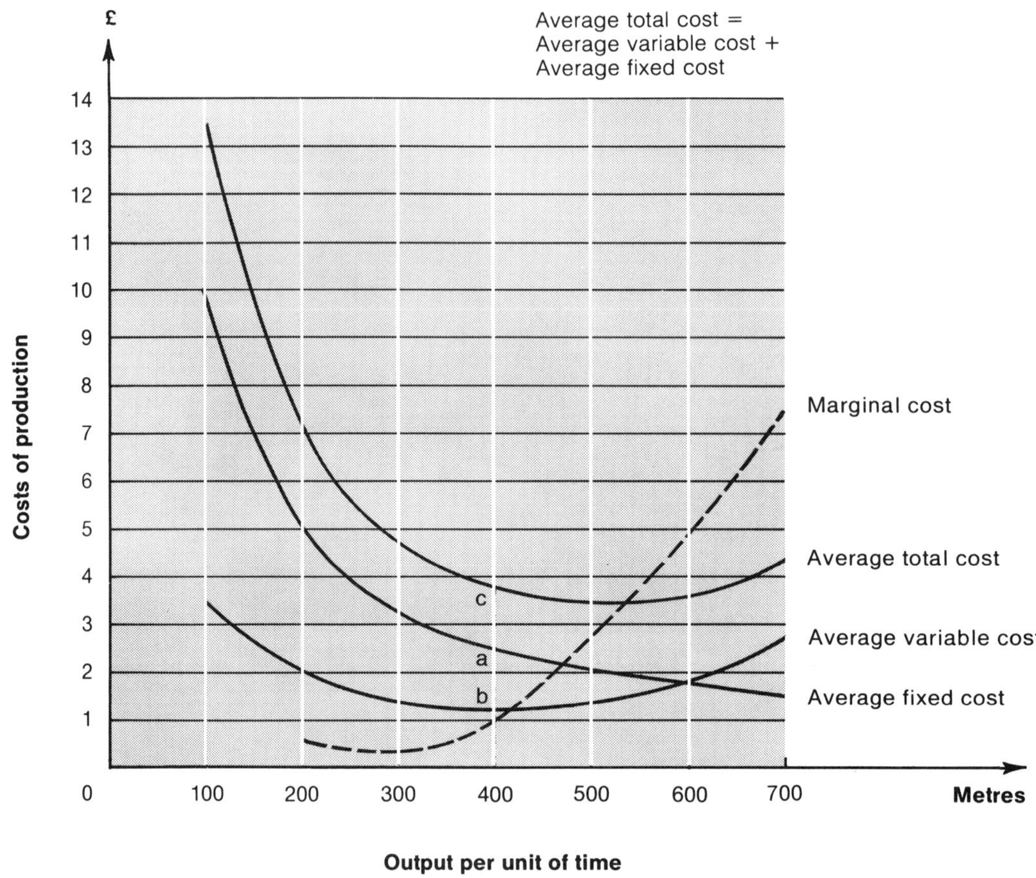

Figure 8.5 Costs of production

in Figure 8.6. Short-run average cost curve 1 (SAC_1) is the enterprise's average cost curve at a particular time. It was producing *a* units of output per week at an average cost of £a_1. Following an increase in demand, the firm decided to increase production. At the time it could only increase production quickly by incurring higher production costs. Figure 8.6 shows that if production were to be stepped up to *b* units within a couple of months, then the only way in which this could be done was by moving along SAC_1. The average cost is £b_1. Given more time, say a couple of years, the firm might be able to produce *b* units per week far more cheaply. It might tear down its present factory, build a larger one and put in new equipment. In Figure 8.6 the costs associated with such a new production plan are shown by a second short-run average cost (SAC_2). With SAC_2 in operation it would be possible to produce *b* units per week at £b_2 per unit. This is substantially lower than the cost of producing *b* units per week under the original system (SAC_1).

At each level of output, such as *a*, there will be a production plan that mimimises average costs. The line that joins these least cost points for each level of output is called the long-run average cost curve (LAC).[2]

The long-run average cost curve slopes downwards from left to right in Figure 8.6. It has been drawn in this way because there is now a great deal of evidence to suggest that such downward sloping average cost

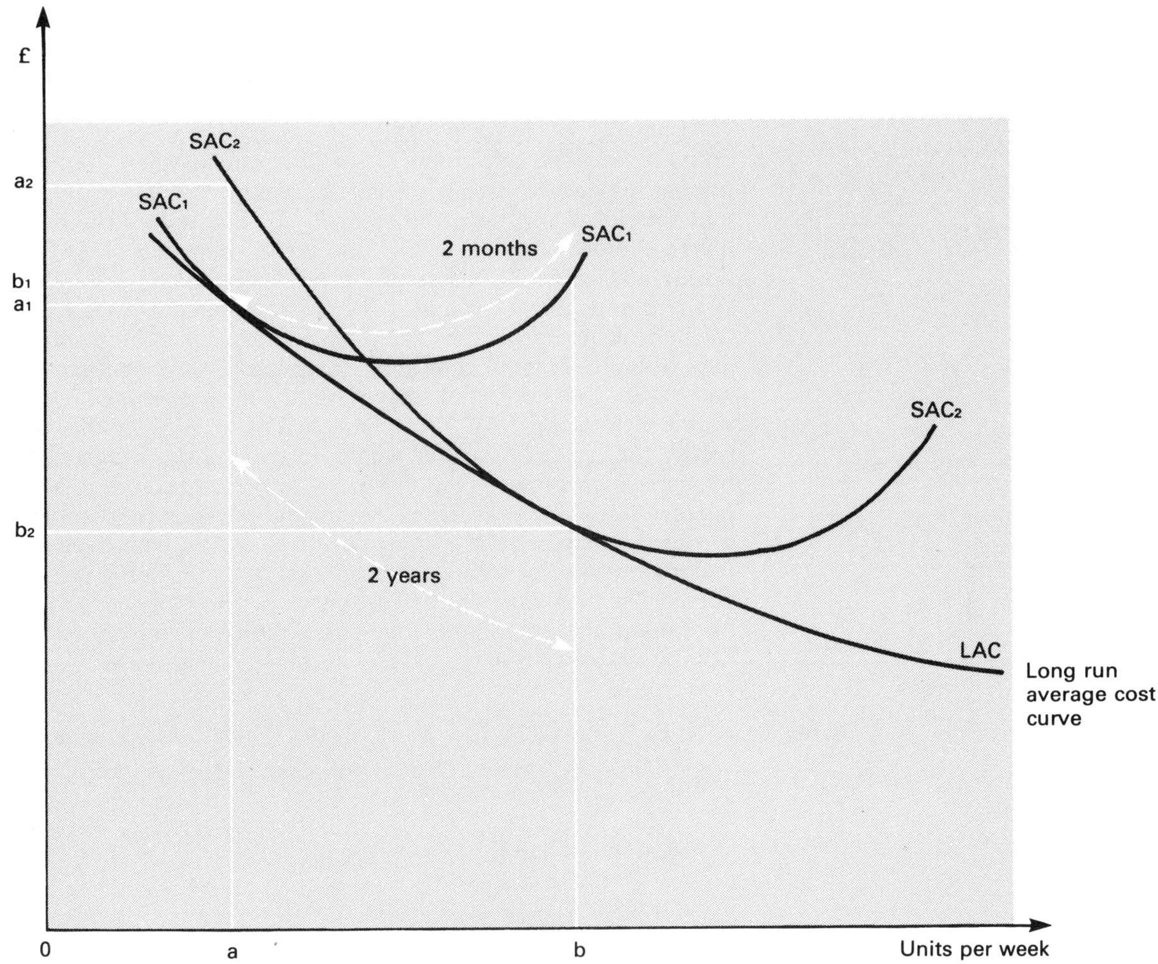

Figure 8.6 Long-run costs

curves are common in manufacturing and in the service industries. Cost reductions come from the technical economies associated with large-scale operations. They also result from the favourable prices that very large businesses can sometimes negotiate for the materials they require. In the UK, industries in which falling costs have been identified include bread making, petroleum refining, banking, brewing and automobiles.

With falling long-run average cost curves in many enterprises in the UK, the opportunity arises for the prices of products to fall with increases in output. Increases in production would bring cost savings and allow price reductions. However, whether this takes place depends upon the size of the market for the product. For example, in volume car production the UK producer is at a disadvantage compared with rival Japanese and European producers, if the demand for British made cars is not high enough to take full advantage of the substantial economies of scale that could be achieved.

Another opportunity for increasing production and reducing costs occurs if there is a possibility of supplementing domestic demand by exporting part of the enterprise's output. The opportunity for exporting is dependent on prices being competitive with existing low cost producers on overseas markets. Variations in exchange rate obviously apply here, as do other trading conditions, such as tariffs or quantitative restrictions that may be imposed by importing countries.

Although the businessman's long-run average cost curve sets the limits to what he can produce, for how much, when he has unlimited time at his disposal, many decisions have to be made in the knowledge that the 'ideal' can never be attained. In Figure 8.6, the business may increase production using the production methods of SAC_1 and may decide not to switch to a second type of production technology, SAC_2. His reasoning may be sound. It would have taken two years to introduce the new technology and by the time the change had been completed, the factory built, demand conditions might have changed again. If demand had fallen, the firm would have found that it was again operating the wrong technology (SAC_2). It might then have taken another two years to rectify the error. No matter where on its long-run average cost curve a business is operating it will find itself restricted because it is also operating on a short period average cost curve at the same time. At any moment of time a business faces a short period situation, with fixed costs, diminishing returns, a U-shaped average cost curve and a rising marginal cost curve. The long-run average cost curve can best be seen as an aid to the business in determining its long-run production strategy rather than for dealing with day-to-day changes in market conditions.

8.5

A local business has established a small textile factory after choosing a factory layout and production system with the following production costs:

Production plan 1

Output ('000 metres per month)	Total variable cost (£)	Fixed cost (£)	Total cost (£)
0	0	20 000	20 000
10	10 000	20 000	30 000
20	26 000	20 000	46 000
30	49 000	20 000	69 000
40	90 000	20 000	110 000
50	150 000	20 000	170 000
60	250 000	20 000	270 000

1 Calculate the average fixed cost, the average variable cost and the average total cost for each level of output. You will need to use the rather crude device for calculating the marginal cost of a metre of the textile product of first determining the extra cost of producing another 10 000 metres of cloth and then dividing by 10 000. Draw these curves on a graph measuring quantities of cloth produced per month on the horizontal axis.

2 Suppose that the business had been faced with an alternative production layout when it started out – one with the production costs given below:

Production plan 2

Output ('000 metres per month)	Total variable cost (£)	Total cost (£)
0	—	50 000
10	15 000	65 000
20	29 000	79 000
30	43 000	93 000
40	58 000	108 000
50	78 000	128 000
60	100 000	150 000
70	125 000	175 000
80	160 000	210 000
90	210 000	260 000
100	300 000	350 000

Is it possible to nominate one of the production plans as superior? If not, what other information might have been used to decide which production strategy to employ?

8.6

Imagine that a business had no variable costs at all, and that the limited size of its factory meant that it was unable to increase production above a certain limit. Draw a graph of its total cost and average cost curves and explain why the average cost curve is not U-shaped. Would a cinema have cost curves similar to those you have drawn; that is, how important are variable costs in that industry?

8.7

In the following diagram the average or marginal cost curves have shifted. Try to put forward plausible explanations of the movement.

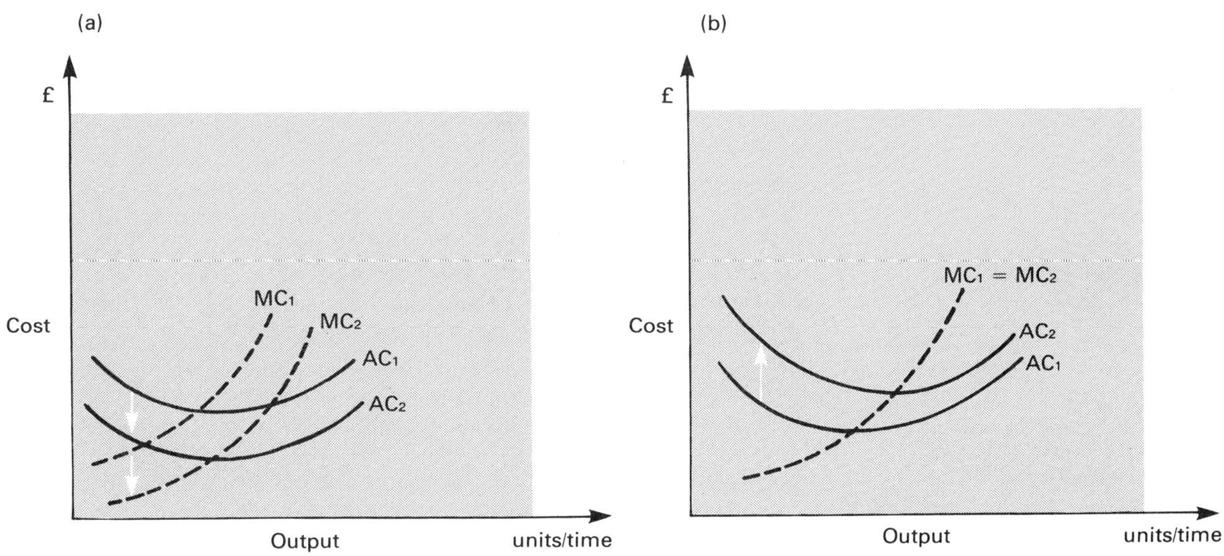

8.8 It is quite common today to hear businessmen talking about having a manufacturing plant which is operating at, say, '75 per cent capacity'. Discuss what might be meant by this term. Does it refer to a short-run or to a long-run situation? It may be that your ideas of what constitutes surplus capacity do not fit in with the idea of a U-shaped cost curve. If not, try drawing a different shaped curve.

Price-takers

In Chapter 7 a distinction was made between businesses that are free to fix their prices (price-makers) and those that have to take the market price (price-takers). In general, the more businesses producing a particular article, the less likely it is that any one of them will be able to charge a higher price than its competitors. Rivals would soon win all the customer support and drive it out of business. Even if there are only a few firms producing what amounts to an identical product, the competition is likely to be fierce enough for a single market price to be established and for all to abide by that price.

Price-taking is predominant in a number of industries in the UK, notably agriculture and other primary industries. The prices of most agricultural products are determined by government price schemes or by demand and supply on world markets. Many basic products have their prices determined by market forces in specially organised centres, such as the London Metals Exchange. The price-taker is faced by price levels and changes in prices which are outside his control. In contrast, the price-maker is able to set a price based on his estimate of how much consumers will be prepared to buy at particular prices.

The decision confronting the price-taker may appear a simple one. He is unable to make a decision about how much to charge, and is concerned solely with what quantity to produce. Nevertheless, his task is just as difficult as the price-maker's because he has fewer options and less room for manoeuvre. He has to make an estimate of the likely price of the product and the costs of producing alternative levels of output. Figure 8.7 shows the sort of result that making such estimates might yield.

In Figure 8.7 the price-taker's estimate of the market price for his product is shown by the horizontal line (fixed price). This line also indicates the average revenue because the price paid by the consumer must equal the average revenue received by the producer. In addition, it indicates the marginal revenue coming from each unit sold. The businessman's cost estimates are shown in the form of average and marginal cost curves (AC and MC respectively). Profit is defined for our purposes as the difference between average revenue and average cost, multiplied by the quantity sold (average profit × quantity). In Figure 8.7 total profit from the sale of a units of the product is $(b - c) \times a$. Profit is therefore Total Revenue less Total Cost.

Definition of profits

Having estimated market price and production costs, the businessman then has to decide how much to produce if he is to maximise profits. This can be determined by equating marginal cost with price. In Figure 8.7 the marginal cost curve cuts the price line at d, indicating that the profit maximising output per given period of time is a. For levels of output below a the increase in total revenue (price, average revenue,

The price-taker maximises by equating marginal cost and price

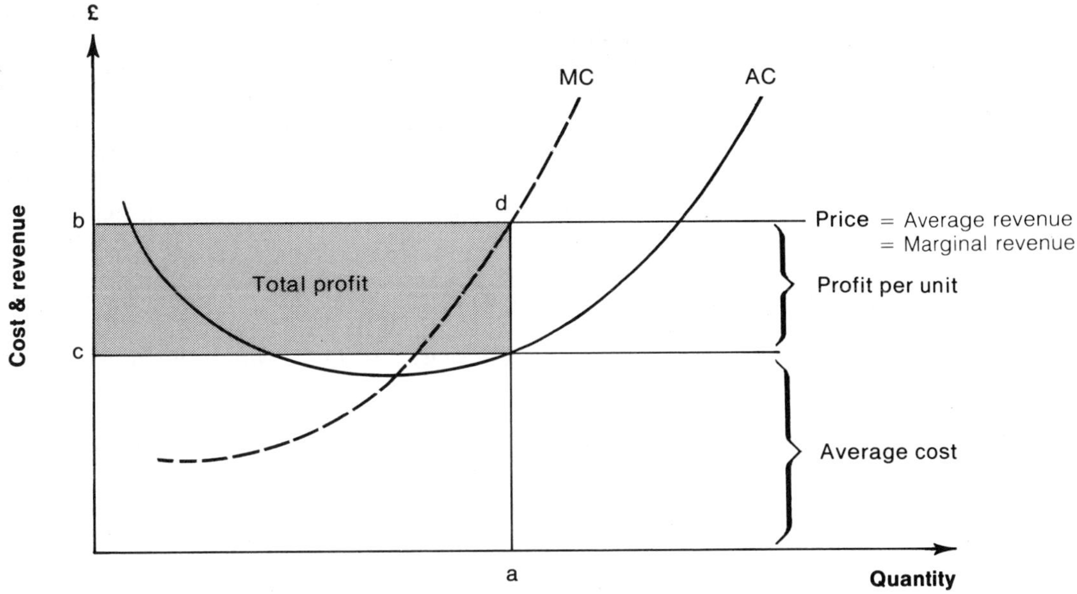

Figure 8.7 Profit maximising for the price-taker

or marginal revenue) from the sale of an extra unit of output is greater than the increase in total costs (marginal cost) from the production of that extra unit. Hence total profit increases as the quantity produced and sold increases.

But for levels of output above *a* the reverse is true. The increase in total revenue from the sale of each extra unit of output is less than the increase in total costs incurred in the production of the extra unit – total profit falls as the quantity sold increases. Thus, if the business is producing an output less than *a* it can increase profits by increasing output, and if it is producing an output of more than *a* it can increase profits by reducing output. It follows that profits are maximised when *a* units are produced and sold; the increase in total revenue from the production of the ath unit is matched by the increase in total costs incurred.

Many businessmen have never heard of marginal costs

You may know someone in business, perhaps a farmer, who can fairly be described as a price-taker. The probability is that if you described to him the profit-maximising procedure outlined above, he would object and point out to you that he did no such thing. The majority of businessmen do not consciously equate marginal cost with price; many have never heard of marginal cost. The economist's use of the term marginal cost is the result of his desire to express in a neat fashion what often goes on in practice. Actual decisions about how much to produce are based on guesses, past experience, the knowledge of other people's mistakes, and also upon an intuitive understanding. (Many activities, such as playing snooker, involve solving complex relationships such as working out the angles needed to play certain shots successfully. The expert player may know no formal physics but he achieves the results.)

The relevance of the economist's use of the idea of the margin can be appreciated if it is asked: How will the price-taker respond to a sudden increase in the price of his product? The probable answer is that he will increase production, provided the new price is greater than the costs he will incur in increasing production. In the economist's language, he is expanding production until marginal cost is equal to the new price.

The price-taker's marginal cost curve can be regarded as his supply curve because it indicates the maximum quantity the business will be prepared to supply at any price (average revenue). The exception to the price equals marginal cost rule for profit maximisation is when the price falls below average costs, for here the business is making losses. Even then, the firm may decide to continue production in the short run, equating marginal cost with price if it can cover its average variable costs and pay off part of its fixed contract costs. In the long run the firm will go out of business, or shut-down, if the price remains below average costs.

Perfect competition

The position of the price-taker in the market is also referred to as a situation of perfect competition. As a theoretical model, perfect competition assumes a number of conditions which have been discussed above in relation to the price-taker. More specifically, these assumptions are: many producers and consumers such that no single producer or consumer is able by his own actions to influence the market price; free entry to, and exit from, the market by producers; perfect knowledge and information in the market so that no producer or consumer has an advantage over any other firm or buyer in the market. The resulting effect of these conditions is to produce the model of the price-taker where each producer is in effect faced by a horizontal demand curve at the ruling price in the market. Decisions are then taken on the basis of what quantity to produce and are taken at the margin. Profits being maximised where marginal costs equal marginal revenue.

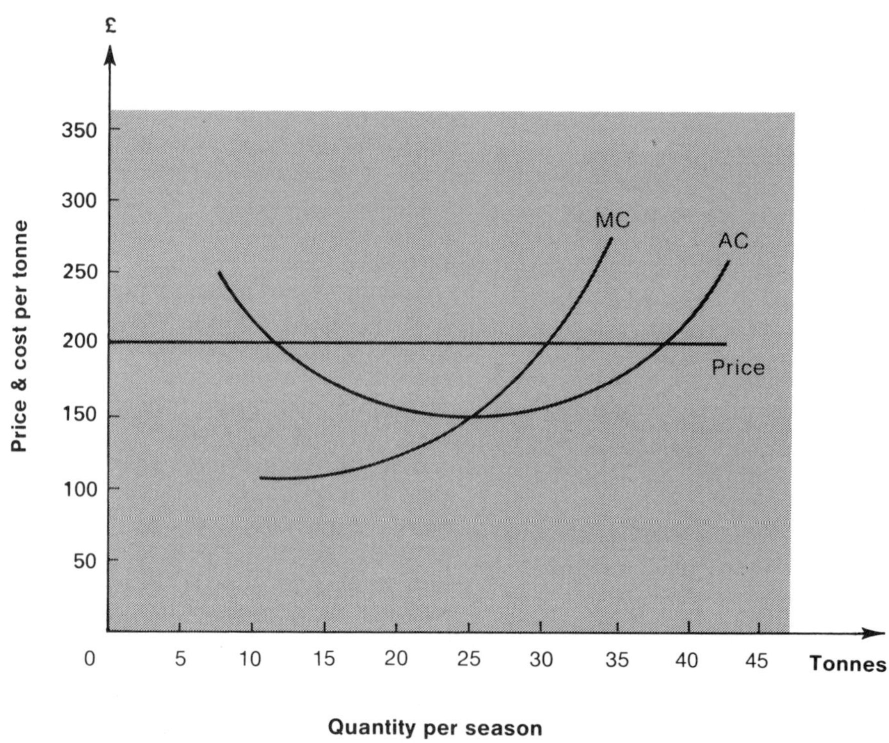

8.9

The diagram on page 134 presents information available to a farmer who is thinking about producing a particular cash crop the following season. He has calculated his average costs and marginal costs and anticipates that the price he will receive will be £200 per tonne.
1 Mark on the diagram the most profitable output and explain in your own words why it is the most profitable output.
2 If the farmer produces 25 tonnes of the crop he maximises profit per unit. Explain why maximising profit per unit of output does not necessarily mean that total profits will be maximised.
3 Suppose the farmer estimated that the price would be £250 per tonne. What quantity should he attempt to produce and what profit would he expect to earn?
4 Suppose the farmer estimated that both the average and marginal cost of each tonne of the crop would be £50 per tonne lower. What quantity should he attempt to produce and what profit would he expect to earn?

Price-makers

The second group of businesses are those which have some degree of control over the price they receive. Usually they are faced with the choice of selling a given output at a particular price or of selling a larger quantity at a lower price. The problem is one of selecting the pricing policy that will maximise profits, a task that is often complicated by the need to take into account the policies of competing businesses, the development of new products and the establishment of rival businesses.

Monopoly

Definition of monopolist

The simplest of the price-maker situations is when the business is a monopoly. The *monopolist* is the only producer of a good or service for which there are no close substitutes. The true monopolist can plan his pricing strategy without need to enquire about his rivals' actions and reactions for there are no rivals or potential rivals. Nor is there a good substitute product to which the disgruntled consumer can change. The consumer is faced with the choice: 'Pay up, or go without'. The profit maximising policy of the producer who is operating in a monopoly position is shown in Figure 8.8.

Average and marginal revenue differ

The principal difference between Figure 8.8 and the diagram showing the profit maximising position of the price-taker (Figure 8.7) is that here the average revenue curve slopes downwards instead of being horizontal. As a result, there is a separate marginal revenue curve that also slopes downwards. The reason why the average revenue, or price, and marginal revenue do not correspond is not obvious. When a monopolist lowers his price to increase sales, average revenue falls to the new price because all consumers buy at the new price. But the increase in total revenue (marginal revenue) will be less than the price received from the extra sales because the revenue received from all other sales is reduced. In fact, the situation may arise where a reduction in the price of a good may lead to a fall in total revenue (marginal revenue is negative) because the increase in sales is not sufficient to offset the fall in price.

Profit maximising determined by MR = MC

In Figure 8.8 the monopolist maximises profits by charging *b* per unit because at that price he estimates that consumers will buy *a* units of

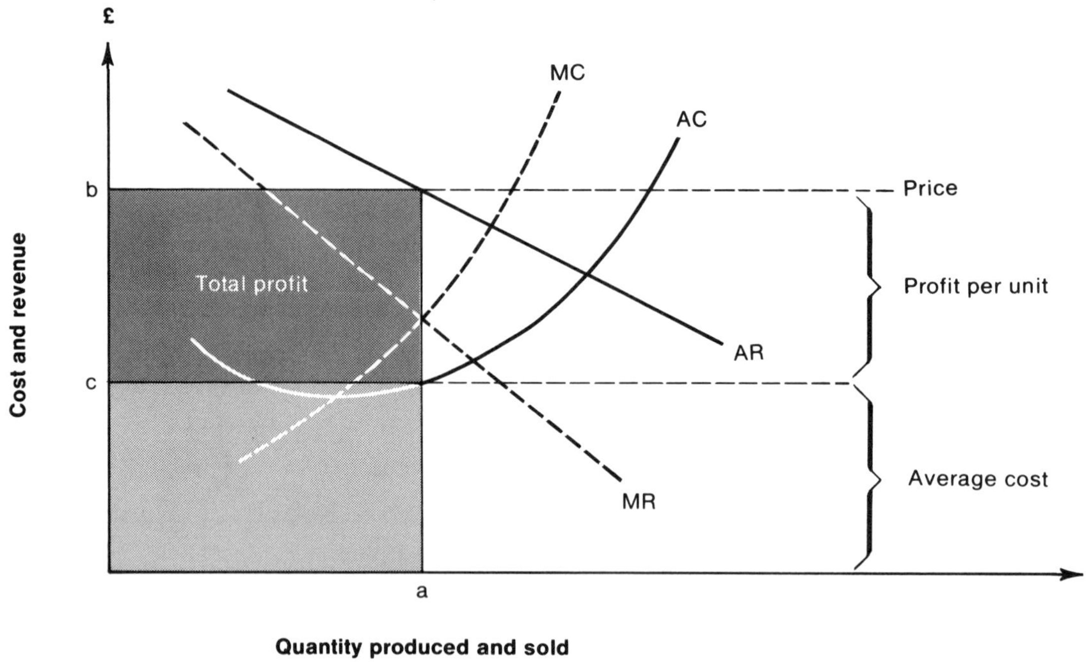

Figure 8.8 Profit maximising under monopoly conditions

the product and that the marginal cost of the ath unit will be equal to its marginal revenue. Again, it can be shown that this is the profit maximising position by using the same reasoning applied in the price-taker case. Total profits are shown by the shaded area: equal to $b - c$ (profit per unit) multiplied by quantity sold.

Being the only business in the UK providing a particular article does not prove that the firm has monopoly power (there may be effective competition from foreign suppliers for example). A true monopoly depends upon having effective power to change prices without worrying about possible competition or hostile government reactions. It is always possible for a new firm to enter into competition so that an effective monopoly is often protected by barriers to entry, such as patents or economies of scale. As far as monopoly legislation in the UK is concerned, a firm may be classed as a monopoly if it has more than one quarter of the market for, or supply of, a good or service in the UK. Firms satisfying the 25 per cent criterion may be referred to the Monopolies Commission for investigation of any possible abuse of that monopoly position.

Monopoly may still exist when there is more than one firm in an industry

Conversely, evidence that there is more than one business in the UK producing a particular article does not mean that monopoly power is absent. First, markets in different parts of the UK may be quite separate and different firms may be sole producers in each region or in isolated localities. Local monopolies may exist in many areas of the UK, for example, in the provision of services. Transport costs may limit possible access to the market by competitors and act as an effective entry barrier. Retail outlets in remote areas are often in a powerful market position. Second, even when there are a number of producers in an area, one may assume a dominant position because of its size and lower production costs. It may be able to determine its price, knowing

Price leaders have effective monopoly power

Monopoly exists where firms practise collusion

full well that the other businesses are in no position to compete successfully, and that in the last resort it could drive them out of business by undercutting them. Such businesses are called *price leaders*. A business which is an effective price leader and accepted as such is also an effective monopolist. A third case of monopoly exists when independent businesses get together to determine joint pricing and marketing policies. Such collusion enables them to overcome all difficulties involved in guessing what rivals will do. A monopoly price can be charged by all or the market split in some predetermined way. Such restrictive practices are discussed in Chapter 18.

It is apparent from these comments that the identification of businesses which have or make use of monopoly power is difficult. *Concentration ratios* are sometimes used in this context as an indicator of possible monopoly power. Concentration refers to the extent to which an industry is dominated by the largest firms (usually three or five firm ratios are calculated) and measures the percentage of sales, employment or capital employed held by those firms. A high degree of concentration in itself however is not indicative of the abuse of monopoly power as has already been pointed out.

The Fair Trading Act of 1973 defines monopolisation as at least a one quarter share of total sales in a relevant market, including the possibility of defining a market in a particular local area as well as at a national level. The scope of the Act also covers other types of anti-competitive practice by a single firm or group of firms. (For a fuller discussion, see Chapter 18).

Any government decision that removes monopoly power and compels a business to reduce its price involves a value judgement. Is it better that someone (the producer) should be made relatively worse off and that someone else (the consumer) should be made better off? The problem governments face is in deciding when to make one group better off and another group worse off. When is a business making excessive profits? How can a government be 'fair' to both consumer and producer? Having a monopoly is no guarantee that a firm will be making profits in the first place.

Making monopoly illegal

An alternative approach is the more radical one of banning monopoly altogether and of fostering competition. This has been the idea behind anti-trust legislation in the United States. The Sherman Act of 1890 included the provision that: 'Every person who shall monopolize, or attempt to monopolize, or combine or conspire with any other person . . . to monopolize any part of trade or commerce among the several states, shall be deemed guilty of a misdemeanour, and on conviction thereof shall be punished by fine not exceeding five thousand dollars, or by imprisonment not exceeding one year, or . . . both.' In practice, it has been difficult to implement and may not necessarily work in the consumer's interest.[4]

In an economy such as the United Kingdom, the effect of competition from overseas and the size of the market may effectively deny to some firms the benefits of cost saving that come from producing large quantities. The more firms the higher the production costs. Monopoly may thus offer the cheapest way of producing an article in a country, and it may therefore lead to cheaper prices than would rule in a competitive situation. The consumer's interests are best served if the product is produced as cheaply as possible (maybe by a single firm), and the firm's power to set prices is checked by the threat of government intervention or foreign competition.

8.10

It is quite possible that a monopoly may be maximising profits while charging a price that only just covers its costs of production. In the language of the accountant it is just 'breaking even'. Draw a diagram of this situation with average and marginal cost and revenue curves, and explain the main features of the diagram.

8.11

The system of patents has been developed to protect inventors and developers of new products from other firms copying the ideas. Thus, it makes it possible for the originator to profit from his discovery and to recover development costs. But it also establishes a legal monopoly for a period, which it may be difficult to break by the development of substitute products. This may result in high prices being charged for the protected article. In your opinion, does this fear of consumer exploitation provide a case for abolishing the patent system? Is there an alternative system that might be introduced that would reward inventors but overcome the monopoly problem?

8.12

Imagine that you were appointed a member of a Monopolies Commission panel charged with establishing whether or not a particular firm was operating against the public interest. What set of rules or criteria would you adopt as an indicator of abuse of the public interest by a firm, or group of firms acting collectively? If you had to choose all the members of such a panel, whom would you select – industrialists, civil servants, lawyers, politicians, trade unionists, accountants, economists or the general public? What difference does it make where they come from?

8.13

Prices of drinks, ices, chocolates, etc. at cinemas and theatres are often much higher than shop prices in towns. To some extent the cinemas are taking advantage of their monopoly power in selling to audiences with no option but to pay the higher prices. Discuss the arguments for and against the government taking action to prevent the suppliers from selling products above the price ruling outside the cinemas. Three questions are relevant: is the business a monopolist; is the business abusing monopoly power to charge high prices; is it making profits?

8.14

Imagine that the British government puts forward a set of proposals that would make it illegal for a business to be the only business in an industry. Present a formal submission to the government in your capacity as a spokeman for British industry, opposing the proposal. As an intelligent industry leader, you will attempt to show that the effect of making monopoly illegal will harm both business and the people of the UK in general.

Monopolistic competition and oligopoly

Both of these market forms fall within the general price-maker category. *Monopolistic competition* is a situation in which an industry is made up of many firms which are not price-takers because they do not produce identical products. They have some latitude to raise or lower their prices because the consumer is able to distinguish each business's products.

Differentiated products give firms some scope for price fixing

The products are similar to one another, differentiated by brand name, colour, minor design features or packaging. Alternatively, the businesses may be offering a service rather than a good, in which case it is not hard to convince consumers that the services offered by competing firms differ in some way.

The consequence of goods being close but not perfect substitutes is that a business can set a new price for its good if it desires. If it raises the price then it will lose sales – possibly heavily – but it will retain some of its customers who are convinced of the superiority of its product. Similarly, it can gain sales by lowering its price, though there will be resistance from consumers who remain 'loyal' to the other brands. Monopolistic competition exists when there are many firms, because only then can the individual firm be certain that the other firms will not react when it changes its price, or the colour of its packet, or whatever. It is too small to affect their sales. The firm can thus equate marginal cost and revenue and select the price within the narrow range that promises it most profits.

Uncertainty about rivals' reaction

Oligopoly exists where there are only a few firms in an industry, or where an industry is dominated by a few firms (although there may be other small firms). The unique problem facing the oligopolist is uncertainty about how its rivals will react to changes in its policy. This uncertainty is reflected in an inability to determine what the firm's average revenue curve will be. The quantity a firm sells at any price will be influenced by the prices of substitute products put out by competing firms. The business owner may be in a complete dilemma. 'If I put up my price, will firm X increase its price also?' 'If I cut my price, will the others follow suit?'

8.15

To what extent do you consider that there is a case for having price controls on firms and a government Prices Commission requiring firms to justify price increases for their products? How would you determine criteria on whether to allow price increases or not? Are there any types of goods or services where price controls would not be feasible to operate for the UK market? What do you see to be the advantages and disadvantages of such a policy?

Oligopoly strategies

Faced with this uncertainty about its marginal and average revenue curves, and the consequential inability to determine a profit maximising price or output, the oligopolist has four possible courses of action. It may:

ignore rivals' reactions,
do nothing,
agree with other firms on a common policy,
wait for a lead from another firm – be a price follower.

Ignore the other firms

First, it can assume that other firms will not react to its policy decisions. It will ignore them, will make an estimate of the average revenue curve and decide the pricing policy accordingly. Obviously, by so doing it takes a big risk. If it increases its price and others accept its lead and increase prices too, it establishes itself as a price leader and *therefore* as an effective monopolist. But if it increases its price and the other firms do not follow it may lose its share of the market. If it lowers its price it may initiate a vigorous round of price-cutting that continues until some firms are driven out of business, or pricing policies are revised and prices increased again.

Do nothing

Second, the oligopolist may follow a cautious or pessimistic policy. A pessimist sees the worst possible outcome in any decision and plays safe. Such an oligopoly will recognise that increasing its price may lead to a sharp fall in sales, and will recognise too that a cut in prices may lead to a price-cutting war that brings little increase in sales. Consequently, it sees itself operating on what amounts to a 'kinked' average revenue curve. It is unwilling to increase price; reluctant to drop it. In Figure 8.9 the price of *b* is the ruling price from which the oligopoly is loathe to move.

Kinked sales curve

Third, the oligopoly may agree with other enterprises on a common policy to charge a common price, to divide up the market between them, to restrict output and so on. This is a tempting solution when the problems of competition appear difficult. When collusion occurs the market form again reverts to monopoly, or rather to one with the bad features of monopoly and none of the good. Such restrictive trade practices can work against the public interest without bringing the cost savings sometimes associated with large-scale enterprise.

Collusion and restrictive trade practices

The fourth possibility is that a firm will wait for a lead from another firm, which is the price-maker. If it does this, then it solves the problem by becoming a price-taker and following the established market price.

The conclusion to be derived is that it is extremely difficult to identify which firms are monopolists, monopolistic competitors, oligopolists and price-takers in the UK. The number of firms in an industry is some help. However, the number of firms in an industry is not a certain guide to the policies they may follow. Businesses operate in a changing environment. Government policies vary, management changes, new products are developed and with these changes the business policies of firms change too. A business that was once content to follow the lead

A firm's policies change with changes in business conditions

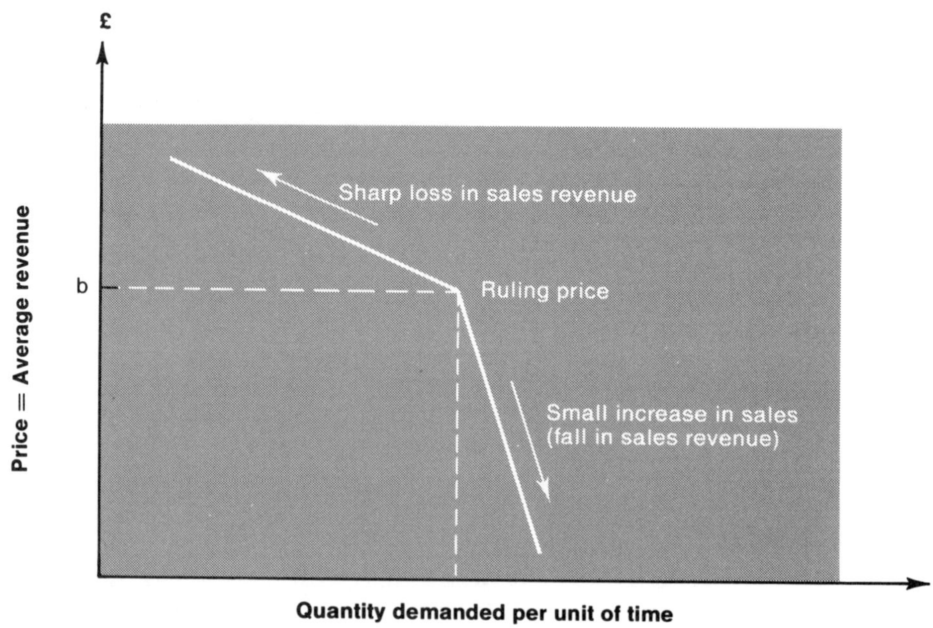

Figure 8.9 The pessimistic 'do-nothing' oligopolist

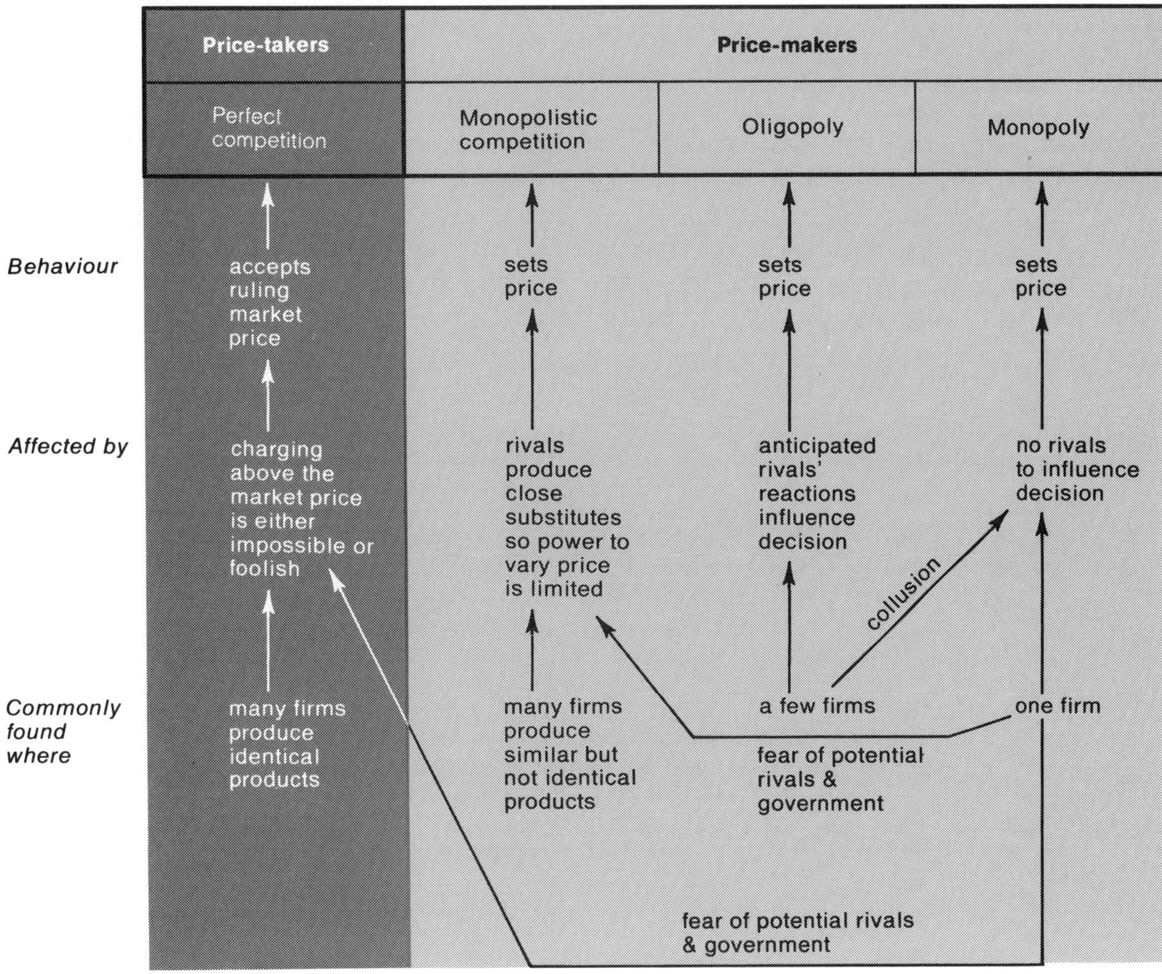

Figure 8.10 Business behaviour and market forms

of others becomes dynamic and aggressive. It institutes policies that others recognise and accept, so that instead of being a price-taker it becomes an effective monopolist, the other firms following its lead.

Figure 8.10 summarises this section. It links the four market forms discussed with the business behaviour that characterises each form.

8.16

1 An industry consists of two firms. Firm A is making an annual profit of £500 000, selling its principal product at £24. Firm B is making a profit of £100 000, selling a similar product at £30. Firm B's management is not happy about the profit performance but is undecided on whether to raise the price, lower the price or carry on as before. Its uncertainty stems from an inability to guess how Firm A will react to changes in the price of its product, or indeed an uncertainty about whether Firm A is about to change its price anyway. Firm B's management consider that three possible courses of action are open to it:

To raise the price by £5,

to leave the price as it is,
to lower the price by £5.

It then estimated the possible reaction by Firm A to each of these policies. Firm A might:

raise the price by £5,
ignore Firm B,
lower the price by £5.

Each reaction would affect Firm B's profits. As there were three possible reactions to each choice open to Firm B, Firm B's management estimated the nine possible profit situations it was faced with. These estimates are given in Table 8.3.

Firm B's policy decisions	Firm A's reactions		
	Raise price £5	Ignore Firm B	Lower price £5
Raise price £5	£150 000	£ 60 000	–£40 000
No price change	£120 000	£100 000	£70 000
Lower price £5	£220 000	£160 000	–£ 5 000

Table 8.3 The effects on Firm B's profits of different policies of Firm B and reactions by Firm A

After preparing these estimates, Firm B's management decided that they were prepared to increase the price of their product by £5. Do you think that this was a sensible suggestion? Explain why you agree or disagree. If you disagree, what would you have proposed in the circumstances?

2 Eventually Firm B's management had second thoughts about making a decision on the information before them and decided to seek more. Being quite unscrupulous, they employed an agent to carry out industrial espionage. The agent's job was to infiltrate Firm A and to discover estimates of how Firm A's profits would be affected by B's proposed policies. The results of his investigations are shown in Table 8.4.

Firm B's policy decisions	Firm A's reactions		
	Raise price £5	Ignore Firm B	Lower price £5
Raise price £5	£490 000	£530 000	£550 000
No price change	£450 000	£500 000	£440 000
Lower price £5	£380 000	£470 000	£630 000

Table 8.4 Effect on Firm A's profits of the different policies of Firm B and reactions by Firm A

It is also known that Firm A is keen to maximise profits.

1 With the use of this additional information, recommend to the management of Firm B an appropriate policy and explain why you make the recommendation.

2 From the data before it, Firm B may have serious grounds for concern about the policies Firm A is likely to adopt in the future. Comment on these worries.

Price elasticity of demand

Elasticity of demand is a concept that economists use when investigating the relationship between the quantity of a good demanded and the various determinants of demand. *Income elasticity of demand*, which measures the relationship between quantity purchased and income, was discussed in Chapter 5. *Price elasticity of demand* measures the responsiveness of the quantity demanded to changes in the price of the good. It is determined by dividing the proportionate change in quantity demanded by the relative change in price. Formally, it can be expressed as either,

Definition

$$\text{Price elasticity of demand} = \frac{\text{Percentage change in quantity demanded}}{\text{Small percentage change in price}}$$

or

$$\text{Price elasticity of demand} = \frac{\text{Change in quantity demanded}}{\text{Original quantity demanded}} \div \frac{\text{Change in price}}{\text{Original price}}$$

The measure involves the use of *small* percentage price changes and for such changes both definitions give exactly the same result.

Elasticity is a pure number

As with income elasticity of demand, the calculation of price elasticity yields a pure number: that is, a number not given in units of something. For example, if 10 000 kg of sugar are sold at a price of 20p per kg and 9000 kg are sold when the price rises to 21p per kg, the price elasticity of demand is calculated as:

$$\frac{-1000}{10\ 000} \div \frac{1}{20} = \frac{-1000}{10\ 000} \times \frac{20}{1} = -2.0$$

The units of kg of sugar and pence disappear, leaving only a number: –2.

By convention, the negative sign of an elasticity is dropped

The answer to this calculation reveals a difference between price and income elasticity of demand. Normally, a person will consume more of a good as his income rises and the elasticity calculation yields a positive number. But normally he will purchase less of a good as its price is increased and therefore the calculation of price elasticity of demand will yield a minus number: –2.0 in the example. However, it has become conventional to drop the minus sign and simply refer to the numerical value of the elasticity: 2.0, and so on. Almost certainly the convention grew up because of the confusion caused when non-mathematical economists had to make up their minds what they meant by expressions such as more than –1 and less than –1. In this book convention is followed and all elasticities are expressed in numerical values only; the minus sign is ignored.[5]

Elastic and inelastic

If the price elasticity of demand calculation yields a figure greater than 1, then demand for the good with respect to price is said to be *elastic*. If the number is less than 1, then demand for the good with respect to price is said to be *inelastic*. If the number calculated is exactly 1, elasticity is referred to as *unity*.[6]

Two other values for elasticity are of great importance in the measurement of the price–quantity relationship.

Zero elasticity

1 Elasticity is equal to zero when the demand curve is a vertical line. An increase in price (or a decrease) has no effect whatsoever on the quantity demanded. The change in quantity is therefore zero, which is the number which results from the calculation. It is then said that demand is *perfectly inelastic*.

Elasticity is infinity for the price-taker

2 Elasticity is equal to infinity when the demand curve, or average revenue curve, is a horizontal line. This is the price-taker situation, where any lowering in the price of the good (no matter how small) would produce an infinitely large increase in the quantity demanded, and any increase in the price of the good above the market price would result in the loss of all sales. Demand is then said to be *perfectly elastic*.

Elasticity is also a relative term

The terms elastic and inelastic are also used in a relative sense. For example, a good with a price elasticity of 0.8 is said to have a more elastic demand than one with a price elasticity of 0.7. Likewise, the second good may be referred to as having a *less elastic* demand or a *more inelastic* demand.

8.17

Figure 8.11 is a demand curve for sugar. Table 8.5 is part of the demand schedule from which the curve was drawn. We have already calculated the price elasticity of demand for sugar for a price increase from 20p to 21p (part B on the demand curve).

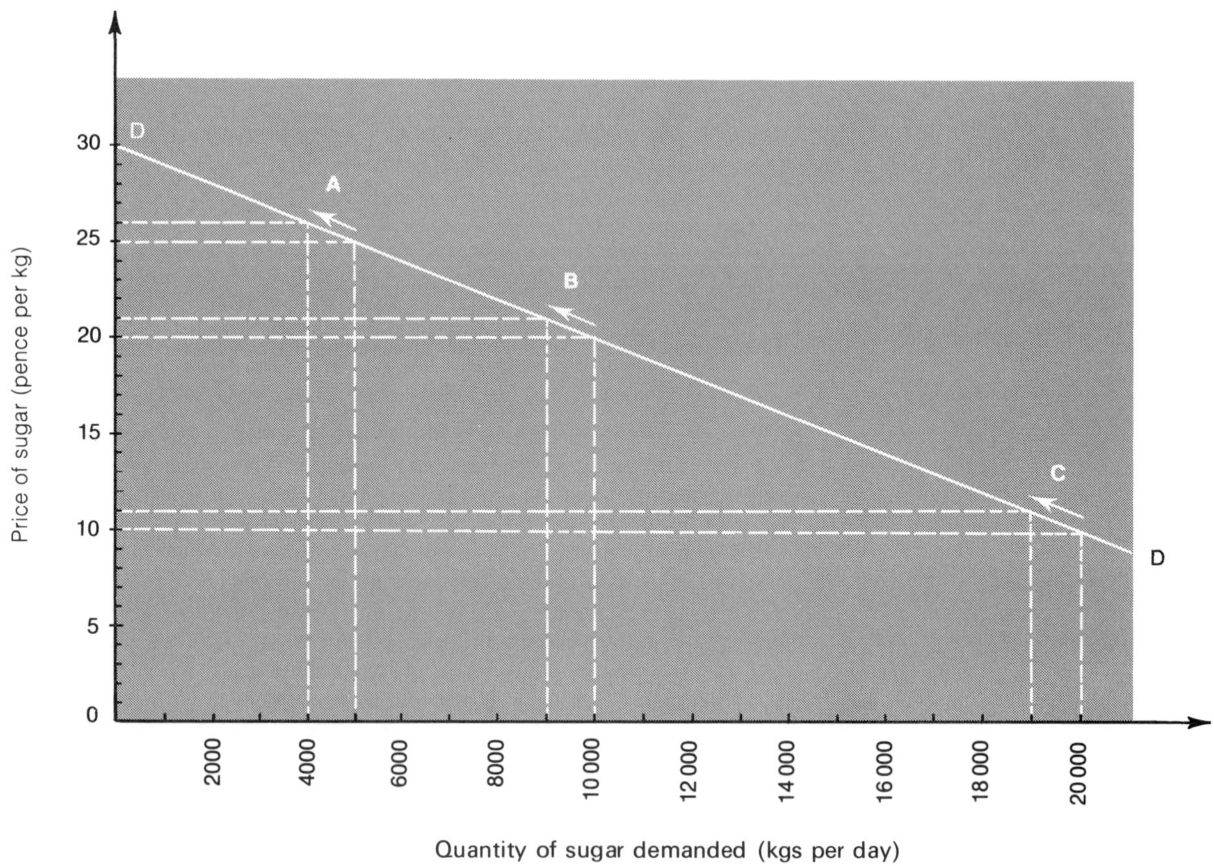

Figure 8.11 Demand curve for sugar

Work out the price elasticity for a price increase from 25p to 26p (part A on the demand curve) and for a price increase from 10p to 11p (part C on the curve). What can you conclude about the price elasticity in the three parts of the curve?

Price (pence per kg)	Quantity demanded (kgs per day)
26	4 000
25	5 000
21	9 000
20	10 000
11	19 000
10	20 000

Table 8.5 Demand schedule for sugar

Cross elasticity of demand

Cross elasticity of demand measures the effect of changes in the price of one good on the quantity demanded of another good. In this case, it is the responsiveness of changes in demand, in relation to the prices of other goods, that is considered. Formally it can be expressed as either:

$$\text{Cross elasticity of demand} = \frac{\text{Percentage change in quantity demanded of good A}}{\text{Small percentage change in price of good B}}$$

or

$$\text{Cross elasticity of demand} = \frac{\text{Change in quantity demanded of good A}}{\text{Original quantity demanded of good A}} \div \frac{\text{Change in price of good B}}{\text{Original price of good B}}$$

It can be seen from the formula that two different goods are referred to, in this case goods A and B. If A and B were substitute goods for each other (for example A might be butter and B margarine) then an increase in the price of B (margarine) would lead to an increase in the quantity demanded of A (butter). In this example, the formula for cross elasticity of demand would give a positive result. If the two goods were complementary to each other, i.e. complements (for example, A might be petrol and B motor cars), an increase in the price of cars could be expected to lead to a fall in the demand for cars and therefore some fall in the demand for petrol. Cross elasticity of demand would then be negative because an increase in the price of one good has resulted in a decrease in demand for the complement good. If the formula for cross elasticity of demand produced an answer of zero, then this would imply no relationship between the two goods. In other words that A and B are neither substitutes nor complements to each other. The value of cross elasticity can also indicate the closeness of the relationship between the two goods. A high positive value indicates the goods are a close substitute for each other; a high negative value that they are closely related complements.

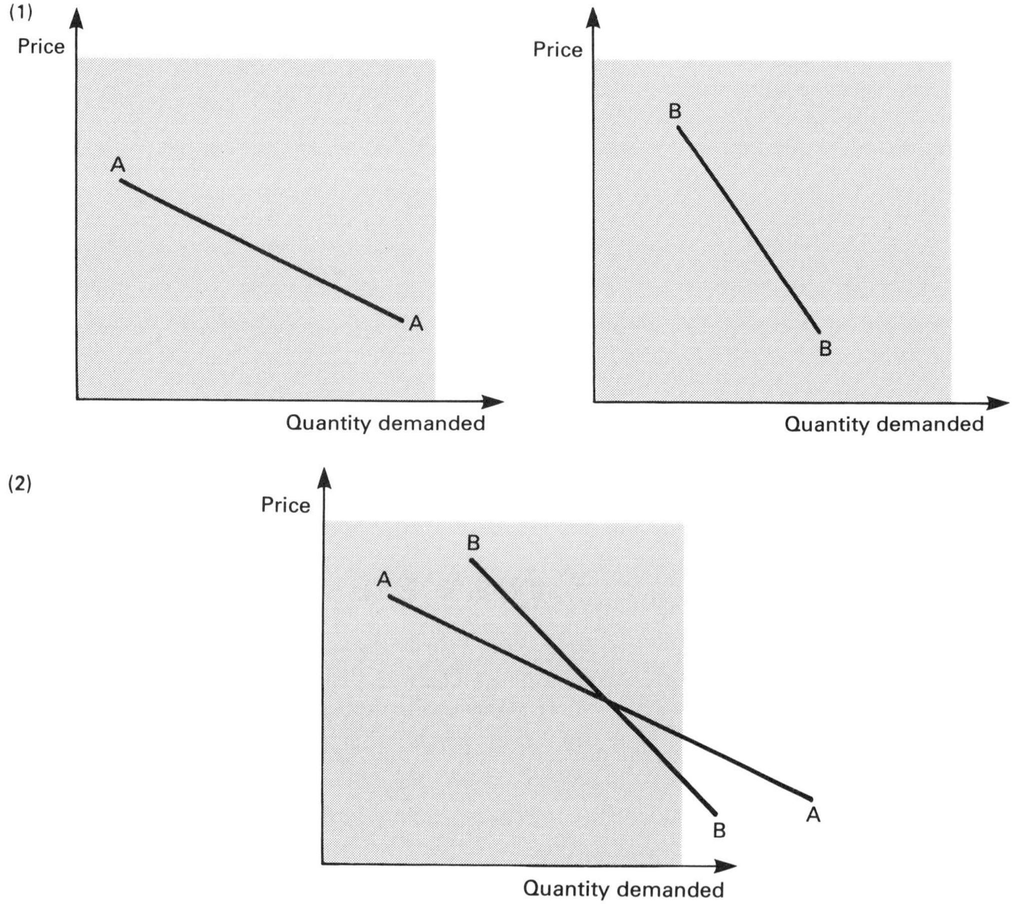

Figure 8.12

8.18

It is common for people to look at sketches of demand curves, such as those above and then to make statements such as, the demand for good B is inelastic and the demand for good A is elastic; or the demand for good B is relatively inelastic. Are either of these statements correct in situation (1) or situation (2)? Explain your conclusion.

Price elasticity of demand and total revenue

It is sometimes of critical importance to be able to estimate whether an increase in the price of a product will lead to an increase or a decrease in total revenue. If the quantity demanded falls by a smaller percentage than the increase in price then revenue will rise. If it falls by a greater percentage than the percentage increase in price, total revenue will fall. There is a link between price elasticity of demand and changes in total revenue, and this is summarised in Table 8.5.

This does not mean that a businessman should always lower his price when the demand for his product is elastic, or increase it when demand

Limits to use of elasticity in profit maximising

is inelastic. If his aim is to maximise profits, he will fix his price only after taking into consideration both his costs and his sales revenue. But, without going into it in any detail, it can be said that a businessman will seldom be justified in producing a good and selling at a price when that price lies on an elastic part of his demand curve.

Price elasticity of demand	Price	Total revenue
Elastic	raised	falls
	lowered	rises
Unity	raised	unchanged
	lowered	unchanged
Inelastic	raised	rises
	lowered	falls

Table 8.6 Price elasticity of demand and total revenue

Notes

1 Public companies are those which may raise funds by inviting the general public to buy shares. These shares can be sold to other people commonly through stock exchanges which are markets for second-hand shares in public companies. They include the word 'limited' in their title, or the abbreviation 'PLC' for public limited company.
2 Notice in Figure 8.6 that the lowest point on each of the short-run curves is not on the long-run average cost curve. If the LAC slopes downwards it is impossible for the minimum point on any SAC to touch it. The slope of the LAC implies that there are other SACs lying between SAC_1 and SAC_2.
3 The monopolist cannot fix *both* the price *and* the quantity consumers will purchase. If he sets the price, consumer reaction determines how much can be produced and *sold*.
4 In contrast, the legislation has been extremely successful in outlawing agreements between firms designed to give them effective monopoly power.
5 People whose job it is to measure elasticities invariably restore the minus signs in the interests of accuracy.
6 A product that has a price elasticity of greater than 1 (elastic) is one for which a given small percentage rise in price results in a more than proportionate fall in the quantity demanded. A product that has an elasticity of demand of less than 1 (inelastic) is one for which a given small rise in the price will result in a less than proportionate increase in the quantity demanded, whilst a good with an elasticity of 1 (unity) is one for which a small percentage price rise results in an equiproportional increase in the quantity demanded.

Chapter 9 Human Resources and Unemployment

Population, production and living standards

Demography, the study of population, is of great interest to economists. An increasing population requires increases in the production of goods and services simply to maintain living standards. People are also resources that can be combined with other resources to provide extra production and to raise living standards. For about 200 years economists have been concerned with these relationships between a country's population, its productive capacity and its living standards. The proposition has been advanced from time to time that an increasing population will sooner or later put such pressure on the world's natural resources that they will be exhausted, or at very least be depleted to a point at which standards of living must decline. At other times, particularly after devastating wars, there has been concern about the lack of population and in particular at the reduced percentage of active producers in the population. The present sharp drop in birth rate in the UK raises the prospect of an increasing number of old people having to be supported by a decreasing number of workers.

Malthus

At the end of the eighteenth century, Thomas Malthus put forward the idea that population, unless checked in some way, would increase more rapidly than available food supplies.[1] Early writings by Malthus expressed the belief that whereas food supplies would increase at an arithmetical rate, 1,2,3,4,5, . . ., population would increase at a geometric rate, 1,2,4,8,16, . . . The outcome would soon be starvation. Later, Malthus modified his theory considerably. Subsequent innovations, agricultural reform, industrial progress and the opening up of new lands led to increases in production which far outstripped population growth, and for many decades Malthus' ideas were discredited. But in recent years the situation in countries such as Bangladesh has revived interest in Malthusian theories.

Population theories

Another idea, the theory of *optimum population*, was based on observations of diminishing returns in production. It was believed that increases in a country's population would only raise production per head to a limited extent, and that additional increases in population would reduce production per head. It was concluded from these assumptions that a nation should aim at limiting its population to the level at which gross domestic product per head was maximised.

The concept of optimum population depends upon the resources available to an economy at any given time, and the level of technology and state of knowledge which the economy has achieved. Changes in technology or in the level of resources, will therefore have an impact on the level at which the economy operates at optimum. As a concept, optimum population may be easier to discuss than to actually measure for a country. Even with this drawback, the theory of optimum population has at least raised the issue of overall population size to resource availability and the role of government policy in this area.

For a country such as the UK, with an already developed industrial structure and a high population density by international standards, the relationship of population size and the theory of optimum population is a very different concern compared with economies such as Canada and Australia, where population may be too low to allow the potential level of output per head to be reached. In consequence different economies adopt population policies appropriate to their own ideas of an optimum level.

The labour force

Activity rate

A sensible way of investigating conflicting population theories is to examine the relationship between population, the labour force and production. The labour force is that section of the country's population that is able and willing to work. The activity rate (also known as the participation ratio) measures the proportion of the population who are of working age and are economically active as part of the labour force. The working population includes those actually working and those available for work but registered as unemployed. In mid-1979 the working population in the UK was about 26$\frac{1}{3}$ million – including 1$\frac{1}{3}$ million unemployed. The numbers unemployed represent those registered as unemployed at local offices of the Department of Employment or, in the case of young people, at careers offices of local education authorities, on a certain day each month. Those registered are deemed to be available for and capable of work on that day. From November 1982 the unemployment count is taken as the number of people entitled to claim unemployment benefit on a particular day each month. Unemployment fluctuates with overall economic conditions and many other factors. For example, by mid-1983 unemployment had risen by about 2 million over the mid-1979 figure. People not in the labour force or working population, therefore, comprise those who are without a job and are not actively seeking one.

The labour force therefore excludes all persons under the age of 16 years (in compulsory full-time education), all retired persons not seeking work, and those of working age who do not seek to work. Principally, this group includes housewives working full-time in the home, full-time students over 16, those handicapped and severely disabled, and those who choose not to work.

	Under 16	16 years and over				Total population
		Employed (a)	Unemployed	Total labour force	Not in labour force	
Males	6 786	15 171	1 023	16 194	4 190	27 170
Females	6 427	9 743	423	10 166	12 073	28 666
Total	13 213	24 914	1 446	26 360	16 263	55 836
%	23.7	–	–	47.2	29.1	100

Note (a) Employed includes employers and self-employed.
All figures are in thousands.

Table 9.1 UK Labour force 1978 (mid-year estimates)

Source: *Annual Abstract of Statistics 1980*, Tables 2.6 and 6.1, HMSO

Table 9.1 gives details of the labour force in the UK in 1978 based on mid-year estimates of population. Out of a total of almost 56 million people, about 47 per cent were contributing to or available to contribute to production. Almost 24 per cent of the population was under 16 and the remaining 29 per cent had either retired, or had chosen not to work, at that particular time.

Determinants of the labour force

Size of the population

In 1978 the population of the UK was a little under 56 million persons. In 1901 the population was about 38 million, increasing by 1950 to around 50 million. In the first decade of this century the population increased by over 10 per cent – a rate of around 1 per cent per annum. In the decade 1971 to 1981 population in the UK was forecast to increase by 1.3 per cent. The marked decrease in the annual growth rate in the 1970s is in marked contrast to the rate of about 0.5 per cent per annum from 1945 to 1970. Forecasts for the rate of population increase at the end of this century are in the order of 0.25 per cent per annum.

Elements of population growth

The two elements in the growth of population are the rate of natural increase of the population and the rate of net migration. Table 9.2 shows how these rates of growth have varied from 1951 and how they are projected to change to 1991. The decline in the rate of natural increase is most noticeable. Migration after 1961 shows a net outflow which reduces the rate of population growth in total. In 1971 to 1978 net migration has halved the annual overall population growth. Significant also is the very small change in the total population, forecast after 1978.

Average annual changes

	Natural increase (%)	Net migration (%)	Total increase (%)	Population at end of period ('000s)
1951–61	0.49	+0.01	0.5	50 290
1961–71	0.61	–0.08	0.53	52 807
1971–78	0.12	–0.06	0.06	55 610
*1978–81	0.067	–0.055	0.012	55 903
*1981–91	0.26	–0.07	0.19	55 922

*Projected figures

Table 9.2 Components of UK population growth, actual and projected 1951–91

Source: *Annual Abstract of Statistics, 1980*, HMSO

In the chronic economic depression of the 1930s the birth rate in the UK fell to as low as 16 per 1000 (1.6 per cent) compared with 23 per 1000 in the previous decade. In the 1970s the birth rate has fallen dramatically from 16.3 per 1000 in 1970 to as low as 11.8 per 1000 in 1977 and recovering to approximately 13 per 1000 in 1979. As a consequence the population in the UK has remained stagnant and even declined slightly over the last few years. (Death rates have remained at around 12 per 1000 and there has been net outward migration from the UK over this period).

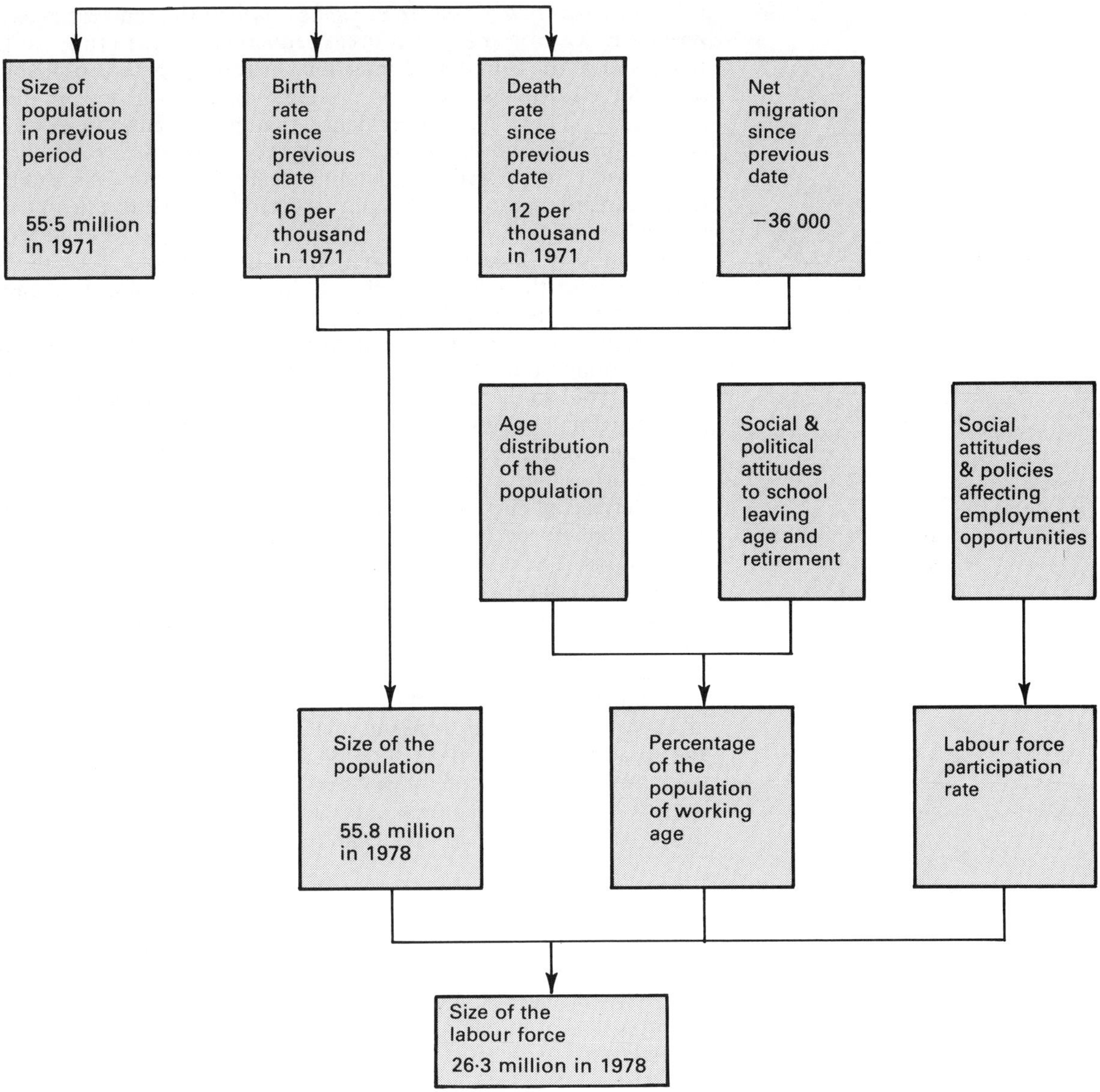

Figure 9.1 Determinants of the size of the labour force

The rate of natural increase is determined of course by the crude birth rate (number of live births per 1000 of population) and the crude death rate (number of deaths per 1000 of population). These together are likely to be influenced by a number of factors.

1 *Changes in social attitudes* to birth control and abortion will affect the crude birth rate. So too may war, or economic conditions
2 *Government policies* may also have an effect on people's decisions to have families, how soon to have families and how many children to have. Social services, taxation concessions, job-sharing arrangements and the provision of childcare facilities may all have some effect on desired family size.

3 *Improvement in the standard of public health* in the nineteenth and early twentieth centuries produced great reductions in the crude death rate as a result of the conquest of infectious diseases. There is probably little scope for medical discoveries to produce similar reductions in the death rate today. There is some evidence that health education leading to changes in diet and life style may be able to produce some reduction in the death rate by reducing fatalities from the major causes of death – heart disease and cancer – but spectacular improvements are not feasible.

Migration

Migration is an important component of population growth. Recent experience for the UK has been a net loss of population through migration as the figures in Table 9.2 demonstrate. The level of net migration is stressed in these figures and does not reveal the extent of the flow of immigration to the UK, or the flow of emigration. Over the decade from the late 1960s to the late 1970s, the UK has experienced an annual flow of approximately 250 000 emigrants and 200 000 immigrants so that, over those years, the net migration loss to the UK was somewhere in the region of half a million people.

The effects of such migration flow depend not only on the net figure, whether inflow or outflow, but also on the composition of migrant populations. The much publicised 'brain drain' highlights the particular problems caused by the exodus of highly skilled and qualified workers. If the immigrant population has a marked difference in the birth rate and average age to the indigenous population, then this will obviously have an impact on the host country's population structure.

The main economic benefits and costs of immigration are summarised in Table 9.3. It is clear from this analysis that there are both advantages and disadvantages involved through immigration to a society. It is far too simple an argument to say that immigration should be prevented because this involves immigrants taking jobs when unemployment is high. The UK has also political responsibilities for Commonwealth

Benefits	Costs
1 Increases the supply of labour	1 Direct and indirect costs of absorbing extra people – e.g. on social services, transport, housing, etc.
2 Effects on mobility of labour which will increase if a high proportion of immigrants are single male workers prepared to move around to find work	2 May lead to more problems of congestion and overcrowding with higher population growth
3 May help eliminate particular labour shortages, e.g. trained medical personnel	3 Increasing population leads to a greater increase in imports and adds to strain on balance of payments
4 Increasing population stimulates demand and investment	4 Immigration accentuates the unemployment problem during business recessions
5 Market increases for goods and services; greater potential to benefit from economies of scale	
6 Immigration brings cultural benefits from other traditions, skills, life-styles, etc.	

Table 9.3 Benefits and costs of immigration

immigration resulting from historical and colonial links with other nations. Often in this debate over immigration, it is forgotten that the UK commonly exhibits a net loss in migration. For countries such as Australia, immigration is a much more vital component in population growth and the analysis in Table 9.3 becomes more crucial to them.

In conclusion, it must be stressed that, with individual variations according to each economy's own population history and structure, the list of benefits and costs for a country may differ significantly to that shown in Table 9.3.

9.1

Characteristic of mid-Victorian attitudes to Malthus, to the increasing population and to the growth of production, is the following statement.

> We shall next proceed to show how [the alleviation of poverty] may be brought about, regardless of the system of Malthus and all that legion of overpopulationists; for a greater than they hath said, 'Be fruitful and multiply and replenish the earth, and subdue it'. The Divine Economist has so provisioned the earth that if men employ the means which he has blessed them with for subduing it, their mouths will be 'filled with food, and their hearts with gladness' (Robert Watt, *The Practical Elucidation of National Economy*, 1848)

Discuss the point of view put forward by Mr Watt. Do his ideas on economics have any value in the twentieth century?

9.2

The theory of optimum population (which fell into disrepute many years ago) implied that there was some level of population at which gross domestic product per head was maximised. The basic assumption was that if a country's population continued to increase, but its supplies of other productive resources and its production methods were unchanged, then at some stage the marginal product of labour would fall, leading later to a fall in the average product.

What do you see as the principal reasons for believing that it is unrealistic to attempt to define an optimum population for the UK for the year 2001? Given that it is unrealistic to attempt to determine an optimum population, what general recommendations might a national population enquiry make, if it was asked to give government some guidance on the future size, composition and distribution of population of the UK?

9.3

What are the main arguments employed by advocates of zero population growth for the world? How would you make up your mind whether their arguments are conclusive, or are strong enough to be accepted by you?

9.4

Advocates of zero population growth say that countries should aim at ZPG, even though population problems here do not appear to be as great as they are in other parts of the world. To achieve ZPG, it would be necessary to halt migration. But it can also be argued that if host countries increased immigration, this would distribute the world's population more evenly and help to alleviate pressures on resources, where the pressures are greatest.

Do you think the policy of the ZPG movement should be zero population growth for individual countries irrespective of social and economic conditions in those countries, or, ZPG for the world as a whole coupled with a redistribution of population?

9.5

The following passage, which is a quotation from Kenneth Boulding's *Economics as a Science*,[2] suggests one solution to the population problem.

> There must, for instance, be stability of population, or at least a rate of increase which is commensurate with any increase in the carrying capacity of the world. This could be achieved, as I have suggested earlier, through a market mechanism which I have sometimes called the Green Stamp Plan for population control, according to which each human being would receive in adolescence, say, 110 green stamps, 100 of which would entitle the owner to have one legal child. A market would then be set up in these instruments so that those who had a strong desire for children could buy stamps from those who did not want to have children. Individual preferences in this matter could thus be expressed, while at the same time society could maintain overall social control of the rate of growth of population. There would presumably have to be mild sanctions for having illegal children which might entail temporary sterilisation until the illegal children are paid for in green stamps. This scheme has met with a good deal of disapproval. The alternative, however, would surely be authoritarian control, with a set number of children allowed per family and severe sanctions for violating the alloted number.

Discuss in class the merits and drawbacks of Boulding's plan.

Percentage of the population of working age

This depends on the age distribution of the population and also on what society regards as the working age group. In the UK the normal working age period has been regarded as between sixteen years and sixty-five for men and between sixteen and sixty for women. It is possible that these ages may differ as society reconsiders what are appropriate ages to leave school or to retire. There is a growing tendency for men to leave their jobs and to retire before sixty-five. The proportion of the population that continues to work after the normal retirement age is small.

Population structure

Figure 9.2 is a bar chart showing the population structure of England and Wales in 1976. This diagram, also known as a population pyramid, further shows the proportion of the age distribution economically active within the age distribution. Since the diagram measures the numbers of males and females separately on a scale from a central axis, the breakdown of population by sex is also shown.

In 1978, 22 per cent of the UK population was under 15 years and 14.5 per cent was over 65 years. With falling birth rates, and projections of a very slow rate of population growth in the future UK population, the age distribution by the year 2011 will alter to less than 20 per cent under 15, and 14 per cent over 65. (In the year 1911 the figures were 31 per cent under 15, and 5 per cent over 65.) As a proportion of total

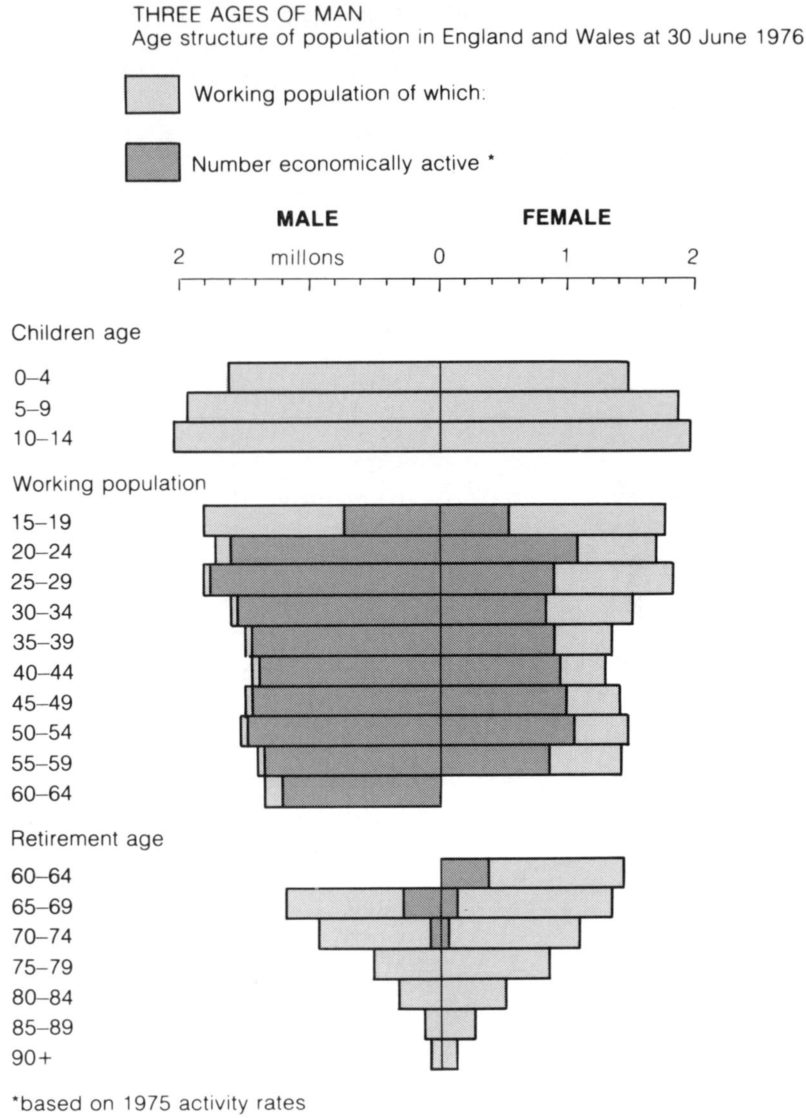

Figure 9.2 Age structure of population in England and Wales, 1976

Source: The Economist, 24 December 1977

population the numbers of old people over 65 has increased from 1 in 9 of the population in 1951, to 1 in 7 of the population in the mid 1970s.

Such changes in the age distribution have effects upon consumption expenditure, as mentioned in Chapter 5. A persistent reduction in the rate of growth of the population will eventually have the effect of gradually reducing the proportion of the population in the working age groups, although in the short run it increases it. Why is this so?

Labour force participation rate

This refers to the proportion of the population in the working age group able and willing to work. Table 9.4 provides information about the labour force participation rates for males and females by age in 1971.

Males (aged 15 and over)		Females (aged 15 and over)	
Total population	19 496 000	Total population	21 439 000
Total economically active	15 884 000	Total economically active	9 138 000

Activity rates by age groups (%)

Males		Females	
15–19	61.4	15–19	56.1
20–24	90.3	20–24	60.2
25–34	97.7	25–34	44.0
35–44	98.4	35–44	57.2
45–54	97.7	45–54	60.4
55–59	95.4	55–59	50.1
60–64	86.6	60–64	27.9
65 and over	19.3	65 and over	6.2

Table 9.4. Activity rates UK 1971 by age and sex

Source: *Annual Abstract of Statistics 1982*, Table 6.16, HMSO

Together with Figure 9.3, the information in Table 9.4 gives a detailed picture of the distribution of the labour force by age, and by marital status, for the female population. There are marked variations for both males and females in the 15–19 and 20–24 age groups as a result of those students remaining in education and out of the labour force. For males, activity rates then increase to levels of 97 and 98 per cent until retirement begins to lower the rates. For women, the pattern is more complex, with the 20 to 35 age groups affected by those bringing up families as an occupation outside the labour force. This shows up more clearly in the figure demonstrating the effects of marital status on activity rates.

9.6

Comment on the probable effects of the following policies and events on the size of a country's labour force: within three months, and in 20 years time.

1 A fall in the birth rate.
2 Abolition of the means test on aged person's pensions.
3 Introduction of job sharing in the public service.
4 Provision of more child-care facilities.
5 Reduction in the retiring age to 55 years for men and women.
6 Introduction of policies giving job preference to unmarried before married women.
7 Restriction of immigration to the families of skilled and professional workers.
8 Legalisation of abortion.
9 Introduction of a shorter working week.
10 The development of a national retraining scheme for those displaced by structural change, or those wishing to change their jobs.

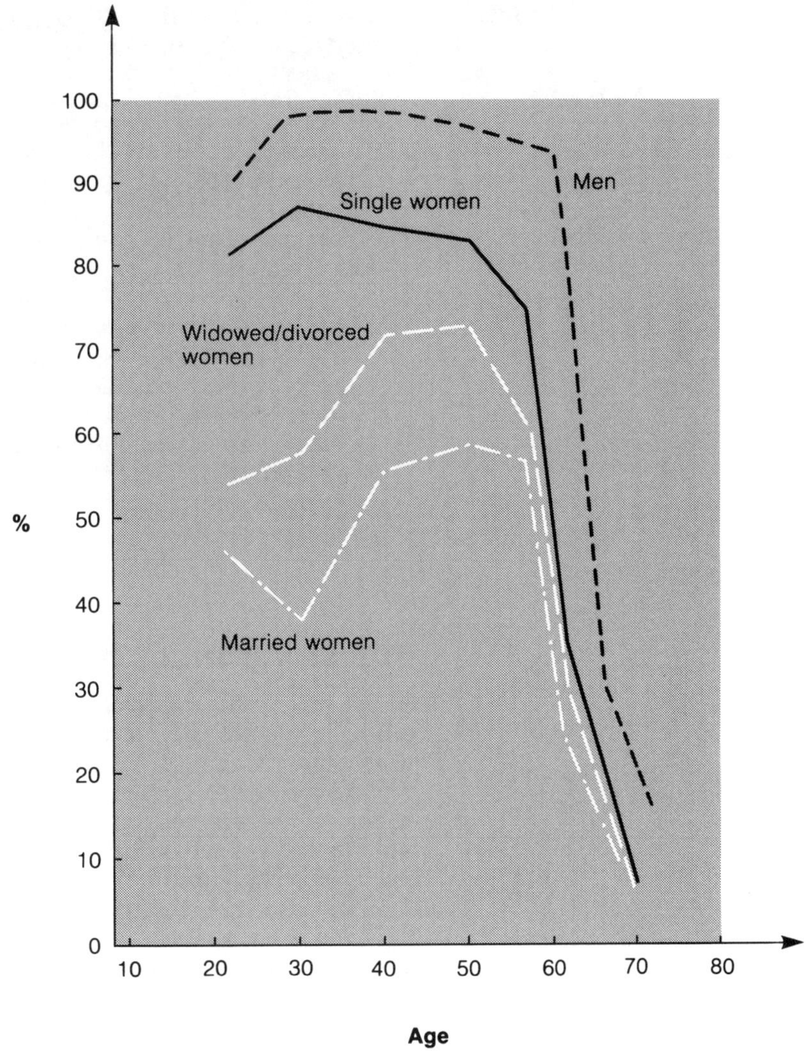

Figure 9.3 Activity rates, 1971

Source: Economic Progress Report, November 1974

9.7

Study Table 9.4 and Figure 9.3 carefully.

1 What explanations can you give for the variations in activity rates shown?

2 Why are activity rates never 100 per cent?

3 Explain the variation in activity rates for married women compared with single women in the figure.

4 Explain what events, or changes in attitude, have contributed or, are likely to contribute to, changes in the pattern of activity rates in the UK.

9.8

With the help of the following information, make a projection of the UK's labour force in 1979, 1980 and 1981.

Population in 1978	55.8 million
Crude birth rate	12.3 per 1000
Crude death rate	11.9 per 1000
Net migration outflow	32 000 per year
Percentage of population 16 years and over	76.3 per cent
Activity rate	61.8 per cent

Use of a calculator will ease the chore of calculation. Compare your projection with the actual estimated labour force published by the Central Statistical Office in the official statistics. Try to discover reasons for any variations between the figures by investigating actual figures for birth rates, death rates, migration levels and so on. Why are projections for the labour force for several years in the future more likely to prove inaccurate compared with actual results?

The structure of the labour force

Employment by sector

In Chapter 5 the principal forms of private final consumption expenditure in the UK were investigated. In Chapter 6 the value added to production by each of the industries of the UK was considered. Table 9.5 analyses the percentage of the labour force employed in the different sectors of the economy. For many decades, there has been a notable shift out of primary employment, initially into the secondary sector: manufacturing, construction, gas, water and electricity. Since 1961 the services sector in the economy has expanded while the secondary sector has contracted. In parallel with these changes, the proportion of manual workers in total employment has fallen.

% of employment in:	1961	1971	1981 (projected)
Primary	6.6	4.3	3.2
Secondary	44.3	42.9	39.4
Services	48.7	52.8	57.3
Manual	56	51	46
Non-manual	38	43	48
Unclassified	6	6	6

Table 9.5 Distribution of employment in the UK

Source: *The Economist*, 1 January 1977

The decline in employment in the manufacturing sector is highlighted in Table 9.6, which also looks at the distribution of male and female employment in the UK. The growth of the services sector and of female employment is particularly noticeable. In 1976 about 37% of the UK labour force were females of whom some two-thirds were married. Of the total employed population in 1976, about one in six were women engaged in part-time employment.

	Thousands		
	1951	1976	% change
Manufacturing			
Males	5 761.5	5 131.0	−10.9
Females	2 984.4	2 114.7	−29.1
Total	8 745.9	7 245.7	−17.2
Services			
Males	4 864.1	6 134.9	+26.1
Females	4 009.4	6 745.7	+68.2
Total	8 873.5	12 880.6	+45.2

Table 9.6 Employees in employment in manufacturing and services in the UK.

Source: *NWBQR*, November 1979, p 59

Unemployment

From Table 9.1 on page 149 it can be seen that the United Kingdom had 1 446 000 persons unemployed in 1978. This represented about 6.2 per cent of the labour force. By the end of 1980, the number unemployed had risen to 2 150 000, or about 9 per cent, and was continuing to rise. By the end of 1982 over 3 million were unemployed.

Changes in unemployment in recent years

There have been great changes in the magnitude of unemployment in recent years. During the 1950s and 1960s the unemployment rate in the UK seldom rose above 2.5 per cent of the labour force. Full employment was said to be one of the UK's principal economic objectives and there was general feeling amongst governments and their economic advisers that the operation of the economic system was sufficiently well enough understood to prevent more than a temporary departure from these low unemployment levels. Any government that permitted unemployment to rise above such levels at that time probably would have found considerable electoral reaction to its policies.

During the 1970s the unemployment rate altered significantly in the United Kingdom. Unemployment levels have risen beyond those experienced in the 1950s and 1960s.

Unemployment rose sharply in 1971 and 1972, fell again in 1973–74 and then rose to 6 per cent in 1976. Since then the unemployment rate rose again to levels approaching 10 per cent by early 1981.

Figure 9.4 illustrates for Great Britain the distribution of the registered unemployed by age and by sex. As can be seen, there is considerable variation in unemployment in different age groups. The largest registered unemployed male age group is for 20–24 year olds with the 60–64 year age group second largest. For females the largest age groups unemployed are seen to be the under 20s and the 20–24 year olds. In interpreting these figures, it should be remembered that these are measures of the absolute numbers unemployed. The proportionate, or relative, distribution of unemployment by age, of the total number unemployed, will be affected by factors such as activity rates, which vary with age also. The full extent of the age differences in unemployment rates is shown by the statistics of unemployment as a percentage

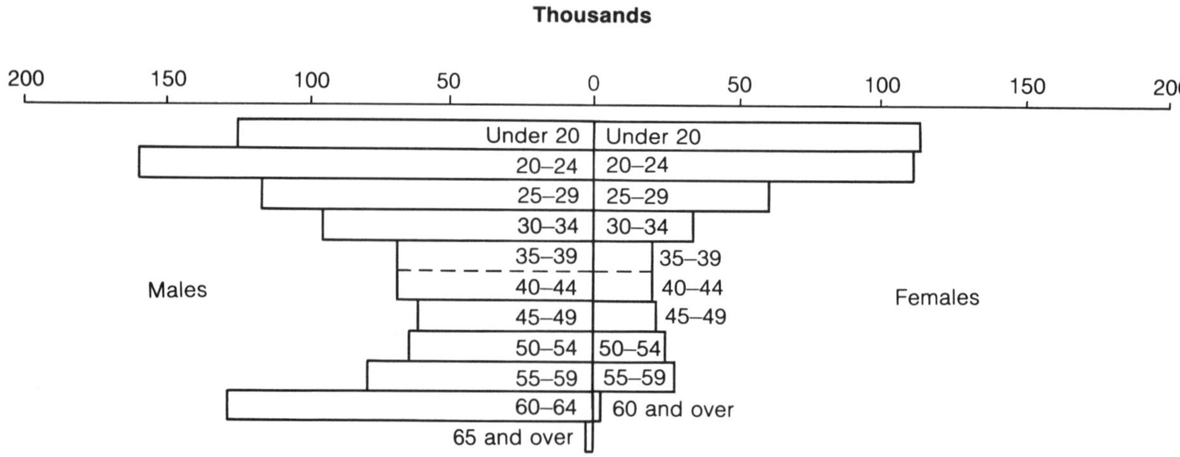

Figure 9.4 Unemployment by age, 1979

Source: Department of Employment News, No. 74, June 1980

of the labour force within a particular age group. This allows comparisons to be made of unemployment when there are differences in the numbers in each age group due to population change and other demographic factors.

One measure of the seriousness of unemployment from an economic and social point of view is the length of time people are out of work. This is shown in Table 9.7.

Unemployed for:	4 weeks or less	4–13 weeks	13–26 weeks	26–52 weeks	Over 1 year
Percentage of total	16	24	19	18	23

Table 9.7. Duration of unemployment: April 1980, Great Britain

Source: Employment News No. 74, June 1980

From the total, it can be seen that in April 1980 more than 40 per cent of the unemployed had been out of work for at least six months and a considerable proportion, 23 per cent, had not worked for over a year. Long periods of unemployment are likely to have a devastating effect on morale. The individual may despair of finding a job, become depressed and ultimately unemployable. The problems of long term unemployment are not easy to find solutions to. Moreover, the numbers of long term unemployed have been increasing; for example, between 1967 and 1977 the numbers unemployed for more than six months have increased by about four times.

Types of unemployment

A common classification distinguishes four types of unemployment:

1 *Frictional unemployment* This is created as people move between jobs. Some frictional unemployment is always present.

2 *Hard-core unemployment* This is caused by age, physical or mental handicaps or personal characteristics that make it difficult for the individual to get or retain a job. Such people are likely to be out of work for

long periods. To reduce the numbers of this type of unemployment may be extremely difficult.

3 *Structural unemployment* This term refers variously to a number of situations. They include where there is a lack of employment opportunities in a particular district or where there is a shortage of jobs in an industry which is in decline. It is also used to refer to a situation where unemployment is the result of the unemployed person lacking the suitable qualifications to perform the jobs that are available.

4 *Cyclical unemployment* This is a term that is sometimes used to refer to unemployment resulting from a reduction in the level of business activity generally. It is argued by many that the unemployment affecting the UK at present is of this type.

Such attempts to categorise unemployment have limited value. They are useful if they assist in diagnosing the problem of unemployment, and particularly if they assist in overcoming it. But the boundaries between the types of unemployment listed above are necessarily vague. For example, a general down turn in the level of economic activity is likely to be felt in those areas and industries that have particular structural problems. It is difficult to determine whether unemployment amongst workers in the automobile industry is structural or cyclical. Certainly that industry has specific structural problems. So too does the ship-building industry. But both are accentuated by adverse economic conditions. Similarly it is difficult to distinguish between structural unemployment and hard-core unemployment. A person who is laid off, who lacks the necessary skills, who comes from an area where there are no employment opportunities may find it impossible to get a job. In this environment his age, or his reaction to the situation in which he finds himself may then make him unacceptable to employers and to the conventions they require from prospective employees.

Regional unemployment

Within the United Kingdom, there is considerable variation of unemployment on a regional basis. This is only one source of the disparity between the regions that comprises the 'regional problem' in the UK. Other variations occur in the level of income per head, the level of social

Region	Number unemployed ('000s)	% in region unemployed	
	1979	1979	1982
North	117.7	8.5	17.6
Yorks and Humberside	117.8	5.6	14.6
East Midlands	73.8	4.6	12.1
East Anglia	30.7	4.3	11.2
South East	267.6	3.5	10.4
South West	93.4	5.6	11.8
North West	199.3	7.0	16.6
West Midlands	126.3	5.4	16.6
Wales	85.2	7.7	17.4
Scotland	180.3	8.0	15.8
Northern Ireland	63.4	11.0	21.7
UK, total	1 355.5	5.6	13.8

Table 9.8 Unemployment by region: UK, December 1979 and October 1982

Source: *Employment News* No. 74, June 1980 and Department of Employment amenities, the age and dereliction of the housing stock and so on. As regards unemployment, the causes of regional variation are primarily historical, such as the decline of old consumer and heavy industries, which creates above-average unemployment in those regions traditionally heavily dependent on these industries. Table 9.8 shows for December 1979 the variation of unemployment rates by region in the UK.

Table 9.9 gives a much wider view of unemployment in the regions. For 1970 to 1978 the level of unemployment in each region is expressed in terms of an index number, with the level for the UK equal to 100 throughout. From these figures, it is clear that Scotland, the North, Wales and the North West face considerable regional unemployment while the South East and the Midlands fare much better than the national average. The problem of regional differences is shown to be a continuing one, but the degree of variation between regions has altered.

Region	1970	1971	1972	1973	1974	1975	1976	1977	1978
Scotland	162	166	168	167	154	124	121	134	137
North	177	163	166	174	177	140	129	135	142
Wales	150	126	126	126	142	133	128	131	134
North West	104	111	126	133	135	126	121	121	119
Yorks/Humbs	108	109	111	104	100	95	97	94	95
South West	108	94	89	81	100	112	110	113	110
East Midlands	85	83	79	74	85	86	83	82	82
East Anglia	81	91	76	70	73	81	84	87	85
West Midlands	73	83	95	81	n/a	98	102	94	87
South East	62	57	58	56	58	67	72	73	69
GB percentage	2.5	3.4	3.7	2.6	2.6	4.1	5.6	6.0	6.0

Note GB = 100 throughout

Table 9.9 Relative unemployment rates GB 1970–78

Source: *Annual Abstract of Statistics, 1980*, HMSO

Full employment

It was said earlier that during the post war period successive British governments have been committed to the objective of full employment. This concept of *full employment* needs some comment. Clearly, it does not mean the employment of every person in the labour force. It is recognised that to achieve this would be impossible and in one important sense, undesirable. Unemployment can only be reduced below a certain point by producing conditions in which the rate of inflation will accelerate. These conditions may also worsen the balance of payments position and may well produce a redistribution of income in an unacceptable form. Paradoxically, the very increase in unemployment might then produce circumstances in which the level of production might be reduced and living standards depressed. Consequently, even in the late 1960s it was conventional to define full employment as 'the highest rate of employment capable of being sustained', without the emergence of these undesirable effects.

Today, many economists believe that the full employment level, or zone, is a great deal higher than it was in the 1960s. In other words, any attempt by government to introduce short-term policies that brought unemployment down to 1.5 per cent or even 2 per cent of the labour force would bring with them a high rate of inflation. It may well be that the appropriate full employment level for the 1980s is 5 or 6 per cent of the labour force. Other economists refuse to accept such a pessimistic outlook. They believe that selective policies can be introduced that will reduce unemployment significantly without increasing the rate of inflation. However, few would see a return to the full employment zone of the 1960s as a realistic possibility in the short term.

Country	1973 (%)	1976 (%)	1980 (%)	1982 (%)
Australia	1.5	4.7	6.1	—
Canada	5.7	7.1	6.8	—
Germany (Federal Republic)	1.3	4.6	4.2	7.7
Italy	3.5	3.7	8.3	10.2
Sweden	2.4	1.6	—	—
United Kingdom	2.6	5.4	10.0	12.2
United States	4.9	7.7	7.1	9.5

Table 9.10 Rates of unemployment in various countries

Sources: *Main Economic Indicators*, July 1977, OECD, Paris, 1977; *Employment Gazette*, June 1982

It should be clear that the reduction of unemployment is inextricably bound up with the problem of how to reduce inflation. On this there is general agreement. The relationship between unemployment and inflation and the controversy about what policy the British government should follow to deal with these problems is discussed in the following chapter and in more detail in Chapter 16.

The higher levels of unemployment experienced by the UK in the 1970s have also occurred in other western industrial countries. Table 9.10 shows the rates of unemployment for a number of countries in 1973, 1976, 1980 and 1982.

The figures for the various countries are not precisely comparable. Different dates and methods of estimation were used. Nevertheless they provide a reasonable comparison and the change in the UK's position relative to the others is particularly significant.

9.9 As unemployment increased during the 1970s it was common to read letters to the editors of newspapers written in the following terms.

Dear Sir
The claims that we in Britain hear about there being a serious unemployment problem are grossly exaggerated. You look at who it is that is without work. It's these youngsters straight from school. I say that they are more interested in living off the rest of us than in getting down and doing a solid job. If they got out and buckled down there would be no unemployment to speak of. What's more I can prove what I am saying. Last week my business offered jobs to two unemployed lads. One didn't bother to turn up and the other left after two days saying he didn't like the work. They're not worth bothering with under these cirucmstances.

Disgusted businessman

Discuss this letter in the light of the information about unemployment presented in this section. To what extent does it appear that unemployment is self-inflicted and to what extent could unemployment in the UK be attributed to structural problems in the economy?

9.10 What explanation can you provide for the current level of unemployment in your regiόn and the difference between that and the levels of current unemployment in other regions?

9.11 Explain why it is that unemployment is frequently higher in rural areas than in metropolitan centres. Should government endeavour to reduce the disparity? If so, what sorts of policy measures might it consider?

Notes

1 T R Malthus 1798 *Essay on Population* 1st edn. repr Penguin. 1971 (ed AGN Flew).
2 K E Boulding 1970, *Economics as a Science*, McGraw-Hill, New York, 1970, pp 149–50.

Chapter 10

Wages and Unemployment

The previous chapter investigated some of the more important determinants of the supply of human resources in the UK. It also explored the serious social and economic consequences that unemployment has had for UK citizens in recent years. This chapter deals with a closely related topic: the relationship between the level of wages and the unemployment rate. Wages can be regarded as the price that employers pay to hire human resources. Consequently, it seems logical to look for a connection between wage levels and the number of persons employed. As we shall see, there is a connection, but it is by no means a simple one. Indeed it is far more complicated than the initial discussion of demand and supply in Chapter 7 might lead one to suppose.

Wages – the price of human resources

The relationship between the level of wages and unemployment is one of a number of related questions that interest economists. Another is the link between productivity changes, technological innovation and the demand for labour. In the past few years such questions have been considered against a background of general increases in the price level. To understand these and the associated problems, it is necessary also to understand how wages are determined in the UK and to appreciate the respective parts played by employers, unions, the government and the various institutional bodies such as the Advisory Conciliation and Arbitration Service (ACAS) and Wage Councils.

Wage rates and earnings

At the outset it is important to distinguish carefully between some of the principal terms that are used. The *wage rate* is the amount of money to be paid to a worker for working for a specified period, or for performing a specified number of tasks. Thus a wage rate may be expressed in the form of £5 per hour, or say £30 a day, or maybe £150 per 40 hour week. Alternatively, the rate of pay may be expressed as a fixed salary per month or per year, e.g. £8000 per annum. The wage rate may be paid on a piece rate basis, that is directly related to the level of output of the worker, such as £5.00 per 100 production units. These forms of payment are commonly referred to as incentive payments or 'payment by results' schemes. Normally, wage rates are fixed by agreement between workers and management. Alternatively, they may be determined by a third party such as ACAS, or in the context of government policy on incomes if currently in operation. The actual wage contract may utilise a number of different forms of wage rate. There may be a basic wage rate for a 35 or 40 hour week, with additional incentive payment rates, such as a piece rate and a separate overtime rate for occasions when the employee is required to work other than the standard hours. Additional payments for 'unsocial hours' may be payable for shift work, work at weekends or on public holidays. Specific loadings may be added for carrying out specified tasks of working in special conditions.

Earnings are the *amounts actually earned* by the employee during a specified period. The earnings for a week may differ from the determined weekly wage rate for the job because the employee worked overtime, or earned bonuses, or alternatively was on short time. It is also important to distinguish between the wage rate that the employer is *bound* to pay employees, as the result of a determination of a wage-fixing authority, for example a wages council, and the wage rate which the employer *agrees* to pay the employee.

About one-third of the employed population of the UK have a minimum wage level established for them by a wages council or similar statutory body. Wages tend to be lower than actual earnings for many workers because wage rates relate only to earnings per hour, or working week, and many workers will have additional payments for overtime, productivity, bonuses, shift-work and other allowances. The difference, or gap, between wages and earnings is referred to as wage-drift or earnings-drift. Bargaining at plant-level or in an individual firm by the local union and management may also produce wage-drift above a nationally agreed minimum level of payment for the industry.

Wage-drift

Earnings tend to reflect the overall market for labour. Thus in a time of full employment the gap between earnings and the agreed wage rate may be increasing; in a recession when unemployment is high the gap is likely to narrow.

Each of these sets of figures is valuable when attempting to discover a connection between wages and unemployment. The wage rate is probably more important to businesses as they consider the costs of employing extra staff or of retaining their existing staff. The wage rate is the effective price that they will be required to pay when they take on an extra worker. Weekly earnings are likely to be of more relevance to the employee than the wage rate. Actual take-home pay will be influenced directly by changes in earnings, and the changes in income will affect the capacity to purchase goods and services.

Wages and prices

Figure 10.1 illustrates the very strong upward movement in average earnings in the United Kingdom during the 1970s. This increase in earnings was accompanied by an increase in the money incomes of households. Wage earners had more money to spend. It is not possible to say that households were better off in real terms without considering the increases in prices that also occurred. Figure 10.1 shows the index of retail prices over the same period. It should also be borne in mind that wages form an important element of total costs and that an increase in money wages will tend to feed back into increases in prices. In Chapter 7 wage costs were identified as one of the determinants of supply and income as one of the determinants of demand. The possible effects of a related increase in the wage costs of a representative industry and the incomes of its customers are shown in Figure 10.2.

An initial equilibrium position for the industry is at E_1; the intersection of demand curve D_1D_1 and the supply curve S_1S_1. An increase in wages to the industry can be expected to raise costs and to thus lead

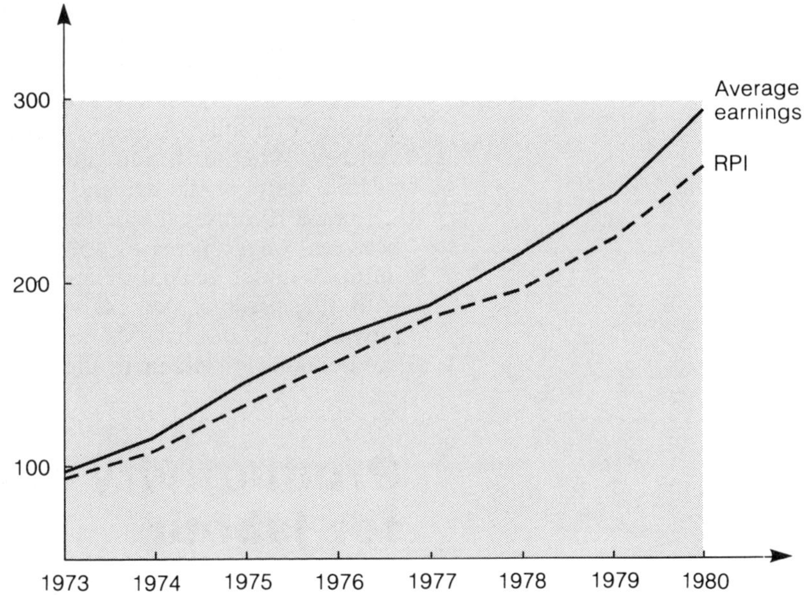

Figure 10.1 Index of average earnings and retail prices index, 1973–80
Source: Department of Employment News, No. 74, June 1980

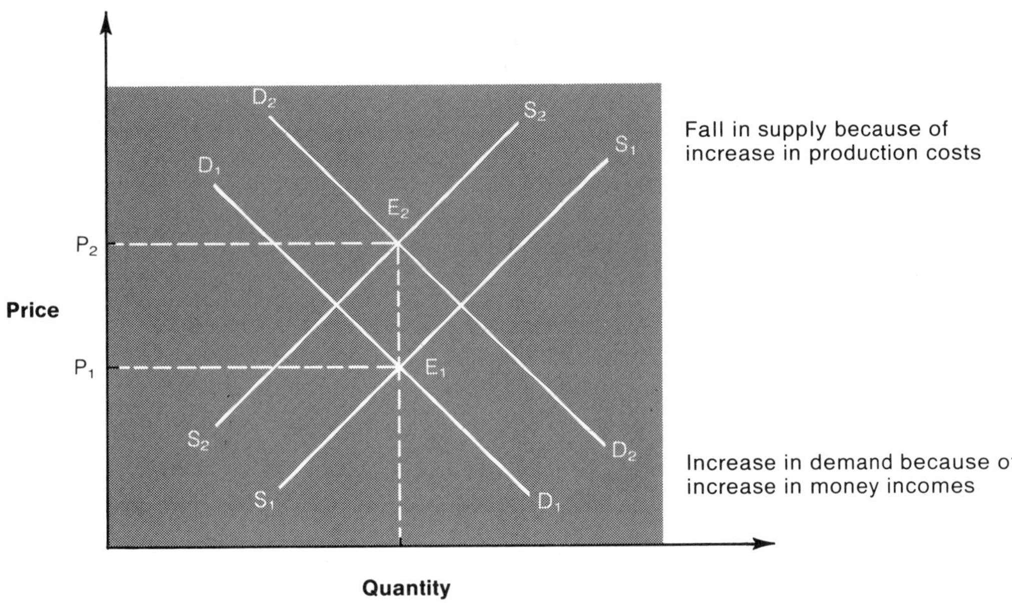

Figure 10.2 Possible effects of an increase in wages

to the formation of a new supply curve S_2S_2. *Other things being equal* the resulting adjustments would lead to the industry selling a smaller quantity at a higher price.

However, if wage increases are general then the industry is likely to benefit because its customers are likely to have higher incomes, and are likely to spend some proportion of these higher incomes on its products. Consequently the initial demand curve D_1D_1 is replaced by a new demand curve D_2D_2. The net effect is that a new equilibrium position occurs at E_2; the intersection of S_2S_2 and D_2D_2. The price of the industry's product is higher along with the prices of other goods and services. Whether production is increased or reduced depends on the relative shifts of the demand and supply curves.

Figure 10.2 uses the tools acquired in Chapter 7 to examine the link between wage increases, prices and production in a representative industry under general inflationary conditions. It does not deal directly with the effect of general wage increases on employment, or unemployment. To do that it is necessary to consider the factors which affect the demand for labour in the UK.

Productivity and the demand for labour

If a business is seeking to operate as profitably as possible, the number of people that it will be prepared to employ will be influenced by three major considerations:

the productivity of its workers,
the price at which its product is sold, and
the wage rate it has to pay to obtain workers.

The *productivity* of its workers is the measure of the contribution that the labour force makes to the firm's physical output when working with given plant and equipment. In Chapter 8 an important relationship between the use of resources and their product was discussed. It was shown that as additional workers are employed in a given production environment, with no increase in plant and equipment, their average and marginal product will decline. This is the operation of the law of diminishing returns. In such circumstances employing extra workers leads to an increase in total physical output, but the average productivity of the workers will be reduced. We noted that in the short run it is often difficult to change plant and equipment.

Diminishing marginal product of labour

The firm's demand for labour will be influenced by the *market price* it obtains for its products. If the firm can first estimate the *physical* contribution made to output by employing each additional worker, then it will be able to put a *monetary* value on the additional production. Suppose that the firm is unable to influence the price of its product on the market. In this situation the monetary value from employing one more worker will be the marginal physical product of that worker multiplied by the price of the product. Thus, where the marginal product is diminishing, the monetary contribution that each additional worker makes to production will decline.[1]

The third influence on a firm's decision about how many workers it can profitably employ is the wage rate it must pay. If the firm wants to maximise profits then the appropriate policy is to take on additional workers as long as the increase in the firm's revenue that results is greater than, or equal to, the extra cost in employing them.

The relationship between these three influences in determining the number of persons a firm is prepared to employ is set out in Figure 10.3. The downward sloping line, DD, measures the additional revenue

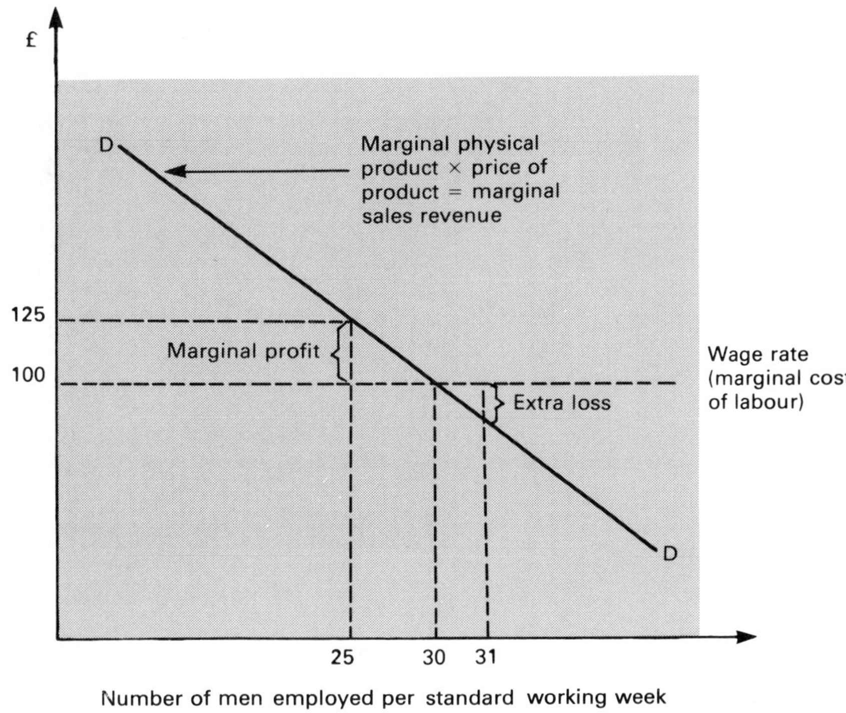

Figure 10.3 Marginal costs and revenue of labour

the firm can obtain from the sale of the additional output obtained by employing each extra worker. It therefore incorporates both the influence of diminishing marginal productivity of labour and the price the firm obtains for that product in the market place. The influence of the ruling wage rate is also shown. It shows the additional labour expense incurred by employing one extra worker. Suppose the wage rate is £100 per week. An additional employee will cost the firm an extra £100. In Figure 10.3 it will be to the firm's advantage to employ 30 workers because the 30th worker adds £100 to revenue and costs £100. The employment of the 30th worker then brings in just enough revenue to meet the cost of employing him. To employ a 31st worker would not be profitable, because the increase in revenue would be less than £100. Alternatively, if the firm employed only 25 workers it would be foregoing the chance to gain more in sales revenue than it incurred in production costs. It would not be maximising profits.

If the current wage rate happened to be £125 then the appropriate decision would be to employ only 25 workers because the wage rate, the marginal cost of an extra worker, just equals the additional revenue earned by employing the 25th worker. Notice that it has been assumed that the firm is required to pay the same wage rate to all the workers it employs and that the wage rate line is shown as horizontal.[2]

Industries that find themselves in the position of not being able to pass on the cost increases flowing from higher wages in the form of higher prices, will reduce their demand for labour as Figure 10.4 demonstrates. The resulting unemployment will be the consequence of the wage increase. However, many industries will be able to pass on some, or all, of any wage increase with correspondingly less effect on

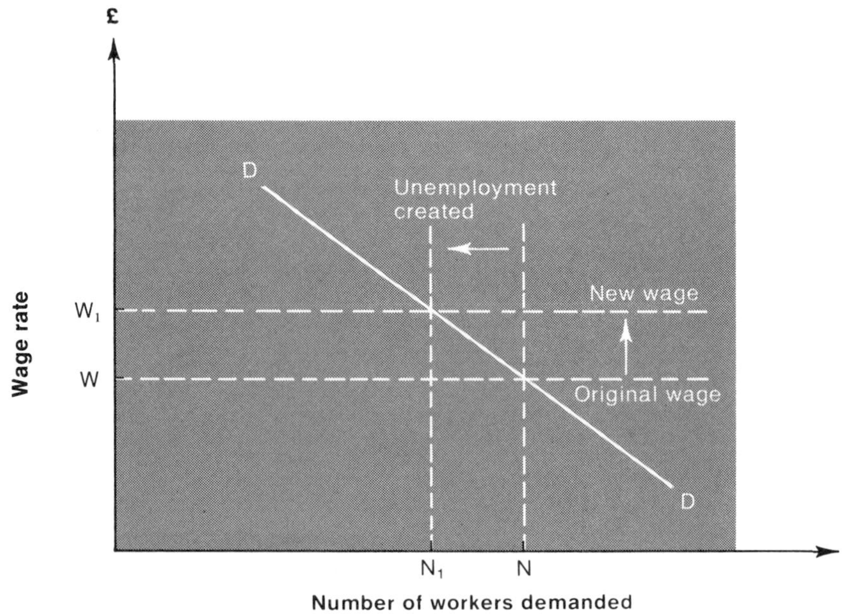

Figure 10.4 Effects of wage increase on employment

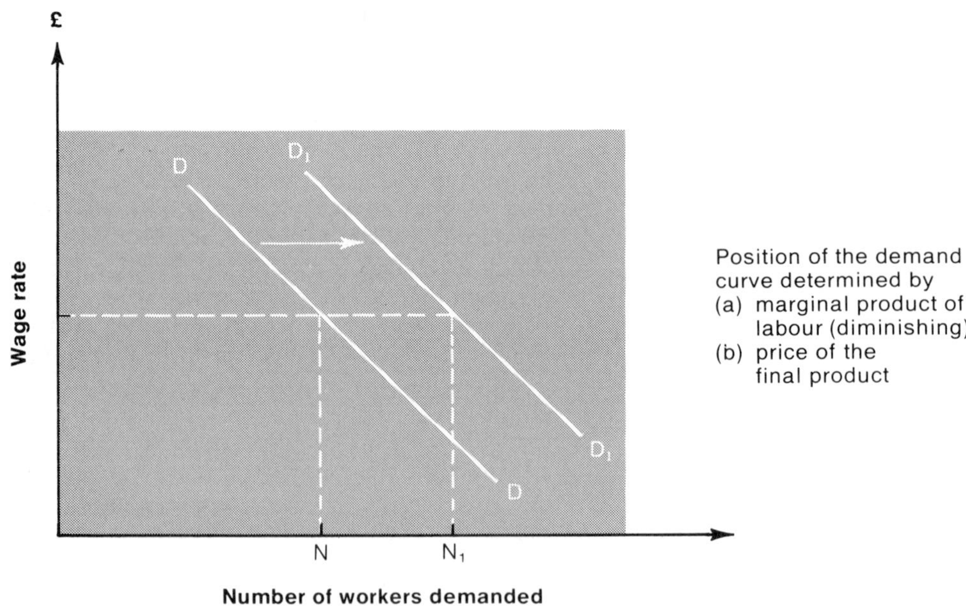

Figure 10.5 Effects of an increase in product prices or labour productivity on the demand for labour

the level of unemployment. The effect of an increase in labour productivity is to move the demand curve to the right as shown in Figure 10.5.

The downward sloping line, DD, in Figure 10.3 can be regarded as the firm's demand curve for labour in the short run. It shows the quantities of labour that the profit-maximising firm will seek to employ at different wage levels. By adding together the quantities of labour that each of the firms in an industry is prepared to employ at each wage level, it is possible to obtain the industry's short-term demand curve for labour. This too slopes downwards from left to right.

It is now possible to consider the effects on a particular industry of changes in wages, product prices and the productivity of labour in that industry. For simplicity, each of the effects is considered initially in isolation. The effect of an increase in wage rates is shown in Figure 10.4. If wage rates rise and there is no change in productivity or in product prices, there is likely to be reduced employment as individual firms adjust their labour requirements.

Wage increases and unemployment

An increase in product prices does this by raising the monetary value of each man's output to the firm. A shift in consumer demand towards a particular commodity will make it profitable for that industry to have more labour at the going wage rate. The rapid expansion of the take-away food industry is an example of such an effect.

If the physical output of each worker is increased, for some reason, then the monetary value of the employees' work is increased even if the price remains the same. In this situation firms within the industry will find it profitable to employ more persons at the ruling wage rate and such changes will therefore be employment creating. Figure 10.5 shows the firm's response to a favourable shift in the value of the marginal product of its workforce. This shift may be due either to an improved price for its product or an improvement in the productivity of the workforce.

As noted earlier, such changes in wage rates, in prices and in labour productivity do not occur in isolation as we have assumed for our exposition. In the 1970s they have been occurring simultaneously. It is the *relative* strengths of demand and supply for a product that will determine whether its production increases or falls when wages and prices are rising. It should now be clear that it is the relative strength of wage increases and of shifts in the demand curve for labour that determine whether employment increases or falls as wage rates rise. Certainly, it should be clear that it is not necessarily true that increases in money wages will lead to growing unemployment.

Money wages and real wages

When prices are rising the usual measures of production and consumption in money terms tell us little about whether the quantity of goods being produced or consumed is rising or falling. The notions of 'real' consumption and 'real' production were introduced in Chapters 5 and 6. Real consumption is final consumption expenditure valued at constant prices. Real production is gross domestic product valued at constant prices. Another very useful comparable measure is 'real' wages. The worker's real wage will be determined by his money wage and by the prices of goods he wishes to buy. If prices of consumer goods are rising more rapidly than his wages then his capacity to purchase is reduced and his real wage falls even though his money wage may be rising. If his money wage is rising more rapidly than the prices he pays, his real wage will be rising. The real wages of the worker are a measure of his capacity to purchase goods and services. If the worker's real

Real wages measure capacity to purchase goods and services

wages are rising then he will be able to purchase a greater quantity of goods and services than before.

The difference between real wages and money wages is also thought to be of importance to employers and to their demand for labour. If the prices an employer receives from the sale of his products are increasing less rapidly than the wages he has to pay, the real wage he has to pay as a cost is increasing. If the prices of his products are rising more rapidly than the wages he pays then the real wage cost to the firm is said to be falling. Increasingly, in recent times, the proposition has been put that there is a clear link between the level of real wages in the UK and the level of unemployment. It is claimed that unemployment increases when real wage levels are 'too high'.

Real wages and unemployment

Year	Index of average earnings	Index of retail prices	Real earnings
1973	97.9	93.5	104.7
1974	116.1	108.5	107.0
1975	147.1	134.7	109.3
1976	170.1	157.1	108.3
1977	187.3	182.0	102.9
1978	214.4	197.1	108.8
1979	247.8	223.5	110.9
1980	294.3	263.5	111.7

Table 10.1 Real earnings as a business cost, UK, 1973–1980

As a first step to testing this proposition, it is possible to calculate measures of real earnings. One such measure is to deflate the index of average earnings by some indicator of changes in the price level. Table 10.1 shows a calculation of real earnings for the period 1973 to 1980 using average earnings as a representative of the level of money wages. It then deflates this to real terms by dividing it by the index of retail prices for the same period.

The justification for calculating the real earnings in this way is partly because the desire to show how real earnings as a business cost changed during the period. Other deflators could be used for this purpose, for example the GDP price deflator. Other measures of wage rates could also be used, such as minimum wage rates rather than the index of earnings.

The table shows that real earnings have not increased at the same rate over the period 1973 to 1980. The level of earnings rose faster than retail prices from 1973 to 1975 and from 1978 onwards. From 1975 to 1978 the rate of increase of retail prices was greater than the rise in earnings so that a greater proportion of the increase in earnings was accounted for by increased prices.

Comparing these results for real earnings with unemployment does not provide conclusive evidence that increases in real earnings lead to unemployment. The rate of increase of unemployment did fall from 1977 to 1978. However, before then, unemployment continued to rise and real earnings had risen. It is probable, of course, that there are lags in the processes whereby firms adjust to changes such as the level of earnings. In practice, an economic relationship such as the one between employment levels and earnings will seldom be straightforward enough to be summed up by a single proposition, no matter how appealing it may sound.

Productivity, technological change and longer term adjustments

Another reason that is given for at least some of the current unemployment is technological change and the problems caused by it when people are replaced by machines.

Earlier, however, it was said that increases in labour productivity often come from the introduction of new plant and equipment and that the greater productivity will increase the demand for labour. It is also said that the capacity of industry to sustain higher wages is dependent upon increasing productivity. Such arguments sound odd. They certainly would not sound convincing to workers made redundant following the introduction of automated processes in industry. Clearly, much depends upon the nature of the innovations that are taking place. There is, for example, the possibility that the skills required after technological change may be unrelated to those needed beforehand. Computer operators may replace clerks. But the effect of innovation will be that the industry's need for manpower to produce a *given* output will be reduced; production per employee is increased. Figure 10.5 was drawn on the assumption that the quantity of non-human resources and the available technology were fixed in the short run. In the longer term, as innovation occurs, it may become profitable to *substitute* machines for men, the productivity of those employed will increase, but the numbers employed may fall substantially. In short, some types of change are likely to lead to a reduction in the demand for labour and for some part of the demand curve for labour to move to the left rather than to the right.

Factor substitution

A critical determinant of the quantities of labour that an industry is able to retain following spectacular technical progress will be the rate of growth of demand for the products and the price elasticity of demand. If the demand for the products is so limited, innovation is likely to lead to a substantial reduction in labour requirements. If demand for the product is increasing and in addition is price elastic, the industry may be able to increase production to such an extent that the effects of innovation on the labour force may be small. Or, it is even possible that the fall in the relative price of the product of the innovating industry is sufficient to induce such an increased demand for the commodity that, despite the increase in labour productivity, more workers are employed. The sharp falls in prices of electronic products and the increase in their usage in the 1970s stands in stark contrast to the rising prices of most other products.

There is also a link between wages, technical innovation and unemployment. In the long run businesses are likely to select the particular technology that offers the best profit potential. Thus even though a business may be able to recoup its higher wage costs by charging higher prices so that its real wage levels are unchanged, or maybe fall, it may find that the relative costs of alternative production techniques are lowered. As wages rise relative to the costs of other resources, the increases may tip the balance in favour of alternative production techniques. These may take time to implement, but may eventually lead to the replacement of labour and to unemployment. The increased use of self-service petrol distribution is an illustration of their effect.

10.1

Table 10.1 calculated real earnings by deflating the index of average earnings by the retail price index. Average earnings are higher than wage rates for a number of reasons, for example, overtime pay, bonus payments. There are other labour costs that businesses have to face which are appropriate to consider when assessing the impact of labour costs to businesses on the level of employment. If you had the available information, which of the following cost influences would you include when determining an appropriate labour cost series?

employers' contributions to national insurance and graduated pensions
employers' contributions to superannuation.
shorter working hours
increased number of public holidays
the effects of implementing equal pay legislation

10.2

1 Use a demand and supply diagram to show the effects of a spectacular technological improvement in an industry. What effect would you expect this to have on production and the price of the product?
2 Draw a diagram of the demand for labour by the industry before and after the innovation. Assume that the wage rates are unchanged. How do the effects illustrated by your diagram of (1) influence your diagram (2)?

10.3

There is very little evidence that dramatic technological improvement in some western-type industrial countries such as Japan and West Germany in recent years has led to large-scale unemployment in those countries. How does this reflect upon the claims that unemployment is caused by technological change, rather than an inadequate level of economic activity, or by an excessively high level of real wages?

Wages share

That part of the aggregate value of production which goes directly to households through wages and salaries is referred to as the *wages share*. One simple definition is:

$$\text{Wages share} = \frac{\text{aggregate of wages, salaries and supplements}}{\text{gross domestic product at factor cost}} \times 100$$

The remainder of GDP at factor cost is gross operating surplus from which comes dividends and undisturbed profits, income from self-employment and rent. Table 10.2 gives the wages share of GDP at factor cost for 1970 to 1978.

Year	Income from employment (%)
1970	69.5
1971	68.7
1972	68.5
1973	68.6
1974	72.5
1975	73.9
1976	71.9
1977	69.6
1978	69.6

Table 10.2 Wages share as a percentage of GDP at factor cost, UK, 1970-78

Source: *Annual Abstract of Statistics 1980*, Table 14.2, HMSO

Table 10.2 shows that income from employment rose sharply after 1973 until 1976 in line with the increases in money wages and real wages already noted. Generally, the wages share of GDP at factor cost is in the order of some 70 per cent. Of the remaining income to be distributed, the share going to enterprises as a profit, or a surplus, is particularly susceptible to influences from the level of economic activity in the country.

It is important to realise the limitations of the wages share indicator. It simply describes how income from production is being distributed between businesses and the labour force. An increase in wages share does not necessarily mean that total business profits are declining. This, in aggregate, will depend on whether gross domestic product at constant prices is increasing sufficiently rapidly to meet the rising wages share and to provide a greater aggregate gross operating surplus. The sharp increase in the wages share in 1974 and 1975 was accompanied by a decline in GDP at constant prices. In fact the real gross operating surpluses of companies, and particularly of unincorporated enterprises, fell sharply during this two-year period. Their subsequent recovery coincides with the reduction in wages share and an increase in GDP at constant prices.

Real wages and wages share

Likewise, increases in real wages and increases in the wages share should not be confused though they may well occur together. If real wages are rising then the wages share is also likely to rise provided GDP at constant prices is rising less rapidly than real wages. However, in a strong growth situation total real wages may be increasing. Yet their share of income may actually be reduced whilst the share going to businesses and their shareholders increases. In general, when the economy moves into the recession phase, the wages share increases even though employment may decline and wage rates may increase more slowly. The explanation is that the recession has a disproportionately severe effect upon profits. Conversely, in the upswing, although employment and wage rates will accelerate, the share of wages is likely to decline because profits increase more rapidly than wages.

10.4

Discuss the prospects for a reduction of unemployment in the following situations, where:
1 real wages are rising, but the wages share is falling,

2 real wages are rising and the wages share is rising,
3 real wages are falling, but GDP at constant prices is rising, and
4 real wages are falling, wages share is falling and GDP at constant prices is falling.

Do you think that situations such as (3) and (4) are likely to happen in the UK? If so, under what circumstances?

Alternatives views on real wages and unemployment

It has been suggested that, although many economists hold the view that unemployment exists because the real wage is too high, there are dangers in accepting such a simple proposition without reservation. In fact, large numbers of economists in the UK take a very different view of the unemployment problem and its remedy. Such economists argue that the main cause of unemployment is the low level of economic activity. They hold that if real consumption, investment, government expenditure or exports can be increased, the level of production will rise, profits will increase and employment will be increased. The ways in which this might occur, are outlined in Chapter 15 on aggregate economic activity.

The practical problem these economists face is what specific policies should be tried. A typical suggestion is:
1 recognition of the need for restraint in wage increases to prevent unemployment rising;
2 the adoption of demand-creating measures such as cuts in personal income tax or in taxes on expenditure.

They argue that unions might accept such tax cuts as a substitute for higher wages and that businessmen would benefit from reduced cost pressures as well as increased spending by the community. This group of economists does not see restraint in increases in money wages *by itself* as sufficient to stimulate the demand for labour.

Much of the debate between the two groups turns on whether the latter approach can be adopted without there being a serious acceleration in the rate of inflation. This question is discussed in Chapter 16.

Wage determination

Trade unions and the supply of labour

In our discussion on the relationship between employment and wage levels it was taken for granted that the wage rates employers had to pay were already determined. It is now necessary to look at how wages are determined in the UK.

The principal determinants of an industry's demand for labour have already been considered. But any explanation of what determines the wage paid by an enterprise, or an industry, and the quantity of labour resources hired, will need to take into account the supply of labour. The shape of the supply curve of a specific type of labour for a particular enterprise, or industry, will depend on the worker's need and attitudes

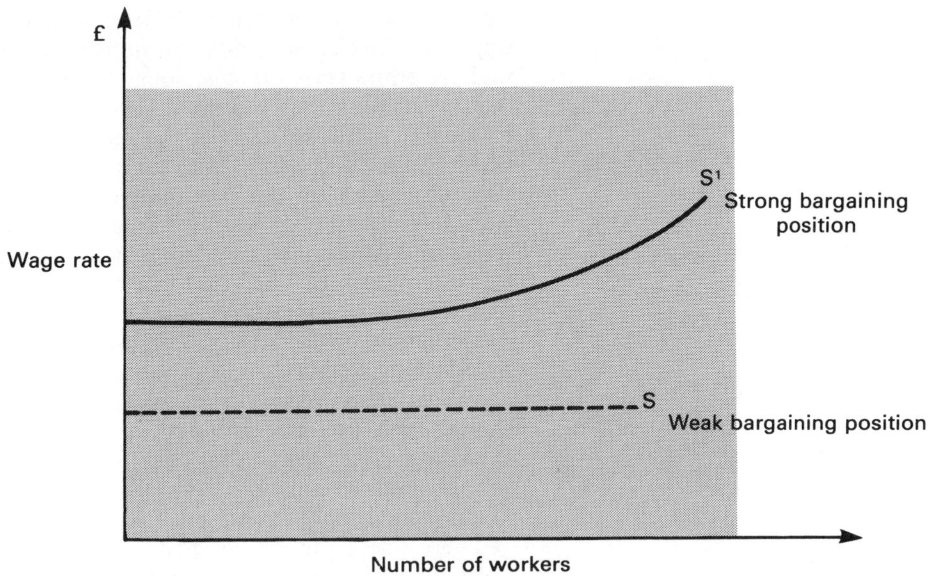

Figure 10.6 Supply curves of a particular type of labour to a specific industry in differing bargaining positions

to work, the wages offered by other enterprises and by other industries and the bargaining strength of the prospective employees. If employers have ample workers to choose from, if alternative job opportunities are scarce and if the workers are poorly organised, the individual worker will be in a weak bargaining position. The supply curve is likely to be a horizontal line. The rate will be lower than it would be if there were little unemployment and a high level of unfilled vacancies. A comparison of the two situations is shown in Figure 10.6.

The weak bargaining position of the individual employee led to the formation of trade unions. A principal objective of trade unions is to provide a united front of workers to employers, and a power-base from which to bargain. The existence of a trade union in an industry may lead to agreement by the members of the union not to work unless a certain minimum wage is paid. The effect is that the trade union sets a minimum level for wages. The actual supply curve may then rise from this level as in Figure 10.6. For example, the supply of bricklayers appears to be related to the wage in this way. In practice, unions may make a wage claim for their members and subsequently agree to a somewhat lower wage after negotiation or the settlement of a dispute. Relative wages in different occupations and industries may well be influenced by the relative bargaining strength of the unions.

10.5 Draw supply curves for the following occupations in the UK:
1 airline pilots
2 typists
3 oil tanker drivers.
In what ways do these supply curves differ and for what reasons?

In the nineteenth century British unions fought some fierce battles with employers and lost. Their members were unable to remain on strike for a sufficient length of time to gain the increases in wages and improvements in working conditions they sought. Nowadays, it is often said by employers' organisations that trade unions are 'too powerful': that by striking they can obtain ever higher wages. But there are limits to the extent to which even the most militant trade unions can secure better wages and conditions, because the demand curve for labour is still influenced by the productivity of labour and slopes downwards from left to right, as we saw earlier. No union can determine *both* the wages and conditions its members will receive and the *number* of persons to be employed. There is always the possibility that the effect of increasing wages may be to force employers to reduce their labour force immediately. Alternatively, employers may respond in the longer run by adopting labour-saving production techniques.

Reasons for union pressure during inflation

To many people, it is perplexing that the trade union movement should exert pressure to obtain higher wages, particularly when prices are rising. They argue that such actions are shortsighted because they simply produce inflation, with all its problems and do not improve the living standards of the union members.

There are a number of reasons why individual unions continue to press for higher wages and better conditions, and some of these at least are entirely rational within the framework of our type of economic system.

First, increases in money incomes are the means by which individuals come to benefit from increases in the production of goods and services in UK. Real wages *did* increase in 1974.

Second, it does not necessarily follow that the increases in the wages of one group will be reflected directly in the prices of the goods they buy. A wage increase for a particular group of workers in itself will increase their real wage because they are not themselves making the products they purchase.

Third, it is misleading to see wage increases as the sole cause of UK's inflation. Many wage claims are based on earlier price increases. They result from a desire to maintain real wages. In addition, the *expectation of future price increases* may cause unions to seek increases that not only help their members to catch up with past price rises but prepare them for the future.

Fourth, most people are concerned with the *relative* size of their money income. They compare it with incomes of persons in other occupations. Even though they may be well aware that by basing wage demands on inflationary expectations they are adding to inflationary pressures they may find it necessary to pursue such a course of action. They reason that if they show restraint, and others do not, they will become worse off in absolute and relative terms.

The willingness of unions to press for higher wages and better conditions can be measured by the number of industrial disputes. Table 10.3 gives the number of industrial disputes, the working days lost as a result of stoppages and the level of unemployment in the UK from 1970 to 1980.

The analysis of strike statistics requires some explanation. Disputes involving less than 100 workers or lasting less than one day are excluded. The number of working days lost through disputes can be much distorted by the disproportionate effects of one or two major national stoppages involving a whole industry for a period of weeks. Examples of such disputes in the past have involved the steel workers

Year	Number of disputes	Working days lost ('000s)	Unemployment (%)
1970	3 906	10 980	2.6
1971	2 228	13 551	3.5
1972	2 497	23 909	3.8
1973	2 873	7 197	2.7
1974	2 922	14 750	2.6
1975	2 282	6 012	4.1
1976	2 016	3 284	5.7
1977	2 703	10 142	6.2
1978	2 471	9 405	6.1
1979	2 080	29 474	5.7
1980	1 330	11 964	7.4

Table 10.3 Industrial disputes, UK, 1970–80

Source: *Annual Abstract of Statistics, 1982*, HMSO

and the mineworkers. The majority of strikes in the UK are relatively small and short. It is easy to over-estimate the 'strike problem' in the UK, for example from 1967 to 1976 the average annual working days lost per 1000 employees was 788, which represents 0.33 per cent of the total working days per year. Moreover in 1972, when almost 24 million days were lost due to disputes, the number of days lost due to sickness was over 300 million. Compared with other countries, the strike record of the UK is generally in the middle of any international statistics ranking countries in terms of stoppages or working days lost. It is not clear from such figures that the UK has a worse industrial relations record as is sometimes claimed. However, it is difficult to measure the actual impact of strikes on an economy which goes beyond the immediate number of days lost.

Industrial disputes and unemployment

Many people think that there is a relationship between the number of industrial disputes and the level of unemployment. It is argued that as unemployment falls and production rises trade unions become more militant and press for higher wages through collective bargaining processes including strike action. Likewise, it is claimed that when unemployment is rising there is more awareness amongst trade union leaders that wage claims are likely to raise production costs and accentuate unemployment. Table 10.3 provides information about unemployment in the UK in the 1970s. Comparing this information with the number of strikes shows some support for this argument. The number of disputes was high in 1970, 1973 and 1974 when unemployment was low. The number of disputes fell in 1971 and 1972, in 1975 and 1976, and in 1980 as unemployment was rising. Note that the trend of working days lost does not follow this pattern too exactly, because of the effect of a small number of long lasting national strikes which involved a large number of workers. In 1980 of almost 12 million working days lost, 8.8 million were accounted for by the steel strike in that year.

Another suggestion is that union strike activity is also a response to the rate of inflation. Unions seek higher wages to maintain real wages. The more rapid the rate of price increases, the more pressing are they in their claims for higher money wages. Industrial disputes arise over a number of issues. From 1973 to 1977 pay issues were on average responsible for 55 per cent of disputes and 73 per cent of working days lost. Issues related to manning levels and work allocation accounted for 13.5 per cent of disputes and 7 per cent of days lost. Other causes of disputes involve working conditions, redundancy, dismissal and disciplinary measures, duration and pattern of hours worked.

Disputes may also arise because of the employment of non-union labour. The issue of compulsory unionism or preference for union members is considered a fundamental one by most trade unionists, for it is claimed that only by compelling all workers to join the union can it have a strong bargaining position. Not only might the presence of non-union labour weaken this position, but it is argued that it would be unfair for non-union labour to share in the benefits won by the union without paying union subscriptions and without being bound by union rules.

In addition to this function of securing economic benefits for members through a combined approach to employers, trade unions also have a political objective – the improvement of the economic and social conditions of members through legislation.

The trade union movement is closely involved with the Labour Party and plays a major part in the policies and running of the party. Unions also have attempted to provide social welfare assistance for their members in the past, but with the increase of government social services the need for union welfare schemes has declined.

Union membership

In December 1977, the United Kingdom had 480 trade unions with a combined membership of 12.7 million, about 48 per cent of the total working population. The largest union, the Transport and General Workers' Union has a membership of over 2 million. The 26 unions with more than 100 000 members in 1977 accounted together for more than 80 per cent of total membership. In recent years the number of trade unions has fallen as amalgamations have occurred. The average size of unions has increased as a result. (In 1979 there were 454 unions with a total membership of almost 13.5 million).

Unions can be characterised by the type of membership that they cater for. In some unions, membership is limited to members of a particular trade or craft, for example engineers, carpenters, printers. Other unions are organised on the basis of serving a particular industry. Examples of such industrial unions can be found in the railways, coal-mines and among merchant seamen. General unions have a much more open approach to recruitment, and have a broader membership base as a result, covering a wide variety of crafts and industries. Consequently, many of the largest unions are in this category; the TGWU, General and Municipal Workers' Union, the National Union of Public Employees provide examples. A more recent development has been the growth of unions representing white-collar workers such as teachers, clerical workers, managerial and supervisory workers and civil servants. Conflict between unions over whose members should do a particular job (demarcation disputes), or to which union a particular group of workers should belong, can lead to disruption of production.

10.6

If trade unions are supposedly less militant at times of high unemployment what logic is there in going on strike when retrenchments are announced by businesses?

10.7

In the 1950s, Dutch employers of agricultural labour used the argument that they should pay their employees lower wage rates for overtime work because the workers were then tired and did not produce as much as when they were fresh. Suppose you are a trade union representative. How would you reply to this argument and at the same time present a convincing case for higher rates of pay for overtime work?

10.8

'More production is lost in one day's public holiday than in all the industrial disputes in a year.' Discuss this controversial statement, with the help of Table 10.3.

10.9

Imagine you are a trade-union leader and that negotiations with employers have broken down. What criteria would you use in deciding whether to recommend strike action to the members of the union?

10.10

Discuss in class the argument that the bargaining power of trade unions would be reduced if compulsory secret ballots were introduced as the means of determining the wishes of trade-union members during an industrial dispute.

10.11

A strike that lasts 2 weeks involves workers in a loss of 4 per cent of their annual wage, so that even with a 5 per cent wage increase it will be almost a year before they have even restored their lost wages. Why then do workers strike?

10.12

Study carefully a recent industrial dispute relating to wages or to conditions of work.

1 What were the unions seeking and what was the reaction of employers?

2 What part in the eventual settlement was played by the arbitration and conciliation institutions?

3 What part did the government play in the dispute? Do you think that its action, if any, contributed towards the resolution of the dispute?

4 Explain whether there were any aspects of the final settlement that you were unhappy with because of effects on:

(a) future industrial relations
(b) the rate of inflation
(c) the level of unemployment.

Wage fixing – arbitration and conciliation

The first two influences on the determination of wages and salaries in the UK to be distinguished were the demand for labour and the effect of trade unions on the supply of labour. The third important element in the UK is the system of arbitration and conciliation. The essential feature of *arbitration* is that the representatives of employers and employees present their cases before an independent third party and agree to accept his decision. A distinction can be made between

Compulsory arbitration and voluntary arbitration

compulsory arbitration, where the arbitrator can act on the request of one of the parties of the dispute, and voluntary arbitration, which calls for the prior agreement of both employers and employees that they will seek an independent determination.

Conciliation is a procedure whereby the employers and employees (or it may be two unions during a demarcation dispute) use the good offices of a third party, without being bound by his opinions.

The purpose of arbitration and conciliation is to provide an alternative to bargaining strength in the determination of wages and to assist in the prevention or resolution of industrial disputes. It can thus be used to protect those workers in a weak bargaining position who would earn very low wages if it were not for an independent judgement. Likewise, it can give employers a measure of protection from strong and militant trade unions.

10.13

It has been argued that the democratic rights of each employee should be safeguarded. Compulsory membership of a trade union is said to infringe those rights.

Suppose you were a trade union leader. What arguments would you put forward to government and to workers in support of compulsory unionism? How would you react to the suggestion that those not wishing to join should be required to donate an equal amount to a charitable institution?

10.14

The following statements are grouped in pairs and relate to wages and employment. In each case there is conflict between arguments or statements. Imagine that you were an arbitrator with the responsibility of deciding which arguments to accept. Examine the statements and determine which, if any, are correct, and what the implications of accepting any particular claim would be. Attempt to distinguish between the positive and normative elements of each statement.

1 (a) Increases in public servants' wages should be granted because they do not lead to increases in prices.
(b) Increases in public servants' wages should not be granted because the productivity of public servants does not increase.

2 (a) Businesses that make higher profits should pay their workers higher wages.
(b) Businesses that make large profits should not have to pay higher wages because the higher profits reflect their efficiency.

3 (a) Women should be paid the same wage as men, whenever they do work of equal value to that performed by men.
(b) If women are paid the same as men this will make it unprofitable to employ them in many occupations and deny them the chance of working.

4 (a) Wage rates should be increased automatically whenever there is an increase in the general level of prices.
(b) Automatic wage rate increases must be resisted because they are inflationary.

Notes

1 If a firm is a price maker the price of the product may have to be lowered if larger quantities are to be sold. In this situation the value of employing an additional worker is calculated by determining the marginal revenue obtained from the additional output so produced.

2 It is seldom practicable to pay different wages to people doing similar jobs. Moreover the effects of industrial wage determinations and the insistence of trade unions are that the same wage is paid to all workers in a trade or occupation even if the last man taken on happens to be less proficient.

Chapter 11

The Financial System

Principal features of the system

In Chapter 4 the use of money was identified as one of the distinguishing features of a modern economic system. Money is essential for efficient exchange and makes possible borrowing and lending on a large scale. This chapter examines the financial system in the UK. It describes how each of the principal financial institutions operates and fits into the system. It also explains how the Bank of England controls the activities of the financial institutions and why it is necessary for it to do so.

The principal institutions operating in the money and capital markets are:

the Bank of England, the Commercial Banks, the discount houses, finance companies, life assurance companies, building societies.

In addition, the Stock Exchange, public and private pension funds, non-life insurance companies, merchant banks, savings banks and other institutions play a significant part in the operation of the system.

Essentially, the task of the financial institutions is to attract funds from households, businesses and overseas, and to channel them to other households, businesses and government. Most financial institutions have a specialist role. For example, building societies use their funds to provide housing finance. Finance companies provide funds for hire purchase of consumer durable goods. There is, however, some considerable overlap of functions. Households have a large choice of types of institutions (banks, building societies, life assurance companies and so on) when deciding how to save, where to deposit funds and from whom to seek loans.

The principal lending and borrowing relationships between the institutions and the other sectors of the economy are set out in Figure 11.1. The arrows indicate the direction of the flow of funds from lenders to users. For example, the two arrows on the line linking households and finance companies show that, as a group, households both lend to finance companies (by purchasing the debentures they issue) and borrow from finance companies. The single arrow on a line, such as that between households and the Bank of England, indicates that the government borrows from households through the Bank of England, but households do not borrow from the Bank of England. Notice this link between the government and the other sectors of the economy through the Bank of England.

Most financial institutions are private enterprises seeking to make profits for their owners in precisely the same manner as other businesses in the economy. Interest rates and service charges are therefore very competitive in the financial system between different institutions.

Rate of interest is the price of funds

The rate of interest can be regarded as the price of loanable funds.

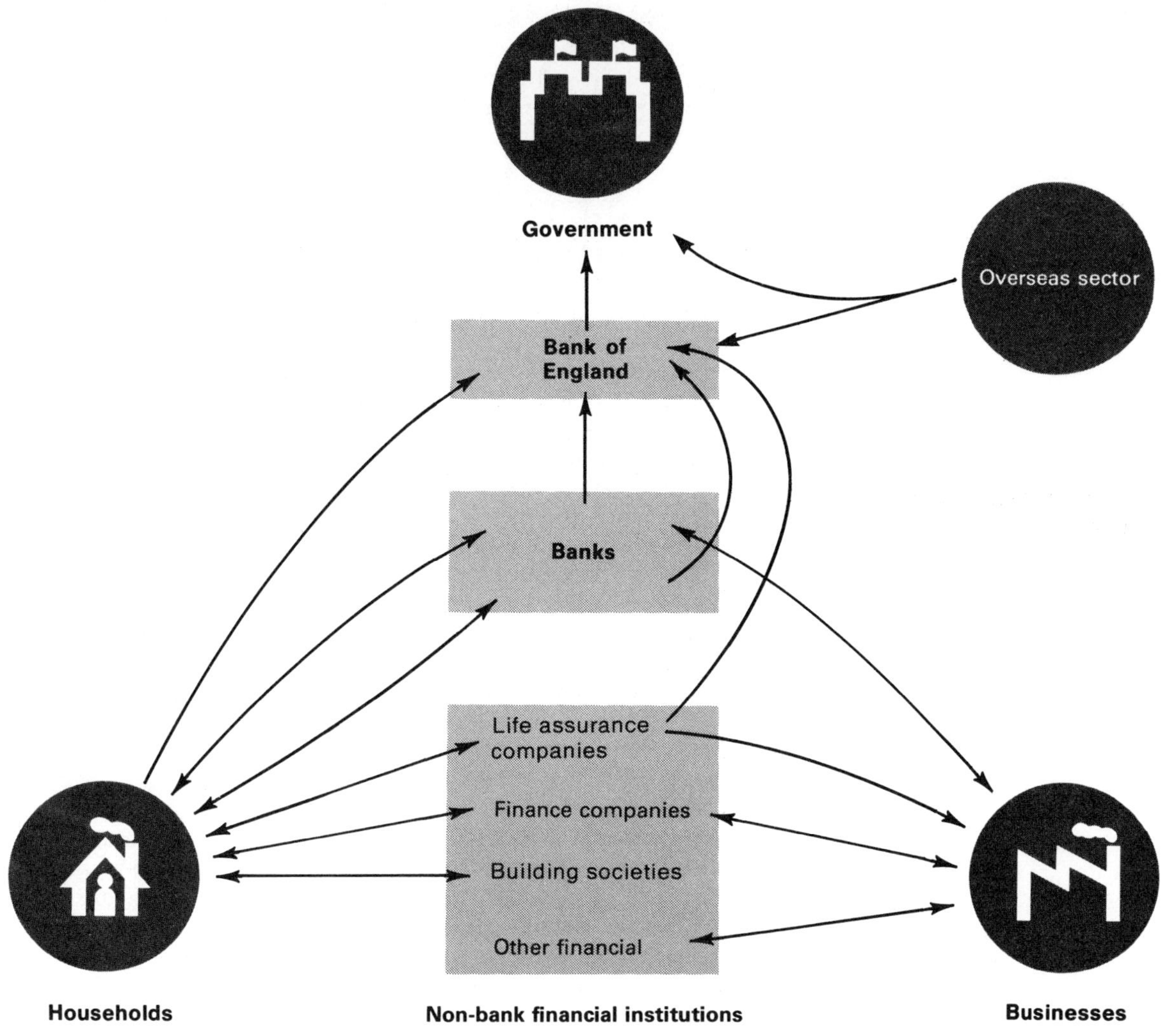

Figure 11.1 Principal financial institutions

It is expressed as a percentage of the sum borrowed and thus represents the cost of borrowing that sum for a specified period. Usually the interest rate for a loan is calculated as a specified percentage per annum. It is important not to confuse the rate of interest (*x* per cent per year) and the term of loan (the period over which the loan is being made). Thus a 3 month loan of £10 000 made at an interest rate of 10 per cent per annum will require an interest payment of £250, not £1000. The relative rates of interest payable on different loans depend upon a number of influences. In general, the rate of interest is greater on a loan for a longer term.

A finance company seeking to borrow funds from the public may offer, say, 9 per cent per year on three year loans, but may have to offer 10 per cent per year on six year loans. This reflects the greater uncertainty and risk associated with loans of a longer period.

The rate of interest payable on loans made for a specified period is also influenced by the relative riskiness of use to which the funds are to be put, or from the lenders' viewpoint, the relative security the various borrowers can offer them. For this reason, government securities and loans to local authorities often carry a lower rate of interest than do loans of the same term to finance companies and other commercial enterprises. Interest rates for funds borrowed by different financial institutions and for varying periods bear a close relationship to one another. Length of the term and riskiness of the loan clearly are important determinants of the relative rates.

Although most of the funds placed with financial institutions yield interest, there is usually no interest paid on current account deposits in the commercial banks. This is because these funds can be withdrawn on demand and are extremely safe. People find that there are other very considerable advantages in holding part of their assets in bank deposits. They provide a convenient form of saving and a suitable way of holding funds needed for regular purchases or unforeseen expenses. Current accounts are also very useful for cheques can be drawn against them as a convenient means of making payments.

How financial institutions make profits

By and large, the financial institutions make profits by borrowing surplus funds at a specified rate of interest and lending funds at a higher rate of interest. The higher the rates of interest the institutions need to pay to attract funds, the higher the rates they have to charge to borrowers if they are to operate profitably. For example, if permanent building societies are offering rates varying from 8.5 per cent to 10 per cent to depositors, they are likely to be charging 11 or 12 per cent to prospective home buyers.

A common way by which government or private commercial enterprises obtain funds is by selling securities. A security, such as a government bond, usually carries a specified rate of interest, payable at regular intervals, and is redeemed by the enterprise on the due date. For example, suppose a bond is offered for sale which matures in 2000 and carried a rate of 8.5 per cent interest. The subscriber is not required to hold the bonds until maturity date, for the bonds are transferable. They can be bought and sold daily on the open market. However, the market price at which a bond with a maturity value of £100 and paying £8.50 per year sells depends on current market conditions and the ruling rate of interest. Suppose that the government later determines that the interest rate on newly issued £100 government bonds that will also mature in 2000 will be 10 per cent (£10.00 per year). No one will then be prepared to pay £100 for the 'secondhand' bonds because they offer a yield of only 8.5 per cent. Their market price will fall to £85 because this offers buyers an effective yield of 10 per cent, that is, £8.50 on the market price of £85.00. Conversely, if the interest rate on current issues of bonds maturing in 2000 falls to 7 per cent, then the

Price of bonds

8.5 per cent bonds issued earlier will become worth more than £100. Their price will rise to £121.43, since:

$$\frac{\pounds 8.50}{\pounds 7.00} \times \pounds 100 = \pounds 121.43$$

In short, the secondhand price of bonds issued at a fixed rate of interest varies inversely with the ruling market interest rate of equivalent securities.

Although the objective of each of the financial institutions is to make profits, there is conflict between the temptation to make large short-term profits and the need to avoid the financial dangers that such a policy may bring. Since lending for long periods and on relatively risky

'Borrowing short, lending long'

projects commands higher rates of interest, a financial enterprise can make larger short-term profits by borrowing for short periods (at the lower rates of interest) and lending for longer periods (at the higher rates).

The dangers inherent in this practice of 'borrowing short, lending long' are twofold. First, there may be a temptation to lend money at high rates for projects with a high degree of risk. For example, luxury hotels may take years to build and then prove unprofitable. The failure of such projects may endanger the profitability of the enterprise lending the funds. Second, an enterprise that lends long but borrows short, runs the risk of not being able to repay loans as they become due because it lacks assets that can be turned easily and quickly into cash. It depends on the availability of a continuing stream of short-term funds. Should these funds dry up, the enterprise will soon find itself with a liquidity crisis. The very success of financial enterprises depends on maintaining public confidence in their ability to repay loans. If this confidence is damaged, there is likely to be a rush to withdraw funds and place them with a safer institution. The 'runs' on banks during the early days of banking and subsequently during economic crises serve as a reminder that financial institutions need to keep an adequate proportion of funds in a form that can be turned into cash at relatively short notice.

The task facing banks, and other financial institutions, is to maintain a suitable balance between liquidity and income earning. Later in this chapter this problem will be examined.

The government through the Bank of England regulates the conduct of the commercial banks and other financial institutions. Monetary policy measures are applied using the Bank of England and its functions in the money markets. In 1971, in a document called *Competition and Credit Control*, the Bank of England detailed proposals for the operation of, and control over, credit conditions. These conditions applied not only to commercial banks but to discount houses and finance houses as well. The implications of these and other measures for financial institutions are discussed later in this chapter.

Government control over the operations of the financial institutions is vital because of the importance that money and the monetary system have in the overall operation of an economic system. At the most basic level, government control over the note issue is essential. A financial system that allowed any enterprise to issue to the public unlimited quantities of its own bank notes would not run as efficiently as a system with all notes issued by the central bank – the Bank of England. Its operation would be limited by the confidence that buyers and sellers were prepared to put into any particular enterprise's note issue. The unrestricted issue of bank notes by any particular enterprise would soon lead to a loss of confidence in its note issue and to the collapse of the institution.

The quantity of money

Even where the note issue is the responsibility of the central bank, a rapid increase in the quantity of money is likely to have undesirable effects. Many years ago, economists came to see a relationship between the quantity of money and the price level. It appeared self-evident that if the supply of money to the system was increased, but the production of goods and services remained constant and money changed hands at about the same rate, the general price level would also rise. It was said that if the money supply increased by 10 per cent then prices would rise, on average, by 10 per cent within a short time.

At times a country's inflation may reach catastrophic levels. The hyperinflation suffered by Germany and Austria 1922–23 was characterised by price increases of thousands of per cent overnight, of central banks printing more money and overprinting notes with higher values and of an understandable public unwillingness to hold money at all.

The inflation of the 1970s in much of the world has focussed attention once more on this link between the quantity of money and the general price level. Many economists argue that there is a need for government to control the rate of growth of the money supply if inflation is to be controlled and reduced. This is a strong argument for government regulation of the money system but it does not mean that the government has the means of controlling the money supply. Nor does it mean that there is agreement about how to control the money supply. It is not simply a question of the government refusing to print more money, as we shall see later in the chapter. To explain inflation solely in terms of the growth of the money supply is altogether too simple because it ignores the underlying reasons for that growth.

An associated reason for the need for government control of the monetary system is that variations in the availability of funds and changes in the level of interest rates may affect the level of aggregate economic activity; that is, of production and employment. Additional funds offer businesses the opportunity to undertake new investment projects, to increase production and thus to employ more workers. Lower interest rates mean a reduction in the cost of funds and hence in the cost of implementing new projects. A reduction in the rate of interest may make all the difference to the profitability of a project and result in a business taking the decision to increase capital formation. Conversely, restrictions in the availability of funds or an increase in interest rates may lead to a fall in economic activity as projects are deferred or curtailed. A reduction in funds available for housing may have the effect of reducing building construction. Higher interest rates for housing loans will make the repayments too high for some prospective home buyers.

A financial system in which interest rates and the supply of loanable funds are not properly regulated may generate undesirable fluctuations in the level of economic activity. A government with effective powers to determine the availability of funds and interest rates may use these powers to counter any changes in the level of activity it considers undesirable.

Effects of reduction in interest rates

Government policies that make more funds available and reduce interest rates may offset a potential recession by making investment more profitable and by encouraging businesses to increase production. But one cannot assume that an increase in funds or a fall in interest rates will automatically lead to an increase in investment. Businesses may lack the confidence to increase production once a recession has begun. It may be possible to stop people investing by raising interest rates, but they cannot be made to borrow.

Effects of increase in interest rates

Alternatively, an inflationary situation may develop in which low interest rates and plentiful supplies of loanable funds help to produce circumstances in which the demand for goods and services by the country's residents is greater than its ability to supply those goods. Shortages and/or price increases occur. Government controls over the financial system offer some possibility of controlling such a situation. Measures that restrict the supply of funds or increase interest rates are likely to have some effect in restricting demand and reducing the inflationary pressures. Just how quickly or how successfully such policies are likely to work is discussed in Chapter 16.

Government controls permit redistribution of wealth

A less obvious reason for government control of the financial system is that the controls provide a means of redistributing wealth amongst members of the community. Borrowing offers to household and business enterprise alike the means of spending more than their current income. But an unregulated financial system makes it difficult and expensive for lower income groups to borrow for major items such as housing because they often cannot offer as much security on loans.

Bank of England

The Bank of England is the institution through which the government implements its monetary policies. These are designed to assist in the economic management of the economy. The Bank is also the British government's agent in the money market for obtaining funds. The government is in the unique position of determining the volume of funds that it can borrow because the Bank of England meets all its requirements. It also can influence the amounts the banks and life offices invest in goverment securities. However, it lacks complete control on the amount that it can borrow at the determined interest rate because the financial enterprises determine their total holdings of government securities only after comparing all interest rates in the various markets.

11.1

A £100 bond maturing in thirty years time is issued at par and pays 5 per cent interest per annum. Calculate the resale price of the bond if the market interest rate for equivalent bonds changes to:

10 per cent,
3 per cent,
7.5 per cent.

11.2

From a recent issue of the Financial Times, or from a business news supplement of a Sunday newspaper, find out the current structure of interest rates to be earned from various types of investment; e.g. from government bonds which mature in 2 years, in 5 years and in 10 years, local authority stocks, etc. Compare these with rates of interest offered by the finance companies for borrowings of similar terms. Do your findings confirm the general rule that interest rates increase as the term of the loan increases and are less the more secure is the loan?

11.3

In the late 1970s and early 1980s, prices in the UK rose in some years at a much higher rate than the interest rate offered to depositors by banks, building societies and other financial institutions. Can you suggest why households continued to lend money to financial institutions when the purchasing power of those funds after the addition of interest was falling?

11.4

It is common to find in the UK that the building societies offer a range of interest rates to depositors for different types of accounts. Obtain information on these different types of accounts from a local branch of a building society and compare the rates of interest paid with the conditions of the deposit account. Explain how the structure of the interest rates confirms the general principles established in this chapter.

11.5 What advice would you offer a saver, with £500 to deposit for a minimum period of 6 months, as to the range of institutions and types of account available. Consider banks, building societies and national savings, etc. as possibilities and obtain details of current interest rates. If the deposit was for £5000 and for at least 1 year, what other savings advice could you give?

Commercial banks

The commercial banks are also known as joint-stock banks. They are owned by their shareholders as are many other examples of private sector enterprises. The best known of these banks are the 'big four' – Barclays, Lloyds, Midland and the National Westminster. As clearing banks, the commercial banks are all members of the London Bankers' Clearing House, which enables them to handle and exchange cheques drawn on the banks by their customers. The other main feature of these banks rests in their structure and organisation as branch banks, with thousands of branches all over the country providing a national and comprehensive banking service for customers.

Functions of commercial banks

The commercial banks accept deposits from customers and provide a large range of services, including operating the cheque system for making payments, giving advice on investment, making loans and overdrafts, safe-keeping of documents and valuables, acting as executor and trustee, handling foreign exchange and travellers' cheques, and many more.

Types of accounts

There are two major types of accounts in which customers' deposits are held. Deposit or savings accounts earn interest at a rate determined by the banks' own base rate. Notice of withdrawal is often required for such accounts for any reasonably large withdrawal of deposits. They are also often referred to as time deposits. Current account deposits are non-interest bearing but allow the depositor to use a cheque book to make payments. Deposits can therefore be obtained immediately by depositors on presentation of a cheque drawn on the account. Current account deposits are also known as sight deposits. In addition, the cheque system provides a most convenient way of settling accounts. Widespread public acceptance of the cheque as a means of payment and the use of cheque cards to guarantee payment within specified conditions, has contributed largely to the success of these cheque accounts.

Deposits are banks' liabilities

The deposits held in the banks by customers represent the liabilities of the banks. Funds on deposit may be withdrawn by customers although, as we have seen, notice of withdrawal may be required for some accounts. The banks have to compete with other financial institutions for deposits and therefore have to offer an attractive rate of interest to persuade depositors to deposit funds with them. The banks are in business to make a profit which they achieve by lending these funds deposited with them and charging a higher rate of interest on their loans than they pay on their borrowings, i.e. deposits. (Banks do make charges for the services that they provide and these are an important source of revenue but the chief element of the banks' profits lies in the difference between the interest rates on deposits and loans.) The desire to make profits by lending is constrained by the need to maintain sufficient liquid funds to meet any demands for repayment of deposits placed on the banks. Moreover, the lending policy is constrained by government regulations and controls which specify the proportions of banks' funds to be held in specified forms of assets.

Eligible reserve assets

In 1971 the Bank of England introduced a control on bank lending through a minimum eligible reserve assets ratio of 12½ per cent which banks were required to maintain as a proportion of eligible liabilities. Thus for every £1000 of eligible liabilities, that is bank deposits, the banks were obliged to keep at least £125 in some form of specified reserve assets. The remainder of any deposit after the reserve asset ratio requirement has been met is therefore available for the bank to use, to invest or to give loans or overdrafts. Eligible reserve assets consist of the following: cash balances held at the Bank of England (at least 1½ per cent of eligible liabilities), money at call and short notice, treasury bills, other bills of exchange and British government stocks with less than one year to maturity. The essential feature in common with all these forms of asset holding is that they represent assets which are highly liquid, that is readily transferable and convertible into cash to meet liabilities. To understand the significance of these forms of assets it is necessary to consider the overall balance sheet of the banks which is given in Table 11.1.

Liabilities	Assets	
37 979 deposits (of which 17 264 sight deposits)	854	Notes and coin
		Eligible reserve assets
	599	Cash balance and Bank of England
	1 844	Money at call and short notice
	369	Treasury bills
	700	Other bills
	348	British government stock to 1 year
	3 860	Total reserve assets
	2 545	Investments
	6 809	Loans to money market etc.
	25 814	Advances
	22	Special deposits

Note: Figures refer to London clearing banks only and to dealings in sterling

Table 11.1 London clearing banks: sterling assets and liabilities as at 16 January 1980 (£ million)

Source: *Bank of England Quarterly Bulletin*, March 1980

Liabilities and assets

As in any balance sheet, total liabilities must equal total assets. In Table 11.1 a simplified picture is given of the balance sheet for the London clearing banks and concentrates on sterling accounts only.

Liabilities consist of deposits held in bank accounts by customers; eligible liabilities are deposits in sterling of not more than two years maturity. In detail, the assets structure can be explained as follows. Notes and coins represent the money held by the Banks as 'till money' to meet the needs of depositors who wish to withdraw cash at any one time. In practice this represents a small proportion of total deposits and the banks will keep this proportion as low as possible for money in the till cannot be put to use as loans and therefore earn interest. On 16 January 1980 total eligible reserve assets amounted to £3860m. Cash balances at the Bank of England enable banks to settle debts between each other that arise in the course of cheque clearing. It is much easier and more convenient if each bank settles the overall indebtedness with the other clearing banks at the end of each day's clearing through a transfer of the cash balances that each is required to keep with the Bank of England. Money at call and short notice represents short-term loans to financial institutions, particularly discount houses, and which can be called in very quickly. Frequently these loans are on an overnight basis. Such loans do earn interest and allow the Banks to ensure that all available funds can be put to use even on a very short term basis. Treasury bills are a form of Government short-term borrowing and are issued for 91 days, three months. The role of Treasury bills is discussed below under the topic of discount houses. Other bills of exchange, and British Government Stock with less than one year to maturity, make up the remainder of the required reserve assets ratio. These are highly marketable securities which can be readily converted into cash. Since this ratio is a required minimum, the Bank of England is able to influence the level of liabilities–deposits, in the banking system by changing the reserve ratio, or by operating on the availability and structure of the reserve assets held. For example, the amount of treasury bills available in the money market can be increased or decreased as part of the Bank of England's monetary policy measures. Buying and selling treasury bills, by changing the overall level of reserve assets will have a consequent effect on the level of deposits that the banking system can make available.

Credit creation

Credit multiplier

The reserve asset ratio requirement enables the banking system to create deposits up to a multiple of the amount of reserve assets held in the following manner.

If a bank has £1m of reserve assets which must be a minimum of $12\frac{1}{2}$ per cent of total liabilities, then the bank can increase the level of deposits up to a maximum of £8m and maintain the reserve ratio. For £2m of reserve assets, liabilities to a limit of £16m are available to the bank. An increase in the amount of reserve assets held will therefore permit deposits to be increased in the proportion of $\frac{1}{\text{reserve ratio}}$. In the example, this is $\frac{1}{12\frac{1}{2}\%}$, which equals 8. Thus the bank credit multiplier, the amount by which banks can make deposits available, is equal to the reciprocal of the reserve ratio.

Changes in the reserve ratio are therefore a means by which the government may influence bank lending policies and thus the money supply. In the UK, the Bank of England has not resorted to changes in the statutory reserve requirement as a means of monetary control. Since Competition and Credit Control was adopted in 1971 the rate has stayed at 12½ per cent. This does not mean that the ratio has not had a direct effect on bank lending, but in the UK the influence has come through changes in the items that constitute the ratio rather than in changes in the ratio itself.

Monetary control 1980

Significant changes have been made in the system of banking controls introduced by Competition and Credit Control in 1971. The Banking Act 1979 and a green paper *Monetary Control 1980*, together with other documents, have been published on a wide range of monetary issues including the problems of liquidity of the banking system. The main proposal that concerns us here is that the 12½ per cent minimum reserve ratio was dropped as it is no longer felt to be a necessary instrument of monetary policy and other more appropriate measures were adopted instead. The ratio requirement was abolished in August 1981. A distinction is being made between monetary control measures on the one hand and prudential controls, designed to protect the interests of bank depositors and the general public, on the other. These prudential controls are felt desirable to avoid the possibility of any banking crisis or collapse and are commonly adopted in other countries within the EEC. These are quite separate from the issues and concerns of direct monetary control.

Types of liquid assets

Liquid assets are distinguished into primary and secondary types. Primary liquid assets are cash, or a ready source of cash, because the authorities will in all circumstances buy them. (They constitute the same items as classified as eligible reserve assets.) Secondary liquid assets are near-cash or readily marketable and may be in sterling or in foreign currency, unlike primary assets which are only sterling.

Prudential controls require a level of liquidity expressed as a norm and not as a compulsory minima. The idea of a norm implies a degree of flexibility in the daily operation of the banking system which the minimum requirement did not allow to the same extent. Further, an imposed minimum itself required a surplus to be maintained above the minimum to ensure that the minimum is not breached.

Special deposits

These are a monetary control measure which operate as a compulsory deposit requirement by the Bank of England of the banking system and can be used to reduce the level of credit created. Special deposits may not count as part of the reserve assets ratio and are in essence a frozen asset held by the Bank of England for such time as the Bank deems necessary. Special deposits act as a control mechanism because the banks, in order to pay the Bank of England, have to adjust their other holdings of liquid assets and consequently this reduces the level of deposits that the banks can maintain.

Advances

Loans and advances to customers amount to about two-thirds of deposits as the figures in Table 11.1 show. Advances may take the form

Loans and overdrafts compared

of either overdrafts or loans. The overdraft is a very common method of advancing money to customers and involves setting an overdraft limit on the customer's ordinary cheque account, literally an amount to which the account can be overdrawn or 'go into the red'. Interest is then calculated on any negative balances that occur in the account on a day to day basis. This represents a convenient system for borrowers who have receipts to deposit in the course of business. Such payments reduce the amount by which the borrower is overdrawn and therefore reduce the amount of interest payable. This is more convenient than a system in which two accounts are established with full interest payable on a specific loan in the loan account and with any positive balance held in a separate cheque account. Overdrafts are also an important source of finance for private industry, particularly for the relatively small-scale businesses.

Bank loans, such as personal loans, are different from overdrafts in a number of respects. First they are made for a fixed term, normally for personal loans for periods of one or two years. A fixed sum is advanced to the customers. This sum is repaid in instalments and carries a flat rate of interest. Consider the following example which takes the rate of interest to be 8 per cent.

The rate of interest

A personal loan of £1000 for one year would require the borrower to pay interest of £80 in addition to regular repayments of the principal borrowed. A flat rate of interest of 8 per cent looks attractive compared with an overdraft rate of say 11 or 12 per cent. However, the quoted flat rate of interest is not the true cost of borrowing money. The effective rate of interest is approximately 16 per cent. Over the year of the loan, the amount outstanding is progressively reduced. For the second quarter only £750 is owing, for the third quarter only £250. For the year as a whole, the average sum outstanding is only £500. The flat charge of 8 per cent is made on the maximum amount of the loan, that is £1000. The effective rate of interest differs from the flat rate wherever the instalment system is used. Hire purchase by finance companies is the most familiar form of instalment credit.[2]

Advances are the most profitable asset of the commercial banks but since they represent money lent for a specific term in the form of a loan, or amount lent on overdraft, they are not particularly liquid for the bank. To call in loans, or reduce the amount of credit on overdraft, would require a certain amount of time to be effective. On the other hand, reserve assets are very readily converted into cash but are not as profitable. Liquidity and profitability can be seen to be oppositely related to each other.

Bank of England

The Bank of England operates in the UK as the central bank to the banking system. Established in 1694 the Bank of England was acquired by the government in 1946. The Bank has two main departments dealing with its unique position and role in the financial system. The Issue Department is concerned with the issue of bank notes in England and Wales, for which it has the sole right. In Scotland and Northern Ireland the banks have a limited right to issue bank notes but these have to be covered by holdings of Bank of England notes. The note issue nowadays is fiduciary, that is backed by government securities and not by gold. This position is illustrated in Table 11.2.

Liabilities	£m as at 20 February 1980
Notes in circulation	9651
Notes in Banking Dept	24
Total	9675
Assets	
Government securities	8042
Other securities	1633
Total	9675

Table 11.2 Bank of England: Issue Department

Source: *BEQB*, March 1980, Table 1, Vol 20 No. 1

The Banking Department of the Bank of England deals with the other wider implications and operations of the central bank in the UK.

Functions of the Bank of England

1 to issue notes for circulation in the UK
2 to act as the Government's bank
3 to act as banker to the banks
4 to carry out the Government's monetary policy
5 to act as lender of last resort
6 to manage the National Debt
7 to handle foreign exchange and to deal with international agencies, foreign banks and institutions, etc. on behalf of the Government

As banker to the Government, the Bank of England handles the Government's accounts for its taxation revenues and its spending and also Government borrowing and lending. As banker to the banks, the Bank of England holds accounts for the clearing banks as part of their reserve assets and assists in the day to day settling of debts between banks in the course of clearing. The role of the Bank of England in monetary policy is discussed later in this chapter.

Lender of last resort

Lender of last resort in effect means that the Bank of England will act to support the banking system in the UK in meeting its obligations. This particular function is operated in connection with the Discount houses such that the Bank of England is prepared to make funds available to them in times of need and thereby prop up the banking system. More detail is given later on this aspect when the Discount houses are explained more fully. The National Debt represents the amount of borrowing by the Government which has been used to finance public spending on a wide range of activities and services. The Bank of England manages the Debt by paying the interest to holders of securities when it falls due, the repayment of loans and securities when they mature, and the issue of new loans when the Government is obtaining additional finance. The National Debt at the end of March 1979 was estimated at some £87 000 million. Most of this total was in the form of internal debt, representing borrowing by the Government from banks, institutions, the general public and so on. In this sense the National Debt, and the payment of interest due on it, represents an internal transfer of funds and a redistribution of incomes within the economy. For example, money paid as interest to a government stock-holder is financed out of general government spending but is then redistributed to the recipient of interest and is available for him to spend or save as any other form of income. Looked at in this way, the National Debt does not represent in any sense a burden to the economy or a debt that must be repaid. The government has used its borrowings to finance all manner of services which the community has benefitted from and in this way has increased its level of provision of welfare and so on, beyond that which current taxation and other revenues would permit. There are problems, however, if the debt is external, since payments of interest and loan repayments mean a net outflow of capital from the UK in the official financing and currency flow accounts. Such domestic borrowing from overseas and payments out of the economy may have less desired effects on the value of the exchange rate, on the level of inflation and interest rates in the domestic economy, on the balance of payments and other dealings with international banks and institutions.

Managing the National Debt

Servicing the National Debt when interest rates rise, or reach high levels, presents a potential problem to the Government in that the greater amounts of interest that have to be paid are at the expense of other current claims on government revenue. Governments may find themselves doubly committed to borrowing by issuing new debt to pay increased interest payments as well as to expand services and welfare.

The Bank of England is responsible for the holdings of gold and foreign currency reserves. With these funds held in the *exchange equalisation account* (EEA), the Bank may intervene in the foreign currency market to influence the value of sterling if, for example, speculation was causing the rate to fluctuate too widely. The Bank has other duties and responsibilities with bodies such as the International Monetary Fund

Liabilities	£m as at 20 February 1980
Public deposits	26
Special deposits	104
Bankers deposits	579
Reserves and other accounts	667
Total	1376

(Certain small items have been omitted, total liabilities are 1390 including these)

Assets	
Government securities	730
Advances and other accounts	199
Notes and coins	24
Premises, equipment and other securities	437
Total	1390

Table 11.3 Bank of England: Banking Department

Source: as for Table 11.2

(IMF), the World Bank, other governments' central banks and so on. This involves not only acting as the British government's agent or spokesman, but also in advising and formulating policies for appropriate action in foreign money, capital and exchange markets. In like manner, the Bank is also intimately involved in the formulation of domestic monetary policies as well as taking on the responsibility for their implementation. The figures for the Banking Department's activities tend to vastly underestimate the flow of funds which passes through the accounts in, for example, the public deposits or the balance in the Government's accounts.

Discount houses

Market for short-term funds

These institutions are unique to the UK financial system and the City of London. The discount market has a special function in the monetary system to provide a market for short-term funds. The discount houses borrow money at call and short notice and lend for longer periods of time. They undertake to cover the tender for the Government's weekly issues of treasury bills so that the Government is always able to raise the cash it requires from selling 91-day bills. These treasury bills may be resold to other institutions, such as the commercial banks, by the discount houses. From the banks' point of view the discount market provides a very flexible means of earning a return on surplus funds which can be easily recalled. If discount houses were to find themselves short of funds, which is a distinct risk in a market that borrows for such short periods of time, then they have recourse to the Bank of England as lender of last resort. The Bank of England will provide funds at the minimum lending rate (MLR), although it may charge a higher rate. In this event, the close inter-relationships between the financial institutions in borrowing and lending to each other would lead to a general increase in interest rates throughout the money market.

The Bank of England, by varying the amounts of treasury bills sold in relation to the bills that mature each week, is able to use the discount market as a means of influencing the amount of credit and money supply in the economy by operating on the banks' reserve assets holdings. The discount market has shown itself to be highly efficient in providing a convenient market in short-term funds and treasury bills for both the banks and the Bank of England. In the dealings between the banks and the Bank of England, the discount houses can be seen to be a kind of buffer, or shock-absorber, within the system. The discount houses first feel the effect of an increase in interest rates during a period of monetary squeeze and contraction, which is then passed through to the commercial banks through the workings of the money market.

The discount market also deals in local authority bills and commercial bills as well as treasury bills. These operate in a very similar manner and represent a means of short-term borrowing by the bill-issuing body. The rate of discount offered on a bill will depend upon the length of time before its maturity and the degree of confidence and security that the bill reflects. Negotiable certificates of deposit (CD) in both sterling and in US dollars are also dealt with by discount houses. The CD represents a receipt for a deposit made with a bank, stating the amount of the deposit and any interest that might be payable at a fixed date to the bearer. These CDs can be bought and sold for cash at anytime before maturity on the discount market since the maturity date and value of the CD are clearly stated and their acceptance by a bank, or discount house, acts as a guarantee of payment.

Rate of discount

The rate of discount on a bill represents in percentage terms the yield on holding a bill till maturity over the price paid for it. For example, a £100 treasury bill newly issued will be repaid in 91 days' time. If £97 cash is offered for the bill on issue, then in 91 days that bill will return £3 to the buyer. £3 for 3 months is equivalent to an annual rate of interest of 12 per cent. A similar bill bought new for £98 cash would yield 8 per cent per annum. Changes in the cash price offered therefore change the percentage return or rate of discount; the discount being the difference between price paid and maturity value. As a bill nears its maturity date, the cash value will increase (the rate of discount will fall) because a shorter time has to elapse before repayment. By thus adjusting the rate of discount on bills in relation to the time required for maturity through altering the prices paid for buying and selling them, the discount market is able to provide the financial system with a whole range of short-term assets of varying liquidity.

Non-bank financial institutions

Life assurance companies

Some part of the savings of the community are mobilised through the activities of the life assurance companies. Under the terms of an endowment policy the individual pays a regular sum of money (a premium) to the company, which in turn guarantees to pay not less than a specified sum to the policy holder or other beneficiary, either at the person's death or at an agreed date. The company either invests or lends the funds it obtains in this way to obtain income and then uses this income to credit the contributor's policy with bonuses. The bonuses increase the amount payable on death or maturity of the policy. Life policies provide a means of making provision for death, but they also offer an interest bearing but secure means of saving money over a long period. Frequently life assurance is the means people choose to provide for their retirement. Frequently superannuation schemes operate through life assurance policies.

The UK government has encouraged taxpayers to prepare for retirement and to save over the long-term by taking out life assurance policies. The incentive has taken the form of allowing premiums on life assurance policies to be set against income tax liability. This tax relief benefit was allowed on half of the annual premium paid, the policy holder then receiving as relief the amount of tax he would otherwise have had to pay. This position has been much simplified in recent years by the life assurance companies now charging premiums net of tax-relief; that is a lower premium to the policy-holder and with no necessity anymore for the life assurance premium to be claimed against income tax.

The life assurance companies are important as institutional investors with very large resources and funds to invest in long-term projects, government stocks, industrial companies shares and debentures. The companies need to maintain a flow of liquid funds necessary to meet their operating requirements and the expected payments on policies at any one time, but also require long-term security and adequate yield to cover their commitments in the future on the policies carried. In more recent years, life assurance companies have been more involved in making long-term loans on mortgages to house-buyers against the security of an endowment policy.

Finance companies

Finance companies provide funds for households and private businesses for terms ranging from 'at call' and 90 days to several years. One of their most familiar activities is the granting of instalment credit (hire purchase) for retail sales. Legally, the goods become the property of the finance company until all payments have been made, and failure to repay the loan may result in the company repossessing the article. Instalment credit on retail sales accounts for most of finance company lending. Other important uses of funds are wholesale credit (such as the financing of the stock of cars held by used car dealers), short-term commercial loans and personal loans not identified with the purchase of specific items.

Building societies

There are about 230 building societies in the UK (1982) but the largest 10 deal with more than half of the total of deposits and loans. They exist to make loans available for the purchase of housing on mortgage. Borrowing on mortgage to buy a house is often for a period of twenty to thirty years. In the UK they dominate the home loan market and are specialised, non-profit making institutions subject to strict controls and regulations. The building societies attract funds from savers which are held on deposit and are repayable on demand (or at very short notice). These funds are then used to provide loans secured against the property that they are obtained to purchase. Mortgages are commonly for long periods and this presents a problem to operating the societies in terms of borrowing short and lending long. Mortgage funds are charged at a rate of interest which has to cover the rate of interest paid to depositors and cover administrative costs, running expenses and maintain sufficient reserves.

Building societies have proved very responsive to interest rates offered by other institutions to depositors since they are competing directly in the market for depositors' funds. They cannot afford to be out of line or uncompetitive for long and generally respond very quickly to changes in interest rates. The mortgage rate of interest is also very responsive to the general level of interest rates and the money market because of the need to maintain a sufficient margin between interest received and that paid out to depositors. Failure to attract new depositors' funds or to keep deposits directly influences the amount of mortgage loans that societies are able to offer. Setting mortgage rates of interest too high will also restrict the numbers applying for loans, either first-time buyers or owner-occupiers buying a different property. The housing construction industry has shown itself to be very susceptible to changes in demand for new housing, resulting from changes in mortgage availability and in interest rates.

One particular feature of mortgage interest paid to a building society is that it is allowable for relief against income tax. Thus the real rate of interest actually paid on a mortgage depends on the interest rate charged less the value of the rate of income tax that would otherwise be paid by the owner-occupier. (An option mortgage scheme allows those on low incomes to pay a reduced rate of interest if they are not earning sufficient income to get the full benefit of the tax relief.) Since 1983 the tax relief on mortgage interest payable to building societies has been deducted at source so that the tax-payer pays interest net of the tax relief. The rate of interest to depositors is paid net of tax for the buildings societies pay the Inland Revenue directly at an average rate on the gross interest that they pay out. Comparing interest rates between building societies and other forms of savings requires consideration of the position relative to income tax liability and the gross and net rates paid.

Development finance

In recent years there has been a growth in the number of bodies providing finance for development in industry. Merchant banks have for many decades been active in providing funds for companies dealing in property, shipping, exports and foreign trade and development. They have also been much involved with issuing new securities and shares for firms going public, with the merchant bank often underwriting, or guaranteeing, the sale of shares. Buying any surplus shares up after they have been offered to the public is undertaken by the institution acting as underwriter.

To these institutions have been added foreign banks and other UK banks besides the clearing banks, which have also become heavily involved in providing finance for investment such as leasing of equipment.

The state has also become more directly involved in this aspect of finance through bodies such as the National Enterprise Board (NEB). The NEB is intended to make funds available by loan or share capital for projects which are regarded as particularly important or would otherwise not be fully funded. The NEB also acts for the government in the companies where the state has a direct holding.

Finance for Industry is a specialist provider of finance for private enterprise, operated and owned by the Bank of England and the clearing and other banks. The Industrial and Commercial Finance Corporation (ICFC) and the Finance Corporation for Industry (FCI) provide loans on a long-term basis to companies and are subsidiaries of Finance for Industry.

State involvement in the small firms sector of the economy was an important feature in the 1979 budget, and later budgets, of the Conservative government that came to power then. The provision of funds particularly for this sector is a key element in the policy measures introduced. The business start-up scheme, for example, designed to provide small businesses with capital to enable new ventures to take place was introduced in the 1981 budget.

The European Investment Bank and the Regional Development Fund of the EEC are also sources of finance for the government and local authorities for specific projects such as developing infrastructure (i.e. roads, bridges, ports and harbours etc.) and providing aid for industry in the form of cheap loans, grants, financing retraining of workers, re-equipping with new technology.

The Bank of England and monetary policy

The functions of the Bank of England were discussed earlier but more concentration is given here to the Bank's function in implementing policy.

The UK government's monetary policies are carried out by the Bank of England in a number of ways. The measures that are adopted influence, in various ways, the supply of funds available to businesses and households through the financial system. Alternatively, the cost of funds may be altered through changes in the interest rate which is, in effect, the price of money. A reduction in the supply of funds, or an increase in the cost of borrowing, may deter some businesses or households from spending; whilst an increase in funds, or lower interest rates, may encourage economic activity by increasing the profitability of investment projects or encouraging additional spending.

Controls on supply of money

The Bank of England uses quantitative controls to influence the supply of money and the level of activity. The minimum reserve assets ratio acts as a constraint on the power of the banking system to make credit available by creating deposits. The effect this has on the workings of the bank credit multiplier was discussed earlier. Using the same mechanism to expand or contract bank deposits through operating on the reserve assets structure, open-market operations by influencing the availability of liquid reserve assets in the money market are also a Bank of England control measure. When the Bank of England sells securities, liquidity in the banking system is reduced, with consequent reduction in the money supply. If the Bank buys government securities from the market, the overall level of liquidity in the banking system increases and bank deposits and lending can also be expanded.

Special deposits are another quantitative control which operate directly on the level of assets held by the banks, as was outlined earlier. Supplementary special deposits were another form of money supply control which took a certain percentage of any increase in deposits beyond specified levels in the form of an additional special deposit. This scheme, also known as the corset, was deliberately aimed at restricting too rapid a rate of growth of bank deposits. Any call for special deposits or additional deposits has a multiplied effect in contracting the overall level of bank credit. This is because the special deposit has to be met by reducing the level of assets held by the banking system and therefore reduces the asset base to support a given level of deposits. The amount of deposits must fall in line with the ratio of assets held to total liabilities. Special deposits are applicable to other financial institutions, such as finance houses, as well as the commercial banks.

Interest rates

The Bank is able to influence interest rates in the financial sector in two main ways.

1 Interest rates in the short-term money market (such as MLR) can be set by the Bank and will be closely matched by changes in the basic rates which the commercial banks charge to borrowers and pay to depositors. Interest rates throughout the financial system will also be influenced by changes in MLR. For example, if the banks increase interest paid on deposits, this is likely to force building societies to raise

their rates to sustain the inflow of funds, or to stop an outflow of funds. MLR, when first introduced, was set by formula which was closely related to, but above, the rate of interest determined by the rate of discount on treasury bills. In this way whenever discount houses borrowed from the Bank as lender of last resort, interest rates were forced up above the market rate obtained from Treasury bills. The formula has been suspended by the Bank when particular requirements of monetary policy demanded. In August 1981 the practice of posting the MLR by the Bank of England was ended. In future the Bank of England will keep interest rates for short-term lending within an undisclosed band which will be moved from time to time. The Bank, in interest rate policy, is now relying on market forces rather than on direct lending. (See Figure 11.3 on page 205.)

2 Interest rates are also influenced through market forces by open-market operations. The purpose of these buying and selling operations is to maintain orderly markets, balance out peaks and troughs in the level of liquidity and to influence the price and availability of funds in the money market and thus the the ability and willingness to lend, borrow and spend.

The Bank by planning its sales and purchases of securities, can maintain the desired market interest rate on bonds. By doing this it is relying on demand and supply to influence interest rates; using quantity in the market to influence price. By selling bonds, the market price is depressed and the market interest rate is increased. Buying bonds will increase the market price but reduce the market interest rate. There are indications that companies planning to borrow money pay close attention to the ruling bond rates when determining the interest rates they will offer on debentures.

The day to day operations of the Bank in buying and selling securities act as a stabilising influence on bond prices and interest rates rather than producing changes in liquidity.

With regard to interest rate policy, the monetary authorities are in a position of either determining directly the interest rate as the price of money, or determining the quantity of bonds in the market and influencing, through the market, the level of interest rates.

Funding means the conversion of short-term debt into longer-term debt by the Bank of England. This would result if the Bank sold bonds in place of Treasury bills in the money markets. Funding has a direct influence on the asset structures of the commercial banks and on the structure of the National Debt.

Directives

The other ways in which the Bank of England is able to influence the borrowing and lending policies of the financial institutions is by the directions it gives to the institutions about lending and borrowing policies; to whom they should lend and how much they should lend. For example, a limit may be put on the level of advances made by a bank, known as a ceiling on advances. Other qualitative controls may be imposed on the nature of lending, for example to give exporters or manufacturing industry priority for funds. Other examples of Bank of England controls come in the form of suggestions or requests to financial institutions. Generally the Bank is more reluctant to use direct measures or orders to control the monetary system. Competition and credit control started a move towards relying on the market mechanism acting as a means of control through rationing credit accordingly by its price. A different policy regime that demands stricter control over the money supply and its growth has led to a more deliberate attempt to use higher interest rates to curb credit in the economy.

UK monetary policy since August 1981

The Bank of England manages the banking system in the country through its ability to dictate the terms at which it will make cash available to the money market. In this way the Bank of England is able to determine the level of short term interest rates in the economy. Until August 1981 this was indicated by MLR (prior to that by the Bank Rate) as the level at which the Bank was prepared to provide funds to the banking system. In the days of MLR, which was formally determined by the use of the formula linking the rate to the treasury bill rate, the Bank of England was able to abandon the formula for the MLR when it was felt that conditions required direct action, such as pressure on the exchange rate from international competition for funds with countries competing through interest rates. Figure 11.3 shows the links between the official rate of interest and the rates for lending by the clearing banks and the changes of interest policy from bank rate, and then MLR, until MLR was suspended.

Emphasis on market forces

The use of the reserve asset ratio was abolished as a means of monetary control in August 1981 and policy shifted in favour of the flow of cash in the system which determined the level of interest rates and the monetary authorities' operations in the market. The emphasis for control has in consequence altered to the level of interest rates and the operation of market forces.

> The new system involves those institutions within the expanded banking sector holding ½ per cent of their eligible liabilities (basically customer deposits) as balances at the Bank of England. Although this balance is intended only to provide the Bank of Engalnd with the funds it needs to carry out its operations, the central bank's influence on interest rates still turns on the terms at which they provide funds to the banking system. The abolition of MLR means that for most of the time the influence on interest rates generally will be seen in their day to day bill transactions. These sales and purchases of bills are the preferred way of providing assistance to the money markets and are usually for periods of less than one month. In order that the Bank may continue to provide assistance through the discount market, 'eligible' banks must maintain not less than 4 per cent of their eligible liabilities with the discount houses to enable them in turn to maintain a broad market in bills. (UK Monetary System, *Barclays Bank Review*, November 1981)

The eligibility requirements of 4 per cent secured with the London Discount Market and an overall daily average of 6 per cent to be loaned to the discount market and the money brokers and gilt-edged-jobbers, has therefore replaced the previous liquidity ratio requirements. The new requirements ensure that the discount market as a whole has a pool of liquidity which provides the Bank of England with the mechanism for operations and control in the money market and ensures that the discount market will continue to provide a highly developed market in short term bills. The Bank of England, in shifting more emphasis to money market operations, is therefore continuing its traditional practice of dealing via the discount houses.

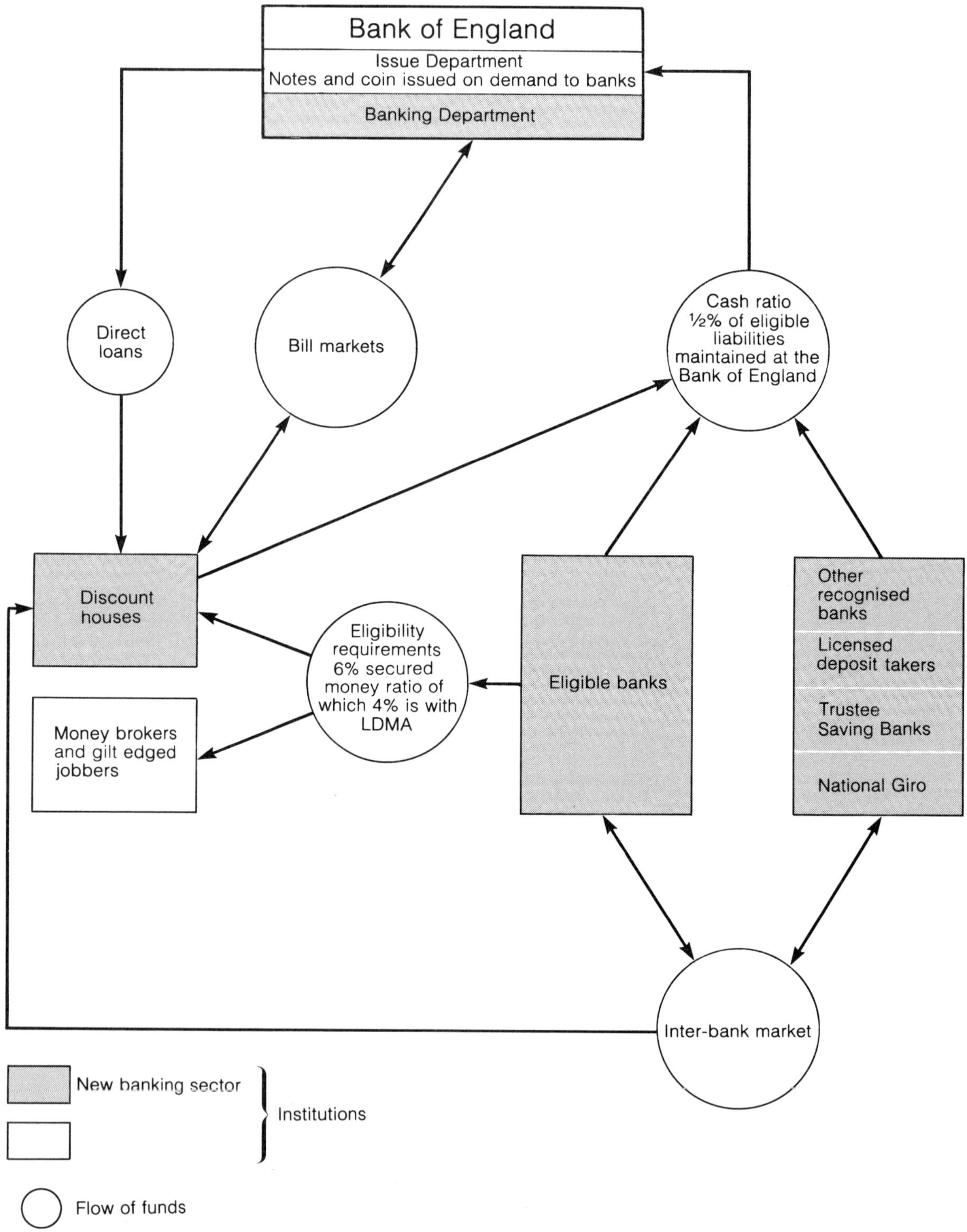

Figure 11.2 The UK banking sector

Source: Barclays Review, November 1981

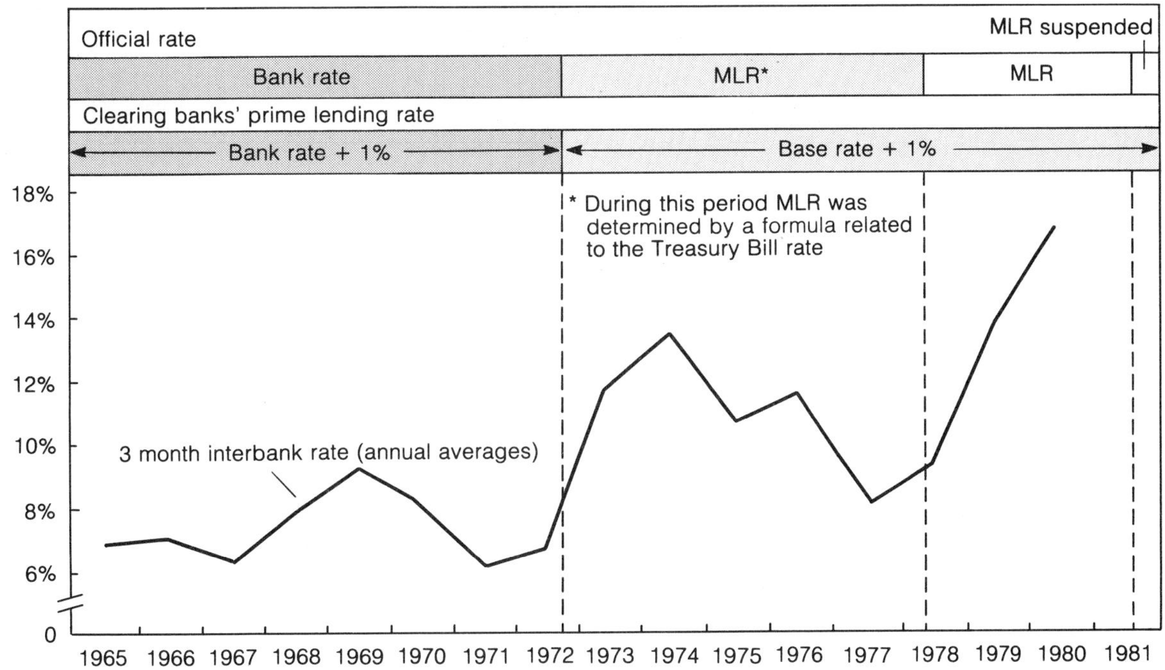

Figure 11.3 Interest rates

Source: Barclays Review, November 1981

11.6

What effects, if any, would you expect an increase in the rate of interest payable on a mortgage extended by a bank or a building society to have on:
the price of houses,
the UK building industry,
the level of deposits in banks and building societies,
the demand for 'second-hand' as opposed to new houses?

11.7

Compare and contrast a bank loan and an overdraft as alternative ways of borrowing money from a bank for a short-term loan.

11.8

Assume the banking system in an economy operates on a reserve ratio of 12½ per cent of assets to liabilities.

1 What would be the effect on total liabilities if deposits increased by £5m?

2 If the monetary authorities reduced the reserve ratio to 10 per cent, what would be the effect on total liabilities of the same increase in deposits of £5m?

3 If the reserve ratio was 15 per cent what would happen to the level of liabilities with the same increase in deposits?

4 Using the results obtained above, explain how different reserve ratios imposed by the monetary authorities influence the level of credit created in the economy.

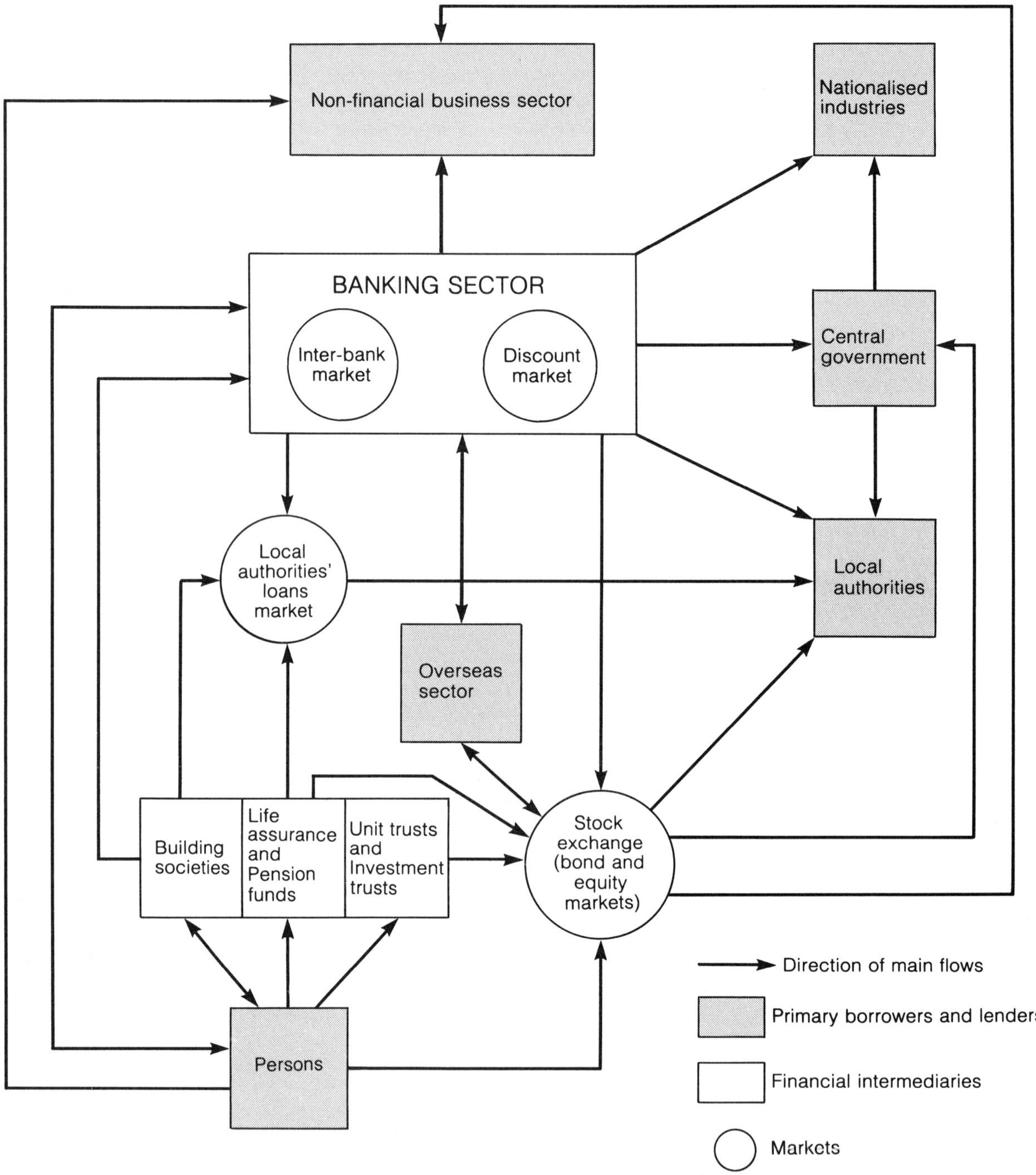

Figure 11.4 The financial system – principal flows and operators
Source: Barclays Review, November 1981

11.9

If the reserve ratio was $12\frac{1}{2}$ per cent and total liabilities and assets in the banking system were £5000m; what amount of assets would be held as reserves? If the central bank then called for a special deposit of £100m from the banking system to be met immediately from reserve assets, what effect would this have on total liabilities and why? If at a later date the special deposit was repaid, what would be the impact on credit creation in the economy by the banking system?

11.10

The Bank of England by 'open-market operations', that is buying and selling treasury bills to discount houses, is able to influence the level of reserve assets held by the banks in the banking system and through this the level of credit creation or money supply. Outline the consequences of the Bank's actions in selling more treasury bills on the money supply and explain whether credit would expand or be restricted. In like manner, examine what happens when 'open-market operations' have a net effect of reducing the amount of bills in the market, i.e. buying securities, and explain the changes in the money supply as a result.

11.11

Consider the implications for the money supply if the Bank of England sells stock to
1 the general public
2 the commercial banks
3 companies and non-bank financial institutions
4 foreign banks and financial institutions overseas

11.12

What are the implications to the money market of a shift in monetary policy from interest rates set by the Bank of England to rates determined by market forces? Are interest rates more or less likely to fluctuate as a result?

11.13

In what senses can it be argued that the National Debt does not constitute a 'debt' at all and therefore need not be repaid? It will help to consider what the debt is used to finance and also who holds the debt.

Notes

1 This relationship between the interest rate, yield and the price of the bond will only take this precise form if there are many years to go to maturity. If the bond is to mature soon any reduction in its price offers the buyer the possibility of a capital gain.

2 The effective rate of interest can be calculated approximately using the formula,

$$E = \frac{2n \times R}{1 + n}$$

Where E = effective rate of interest
R = flat rate of interest
n = number of repayment periods.

Chapter 12

International Trade

Overseas Trade Statistics of the United Kingdom, published monthly and annually, and the *United Kingdom Balance of Payments* (the '*Pink Book*') published annually by the Central Statistical Office, indicate the great complexity of the UK's trade with other countries. As an island economy, the UK is very heavily dependent on trade. In 1978 total exports amounted to £53 767m and imports were £52 735m in total. Gross domestic product at market prices in 1978 was £161 639m. One of the tasks of the economist is to provide an explanation of why this trade takes place. In this chapter trade in merchandise (i.e. imports and exports of goods) is discussed and trends and developments in the value, volume and directions of trade in the UK are outlined.

The second task of the economist is to assess the effects that changes in trade may have on aggregate economic activity. He may be called on to advise government of the likely effects of a reduction in trade on the levels of production, unemployment and the rate of inflation. This chapter examines the questions:

Why does trade occur?

What are the effects of changes in trade?

Reasons for international trade

A common explanation of the benefits that come from international trade was given in Chapter 4. It was demonstrated in some detail that specialisation can bring benefits to either an individual or a country by making it possible for them to acquire a greater quantity of goods and services than they could obtain by their own activities. The conditions that are necessary to achieve these benefits are, first, that the country's residents should specialise in the production of those activities in which they hold a comparative advantage and, second, that exchange must take place at prices that bring the benefits of increased production to both countries.

Comparative advantage

The existence of a comparative advantage in a particular activity was explained in terms of opportunity cost. It was said that a country holds a comparative advantage in the production of an article if its opportunity costs of producing that article are lower than the opportunity costs of other countries. This comparative advantage can be illustrated by using a further example. Table 12.1 sets out the hypothetical opportunity costs of producing a bale of wool and a tractor in Australia and Japan. It shows that the opportunity cost of a bale of wool is lower in Australia (in terms of the tractors that might have been produced with those resources). Similarly, the opportunity cost of a tractor is lower in Japan than in Australia. There are potential benefits to both countries if Australia specialises in producing wool and Japan in the manufacture of tractors. Normally, these benefits are illustrated in terms of two country examples. In the real world, trade consists of transactions between many countries. The principle of comparative advantage still holds when many countries are trading many products, though it is a much more difficult task to demonstrate in simple terms.

	Australia	Japan
Opportunity cost of 1 bale of wool	0.25 tractor	1 tractor
Opportunity cost of 1 tractor	4 bales of wool	1 bale of wool

Table 12.1 Opportunity costs: a two country example

Table 12.2 extends the example to a situation in which there are three goods and three countries. In this example the country with the lowest opportunity cost for each product is indicated.

	Australia	Japan	United Kingdom
Opportunity cost of 1 bale of wool	0.25 tractor 700 metres cloth	1 tractor 1400 metres cloth	0.5 tractor 2100 metres cloth
Opportunity cost of 1 tractor	4 bales of wool 2800 metres cloth	1 bale of wool 1400 metres cloth	2 bales of wool 4200 metres cloth
Opportunity cost of 100 metres of cloth	1/28th of a tractor 1/7th of a bale of wool	1/14th of a tractor 1/14th of a bale of wool	1/42nd of a tractor 1/21st of a bale of wool

Table 12.2 Opportunity costs: a three country example

Each country can benefit from trade

Australia has the lowest opportunity cost for a *bale of wool* when measured either in tractors or cloth. Japan has the lowest opportunity cost for *tractors* in terms of either wool or cloth. The UK has the lowest opportunity cost for *cloth* when measured in tractors or wool. Each country can derive a potential benefit from trade, and three-way trade might be developed advantageously in the directions indicated in Figure 12.1.

It would be possible to extend the example to cover many countries and many goods. However, little would be gained by the exercise. The figures in Table 12.2 are sufficient to indicate the general principle and also complicated enough to suggest that including more countries only increases the number of calculations that have to be performed.

Of more value is the inquiry into the underlying reasons of why opportunity costs differ from one country to another. Three possible causes have been identified:

differences in productivity of resources,
differences in resource endowments,
differences in demand conditions.

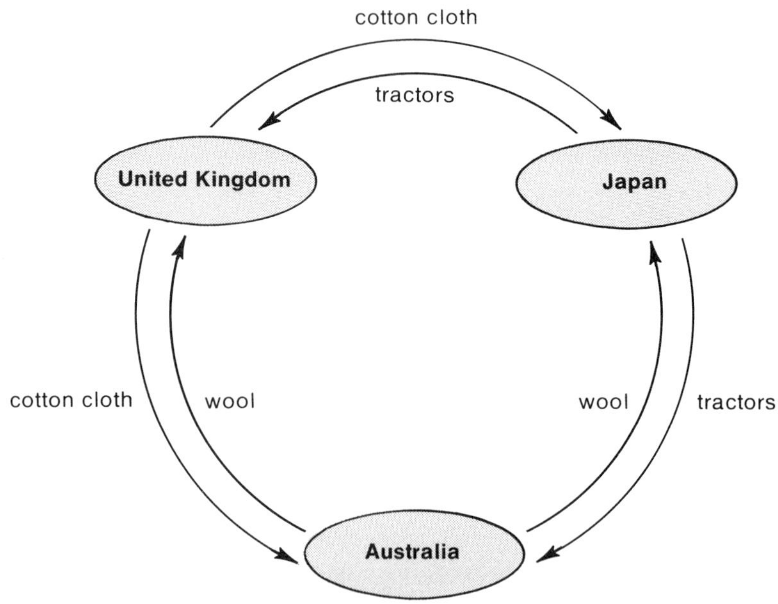

Figure 12.1 Three-way trade

Differences in productivity of resources

One of the earliest explanations of how countries gained from trade was based on the recognition that production techniques and the productivity of resources varied from country to country. It was said that the residents of a country specialised in a particular activity because they were relatively more productive than the residents of other countries.

This argument has value, but it cannot be accepted as a complete explanation of why opportunity costs differ. With the rapid transfer of information today, fostered by international investment and the development of multinational corporations, knowledge of many production techniques is becoming universal. When this happens, it becomes possible for a given quantity of resources of the appropriate quality to be used as productively in one country as another.

Differences in resource endowments

Probably of greater significances than 'differences in productivity' is the fact that the quantity of resources available for production differs between countries. Differences in climate, soil, land area, size of the labour force, human skills, capital stock and so forth play an important part in determining the relative opportunity costs of products in various countries.

In the UK land is relatively scarce compared with Australia or Canada and this accounts for their lower relative opportunity costs of wheat production and in other agricultural products. Taking the comparison with Australia further, many categories of skilled human resources and other endowments of capital are relatively scarce there and consequently the opportunity costs of products that use these resources (such as colour television sets, computers) is high. The argument can be summarised in this way. Countries tend to export those products that are heavy users of those types of resources that are relatively abundant. They tend to import those commodities that are heavy users of resources that are relatively scarce.

Differences in demand conditons

The strength of consumer demand may be quite different in countries that have a similar range of production techniques to choose from and have similar resource endowments. If one country has a high demand for a product, the price, and also the opportunity cost, of that product may be higher than the price in a second country in which demand for the product is low. With the difference in prices and opportunity costs a potential gain is to be had if production is increased in the low demand, low cost country and exported to the high demand, high cost country. This is demonstrated in Figure 12.2. The greater demand in country A leads, initially, to a higher price in that country for a particular product (OP compared with OP_1 in country B). Country B then possesses a price advantage and is able to increase production and export its surplus to country A. In the diagram, the trade continues to increase until the price differential disappears. (OP^* is then the ruling price in both countries.)

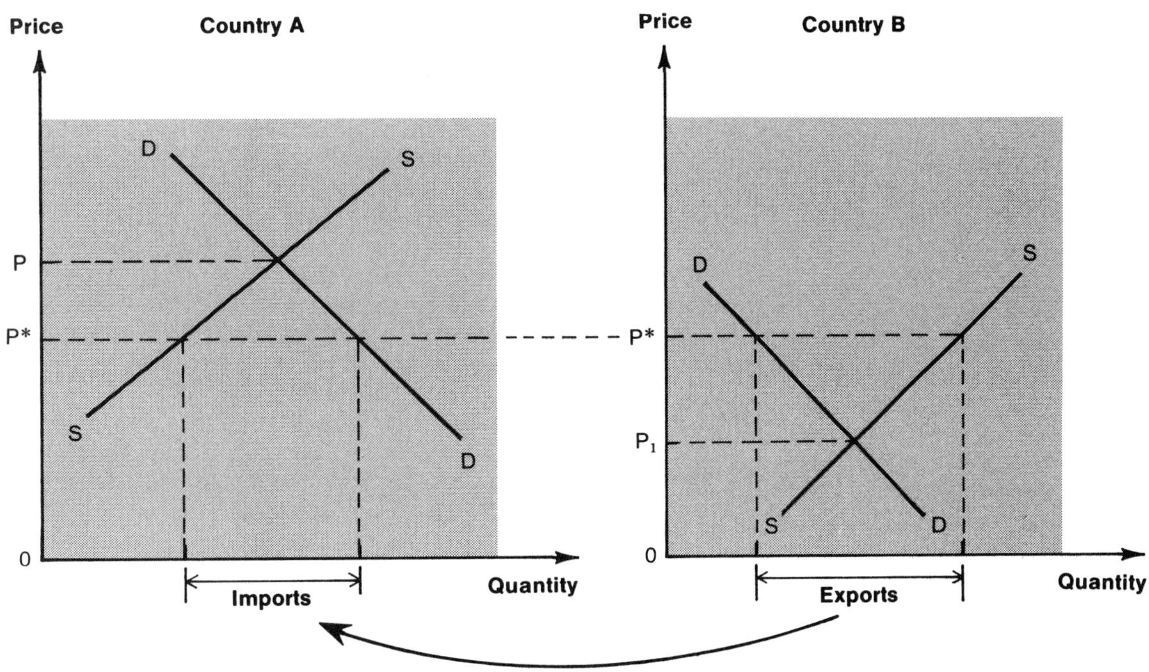

Figure 12.2 Trade possibilities between high and low demand countries

Exchange rates

The precise gains obtained from specialisation depend on the terms on which goods are exchanged in a barter situation, or on their relative money prices when the goods are bought and sold at a market. One of the special features of international trade is that each country has its own currency, for example, dollars, pounds, yen, rupees and marks. Any producer or consumer must have some idea of the exchange rate between his own country's currency and those of the countries he proposes to deal with before he engages in overseas trade. In general, it is necessary for these international exchange rates to settle at levels that offer residents of each country the opportunity of profitable trade.

	Cost of 1 bale of wool	Cost of 1 tractor
Australia	A$700	A$2 800
Japan	420 000 yen	420 000 yen

Table 12.3 Money costs: a two country example

Suppose that production costs of wool and tractors in Australia and Japan are those given in Table 12.3. Price quotations in Japanese yen will be meaningless to Australia tractor buyers, but if an exchange rate between dollars and yen of, say, A$1 = 300 yen is established in some way, yen prices can then be converted into Australian dollars and vice versa. As A$1 = 300 yen, the cost of 1 bale of wool and 1 tractor in Japan are each A$1400. Australia can produce wool more cheaply and Japan tractors more cheaply in money terms. However, if the exchange rate happened to be A$1 = 1000 yen, the cost of 1 bale of wool, or 1 tractor, would be A$420 in Japan, and Japan would be able to produce both goods more cheaply in money terms. In practice, such a situation would be to no one's advantage, because, although Japan could produce both goods more cheaply, Australia would have nothing it could sell to Japan whereby it could earn the necessary yen to buy the Japanese products. For this reason, exchange rates tend to settle at levels at which a country's total payments on overseas transactions more or less balance its total receipts from overseas tranactions. There is, however, no need for receipts and payments from transactions with each country, individually, to balance. In a multilateral system, debts in trade with one country can often be offset against credits with another.

In recent years, there have been many changes in international exchange rates as countries have tried to balance payments and receipts by devaluing or revaluing their currencies, or simply allowing them to fluctuate under the influence of international demand and supply. Such changes have had important effects upon the profitability of trade. Export markets have been lost overnight and countries that previously imported a product have suddenly found themselves with profitable export markets.

The gains from trade

Trade benefits the residents of a country because it brings them, in aggregate, greater quantities of goods and services, and provides some goods that could not be produced at home at all, thus making it possible to sustain higher living standards. Although these benefits spread through the community, it does not follow that all groups benefit to the same extent. For example, businesses that have to compete with imports may claim that their profitability is damaged and local employment opportunities are threatened by the competition. They argue that more trade redistributes wealth to those groups actively involved in the production of exports.

Individual enterprises engaging in trade measure the gains in terms of the profits the trade brings. Exporters often attribute those gains to such influences as energetic sales promotion, skilful bargaining and initiative, or ignorance and poor presentation by their competitors. Consequently, it is sometimes suggested that explanations of the gains from trade based on the benefits of specialisation are irrelevant. Certainly, there can be no denying that many contracts are only finalised after energetic sales promotion and that others are lost through ignorance and inertia, but it would be an exaggeration to suggest that these influences are all important. Many critical factors are beyond the control of the individual businessman. No amount of hard selling will overcome the fundamental disadvantages of low productivity, lack of suitable resources or an unfavourable exchange rate. All affect the cost of selling the product in a foreign country and the ability to trade profitably.

Obstacles to trade

Commercial policies

Tariffs and quotas restrict trade

Governments commonly use economic policy instruments such as tariffs and quotas to restrict trade. Tariffs restrict trade by raising the foreign producer's costs of supplying goods to the local market, making it more difficult and often impossible to compete with local producers. Quotas are more direct; they limit the quantity of a good that can be imported or exported. The reasons why governments use these measures to prevent a great deal of otherwise profitable international trade and also the international attempts to reduce such restrictions, including across-the-board tariff reductions, are discussed later.

Customs unions

Commercial policies are also used to divert international trade from one country to another country, or group of countries. Customs unions, such as the European Economic Community (EEC) promote free trade between members and associate members, but discriminate against non-members by adopting common external tariffs. Trade is therefore created between member states but diverted from countries that are not in the customs union. The extent to which such customs unions expand or restrict trade depends to a large extent on whether the members of the customs union are capable of producing goods demanded by the residents of fellow members.

Free trade associations have similar, but somewhat more limited aims. They seek to establish free, or freer, trade between members without prescribing what protective barriers shall apply to trade with non-members. The European Free Trade Association (EFTA) was established in 1959 by the UK, Norway, Sweden, Denmark, Austria, Portugal and Switzerland. In 1961 they were joined by Finland, and Iceland became a member in 1970. The UK and Denmark left the Association in 1973 on becoming full members of the EEC. Agreements have been made between the EEC and EFTA to extend free trade and eliminate import duties on goods given certificates of origin if 'wholly produced' or 'sufficiently processed' within member countries.

Transport costs

Transport costs can have a decisive effect in restricting international trade. They reduce the cost advantage for the exporting country. The Australian apple and pear industry used to export about 30 per cent of its production to Western Europe. Its productivity per hectare and per person was high, the necessary resources were plentiful and the quality of the fruit excellent. Steadily rising costs of the essential refrigerated shipping placed the industry at an increasing cost disadvantage and exports dwindled to about 10 per cent of production. In 1979 the cost of shipping a carton of apples to the UK was about $6.00 compared with a cost of less than $3.00 to produce the apples in the first place.

In general the sharp increases in oil prices by the OPEC members in the 1970s has led to general increases in sea freights. Such cost increases fall heavily on those products with a low value to volume ratio.

Social, political and industrial conditions

Social and religious customs may have a restricting or diverting effect on international trade. For example, exports of carcass meats to the Middle Eastern countries have been subject to the requirements of the Islamic countries and the rites practised in the slaughter of animals. Restrictions have also been placed on the export of live animals.

Political affiliations have a strong bearing on the direction of international trade, though in the last decade there has been a steady increase in trade between Communist and non-Communist countries. Economic sanctions are still common and in recent years have included the United Nations sanctions on trade with Zimbabwe and individual countries' trade boycotts that have included Chile, South Africa and Cuba.

12.1

Production of wheat per hectare is much greater in the UK than in Australia, but in 1971–72 Australia exported over half a million tonnes to the UK. Try to suggest a reason for this trade. If UK wheat-growers are so efficient, why is it that they do not export wheat to Australia instead?

12.2

> 'If wages go up and inflation occurs, we shall price ourselves out of world markets.' (Anxious businessman)
>
> 'No matter what happens to money costs of production, a country will be able to trade profitably if it specialises in those products for which its opportunity cost is relatively low.' (Confident economist)

Put yourself in the position of the 'confident economist' and attempt to explain to the businessman that even if money costs rise, trade will still be profitable if a suitable exchange rate exists.

The United Kingdom's overseas trade

Figure 12.3 shows the contribution to exports and imports made by the various categories of goods in 1978. The outstanding feature of the

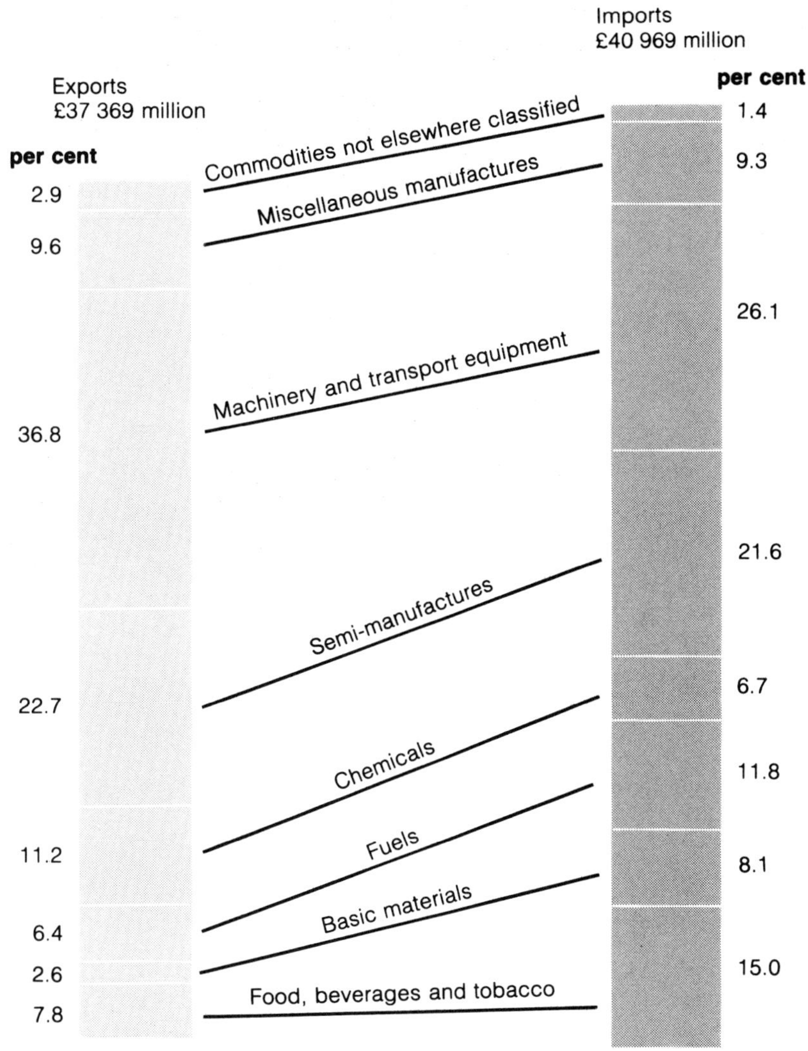

Figure 12.3 United Kingdom external trade by commodity, 1978

Source: Annual Abstract of Statistics 1980

diagram is the proportion of trade taken up by manufactured goods both exported and imported. Manufactures in 1978 accounted for 80.3 per cent of exports and 63.7 per cent of imports. Within this broad group of manufacture, machinery and transport equipment accounted for 36.8 per cent of exports and 26.1 per cent of imports alone. Food, beverages and tobacco made up 15.0 per cent of imports in 1978, goods which the UK is largely dependent upon overseas countries to supply. However, a large proportion of trade of the UK is in similar products both exported and imported.

The breakdown of the trade of the UK for 1978 in Figure 12.3 demonstrates the relative importance between classes of goods, but it would be wrong to conclude that the share of each class of goods in total trade is fixed. Fluctuations occur from year to year, and when examination is made of trade in particular products it is evident that these changes can be considerable. Measurement of trade by value is subject to the influence of price changes, for example, the rapid increases in oil prices during the 1970s after 1973 have had a marked effect on oil imports.

Trade statistics can also be represented on a volume basis, i.e. in terms of the actual physical quantities of goods traded. Increases or decreases in the level of trade clearly show up in volume terms without the distorting effect of price changes of goods on the value of trade. Alternatively, trade statistics by value can be measured in terms of constant prices using index numbers to indicate changes from a selected base year. The base year is taken to be equal to 100 and values for different years are expressed as index numbers relative to the base. In similar fashion, changes in volumes of trade can be represented by index numbers relative to a base year.

Products traded are grouped into commodities in the official statistics in the sections and divisions of the revised Standard Industrial Trade Classification (SITC). This distinguishes goods into sections 0 to 9 with divisions in each section subdividing into different product groups and types. For example, section 5 classifies chemicals and related products and, within this grouping, 51 refers to organic chemicals, 52 inorganic chemicals, 54 medicinal and pharmaceutical products, 56 fertilisers, manufactured, and so on. In most of the categories a distinction is made between primary products, semi-finished and finished manufactured goods.

	1960	1965	1970	1975	1978	1982
Food, beverages and tobacco	33.9	29.7	22.7	18.0	15.0	12.7
Basic materials	23.8	19.3	15.1	9.2	8.1	6.9
Fuels	10.6	10.6	10.4	17.8	11.8	13.0
Total non-manufactures	68.3	59.6	48.2	45.0	34.9	32.6
Manufactured goods	31.4	39.2	50.6	53.0	63.7	65.1
Other commodities	0.3	1.2	1.2	2.0	1.4	2.3

Table 12.4 United Kingdom imports, percentage share of total by value, 1960–82

Source: *Annual Abstract of Statistics*, various issues

Structure of import trade has changed

The structure of import trade has altered considerably over time as Table 12.4 shows. There has been a shift in the balance between non-manufactures and manufactured goods so that by 1978 almost two-thirds of imports were in manufactures compared with less than one third in 1960. The import of non-manufactures such as food, beverages and tobacco although declining in terms of its percentage share of total trade has, in fact, maintained or increased in volume but is taking a smaller proportion of a rapidly expanding trade in total. Imports measured by volume give a ready indication of the growth in trade by category of goods as demonstrated by Table 12.5.

Comparing the relative performance of each class of commodity imported with the index for total trade, highlights changes in the structure of trade. Imports in 1968 were 77.8 per cent of the volume of imports in 1975 and by 1978 had increased by a further 17.2 per cent from that level. Finished manufactures were only 47 per cent of their

	1968	1969	1970	1971	1972	1973	1974	1975	1976	1977	1978	1979	1980
Food, beverages and tobacco	104	101	101	100	102	103	100	100	102	102	101	103	96
Fuels	101	109	117	128	127	131	123	100	100	83	81	78	66
Basic materials	129	126	131	119	120	136	120	100	123	119	124	130	112
Chemicals	61	69	83	85	97	114	123	100	122	132	158	180	153
Other semi-manufactures	71	71	75	77	86	100	112	100	108	109	121	134	132
Finished manufactures	47	51	56	64	81	103	106	100	109	123	141	170	168
Total	77.8	79.0	82.9	87.2	95.8	109.1	109.4	100.0	106.4	108.8	117.2	126.7	121.3

Table 12.5 United Kingdom import volume index numbers, 1968–80 (*1975 = 100*)

Source: *Annual Abstract of Statistics 1980 and 1982*, CSO, Table 12.4

1975 volume in 1968, and increased by a further 40 per cent from 1975 to 1978.

Particularly interesting to note is the performance of fuels in the table. Volumes increased to 131 in 1973, compared with 1975 = 100, but had fallen to 66 in 1980. The impact of domestic supplies of oil substituting for imports can be seen at work.

	1960	1965	1970	1975	1978	1982
Food, beverages, tobacco	5.7	6.6	6.4	7.2	7.8	7.1
Basic materials	3.6	4.0	3.4	2.8	2.6	2.4
Fuels	3.7	2.7	2.6	4.1	6.4	20.2
Chemicals	9.0	9.2	9.7	10.9	11.2	11.0
Textiles	7.2	5.8	4.9	3.5	3.3	2.1
Metals	13.0	11.8	11.9	9.2	8.3	7.1
Other semi-manufactures	5.0	7.8	7.9	8.7	11.1	(a)
Machinery	26.1	26.5	27.6	29.0	24.7	23.3
Transport equipment	17.0	14.9	13.4	12.3	12.1	9.3
Other manufactures	6.2	7.6	9.0	9.0	9.6	14.4
Other commodities	3.5	3.1	3.2	3.3	2.9	3.1

Note (a) Included with 'Other manufactures'

Table 12.6 UK exports, percentage share of total by value, 1960–82

Source: *Annual Abstract of Statistics*, various issues

Major changes in export trade are apparent in Table 12.6, showing percentage shares by value from 1960–82. Long-standing traditional export industries, such as metals and textiles, can be seen to have declined in terms of their relative proportion of total trade. Transport equipment similarly shows a decline while other areas of trade in semi-manufactures and other manfactures have increased their share. Export trade as whole has expanded considerably in value terms over the period so that a decline in proportionate share by value of an export does not necessarily mean a decline in terms of volumes exported. Table 12.7 shows a breakdown of exports from the UK measured by volume from 1968–80. The example of textiles, reveals that although the share of

	1968	1969	1970	1971	1972	1973	1974	1975	1976	1977	1978	1979	1980
Food, beverages and tobacco	59	59	65	71	74	88	91	100	103	111	132	124	131
Basic materials	87	90	92	92	100	106	111	100	117	126	134	147	165
Fuels	90	95	110	110	112	117	109	100	120	165	209	277	290
Chemicals	63	69	73	80	85	103	122	100	124	141	154	157	149
Textiles	82	91	96	101	107	124	118	100	117	120	117	n/a	n/a
Metals	89	94	97	104	105	120	112	100	109	116	117	n/a	n/a
Machinery and transport equipment	66	75	75	83	82	91	95	100	101	106	105	n/a	n/a
Other manufactures	62	73	71	81	84	98	104	100	116	134	139	n/a	n/a
Total	68.4	75.9	77.8	84.5	86.1	98.1	102.7	100	108.7	118.7	124.0	123.8	126.0

Table 12.7 United Kingdom export volume index numbers 1968–80 (1975 = 100)

Source: *Annual Abstract of Statistics 1980 and 1982*, CSO, Table 12.4

textile trade by value fell from 4.9 per cent in 1970 to 3.3 per cent by 1978 the volume of textile trade increased from 96 in 1970 to 117 in 1978 (as compared with the 1975 volume taken as equal to 100).

The major share of UK export trade is taken up by manufactured goods, over 80 per cent; and in recent years they are also responsible for a growing proportion of imports. To an increasing extent, the economy is selling exports in world markets such as cars and other vehicles, machinery, aircraft and engines, chemicals, electrical goods and more recently oil, in order to finance the import of a similar range of commodities. Particular concern has been expressed, for example, in the motor industry over the increasing share of the car market taken up by foreign manufacturers' models principally from the EEC and Japan. However, this may be the result of the increase of choice for the consumer and consumer sovereignty at work.

Changes in direction and pattern of trade

The direction and pattern of trade has also changed in the UK along with changes in structure. The most notable feature is the increasing trade with Western Europe, particularly the EEC both before and after United Kingdom membership of the community in 1973. At the same time the Commonwealth has declined in importance as a supplier to and market for the UK. Traditional markets based on 'empire' links and the Commonwealth have declined as the historical ties have weakened and the UK no longer benefitted from the special preference shown to her by such countries.

Figure 12.4, of UK merchandise trade by area, demonstrates that import and export trade from 1955 to 1973 has shifted from the overseas sterling countries in favour of the EEC and Other Western Europe. Figure 12.4 is based upon the classification of trade used in the official statistics until 1973. From 1973 the analysis has been based upon a new grouping of trading areas following UK membership of the EEC. This new classification is used in Tables 12.8 and 12.9 and reflects the declining importance of the sterling area and the Commonwealth, and other changes in the structure of trade. Notable is the inclusion of a category for oil exporting countries. Resulting from the increase in oil

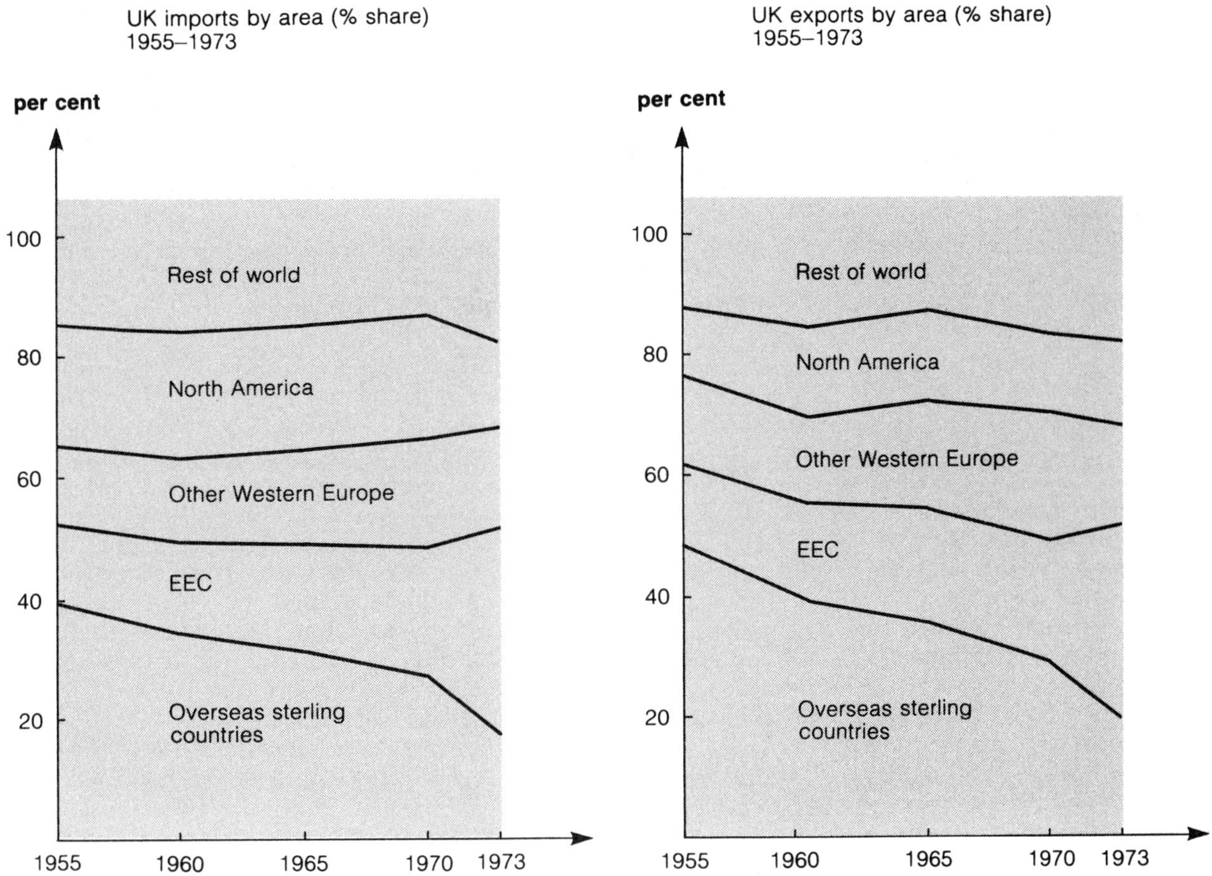

Figure 12.4 UK merchandise trade by area, 1955–73

Source: Annual Abstract of Statistics 1980, HMSO

prices from 1973, the oil exporting countries have taken an increasing share of UK trade, doubling from 6.4 per cent in 1973 to 12.8 per cent in 1978. Imports from the oil exporting countries increased dramatically from 1973 to 1974, 9.4 per cent to 16.2 per cent but since then the percentage share of imports has fallen to a level of 8.5 per cent in 1978. Other new classifications involve the developed countries and the developing countries (which include the former sterling area countries), and the centrally planned economies.

Other developed countries are South Africa, Japan, Australia and New Zealand. Oil exporting countries are Algeria, Libya, Nigeria, Gabon, Saudi Arabia, Kuwait, Bahrain, Qatar, Abu Dhabi, Dubai, the United Arab Emirates, Oman, Iraq, Iran, Brunei, Indonesia, Trinidad and Tobago, Venezuela and Ecuador. Other developing countries are Egypt, Ghana, Kenya, Tanzania, Zambia, Cyprus, Lebanon, Israel, Pakistan, India, Thailand, Malaysia, Singapore, Taiwan, Hong Kong, South Korea, Philippines, Jamaica, Mexico, Chile, Brazil, Argentina and other countries. Centrally planned economies are the Soviet Union, German Democratic Republic, Poland, Czechoslovakia, Romania, Hungary, Albania, Bulgaria, China, North Korea, Vietnam and Mongolia.

Imported from:	1973	1974	1975	1976	1977	1978	1979	1980	1981	1982
European Economic Community	33.0	33.2	36.4	36.6	38.4	40.5	44.6	41.4	42.5	44.4
Rest of Western Europe	17.0	14.9	14.7	14.7	15.1	17.1	15.4	14.6	15.3	14.7
North America	14.9	13.9	13.3	13.5	13.4	13.1	13.2	15.0	14.8	14.3
Other developed countries	9.2	7.2	7.9	6.8	7.3	6.9	6.5	6.8	7.2	7.8
Oil exporting countries	9.4	16.2	13.5	13.6	10.3	8.5	6.9	8.6	7.2	6.1
Other developing countries	12.8	11.4	11.2	11.3	11.8	10.7	10.9	11.4	11.0	10.4
Centrally planned economies	3.7	3.2	3.0	3.5	3.7	3.2	2.5	2.2	2.0	2.3

Table 12.8 United Kingdom imports, analysis by source; percentage share of total value

Source: *Annual Abstract of Statistics, 1980, 1984* HMSO

Exported to:	1973	1974	1975	1976	1977	1978	1979	1980	1981	1982
European Economic Community	32.5	33.3	32.3	35.6	36.6	37.8	43.0	43.4	41.4	41.7
Rest of Western Europe	18.2	17.7	16.9	16.5	16.9	15.3	13.7	14.5	12.4	12.1
North America	15.5	13.7	11.9	12.0	11.5	11.4	11.8	11.3	14.0	15.0
Other developed countries	9.7	10.2	9.4	7.6	6.3	6.3	6.4	5.6	5.8	5.9
Oil exporting countries	6.4	7.3	11.4	12.4	13.2	12.8	9.0	10.1	11.6	11.6
Other developing countries	14.4	14.6	14.8	13.1	12.8	13.5	13.2	12.3	12.3	11.9
Centrally planned economies	3.3	3.2	3.3	2.8	2.7	2.9	2.9	2.8	2.5	1.8

Table 12.9 United Kingdom exports, analysis by destination; percentage share of total value

Source: *Annual Abstract of Statistics, 1980, 1984* HMSO

Figure 12.5 concentrates on the share of UK trade with Europe which since 1976 has accounted for more than half of both exports and imports. The EEC countries referred to are the other eight member nations from 1978: France, Belgium, Luxembourg, Netherlands, Federal Republic of Germany, Italy, Irish Republic and Denmark. Western Europe involves the rest of the European nations, with the

1970		1978	
	%		%
1 United States	12.9	West Germany	11.0
2 Canada	7.5	United States	10.3
3 West Germany	6.2	France	7.8
4 Netherlands	5.1	Netherlands	6.2
5 France	4.1	Switzerland	5.3
6 Sweden	4.0	Italy	4.7
7 Irish Republic	3.7	Belgium and	4.5
8 Denmark	3.0	Luxembourg	
9 South Africa	2.9	Irish Republic	3.9
10 Australia	2.8	Norway	3.5
11 Italy	2.7	Sweden	3.3
12 Soviet Union	2.3	Japan	3.1
		Canada	2.7
Total	57.2		66.3

Table 12.10 The United Kingdom's principal import suppliers

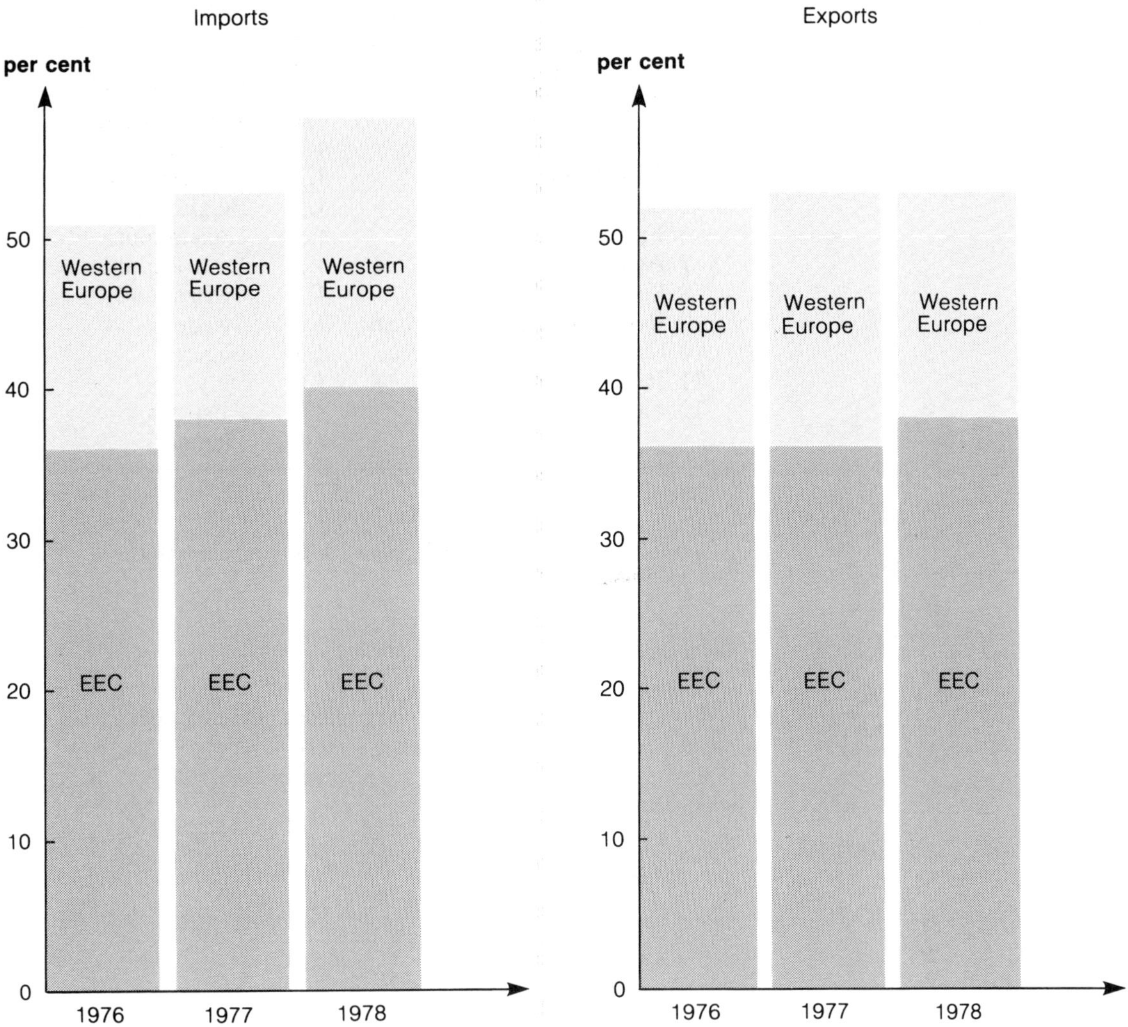

Figure 12.5 Share of UK trade with the EEC and Western Europe

Source: Annual Abstract of Statistics 1980, HMSO

major nations of Norway, Sweden, Finland, Switzerland, Austria, Portugal, Spain, Yugoslavia, Greece, Turkey being the most important.

Tables 12.10 and 12.11 concentrate on the relative importance of individual countries to the UK as principal suppliers or top export markets. Changes in positions in the lists and in the inclusion of new countries and the absence of former important trading partners are a consequence of trading and political realignments and affiliations. The influence of EEC membership can be seen in the improved positions of member countries in UK trade. West Germany especially has become the UK's major trading partner alongside the United States.

In 1978 the UK ranked as fifth in the list of the world's major trading nations (based on the trade of all industrial countries). This share of trade is approximately a half of the share of the trade of the United States. West Germany can be seen in Figure 12.6 to be the closest rival for top position as a trading nation.

1970		%	1978	%
1	United States	11.6	United States	9.3
2	West Germany	6.4	West Germany	8.3
3	Netherlands	4.75	France	6.8
4	Irish Republic	4.7	Netherlands	6.0
5	Sweden	4.5	Belgium and Luxembourg	5.9
6	France	4.3	Irish Republic	5.5
7	Australia	4.2	Switzerland	5.1
8	South Africa	4.1	Sweden	3.1
9	Belgium and Luxembourg	3.6	Nigeria	3.05
10	Canada	3.55	Italy	3.0
11	Italy	3.0	Australia	2.3
12	Denmark	2.7	Denmark	2.25
Total		57.4		60.6

Table 12.11 United Kingdom's top export markets

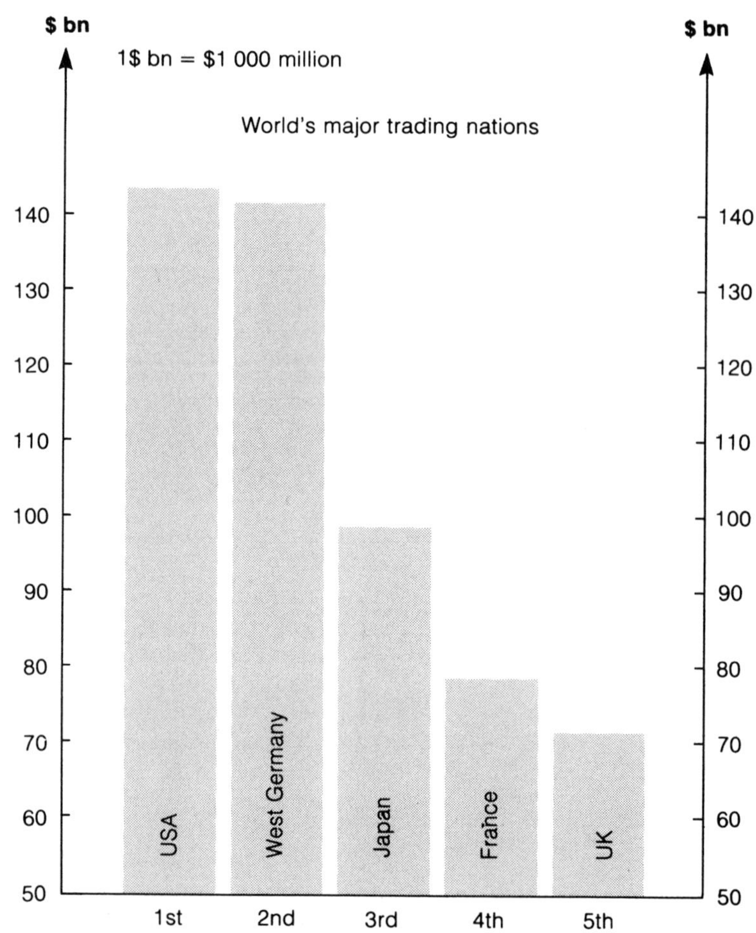

Figure 12.6 Shares of world trade, 1978

Source: Annual Abstract of Statistics 1980, HMSO

In the mid-nineteenth century the UK was unchallenged in world trade, but by the end of the century the United States and Germany were close rivals for overseas markets. Trade at that time largely followed a pattern of industrialised countries selling manufactured goods and obtaining primary products in return from non-industrialised nations. Trade between industrialised countries in manufactures has become a dominant feature of trade since the Second World War. It is not surprising that the UK has slipped back in relation to other nations in its share of world trade; it is important to remember that the volume of world trade has also increased at the same time that the percentage share has fallen.

12.3

Up to the 1 January 1970, in the UK trade statistics, re-exports were separately distinguished as a class on their own. Since then re-exports have been included with exports of UK produce.
1 Why might it be useful to distinguish between exports and re-exports in the trade figures?
2 What goods do you think are most likely to come into the category of re-exports?

12.4

From Figure 12.3 comment upon the relative shares of the commodities named as a proportion of imports and exports.

12.5

Compare the data in Table 12.4 and Table 12.5 on UK imports measured by value and by volume for the years 1970, 1975 and 1978. Does the data reveal any important differences between changes in import trade as measured by value and volume?

12.6

Explain why changes in trade value and in trade volume for the same years vary.

12.7

Compare the data on UK exports in Table 12.6 and Table 12.7 and comment on changes in value and volume.

The effects of sudden changes in trade

The loss of a source of imports or of an important export market can have far-reaching repercussions on a country's economy. Initially, its residents may suffer because of the time it will take to adjust to the new situation: moving perhaps from specialisation to self-sufficiency. Second, it may suffer in the long run because it may lose the gains it formerly enjoyed from trade. During the two world wars the population of the UK was threatened with starvation because of enemy attacks on merchant shipping which reduced imports of food and essential raw materials. Many people believe that an economy should be diversified to some extent as a precaution against such eventualities.

Effects of a fall in exports

The effects of a fall in the value of exports can be severe also. In the UK after 1929, the level of export trade declined in volume terms by over 2% per year on 1921–29. The return to the gold standard in 1925 created extra difficulties for exports, for the overvalued exchange rate meant that they were priced out of world markets. When the level of prices fell with the depression of the 1930s the effect of a falling volume of exports was to cause a dramatic fall in the value of exports. In the years 1925–29 exports and re-exports averaged £854 million. In 1930 the value fell to £666 million and continued to fall to £461 million in 1931 and £422 million in 1932 and 1933. Thus, in the years 1929 to 1932 the value of exports fell by a half. From 1934 to 1937 exports increased in value but only to a level of £606 million in 1937.

The major part of the decline in exports fell initially upon the two basic commodities cotton and coal, and the level of employment in those industries. Unemployment as a consequence rose in step with the fall in the level of demand, reaching unprecedented levels as world trade continued to slump and the effects became widespread throughout the economy.

An associated effect of a fall in the value of exports is that it is likely to reduce the size of a country's foreign exchange reserves and thus deprive it of the means to purchase the desired quantities of imports. This also occurred during the years of the depression. The problem in the UK was further heightened by the return to gold at far too high a level, with resultant pressure on reserves and a loss of confidence in sterling. Imports did decline in value after 1929 but were still at a much higher level than the value of exports. Consequently, the balance of trade was in deficit, which was not a new feature, but in the inter-war period, unlike the years before the First World War, invisible export earnings from the sales of services and from the returns from foreign investment were no longer sufficient to cover the trade deficit. Surpluses that previously had been available for reinvestment abroad were no longer made in the 1930s. The growth of invisible earnings was not able to meet the larger trade deficits resulting in the UK having to live on her capital.

Effects of a rise in exports

A sudden increase in the value of exports is likely to have the opposite effect. The export industries will derive an immediate benefit, with increasing incomes and profits. The effect of increased incomes depends upon which industries are the principal beneficiaries but bank deposits, the level of expenditure on capital formation, production levels and consumption expenditures are likely to increase. However, the increase in aggregate demand is likely to lead to a general increase in production and to the employment of any unused resources. Equally important, the level of bank liquidity is likely to increase and the capacity of the banking system to lend funds to those wishing to invest. Furthermore, the increase in foreign exchange may make it possible for imports to be increased.

It can happen that a country's economy may not be able to respond to the demands placed upon it for more goods and services following an increase in the value of exports. In such circumstances, the immediate effect will be to generate inflationary pressures and the extent to which these can be avoided will depend on the opportunities that exist for importing the required goods and services from abroad.

12.8

The value of UK trade for selected countries in 1970 and 1978 is shown below.

	1970 (£ million) Exports to:	Imports from:
USA	944.1	1186.4
West Germany	522.9	569.8
France	305.6	379.4
Irish Republic	328.7	343.6
Australia	346.1	260.2
Japan	148.6	134.7
Saudi Arabia	36.5	106.1
India	73.8	105.4
Total trade	8169.1	9163.3

	1978 (£ million) Exports to:	Imports from:
USA	3 477.2	4 222.6
West Germany	3 104.9	4 512.8
France	2 530.4	3 211.8
Irish Republic	2 044.8	1 606.3
Australia	856.3	349.1
Japan	542.3	1 283.2
Saudi Arabia	786.3	870.5
India	348.6	322.1
Total trade	37 362.7	40 969.1

1 From the information in the table, calculate the visible trade gap (surplus or deficit) for each of the countries listed for 1970 and 1978. Then list the countries in order of the amounts of surplus or deficit in trade for 1970 and 1978.
2 Comment on the changes in relative position of the countries revealed and also on changes in the amounts of the trade gap. These can be compared with the overall changes in import and export trade using the figures quoted for total UK trade.
3 What particular problems are posed for the UK in its trade with the countries in the list?

12.9

The share of imports as a percentage of total UK sales measures the degree of import penetration in the market. The table below shows imports as a percentage of total British sales 1975 for selected manufacturing industries

Electronic computers	68
Construction and earth-moving equipment	59
Paper and board	54
Radio and electronic components	44
Scientific and industrial instruments	43
Metal-working machine tools	41
Mechanical machinery	36
Man-made fibres	33

What explanations can you offer for the degree of import penetration revealed in the above figures? What factors will influence the amount of imports in the UK market?

12.10 Explain why a distinction is made in the analysis of UK trade by source between the developed countries, oil-exporting countries, developing countries and centrally planned economies.

12.11 From the data in Table 12.10 and Table 12.11, comment upon the major changes revealed in the importance of individual countries as UK suppliers and as UK markets. Compare the results with those obtained from question 12.8 which considered the visible trade gap between the UK and several selected countries.

The terms of trade

The benefits from international trade depend on the rate at which the goods and services produced by one country exchange for those produced by other countries. The more goods that can be imported in exchange for a quantity of home-produced goods the more favourable will be a country's terms of trade. If the trading situation changes so that the country's residents can obtain a larger quantity of imports for this given quantity of exports, the terms of trade are said to have improved, whilst if the quantity of imports that can be obtained for the given quantity of exports is reduced, the terms of trade are said to have deteriorated.

A common measure of changes in the terms of trade is the relative movement of export and import prices, for ordinarily, if the prices of imports fall relative to the prices of exports, the export receipts will allow the country's residents to purchase more imports. Alternatively, if the price of imports rises relative to the price of exports, receipts will finance a smaller quantity of imports.

Export and import price indices

In practice, a problem to be overcome when measuring the terms of trade is how to aggregate the prices and quantities of the many commodities that enter trade. Export and import price indices are constructed by weighting the various exports and imports based on their relative importance at some specified time or over a specified period. Changes in the actual prices of individual exports and imports are then reflected in movements of the relevant export price index or import price index. The terms of trade itself are expressed as an index number by dividing the export price index for any moment of time by the import price index number and multiplying by a hundred.

$$\text{Terms of trade} = \frac{\text{export price index}}{\text{import price index}} \times 100$$

Table 12.12 gives the export and import price indices and the terms of trade for the UK and the United States for the years 1970 to 1978. In the table the value for each export and import index for 1970 is 100. 1970 is the base year and all subsequent changes are measured against that year, which provides the basis for comparison. The fact that each index is 100 does not imply that prices 'were the same' in that year. There is no way in which they can be same. The selection of an appropriate base year for an index is extremely important. If prices are unusually low in the base year, this can give a misleading picture of subsequent events. One way of overcoming the problem is by selecting the average of a number of years as the base.

During the period 1970–72, the UK export price index increased by more than the import price index so that the terms of trade increased slightly. After this time, the import price index rose more rapidly than export prices resulting in a substantial deterioration in the terms of trade index. The United States' terms of trade over the same period fell also.

	United Kingdom			United States		
	Export price index	Import price index	Terms of trade	Export price index	Import price index	Terms of trade
1970	100.0	100.0	100.0	100	100	100
1971	105.6	104.7	100.9	103	105	98
1972	111.1	109.7	101.3	106	113	94
1973	126.0	139.9	90.1	124	133	93
1974	162.7	217.2	74.9	158	200	79
1975	198.5	246.1	80.7	176	217	81
1976	240.6	300.3	80.1	183	224	82

Table 12.12 Export and import price indices and terms of trade (1970 = 100)

Improvements in terms of trade does not necessarily mean improvement in international payments position

It is tempting to conclude that an improvement of a country's terms of trade must indicate that the country's international payments position is improving (that receipts are rising relative to payouts). Likewise, one might be led to think that a deterioration in a country's terms of trade must indicate that it faces international payments problems. Often this is not the case. For example, during the period 1963–70 the terms of trade index in the United States rose from 1963 = 100 to 108 in 1970. The terms of trade index for Australia in the same period declined from 100 in 1963 to 87 in 1970. Despite this movement, in Australia international trade increased and exports in volume rose more than imports and the Australian balance of payments improved. In contrast, the United States' terms of trade rose but was accompanied by rapidly rising foreign payments and an increasingly severe balance of payments problem.

Quantities exported and imported are every bit as important as prices when determining overall export receipts and import payments. The terms of trade index in Table 12.12 tells us nothing about the quantities actually imported and exported.

The reason for a country's payments problems may be the fact that the terms of trade are too much in its favour. If export prices are high relative to import prices, compared with some previous period, the country may be losing its competitive position. Its manufacturers may be pricing themselves out of world markets and the high prices that make the terms of trade appear so favourable may be the reason why the value of exports is falling.

Another reason why the terms of trade are not a good indicator of a country's overseas payments position is because of the many types of overseas receipts and payments it leaves out entirely: payments for services and movements of funds from one country to another are ignored.

A devaluation of a country's currency will have the effect of increasing its import prices and reducing its export prices thus producing a deterioration in the terms of trade. A rising exchange rate on foreign currency markets will have the opposite result on the terms of trade with the increase in export prices relative to the prices of imports. Although this may be a favourable movement in the terms of trade, too high a level of export prices may reduce competitiveness as outlined earlier.

12.12

The table provides information about the UK terms of trade index for 1970 to 1976, on the basis of 1970 equals 100. Compare these results with the figures for terms of trade in the following table on a basis of 1975 equals 100. Graph the terms of trade for 1970 to 1976 for both base years. What difference, if any, does this make to the results?

UK (1975 = 100)

	1967	1968	1969	1970	1971	1972
Exports price index	42.9	46.2	47.7	50.9	53.8	56.9
Imports price index	35.0	39.2	40.4	42.2	44.3	46.7
Terms of trade	122.7	117.9	118.1	120.6	121.7	121.8

	1973	1974	1975	1976	1977	1978
Exports price index	64.0	81.7	100.0	120.7	142.5	155.1
Imports price index	59.6	87.4	100.0	121.8	141.3	146.4
Terms of trade	107.4	93.5	100.0	99.1	100.8	105.9

12.13

For much of the 1950s and 1960s the terms of trade of countries exporting principally primary products fell. In contrast the terms of trade of industrial countries exporting manufactures rose. What are the underlying reasons for these trends in the terms of trade?

12.14

The UK motor industry

UK car output and exports 1967–1976, as number of vehicles, are shown in the table below.

	Output ('000s)	Exports ('000s)
1967	1552	503
1970	1641	690
1973	1747	599
1976	1333	496

1 Comment on changes in the figures for output and export of cars in the UK, and on changes in the proportion exported.
2 Research the latest figures for UK car output, exports and imports. (The Society of Motor Manufacturers and Traders regularly publish this information.)

1978 UK road vehicles exports and imports are shown (in £ million) by area in the table below.

	EEC	Rest of Europe	North America	Rest of world	Total
Exports to	1144.8	391.1	333.3	1200.4	3069.6
Imported from	1959.1	286.6	60.1	489.3	2795.1

3 What do the figures reveal about the pattern and nature of UK trade in 1978 for road vehicles? Is the UK a net exporter or importer of road vehicles in all areas?
4 The following tables measure the changes in volume and in unit value of UK road vehicle exports and imports (1975 = 100). Compare and comment upon the changes in export and import trade revealed. Are there any marked differences in volume and value of exports and imports?

	1970	1971	1972	1973	1974	1975	1976	1977	1978
Volume									
Exports	84	90	81	90	94	100	104	105	112
Imports	39	58	90	105	90	100	127	160	165
Unit Value									
Exports	53	59	62	67	79	100	123	153	163
Imports	50	54	62	71	83	100	128	155	194

12.15

During the period 1968–71, the United States' balance of payments situation changed from a small surplus (receipts exceeded payments) to one of heavy deficit. One of its principal trading partners, Japan, showed an increasing surplus in its balance of payments, largely as a result of its trade with the United States. The table below gives information on export and import prices in the countries during the period.

	United States			Japan		
Year	Export price index	Import price index	Payments surplus (+) deficit (–)	Export price index	Import price index	Payments surplus (+) deficit (–)
	1963 = 100		(US $m)	1963 = 100		(US $m)
1968	111	103	+1 641	102	100	+864
1969	115	106	+2 702	104	103	+800
1970	121	112	–9 839	110	106	+1 130
1971	125	118	–29 766	113	109	+10 336

Source: International Financial Statistics, International Monetary Fund, March 1973, Washington DC, 1974.

To what extent, if any, can the surplus and deficit in the two countries be explained by absolute or relative movements in their terms of trade?

12.16

Consider the following pairs of statements carefully, then explain how the two statements can be reconciled. Under what circumstances might such events occur together?

1 (a) a rise in export prices,
(b) a deterioration in the terms of trade.

2 (a) an improvement in the terms of trade,
(b) a deterioration (surplus to deficit) in the balance of payments situation.

3 (a) an improvement in the terms of trade,
(b) an improvement (deficit to surplus) in the balance of payments situation.

Chapter 13 The Balance of Payments

The discussion of trends in international trade in Chapter 12 ignored other types of overseas transactions. The level of these transactions has an important effect on the level of economic activity within a country and upon its capacity to buy goods and services from the residents of other countries. A full statement of UK residents' transactions with the residents of overseas countries is published annually by the Central Statistical Office, *United Kingdom: Balance of Payments*, also known as the '*Pink Book*'. Table 13.1 presents the main elements in the UK balance of payments statement for 1977 to 1980.

	1977	1978	1979	1980
Current account				
Exports (f.o.b.)	32 148	35 432	40 678	47 389
Imports (f.o.b.)	33 892	36 607	44 136	46 211
Balance of trade	–1 744	–1 175	–3 458	+1 178
Invisible credits	16 413	18 335	23 694	25 764
Invisible debits	14 376	16 128	21 099	23 736
Invisible balance	+2 037	+2 207	+2 595	+2 028
Balance on current account	+293	+1 032	–863	+3 206
Investment and other capital flows				
Official long term capital	–319	–348	–401	–125
Overseas investment in UK public sector	+2 182	–81	+4 307	+4 649
Overseas investment in UK private sector	+3 067	+2 770		
UK private investment overseas	–2 222	–4 087	–6 555	–6 891
*Other transactions	+1 846	–337	–	–
Import credit	+351	+243	+72	–238
Export credit	–613	–685	–849	–907
*Other short-term transactions	+114	–406	–	–
Total investment and other capital transactions	+4 406	–2 931	+2 177	–1 475
Balancing item	+2 662	+773	+396	–539
Balance for official financing	+7 361	–1 126	+1 905	+1 372

* Classified on a different basis in 1979, 1980 balance of payments accounts.

Table 13.1 UK balance of payments 1977–80 (£ *million*)

Source: *Annual Abstract of Statistics 1980, 1982;* Table 13

From Table 13.1, the UK can be seen to have experienced a marked difference on the balance of payments in 1977 and 1978. In both years a deficit on visible trade was converted into a surplus on current account through the positive invisible balance. In 1977 a large investment and capital inflow produced a balance for official financing of £7361m. In 1978 a capital outflow reduced the current account surplus leaving a deficit balance for official financing of £1126m. A deficit balance on official financing reduces foreign exchange reserves or incurs foreign borrowings and loans. This situation of a balance of payments deficit is therefore matched by a total net currency outflow. Conversely, a balance of payments surplus produces a net inflow of currency. The total currency flow is important because it represents the amount of foreign currency becoming available to a country.

Occasionally, one comes across statements to the effect that 'a country's balance of payments must always balance'. They refer to a particular way of presenting the accounts that requires that debits and credits offset one another. They do not mean that a country cannot spend overseas more than it receives from overseas sources or vice versa. If a country spends more overseas than it receives from overseas, the deficit must be accounted for in some way – by a reduction in its international reserves.

1 Balance of trade = exports of goods – imports of goods
2 Balance on current account = balance of trade + invisible balance
3 Balance for official financing (or total currency flow) = balance on current account + total investment flows + balancing item
4 Balance for official financing must be matched by official financing so that debits and credits offset each other

Table 13.2 Relationships in the balance of payments

Balance of payments problems

If a country has a persistent balance of payments deficit, it can be said to have a balance of payments problem. Its foreign exchange reserves will be falling and government will need to take action to prevent them becoming exhausted and to raise them to an acceptable level. The particular measures a government may adopt to deal with a balance of payments deficit will depend on the causes of the deficit. The deficit may have arisen because the country's residents are importing more goods and services than they are exporting, or it may be the result of an outflow of investment funds. In terms of relationship 3 (Table 13.2), the balance for official financing or the total currency flow may be in deficit because of the current account balance or because of a net capital outflow. This was the case in 1978 as Figure 13.1 shows.

Figure 13.1 shows the 'balance' between debits and credits on the UK balance of payments in 1978 yet still identifies the overall deficit.

If a country has a persistent balance of payments surplus it can also be said to have a balance of payments problem requiring government attention. It will be in the country's interests to resolve the problem, if possible. The continuing build-up of foreign exchange reserves is an indicator that while productive resources are being used to supply goods and services to foreign countries, the gains are not being used to obtain goods and services from other countries, which might raise living standards within the country experiencing the surplus. Figure 13.2 shows that the UK has experienced both types of balance of payments prob-

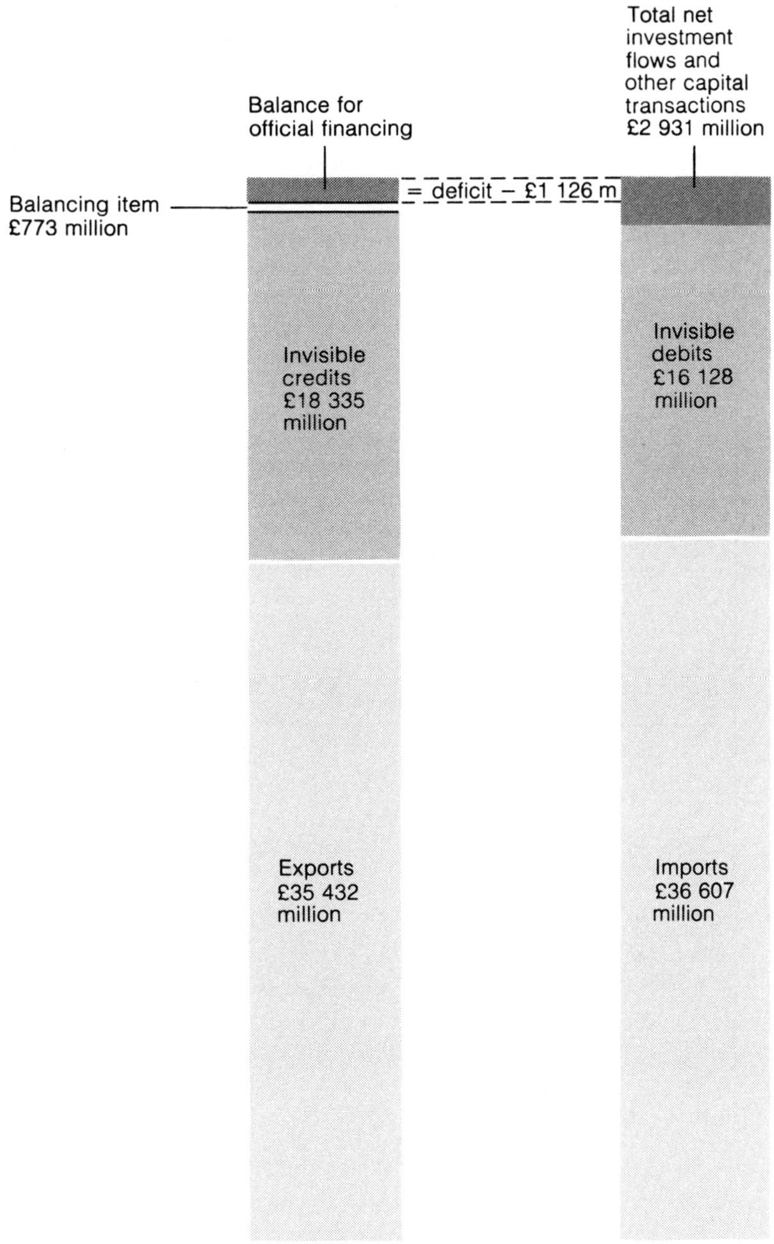

Figure 13.1 UK balance of payments, 1978

lems since 1967. In the early part of the period from 1967 to 1968 the total currency flow was outwards; from 1969 to 1971 a net inflow of currency was recorded; 1972 to 1976 saw a net outflow once more. The balance for 1977 and 1978 was shown in full in Table 13.1. The UK experience has more commonly been one of problems of balance of payments deficits.

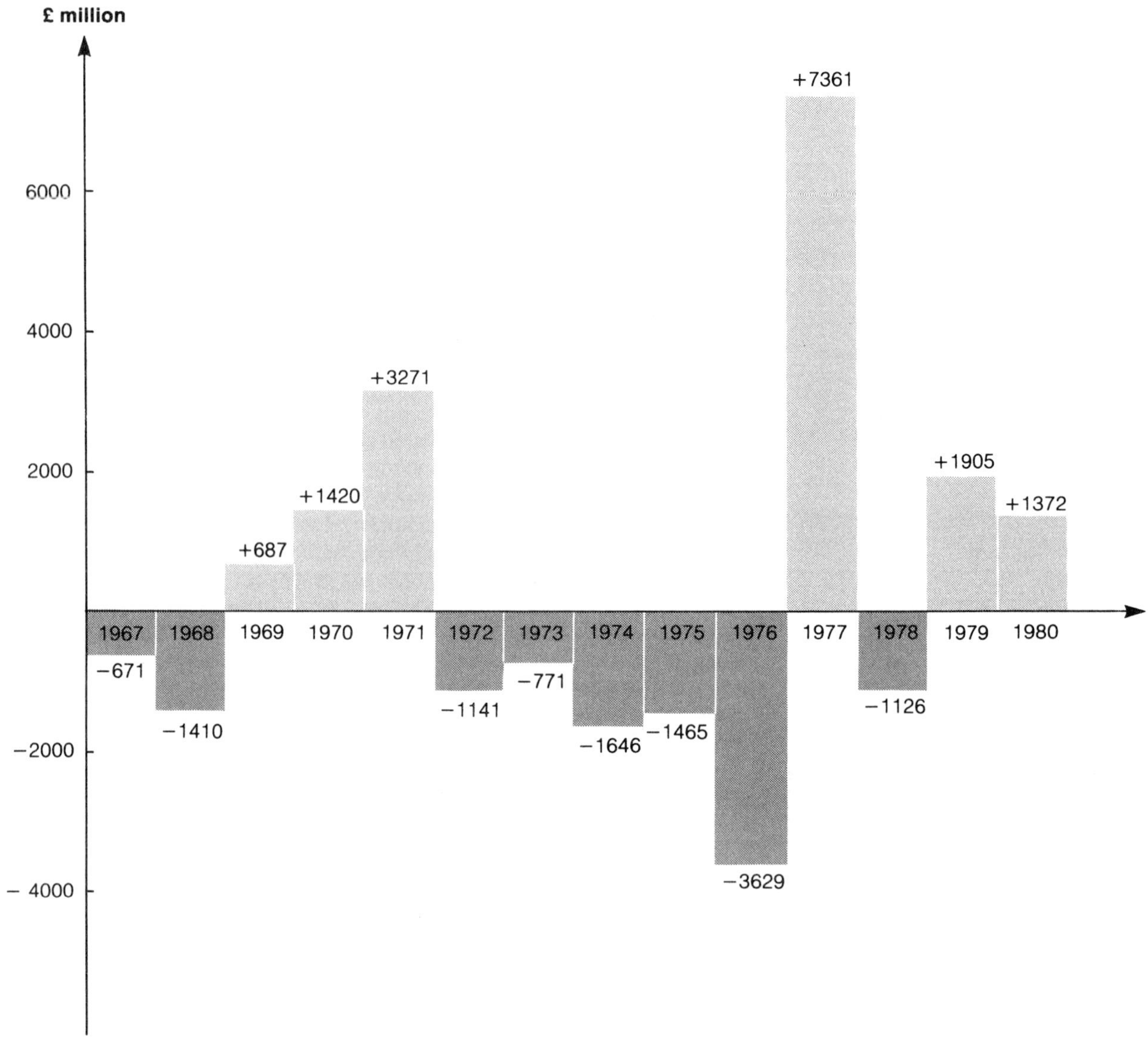

Figure 13.2 UK balance for official financing, 1967–80

Source: Annual Abstract of Statistics 1980, HMSO

Balance of trade

This is the difference between the value of merchandise exports (f.o.b.) and the value of merchandise imports (f.o.b.); f.o.b. stands for 'free on board' which is a term that indicates none of the freight and insurance costs and charges associated with the transportation of the product are included in the declared value. The term c.i.f. (cost, insurance and freight) is used whenever the transportation component is included in a declared value.

For the UK it is common to find that the visible balance, or balance

Importance of changes in balance of trade

of trade, is in deficit. In 1978 the deficit was £1175 m. Although merchandise trade is only one element in the balance of payments and it is therefore not necessary that it should be in surplus, governments normally pay particular importance to changes in the balance of trade. First, merchandise trade is by far the largest single item in total overseas transactions. Second, provisional statistics on exports and imports become available very soon after each trading period and thus provide an early indication of fluctuations in a country's current account balance and in its overall balance of payments position. Third, exports and imports are sensitive to, and reflect changes in, costs, prices and demand conditions within the country's economy and overseas. They thus assist government in the selection of internal economic policies.

In 1978, total receipts from overseas amounted to over £53 000m, of which over £35 000m was from merchandise exports, therefore comprising some two-thirds of the total.

Balance on current account

Relationship 2, Table 13.2, shows that this is obtained by adding the balance of trade (relationship 1) to 'net invisibles'. Net invisibles, or invisible credits less invisible debits, or invisible exports less invisible imports, is the positive, or negative, balance of receipts over payments from current transactions involving services and transfer payments. The term 'invisible' distinguishes such transactions from 'visible', that is, material or tangible, merchandise trade.

The invisible balance or, net invisibles, consists of three main items: services; interest, profits and dividends; and transfers. Services consist of items such as finance, banking and insurance, transport and travel, and many others provided by the government, private companies and

	Credit	Debit	Net
Services			
General government	318	1 015	− 697
Sea transport	3 163	3 334	− 171
Civil aviation	1 448	1 100	+ 348
Travel	2 503	1 548	+ 955
Financial services	1 488	–	+1 488
Other	3 284	1 918	+1 366
Interest profits and dividends			
General government	766	1 222	− 456
Private sector and public corporations	4 281	2 989	+1 292
Transfers			
General government	454	2 154	−1 700
Private sector	630	848	− 218
Total	18 335	16 128	+2 207

Note Financial services separately classified as a credit item but not as a debit item

Table 13.3 Principal invisible credits and debits in UK balance of payments current account 1978 (£ million)

Source: *Annual Abstract of Statistics, 1980* and *1982*, HMSO individuals and public corporations. Services are the most important element of the invisibles account and contribute about two thirds of invisible earnings or credits, and over a half of invisible debits. Interests, profits and dividends represent earnings from direct investments overseas and interest received on official reserves on the credits side. The main debit items are profits of foreign companies in the UK and interest payments to foreigners. Transfers represent, for the central government, payments to and receipts from the EEC budget and also aid grants to developing countries. Private transfers refer to such items as donations, gifts, migrants' transfers of assets and so on.

Importance of invisibles

The traditional pattern of the UK current account has been a visible trade deficit partly or wholly offset by a surplus on the invisibles account. From 1947 to 1979 there was a visible trade surplus for only three years, but there has been a surplus on invisibles every year since 1947. More recently the invisibles surplus has declined as a result of increased payments made overseas, which has meant that invisible debits have increased faster than the continuing increase in invisible credits. Invisibles as a whole now amount to approximately one third of all trade earnings and payments

A large part of the invisibles surplus is due to the earnings of UK financial, banking, insurance services and from transport and travel. As a result of these and other net invisible earnings, the UK has the second largest invisible surplus in the world after the United States. Some countries with traditionally large visible trade surpluses, such as the German Federal Republic and Japan, also have deficits on invisibles which to some extent offset the trade surplus.

Current account equilibrium

Large deficits on the current account were recorded in 1973 to 1976 in the UK as a direct result of increasing oil prices. With the development and production of North Sea oil supplies, the UK is faced with the prospect of being able to record a balance of trade surplus rather than the customary deficit, which, with the surplus on the invisible balance presents a current account surplus. This reduces the policy constraint on governments which have been imposed in the past with current account deficits. A deficit on the current account can be viewed in different ways. In the short term, the deficit need not be a cause of worry or alarm. If the problem is one of recurring deficits, then this is more serious in its implications for the structure and level of demand in the economy, the competitiveness of home producers with those overseas, the employment prospects and investment in domestic industries and so on. Some economists have maintained that it is the total currency flow position that is important, for this represents the overall balance of payments position. This is discussed later.

Exchange rates

Restoring equilibrium on the balance of payments from a position of surplus or deficit is much influenced by the system of exchange rates in operation. With a fixed exchange rate, the level of official reserves, borrowings or loan repayments, are directly affected by the balance of payments overall position. A floating exchange rate is determined by the relative supply of and demand for the currency on the exchange markets. Deficits and surpluses on the balance of payments have an immediate bearing upon the amounts of currency made available on the exchange markets and therefore on the value on the exchange rate. This is discussed more fully in Chapter 17.

Balance for Official Financing

Relationship 3 in Table 13.2 introduces investment and capital flows and the balancing item to the consideration of a country's overall position relative to its dealings with the rest of the world. The Balance for Official Financing indicates the overall flow of currency to the economy. It is this balance which has to be met or accounted for in some way. The way in which a deficit has been financed, or a surplus disposed of, is revealed in the figures for Official Financing.

	1975	1976	1977	1978
Borrowing from IMF and other monetary authorities (loan (+)/repayment (–))	–	+984	+1 113	–1 016
Foreign currency borrowing	+810	+1 792	+1 114	– 187
Official reserves (drawings on (+) additions to (–))	+655	+ 853	–9 588	+2 329
Official Financing	+1 465	+3 629	–7 361	+1 126
Balance for Official Financing	–1 465	–3 629	+7 361	–1 126

Table 13.4 Official Financing, UK, 1975–78 (£ million)

Source: Annual Abstract of Statistics, 1980, HMSO

Table 13.4 provides information on the total currency flow for the UK from 1975 to 1978 as shown by the Balance for Official Financing.

That balance has then to be provided for in the Official Financing figures. Any loans from bodies, such as the IMF and other monetary authorities, are shown as a positive item; repayments of past borrowings are a negative item. If the official reserves have to be drawn upon to meet a net currency outflow then this appears as a positive item, showing that the reserves are providing the necessary funds. A net currency inflow allows the possibility of increasing the official reserves, which is shown by a negative sign in Official Financing. Therefore Official Financing matches by an equal amount, but an opposite sign, the balance representing the total currency flow. Thus, in 1978 the deficit of £1126m was accounted for by drawing £2329m from the official reserves, after repayments of loans of £1016m and of £187m of foreign currency. In 1977 the surplus of £7361m was used to build up the official reserves by £9588m, with the UK borrowing £2227m.

Investment and capital flows

Table 13.1 shows clearly the importance of investment and capital flows in determining the total currency inflow or outflow, which may be in marked contrast to the current account balance. In 1977 a current account balance of £293m became a currency flow of +£7361m, but a current account surplus of £1032m in 1978 resulted in a net outflow of –£1126m. Table 13.1 highlights the importance of foreign investment flows, whether overseas investment in the UK public and private sectors, or investment by UK citizens in firms and projects overseas. A net inflow of investment in 1977 was largely responsible for the large currency inflow recorded. In 1978 the inflow of investment was much reduced, particularly in the UK public sector, while investment overseas by UK citizens increased and this was largely responsible for reversing the current account surplus.

Two points of explanation are necessary here. First, the term 'capital' is used here, and elsewhere in the balance of payments statement, to refer to a money flow and not to a movement of man-made resources or to a monetary measure of such a movement. Second, the inclusion of the 'balancing item' needs explanation. The accounting system adopted requires that surpluses and deficits on the current account and capital account should balance, in a formal manner, the monetary movements in the official financing statistics.

The figures for Official Financing can be measured accurately, but recording many of the items in both the current account and the capital account is much more difficult. Estimates are required, errors and omissions occur and problems of when to record transactions result in discrepancies in the official record. Consequently, it is necessary to add a balancing item so that relationship 4 in Table 13.2 holds.

Foreign investment

There is some controversy as to whether the effect of foreign investment in the UK has in recent years been of net benefit to the balance of payments. The recycling of oil surpluses from oil exporting nations in the 1970s and the influx of foreign capital in the North Sea oilfields, for example, has had important consequences for the balance of payments in the UK. The outflow of funds representing profits earned by foreign investors may cause problems in years to come after the initial benefit of the inflow of capital. Private sector capital has been exported from the UK and has caused some concern resulting in restrictions and controls on such capital investment overseas, from time to time.

Costs and benefits of foreign investment

The effects of foreign investment are quite complex in the economy. They go beyond the purely nationalistic concerns of ownership of assets and control by foreign companies and non-residents of the UK. A net outflow of investment will mean that domestic investment is lower than would otherwise be the case if the direct investment overseas is at the expense of domestic investment. This situation leads to a reduction in the level of economic activity in the economy and consequent potential harmful effects on the level of output and employment. Substantial investment flows, both long term and short term, have an effect on the exchange rate and may be destabilising. Short-term capital flows may be purely speculative in nature and put strain on the official reserves as investors react to their expectations of changes in the value of currency.

Overseas investment stimulates demand in the economy as multina-

Multinational corporations

tional corporations and foreign companies set up subsidiaries in the UK. This will obviously benefit output and employment directly as well as allowing the importation of new technologies and management skills. There may be at the same time, undesirable aspects of increased foreign ownership and control of capital and enterprises, for the multinational corporation will make decisions to bring maximum benefit to the overseas parent company and its shareholders. Consequently, decisions are less likely to be in the general interest of the UK than if the company were UK-owned and controlled. For example a multinational corporation may decide to allocate export markets between its various subsidiaries and the parent company, thus restricting the opportunities of its UK subsidiary to develop export markets as fully as might otherwise be possible. Worse still, in the event of world recession, the multinational corporation might decide to maintain full production in the parent company and cut back the operations of the subsidiaries, thus exporting unemployment. Then again, the multinational company may compel its subsidiaries to purchase materials from the parent, or another subsidiary, and this may restrict trade opportunities for other UK firms. It has also been suggested that multinational corporations are in a position to minimise taxation obligations by arranging their trading profits in each country in an appropriate manner; by perhaps importing materials from one subsidiary at a high nominal cost, making a low profit on the UK operation and therefore paying low company tax, but making a high profit in the country from which materials were imported and in which company taxes are low. This 'transfer pricing' is very difficult to determine in practice and to control. By such arranged prices, foreign firms may gain an additional competitive advantage over local firms.

13.1

Table 13.1 compares the main components in the UK balance of payments for 1977 to 1980.
1 Summarise the major changes in the table in the balance of trade and in the balance of payments on current account.
2 What evidence is there to support the view that the balance of payments had improved in 1980?
3 Research more recent balance of payments figures for the major items of balance of trade, invisible balance, current balance, total investment and capital flows, balancing item and the balance for official financing. Compare these figures with Table 13.1 and consider the changes since the 1980 position. Have the balance of payments positions improved or deteriorated since then?

13.2

Figure 13.1 shows in diagram form the balance of payments position in 1978 as given in Table 13.1.
1 Using the 1980 figures in Table 13.1 draw a similar diagram to Figure 13.1.
2 Draw a diagram of the balance of payments for the most recent year available as researched in question 13.1.

13.3

When trade issues are discussed in the press and the external balance of payments situation considered it is often the case that popular attention rests almost exclusively on the trade in merchandise (ie. trade in visibles) and ignores trade in services (invisibles). Write a short, clear statement outlining the relative importance of the 'invisibles' account to the UK balance of payments.

13.4

Using concepts of opportunity costs and comparative advantage, explain the nature and structure of the balance of payments accounts in the UK in terms of the surpluses and deficits recorded. From a study of the balances recorded, where does the UK's comparative advantage appear to lie?

13.5

To what extent do deficits in visible trade mean that a country is unable to pay its way in international trade?

13.6

Consider the following solutions to long term deficits on the balance of payments and explain how, in practical terms, these changes may be encouraged or brought about.

1 increasing exports of merchandise from the UK
2 increasing invisible earnings by the UK
3 increasing foreign investment in the UK
4 decreasing capital outflow from the UK

Consider the relative advantages and disadvantages of the suggested changes and make out a reasoned argument for a change in government policy to incorporate the measures you favour. Are there any other practical policy suggestions that you could make as alternatives to those above?

13.7

Overseas investment in the UK can take the form of foreign takeovers of existing UK owned and controlled firms, or new investment establishing new industries. Try to think of the relative advantages and disadvantages of each form of investment. Are there any circumstances in which a foreign takeover of an existing firm might be beneficial? Are there any circumstances in which the establishment of a new industry under foreign control might not be beneficial?

13.8

Discuss the proposition that too much foreign investment will lead to too much foreign ownership and control. If this is the case, then does this mean that foreign investment should be discouraged if not prevented?

13.9

Does the operation of multinational corporations differ markedly from that of any large-scale commercial enterprise in a single country? How might a multi-national corporation act against the public interest? In what ways could the operation of a multinational company in a single country be controlled or made more responsible to that country's domestic policies?

13.10

Explain briefly how a multi-national corporation could use a policy of 'transfer pricing' to maximise its profits in one country to the detriment and disadvantage of another country.

Chapter 14

Government in the UK

The part a government can play in the operation of a modern economic system was outlined in Chapter 4 (see page 59). This chapter deals in more detail with a number of aspects of the economic role of government in the UK. In addition to the fundamental tasks of being responsible for the defence and security of the nation and for maintaining law and order, government influences the operation of the economy in three main ways:

The government and the economy

by engaging in productive activity,

by redistributing income through taxation and social welfare programmes,

by assuming responsibility for the overall management of the economy.

The government sector engages in the production of goods and services. For example, in the UK, local and central government provide postal services, electric power, transportation, water supplies and sewerage, refuse collection and disposal, broadcasting, and produce aircraft and defence equipment. Some of these activities, such as railways and postal services, are administered by nationalised industries and public corporations. In general, these bodies have a much greater degree of autonomy, and are not as directly accountable to Parliament in the way that government departments are. The criteria under which state-run industries operate vary from industry to industry but they seldom operate on the same profit-maximising lines as private business enterprises. In particular there is an emphasis on the quality of services provided to customers. The operation of these publicly-owned businesses was referred to in Chapter 8.

Social welfare

Government policies have an important direct effect on the living standards of the population of the UK. Governments have gradually responded to appeals that the living standards of the less affluent should be increased and have instituted social welfare policies designed to improve health, education and living conditions. To enable it do this the government has increased government spending as a proportion of gross domestic product and has increased taxation to raise the necessary funds. The result has been a redistribution of income from more affluent to less affluent groups in the population. Much of this chapter deals with the ways government spends money in the UK, how it raises this money and the conflicts produced by the claims of competing groups in the community.

Management of the economic system

Governments since the 1940s have taken responsibility for the management of the economic system. Today the government of the UK places a high priority on the reduction of the rate of inflation. Other closely related objectives include the reduction of unemployment and an increase in living standards, a faster rate of economic growth and a satisfactory balance of payments position.

With an increasing understanding of the way in which an economic system operates came a growing awareness of the ways in which economic stability could be achieved and economic growth promoted.

This led successive UK governments to seek and use a variety of economic policy instruments, ranging from direct wartime controls to monetary and fiscal weapons such as changes in interest rates, the regulation of borrowing and lending, changes in taxation rates and in the level of government spending. In recent years much attention has been paid to the use of direct government price and income controls as a means of controlling inflation at an acceptable level.

The effectiveness of the various instruments and economic policies used to control the level of economic activity cannot properly be appreciated without first understanding the way in which the UK economy operates, and this in turn calls for an understanding of the relationship between consumption, investment, production and employment. This set of relationships is discussed in the following chapter. Government economic policies are discussed in Chapters 16, 17 and 20.

Local and central government

Government in the UK operates at two levels. Central government at national level works through Parliament, government departments and the civil service making decisions and implementing policy for the UK as a whole; local government is more concerned with the direct local needs of the community through the local authority, whether at district, county or metropolitan area level. Local government is partly independent of central government in being able to raise revenues for its spending in its own right through the rates and fees and charges for its services. Central government also makes available additional finance through grants to the local authorities known as rate-support grants. Local authorities are also constrained by law to provide certain services and forms of welfare such as education, law and order and so on.

Any discussion of the economic role of government is largely concerned with the activities of the central government because of its financial importance and because of the powers it possesses to influence the aggregate level of economic activity. The government is able to use these powers to manage the economy, such as in determining fiscal and monetary policies, or even to control the level of incomes and prices.

Public goods

There are a number of goods and services provided in the economy by the public sector which are known as *public goods* or collective consumption goods. Perhaps the best example of such a good or service is that of national defence but the same principle would also apply to street lighting, lighthouses, waterworks and sewage plants and so on. In each of these examples, the problem of provision is only solved by a public body of some sort since, under the private sector and a profit motive, it is unlikely that these facilities could be provided. There would be problems of how and what to charge for such provision, how to prevent 'non-payers' from benefiting from the services provided for all and how to ensure an adequate level of provision if left to the market mechanism. Consequently, central or local government takes on the responsibility for these goods and services and the attendant obligation of providing the necessary finance through taxation or rates.

Merit goods

There are, in addition, other goods and services such as health care and education which could, in some circumstances, be provided for by the price mechanism and indeed are to some extent by private sector medicine, hospitals and schools. Provision of these services by private insurance schemes is common in some countries eg. USA, Australia, and the private medical insurance sector in the UK is growing through schemes such as BUPA. The central problem for the authorities in the case of these *merit goods* is to ensure sufficient and adequate provision for all citizens. If left entirely to the price mechanism, a situation could arise where the poor and less advantaged might be prevented by lack of income from benefiting to the extent deemed necessary. In such instances the state takes on the role of provider in full or part because these goods or services are felt desirable, or of merit. Alternatively these services can be provided by the state or privately but heavily subsidised and financed out of taxation. Clearly the results of such activities are to redistribute income and ensure a more equitable distribution of welfare than would otherwise be the case.

14.1

In the UK, policy decisions are made by Parliament and unlike other advanced industrial nations there is no written constitution which sets the powers of government within a specific legal framework. On rare occasions, the UK has made use of the referendum for settling issues – on the decision to enter the EEC for example. Generally, the UK political system is not in favour of the regular use of referenda to determine government policy on important matters. What arguments might be advanced for and against the use of referenda to determine policy on national issues?

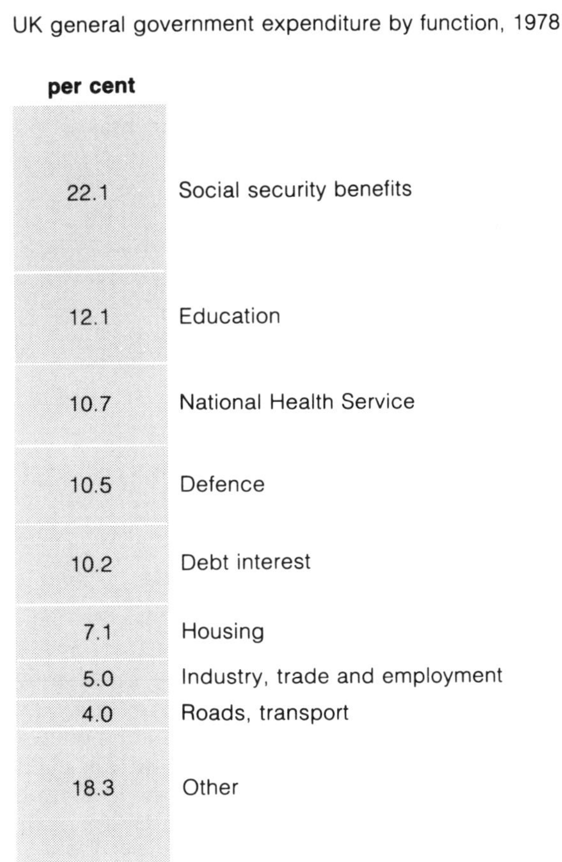

Figure 14.1 UK general government expenditure by function, 1978

Government spending

In 1978 the UK government spent in total about £71 000 million which represented about 50 per cent of GDP. Figure 14.1 shows the principal ways in which government spending was allocated to different items of state activity. About a half of government expenditure consists of transfer payments such as pensions and grants, subsidies and debt interest which are eventually spent by the private sector on goods and services. The major items of government expenditure are social security benefits, defence, education and the National Health Service. Debt interest represents the payments that the government makes to holders of government stock as part of the borrowing by the government when its expenditures exceed its revenues. The National Debt represents the total amount of such borrowings and the payment of interest due on this amount is known as servicing the National Debt.

	£ million
Social services:	
Social security	15 361
Education, libraries, science, arts	8 722
Health and personal social services	8 233
Defence and external relations (UK):	
Defence	6 868
Overseas aid and services	1 762
Commerce and industry:	
Agriculture, fisheries, food, forestry	845
Trade, industry, energy, employment	3 232
Environmental services:	
Roads, transport	2 782
Housing	5 006
Other	3 047
Law, order, protective services	2 092
Other services	1 889
Government lending to nationalised industries	1 100
Northern Ireland*	2 020
Total programmes	62 958
Contingency reserve	41
Debt interest	2 200
Total public Expenditure	65 199

*Including the other services shown above except defence and external relations

Table 14.1 Public expenditure 1978–79

Source: Britain: An Official Handbook, 1980, HMSO

Social security

National Insurance

Government policy over the years has been to improve the level of welfare, health standards and the standard of living of disadvantaged groups in the community. Table 14.1 indicates the level of spending in this area by the state. The principal cash social services payments are pensions, sickness benefit, unemployment benefit, supplementary benefit and child benefit. The National Insurance scheme covers many benefits by payments from a national insurance fund provided from contributions from employed people and their employers, the self-employed and the government. Other benefits are financed from general taxation.

Pensions

State retirement pensions are payable to women at the age of 60 and to men at the age of 65. Since 1978, a graduated pension scheme has also been in operation to provide an earnings-related pension in addition to the basic pension. Changes in pensions, which are paid at single and at married rates, are announced in the annual budget. Since 1975 retirement pensions and certain other benefits have been 'index-linked', i.e. increased annually in line with increases in the level of retail prices, or average earnings whichever was the greater. This has been done to protect the real value of the benefit given.

Sickness benefit and unemployment benefit

Contributory benefits are payable to those who are unable to work because of sickness or who find themselves unemployed. The rates of benefit actually payable are similar whether for sickness or unemployment. Various regulations and restrictions determine for how long benefit may be paid and the conditions for claiming them. Since these are contributory benefits, certain conditions regarding the level of contributions made within a specified period determine the entitlement to benefit.

Supplementary benefit

In cases of absolute need anyone who does not have enough money to live on may be entitled to supplementary benefit. The amount of benefit paid is determined by calculation of needs, as defined by certain rules and conditions, and is paid to supplement other income or benefits such as pensions or sickness benefit. Family income supplement (FIS) is a cash benefit payable to families on low incomes as defined by the current rules and conditions. Other benefits are automatic with the payment of FIS such as free school meals, free milk for children under school age, exemption from prescription charges etc.

Child benefit

The main form of benefit for children is in the form of a non-contributory payment for each child, paid weekly at post offices to the mother of the child or children. Special provisions are made for single-parent families, or for payment to whoever is responsible for bringing up a child whether the mother or another person. Child benefit is payable up to the age of 16 and for those up to 19 if still in full-time education. This benefit is payable for all children irrespective of the level of parental income or need, and is also tax-free.

Other benefits

There is a wide range of other benefits payable to people in particular circumstances or need, such as maternity benefit, widows' benefit, industrial injuries benefit, mobility allowances for disabled people, attendance and invalid care allowances for those looking after the disabled, war pensions, invalidity pensions and so on. Together all these forms of benefits and welfare payments provide a basic social security system which deals with many of the problems of disadvantaged people in society. The social security system therefore provides a basic standard of living for people in financial need. Other social services provide for other cases of need and care such as for the elderly, disabled people, the handicapped, children in need, and so on. The National Health Service provides medical facilities and treatment. In all, the social welfare system in the UK provides a comprehensive coverage for many different aspects of need.

In 1978 total spending on social welfare in the UK was: social security £15 786m, health £7615m and personal social services £1390m.

National Health Service

The National Health Service (NHS) in the UK is based upon the principle that medical care and treatment should be freely available to all at little or no cost. The only qualification for treatment is that of need. Financing the NHS is partly on a contributions basis as the rest of the National Insurance scheme, but most of the funds come from general taxation. Some items, prescriptions for example, are charged for by the NHS which makes a small addition to revenue. The NHS has encountered many problems: shortage of resources, an increasing demand for services and medicines, disparities in health provision in different regions and increasing costs with more advanced equipment and drugs.

14.2

The NHS makes a charge for its items and medicines provided on prescription. Exemptions are made for children, old people, expectant mothers and the long-term sick. It has been argued that imposing prescription charges, rather than providing items entirely free, encourages a more efficient use of resources. How would you as an economist discuss and demonstrate this argument? Can you show by a simple demand and supply diagram the main point of the argument involved here? Explain the likely nature of the supply curve for medical care if provided entirely free.

14.3

As an economist, what contribution can you make to the discussion of the advantages and disadvantages of a private health care system in the UK operating alongside the NHS?

1 What type of health care system would develop if left solely to private enterprise?

2 On what criteria would health care be provided?

3 What effect would there be on the allocation of resources and on efficiency in the health care industry if a free enterprise system replaced the NHS?

14.4

Child benefit is payable for every child in the UK by the State. Discuss the argument involved in providing a benefit such as this regardless of the family's level of income as opposed to paying a higher rate of benefit on a selective basis to families who can be identified as in special need or disadvantaged.

14.5

To what extent do you consider that the payment of unemployment benefits may act as a disincentive to the unemployed to find employment? What arguments can you find to support or refute this view? Which can be said to have economic substance? Which depend on value judgements and opinion? What data or evidence would be required to analyse such a proposition rigorously?

14.6

Consider the arguments for and against each of the following proposals for social welfare measures:
1 that unemployed persons be required to work on projects for voluntary agencies
2 that pension increases be index-linked to changes in the Retail Prices Index
3 that all forms of benefits be index-linked
4 that an income test be introduced for child benefits to make the benefit a selective one
5 that benefits be not paid to workers and their families when on strike
6 that abortions should not be provided on the NHS.
Which of the arguments can be said to have economic substance? Which depend on an appeal to social or moral values?

Government revenue

Taxation is main source of revenue

Taxation, of one sort or another, is the principal source of revenue for the government. In 1980–81 the forecast receipts of general government were as given in Table 14.2. Income tax can be seen as an important source of revenue providing approximately one third of all receipts. Expenditure taxes (including rates) contribute about 42 per cent of forecast receipts and include VAT, excise duties, custom duties, rates etc. Over the years, there have been changes in the tax balance representing the proportions of taxation accounted for direct taxes, i.e. taxes on income and indirect taxes, i.e. taxes on spending.

	£'000 million
Taxes on income	31.5
Taxes on expenditure (including rates)	40.0
National Insurance contribution	14.5
Taxes on capital	1.0
All other receipts	8.0
Total	95.0

Table 14.2 General government receipts, 1980/81, UK

During the early and mid 1970s, taxation on income tended to increase relatively and taxation on expenditure decreased relatively, in other words the tax balance shifted in favour of direct rather than indirect taxation. With tax changes in the budget of 1979 the balance was deliberately shifted the other way towards a greater proportion of indirect taxation as part of government policy. The implications of such a shift from one form of taxation to another are considered later in this chapter.

Purposes and principles of taxation

Four main purposes of taxation can be distinguished:
to raise revenue, in order
to provide services and public goods,
to permit the redistribution of incomes,
to allow government to increase or reduce aggregate demand for goods and services by altering the disposable income available.

Adam Smith's canons of taxation

One of the earliest attempts to frame a guiding set of principles on which to base a taxation system was made by Adam Smith in *Wealth of Nations*.[1] His principles, or 'canons' of taxation were designed to allow a given sum of money to be collected with as little disturbance to economic activity as possible. He emphasised:

1 *equity* – that residents of a state should contribute taxes in proportion to their income and hence their ability to pay;

	£ million
Total Inland Revenue	*26 590*
Income tax	19 655
Surtax	10
Corporation tax	4 850
Petroleum revenue tax	730
Capital gains tax	390
Development land tax	20
Estate duty	25
Capital transfer tax	360
Stamp duties	550
Total Customs and Excise	*18 250*
Value Added Tax	8 325
Oil	2 900
Tobacco	2 550
Spirits, beer, wine, etc	2 400
Betting and gaming	410
Car tax	510
Other excise duties	10
Customs duties etc	860
Agricultural levies	285
Other taxation – vehicle excise duties	1 148
National Insurance surcharge	2 952
Miscellaneous receipts	
Broadcast receiving licence	383
Interest and dividends	310
Other	1 380
Total	51 013

Table 14.3 Taxation and miscellaneous receipts, UK, 1979–80

Source: *Britain: An Official Handbook, 1980*, HMSO

2 *certainty* – of the time at which the payment is due, the amount to be paid and the way in which the assessment is made;

3 *convenience* – so that time of payment and manner of payment are selected in such a way that disadvantage to the taxpayer is minimised;

4 *economy* – in collection, so that the taxes selected are those that bring in the required revenue with as little administrative cost as possible.

These canons of taxation remain a useful guide when the essential purpose of taxation is solely to raise revenue. In general, tax-collecting authorities have adopted the second, third and fourth principles. Collection of income tax in the UK by the Inland Revenue is mainly operated through the pay-as-you-earn system (PAYE), whereby the employer deducts the income tax payable from the wages and salaries of employees and pays the tax authorities. Self-employed persons and businesses deal direct with the Inland Revenue. Expenditure taxes, such as VAT and excise duties, are paid by producers, wholesalers and retailers, where appropriate, which minimises the disadvantage to the tax-payer and economises collection costs.

The extent to which the first principle is accepted today needs to be interpreted rather carefully and related to the other main taxation purposes – income redistribution and the control of aggregate demand. It is accepted that the more affluent members of society should, in general, pay higher rates of taxation than the poor; the extent to which they do so in a modern system makes possible some redistribution of income.

Proportional and progressive tax

It is normal to distinguish between the proportional taxation referred to by Adam Smith and *progressive* and *regressive* forms of taxation. A *proportional tax* is one for which the total tax paid by the person, or company, varies in direct proportion to the income or amount on which the tax is assessed. Thus, a person on double the income will pay double the tax. Another way of defining a proportional tax is by saying that the

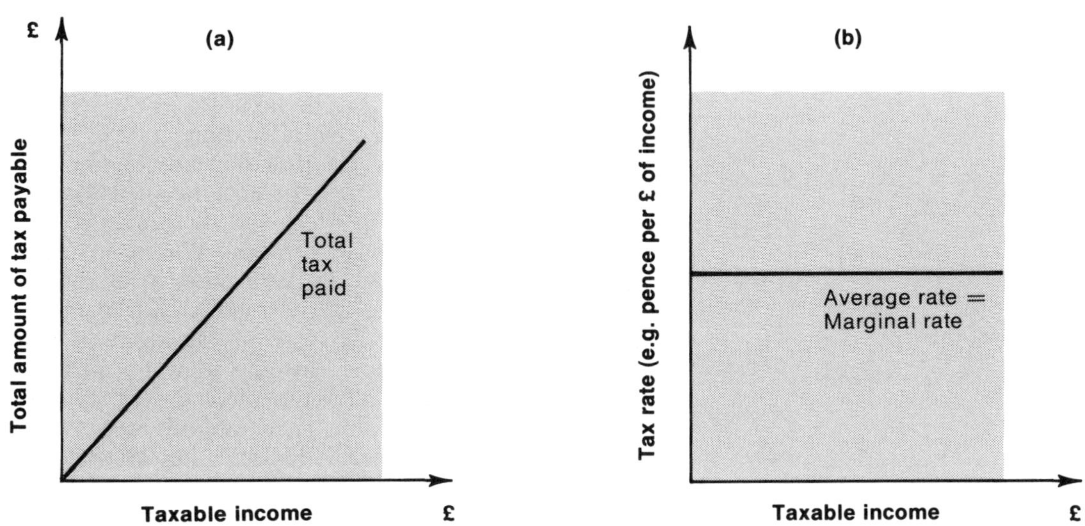

Figure 14.2 Proportional taxation

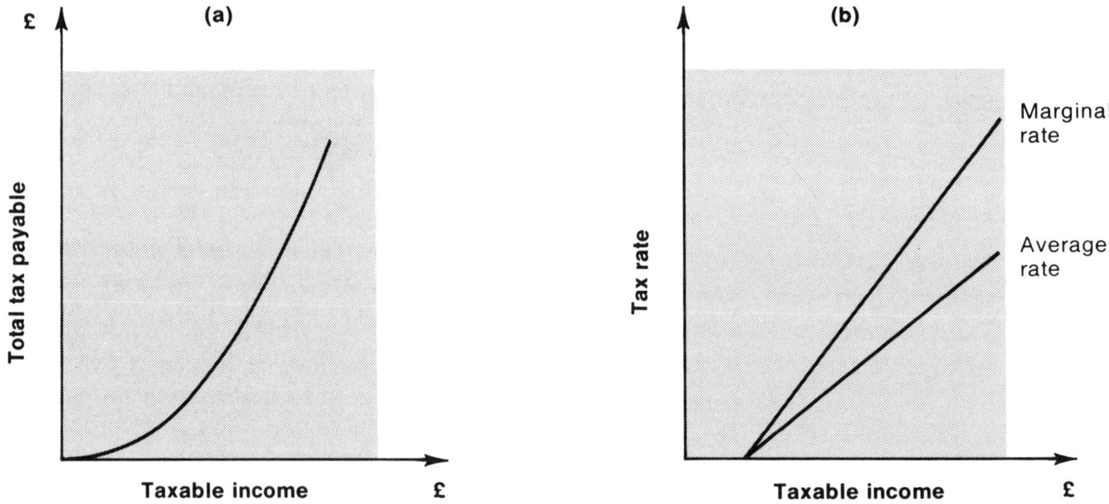

Figure 14.3 Progressive taxation

marginal and average rate of tax payable are constant. Figure 14.2(a) and 14.2(b) illustrate this definition.

In the UK corporation tax, a tax on company income (i.e. profits) is a proportional tax. Companies are required to pay a tax on profits of 52 per cent, irrespective of the amount of profits earned. Small firms pay at a rate of 42 per cent (rates of tax at 1981).

The principal objection to a system of proportional taxes on incomes is that a tax of a set percentage of income will weigh more heavily on a low-income earner than a high-income earner.

A *progressive tax* is one in which the average rate at which the tax is paid increases with the taxpayer's assessable income. Thus a person on double the taxable income will pay more than double the amount of tax. If the tax schedule incorporates marginal rates of tax that increase steadily then the relationship between total tax payable and taxable income will be as shown in Figure 14.3(a). The relationship between the marginal rate and average rate will be as shown in Figure 14.3(b). Income tax in the UK is a progressive tax but is rather different from that shown in Figure 14.3. The tax rates in the 1980 budget made for a system of tax bands whereby the marginal rate of tax rises in a number of steps. The amount of tax paid depends on the amount of taxable income and on the rates of tax. Taxable income is less than gross income because the tax system provides for allowances to be deducted from income before tax. There is a personal allowance (single £1375, married £2145 per annum, in 1980, by 1983 raised to £1565 and £2445) for all taxpayers, dependent on marital status. For a married couple both working, only one married rate of allowance is claimed, the wife normally receiving an earned income allowance of the same amount as a single person. Other allowances recognised by the tax authorities include the interest payable on a building society mortgage, certain expenses connected with a job, profession or trade; additional allowances may be claimed in special circumstances e.g. for blind persons, and for aged people. Taxable income is then taxed at a basic rate of 30 per cent with higher rates applying to bands of income at certain levels.

The rates for the tax year 1981–82 were as follows:

Rate		Taxable income
Basic rate	30%	£ 1 – £11 250
Higher rates	40%	£11 251 – £13 250 (next £2000)
	45%	£13 251 – £16 750 (next £3500)
	50%	£16 751 – £22 250 (next £5500)
	55%	£22 251 – £27 750 (next £5500)
	60%	Over £27 750

No tax is payable by a person until annual income reaches the amount of tax allowances. For the first £11 250 of taxable income, the marginal rate of tax was 30p in each pound (rates of tax as at 1981–1982). On the next £2000 the marginal rate rises to 40p in each pound; on the next £2000 the marginal rate is 45p, then 50p on the next £5500, 55p on the next £5500, finally reaching the rate of 60p in each pound of taxable income over £27 750. Clearly the average rate of tax lies below the marginal rate of tax but continues to rise as income increases. Thus income tax is a progressive tax on taxable income. Figures 14.4(a) and 14.4(b) demonstrate the effects of the UK tax system for a single person claiming only the personal allowance against tax liability. The general principle of the progressive nature of the tax is easily seen from Figure 14.4(b) which shows the marginal rate of tax as a series of steps on successive higher levels of income. The marginal rate of tax is also higher than the average rate of tax. Figure 14.4 illustrates the effect of the UK income tax system on a single person in 1981–82. The amount of tax allowance of £1375 is shown on the diagram as being the level of income at which tax is first paid. The diagram can easily be adapted to show taxation on incomes for any other taxpayer's individual circumstances. In the event of a taxpayer with a total, say, of £4000 of allowances against tax, the schedules would start at the £4000 income limit for both the amount of tax paid as shown in 14.4(a) and the rates of tax in 14.4(b).

Alternatively, a tax can be regressive. A *regressive tax* is one in which average and marginal tax rates fall as taxable income increases; the taxpayer contributes a smaller proportion of his income as his taxable income increases. Such a situation is shown in Figures 14.5(a) and 14.5(b) on page 252. In Figure 14.5(a) total tax payable increases despite the decline in the tax rates (Figure 14.5(b)).

It is sometimes said that taxes on expenditure are regressive because all who purchase the product on which the tax is levied pay the same amount, irrespective of their income. As a result it can be claimed that government policies that aim at a redistribution of income through a progressive income tax system are, to some extent nullified by regressive sales taxes, particularly if these taxes fall on products for which there is a low price elasticity of demand. The extent to which a tax is burden to rich or poor depends on which group normally purchases the article.

Direct and indirect taxes

A distinction is frequently made between direct and indirect taxes. A *direct tax* is one which is levied on the person whom it is intended should pay it. Thus, income tax, probate duties and company taxes are examples of direct taxes. *Indirect taxes* are taxes that are levied on one person and paid by him, but subsequently recouped from someone else. For example, the impact of VAT is borne by the producer, then shifted to wholesaler and retailer and, finally, to the consumer on whom it is said the incidence of the tax falls. VAT is levied on goods and services and is imposed at each stage of the production process. It is, however,

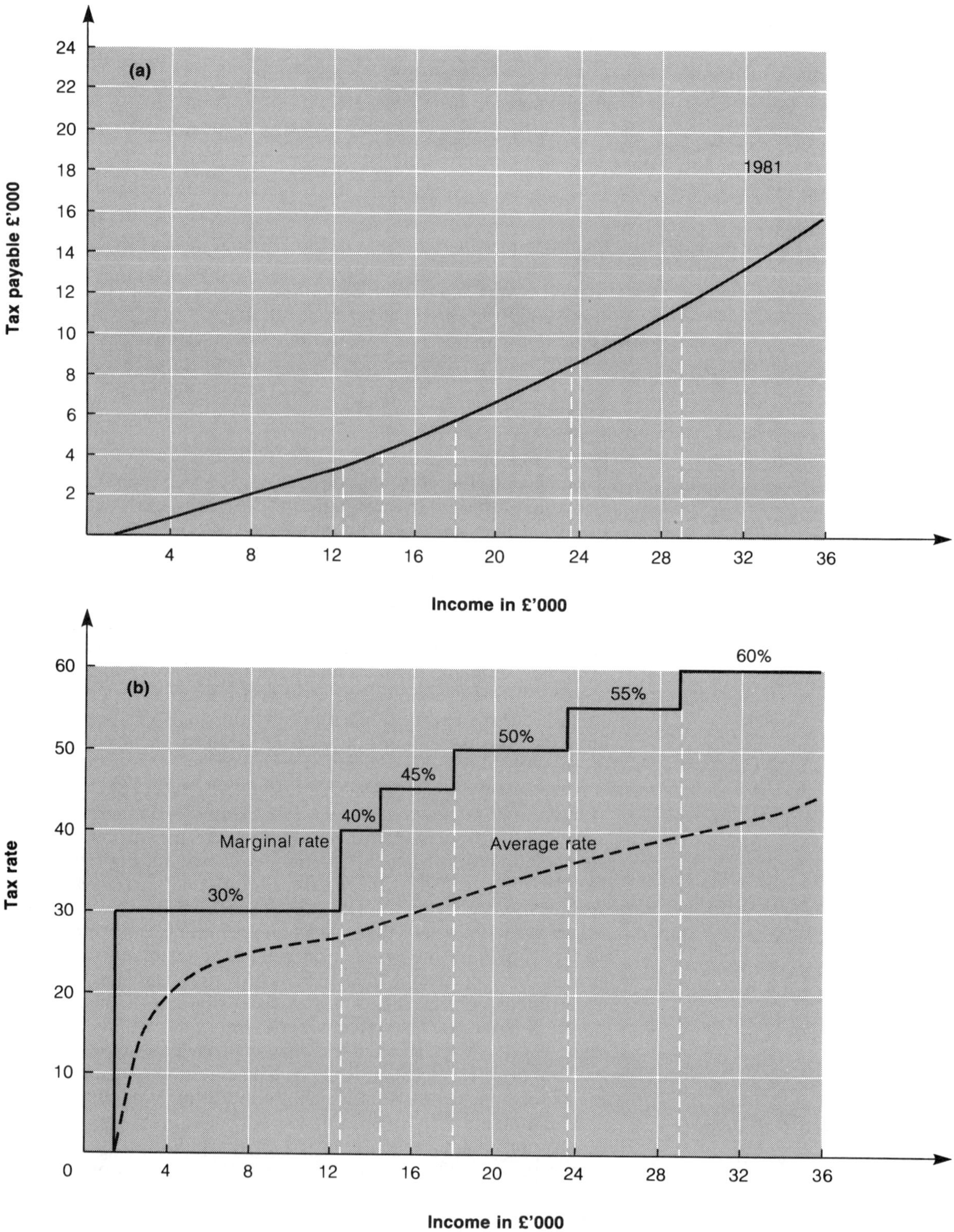

Figure 14.4(a) *The UK personal income tax schedule*
(b) *UK average and marginal rates of tax*

Source: Annual Abstract of Statistics 1980

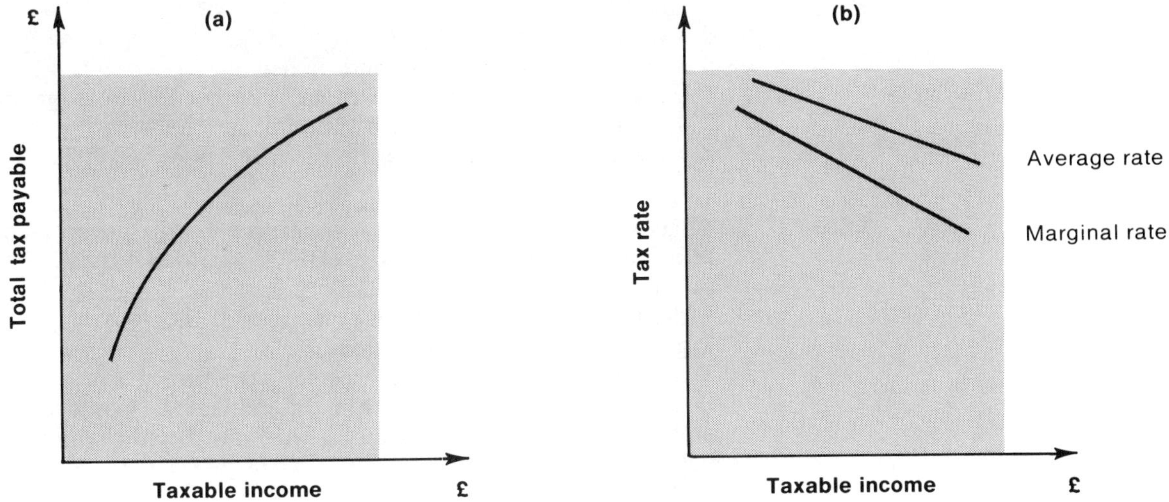

Figure 14.5 Regressive taxation

levied only on the amount of value added at each stage of production. Any intermediate stage of production or distribution of a good or service is liable to charge the rate of VAT on the value of output produced but is able to claim back any VAT already paid on inputs to that stage of the production process. The consumer bears the full amount of the tax, being unable to reclaim any of the VAT paid. The effect of the tax is then spread throughout its production rather than being imposed on the wholesaler or retailer alone. Certain goods are zero-rated for VAT purposes such as most foodstuffs, exports, domestic fuels (other than petrol for motor vehicles) books, newspapers and magazines. Since no VAT is chargeable on the value of the output of these goods any VAT paid on inputs can be claimed by the producer. In effect this is a subsidy on production. Exempt goods are also free from VAT but do not permit VAT on inputs to be reclaimed. Examples of goods exempt from VAT are insurance, health-care and education, postal services, finance, burial and cremation.

Consumers ultimately bear excise duties, such as the taxes on alcohol, tobacco and petroleum products, and import duties met initially by importers.

14.7

In 1980 the basic rate of income tax was 30 per cent. Higher rates of tax then applied at different higher bands of income. What arguments can be put forward in favour of a system in which all taxpayers pay the same marginal rate of tax (i.e. if all taxpayers paid tax at the basic rate)? Is it, for example, consistent with Adam Smith's principles of taxation?

14.8

Adam Smith's principles of taxation can be generally applied to test whether a tax is a good one or not. Discuss the merits and weaknesses of the following types of taxes in the light of these principles.
1 death, or estate, duties
2 a tax on annual expenditure of the individual or household

3 land tax
4 a tax on capital gains
5 a tax on gifts of property and money
6 a tax on each tonne-mile of freight conveyed by road hauliers
7 a tax on mileage travelled by the private motorist
8 a tax on private residential housing, the rates.

14.9

What effects would you expect a decision by the government to levy income tax, at the present rates, on households rather than on individuals to have on:
1 the activity of the individual members of the household?
2 government taxation revenue?
What advantages would there be for government and society in taxing the household rather than the individual. Would there be any problems in switching from the individual to the family as the basis for taxation?

Income tax and the distribution of income

The second purpose of a taxation system is that it can be used as part of a policy to redistribute income. If the desire is to redistribute from rich to poor, a progressive system of direct taxation on income will take proportionately more from those on higher incomes. The market mechanism produces an unequal distribution of incomes within society and a progressive taxation system provides part of the means of achieving a redistribution of income and reducing this inequality.

Range of income (lower limit)	Number of incomes ('000s)	Percentage of all incomes	Cumulative percentage of incomes	Percentage of income before tax	Cumulative percentage before tax	Percentage of income after tax	Cumulative percentage after tax
£ 750–	944	4.2	4.2	1.0	1.0	1.2	1.2
£ 1 250–	2 060	9.2	13.4	3.1	4.1	3.6	4.8
£ 1 750–	2 500	11.1	24.5	5.3	9.4	5.8	10.6
£ 2 000–	2 540	11.3	35.8	6.9	16.3	7.3	17.9
£ 2 500–	2 300	10.2	46.0	7.6	23.9	7.9	25.8
£ 3 000–	4 070	18.1	64.1	17.1	41.0	17.6	43.4
£ 4 000–	3 330	14.8	78.9	17.9	58.9	18.2	61.6
£ 5 000–	2 070	9.2	88.1	13.6	72.5	13.6	75.2
£ 6 000–	1 650	7.3	95.4	13.5	86.0	13.1	88.3
£ 8 000–	501	2.2	97.6	5.3	91.3	5.0	93.3
£ 10 000–	216	1.0	98.6	2.8	94.1	2.5	95.8
£ 12 000–	135	0.6	99.2	2.1	96.2	1.8	97.6
£ 15 000–	80	0.4	99.6	1.6	97.8	1.2	99.8
£ 20 000–	56 }			1.8	99.6	1.1	99.9
£ 50 000–	3 }	0.4 }	100.0	0.3	99.9 }	0.1 }	100.0
£100 000–	1 }			0.1	100.0 }		
Total	22 456	100.0		100.0		100.0	

Note: The figures cover incomes for tax purposes above £750, information is incomplete on incomes below £750. Figures are subject to rounding.

Table 14.4 Distribution of incomes in the UK before and after income tax, 1976–77

Source: *Figures compiled from Annual Abstract of Statistics, 1980* HMSO

Table 14.4 shows UK taxpayers grouped into various income ranges, the percentage of taxpayers in each group and the percentages of income, before and after tax, earned by each income group. The table shows that in 1976–77, 944 000 taxpayers had incomes from £750 to £1249, accounting for 4.2 per cent of all incomes and in total 1.0 per cent of income before tax and 1.2 per cent after tax. Further information about the distribution of incomes in the UK is given in the columns showing the cumulative percentage figures for all incomes, incomes before tax and after tax. Look at the income group £3000 to £3999, for example. Of all incomes 18.1 per cent were in this group; the cumulative percentage shows that 64.1 per cent earned less than £4000. Before tax the cumulative incomes of this group amounted to 41.0 per cent and after tax earned 43.4 per cent of all incomes. The previous income group £2500 to £2999 reveals in the cumulative percentage columns that 46 per cent of income earners earned less than £3000 and accounted for a little more than a quarter, 25.8 per cent, of incomes after tax. Interpreting the figures in this manner, a clear picture can be gained of the distribution of incomes in the UK.

The Lorenz curve

Figure 14.6 is an example of a diagram called a *Lorenz curve*. The curved line in the box is the plotted relationship between the cumulative percentage of taxpayers and the cumulative percentage of actual incomes.[2] The horizontal and vertical sides of the box measure the cumulative percentages of taxpayers and actual incomes respectively. The diagonal straight line drawn from the bottom left-hand corner of the box to the right-hand corner is the line that the Lorenz curve would take if there were a perfectly equal distribution of income (if 10 per cent of taxpayers had 10 per cent of total income, 20 per cent had 20 per cent of income, and so on). The further the actual curve 'sags' from this straight line the greater the inequality in the distribution of income. A Lorenz curve that keeps close to the sides and corner of the box indicates that nearly all income is earned by a very small proportion of taxpayers. The figure shows a hypothetical situation in which 80 per cent of taxpayers obtain 40 per cent of total income, a less equal distribution of income than prevailed in the UK in 1976–77.

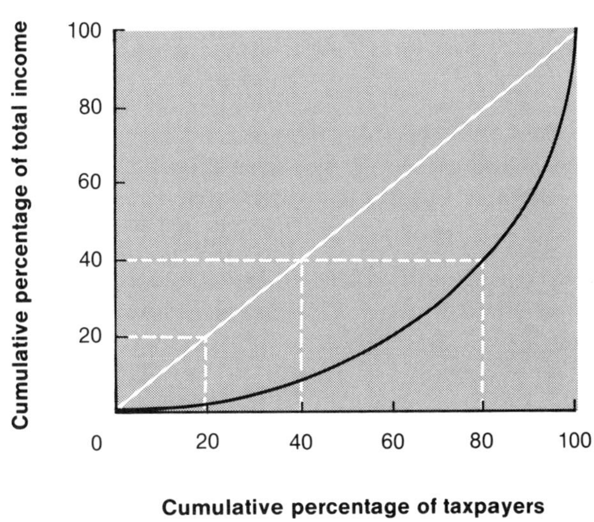

Figure 14.6 *Lorenz curve*

14.10

Use the information given in Table 14.4 to construct a Lorenz curve showing the distribution of actual incomes both before and after tax in the UK for 1976–77. What evidence is given in the diagram to support the proposition that the UK income tax is progressive? Try to obtain more recent figures to construct a similar Lorenz curve.

Inadequacies of the Lorenz curve

Unfortunately, the Lorenz curve in Figure 14.6 fails to give an accurate picture of the inequalities of either wealth or income between households in the UK for several reasons:

1 The statistics relate only to taxpayers. In 1976–77 those who earned less than £750 did not pay tax, and so the statistics excluded many part-time workers, or people who worked for only part of the year, and most retired people.

2 The figures relate to individual taxpayers, not to households. A household in which both husband and wife are in full-time employment may enjoy a higher living standard than one with a single wage earner whose income is higher than either the husband or the wife, although the single man slots into the Lorenz curve of taxable income at a higher position.

3 No distinction is drawn between the ages of taxpayers. Some of those in the lowest income brackets are young people who have just entered the labour force and who will move rapidly to higher incomes. Their position is quite different from a middle aged person in a low-income group because of the latter's inability to gain better paid work.

4 Another determinant of the welfare of a family, the number of dependants, is not taken into consideration in this measure. A single man is better off, at least materially, than a man on the same income who has a family to support.

5 Actual income is not such a good indicator of an individual's or a household's affluence as its disposable income – its income after tax.

The UK income tax system helps to change the distribution of income in two ways. First, by permitting taxpayers to deduct certain expenses from their incomes or giving them a tax rebate for a dependent wife or relative under certain circumstances. Second, by the adoption of a progressive tax system in which the average rate of tax increases as income rises.

The progressive income tax system works to reduce inequalitites but it does not remove them. Few people would support a system of taxation and social service payments that removed all income inequality, even if such a system could be devised. It is widely believed that incentives play an important part in the operation of the UK economic system. If all individuals (or should it be all families?) had the same income, then the incentive to work harder, to do dirty or dangerous jobs, or to train for jobs requiring special skills would disappear and production would be reduced.

If the tax system is progressive and marginal rates of tax are thought to be too high, there may be little incentive to work harder. In 1979 the Chancellor of the Exchequer in the budget announced reductions of the rates of income tax, for example, at the highest level from 83p to 60p in the £ and a reduction in the basic rate from 33p to 30p. By doing so the intention was to restore incentives to the income earner. The reduction in marginal rates of tax was much greater for those on higher incomes and it could be argued that such a change in the system highlighted income inequalities in the UK.

The effects of inflation on the income tax system are such that higher incomes have the effect of increasing the tax yield in two ways. At the lower end of the income scale more people find themselves over the tax threshold as incomes rise and are now liable to pay tax. While for other tax payers, inflation may move them up to higher tax bands and higher marginal rates of tax. In this way progressive income tax is said to act as an automatic stabiliser in that, as a consequence of inflation, the yield from tax will increase more than proportionately to the increase in incomes. In terms of real incomes, if no corresponding adjustment to the income tax system is made with inflation, then they will fall. To prevent this occurring the average rates to tax have to be reduced, a move that is equivalent to shifting the average and marginal tax curves to the right. This is done by increasing the level of personal allowances of income before tax and increasing the income thresholds at which the higher marginal rates of tax apply. The amount by which these increases take place is calculated by the percentage change in average incomes or in retail prices. This process of indexation permits the adjustment of a progressive tax system to ensure the government continues to receive the same proportion of income in direct taxation as before. If allowances and tax bands are not indexed, then the government will take an increasing proportion of income. A proportional tax system, one for which there is only one average and marginal rate, does not require indexing as the government taxes a fixed proportion of incomes as they increase.

Automatic stabiliser

14.11

Taxable income (£)	Tax paid (£)	Taxable income (£)	Tax paid (£)
500	210	3000	1050
1000	400	3500	1185
1500	585	4000	1300
2000	750	4500	1405
2500	910	5000	1500

1 Calculate the average rates of tax in the above table and from them determine whether the taxation schedule is proportional or regressive.
2 Reconstruct the 'tax paid' column of the table so that the tax system is progressive.

Table 14.3 mentions other forms of direct taxation on capital and wealth as opposed to income. The distribution of wealth in the UK is far more unequal than the distribution of incomes. Capital gains tax, capital transfer tax and estate duties are progressive taxes on the value of gains made or wealth inherited or received as a gift. Their yield is very small in comparison with taxes on personal and corporate incomes. The effective taxation of wealth has proved to be far more difficult to achieve than the taxation of income.

Taxes on expenditure

Table 14.3 illustrates that the most important taxes on spending are VAT and the excise duties on tobacco, oils and alcoholic drinks. VAT is levied on most goods and services and was discussed earlier. Excise duties can be seen to be particularly high yielding in revenue and, because of the inelastic nature of demand for products such as cigarettes, petrol and alcoholic drinks, the imposition of high rates of duty does not lead to large reductions in the quantity demanded. Such products are therefore useful to the Chancellor if he wishes to raise high revenue, and involve less disruption to the market and to the allocation of resources used in production, than would be the case if the amount of revenue was to be found elsewhere on other forms of expenditure. The tax system could also be used in a regulatory sense to penalise certain forms of behaviour which may involve social costs, through the imposition of high rates of duty.

Expenditure taxes are inflationary but the extent to which they can be passed on in terms of higher prices to the consumer depends upon the relative elasticities of supply and demand. The effect of expenditure tax is determined by changes in the market price and quantity of a good or service. They do lead to a reallocation of resources depending upon the degree of response from suppliers and the nature of the supply curve.

Other forms of tax and duties cover a wide range of goods and activities: vehicle excise duties, which owners of vehicles have to pay, betting and gaming taxes on forms of gambling are examples. The revenue they yield is of course important to the exchequer but they are not major providers of finance generally.

Local government finance

Table 14.2 presented figures for general government receipts which includes both central and local government revenues. The main sources of finance for local government are grants from central government, loans, rents and charges for housing and trading services, and the rates.

Rates

Rates are local taxes levied on the value of property by the local authority within its boundaries. The rates charged are a function of the rateable value of the property and the amount of rate in each pound of rateable value declared by the authority. Thus a householder living in a property with a rateable value (RV) of £300 and a declared rate of 60p in the £ would have to pay £180 in rates. The RV is determined by the rating officer and is a notional value representing the approximate annual rent that the property is worth. Size, location, age and condition, amenities (such as a garage), are all factors to be taken into consideration in assessing the RV. The rate per pound charged by the authority is decided in relation to the cost of the services to be provided by the authority and the extra revenue required above that received from rents, loans, the rate support grant from central government and any other source of revenue.

Criticisms of the rates

Rates have been severely criticised for a number of reasons. They are said to be regressive and not related to the ability to pay. The amount of rates paid does not reflect the usage of local services and benefits received by different households, e.g. households without children are still contributing towards the local authority's education spending. Rates vary from area to area and RVs tend to be especially low in areas with older and poor quality property which require heavier amounts of expenditure to improve amenities and the environment. House improvements and extensions lead to higher RVs and rates payable.

There are variations in the level of provision of services in different areas which leads to dissatisfaction among rate payers. As a source of local finance for local services, the rates are particularly useful and easy to administer at the local level. It has proved difficult to come up with a valid alternative to the rates which would allow as much local control over finance and collection. A local income tax or sales tax could replace the rates, as happens in other countries and states, but this would involve problems of administration, with the cost of collection and with variability from one local area with another. Abolition of the rates would involve finding the revenue from elsewhere and would reduce the degree of autonomy that the local authority has in finance.

Notes

1 Adam Smith 1961 *An Enquiry into the Nature and Causes of the Wealth of Nations.* 6th edn, Methuen, vol 2, book VI, ch 2, pp 350–2.
2 A Lorenz curve can be used for showing the relationship between the cumulative percentages of any two variables, for example, the percentage of farms producing wheat that grow a particular percentage of the wheat crop.

Chapter 15

Aggregate Economic Activity

National income aggregates

The aggregates 'total domestic expenditure' and 'gross domestic product' were defined and explained in Chapters 5, and 6 respectively.

Total domestic expenditure is the total expenditure by the UK's residents on final goods and services in a specified period. *Gross domestic product* is the value of production of all goods and services produced in the UK in a specified period.

Analysis of simple closed economy

These aggregates are closely linked. Consider an imaginary simple closed economy composed of only a household sector and a business sector. There will be no government sector, no financial institutions and no overseas trade. In this imaginary economy, the two aggregates total domestic expenditure and gross domestic product will be equal.

Total domestic expenditure = Gross domestic product

Equality between gross domestic product and total domestic expenditure

They are necessarily equal because of the way in which these aggregates are defined. We saw in Chapter 5 (on page 83) that total domestic expenditure was the sum of all purchases of final goods and services, plus any increase in stocks. In our imaginary economy, total domestic expenditure is the aggregate of spending by households on final goods and services (consumption), plus spending by households on final goods and services, plus the increase in stocks. In Chapter 6 (on page 87) we saw that if sales (spending) fall short of production in any period, then stocks will increase by the precise amount by which spending falls short of production. (This increase in stocks can legitimately be regarded as expenditure, since it constitutes involuntary investment expenditure.) Consequently, gross domestic product is equal to total domestic expenditure. Similarly, if spending is greater than production in a period, stocks are reduced by the amount by which spending exceeds production. Once more, gross domestic product and total domestic expenditure are equal.

This relationship is important because understanding it is the key to appreciating how the level of aggregate economic activity is determined in a market economy. The relationship is illustrated in Figure 15.1.

In reality the UK economy is a great deal more complicated than this simple closed economy. Although the aggregates total domestic expenditure and gross domestic product are still closely related, they are not identical. In 1978 for example, the aggregates were:

	£ million
Total domestic expenditure	159 525
Gross domestic product	161 639

Reason why national aggregates not equal in open economy with government sector

They are not identical in an open economy with a government sector. Total domestic expenditure is defined in the national accounts as expenditure by residents. This includes spending on imports. Gross domestic product measures the value of goods and services produced in the UK.

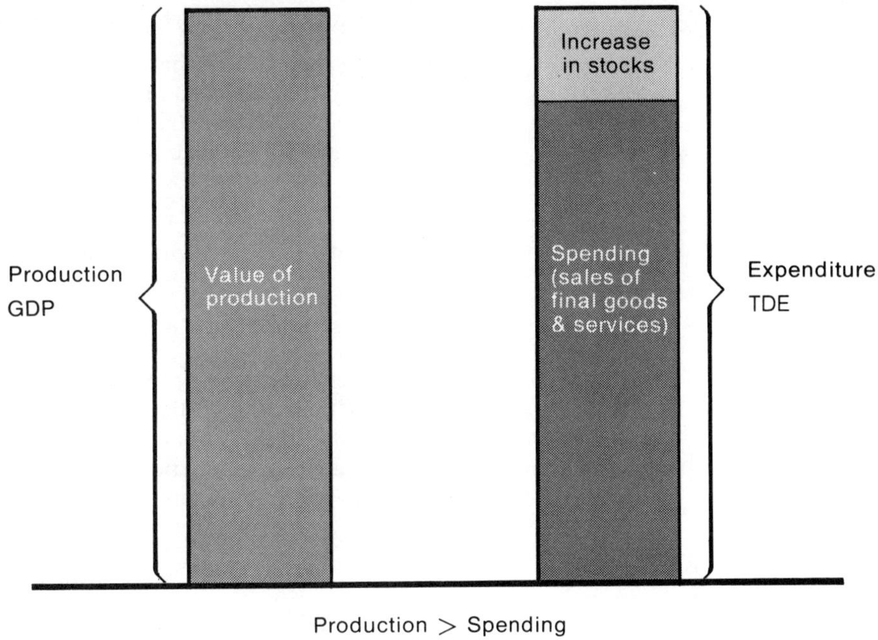

Figure 15.1 Gross domestic product and total domestic expenditure in the two sector economy

It therefore includes exports but excludes imports.

In addition, Chapter 6 distinguished between gross domestic product measured at market prices and at factor cost. The two differ because government indirect taxes and subsidies create a wedge between market prices and the incomes received by the owners of factors of production.

Figure 15.2 shows the relationship between GDP at market prices, GDP at factor cost and total domestic expenditure in the UK in 1978. These different aggregates are related by formal accounting identities in Figure 15.2. The figure introduces another aggregate, total final expenditure, defined as the total flow of goods and services produced within the UK, together with imports, that is:

Figure 15.2 Relationship between GDP and total domestic expenditure in the UK, 1978

Total final expenditure = GDP + Imports

GDP plus imports is the aggregate of supplies of goods and services available to the UK economy and these supplies are either used at home or exported. That part used at home by UK residents is total domestic expenditure. So we have:

Total final expenditure = Total domestic expenditure + Exports

By comparing the two statements of total final expenditure, it can be seen that:

GDP + Imports = Total domestic expenditure + Exports

This rather formal study of the national aggregates can usefully be taken a little further. Recall that in Chapter 5 total domestic expenditure was divided into three components: consumption, investment (capital formation) and government expenditure. These aggregates can also be incorporated into the expression. It can then be said that:

GDP + Imports = Consumption + Investment + Government expenditure + Exports

which can be rewritten as:

GDP = Consumption + Investment + Government expenditure + Exports – Imports

A simple form of algebraic notation is of great assistance in providing a shorthand method of writing this. Let:

GDP be represented by the letter	Y
Consumption	C
Investment	I
Government expenditure	G
Exports	X
Imports	M

The expression can then be written as:

$$Y = C + I + G + X - M$$

In this first section we have revised the national accounting measures of gross domestic product and total domestic expenditure. The major purpose of the chapter is to explain what it is that determines the level of aggregate production in the UK. As we have seen, the definitions used in the national accounts mean that recorded expenditure must coincide with actual production. In the following sections we turn our attention to the spending plans of households and business and see that it is in these plans that the answer to the critical question 'What determines the level of GDP?' is to be found.

Gross domestic product is related to gross national product through the addition of net property income from abroad. Net property income from abroad represents interest profits and dividends received from overseas by UK residents less corresponding payments from the UK to foreigners. Thus, GDP + net property income from abroad = GNP. In some national statistics, figures for exports and imports include payments for property income within those totals and in these instances an aggregate measure for GNP is produced.

15.1

Figure 15.2 shows that gross domestic product at factor cost was much less in 1978 than total domestic expenditure. Does this mean that UK citizens were spending more than they produced? If it does not mean this, explain the difference between the two aggregates. Should such a difference give any cause for concern?

15.2

One of the reasons why economists study the national income aggregates is that changes in GDP are said to give an indication of a country's economic growth. Do you think that the total final expenditure aggregate is an equally useful measure for this purpose? Give your reasons.

15.3

In different parts of this chapter we have said that:
TDE = spending plus increase in stocks, and
TDE = C + I + G.
1 How can these two definitions be reconciled when stocks are increasing?
2 Can they still be reconciled if stocks are falling?

Business behaviour and the level of economic activity

How production is determined

The task of discovering how the level of aggregate production is determined in a market economy has been one of the main concerns of economists in recent times. The more clearly we understand how production is determined, the better are our chances of being able to manage the economy in such a way as to achieve full employment and price stability.

The method economists use in their investigations is to develop a theory that provides a plausible explanation of economic activity. Having developed such a theory, they can then test it to see how well it predicts changes in aggregate economic activity. The search for a theory with which economists are completely satisfied goes on. As their understanding of the way in which an economy works grows, so they attempt to obtain answers to even more specific questions. These include how great particular changes will be and precisely when they will occur. Fortunately, for our purposes, they have already been able to provide a fairly simple explanation of how production and employment are determined.

The business response to changes in market conditions

Consideration of how businesses respond to changes in market conditions provides a convenient starting point. Take as an example the activities of a single textile manufacturer. Suppose that during a particular month the firm expected to sell 10 000 metres of cloth and it produced that amount, but sales of cloth in that month were actually 12 000 metres. The enterprise would probably have some stocks from which it could supplement production to meet the unexpectedly large sales demand. The firm would keep a close check on the level of stocks, for this would provide the buffer to meet unexpected sales demand. If the firm expected sales to continue at 12 000 metres per month it would be likely to increase production in the following period.

When the firm's sales fall short of the expected production level,

Sales	Production	Change in stocks	Response
12 000	10 000	–2000	Increase rate of production
10 000	10 000	no change	No change in rate of production
8 000	10 000	+2000	Reduce rate of production

Table 15.1 Business responses to stock changes

stocks will increase. The enterprise would be likely to respond by reducing the rate of production in the following month. Should sales coincide with production, stocks would be unchanged and the enterprise likely to maintain the existing rate of production. These business reactions are summarised in Table 15.1.

Implications for the economy

These are common business responses, particularly in manufacturing industries. Such behaviour has important implications for the economy as a whole. It suggests that if the sales of businesses in the aggregate exceed their aggregate production, the level of stocks in the economy will be reduced and businesses will then try to increase production in a subsequent period. If aggregate production exceeds aggregate sales, businesses will then try to reduce production. Finally, if aggregate sales are equal to aggregate production, the overall level of production is likely to be maintained in subsequent periods. If sales equal production, and there are no other forces working to cause the production level to change, total production in the economy is at the equilibrium level. That is, the rate of production planned by business matches the rate of people's spending.

Link beween aggregate production and employment in short run

There is an important link between the level of aggregate production and the level of employment in the short run. A decision to increase production is likely to cause businesses to hire more workers, whilst a decision to reduce production means a reduced demand for labour. In other words, the forces that determine the level of production also determine the level of employment.

Sales may differ from the rate of production at any time because the plans of households and businesses to buy goods and services are made *independently* of the plans of businesses to produce goods and services. Sales to households and firms are determined by the decisions of these purchasers. The term used for this planned expenditure on goods and services is *aggregate demand*.

The level of production, on the other hand, depends on businessmen's expectations of future sales. As we have seen, experience in the immediate past is likely to influence these expectations of future sales. There is no mechanism to guarantee that businesses' planned production will coincide with buyers' aggregate demand: there is no reason why production should equal sales. When they differ, this will generate a change in production and accordingly in the level of employment.

Suppose aggregate sales (aggregate demand) is greater than aggregate production. The excess of sales will be accompanied by a fall in stocks and a business will respond by increasing the rate of production. At first sight it may appear that the consequent increase in production will simply match the excess of sales over the previous level of production. This is not so. The *initial* change in production, in response to the fall in stocks, gives rise to a number of *secondary* effects.

When businesses increase production, they must hire more workers or offer more overtime to existing employees. These additional wages will largely be spent on consumer goods and services, and sales will be increased further. If the initial increase in production is sufficient merely to raise production to the level at which it equals sales previously made, then production will still fall short of the amount required to meet current sales. Stocks will be reduced further and it will be necessary to revise production plans again and to increase production again. The initial difference between sales and production triggers the decision to increase production, and this decision sets off a sequence of additional incomes and additional sales that further stimulates production.

Increase in spending less than increase in income

This chain is not an endless one, because, as we saw in Chapter 5, only part of any increase in incomes is spent on final goods and services. Sales do not increase as rapidly as production and income. Accordingly, the increase in production initiated by the excess of sales over production eventually leads to an equilibrium situation in which sales and production are equal, and in which stocks are no longer falling.

The opposite process occurs if aggregate demand is less than production. Stocks rise, production is reduced, employment is cut and incomes fall. The decline in incomes causes some (lesser) fall in spending. Because sales do not fall as rapidly as production and incomes, the gap between production and sales is narrowed, until equilibrium is restored.

Existence of equilibrium not evidence of optimum production

However, the existence of equilibrium between aggregate demand and aggregate production does not necessarily mean that the economy is producing as many goods and services as possible with available resources. We have just considered the case in which an economy moves towards equilibrium after a succession of cuts in production and reductions in employment. An economy may be in equilibrium but unemployment may be high and actual production far short of the potential gross domestic product. The UK, together with many other countries, found itself in just such a position during the depression of the 1930s. Aggregate production was low and consumption was also low.

Since the war the UK has generally avoided a similar severe economic depression, but there have been occasions when production has been significantly below potential and unemployment has been unacceptably high. The end of the 1970s and the early 1980s have seen unemployment rise to post-war record levels and have been likened by some to the 'thirties' depression. Although unemployment has risen, there are still important differences in the nature, impact and severity of the problem compared with the thirties.

15.4

We have said that a business will respond to an unforeseen increase in stocks when sales fall short of the expected level by cutting production and employment. Suppose that instead of cutting production, the business increased production and hired more workers to do so. Explain why this response (no matter how socially desirable) would not prove profitable. Would the business be able to sell this increased production?

15.5

A common reaction by businesses to falling sales during the depression was to reduce the wages of their workers. Do you think that this policy:

1 Benefited the individual firms concerned? (What would happen to prices when all firms had lower wage costs?)
2 Stimulated aggregate production and reduced unemployment? (Would the wage cut stimulate spending?)
3 If you have concluded that the wage cuts did not bring benefits either to individual firms or the population in general, why did individual businesses cut the wage rates offered?
4 If you have concluded that the wage cuts should have brought benefits to individual firms and the population in general, why was it that the depression and the high level of unemployment continued for so long?

Equilibrium and the economy

Total spending = consumption + investment

The relationship between aggregate demand and aggregate production deserves further explanation. The relationship becomes clearer if total spending is divided into two parts: consumption spending by households and investment spending by firms. The link between the level of aggregate consumption and aggregate income (aggregate production) depicted in Figure 15.3 was explained in Chapter 5. The horizontal axis measures aggregate production of goods and services and the vertical axis measures aggregate consumption spending. As before, the 45° line relates aggregate production on the horizontal axis to aggregate spending on the vertical axis. It can also be conveniently referred to as the aggregate production, or aggregate supply line. The aggregate consumption line measures consumption spending for each level of aggregate production.

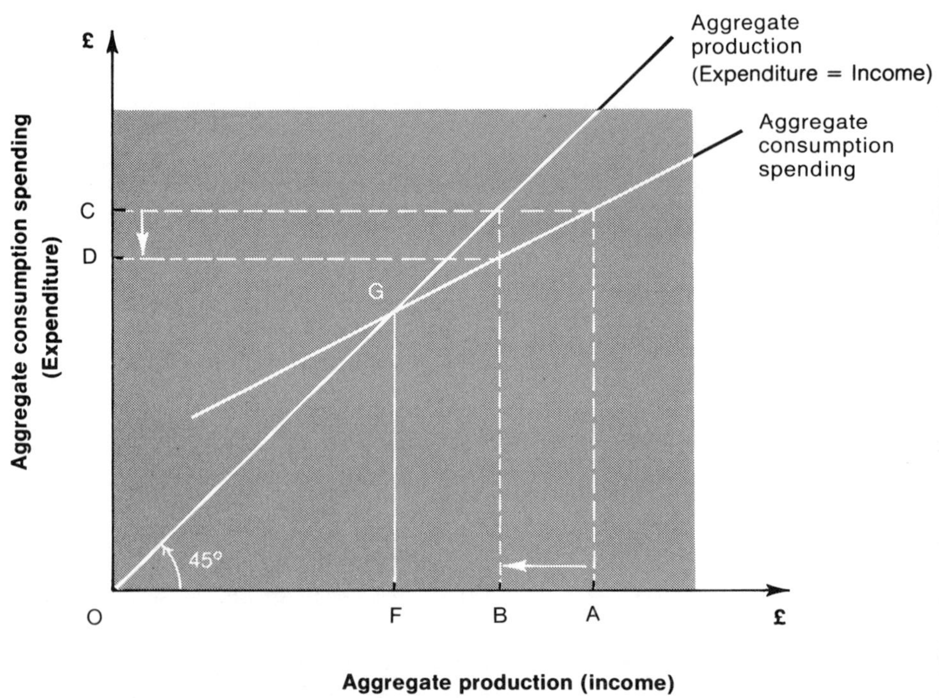

Figure 15.3 Aggregate consumption and aggregate production

Effect of change in income on consumption

Figure 15.3 shows the effect on aggregate consumption of a change in aggregate production (and hence aggregate income). For example, a reduction in aggregate production from OA to OB will result in a reduction in aggregate consumption spending from C to D. The slope of the aggregate consumption line measures the marginal propensity to consume. It indicates what proportion of a change in production (income) is consumed. Thus, if the marginal propensity to consume is 0.6, a reduction in production of £100 million will lead to a fall in consumption expenditure of £60 million. Notice that as aggregate production falls, the distance between the aggregate production line and the aggregate consumption line is reduced, and then eliminated at G. If production fell below OF, consumption spending would actually exceed income. It is this relationship between consumption and production (income) that helps to explain why a series of production adjustments and changes in aggregate demand can lead ultimately to a state of equilibrium.

Level of investment constant in short run

The other component of aggregate demand is investment spending. The level of investment that a business intends to carry out over the next few months has already been planned. For example, new factories that are now being built were planned perhaps three years ago and the contract signed with the builder over a year ago. Accordingly, in the short run, the level of investment spending is inflexible. To simplify the argument, we will assume it is unchanged despite changes in the level of aggregate production over the next few months. This relationship between production on the one hand and the aggregate of planned consumption and investment spending on the other is shown in Table 15.2.

Production (£00m)	=	Consumption (£00m)	+	Investment (£00m)	=	Aggregate demand (£00m)	
25		23		6		29	
30		26		6		32	
35		(29		+ 6)		= 35	Equilibrium
40		32		6		38	
45		35		6		41	
50		38		6		44	

Table 15.2 Production, consumption, investment and aggregate demand

In the example shown in the table, investment spending for the next few months is assumed constant at £600 million per month. Consumption rises as production increases. In this case we assume that 60 pence of each extra pound of income (generated by production) is spent by consumers. Aggregate demand is the sum of consumption and investment spending. When production is £3000 million per month, households spend £2600 million, and this, together with the investment of £600 m, explains why production is less than aggregate demand. When production is increased by £1000 million to £4000 million, households increase consumption by £600 million. Their consumption is then £3200 million, and this, together with the investment of £600 million, gives total spending of £3800 million. Production now exceeds sales by £200 million. However, when production is £3500 million, consump-

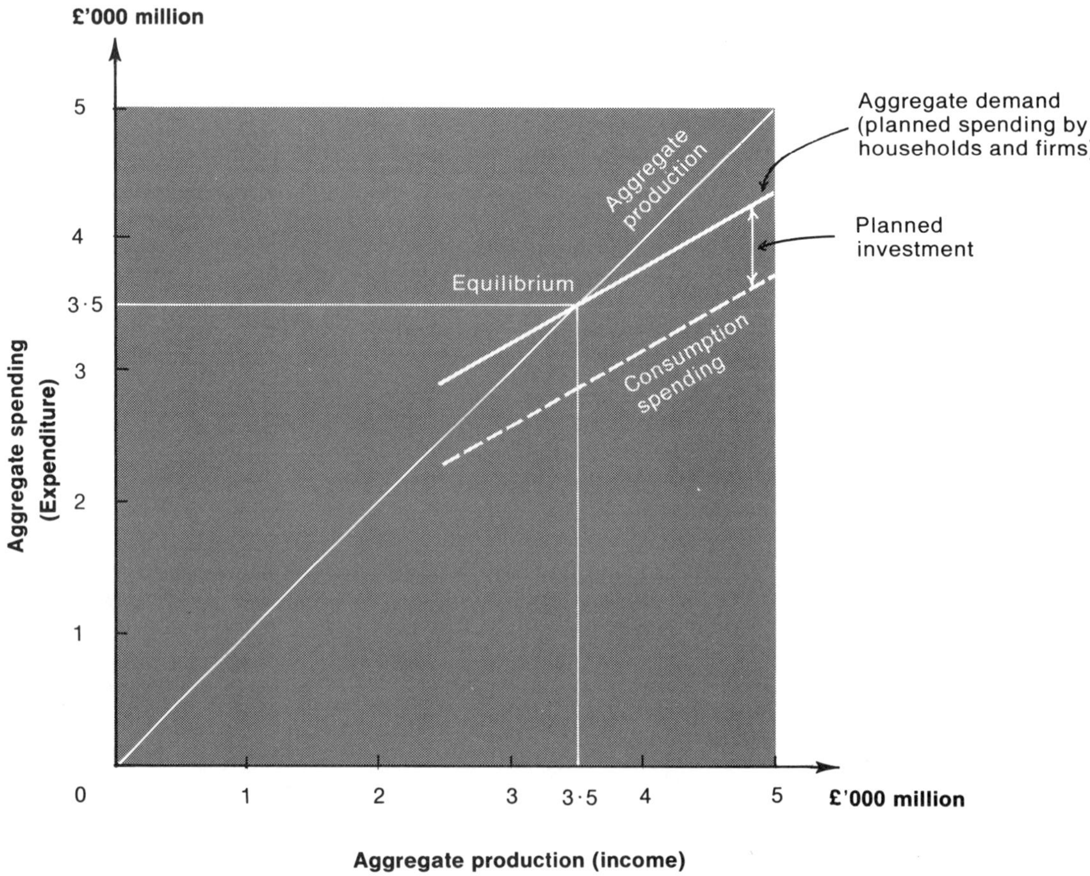

Figure 15.4 Production, consumption, investment and aggregate demand

tion is £2900 million, investment is £600 million and thus production is equal to aggregate demand. This information has been plotted in Figure 15.4.

How the economy moves from disequilibrium to equilibrium

The aggregate demand and aggregate production lines intersect at an aggregate production level of £3500 million. At that level of production, consumption spending of £2900 million and investment of £600 million match the production, so that the economy is in equilibrium. Study of the diagram helps to show how the economy moves from disequilibrium to equilibrium. For example, when aggregate production is £4000 million, aggregate demand is £3800 million (made up of aggregate consumption, £3200 million and investment, £600 million). Sales fall short of production and stocks rise by £200 million. Accordingly, production is cut in the following period. The effect of the reduction in production and income is to produce a reduction in consumption (a movement down along the consumption line), and this reduction in consumption reduces the level of aggregate demand. Notice that investment is unchanged at £600 million. Gradually the gap between aggregate production and aggregate demand is reduced until equilibrium is reached. The number of production periods it will take to achieve equilibrium in the example given above using the data from Table 15.2 will depend on the amount by which aggregate production is reduced on each occasion.

15.6

Consider the data given in Table 15.2 and Figure 15.4. Suppose current aggregate production was £3000 million. This would not be an equilibrium situation.

1 Explain in your own words the processes by which the economy moves to equilibrium.

2 Suppose that when businesses increase or reduce production they do so by making a change of £100 million. Write down the aggregate production, aggregate consumption spending, investment spending and aggregate demand for the following month and for each month as the economy moves towards equilibrium. How many months will it take the economy to achieve equilibrium?

3 Suppose that businesses always change the level of production for the coming month by the precise amount by which stocks changed over the previous month. Will it take more or less time to reach equilibrium than in the case where adjustment was made in units of £100 million? How many production periods will it take?

15.7

A second factor influencing the process of adjustment is the marginal propensity to consume (the slope of the aggregate consumption line in Figures 15.3 and 15.4). In Table 15.2 the marginal propensity to consume was 0.6 because 60 pence in each extra pound of income was spent on consumer goods and services. Table 15.2 shows that when production was £3000 million per month, consumption was £2600 million, investment spending was £600 million and that aggregate demand was greater than aggregate production. We then considered the movement to equilibrium.

But suppose the marginal propensity to consume had been 0.8 rather than 0.6 (80 pence of every additional pound was spent on consumer goods). Would equilibrium have been achieved more quickly, or less quickly than when the marginal propensity to consume was 0.6? As before, assume that production is changed by £100 million each month until equilibrium is reached. You will find it helpful to construct a table similar to Table 15.2 and will need to pay particular attention to the level of consumption spending. You may also find it helpful to draw a diagram similar to Figure 15.4.

Changes in the equilibrium level of production

It has already been noted that equilibrium exists in an economic system at the level at which aggregate demand equals aggregate production. It was also said that the prevailing level of production and employment may be far below what is considered desirable. Other things being equal, the higher the current level of aggregate demand, the higher will be the equilibrium level of production and employment. In the previous section our discussion was of a two-sector economy (without government or overseas sectors) and aggregate demand was divided into two parts: consumption spending and investment spending. But as we saw on page 262, aggregate demand for the UK economy's product can be broken down even further to include government spending and spending by foreigners on the country's exports. Changes in the level of any of these four components of aggregate spending will produce a change in the level of aggregate demand.

Effects of changes in level of investment

In the previous section (see Table 15.2) it was assumed that the level of investment that a business planned was fixed in the short run. Changes in production did not affect the amount they were able to invest. But suppose some event occurs that leads a business to take a more optimistic view of future prospects, and it responds by increasing the level of aggregate investment. For example, it may be decided to raise it because the government has offered some form of investment concessions. Aggregate demand is increased and the immediate result is that aggregate demand has become greater than aggregate production – a disequilibrium has been created. Eventually the system adjusts, production and consumption increase, and a new equilibrium position is reached at which the level of production and employment is higher than the level that operated before the increase in investment. The effects of this increase in investment are shown in Table 15.3, where for simplicity we again consider aggregate demand as comprising only two parts: consumption and investment spending.

1 Initial situation

	Production		[Consumption	+	Investment]	=	Aggregate demand
Initial equilibrium E_1	35	=	[29	+	6]	=	35
	40		32		6		38
	45		35		6		41
	50		38		6		44

2 Situation after increase in investment spending

Production		[Consumption	+	Investment]	=	Aggregate demand	
35		29		10		39	
40		32		10		42	
45	=	[35	+	10]	=	45	New equilibrium E_2
50		38		10		48	

Table 15.3 Effects of a change in investment spending (£00 m)

Part 1 of the table shows the relationship between aggregate demand and aggregate production at various levels of production in the initial equilibrium situation. It shows:

1 investment of £600 million (irrespective of the level of production)
2 that as production (income) increases, consumption spending increases by 60 pence for every pound increase in production;
3 that the equilibrium level of production is £3500 million, because at that level, aggregate demand equals aggregate production.

Part 2 of the table shows the effect of an increase in investment. (Note that investment spending has increased from £600 million to £1000 million per month.)

1 The consumption *schedule* is the same as before.
2 At the initial equilibrium production level of £3500 million, aggregate demand has now increased to £3900 million, because investment spending has increased by £400 million.
3 The adjustment process already described then operates, because aggregate demand is greater than production. Production and consumption increase until eventually a new equilibrium is reached.
4 This new equilibrium level of production is £4500 million. Consumption expenditure has increased from £2900 million to £3500 million and investment spending is £1000 million instead of £600 million.

This increase in investment has been responsible for increasing production and employment. The increase in aggregate production is much greater than the increase in investment spending. It has generated an increase in consumption spending leading to:

Increase in investment	£ 400 million
Increase in consumption	£ 600 million
Increase in production	£1000 million

In short, the increase in production is two and a half times the increase in investment in this example.

This movement from one equilibrium to another is shown in diagrammatic form in Figure 15.5. The initial equilibrium is indicated by E_1.

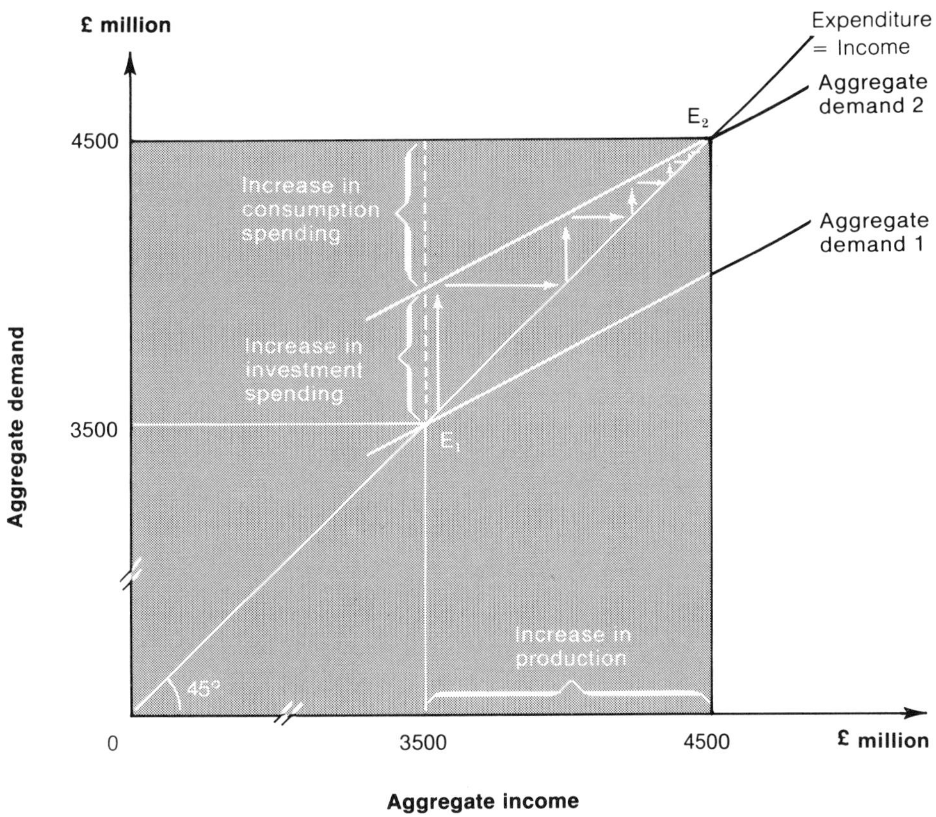

Figure 15.5 Effects of an increase in investment spending on total spending and income

The effect of the increase in investment is depicted as an upwards shift in the aggregate demand curve. A series of adjustments take place (represented by the zig-zag arrows) until the new equilibrium is achieved at E_2.

Effects of changes in government expenditure

It was said earlier that government expenditure is also a component of aggregate demand. For the period covered by each budget, the level of government spending is given (like investment spending) and changes in the level of production do not influence the level of government spending. A budgetary decision to increase the level of government spending will thus have a similar effect to an increase in investment. For example, a public housing project will have similar effects to one undertaken by a private property developer. Both will increase the level of aggregate demand and lead to an increase in production which is some multiple of the initial increase in spending. On this occasion, it is the increase in government investment rather than an increase in private investment that leads to increases in consumption.

Importance to government of general theory of production and employment

This general theory of production and employment has been of very considerable assistance to governments as they have attempted to achieve the economic objective of full employment. If it is known that an increase in investment by businesses or an increase in government spending will lead to an increase in the level of aggregate spending and employment, a government can then introduce policies that will engineer such an initial increase. The relationship between aggregate demand and aggregate production is known fairly precisely, and it is also known at what level of production full employment conditions will prevail. It is thus possible for a government to estimate the size of the increase in private investment or government expenditure necessary to produce full employment. Some of the policies a government can adopt in its attempt to reach full employment were mentioned in Chapter 11. A fuller account of the range of policies is contained in the next chapter.

The multiplier

It is possible to calculate the effect of an initial increase in investment on the aggregate level of production. In Table 15.3, it was shown that £400 million of extra investment led to production increasing by £1000 million and consumption increasing by £600 million. At the same time the example assumed that the marginal propensity to consume was 0.6, that is, for every £1 of increased income, 60p was increased consumption.

Therefore, consumption of £600 million represents 0.6 of the increase in income (production) of £1000 million. If consumption accounts for 0.6 of the extra income then 0.4 must represent investment. Thus an extra £400 million of investment will be equal to 0.4 of the extra production generated by the additional investment spending. Production must increase by £1000 million in order to maintain the MPC at 0.6 and the ratio of extra investment to extra income at 0.4. The amount of extra investment is determined by 1 – 0.6, or in the general case, 1 – MPC. The value of the reciprocal of 1 – MPC in the example is found to be $2\frac{1}{2}$, ($1 - 0.6 = 0.4$ and $\frac{1}{0.4} = 2\frac{1}{2}$) which is actually the amount by which increased production was in excess of the increase in investment. This figure, expressing the amount by which production (income) increases as a multiple of the increase in spending that generated it, is known as the multiplier. Its value can readily be determined by the formula $\frac{1}{1 - \text{MPC}}$ or alternatively $\frac{1}{\text{MPS}}$.

Production and inflation

The previous section described the way in which an increase in private investment spending, or an increase in government spending, might lead to an increase in production and a fall in unemployment. The account may have given the impression that there is no limit to the growth of production that can be achieved in this way provided businesses and government increase spending, and businesses react to falling stocks by seeking to increase production. There is some logic in the reasoning. Increases in the stock of capital goods, plant and machinery will raise the productive capacity of a country and incomes can be spent on the additional goods produced with the assistance of the extra capital equipment.

The problems with this line of reasoning are twofold. Firstly, a country's productive capacity is limited at any particular time by both its labour force and the supplies of capital equipment. As we saw in Chapter 8, the ability of businesses to increase production in the short run is limited. For example, a business that has sales running at a record level, falling stocks and maybe a lengthening order book may be frustrated in its efforts to increase production because it is unable to obtain enough suitable workers. Overtime may be of some assistance, but there is a limit to the amount of overtime that can be worked. The business may well find that an attempt to increase production raises costs of production. In the short run there may be effective limits to the extent to which production can be increased through government spending or private investment without producing general cost increases and inflation.

In the late 1970s governments were reluctant to increase the level of government spending to stimulate production and employment because, it was argued, that this would have led to an increase in the rate of inflation.

Moreover, it has been said that such policies would have had little effect on the level of production or the rate of unemployment. The merits of these arguments are considered in the following chapter.

The second difficulty surrounding the proposition that production and employment can be increased by raising government spending, is that if inflation is sufficiently great, there may be great reluctance on the part of businesses to increase production in response to falling stocks. Indeed during a period of inflation general uncertainty may prevail. If consumers and producers alike take a pessimistic view of the future, savings may increase with the result that the economy may not respond to the stimulus in the way described earlier.

Circular flow of income

The relationship between the level of income (production) in the economy and the level of aggregate demand (expenditure) was illustrated earlier in Chapter 4, in Figure 4.6 showing the market economy. In that model attention is drawn to the principal monetary flows in the economy between the different sectors identified: the business sector, households, government, the financial sector and the overseas sector. Similarities can be seen in terms of the effects of these flows of expenditures and money. The analysis in Figure 15.5. shows the effect of an increase in investment spending on the level of total expenditure and income. An increase in the level of investment clearly increases the level of income and, using the concept of the multiplier, it is possible to calculate the eventual increase in income in relation to the initial increase in investment expenditure. Investment in this instance can be seen as an injection of spending in the economy. In like manner, spending on exports, or by the government on goods and services, will also act as an injection of expenditure and raise the level of income. Reductions of expenditure can occur, not only in the form of increased savings, but also through taxation and spending on imports. Savings, taxation and imports are described as withdrawals or leakages from the circular flow of income. Investment, government expenditure and exports are injections or additions to the circular flow of income.

Figure 15.6 presents a simplified picture of these flows of income in the economy. In the figure the direction of withdrawals and injections in terms of their effects on the flow of income is shown by the arrows as indicated. If the overall effect of these flows is considered, then the total level of injections in relation to the total level of withdrawals will produce either a net injection or a net withdrawal, in the event of total injections not being equal to total withdrawals. If there is a net injection of spending in the economy, then the level of income will increase; a net withdrawal will cause income to contract.

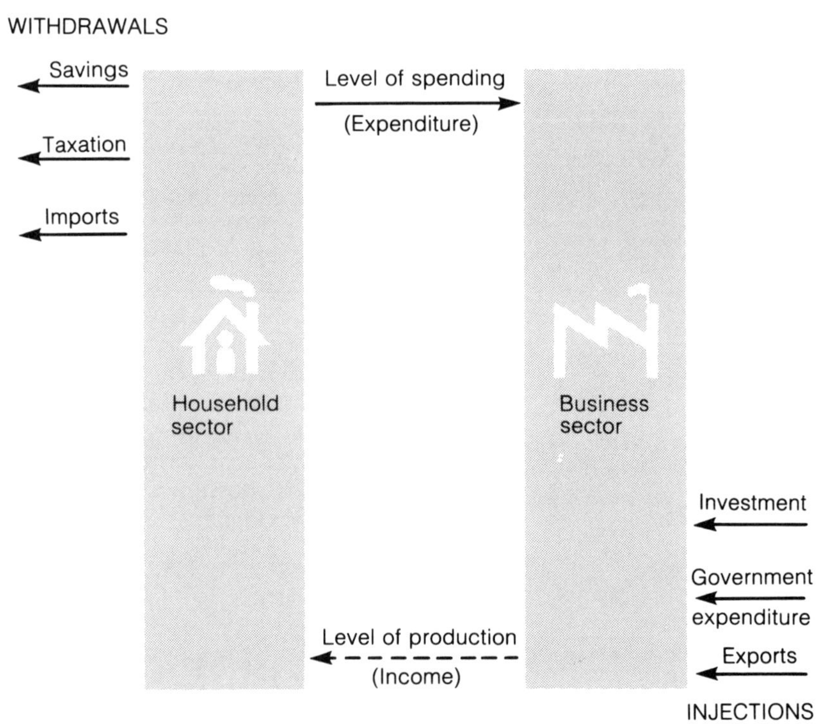

Figure 15.6 Circular flow of income

The extent to which income will increase in response to a net injection of expenditure will depend upon the value of the multiplier. In the reverse instance of a net withdrawal, the amount by which income contracts is similarly dependent on the multiplier. The discussion of the multiplier given earlier produced the formula that the multiplier equals $\frac{1}{1 - \text{MPC}}$ or $\frac{1}{\text{MPS}}$. Taking the formula given, in the general form of the reciprocal of the level of savings, the effect of additional withdrawals in the economy (taxation and imports) can be demonstrated. The proportion of extra taxation in the economy from an increase in the total level of income or expenditure, can be described as the marginal propensity to tax or MPT. The amount of extra spending on imports in the economy, as a proportion of an increase in total expenditure, is the marginal propensity to import or MPM. Then an increase in income in the economy will lead to an increase in imports and taxation as well as in the level of savings. (In the event of a decrease or contraction in the level of income then taxation, imports and savings will fall.) The eventual increase in income, the multiplied effect, will correspondingly be smaller if the level of withdrawals is greater as the multiplier in this instance is equal to

$$\frac{1}{\text{total leakages or withdrawals}}$$

or

$$\frac{1}{\text{MPS} + \text{MPT} + \text{MPM}}$$

Stage three

Economic Problems

Chapter 16

Inflation

The principal economic objectives of successive British governments have been full employment, price stability, a satisfactory balance of payments position and a high rate of economic growth. In recent years the inability to keep the rate of increase of prices to an acceptable level has led to great emphasis on the need to control inflation.

This chapter is devoted to the problem of controlling inflation and the policies that the UK government considers when attempting to do so. Of particular concern is the relationship between the level of inflation and the amount of unemployment, because a number of policy measures impinge upon both of these objectives. More specifically, there are occasions when conflict will arise between these objectives. For example, we noted in the previous chapter that policies designed to increase production and employment may create a situation in which excess aggregate demand leads to price increases. Conversely, there is good reason to believe that measures that attempt to reduce inflation by reducing aggregate demand, are likely to have an initial effect of reducing production and creating more unemployment. Some actions by government taken to achieve one objective may make it impossible to attain the other.

There is also a rather complicated link between inflation, the balance of payments and external economic policies. This link is explored more fully in Chapter 17. The discussion of the fourth objective, a high rate of economic growth, is deferred until Chapter 21.

What is inflation?

Definition of inflation

Inflation has been defined in various ways. Two of the commonest definitions are expressed in terms of aggregate demand or rising prices. The first says that inflation exists when there is excess demand for goods and services in the economy as a whole.

The second defines inflation as a situation in which there is a readily identifiable upward trend in the general price level as measured by an appropriate price index number.[1]

In this chapter we use the second definition; inflation involves an upward trend in the general price level. This particular definition has been adopted because it is rising prices and their undesirable effects that cause concern in the UK and provoke policy responses.

However, both definitions have their weaknesses and one may be more suitable for a particular situation. It is possible to have rising prices without excess aggregate demand – a condition experienced in many western industrial nations in recent years. Conversely, a government that implements rigid price controls may be able to prevent inflation, measured in terms of the movement of some price index, but such policies may still leave a situation of excess aggregate demand.

This may produce other undesirable consequences, which are considered later in the chapter.

Measuring inflation

The commonest index for measuring inflation in the UK is the Retail Price Index (RPI). It is calculated by the Department of Employment and published monthly in various government publications. The RPI measures changes in the price of a basket of goods and services. This basket is chosen to include those items on which a high proportion of household expenditure occurs. Items come from a number of broad groups including food, clothing, household durables, housing, transportation, tobacco and alcohol, health and personal services, leisure services and so on. Prices are collected on a regular monthly basis for various individual items in each group and these in turn are weighted so that their relative importance is reflected in the calculation of the index number. The weights are determined from the Family Expenditure Survey which collects data showing how households allocate their expenditure on different items. The weighting given to each group then represents its proportionate share in total spending.

Price information is collected from different areas in proportion to the population living there so that the index can allow for regional variations. Since prices for consumer goods vary between different retailing establishments, a wide range of price collection points are used to achieve a more representative weighted average. Average prices for each item are then calculated from the many price quotations taken and built into the calculation of the monthly index. Figure 16.1 shows the RPI for the UK from 1966 to 1974 in (a) and from 1974 onwards in (b). Two graphs are shown being calculated on different base dates, for (a) the index = 100 on 16 January 1962 and for (b) the index = 100 on 12 January 1974. The values given for each year are the monthly averages of the index. The two graphs can be compared to show changes in the index over the whole period, provided that the effect of changing the base year in 1974 is considered. The index in Figure 16.1(b) indicates changes relative to 1974.

Note the sharp increase in the index since 1973. Great care must be taken when interpreting graphs such as Figure 16.1. An elementary mistake is to infer that when the index is increasing, inflation is also increasing. The increase in the index tells us that prices are rising and that there is inflation. The rate of inflation tells us how fast prices are rising. This rate of inflation is conventionally expressed as the percentage increase in the index over a specified period, such as a year, or three months.

Figure 16.2 shows the annual rate of inflation as measured by the rate at which the RPI increased from year to year. This figure shows a sharp increase in the rate of inflation in the UK in 1973 to 1975, followed by a reduction in the rate since then. Discussion on inflation in the 1960s was quite different from the problem of the mid 1970s when the main concern was to bring the rate down from over 20 per cent. Since then the UK government has stated its intent to bring the rate of inflation down to less than 10 per cent per annum. For various reasons, this objective remains a major policy goal of the early 1980s. Policies introduced in relation to this goal have produced a fall in the rate of inflation through a reduction in the level of economic activity; there have been cuts in public expenditure, reductions in the money supply, which have contributed towards a fall in the level of aggregate demand, and increasing unemployment as a result.

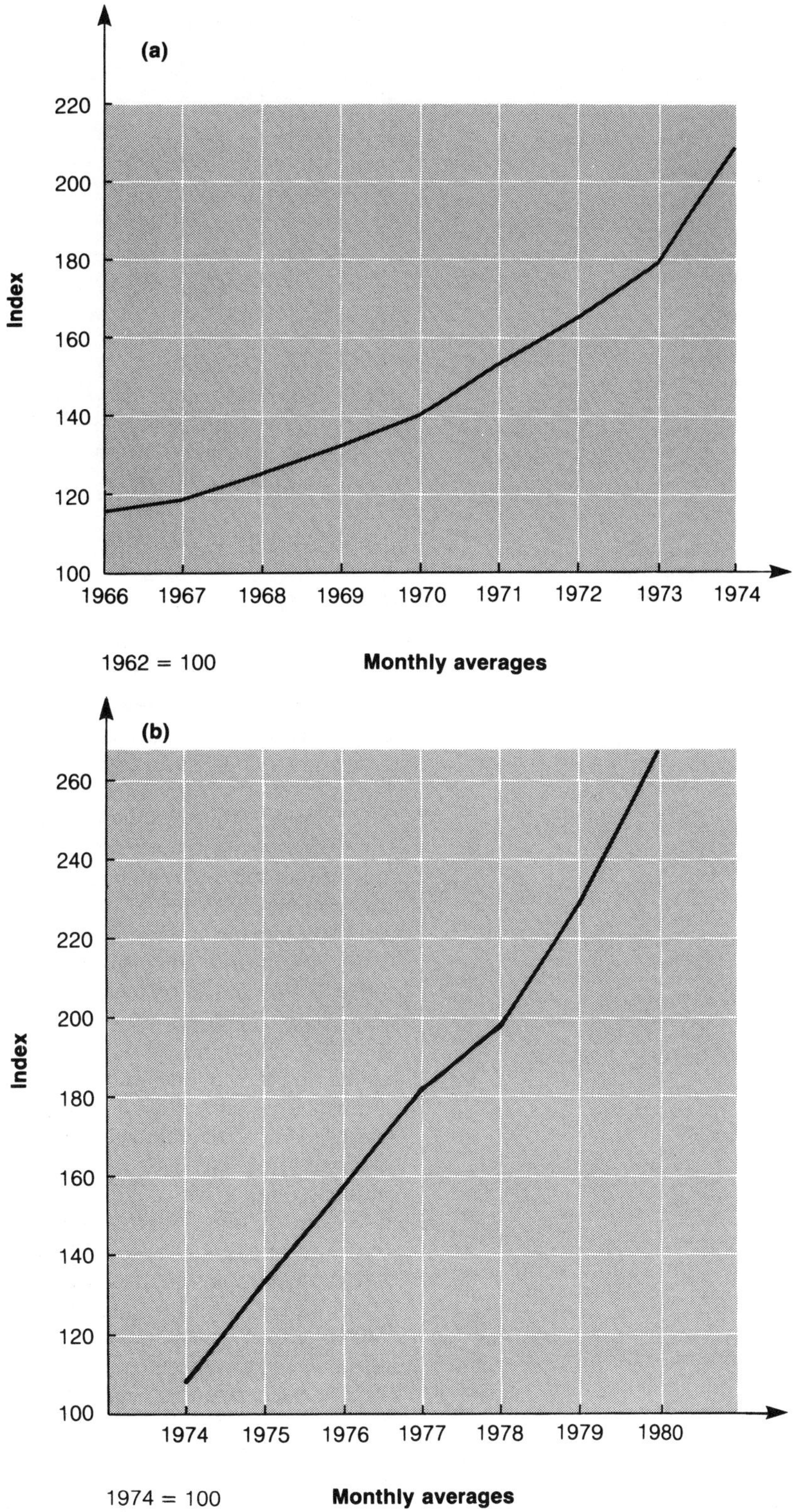

Figure 16.1 Index of retail prices: (a) 1966–74 (b) 1974–80

Source: Annual Abstract of Statistics 1980, HMSO

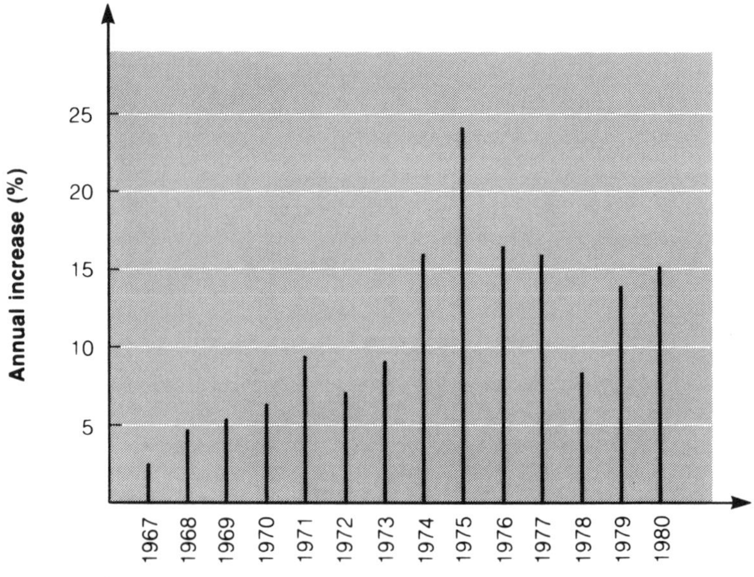

Figure 16.2 Annual percentage increase in retail price index 1967–80
Source: Annual Abstract of Statistics 1980, HMSO

The retail price index is only one of the number of price indexes that are used to measure inflation. It is commonly used because it relates to consumer goods and is available soon after the end of each month. It is easier for the general public to gain a broad understanding of the retail price index than most of the alternative measures. Its principal disadvantages are that it relates only to consumer goods and to what the statistician judges to be a representative group of these goods. A sudden movement in the price of one heavily weighted item such as meat may have a substantial effect on the index.

An alternative that can be used to measure inflation is the implicit deflator that is used to convert gross domestic product at current prices to gross domestic product at constant prices. The deflator is found by dividing the value of GDP at current prices by the value of GDP at constant prices. The implicit deflator has the advantage that it covers a much broader group of commodities and services than does the retail price index. It includes products necessary for businesses but not normally purchased by households. As higher prices to businesses often precede higher prices for consumers, the implicit deflator of gross domestic product may also provide an early indication of the likely trend in consumer prices. This same point can be made for the wholesale prices index which measures price changes of the raw materials and other inputs used by industry in production.

Table 16.1 shows the annual increase in prices as measured by the implicit price deflator of gross domestic product between 1974 and 1978. Comparison of Figure 16.2 and Table 16.1 shows some difference between the RPI measure and the implicit deflator of gross domestic product. Other measures of inflation, such as the Tax and Prices Index, may be used by governments at a particular time and there may be an additional political advantage in emphasising an alternative measure.

However, there is little dispute about the trend in the UK inflation rate during the 1970s. Both measures show rapidly accelerating inflation in 1974 and 1975, some moderation in 1976 and a continuing reduction through to 1978, once more rising to 1980.

Year	Index 1975 = 100	Rate of change (%)
1974	78.5	17.0
1975	100.0	27.4
1976	113.7	13.7
1977	127.2	11.9
1978	140.8	9.7

Table 16.1 Implicit price deflator of gross domestic product, UK

Is inflation undesirable?

Inflation causes redistribution of incomes

Various reasons are given for trying to avoid (or at least contain) inflation.

First, inflation causes a redistribution of incomes. Pensioners and those groups of workers within the community who are in a poor bargaining position often find it difficult to gain the increases in money incomes necessary to prevent reductions in their real incomes.

Means money losing value

Second, inflation means that money is losing value and it whittles away the real value of existing savings. Inflation may make people reluctant to hold savings in the form of money; it may take away the incentive to invest in life assurance policies in preparation for retirement. But, paradoxically, it may also lead to uncertainty that results in many people saving more of their incomes. This appears irrational, but can be explained in terms of the need to take precautions against the effects of difficult economic conditions that may occur in the future. In the 1970s the ratio of savings to income rose sharply as inflation and unemployment increased. It seems likely that this increased saving was an attempt by individuals to protect themselves in a more uncertain world.

Inflationary expectations produce more rapid inflation

Third, loss of the value of money may generate an even more rapid rate of inflation. Several factors contribute to this. There is a great deal of evidence to support the view that if the rate of inflation is increasing, people will come to expect it to increase even more rapidly. In consequence they seek compensation for the expected inflation and this in turn has the effect of raising the actual rate of inflation still further. For example unions may seek higher wages for their workers based on how much they expect prices to rise by. If these wages claims are granted then costs and prices will rise more rapidly than in the previous period. Similarly, business firms may make price increases *now* as a defence against what they see as inevitable wage increases in the next few months. They may also increase prices because of the need to raise sufficient funds to replenish stocks of materials which they expect to be more expensive in the future.

Escalating inflation may reach the stage at which it threatens the operation of the money system itself. Speculation is encouraged. Individuals seek to hold their assets in some form that will increase its monetary value; hence the purchase of land, works of art, antiques, postage stamps and securities. There may be a rush by consumers to buy now rather than later when prices are even higher, and this will increase the pressure on available resources. The higher the rate of price increases the greater this pressure becomes, with the result that greater price increases are stimulated.

Balance of payments problems

Fourth, it is often said that inflation is undesirable because it is likely to produce balance of payments problems by increasing the costs of export industries and import-competing industries, particularly if the pace of inflation in the UK exceeds that of its trading partners. The UK faced severe balance of payments problems in the mid 1970s which were in part made more difficult by the higher rate of inflation experienced in the UK compared with other industrial trading nations.

The world-wide nature of inflation has led to suggestions that inflation is not a problem when all countries are experiencing a similar situation. This view must be rejected. The first three reasons given in this section constitute powerful arguments for controlling inflation. In addition a succession of world monetary crises have been one of the marks of this inflationary period. Most of the western industrial countries including the UK have faced balance of payments problems, which have been more difficult to solve because of the existence of inflation. These problems are discussed in the following chapter.

Causes of inflation

Demand-pull theory

Cost-push theory

Two theories of the inflationary process are the 'demand-pull' and the 'cost-push' explanations. The first suggests that the inflationary process starts as a result of excess demand pressures; these then cause a bidding up of costs and prices. The second suggests that it is the additional costs resulting from pressures such as unions' demands for higher wages that force businesses to increase their prices; these initial increases then generate further wage demands and cost increases. Differing views on the merits of these theories have been put forward. These have ranged from the belief that they describe different aspects of the same inflationary process to the opinion that they are quite separate theories which either provide different and conflicting explanations of the same inflationary process, or that they are each legitimate explanations of quite separate inflationary processes.

There is fairly general agreement that whatever the cause of the initial increase in prices, it will tend to lead to new wage demands and to cost increases which cannot be absorbed by increases in productivity. Consequently, further price increases are inevitable. Attempts to identify a single starting point in this 'chicken and egg' situation are not helpful. It is more useful to indicate some of the possible and probable starting points from which the inflationary process may develop. Some of these are listed in Table 16.2.

	Demand pressures	Rising costs
Internal	(Labour market shortages)	
	Employers offer higher wages	Union demands for higher wages
External	Rising export prices	Increasing import prices
	Capital inflow	

Table 16.2 Possible causes of inflation

Excess demand within the country may mean that businesses are prepared to pay higher wages to attract scarce labour, and that they bid up the price of materials. The excess demand may also present firms with an opportunity to increase their profit margins. They may raise their prices safely knowing that shortages will compel purchasers to pay the higher prices.

In addition, the sharp increase in UK government expenditure in the 1970s without increases in taxes stimulated internal demand pressures.

External influences may play a major part in triggering inflation. In the UK this has come about through increasing costs of imported materials. The UK, like many other countries that relied heavily on imports of petroleum products, experienced substantial cost increases in 1973 and subsequently, following the price increases in crude oil. Increasing export prices are a potential cause of inflation through increasing incomes and aggregate demand in the economy. More investment and capital inflow into an economy would increase demand in the same manner and may result in demand pull pressures on the price level. Higher export prices and the flow of investment will be influenced by the exchange rate. A strong pound may attract investors but there are problems involved if the exchange rate appreciates to such an extent that exporters find that prices of their products are too high to be competitive on foreign markets.

Inflation and wage demands

The idea that inflation is generated by acceding to wage demands is a familiar one. Increases in wage rates are often seen as the immediate cause of price increases, whether the wage rates are increased by some wage fixing authority, by arbitration, as a result of bargaining by unions and employers, or the result of a protracted dispute and a successful wage claim by unions. Granting employees a shorter working week or longer holidays without reducing earnings will have a similar result. Costs are increased and then passed on in higher prices. However, it may be the case that increasing wage rates are responding to underlying pressures in the economic system. Large increases in wages are granted because of excess demand for labour or because prices are rising sharply.

Inflation in the UK in the 1970s has been the result of many causes. Excess demand for certain types of labour contributed to wage push pressures early in the decade. Even more apparent was the wage explosion of the early 1970s when the incomes policies adopted in the late 1960s were abandoned. Throughout the 1970s demands for wage increases have been a major factor and have at times reached unprecedented levels. This, as we will see later in the chapter has led to the reintroduction of incomes policies. Import prices for items such as crude oil, basic plastic materials, foodstuffs and industrial raw materials have risen substantially. The effect of government spending and borrowing in the economy has increased the level of aggregate demand and the money supply in the economy with inflationary consequences. Because inflation is such a complex phenomenon, we must be sceptical of simplistic proposals to solve the problem.

16.1

From appropriate sources, graph movements in the Retail Price Index and the implicit deflator of gross domestic product for recent periods. Compare the results with the information in Figure 16.2 and Table 16.1 (It may be possible to find data for this to be done on a quarterly basis).

1 What can you conclude about the rate of inflation in the UK?

2 Is there any evidence to suggest that changes in the rate of inflation show up sooner in the implicit deflator than in the consumer price index?

16.2

Country	Annual percentage increase Year ended August 1975	1976	1977	1978
Canada	11.1	6.2	8.3	9.4
United States	8.6	5.6	6.6	7.9
Japan	10.0	8.8	8.5	4.2
Australia	16.9	12.3	13.4	7.9
Belgium	11.4	8.8	7.1	4.1
France	11.0	9.5	9.9	9.4
Germany (FDR)	5.9	4.6	3.9	2.4
Italy	15.3	17.0	18.8	12.1
Switzerland	6.7	1.5	1.3	1.2
United Kingdom	26.9	13.8	16.5	8.0
Yugoslavia	24.0	7.7	15.0	13.9
Total OECD	11.0	8.3	9.4	8.4

Table 16.3 Increases in consumer price index: various countries, 1975 to 1978

Source: *Main Economic Indicators*, (various issues), Organisation for Economic Co-operation and Development

1 Is there any evidence in Table 16.3 to suggest that the OECD countries are now capable of controlling their inflation?
2 What additional information would you need to establish whether performance in controlling inflation was better or worse than other OECD countries?
3 To what extent does the information in the table support the view that small countries with strong trading links with others are unable to avoid world inflation so the best they can aim for is to achieve a somewhat lower rate of inflation? Why may such small countries be vulnerable to inflation originating in the major industrial countries?

Policies to control inflation

Problems of selecting economic policies

Governments face considerable problems when selecting economic policies. First, they need to have an understanding of the general effect of applying any particular policy instrument. Second, it is often difficult to predict the precise effects of a policy decision. For example, the government would like to know not only whether a particular increase in expenditure will reduce unemployment, but how great the fall will be and how quickly it will occur. There is an inevitable time-lag between the moment a policy decision is taken and the time when that policy starts to take effect. A third problem is the extent to which various policy measures are politically acceptable, while the fourth problem already mentioned is the effect of the policy on other economic objectives.

It seems logical to suggest that the way to control inflation is to attack its causes. The level of aggregate demand appears to have considerable influence on inflation generated from internal sources. The suggestion that policies need to be developed to prevent internal cost pressures from developing also appears important. Thirdly, it is necessary to devise and implement policies that would reduce the effects of external influences on price levels in the UK.

Table 16.4 lists some of the main types of policy a government considers when attempting to control inflation.

This list of policy instruments is not comprehensive, nor is it meant to indicate that all the measures listed are equally important devices for stimulating employment, nor that they are all used primarily by government for the attainment of the price stability objective. For example, external policies are more commonly used to achieve a satisfactory balance of payments situation, though they can, and have been used to combat inflation.

Short-term policies

Policies are divided into short-term, long-term and background policies. Short-term policies can be regarded as measures that are likely to have an effect on aggregate demand and production within, say, twelve months. For example, it is likely that an increase in interest rates will have some effect on economic activity within a year of the change, particularly in such sensitive areas as housing. On the other hand, a decision by the UK government to reduce capital expenditure will take longer to implement and its full effects may not be felt for several years.

Background policies

Background policies are seldom changed but nonetheless act as a constraining element and complement the various short- and long-term policies. For example, during the 1970s trade practices legislation has been enacted with the aim of fostering price competition between firms. These policies are discussed in Chapter 18. The UK's commercial obligations as a signatory to the General Agreement on Tariffs and Trade (GATT) also provide a background against which specific changes in import duties are made.

	General measures, to change aggregate demand		Specific wage price policies	External policies
	Monetary policies	Fiscal policies		
Short-term	Liquid assets ratio Interest rates Open market operations Bank of England directives Special deposits	Direct and indirect taxation rates (allowances and incentives) Current UK government expenditure	Wage price freeze (price controls) Incomes policies	Quotas Exchange controls Exchange rate variations
Long-term	Public Sector Borrowing Requirement (PSBR)	Government capital expenditure Implications of PSBR on Government expenditure	Wage indexation	Exchange rate Import duties
Background policies	Monetary targets		Industrial legislation Legislation to promote price competition	Foreign investment controls Commercial treaty obligations e.g. EEC, GATT

Table 16.4 Policy instruments that may influence the rate of inflation

Monetary policy

The main types of monetary policy open to the UK government were outlined in Chapter 11. In essence, monetary policy works to reduce inflation when it reduces aggregate demand. Businesses are forced to respond to the more stringent monetary conditions by restricting new investment. Households may be unable to obtain funds for housing or for consumption expenditure.

Availability of funds and costs of funds

It is possible to distinguish between those instruments that are directed primarily at the availability of funds and those designed primarily to influence the cost of borrowing funds. The reserve assets ratio and the Bank of England's directives to banks and the non-bank financial intermediaries are aimed directly at the availability of funds, whereas interest rate controls affect the cost of funds. Open-market operations can directly affect both the availability of funds and the level of interest rates.

The availability of funds and the cost of funds are, of course, related. Measures that are directed primarily at reducing the availability of funds typically produce situations in which market interest rates rise. Conversely, changes in interest rates typically affect the availability of funds.

Monetarism

The UK has seen, in the late 1970s, a marked change in emphasis towards the role of monetary policy in containing inflation. The Conservative government that took office in 1979 declared itself to be committed above all to reducing the rate of inflation. Monetary policy rather than fiscal policy was to be the main instrument in achieving this objective. A marked change in government policy towards a monetarist approach is clearly apparent, shifting away from what had been the accepted traditional fiscal, or budgetary, approach to managing the economy. The role of the money supply in the economy, whether it be expansionary or restrictive, is seen by the monetarist to be a crucial determinant of changes in the level of aggregate demand and in the level of prices. In brief, this can be demonstrated by the quantity theory of money which states in its simplest form that:

Quantity theory of money

$$MV = PT$$

where M is the money supply or stock in the economy
V is the velocity of circulation of money
P is the price level
T is the volume of transactions or output.

From this question, it can be seen that if the velocity of circulation of money remains constant then a change in the supply of money will cause an increase in prices and/or the volume of transactions. From this, the monetarist argument then follows, that inflation can be brought about by increases in the money supply in the economy (in the absence of an accommodating change in the velocity of circulation or the volume of output). The claim then follows that, if the money supply is increased in an economy, then the price level will also increase after a sufficient time-lag for the effects to work through the economy, usually 12 to 18 months. To reduce inflation, implies that the rate of growth of the money supply needs to be restrained and controlled. Anti-inflation policy then takes on the role of monetary restraint in the economy, often expressed by the government as a target rate of growth for the money supply in the economy.

Money supply

It becomes necessary for the government to have a clear definition of the money supply in the economy in order to attempt some degree of control over it and to monitor its rate of growth. Measuring the money supply is more complex than it might appear at first thought. Clearly notes and coins in the economy represent only a small proportion of the money supply; as was seen earlier, bank deposits and the availability of credit in the economy have also to be taken into account.

Definitions of the money supply

In the UK, two official definitions of the money supply are usually referred to, M_1, the narrow definition of the money supply, consists of notes and coins in circulation plus deposits in current accounts held by the private sector in sterling. M_3, is a wider definition and includes notes and coins and all bank deposits, in sterling and other currencies, held in the UK by both the private and the public sectors. Sterling M_3 excludes deposits held in foreign currencies by UK residents from the total for M_3, therefore representing M_3 in terms of sterling only.

The rate of growth of the money supply, as measured in terms of M_3, becomes an important policy target for the operation of monetarist policy. If the money supply expands beyond the desired level the rate of increase in prices will accelerate according to the monetarist view. The difficulty in terms of policy is to determine what the target rate of increase for the money supply should be. Further problems also arise as to whether the money supply measure itself is the appropriate one and if it fully represents the full availability of, and level of money and credit in the economy. Restraint on the money supply to cure inflation may not operate to the extent that the government wishes if other sources of credit and deposits in the economy may finance spending and generate demand.

PSBR

Moreover the government itself plays a major part in determining the size of, and changes in, the money supply through its own activities and expenditure. The Public Sector Borrowing Requirement (PSBR) represents government borrowing to finance expenditure. The PSBR in the form of government stock and securities, when sold to the banks and other financial institutions, will expand the money supply through the mechanism of credit creation by supplying the financial system with reserve assets. The PSBR financed by National Savings, or sales of stock to the private sector, will not have this expansionary effect on the level of credit since it will be provided for out of private savings which would otherwise be lodged in some other form of asset or deposit. The level of the PSBR is clearly important as is the way it is financed.

An increased PSBR necessitated by increased public spending will put more pressures on any government attempt to impose restraint. If more public spending is unavoidable, for example as a result of rising unemployment, then the effect of this on the PSBR will conflict with a government's anti-inflation policy based on monetary restraint.

Control of the money supply

The main instruments of monetary control are first those that influence the price of, and supply of, credit in the economy. The level of interest rates can be increased to reduce credit and the government can use measures such as special deposits, directives, open-market operations to influence the volume of credit. Monetary restraint will also involve public expenditure and tax policies, which will determine the size of the PSBR and its composition. Interest rates will also be influenced by the financing of the PSBR and the sale of government securities. If the government issues long-dated stock to finance the PSBR, sales of the stock will tend to depress the price and increase the rate of interest. This has implications for government expenditure, for the higher interest rates must be paid in future years, and also on the level of private investment from higher interest rates on borrowed funds. Reducing the volume of private sector investment may prove a serious problem arising from the high interest rates that monetary policy imposes during a period of restraint.

The level of aggregate demand in the economy is clearly affected by expenditure and tax policies. From the monetary point of view there are also monetary implications from changes in public spending and taxation to be borne in mind. The impact of the level of the PSBR has already been referred to and changes in the level and composition of taxes in the economy will similarly be reflected in the money supply. Changes in direct and indirect taxation have repercussions on the level of consumption, savings and investment in aggregate. Productivity and output will change if taxation alters incentives in the economy. Obviously the size of the public sector deficit can be reduced by increased taxation, as well as reductions in expenditure and a smaller PSBR. Fiscal policy is then seen by monetarists in a supporting role to the operation of monetary policies in the economy. The problem for decision-makers is the right fiscal and monetary policy mix which is consistent with other government objectives for the distribution of income, the level of employment, the balance of payments and the rate of economic growth.

Fiscal (budgetary) policy

Aggregate demand can also be reduced by employing policies that affect government recepits from taxation and government expenditure. Measures that increase the rates of taxation will tend to reduce disposable income and thereby produce a fall in consumption. Policies that involve increases in the government's own spending often increase aggregate demand directly and may thus make inflation worse. The converse is also true. Reductions in government spending reduce aggregate demand and tend to lessen inflationary pressures, other things being equal.

Historical emphasis on 'balanced budget'

Until the 1940s there was a widespread belief that 'sound financial management' by governments required that they balance their budgets; that they should raise from taxation what they required to spend. If such a principle is strictly observed, a government's opportunities for increasing or reducing aggregate demand are greatly reduced, for an increase in taxation will largely nullify the effects of an increase in government spending.

During the great depression of the 1930s some economists advocated a deliberate policy of not balancing a budget to give government additional means of influencing aggregate economic activity. A budgetary deficit (expenditure exceeds taxation receipts) tends to increase aggregate demand. Such a deficit can be financed by government borrowing; the additional funds may always be obtained from the central Bank without reducing the liquidity of the other financial institutions. Likewise, a budget surplus (taxation receipts exceed revenue) will tend to reduce aggregate demand and to reduce inflationary pressure.

The qualification 'will tend to' in the last sentence is important. The precise effect on aggregate demand will depend on the types of taxation and expenditure measures, because the effects of each vary considerably. It is possible for a government to introduce measures that produce a budget surplus, or increase an existing surplus, whilst at the same time increasing aggregate demand. Such a situation is illustrated in Table 16.5

	Tax receipts (£m)		Welfare payments (£m)	Net change in budget position (£m)
Change in budgetary position	+100	*less*	95	+5 surplus
Marginal propensity to consume	0.9		1.0	
Change in consumption spending of affected groups	–90		+95	+5 (net change in consumption spending)

Table 16.5 Effects of changes in tax receipts and welfare payments on the level of aggregate demand

In this example, an increase in taxation receipts of £100 million and an increase of welfare payments of £95 million generate a budgetary surplus of £5 million, which, other things being equal, would tend to reduce aggregate demand. However, the actual effect on aggregate demand of each measure will be determined by the marginal propensity to consume. If 90 per cent of the income now taken by the government as additional taxation would have been consumed then the effect of this increase in taxation receipts of £100 million will be to reduce consumption spending by £90 million. If the entire increase in the welfare payments is spent by the recipients, as is likely, this will increase consumption spending of £95 million. Overall, there will be a net increase in consumption spending of £5 million, not withstanding the budget surplus of £5 million. If follows that, whilst the existence of a budget deficit or an increase in government indebtedness provides an indication of whether fiscal policy will be expansionary or not, it is not an entirely accurate measure of the effectiveness of such policies.

When the Chancellor of the Exchequer proposes the budget, or presents any package of fiscal measures, it is necessary for him to estimate the likely effects of each measure so that he can determine the likely overall effect. In recent years, the concern has been to reduce the deficit in the hope that this will help to bring inflation down. Reducing expenditure, or even reducing the rate of growth of expenditure has proved difficult because the government's declared policies have committed it to maintaining existing expenditure levels on many items.

Direct taxation

Government attempts to influence aggregate demand take place against the background of a progressive tax system. As personal incomes increase, individuals find themselves in a group that pays a higher marginal tax rate. For this reason alone, the amount of personal income tax paid increases with inflation without any changes in the tax rates. Income tax collections have risen even with reductions in the marginal and average tax rates. The indexation of taxable allowances allows the government the opportunity to offset the effects of inflation on the income tax yield if it chooses to implement the changes.

A policy of reducing income tax rates for each level of income can be regarded as expansionary. It may be, of course, that the net effect of a reduction in tax rates and an increase in incomes is that total receipts from personal income tax will still be higher than the previous year. Nevertheless, the cut in tax rates can be considered expansionary because receipts will be lower than they would have been.

Changing the allowances against income tax means the government manipulates the tax base as distinct from the tax rate. If the government reduces the allowances, or even holds them constant rather than indexing them, government tax receipts will increase with contractionary effects on demand.

Other important direct taxation measures at the government's disposal are the rate of tax on companies and taxable allowances and incentives offered to businesses. An increase in investment allowances or a more generous rate of depreciation of capital against liability for taxation may have the direct effect of encouraging business to increase investment and production.

Indirect taxes

Sales taxes and excise duties can also be used to influence the level of aggregate demand. In the United Kingdom it has been more common to use increases in the general level of sales tax than income tax changes as a policy instrument. Indirect taxes may of course also be used as essentially revenue raising devices but the government has used the rate of VAT in the UK as a more general policy measure to influence the level of consumption and demand. For example, at one time a 25 per cent rate of VAT was levied on luxuries when the standard rate on other goods and services was 10 per cent. Occasionally the tax on a particular product may be changed to increase or decrease output in that industry. A reduction in the rate of tax, or even the payment of a subsidy, may be used to encourage production.

To be effective either as a revenue-raising or fiscal device, an indirect tax is better levied on goods with an inelastic demand. Increasing the tax rate then has a relatively small effect on the quantity purchased, expenditure on the good is increased and consumers are left with less to spend on other goods. A reduction in the tax rate will have the opposite effect.

Government expenditure

Some of the problems associated with the reduction of government expenditure have been mentioned already. Despite attempts to keep government expenditure down, the commitment to social welfare policies, to health, pensions, education and housing, means that reductions in expenditure are virtually impossible and increases hard to restrict. Government faces political unpopularity when prosposals for specific cuts are put forward. The result is that real expenditure cuts tend to occur in those areas of government activity where opposition to the cuts is less organised or less vocal.

Reducing public spending

In recent years, attempts to reduce real public expenditure have involved the use of cash limits on spending by government departments, nationalised industries and local authorities. In local government, this has meant a threat to the level of services provided by the local authority and cut backs on staffing in education (schools and colleges) for example. Services have been affected in other ways through the cuts, which in most instances amount initially to a reduction in the rate of expansion planned so that the relative level of spending has fallen. In particular, such cuts have direct implications on the wage increases that can be afforded in the annual pay and salaries negotiations by the authorities. Limiting pay increases in this manner is a direct response by central government to the problem of wage-push inflation. Political opposition has arisen to planned cuts in public spending and this centres as much on the political issue as to what amount of state intervention and to what level the public sector should be developed in the economy.

Governments may also be overtaken by events. The increase in unemployment from the late 1970s has committed governments to greater amounts of public expenditure to meet the cost of providing welfare for the unemployed. At the same time, this has been in direct conflict to the government's intended cuts in public expenditure.

There is, then, no simple means of effectively reducing expenditure and suggestions that inflation can be controlled by this method have an element of unreality. Even achieving the intended relationship between expenditure and receipts is extremely difficult. Governments have found it impossible to assess accurately levels of receipts and payments in recent years. Estimates of the size of the budget deficit have often fallen well short of actual deficits at the end of each year.

Inflation and unemployment

In general the monetary and fiscal policy instruments used to vary the level of aggregate demand will affect the level of unemployment as well as the rate of inflation. Measures that reduce the level of aggregate demand will tend to reduce the rate of inflation, but they may also lead to an increase in unemployment. Cuts in government expenditure may lead to direct reductions in the number of persons employed in government services and there may be consequential reductions in consumption expenditure. Increases in interest rates and reductions in the supply of loanable funds may have adverse effects on investment and the level of business activity. This too may lead to increases in unemployment.

Conversely, increases in government expenditure, cuts in direct and indirect taxes, reductions in interest rates and a greater supply of loanable funds are likely to lead to an increase in aggregate demand and to a reduction in unemployment. However, such increases in aggregate demand may also lead to more inflation as businesses agree to higher wage demands in response to a tighter labour market. The lower the rate of unemployment the more successful are unions likely to be in persuading employers to increase wages.

This general relationship between inflation and unemployment is shown in Figure 16.3. The curve slopes upwards from left to right suggesting that the lower the rate of unemployment, the higher the rate of inflation.

Conversely, the higher the rate of unemployment, the lower is likely to be the rate of inflation.

Trade-off between unemployment and inflation

For a number of years, it has been conceded that the two objectives of price stability and full employment may well be unobtainable simultaneously. It has been argued that something of one, or the other, or perhaps of both must be sacrificed and that government is faced with a choice or trade-off between the two objectives. Political parties have therefore had to accept that the cost of reducing inflation has been at the expense of a somewhat higher level of unemployment. There has been a tendency for Labour governments to be more concerned with achieving lower levels of unemployment than Conservative governments, even though the consequence might be a higher rate of inflation.

Nevertheless, studies by economists in the 1950s and 1960s appeared to confirm not only that such a relationship between unemployment and inflation existed, but that it has remained stable for many years. Up to

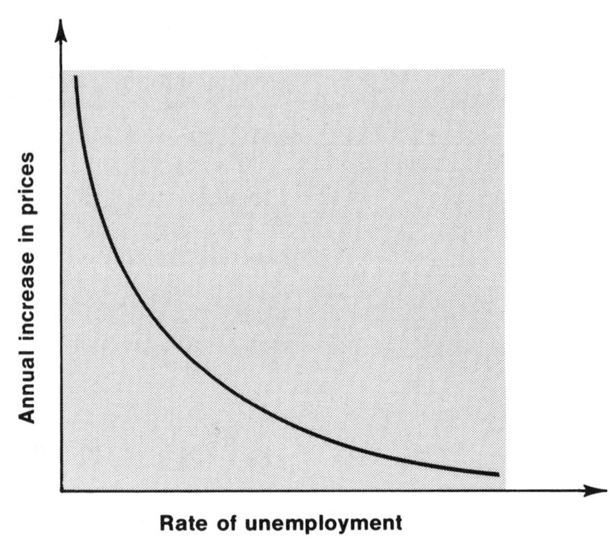

Figure 16.3 A relationship between inflation and unemployment

1967 in the UK, the relationship between the level of unemployment and the rate of inflation was inverse and quite similar to that given in Figure 16.3. This diagram, known as the Phillips curve after the economist who first plotted it, suggested that low levels of unemployment are more likely to permit price increases than higher levels. The relationship was found from actual data relating to the recorded level of wage increases and unemployment in the economy over time, from 1862 to 1958. Since, in the long run, changes in wages are strongly correlated with prices, this produces the trade-off curve as shown in Figure 16.3. From this analysis, it was estimated that an unemployment rate of $5\frac{1}{2}$ per cent would produce stable prices in the economy, more than this level of unemployment and prices would fall. The lower the level of unemployment then prices would rise with the increase in prices becoming greater as unemployment falls, in other words the Phillips curve would become steeper.

Today, these figures for the relationship appear quite unreal, as do most estimates made for other countries in the 1960s and 1970s. Not only have rates of inflation been far greater but they have been coupled with rates of unemployment that were much greater. These combinations of inflation and unemployment cannot be fitted to that inflation–unemployment curve, by any stretch of the imagination.

It is now apparent that a high rate of inflation cannot be overcome simply by taking measures that increase the amount of unemployment. Attempts to reduce inflation by the traditional monetary and fiscal policies have led, in other market economies, to a continuing undesirably high rate of inflation, and distressingly low levels of aggregate economic activity and employment. *Stagflation* is the name coined for this situation. The failure of traditional policies to keep inflation within bounds has led to the suggestion that the inflation–unemployment curve had ceased to exist. Many politicians and some economists have concluded that it is impossible to reduce unemployment without first reducing the rate of inflation.

Stagflation

The likely explanation is that the inflation–unemployment relationship of the type shown in Figure 16.3 still exists, but that it has shifted upwards and that it is a description of a short-term relationship. The evidence for this is that traditional policies continue to be employed and still appear to moderate the level of inflation to some extent but at the cost of higher unemployment. Likewise there is not much doubt that measures which increase aggregate demand will still reduce unemployment at least in the short run, though they may lead to higher inflation. Hence the UK government in 1979 was faced with the option of reducing government expenditure and the money supply in an attempt to reduce the rate of inflation. Increasing aggregate demand by more public spending would reduce the rate of unemployment, which was steadily rising, but this would imply a choice of higher inflation as an alternative.

If it is accepted that the curve describes a short-term relationship, and that the curve has shifted upwards during the 1970s, the next problem is to determine the causes of the shift. Many economists believe it is inflation itself that has produced the upward shift. It is argued that when prices rise they produce expectations of further price rises which in turn leads to groups such as unions adopting behaviour patterns that result in even higher inflation (see page 285), and to an upward shift of the curve. It is argued that policies which raise aggregate demand

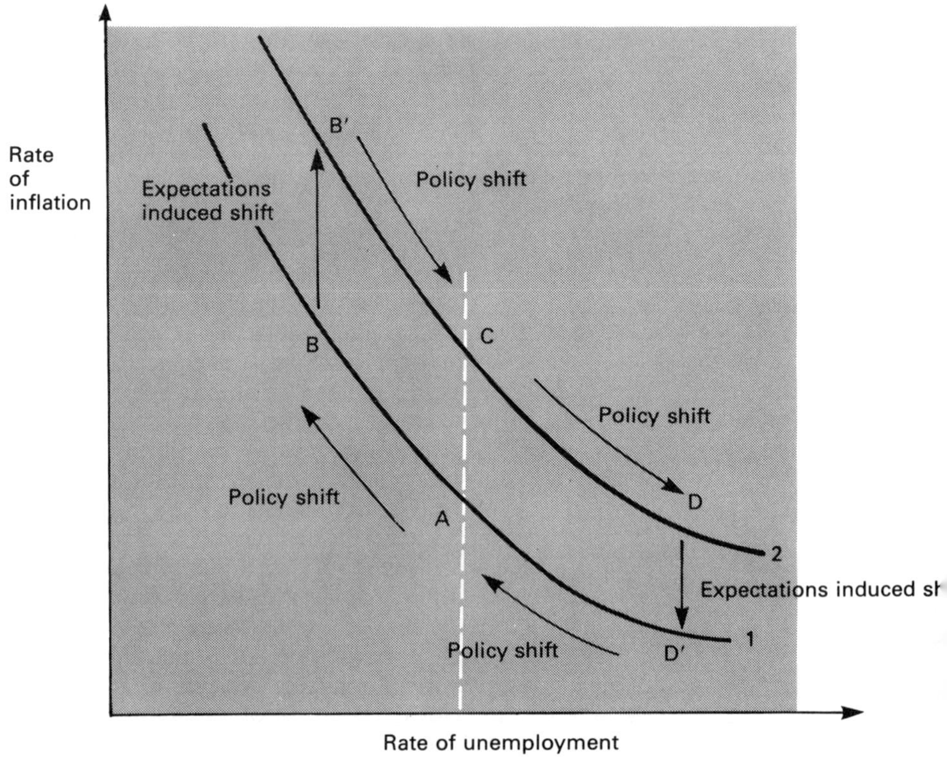

Figure 16.4 Shift of the inflation–unemployment curve following increase in aggregate demand

may produce a temporary reduction in unemployment, but the increase in inflation this leads to will trigger further inflation. Attempts to counter this higher inflation by reducing aggregate demand will only be achieved at the cost of higher unemployment. Such a progression is shown in Figure 16.4. From an initial position at A on line 1, government policy succeeds in moving to B. Unemployment is reduced, but inflation increases. Inflationary expectations outrun the new inflation level and result in the shift of the curve. Unemployment and inflation are now represented by B′ on line 2. As the new level of inflation is considered unacceptable the short-run response is to change policies and to move to C.

Should this view of the long-term relationship between inflation and unemployment be correct, the task facing government is to find some way of shifting the short-run inflation–unemployment curve down again. Many economists believe that, if people's expectations of the future rate of inflation can be reduced below the present level of inflation, they will behave in a different way. Wage demands will be moderated and businesses will not increase their prices by as much in anticipation of cost increases. The overall effect it is said, will be a winding down in the rate of inflation. It may be that sufficiently severe anti-inflationary policies can produce this change in expectations. In Figure 16.4 such a move is represented by the movement from C to D which produces a move to line 1.

16.3

Table 16.4 lists some of the measures a government might adopt in an attempt to control inflation. Which of these types of policy instruments has the government made use of in the last year? Have they been used to reduce inflation or have they been used to stimulate the economy?

16.4

Discuss the two cartoons. Does each one have a serious side?

1 (a) Can a government create a depression and would it lead to the removal of inflation?

(b) In what ways is the current economic situation different from that experienced in 1929?

2 Inflation is sometimes glibly described as too much money chasing too few goods. The UK government has expressed its concern about the growth of the money supply. What then, would be the consequences if the government simply attacked the inflation problem by refusing to print more money?

Australian, 23 August 1974

Mercury, 26 April 1975

16.5

Consider the following information. In the course of one year, a taxpayer's taxable income rose from £6000 to £7000 per annum, an increase of 16.6 per cent. His marginal rate of tax was 30p in the pound. The retail price index rose by 15 per cent during the year. Was he better off or worse off in real terms at the end of the year, and by how much?

16.6

Examine the rate of unemployment and the rate of inflation in the UK for the period 1970 to the present day. Plot the information on a graph similar to Figures 16.3 and 16.4. What evidence is there of an inverse relationship between unemployment and inflation?

16.7

Discuss the possible effects on aggregate demand of each of the following measures:
1 a redistribution of income from rich to poor by means of increased taxation and additional social welfare payments
2 interest payments on house mortgages no longer allowable against income tax.
3 an increase in interest rates
4 a reduction in the rates of personal income tax
5 a reduction in the company tax rates
6 subsidies for agricultural industries

16.8

If a government chose to attack an unemployment problem by increasing aggregate demand, it could reduce taxation or increase government spending. Can you suggest reasons why a government might prefer changes in taxation rates rather than changes in government expenditure as the principal weapon against unemployment?

Specific wage and price policies

So far the discussion has centred largely on policies that influence the level of aggregate demand. The failure of such policies to produce an acceptable level of inflation and unemployment has drawn attention to specific wage and price policies. The argument has been that policies which seek to hold prices down directly, or which hold wages down will be a valuable supplement to policies that regulate aggregate demand. Those policies often referred to as prices and income policies can be divided into basic types:
1 price controls
2 a wage price freeze
3 pay guidelines and limits
4 wage indexation
5 a wage tax trade-off.

Any policy may include elements of more than one of these measures to comprise a policy package of methods to tackle an inflation problem.

In the UK, it has become a regular feature of incomes policies that they are organised into stages or phases introducing new measures and approaches as conditions change. A further distinction has been added to such measures in the UK as to the nature of policies as statutory (i.e. backed by the force of law and legislation) or voluntary (i.e. requiring the agreement and consent of all the parties concerned to accept the limits and controls suggested.)

In the UK, the public sector comprises a major part of the workings of the economy and the state is a major employer in its own right. With respect to the public sector, government policy on prices and wages in effect amounts to a prices and incomes policy even if free collective bargaining exists in the private sector. Controls on public expenditure, such as cash limits to spending, may operate to the same effect as a more formal incomes policy.

Price controls

Various institutional bodies in the UK have at different times attempted to introduce controls over prices. As well as periods when a freeze has been imposed on prices and incomes, the National Board for Prices and Incomes (NBPI), set up in 1965 and abolished in 1971, and the Price Commission, set up in 1973, have established some element of control over prices. The Price Commission introduced a price code which did not allow prices to rise to cover increases in costs except where these were unavoidable. The main aim here was to interrupt the wage–price spiral which had led to continuing inflation in the UK. Employers were not able to grant pay increases that could be paid for by passing on the extra costs in the form of higher prices to the consumer. Firms could therefore only finance higher pay by means of higher productivity or at the expense of their own profit levels.

The Price Commission, through a formal administrative system, was directly involved in interrupting the workings of the market mechanism and establishing restrictions on the determination of prices. On these grounds, the Commission has been challenged and was unpopular with manufacturers and business. Apart from an administrative cost in operation, the Price Commission was also unable to control every price and tended to concentrate on large firms and major consumer goods. Moreover the controls on prices appeared to do little to halt inflation; many of the cost increases to industry were the result of increases in imported raw materials over which the industries had no control. The Price Commission did however highlight the role of wages and increases in determining prices, the need to justify pay increases by productivity and price increases by cost factors not within a firm's control.

Wage–price freeze

On occasions, the government has resorted to statutory powers to impose a compulsory freeze on wages and prices. In 1972 the Conservative government introduced a freeze for 90 days on prices, pay, dividends and rents and later increased this by a further 60 days. This was felt necessary in order to provide an element of breathing space while a more complex and structured policy was devised to deal with rising inflation at the time. This is obviously the most extreme form of prices and incomes policy and does suffer from problems of administering and policing an absolute freeze. The UK is not alone in using a freeze as a short-term measure; the policy has also been used in the United States and in New Zealand for example. It would appear that the freeze is a convenient short-term device for dealing with rapid inflation and that it is possible to hold prices and wages for 3 or even 6 months. Beyond that time, however, some relaxation is necessary to permit market forces to once more allocate resources in an efficient manner.

Pay guidelines and limits

Many different formulae and norms for pay increases have been used at various times as part of policy in the UK. In the 1970s this has varied from £1 per week plus 4 per cent, £6 a week maximum, a 10 per cent guideline, as allowable increases in wages. Usually these limits have been part of an overall package of measures and can be designed to deal with other problems besides that of controlling wage inflation. For example, an incomes policy which gives all earners the same absolute increase in pay, say £6 a week, has an immediate impact on the distribution of income. For low income earners, the increase is obviously much greater in proportionate terms and such a policy can be seen to favour the lower paid and lead to a narrowing of pay differentials between high and low paid jobs. A percentage limit to pay increases will maintain existing differentials and be seen as more equitable if all workers receive an extra 5 per cent or whatever. It is also possible to devise a policy which would impose a maximum allowed increase per year, or a policy which would freeze incomes above a specified level. The use of such guidelines and limits imposed on an annual basis does allow for more flexibility within an incomes policy and allows the price system to operate, albeit in a modified form, offering incentives, maintaining or reducing differentials, dealing with particular problems such as low pay.

The main difficulty with such policies has been that the policy maximum has generally become the norm for any pay bargaining. Up to £6 a week limit on increases in practice became, for many, an increase of £6 per week. In the pay round of negotiations and bargaining if one group of workers successfully obtained more than a guideline, then this tended to act as a signal to other pay bargainers to try to obtain an equally favourable pay deal. The extent to which these limits can be enforceable depends upon the nature of the policy. A statutory policy has legal backing but may increase resentment among workers and unions and prove in practice difficult, if not impossible, to enforce. A voluntary policy requires consensus between interested parties; the unions, government and the employers. This may not be possible to achieve given a continuing increase in consumer prices or opposition to other government policies. The Conservative government led by Mr Edward Heath in 1964 found to its cost that a statutory incomes policy could not be systematically enforced and lost a general election on that issue. The Labour government that came to power introduced a policy dependent on voluntary agreement and support which initially was given by the TUC. Later the trade unions withdrew support for the measures and policy guidelines were often broken so that voluntary targets on pay increases became meaningless.

Any policy to limit or freeze pay has to deal with the consequences for pay bargaining when the policy comes to an end. If it is not renewed by additional limits then, once the limits have gone, a pay explosion may occur as workers attempt to make up for lost ground while their incomes and earnings have been restrained. The return to market forces, in terms of the free collective bargaining of wages, may result in a rapid increase in wages and a further twist in the wage–price spiral. In this sense, the incomes policy may only delay – not prevent – the inevitable pressure on the price level from higher wages. The expectations of workers also play a part here and the extent to which they are prepared to push for higher wages. Expectations will also be influenced by the wage increases that they see being obtained by other groups.

Wage indexation

Wage indexation, which was discussed in Chapter 10, has been advocated as one means of assisting in the reduction of inflationary expectations. The reasoning is that if workers can be assured that wage rates will be increased in line with increases in the cost of living the temptation to seek larger percentage wage increases will be reduced. Wage indexation thus brings more predictability to inflation and this, in itself, provides an environment it which any attempt to reduce inflation may be more successful. Unfortunately, there is little indication of how such indexation might lead to a reduction in inflation. For wage indexation to succeed there needs to be a general willingness amongst unions to accept indexation and it also probably requires their agreement to take less than full indexation at some point. Agreement to the latter is almost certain to lead to a reduction in real wages.

The principle of indexation was tried in the UK as part of the counter-inflation policies of 1972–74. Stage 3 of that policy introduced a pay limit of up to 7 per cent or a flat-rate increase of £2.25 per week. Indexation came into the policy by means of a threshold agreement. After the retail price index had increased by more than 7 per cent then pay would increase by 40 pence per week for each 1 per cent rise in the index. As a policy to reduce inflation, this did not appear particularly successful. The expectation arose that, because the index had increased, then more pay would be given. Thus rising prices were seen in conjunction with rising incomes, and the connection between inflation and the need to reduce the pressure of incomes on prices was not explicit in the policy. The attempt to produce more stability by increasing more security as to the level of real income did not work apparently. After this policy was tried, UK governments have been more reluctant to the principle of indexation as a general counter-inflation policy. There is no doubt that indexation could prevent some of the arbitary redistribution effects of inflation but as a control mechanism there remains much doubt as to its effectiveness.

Wage tax trade-off

Another approach is to compensate income earners for higher prices by reducing taxes instead of raising wages. After tax income increases just as it would have done had full wage indexation applied. Such schemes have the advantage that they do not produce the cost increases to business that then lead on to further price increases. They appear to offer the possibility of breaking the price rise–wage rise–price rise sequence. There are a number of disadvantages in such an approach. First, the reduction in taxes will produce a budget deficit, so demand pressures replace cost pressures. Second, the benefits of tax cuts, as distinct from wage increases, may not readily be appreciated by all income earners. Third, such prices and incomes policies call for consensus between government, employers and unions. The Labour government in the UK in 1976 introduced the idea of tax concessions in return for lower pay increases as part of the Social Contract. The unions agreed to limits in pay increases and provided their backing for the voluntary Social Contract. Tax concessions were again offered in 1977 but were not adopted and supported by the TUC, which instead called for a return to free collective bargaining. The necessary consensus which is required for any voluntary policy to work was not forthcoming.

Incomes policy in the UK in the 1970s

Table 16.6 gives a summary account of the main features of incomes policies operating in the UK during the 1970s. The Labour government which lost power in 1970 had operated a voluntary incomes policy since taking office in 1964. It had imposed a freeze on prices and pay for 6 months, and a 6 months period of a zero norm on pay from July 1966. The government had also set up the NBPI to report on pay and on cases when special consideration should be given. Later the NBPI was given powers to delay pay increases for three months. The Conservative government that took office in 1970 disbanded the NBPI and the limits on pay and prices.

In the various stages of the policies described in Table 16.6, the aspects and types of measure described earlier can be identified.

	Period	Policy type	Limit	Institutional arrangements
	1972–1974 Conservative Government			
Stage 1	Nov 72–Mar 73	Compulsory	Freeze	
Stage 2	Apr 73–Oct 73	Compulsory	£1 + 4 per cent 12 month rule on pay increase (max £250 per person)	Pay Board and Price Commission with legal powers
Stage 3	Nov 73–Feb 74	Compulsory	7 per cent max or £2.25 pw (max £350 per person). Threshold agreement 40p per week for every 1 per cent rise in RPI beyond 7 per cent	Pay Board and Price Commission
	1974–1979 Labour Government			
	Social Contract (1)	Voluntary	Pay rises to compensate for price increases 12 month rule	Price Commission
	Social Contract (2)			
Phase 1	Aug 75–Jul 76	Voluntary (with TUC support) Some statutory limits	£6 max. Freeze on incomes over £8500 pa	Price Commision
Phase 2	Aug 76–Jul 77	Voluntary	£2.50 min. – £4.00 max and tax concessions	Price Commission
Phase 3	Aug 77–Jul 78	Voluntary (Government sanctions on employers paying more than 10%)	10% guideline	Price Commission
Phase 4	Aug 78–1979	Voluntary	5% guideline	Price Commission

Table 16.6 UK incomes policy, 1972–79

16.9

Suppose a government attempted to fight inflation by fixing all prices, but did nothing to control wages. What effects would this be likely to have on:
the rate of inflation,
profits,
unemployment,
production,
investment,
the balance of payments?

16.10

The following statements are grouped in pairs. The statements in each pair appear to contradict one another. Examine the statements and explain which statement you agree with. It may be, of course, that you can see an element of truth in both statements. In that case which course of action would you recommend?

1 (a) The best way of beating inflation is to maintain an absolute freeze on wages.
(b) The best way of beating inflation is to allow wages to rise by the same percentage as increases in the cost of living.

2 (a) An increase in indirect taxation will help in the fight against inflation because it will help to check aggregate demand.
(b) An increase in indirect taxation will worsen inflation by leading to an increase in the prices of those goods that are taxed, thereby increasing the retail price index.

3 (a) An increase in interest rates will help to reduce inflationary pressures by discouraging expenditure.
(b) A reduction in interest rates will help to reduce inflationary pressures by encouraging businesses to produce more.

4 (a) There is no point in attempting to reduce unemployment. The measures taken will only lead to inflation.
(b) High inflation and high unemployment go together. To reduce unemployment we must reduce inflation.

16.11

Suppose you are a trade union leader. The proposition is put to you that the wage rates of your members will be adjusted by the same percentage as increases in the price index for the next two years provided you agree not to seek wage increases or other concessions that would increase wage costs during that period.

What problems and possibilities would you take into consideration before explaining the proposal to your members or making a recommendation to them? Assume, for the purpose of the argument, that your only concern in this period is to prevent their living standards from falling.

Notes

1 Other definitions include 'a continuous increase in the aggregate stock of money' and 'a continuing expansion of short-term government debt'.

Chapter 17

Balance of Payments Policy

The balance of payments objective

The economic objectives of the government discussed in the previous chapter were full employment and price stability. The third economic objective is to maintain long run equilibrium in the balance of payments between receipts and payments. Disequilibrium can be identified in three situations: when a country has a persistent balance of payments deficit, or a persistent balance of payments surplus, or when it is forced to resort to the use of import quotas or exchange controls to balance payments and receipts.

If it has a persistent deficit, then its payments exceed its receipts; its foreign exchange reserves will decline and the government eventually will have to take action to prevent them from falling below some bench mark, such as the value of three months' imports. If it has a persistent surplus, foreign exchange reserves are accumulating. Instead of domestic production providing a flow of goods and services, this production is exchanged for foreign reserves. In the third case, the level of reserves does not change, but the device of artificially balancing receipts and payments by the use of quotas has undesirable features and these are referred to later in this chapter.

But for the balance of payments restraint it would be possible for a country to purchase and consume more goods and services than it produced; it could meet excess aggregate demand pressures simply by importing more from abroad. Reserves provide a temporary buffer against excess demand, but at some stage a continuing deficit will restrict a country's capacity to use this counter-inflationary weapon. Later in this chapter there is discussion of the possible conflict between balance of payments equilibrium and internal price stability.

Balance of payments equilibrium

One definition of balance of payments equilibrium is 'a situation in which the demand for foreign currencies is equal to the supply of foreign currencies'; that is, no change in reserves is occurring. This particular definition takes account of receipts and payments of foreign exchange for the sale and purchase of goods and services, and also of the borrowing and lending of funds recorded in the capital account of the balance of payments. Any study of the measures open to a government to remove disequilibrium in its balance of payments must take account of the effects of the measures on trade and invisibles and also of their effects on the capital flow.

The problem of what to do about a balance of payments deficit (or how to avoid one) has been more familiar to UK governments than the problem of how to deal with a surplus. Under normal circumstances, a balance of payments surplus tends to be 'self-correcting'; the government will be able to pursue 'easy' monetary and fiscal policies and with high levels of domestic spending more goods will be imported by the country's residents. In contrast, to remedy the deficit situation a government often needs to adopt policies that reduce the level of economic activity, production, employment, consumption and the prospects of economic growth.

External measures to remove a balance of payments deficit

Direct controls

Quotas and exchange controls

Quantitative restrictions on imports (quotas), or exchange controls that limit both the value of imports and the capital inflow have the advantage of being certain in their results. Quotas limit the volume of imports but not the prices, whereas exchange controls limit the value of overseas transactions but not the volume. Both may be used when a government has to take decisive emergency action to stem a drain of reserves. As a short-term measure they are invaluable. But when used for a considerable period of time they have serious disadvantages.

Limitations of quotas

Instead of dealing with the causes of disequilibrium, quotas simply restrict the amount of foreign exchange available for international transactions, or limit the quantity of imports. If the disequilibrium was caused initially by the uncompetitiveness of the country's industries at existing exchange rates, quotas will not correct this. The appropriate permanent solution may be to make the industries more competitive, perhaps by altering the exchange rate. Restricting demand for imports to the existing level of foreign exchange is a short run palliative, but the persistent use of quotas leads to the establishment of domestic producers which supply substitutes for the former imports. These domestic producers are relatively high-cost producers and their existence is evidence of the loss of potential gains from trade.

The administration of quantitative controls creates a number of problems. It usually requires a licensing system and often under such a system, trade channels become fixed, inefficient suppliers prosper, and seldom is the system sufficiently flexible to respond to changes in consumer demand.

Import duties

A common cause of a balance of payments deficit – the uncompetitiveness of domestic industries – can be partially remedied by imposing import duties. The arguments for and against using import duties to improve the balance of payments are discussed later.

Tariffs help to reduce a balance of payments deficit by reducing imports. The protection afforded to domestic industry may encourage overseas firms to establish subsidiaries in the UK. This direct investment will increase the capital inflow and further improve the balance of payments position.

Objection to use of import duties

One objection to the use of import duties to remove a balance of payments deficit is that increases in tariffs are more likely to arouse the opposition of trading partners than is a realignment of exchange rates, because a unilateral increase in tariffs may contravene existing commercial treaties, such as those signed under the General Agreement on

Tariffs and Trade. Such policies invite retaliation, which may then lead to a reduction in exports. It is also argued that frequent changes in the level of a protective tariff would lead to business uncertainty though it must be remembered that frequent changes in exchange rates also will create uncertainty.

Export subsidies

Discouragement of export subsidies by GATT

Export subsidies make local domestic exporting industries more competitive and help to increase exports. One objection to the continuing use of export subsidies is that they are discouraged under Article XVI of the General Agreement on Tariffs and Trade.

Varying the exchange rate

Depreciation and devaluation

This is another way a government may be able to influence the competitivness of its domestic industries. It is often said that devaluation of a country's currency is likely to reduce a balance of payments deficit. A devaluation is a specific government action that produces a depreciation in the value of the country's currency. 'Depreciation' is the more general term that refers to a loss of value of a currency. It may result from a specific government action or from the operation of market forces where exchange rates are not fixed. Revaluation (the appreciation of the currency) is often said to be more appropriate when the problem is one of reducing a balance of payments surplus. Whether a devaluation or depreciation will reduce a deficit will depend upon its effects on:

the value of exports of goods and services,
the value of imports of goods and services,
the net capital inflow.

The demand for exports is determined at a price measured in foreign currency. Suppose the current exchange rate between the pound sterling and the US dollar is \$2 : £1. A 10 per cent devaluation of the £ would mean that thereafter £1.00 would exchange for \$1.80, a ratio of 1 : 1.8. Suppose, too, that the current price of a British export is \$200 in the US, or £100 sterling in the UK. The effect of the devaluation would reduce the US price in dollars to \$180, while still remaining £100 in the UK. This fall in price in dollars to US buyers would lead to an increase in demand for such exports depending on the value of elasticity of demand. The increase in quantity sold will tend to offset the loss of dollar earnings from each sale following the devaluation. If demand for exports is elastic, then total dollar export earnings after devaluation will increase. This will tend to reduce a balance of payments deficit, other things being equal. However, producers may not continue to ask the same price for their exports following a devaluation; they may take the opportunity to increase prices by up to 10 per cent, knowing that this will not cost foreign customers any more than before the devaluation. In this case, receipts for exports in pounds will rise but the advantage of increased competitiveness will have been lost.

The devaluation will mean the imports of US wheat which previously cost say \$200 per tonne or £100, will now cost the UK £111 (each £ now equals \$1.80). The effect of this devaluation on import payments will depend on the reactions of the UK to the higher prices charged.

Generally, if imports rise in price, then less will be imported and the import bill in US dollars will fall, but whether import payments in terms of pounds rise or fall will depend on whether the reduction in quantity purchased is enough to offset the increase in the UK price. If demand for imports is inelastic, import payments will increase, whereas if demand is elastic, import payments will fall.

The UK's attempts to deal with its balance of payments deficit by devaluation have been frustrated because it depends heavily on imported foodstuffs and raw materials. The demand for these products is inelastic and consequently import payments rise when it devalues.

The effect of exchange rate changes on the net capital inflow is hard to determine. In a system in which large exchange rate variations are common, speculative capital will be sensitive to possible changes and will attempt to anticipate them. Successful speculation offers the opportunity for quick profits. A threat of devaluation encourages speculators to move funds out of the country. If devaluation does not occur, speculators can bring the funds in again without loss. If it does occur they make a gain equal to the percentage change in the value of the currency. Accordingly rumours of devaluation encourage such speculative outflows and tend to worsen the balance of payments position further. For this reason governments rarely announce a change in exchange rates before the event. They normally deny it.

Devaluation as a policy to correct a balance of payments deficit will only work if the respective elasticities for imports and exports enable export earnings to increase beyond an inevitably increased import bill. Revaluation will tend to reduce a balance of payments surplus by reducing export prices and lowering import prices. They may also reduce the inflow of capital funds. The effects can be appreciated by applying the type of analysis used to examine the consequences of a devaluation.

Even if the policy maker knows the likely general effects of a devaluation or revaluation of the currency, he is still faced with a number of problems. If his concern is solely the balance of payments he will still be faced with the problem of not knowing how large the change in the rate should be. Second, he cannot be certain how quickly such changes will take effect. Another problem is that he will need to consider the effects of such policy changes on other economic objectives such as price stability.

17.1

It is sometimes said that devaluation will correct a balance of payments deficit because 'it makes exports cheaper and imports dearer'. Explain why this is not an adequate statement of the effects of devaluation. Give a possible case where a devaluation will make exports cheaper and imports dearer.

17.2

Would you expect the impact of a devaluation on a country's balance of payments position to be greater in the short term than in the long term? Similarly, what would be the likely relative short- and long-term effects of an appreciation?

Internal measures to correct a balance of payments disequilibrium

A balance of payments deficit may occur as a consequence of excess demand pressures at home. As expenditure increases within a country, more goods and services are imported. When domestic production approaches the full employment level, there is little scope for meeting additional expenditures from increased home production. In addition to this impact on imports, a high level of spending is likely to reduce the level of a country's exports. Domestic firms will find it easier to sell their products on the home market. They will be under less pressure to maintain export sales or to seek new foreign markets. Accordingly, excess demand pressures are likely to cause a balance of payments deficit, even if the country's industries are competitive in terms of price on world markets.

A balance of payments deficit caused by excess demand pressures can be reduced if the government adopts monetary and fiscal policies that reduce aggregate demand. These measures were discussed in Chapter 16 – reductions in government spending, increases in taxation rates, increases in interest rates and restrictions on bank lending all act to reduce aggregate demand and thereby also reduce the demand for imports and may force business to seek export sales to survive.

Variations in the exchange rate may influence the balance of payments by changing the cost competitiveness of UK producers, whether they be export industries or import-competing industries. Depreciation appears to improve the competitiveness of UK industries as we have seen.

Depreciation and devaluation

Thus, there are two broad means of attacking a persistent balance of payments deficit; by improving cost competitiveness through depreciation or by reducing aggregate demand. The two should not be thought of solely as alternatives. In practice a government may opt for a combination of the two and indeed may decide to supplement such policies by overseas borrowing, import controls and the use of import duties.

A possible relationship between a country's relative cost competitiveness and the level of expenditure on the one hand, and the balance of payments position on the other, is shown in Figure 17.1. It suggests that policies that improve a country's balance of payments deficit can either be of the 'cost-improving' or 'expenditure-reducing' type. For

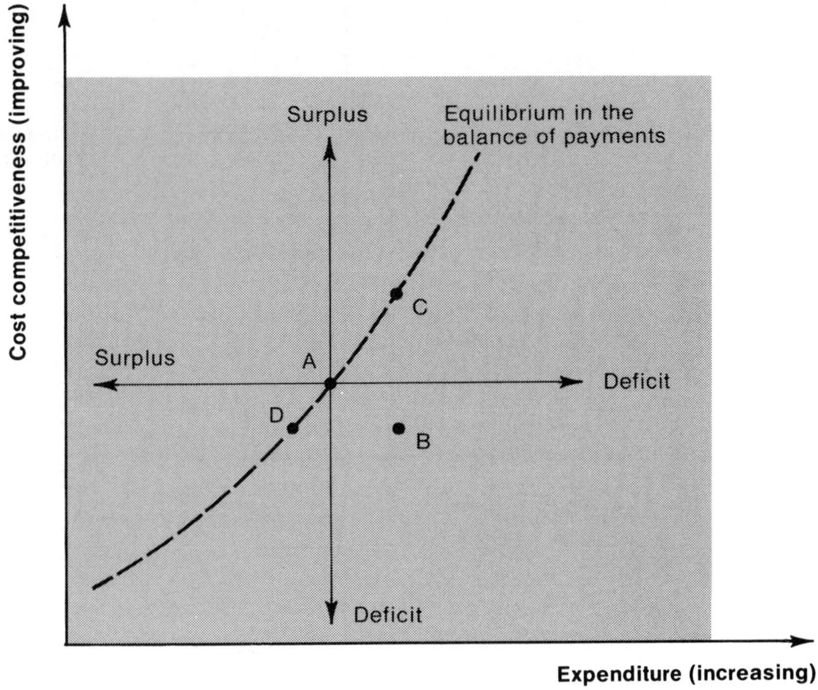

Figure 17.1 External balance

example, consider point B on the diagram. It indicates that, at the particular level of expenditure and cost competitiveness, the country has a balance of payments deficit. The diagram suggests that this deficit can be reduced or removed by improving cost competitiveness (moving from B to C), reducing expenditure (moving B to D), or by operating both types of policies (moving from B to A). In each case the deficit is removed.

Measures that seek to correct a balance of payments problem will also affect the level of unemployment and the rate of inflation. Table 16.4 on page 287 lists some of the policy measures that affect the rate of inflation. They include changes in the exchange rate and the use of import duties. A currency depreciation will tend to be inflationary. Import prices increase and this adds to business costs. Export prices and incomes rise and this has an expansionary effect on the money supply. Some economists even go so far as to argue that the inflationary consequences of a depreciation may ultimately be sufficiently strong to outweigh the initial improvements in cost competitiveness.

Policy measures that affect the balance of payments will also influence the level of economic activity. In Chapter 16 it was noted that increases in expenditure may reduce unemployment, at least in the short run, but they make it more difficult to control inflation. Measures that reduce expenditure tend to increase unemployment, certainly at least in the short run, but they help also to reduce the rate of inflation.

Depreciation and aggregate demand

Likewise, a change in the value of a country's currency, or some other measure that affects the cost competitiveness of its industries will affect production, employment and price stability. An improvement in cost competitiveness, through currency depreciation, is likely to have

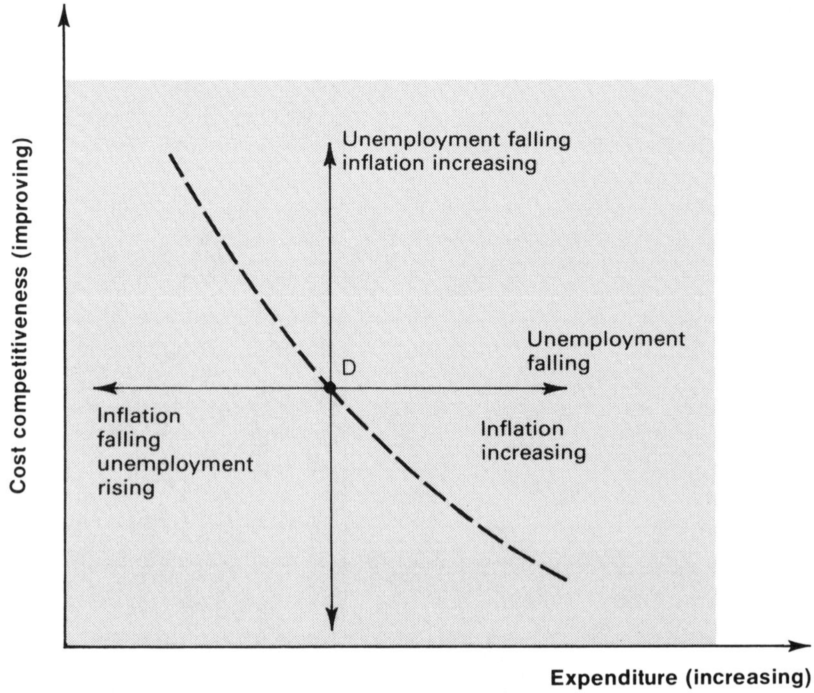

Figure 17.2 Unemployment, inflation, cost competitiveness and expenditure

a direct effect on import prices as we have noted. It may also lead to an increase in demand pressures. Consequently it is likely to have the effect of reducing unemployment, stimulating production but worsening inflation. A revaluation with lower export prices, less protection for import-competing industries and possible outflows of funds is likely to have the opposite effects.

This general relationship between the internal and external policy instruments and their effects on the level of unemployment and inflation is shown in Figure 17.2.

Figure 17.2 suggests that there are various combinations of measures designed to improve cost competitiveness and the level of expenditure that can produce full employment. For many years economists believed that full employment (perhaps a rate of 2 per cent) could be achieved at the cost of a modest annual rate of inflation. It was explained in the previous chapter that it cannot now be taken for granted that governments and their economic advisers will be able to manage this. Achievement of an old-style full employment level, even if it is still possible, is likely to be at the cost of rapid inflation. Once economists thought in terms of choosing policy instruments and applying them in order to achieve a balance of payments equilibrium, full employment and a modest level of inflation. Today, there seems no simple way of attaining these objectives. The sorts of practical alternatives that face the UK government are illustrated in Figure 17.3.

Figure 17.3 effectively combines and augments Figures 17.1 and 17.2. The line U^F represents full employment and shows the combinations of cost competitiveness and expenditure that might achieve it.

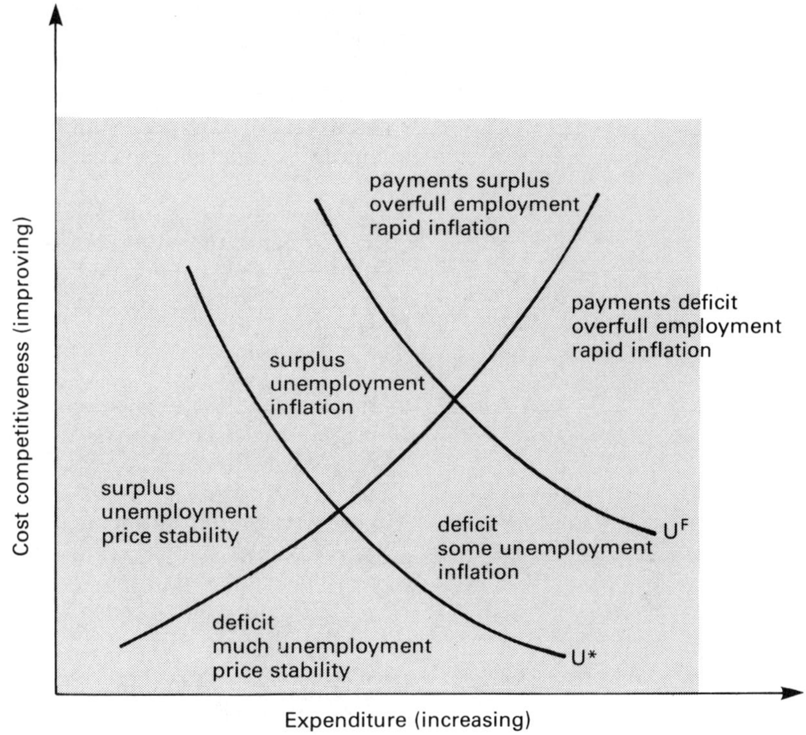

Figure 17.3 External equilibrium and internal objectives

The line U★ shows the combinations of these that might achieve a level of unemployment consistent with price stability. The effect of the introduction of the U★ line is to divide Figure 17.3 into six sectors. The areas below the U★ line are characterised by price stability and high unemployment. Those above U^F have full employment but rapid inflation. Those between U★ and U^F have both unemployment and inflation. A modern government will thus find itself faced with a dilemma because it will be unable to meet the three objectives simultaneously.

In the previous chapter the worsening inflation–unemployment situation in western industrial countries was explained in terms of an upward shift of the inflation–unemployment curve. (See Figure 16.4 on page 296.) The effect on such a shift is to increase the distance on Figure 17.3 between the U★ and U^F lines. In practice, full employment can only be obtained at the cost of higher inflation. Price stability can only be achieved at the cost of higher unemployment. Thus the problem, in Chapter 16, of moving the inflation–unemployment curve to the left has its counterpart in the narrowing of the band between U^F and U★ in Figure 17.3.

An understanding of Figure 17.3 assists in appreciating balance of payments problems. But to use such a diagram for specific policy decisions in our economy it is also necessary to know:

1 how to measure and regulate cost competitiveness and expenditure;
2 how to determine the positions of the balance of payments equilibrium and full employment curves, and a country's current position in relation to these;
3 how to calculate the effects of changes in expenditure and cost

competitiveness on employment and the balance of payments; and how quickly a policy measure will achieve the desired effect.
In short, the diagram in no way replaces the need for economists to find ways of measuring economic relationships. Its value is in providing a framework for comprehending the general nature of the problem of attaining external and internal equilibrium.

17.3

In the early 1970s the UK experienced stagflation and a balance of payments deficit. It was suggested that the best hope for the future lay in an export-led recovery. How could a sudden increase in export earnings be beneficial? What problems, if any, might it bring?

17.4

In Chapter 10 the relationship between unemployment and real wages was discussed. Many economists believe that a fall in real wages will make possible a reduction in unemployment. Suppose the government and the unions were to agree to a system of partial wage indexation that produced a fall in real wages. What effect would you expect this to have on the rate of inflation and the balance of payments? How would these changes be represented on a diagram such as Figure 17.3?

17.5

1 Where would you place the UK on Figure 17.3 at the moment?
2 What specific policies would you advocate to place the economy in a more desirable position?
3 Discuss your conclusions with other members of the class. To what extent are different policy prescriptions based on disagreement about which objectives are more important?

Alternatively they may stem from disagreement about the position of the UK economy at the present time, or alternatively the effects of the policies you are advocating.

World monetary problems

So far the discussion of balance of payments problems has taken no account of the difficulties that international monetary disturbances can create for a country's economy. The late 1960s and early 1970s were characterised by a series of such disturbances, by hurried meetings of finance ministers and bankers, suspension of foreign exchange dealings, an increase in international capital movements for speculative reasons and reversals in many countries' balance of payments position.

Two quite separate influences have been at work. First, there have been strains imposed on the international payments system by the liquidity crisis. Second, there have been payments problems created by the policies of the international cartel of oil-producing countries.

The liquidity crisis

This is the name given to the increasing shortage of acceptable means for completing international transactions. Between 1965 and 1975, the shortage produced a series of breakdowns in the mechanism by which international payments are made. The system that operated after the

Fixed exchange rates

Second World War was one in which countries attempted to maintain fixed exchange rates with one another. They did so by holding gold and foreign exchange reserves from which they could draw when they were temporarily in deficit, and which increased when they ran a temporary balance of payments surplus. The International Monetary Fund (IMF), established in 1947, had as its objectives the maintenance of exchange stability and the establishment of a fund from which countries could draw foreign exchange to help overcome temporary balance of payments problems. Drawing rights with the International Monetary Fund have therefore been regarded as 'second line' international reserves.

For such a system to operate successfully, the means of settling international transactions available to countries must be sufficient, in aggregate, to allow each country to maintain an adequate level of international reserves. The smaller a country's reserves relative to its total of international transactions, the less effective those reserves become as a buffer against a loss of reserves. During the 1960s, world trade increased rapidly but reserves of foreign exchange increased at a much slower rate. Table 17.1 shows that foreign exchange holdings declined from 50 per cent of total trade in 1960 to around 31 per cent in 1970.

In the normal course of trade, deficits and surpluses tended to become larger as the value of word trade increased. It became more difficult for countries to sustain these deficits without taking corrective action. But changing the exchange rate regularly posed a threat to a system that was based on the concept of fixed exchange rates.

Fixed price of gold

The principal forms in which international reserves were held in 1960 were gold, US dollars, sterling and foreign exchange drawing rights with the IMF. These reserves increased slowly and gold holdings, which comprised the greater proportion of reserves in 1960, actually declined. The official price of gold had been fixed at a level that made large-scale mining of the metal uneconomic, except in the Soviet Union and South

	Foreign exchange reserves* (US$ billion)	World trade, imports (US$ billion)	Reserves as a percentage of world trade (%)
1960	60.3	119.4	50.5
1961	62.3	124.6	50.0
1962	63.1	132.4	47.4
1963	66.6	143.5	46.7
1964	68.8	160.9	42.8
1965	70.8	175.2	40.4
1966	72.4	192.4	37.6
1967	74.1	201.7	36.7
1968	77.0	224.7	34.3
1969	77.7	255.5	30.4
1970	91.8	288.0	31.9

* International reserves include gold, foreign exchange and drawing rights with the IMF

Table 17.1 Foreign exchange reserves as a percentage of world trade, 1960–70

Source: *International Financial Statistics*, International Monetary Fund, Washington DC, vol xxi, December 1968 and vol xxvi, December 1973

Africa. The burden of providing additional reserves fell heavily on US dollars and sterling. The willingness of countries to hold part of their reserves in foreign exchange, rather than gold, depends on the confidence they have in the stability of that currency. Continuing balance of payments problems in the United Kingdom led to a decline in the importance of sterling. In the years after the Second World War there was a general willingness by countries to settle international transactions in US dollars and hold their reserves in that form. However, during the 1960s a fundamental disequilibrium developed in the US balance of payments, partly as a result of the Vietnam War and partly from a negative balance of payments with Japan. The initial refusal of the United States to take measures to correct its deficit simply meant that the holdings of dollars outside America increased. Confidence in the dollar weakened, and France began to convert its dollar holdings into gold by selling its dollars back to America. The effect was to reduce the amount of foreign exchange available for financing world trade.

The inadequate rate of increase of international reserves contributed to a series of balance of payments crises in the major trading countries in the late 1960s. The UK devalued the pound in 1967 and France devalued the franc in 1968. The strains imposed on the monetary system were accentuated by the activities of speculators. The possibility of a change in exchange rates offered the opportunity of profit if funds were moved out of a country that was about to devalue. Such speculative movements produced more pressure on reserves and were a destabilising influence. In 1969 the flight by speculators from the French franc to the German mark was directly responsible for the devaluation of the franc. Official government action, buying and selling in the foreign exchange markets, was unable to offset this speculative pressure. For example, speculative demand for gold on the London and Paris gold markets pushed the price of gold above the official price of US$35 a ounce. The United States attempted to hold the price at the official level by selling gold on these markets, but the rapid depletion of its gold stocks compelled it to agree to a two-tier price system that allowed the free gold price to rise above the official price.

United States balance of payments problems

After 1970 the United States balance of payments position worsened rapidly. In August 1971 convertibility of the US dollar was suspended and it was then devalued by 8.5 per cent and a further 11 per cent in 1973. The result was a substantial realignment of world exchange rates as every country was forced to decide a new value for its currency in terms of gold and the exchange rates of its major trading partners.

The crises of the late 1960s had been anticipated, but all attempts to prevent them failed. The principal measures adopted were:

1 The establishment of the 'group of ten' in 1961 (the members agreed to assist one another with foreign exchange when in balance of payments difficulties). Later, an enlarged 'group of twenty' was formed.

2 The introduction of short-term credit arrangements between central banks.

3 The creation of Special Drawing Rights (SDRs) by the International Monetary Fund, to increase world liquidity.

4 The introduction of a two-tier price system for gold.

The measures failed because, with the exception of (3), they merely propped up the existing system. The plan to create SDRs failed to prevent those crises because it was 'too little and too late'.

Special Drawing Rights

Subsequently the rate of creation of Special Drawing Rights has been increased. Countries are issued with SDRs which they can return to the

Fund when in difficulties. The Fund then sells the SDRs to another country in exchange for its own or a needed currency. The system thus allows the IMF to call up particular currencies in short supply.

The root cause of these continuing monetary problems was the failure of world powers to reach agreement on the reform of the monetary system. France suggested a substantial increase in the price of gold, which would make production more profitable. This plan would benefit the Soviet Union and South Africa as the principal producers and it would discriminate against those countries holding most of their reserves in dollars. The United States favoured the demonetisation of gold and the establishment of a separate international reserve currency. This the French objected to.

One response to the continuing uncertainty on foreign exchange markets has been the abandonment of fixed exchange rates by the major trading countries. The United Kingdom, Japan, the Common Market countries and the United States all elected to 'float' their respective currencies.

A *floating currency* is one in which the exchange rate is determined by the forces of demand and supply. If demand exceeds supply for foreign exchange for making payments, and transfers exceeds the supply from receipts and transfers, the local currency is likely to depreciate. If supply exceeds demand, the local currency will appreciate in value. The advantage of having a floating exchange rate that permits demand and supply to match one another is that, in theory at least, it eliminates both the possibility of a balance of payments deficit and the need for international reserves. It has the additional possible advantage that it reduces opportunities for windfall gains from speculation and may therefore reduce speculation.

Advantage of floating exchange rate

Disadvantages

There are also disadvantages in a system of floating exchange rates. Changes in exchange rates may be considerable. These alter the cost competitiveness, alter the price level and cause redistribution of income, make selling hazardous and long-term planning by industries difficult. If the future profitability of export sales is uncertain, businesses may be reluctant to produce for export, or to enter into export contracts.

Devices to overcome disadvantages

Two institutional devices can help to overcome these objections to floating exchange rates. The first is the development of forward exchange markets which enables purchasers to obtain the necessary foreign exchange in advance, and so guarantee payment at a future date. Second, governments have adopted the 'dirty float', a practice of entering the market and buying and selling to maintain exchange rates within an acceptable range.

Floating exchange rates can be illustrated by the use of demand and supply curves as a means of analysis. The demand for currency, in the case of the UK the pound sterling, arises from the requirements of foreign buyers of UK goods and services and foreign investors in the UK. Speculation will also add to the demand for sterling, if sterling is being bought on foreign exchange markets. The supply of sterling to the foreign exchange market arises from the purchases of imports from foreign suppliers by UK residents, investment and capital flows abroad from the UK and from speculators selling sterling.

Figure 17.4 demonstrates the effect of the demand and supply of sterling on the exchange rate. The foreign exchange market establishes the price of a currency in terms of either a single other currency, such as the US dollar or the Deutschmark, or against a 'basket' of currencies (a weighted average of several exchange rates) such as used by the EMS

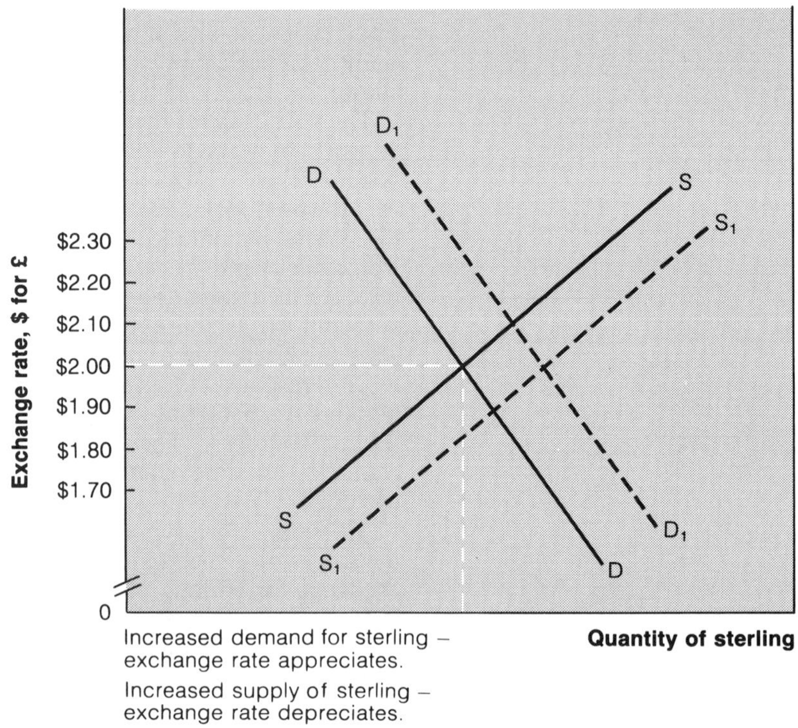

Figure 17.4 Floating exchange rates

(the European monetary system.) In the case of Figure 17.4, the exchange rate is expressed in terms of a sterling: dollar rate.

A free market for currency would establish an exchange rate where supply and demand were equated. In theory this would avoid balance of payments deficits or surplus since the exchange rate would adjust to reach an equilibrium quantity.

Changes in the demand and supply of sterling can be represented by shifts in the demand and supply curves. For example, from the equilibrium position an increase in UK exports overseas would lead to an increased demand for sterling and shift the demand curve outwards to the right. The demand curve would then cause the exchange rate to rise to a new higher level where demand would once again equal supply. The appreciation of the exchange rate would counteract the increased export earnings, creating a balance of payments surplus. A fall in exports would shift the demand curve inwards and the exchange rate would depreciate. In like manner, shifts in demand curve could come about from the effects of investment and capital flows and speculation.

The supply curve of sterling would shift to the right, if the UK increased imports and would shift to the left if imports were cut back. These shifts in the supply curve could also come about as a result of changes in UK investment abroad or from speculation. An increased supply of sterling would cause the exchange rate to fall; a decreased supply would mean the exchange rate would rise, other things being equal. This automatic adjustment of the value of the exchange rate then, in theory, would ensure that the balance of payments was restored to equilibrium without the need for any other policy measure to be adopted by the government.

A floating exchange rate involves changes in the relative prices of goods and services between countries. A rising value of the pound against the US dollar means that UK exports to the US become more expensive to the US buyer. A falling pound and UK exports are relatively cheaper in the US. These relative price changes also affect UK imports. A rising pound means that UK imports fall in price to the UK consumer; a falling pound that imports increase in price. Price adjustments obviously influence the cost competitiveness of one country in relation to another with corresponding shifts in the level of trade. As with the effects of devaluation explained earlier, the impact on the level of export earnings and import payments depends upon the relative elasticities of demand for exports and imports. These changes in relative price as the exchange rate appreciates or depreciates act as an additional equilibrating mechanism to restore the balance of payments. For example, when sterling appreciates against the dollar because the UK has increased exports to the US, relative prices of the exports increase which cuts back on their demand. At the same time, UK imports from the US fall in price, tending towards an increased demand for them. Thus the equilibrium in the balance of payments is more readily achieved.

Oil prices and problems

The second major problem that compounded the difficulties resulting from the collapse of the payments system was the policies of the oil-producing countries. The action of these countries in forming a cartel which more than trebled the price of crude oil between 1972 and 1974 initially had serious effects on the balance of payments of the oil importing countries. The economies were so dependent on oil that the price increases led to sharp increases in the value of their imports and to balance of payments deficits. The demand for oil was so inelastic that such countries had to continue to buy oil even though its price rose. Devaluation of their currencies was no solution because this increased the price of oil still further. Rationing and import controls seemed to be the only immediate solution.

Subsequently, the international economy adjusted to the new situation. It produced a considerable redistribution of income in favour of the oil-producing countries. These countries began to accumulate foreign exchange surpluses and responded to this by investing abroad. Gradually countries that would otherwise have had to face mounting balance of payments deficits and dwindling foreign exchange reserves were able to benefit from the surplus funds available for investment. Capital inflows offset trade imbalances.

The countries to suffer most from the oil cartel's policies have probably been the developing countries which lack oil resources of their own and which find it difficult to attract investment funds. The problems of these countries are considered in more detail in Chapter 24.

Proposals for monetary reform

Jamaica Conference

In January 1976 a conference of Finance Ministers was held in Jamaica to consider a number of measures designed to reform the monetary system. The Jamaica Conference dealt with four main problems,

1 the demonetisation of gold,
2 variation to quotas in the international monetary fund,
3 the position of the developing countries, and
4 an appropriate exchange rate system.

It was agreed that the IMF would sell part of its gold holdings at market prices over several years. A similar amount was to be returned to member countries in exchange for their own currencies. This decision meant that the Finance Ministers were agreeing to the reduction in the importance of gold as a form of foreign reserves. Another part of the proposals was that profits from the sale of the IMF's gold holdings would go to a special fund from which loans could be made to developing countries.

Quotas of IMF members were increased. Of particular importance was the agreement to increase the quotas of the oil cartel countries so that they were required to contribute 10 per cent of total foreign exchange holdings of the Fund. As the voting power of Fund members is related to the size of their quotas this effectively placed more voting power with the oil producing countries.

It was recognised at the Jamaica Conference that many countries employed a system of flexible rather than fixed exchange rates. In recognising this the Finance Ministers agreed that member countries should co-operate with the IMF to prevent competitive exchange rate variations designed to shift economic problems from one country to another.

In addition an IMF council was established to work towards further monetary reform. The monetary system that operated at the end of the 1970s lacks the order and clearly understood principles of the fixed exchange system. Nevertheless the demonetisation of gold, the development of special drawing rights and attempts to adopt a system of managed but flexible exchange rates may help to produce a system more able to cope with international inflation, unemployment and large redistributions of wealth between countries.

17.6

The United States and the United Kingdom resisted exchange rate devaluation wherever possible in the past. It was a matter of national pride that their currencies were strong. Devaluation has been branded as an indication of 'economic degeneracy'. To what extent is devaluation evidence of national weakness? Are people foolish for regarding devaluation in this sense? Does a revaluation or appreciation of an exchange rate indicate strength in the economy and 'economic supremacy'?

17.7

The establishment of the oil-producing countries' cartel has given oil producers monopoly power and has important implications for future world trade. There have already been suggestions that buyers of oil should form a single consumers' group to maximise their bargaining strength. Similarly, there have been suggestions that the producers should establish monopolistic cartels to secure the highest possible price. Faced with such possibilities, do you think that the UK government should:

1 join in consumer buying groups to obtain a better price for the products it buys?
2 join in producer cartels to obtain the best price for its exports?

3 abandon international trade altogether and aim at self-sufficiency?
4 carry on as before?
Explain the likely effects of each course of action. Try to imagine a world in which world prices of each product were determined in bargaining session between producer and consumer cartels, or a world in which there was no international trade at all.

17.8

If a floating exchange rate system operated successfully, the demand for currencies would always equal the supply and individual countries would never have deficits or surpluses and also would not need foreign exchange reserves.
(a) Does this mean that under such a system countries would not have balance of payments problems?
(b) What other problems might they face under such arrangements?

The effects of imposing a tariff

Effect of tariffs on price of imported goods

Import duties normally increase the cost of landing imported goods. The effect is likely to be an increase in the price of the product, an increase in the domestic industry's share of the market and a fall in the foreign competitor's share. Because the price to the consumer is higher, aggregate sales of the product are also likely to be reduced. In other words, the increase in the home industry's sales is likely to be less than the fall in the foreign competitor's sales.

Demand and supply analysis and tariffs

This analysis of the effects of imposing a tariff can be illustrated by using the demand and supply analysis developed in Chapter 7. Indeed, it is very hard to understand how the tariff may affect an industry without using this model. The demand and supply diagram is appropriate because local producers lack effective monopoly power when they are exposed to foreign competition. They have to act as price-takers rather than price-makers and consequently the price they receive is determined by demand and supply forces. However, it is necessary to modify the usual demand and supply diagram somewhat to show both the domestic industry's supply curve and the quantities of the product that will be supplied to the market by foreign competitors. Figure 17.5 sets up these demand and supply curves in a situation in which there is free trade; no import duties are levied.

In the diagram, DD is the domestic demand curve for a product. S_dS_d is the supply curve of the domestic industry. The foreign supply curve is shown as a horizontal line, labelled 'price of imports'. This implies that foreign producers will be prepared to supply unlimited quantities of the good at the ruling international price. As foreign producers are prepared to supply unlimited quantities at this price, £OW per unit, it will become the established price for the product on the domestic market. The domestic industry will have to accept this price of £OW per unit and the maximum quantity that it will be able to produce profitably at that price is OH units. However, the quantity demanded by the local market at the ruling price is OF units, leaving foreign producers to supply HF units (the quantity by which home supplies fall short of demand). Notice from the diagram that the higher

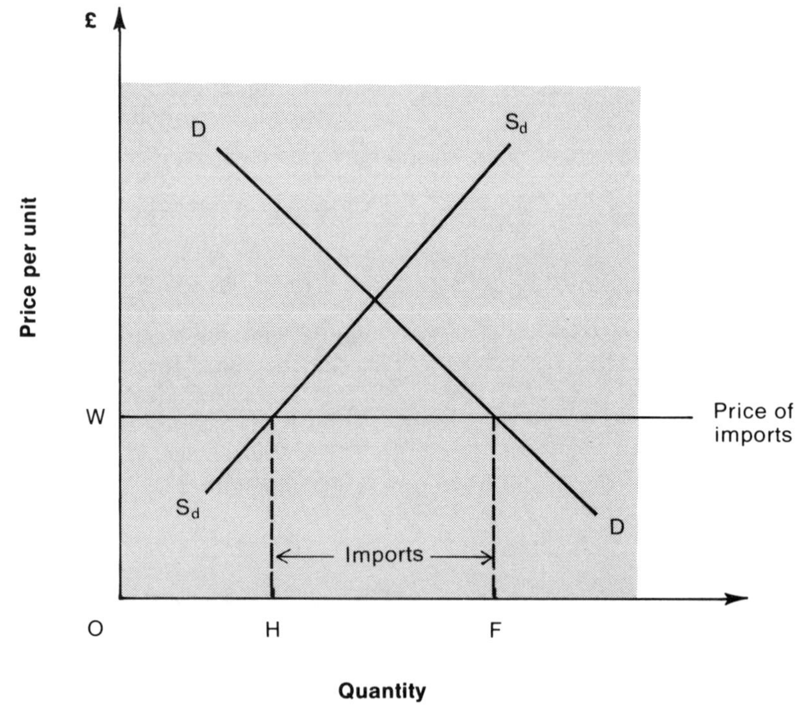

Figure 17.5 Effects of foreign competition in a free-trade situation

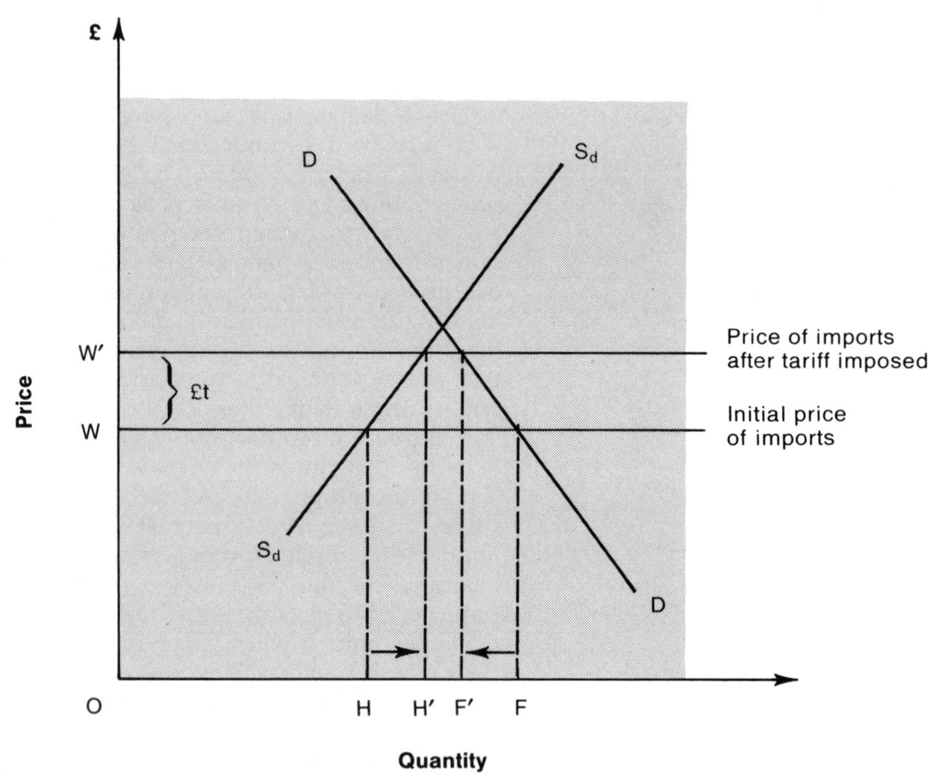

Figure 17.6 Effects of imposing a tariff

the price the larger the quantity the domestic industry would be prepared to supply.

Figure 17.6 shows the effects of the government imposing a tariff on the imports of the good. An import duty of £t per unit will have the effect of increasing the price at which foreign producers are able to supply the product. The foreign supply line is shifted upwards by the amount of the tariff. Foreigners can now no longer supply the local market at prices below £OW′, for this would give them a net return of less than £(OW′ − t); that is, less than £OW. As a result of the imposition of the tariff, £OW′ now becomes the ruling market price, domestic production increases from OH units to OH′ units, total sales shrink to OF′ units and the balance of the sales achieved by foreign producers fall from HF units to H′F′ units.

Tariffs and consumption patterns

The tariff has protected local industry by producing economic conditions in which the industry has found it profitable to expand production. Conversely, a removal of the tariff would have produced conditions that would have forced the domestic industry to contract. Notice that this protection has been accomplished at the local consumers' expense, for there has been a rise in the price of the good and a fall in consumption. Foreign producers also have suffered a cut in their market.

17.9

The following table contains demand and supply schedules relating to an imaginary product on the UK market. Unlike the situation in Figure 17.5 and 17.6, the quantity that foreign producers of this imaginary product are prepared to supply will increase as the UK price of the product increases.

	'000 tonnes per month			
Price per unit (£)	Domestic demand schedule	Domestic supply schedule	Foreign supply schedule	Total supply (domestic + foreign)
40	50	10	10	20
50	45	12.5	17.5	30
60	40	15	25	40
70	35	17.5	32.5	50
80	30	20	40	60
90	25	22.5	47.5	70
100	20	25	55	80

1 Determine the equilibrium price, quantity purchased and quantities supplied by the domestic and foreign industries each month.
2 Suppose that the UK government places an import duty of £20 per tonne on foreign supplies. This will have the effect of raising the price at which the foreign industry will be able to supply the product by £20 per tonne. For example, the foreign industry will not be prepared to supply 10 tonnes per month until the price reaches £60 per unit.
Calculate:
the new foreign supply schedule,
the new total supply schedule,
the new equilibrium price of the good,
the quantity purchased by domestic consumers,

the quantity supplied by domestic producers,
the quantity of the good imported,
the revenue raised by the tariff.

17.10

Study Figure 17.6 carefully.
1 By how much has consumption fallen as a result of the imposition of the tariff of £t per unit?
2 A tariff is a tax on imports and brings revenue to the government that levies it. Is there any way in which it is possible to estimate how much revenue the tariff in Figure 17.6 has brought to the government that imposed it?
3 Suppose that the government had imposed a tariff that was twice as great as that of £t per unit. What would the effects have been on:
the price of the good,
the quantity supplied by the local industry,
the quantity of imports,
government revenue from the tariff?

17.11

In Figure 17.6 it was shown that the effect of imposing a tariff was to increase the market price of the good by the amount of the tariff. In Activity 17.9(2) the effects of the tariff on the price is rather different.
1 In what way is the effect different?
2 How would you explain the difference?

Arguments for tariff protection

Some of the commonest arguments for tariff protection are:
1 foreign countries produce the goods more cheaply;
2 protection can increase the real wages of workers in some circumstances;
3 domestic industries initially require protection;
4 domestic industry should be protected against the dumping of foreign goods;
5 tariffs improve the terms of trade;
6 tariff protection assists the balance of payments;
7 tariffs bring the government revenue;
8 the protection of key industries is essential to ensure survival during military or economic crises.

Foreign countries produce the goods more cheaply

This is one of the most common arguments for tariff protection and economists agree that it is one of the weakest. Of course, it is frustrating for the manufacturer to find that foreign suppliers can land a similar product in the UK more cheaply than he can produce it. This may be because the foreign producers have lower wage costs, or they may have a superior technology or they may enjoy economies of large-scale production. To the UK producer all of these seem 'unfair' precisely because there is often little he can do to become more competitive. Hence he argues that he should be protected.

Economists have countered this argument by pointing out that specialisation and trade bring advantages to a country if its producers concentrate on those goods and services which it can provide more cheaply. In Chapters 4 and 12 it was shown that these are products which have a low opportunity cost.

Counter argument

If we were to protect all possible industries, the benefits of international trade would be lost. In fact, the main purpose of international trade is to obtain goods from abroad precisely because they are cheaper. Scarce domestic resources can be better employed in other productive activities than in trying to compete in the production of items where our opportunity costs are highest.

Protection in such cases benefits the producer, but it reduces total goods and services available to the community. If its result is that many small industries are established, each may not be able to benefit from economies of scale.

Practical problems of reduction in tariff protection

However, it is one thing for a government to be convinced of the academic case for freer trade, but quite another for it to deal with the practical problems that a reduction in tariff protection gives rise to. If a government refuses to continue to protect those industries, the result may be that the formerly protected domestic industries will contract, and some may go out of business altogether.

The eventual result of removing tariff protection is that those productive resources that are released can be channelled into more profitable occupations. But the adjustment may take a long time and the immediate impact is likely to be unemployment, empty factories and even ghost towns. Often governments in the past have decided that the long-term benefits to the nation do not warrant the short-term misery. They also have regard to the electoral consequences of such decisions.

Protection may increase wages

It has been argued by economists that one effect of protecting manufacturing industries here has been to raise wages. It is said that as manufacturers are heavy users of labour, greater domestic production of manufacturers leads to an increase in the demand for labour and this leads to higher wages.

However, protection has an adverse effect on the export industries: the prices they must pay for materials and labour are higher. As a result, their production is less and wealth is distributed away from them. This argument for protection raises the problem already noted: that there is no objective way of assessing whether the gains to one group outweigh the losses to another.

Domestic industries initially require protection

'Infant industry argument'

The other arguments listed are based on the claim that protection brings overall benefits to the whole community. Many economists consider the 'infant industry argument' the most persuasive of these. When an industry is first established it is likely to incur heavy development costs. Its smallness may mean that cost per unit of output are high. In these early stages mistakes will be made and rectified, often at great expense. Businesses, like individuals, learn by doing. An industry's early years can therefore be extremely difficult, even if its prospects for ultimate success appear good. Foreign competition in the development stage may make survival impossible. It is argued that such industries should receive tariff protection throughout the development stage until the point is reached at which unit costs have been reduced so that they can compete openly with foreign firms.

This argument has been widely accepted as valid in principle, though some economists have argued that in a market economy investors should be prepared to bear the risks and carry the temporary early losses if they are confident of the ultimate success of the venture.

Problems in applying infant industry argument

Tariff-making authorities face several practical problems when applying the infant industry argument to any particular case. First, there is the problem of deciding whether an industry has eventual prospects of success. Does it really have a potential comparative advantage? Will it ever reach the stage of not needing protection, or will the promising infant degenerate into a chronic invalid?

Then there is the problem of deciding how much tariff protection should be given to an industry. Some people favour a 'made-to-measure' tariff – one which is high enough to protect the industry regardless of how high that tariff must be. Others say that some common policy should be adopted in all cases; that there should be a uniform tariff or maximum rate of protection. It has also been suggested that time limits should be placed on tariff protection; that no industry should receive permanent protection and that perhaps tariffs should be reduced progressively on a set timetable. Behind these proposals is the knowledge that tariffs may encourage inefficiency; the gradual phasing out of a tariff is seen as likely to have a 'cold-shower' effect on protected industries.

Domestic industries should be protected against the dumping of foreign goods

Dumping

'Dumping' is a rather imprecise term that covers a number of trade practices, but it generally refers to the selling of goods more cheaply in one market than another. For example, a German car-maker may sell cars more cheaply in Australia than in its home market, or a Canadian marketing authority might sell surplus wheat to Egypt at less than production cost.

It is often impossible for the local producer to compete against foreign suppliers who use such practices. Often domestic buyers enthusiastically welcome dumping, but such practices not only create temporary problems for domestic producers, they may be employed deliberately by foreign firms to drive the domestic industry out of existence. When this has been done, the foreign supplier may then raise the price above the original domestic price.

Domestic producers frequently claim that dumping is taking place simply when foreign producers are able to supply the market more cheaply. For example, in 1974 the cattle lobby in the United States claimed that Australia was dumping beef on the United States market and sought protection. It should be clear that in this situation American domestic producers were really complaining that Australian farmers were able to produce beef more cheaply – an argument that has already been dismissed earlier in the chapter.

Tariff protection improves the terms of trade

In Chapter 12 it was said that an improvement occurs in a country's terms of trade if its export price index rises relatively to its import price index. An improvement in this index can occur in many ways: for example, a rise in export prices and no change in import prices, or a fall in export prices accompanied by an even greater fall in import prices. In certain circumstances the imposition of tariffs on a sufficiently wide range of products can have the effect of improving the country's terms of trade (and of causing a deterioration in the terms of trade of its competitors).

This may appear unlikely, because Figure 17.6 demonstrated that the effect of imposing a tariff was to increase the price of imported goods to the consumer. However, none of this increase goes to the foreigner; it goes to the government in tariff revenue. In fact, as Activities 17.9 and 17.11 showed, the local price may well rise by less than the amount of the tariff, and so the price paid to foreign suppliers falls. Thus, if the price of exports of the country imposing the tariff is unchanged, the effect will be an improvement in the terms of trade.

In this case, a given quantity of exports will earn enough foreign exchange to buy a greater quantity of imports than before. However, two or more can play at this game. If one country can improve its terms of trade by imposing tariffs, others can too. Their retaliation will both worsen the home country's terms of trade and also cause a further fall in international trade. If all countries try to improve their own terms of trade by raising tariff barriers higher and higher, the serious reduction of trade is likely to deny to all the benefits of international specialisation and trade.

General Agreement on Tariffs and Trade

Recognition of this problem led to the signing by many countries of the General Agreement on Tariffs and Trade (GATT) in 1947. Liberalisation of trade was the principal objective of GATT and the signatories have held a series of bargaining sessions since then. They have included the Kennedy Round, completed in 1967, and the multilateral trade negotiations (MTN) conducted in Tokyo from 1974 to 1979. The negotiations have resulted in substantial reductions in the general level of tariffs on manufactured goods. Exporters of foodstuffs and primary products have claimed that they have not received similar benefits.

17.12

Use the information given in Activity 17.9 to calculate the improvement that occurred in the home country's terms of trade following its imposition of a tariff of £20 per tonne on imports. Assume that no change occurred in the price of the home country's exports, which may be taken as having an index value of 100. Assume also that this is the only good imported by the home country and that, in consequence, the percentage change in the price received by foreign producers measures the percentage change in import prices. From this you will be able to calculate the price index for imports.

17.13

An often-quoted statement, sometimes attributed to Abraham Lincoln, argues in favour of tariff protection in the following terms:

> I do not know much about the tariff, but I know this much: when we buy manufactured goods abroad we get the goods and the foreigner gets the money. When we buy the manufactured goods at home we get both the goods and the money.

But such a remark might easily have been made by an older-style politician. How would you counter such an argument?

Tariff protection assists the balance of payments

Problems in using tariff protection to assist balance of payments

It is also argued that a tariff will improve a country's balance of payments position by reducing import payments. This arguments is logically correct, but its practical implementation remains difficult.

First, the precise effect on the balance of payments is often difficult to calculate because the change in the value of imports will depend on domestic demand for the products, domestic supply and foreign supply, and it is difficult to estimate precisely, in advance, how quantities demanded and supplied will be affected by the tariff and by higher prices. In consequence, it is usually impossible to calculate the amount by which the value of imports will be reduced.

Second, there remains the possibility of foreign retaliation, which may result in a loss in export receipts. Third, tariffs are not a suitable policy weapon for dealing with frequent changes in the balance of payments situation, because changes in the tariff level mean that domestic producers have to plan production without knowing how much foreign competition they are likely to have to face in the future.

Tariffs bring revenue to the government

Undeniably this is true. However, the more successful a tariff is in reducing imports the less successful it will be in raising revenue. A prohibitive tariff – one so high that it excludes all imports – raises no revenue.

Key industries should be protected to ensure national survival

War, or the hostile commercial policies of former trading partners, can lead to economic isolation, so that the specialist country may be unable to acquire goods on which it has come to depend.

Tariffs which protect a country's key industries enable it to achieve a measure of self-sufficiency in such times of isolation (at the cost of lower standards of living for the country's residents), than might have been possible at other times. If a society decides that the danger of isolation is real, it may decide to protect key industries. Diversification may be justified by the sense of security it brings.

On the other hand, if the danger of isolation is remote and the costs of protection great, the argument will have little appeal. In making such a decision a government will need to consider the alternative strategies of either building up the stocks of vital products by importing more than required for current needs, or the possibility of producing domestic substitutes after imports are terminated.

17.14

UK television manufacturers sought protection against imports of coloured television receivers and components, particularly from Asian countries. Organise a debate on the subject with speakers chosen to present the case for UK manufacturers, foreign suppliers and UK consumers.

17.15

An alternative to tariff protection, as a means of assisting a domestic manufacturing industry to maintain production at a given level, is by subsidising the industry. A subsidy is, in effect, a negative tax and influences supply by reducing the domestic industry's unit costs of producing any given quantity.

1 Suppose that the government decided to subsidise a domestic industry rather than adopt the alternative policy of imposing a tariff on the foreign supplies. What difference, it any, will this make to the price the product sells for in the UK? Will it have a noticeable effect on the total quantity of the product bought by consumers? What will be the effect on the government's tariff revenue?

2 In what circumstances might a government decide to protect an industry from foreign competition by providing a subsidy rather than by imposing a tariff.

Chapter 18

Protecting the Consumer

> Consumption is the sole end and purpose of all production: and the interest of the producer ought to be attended to, only so far as it may be necessary for promoting that of the consumer. The maxim is so perfectly self-evident, that it would seem absurd to attempt to prove it. But in the mercantile system, the interest of the consumer is almost completely sacrificed to that of the producer: and it seems to consider production, and not consumption, as the ultimate end of all industry and commerce. . . .
> It cannot be very difficult to determine who have been the contrivers of this whole mercantile system; not the consumers, we may believe, whose interest has been entirely neglected; but the producers, whose interest has been so carefully attended to . . .[1]

Adam Smith, writing at the end of the eighteenth century, claimed that the economic system of the day distributed income in favour of producers as a group, at the expense of consumers at large. The growth of 'consumerism' in recent years is based on the claim that the modern market economy also discriminates against the consumer, and that governments should adopt policies that specifically benefit and protect the consumer.

Reasons why consumers' position is weak

It has been argued that consumers occupy a weak position in the modern market economy for three main reasons:

1 In many industries there is a lack of competition between suppliers and in consequence consumers have to pay higher prices and consumers have less choice.

2 Consumer sovereignty is a myth. Modern advertising techniques and sales methods have a powerful influence on buying habits. The complexities of both the system, and the products the consumer attempts to purchase, are such that decisions are often made without the consumer being in possession of all relevant information.

3 Consumers have lacked effective means of obtaining satisfaction after a transaction has been completed if the product or workmanship is defective, or if the product falls short of the consumers' expectations. Often the consumer is in a weak legal position, or alternatively has been unable to exercise his legal rights.

This chapter examines each of these arguments which claim that uncontrolled market economies operate against the best interest of consumers. It investigates the extent to which government in the UK and in other market economies has responded to the claims by adopting policies that improve consumers' welfare. The chapter also considers arguments of producer groups against consumer protection. We need to remember that any argument about redistribution of income within a society involves value judgements. Even if it is established that consumers are in a weak position in society, it does not follow automatically that their position must be improved. Such a conclusion requires a value-based decision by society that the claims of consumers are more important than the conflicting claims of producers at the particular time. The argument that consumers should be protected and their position strengthened in the system is analagous to the claims by trade unions that the wages share of gross domestic product should be larger and that working conditions should be improved. There is no way the propositions can be proved.

Producers' arguments against consumer protection

One general argument by producers against a redistribution of income in favour of consumers is that it will have an adverse effect on the operation of the economic system, and that both consumers and producers will suffer. In the short run this will not be so because the supply of goods and services is fixed and thus can be redistributed within the society. But in the long run such a redistribution policy may influence the rate of economic growth.

A common argument is that policies which protect the consumer reduce businessmen's profits and lead to a fall in investment spending and in the rate of economic growth. The argument requires careful attention. Similar arguments have been presented by businessmen when opposing the claims of unions for higher wage rates, or when they have objected to government imposing higher taxation rates. Such disincentive effects may follow a redistribution of income, but they do not necessarily follow every redistribution of income. Whether the argument is valid, then, will depend on the particular circumstances. Even if it is valid, and economic growth is reduced by a particular redistribution of income, society may still decide that the redistribution is preferable to the increase in production.

Adam Smith recognised that government policies that benefit producers also bring advantages to consumers in many instances.

18.1

Consider the following letter to a local newspaper by the owner of a small manufacturing business.

Sir,
The claim that consumer interests are suffering at the hands of businessmen, who exploit them in search of profits, disgusts me. This so-called special class of consumers is in reality the families of the workers I employ in my factory. These workers are constantly seeking higher wages and taking home larger pay-packets. Small wonder I have to get together with other manufacturers and increase my prices if I am to stay in business. Surely the government isn't going to allow them to get at me in both ways. There is no hope for our nation if they do.

Yours etc.
Anon. (name and address withheld)

Does this argument destroy the case put forward by advocates of 'consumerism'. Give your views as fully as possible.

Lack of competition among sellers

It has long been argued that competition tends to benefit the consumer and that its absence works to the advantage of the supplier. It is said that when businesses are forced to compete with one another, prices are likely to be lower and the service better. When there is no competition at all, the producer is a monopolist. In Chapter 8 it was shown that an effective monopolist may be able to set the price for his product at a level that will bring supernormal profits.

Review of arguments against monopolies

It is sometimes claimed that the use of monopoly power works against the consumer in two main ways: by making the price higher, and by reducing the quantity the consumer is able to purchase. In consequence, monopoly leads to aggregate production being less than it would have been in a competitive system. This will not be so in an economy in which the government uses monetary and fiscal policies to maintain full employment, for then the restriction of production by one industry will release resources to other industries. The main objection to the use of monopoly power in these circumstances is that it redistributes income in favour of the monopolist.

The argument that monopolists are less efficient than competitive firms is not conclusive and must be balanced against the argument, referred to in Chapter 8, that monopolies may benefit from the economies of large scale operations and achieve cost savings. Unlike the United States, monopolies as such are not illegal in the UK, though some of their practices are prohibited. The Monopolies Commission may be empowered to investigate large businesses that have effective monopoly power and comment upon whether they operate in or against the public interest. The publicity given to any investigation and report probably acts as a restraint on behaviour.

An agreement between firms in an industry to fix prices, to share the market in some predetermined way or restrict the entry of new firms may operate against consumers' interests just as much as the policies of a monopolist. The effect of many such agreements is that the firms are able, collectively, to act as a monopolist whilst remaining separate legal entities. The term *restrictive trade practices* is used to refer to a wide variety of business policies that reduce competition between producers and limit the freedom of wholesalers and retailers to determine their own selling policies. Several of the more important categories of restrictive trade practice are listed in Table 18.1. It distinguishes two groups of agreement that produce restrictive trade practices: horizontal agreements and vertical agreements. *Horizontal agreements* are made between businesses operating at the same level of production in an industry. For example, a horizontal agreement may exist between textile manufacturers or manufacturers of certain types of building material (businesses that would otherwise be in direct competition with one another). *Vertical agreements* are agreements between firms at different stages of the production process. An agreement between a manufacturer and wholesalers or retailers is a vertical agreement.

	Horizontal agreements	Vertical agreements
Pricing	Price fixing	Resale price maintenance
Size of market	Market sharing	Solo marketing

Table 18.1 Principal types of restrictive trade practice and agreement

Table 18.1 distinguishes between agreements that affect the price of the product (horizontal price agreements and resale price maintenance) and agreements that affect the size and number of competitors (horizontal market-sharing arrangements and solo marketing). The list of trade practices given in the table is far from exhaustive, but a consideration of these four will be sufficient to give an indication of the possible effects of restrictive trade practices on the market economy.

Horizontal price agreements

These can take a variety of forms. There may be a trade association between the businesses in an industry to determine joint policies, or businesses may determine prices during informal discussions. This practice may give rise to monopoly prices being charged by the businesses. A further disadvantage from the consumer's point of view is that the individual firms are each smaller than a single monopolist would have been. Consequently, the practice brings no advantage to society in the form of lower production costs that might have come from large-scale operations.

Collusive tendering

One form of horizontal price agreement that is claimed to be undesirable is *collusive tendering*. Firms tendering for a contract get together and decide either that all should tender the same price for the job, or that one of them should tender a somewhat lower price than the others, with the understanding that one of the other firms will submit the lowest tender for the next job. The practice defeats the whole idea of calling tenders; namely, to obtain the lowest possible price for a job by requiring each business to make a tender without knowing rivals' quotes.

Resale price maintenance

This is a vertical trade practice in which manufacturers or suppliers fix the price at which the retailer is to sell the product. The practice removes price competition between retailers in the sale of the particular branded product. Manufacturers and retailers who favour resale price maintenance claim:

Arguments for resale price maintenance

1 it does not remove competition between brands;
2 retailers are spared the problem of determining what price to charge;
3 the shopper can be certain what the price is, and thus it prevents him being overcharged, and also saves the shopper the time and trouble of seeking bargains.

There is little doubt that most consumers prefer the possibility of active competition between retailers and many are prepared to go from shop to shop in search of lower prices. It is argued that competition between retailers is likely to lead to lower prices and to low-cost retailers benefitting at the expense of those who incur high costs or operate on high profit margins. In many cases it is retailers rather than manufacturers who favour the practice.

The Resale Prices Act of 1964 largely did away with the practice of resale price maintenance in the UK, but it does still remain in a few trades, for instance in the pricing of books. In this case it was demonstrated that the practice was not operating contrary to the public interest.

Horizontal market-sharing agreements

These may determine the quantity of a product each business is to produce. In other parts of the world such agreements have become so

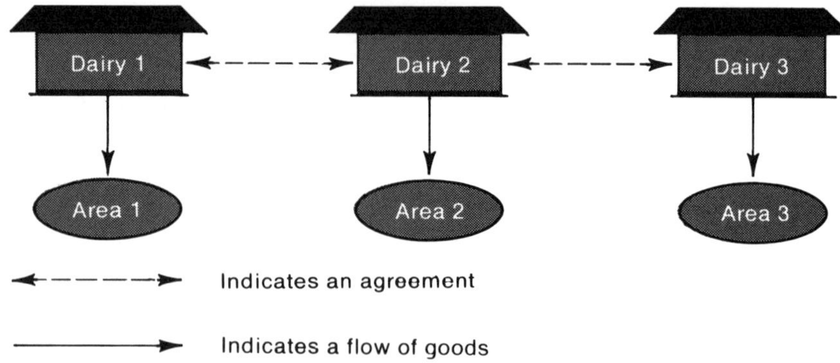

Figure 18.1 Market-sharing agreement between dairies

formal and complete (covering quantity and quality of the product, after-sales service and warranty provisions) that the associated firms are known as a cartel. Their policies are indistinguishable from those of monopolies. Cartels have been vigorously opposed by governments in the European Economic Community countries, where they have been common in basic industries such as coal and iron and steel. International cartels are OPEC (Organisation of Petroleum Exporting Countries) and IATA (International Air Transport Association).

A more common form of agreement is that which divides a market into a series of smaller markets, each supplied by a single firm, thus eliminating competition between them. Familiar examples of market-sharing agreements are those by which different milk vendors and newsagents are solely responsible for deliveries in different parts of a town. Sometimes these market-sharing arrangements are administered by the firm supplying the product to the distributors.

Solo marketing

This occurs when there is an agreement between retailer and manufacturer that the retailer will only sell the manufacturer's product. The

Hobart *Mercury*, 27 March 1974
Copyright Field Enterprises Inc., by courtesy of Alan Foley Pty Ltd, Narrabeen, N.S.W.

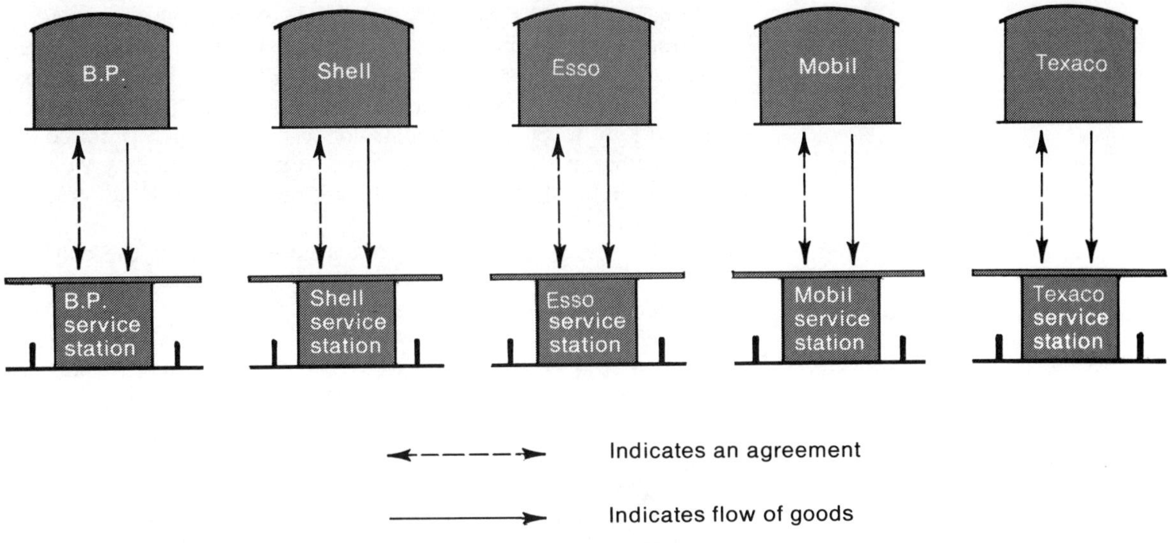

Figure 18.2 Solo marketing of petrol

best-known example of solo marketing in the UK is the sale of petrol through 'tied' service stations. The system is illustrated in Figure 18.2.

Through such agreements, the oil companies are able to obtain sales outlets in particular localities. Each service station can offer only one brand of petrol and the oil company thus acquires a monopoly on that particular site, which, depending on the traffic in the area, can be important.

Solo marketing compared with horizontal market sharing

Nevertheless, there is an important difference between solo marketing and horizontal market sharing. Solo marketing removes competition between brands at a particular sales outlet but does not remove competition within a district, because usually each oil company establishes an outlet for its product. It has been claimed that the solo marketing system has produced a situation in which there are too many service stations, too much competition for the available business, with the result that retail margins are inadequate.

18.2

One argument often put forward to justify many types of restrictive trade practice is that they lead to orderly marketing. It is explained that orderly marketing brings benefits to both producers and consumers by eliminating uncertainty and encouraging continuity of production. Examine this argument as it might be presented in defence of:

a horizontal pricing agreement

resale price maintenance

What arguments would you put forward to counter the 'orderly marketing' arguments?

You may be able to think of some situations in which you believe each of these practices is justified, and other situations in which the practices act against the consumers' interests. Or it may be that you consider that horizontal price agreements and resale price maintenance can never be justified. Explain your thinking as fully as possible.

18.3

1 The following table lists a number of market forms and types of trade practice that can operate against the consumers' interests. It also lists three of the main ways in which trade practices can disadvantage the consumer. Indicate those harmful effects that are most likely to be of particular concern when each practice occurs by placing crosses in the appropriate places. You may well decide that some of the practices can have more than one adverse effect.

	Possible adverse effect on the consumer		
Market form or trade practice	May result in higher prices	Limits the consumer's freedom of choice among existing firms	Restricts entry of new firms
Monopoly			
Cartel			
Solo marketing			
Resale price maintenance			
Horizontal price agreements			
Collusive tendering			
Market sharing			

2 Discuss your results with other members of the class.

18.4

In most Australian cities and towns a single milk vendor delivers to all the houses in a street. In contrast, in England it is common to find as many as three or four dairies delivering to different houses in the same street. These dairies often deliver at different times of the day and the milkmen also carry a limited range of other products: eggs, potatoes and butter. Discuss the advantages and disadvantages of the two systems: market sharing in Australia and competition in England.

Consumer protection legislation

The main protection for consumers in the UK is provided for by the Fair Trading Act of 1973. This act established the office of a Director-General of Fair Trading and brought together the policies relating to competition and to consumer protection. Monopoly and competition policy come under the Office of Fair Trading which can make reference of any monopoly firm to an independent investigatory Monopolies Commission. Restrictive practices and other anti-competitive practices are dealt with by a Restrictive Practices Court which requires parties concerned to prove that any agreement or practice is 'in the public interest' otherwise it is to cease. Under the Fair Trading Act, the scope of this legislation was extended to cover the supply of services as well as the supply of goods. The Office of Fair Trading also has a more general role in the furthering of consumer affairs by such means as publishing information and advice for consumers and encouraging trade associations to set up voluntary codes of practice for their members to protect consumers.

Other legislation increases the position of the consumer in relation to the market place and the producer. Notably the Supply of Goods (Implied Terms) Act of 1973 ensures that consumers have a legal right to goods that are of 'merchantable quality' and are 'fit for their purpose'. Moreover, the consumer is further protected by any guarantee or warranty offered by producers which is additional to the above requirement. The Consumer Credit Act of 1974 ensures that any terms of credit advertised should not be false or misleading and that the true percentage rate of return should be quoted on any hire purchase or consumer credit agreement or offer.

Lack of information among buyers

The second reason for the weak position of consumers in the market place is said to be that they lack the necessary information to make decisions that will bring them the greatest benefit. The economic theory of consumer behaviour has tended to assume that consumers possess perfect knowledge about prices, quality of products and conditions of sale and they act on this information to ensure their satisfaction is maximised in any given situation. But acquiring such information is beyond the capabilities of any consumer in a society in which consumer goods have become increasingly complex. Some of the technical information the consumer would like to know about the merits of rival products cannot be obtained in a form that makes sense. Furthermore, it would take so much time to obtain all relevant information that no sensible person would think it worthwhile to do so.

Consequently, most consumers learn what to buy from experience, or they allow themselves to be persuaded by advertising campaigns. Sometimes they follow such strange rules of thumb as 'if it's expensive, then it must be worth buying'. Inevitably, many consumers end up by paying more than they need for certain goods and services. They do not get the best value for their money. Frequently, they fail to realise that a better alternative exists and so, in that sense, remain satisfied with their decisions. But often the consumer only becomes aware of the mistake that he has made after the event.

Consumers' representatives argue that there are three ways in which the information available to buyers can be improved and their position in the market place strengthened. These are by

1 improving general education on consumer matters;

2 ensuring that more relevant information is available to would-be purchasers; and

3 preventing false and misleading advertising.

Education

Consumer education

Often the basic weakness in the consumer's position stems from a quite irrational attitude to economic transactions. Many of the complaints received by consumer protection authorities in the UK have only arisen because the consumer failed to obtain basic information before committing himself. For example, complaints about the cost of services such as repairs or house painting occur because the consumer failed to find out what the price was going to be before authorising the work, or failed to insist on a written quotation for the job. Many consumer decisions involve weighing up the pros and cons of a particular course of action and sometimes consumers lack the skill to make such a judgement. In recent years there has been an increasing movement to provide consumer education courses in secondary schools. Consumer education is a more common feature in other European countries in the EEC than it is as yet in the UK.

Specific information

Consumers also need information about the ability of a product to perform the function for which it is required. For many years independent organisations such as the British Standards Institute have provided consumers with a guide to the safety of products through the approval they give to articles that meet their safety standards.

Consumers' Association

Voluntary organisations, such as the Consumers' Association, provide information for their members after following a comparative testing programme. The CA has limited funds and its obligations are to its members rather than to the general public. Its detailed findings are published in *Which?* magazine and other publications and are often quoted in newspapers and other media.

False and misleading advertising

In many market economies it is now accepted that any advertisement or description of a product should not contain claims that are untrue, misleading or cannot be substantiated. The Trade Descriptions Act, 1968 makes it an offence to make false representations about the supply of goods or services. The supplier must not offer goods that are claimed to be waterproof, for example, unless they really are waterproof. If a trader offers a good for sale at a reduced price and marks the price down accordingly, then it is required by the Act that the good actually has been on sale at the higher price for 28 days in the previous six months to ensure price comparisons are accurate. (However, some shops now publish a disclaimer to the effect that any price reductions so marked do not necessarily indicate that they have been on sale at the higher price.)

18.5

Each of the following proposals for suggested regulations designed to provide consumers with more information is accompanied by a pair of statements expressing different points of view.

1 *All restaurants and cafes should be compelled to display prices outside.*
(a) This would spare tourists' embarrassment if they found they could not afford a meal when they got inside.

(b) Displaying menus and prices outside would lower the tone of high-class restaurants.

2 *All repair men should be obliged to give a written quote for the job, which consumers would have to accept in writing.*

(a) This would remove uncertainty and prevent overcharging.

(b) It is impossible to determine how much work is involved in repairs until they have been started.

Do you think that either of these proposals should be implemented? What other arguments can you think of to either support or counter the two proposals?

Notes

1 Adam Smith 1776 *An Enquiry into the Nature and Causes of the Wealth of Nations* Book IV ch 8, repr University Paperbacks, Methuen, 1961, vol 2, p 179.

Chapter 19

The United Kingdom and the European Economic Community

Political background

The European Economic Community (EEC) came into being on 1 January 1958 following the signing of the Treaty of Rome in 1957. Under the terms of the treaty France, Germany and Italy joined with the three Benelux countries in a closely integrated economic community which formalised and brought together the six nations and extended the already existing forms of co-operation between them. Benelux was created in 1948 as a customs union of the Netherlands, Belgium and Luxembourg with the aim of free trade between the nations, becoming an economic union in 1960. In 1952 the European Coal and Steel Community (ECSC) was founded to nationalise coal and steel production, particularly in France and Germany, and to establish a free market and a common policy towards prices, investment and trade. Euratom, the European nations' common policy on atomic energy and related development, was established at the same time as the Treaty of Rome brought the EEC into being. Prior to all of these institutional organisations, was the OEEC, the Organisation for European Economic Co-operation, set up in 1947 to organise the distribution of economic aid from the United States to Europe after the end of the Second World War. The OEEC included a wider range of European nations than the Six who were to decide on much closer common links. The body was renamed the Organisation for Economic Co-operation and Development (OECD) in 1961 and was joined by other industrial nations; USA, Canada and later Japan. The nature of the OECD has also shifted towards economic aid for the underdeveloped world.

Although the UK was approached to join the Six in 1957, the UK at that time was not interested in European co-operation, being a major imperial power with a special relationship with the Commonwealth. In 1963 an application by the UK to join the EEC was refused and so was another attempt in 1967. Finally in 1972, the UK's application was accepted and the UK formally became a member on 1 January 1973. At the same time, Denmark and Eire also joined but Norway, although making an application at the same time, decided against membership after holding a referendum on the issue. From 1973 the EEC became an enlarged community of nine countries. Greece, in 1981, was the tenth nation to join; Spain and Portugal are at present making applications.

Aims of the EEC

The basic aims of the EEC are two-fold: (i) to establish a common market with free trade in goods and free movement of people, capital and investment across national boundaries and (ii) to establish common economic policies on such matters as agriculture, energy, industry, competition, transport, taxation and general macro-economic aims such as economic growth, employment, social aims and welfare objectives.

The aims clearly involve the very close unification of the separate member states into a single economic unit but the EEC so far has only developed a customs union, a common agricultural policy and some common policies in the areas of regional, social and industrial policy. Monetary integration, tax harmonisation and general agreement on macro-economic policies are still far from being achieved. At issue here is the important aspect of national sovereignty for the member countries. Any closer form of integration between the member states must involve some loss of sovereignty in individual policy-making. Acceptance of this fact involves the recognition of a European community operating in the wider interests of the community's peoples rather than the narrower viewpoint of any single nation member state.

EFTA

The European Free Trade Association came into being in 1959, as a reaction to the Common Market by several other European nations outside the Six. Britain, Austria, Denmark, Norway, Portugal, Sweden, Switzerland (later Iceland and Finland) agreed to set up a free market between themselves with no tariff on trade between members. On joining the EEC, Britain and Denmark relinquished their membership of EFTA.

Customs union

The EEC is a customs union because member countries have abolished all barriers to trade between themselves, such as tariffs or quotas. Moreover, the community has established a common policy towards trade from outside the member countries by a common external tariff.

A free trade area also abolishes trade restrictions between members but individual countries retain their own tariffs with regard to non-members and do not adopt the common tariff.

The advantages of trade liberalisation for the customs union are principally that it allows the full benefits of comparative advantage to operate. The trade community is able to act as if it were one single economic unit and adopt specialisation fully, leading to an optimal allocation of resources. This creates the possibility of developing new trade within the union and of passing on advantages from lower-cost producers. The trade-creating effect, however, may be offset to some extent by a trade-diversion effect. Such diversions may result from the common external tariff which is applied to all countries outside the customs union and may give an artificial cost advantage for a member producer thereby protected from outside competition. In this case a move away from optimal allocation of resources is apparent.

Other advantages presented by the customs union include the possibility of economies of scale from an enlarged market. The other arguments in the general 'free trade versus protectionism' debate, such as the removal of competition and sheltering inefficient producers behind a tariff wall, are clearly applicable to the discussion of the operation of a customs union. As with any form of trade regulation, or deregulation, the overall effect can only be appreciated fully after a consideration of the relevant elasticities of demand for the imports and exports involved.

Structure and organisation of the EEC

Clearly the problems involved in determining and operating policy for a community of ten nations and a population in excess of 270 million are far from easy to solve. The EEC has developed its own institutional and organisational structure to deal with devising, co-ordinating and implementing policy and legislation. There are four main institutions involved in decision-making for the EEC: the Council of Ministers, the European Parliament, the Commission and the European Court of Justice.

Council of Ministers

Any decision on a major issue in the EEC must gain the unanimous approval of the relevant Council of Ministers, for example, Agricultural Ministers, Foreign Ministers, or Heads of State. Any single country is thus able to prevent a decision by the use of the veto. The Council of Ministers meets on a regular basis in the case of Foreign Ministers and Heads of State, and as required in the case of Industry, Energy, Agriculture and so on as relevant issues affecting them are discussed. Ministers representing all the member countries meet on an equal basis in the Council.

European Parliament

The Parliament is an elected assembly with all European voters able to take part; the first direct elections took place in 1979. Seats in the Parliament are distributed among member nations according to population and size in general terms. France, Germany, Italy and the UK each elected 81 Euro MPs out of a total of 410 in the Parliament in 1979. Luxembourg has 6, Ireland 15, Denmark 16, Belgium 24 and the Netherlands 25 members. Before 1979, the members of the European Parliament were nominated by the individual national parliaments and in the Parliament the members were grouped according to the political parties they represented.

The power of the Parliament lies more in consultation with and general influence over the Commission and the policy decisions of the Council of Ministers, as well as providing a general forum for discussion and debate of issues involving the whole Community.

The Commission

The EEC Commission provides the civil service or bureaucratic organisation for the community. The function of the Commission is to implement the workings of the policy decisions taken by the Councils and provide the administration framework necessary for this. There is also an additional role in the initiation of policy and presenting proposals to the relevant Council of Ministers. The Commission is headed by a number of specially appointed Commissioners who take on the responsibility for a particular function of the Community's affairs e.g. social policy and regional affairs. The Commission is not able to determine policy or act on its own initiative and any policy proposal requires the consent of the appropriate Council of Ministers.

European Court of Justice

The European Court provides for the enforcement, application and interpretation of EEC laws and regulations within the community. The Court of Justice acts quite independently of national self-interests and is therefore objective and impartial in, for example, the settling of disputes between member nations. The Court has the final say in such affairs and member nations agree to abide by the Court's decisions. In the very nature of things the reconciliation of common community policies and rules and regulations with several countries' independent interests and nationalistic aims and objectives will almost inevitably result in conflicts from time to time. The Court of Justice makes for the final adjudication and arbitration in these cases and also acts as a restraint on the other institutional agencies such as the Commission.

The UK within the EEC

The major areas of close involvement of the UK within the community are agriculture, energy, trade policy, regional policy, competition and industrial policy. As discussed earlier, the wider aims of the EEC envisage much closer co-operation in areas of economic policy, monetary integration, tax harmonisation, social policies, but it is in the major areas of agriculture, trade, energy etc. that the closest initial moves towards integration have been achieved. For the rest of this chapter, these issues will be discussed in the light of the problems encountered and the progress made.

Agriculture in the UK

The position of agriculture within the economy of the UK is not the same as that of the other member EEC countries. However, there are certain distinguishing features and characteristics of agriculture which are common to all countries. It is also important to remember that agriculture as a generic title includes a number of quite diffuse activities (e.g. horticulture, dairy farming and fruit growing) each with different problems, production methods, climatic requirements and other difficulties. Therefore, to recognise the separate nature of these components of the agriculture sector, the term rural industries is used in the following discussion.

Although there is a tendency to discuss the rural sector as if it contained a single homogeneous industry this can lead to misleading conclusions. At any one time the problems facing a single rural industry will be quite different from those faced by other rural industries. Examination of the claims for assistance from rural producers in general needs to be related to the problems facing each particular rural industry.

Despite the need for specific investigations, the rural industries have many common characteristics. It is only by a study of these essential characteristics that both the causes of the difficulties of rural industries, and the basis for their claims for assistance can be appreciated.

Common features of rural industries

Characteristics of rural industries:

1 lack of control over production environment
2 price-takers on overseas markets
3 low price elasticity of demand for many products
4 low income elasticity of demand for many products
5 inability or reluctance to leave industry or change the product mix.

Taken together the five characteristics explain why rural industries so often find themselves in economic difficulties and why rural producers experience economic hardship. The nature of rural industry is quite different from manufacturing industry in that the fluctuations to which it is subjected are generally greater and less predictable.

Consider the combined effect of the first three characteristics. The rural producer lacks control over his production environment. He has to cope with adverse weather conditions, pests and diseases and can never predict either the level of his own output or the level of output of the industry as a whole, for a particular season. As a price-taker, he is forced to take the market price for his product, unlike the manufacturer who can usually set the price at a level that will cover production costs.

For most primary products the price elasticity of demand is less than 1. (See Chapter 8 for an explanation of price elasticity of demand). A small increase in production is sufficient to result in a large fall in the price of the product. The effect is illustrated in Figure 19.1.

An industry dependent on foreign markets may face an increase in supply from competing sources, the development of synthetics or other substitute products, or the introduction by importing countries of restrictive commercial policies such as tariffs or quotas. Such factors have a depressing effect on the local industry, as do changes in international exchange rates such as an upward revaluation of the pound sterling or a devaluation of the currencies of the importing countries. These effects spill over on to the domestic market. When prices are low abroad producers tend to sell on the domestic market with the result that prices are depressed there too.

No control of markets

A major weakness in the individual primary producer's position is that as an isolated price-taker he has no control over the marketing environment in which he operates. He cannot charge a higher price to restore his income because he sells in a competitive market. Some growers may be able to set up a roadside stall selling fruit and vegetables

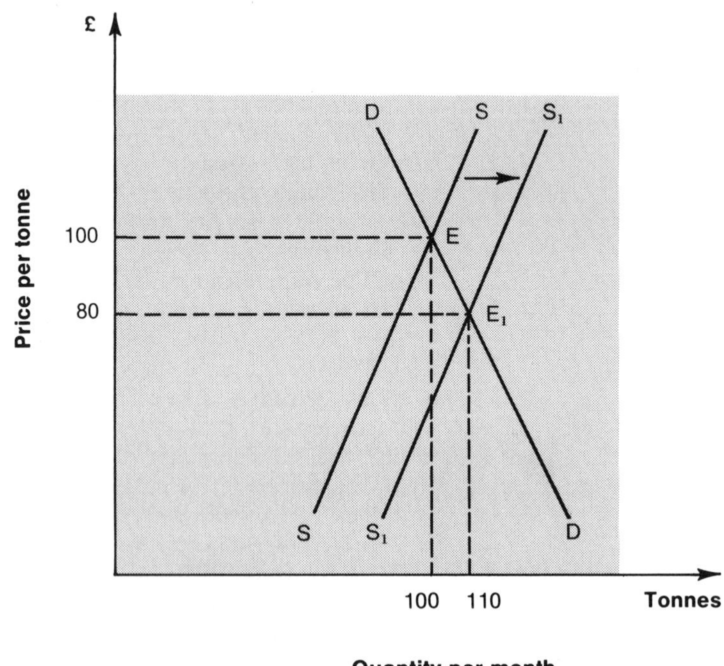

Figure 19.1 Effect of an increase in supply when demand is price inelastic

to the public but the chances are that the prices charged will be close to the market price to attract buyers. Moreover, only well-situated farmers will be able to sell much of their crop in this way.

The significance of the fourth characteristic of rural industries, low income elasticity of demand, is that the demand for farm products is likely to increase relativity slowly. Other things being equal, a gradual increase in demand will bring with it a gradual increase in prices and lead to a slow expansion of an industry. But if foreign supplies are increasing rapidly the overall effect will be one of falling prices. Similarly if the local industry has developed its production technology, and has increased yield per hectare and total output, this too may contribute to falling prices. Any producers who have not improved their efficiency or lowered their production costs will be in difficulty if prices fall.

Economic hardship may result when rural industry fails to adjust to changes in economic conditions. Economic theory suggests that the market mechanism operates to produce an equilibrium situation in which those farmers with the greatest efficiency and hence the lowest costs will be able to make the profits notwithstanding the first four of the special characteristics listed on page 341. The theoretical adjustment process may be illustrated by a simple example. Suppose there is a sharp fall in the demand for cabbages caused by the development and sale of another product, such as frozen sprouts. The effects of this fall in demand for cabbages are illustrated in Figure 19.2.

The fall in demand is represented by the movement to the left of the demand curve. It is assumed that in the short term the quantity of cabbages supplied to the market is fixed and the price falls from 40p per cabbage to 20p. However, 20p per cabbage is not enough to ensure that a permanent supply of cabbages will meet the demand. The long term supply curve for cabbages is represented by the line SS. The least

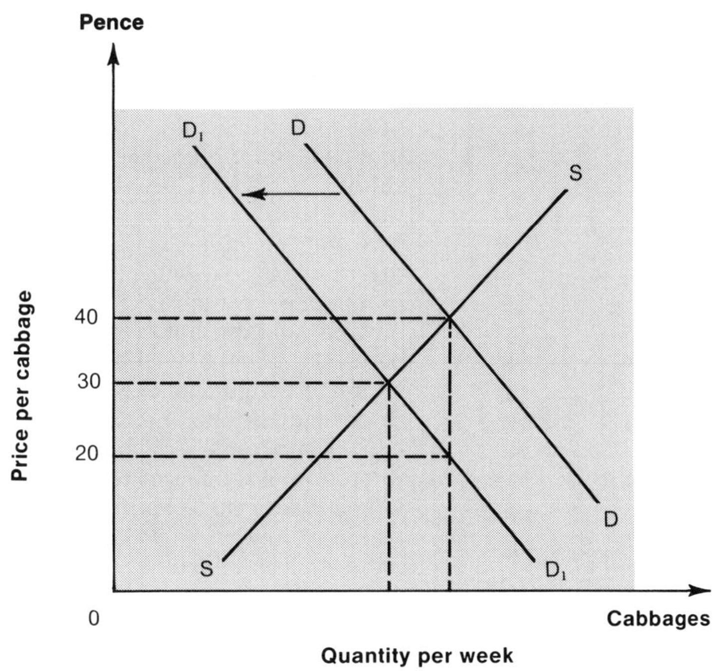

Figure 19.2 Effects of a fall in demand

efficient of the existing producers find 20p an unprofitable price and reduce production, perhaps by switching to other vegetables. The quantity of cabbages supplied to the market is reduced until a new price (30p per cabbage) is established at which demand and supply are equated. The industry is reduced in size but the remaining producers are able to produce profitably.

This is the theory, but it has a number of serious weaknesses, because adjustment seldom takes place without some economic hardship. When, initially, demand is reduced and the price falls, individual farmers respond in a variety of ways. They may do nothing, increase production, reduce production, or alter the product mix. No matter what their response, some hardship may result.

Response to a fall in demand

1 *Do nothing* The individual farmer may respond to lower prices by making no change in his production plans. He may reason that the fall in prices is temporary and that there will be an improvement the following year. If the fall in demand is temporary, maintaining production and taking short-term losses may be the correct decision – even though hardship may result. He may find it difficult to decide why prices are low, and fail to recognise that the fall is likely to be permanent. And of course, even the experts in the industry may be uncertain of future trends in the industry. His appreciation of the position is blurred by the knowledge that weather conditions and other factors outside his control are likely to have a greater influence on future profitability than his decision on how much to produce. If the fall in demand for the product is permanent, and all farmers decide to maintain production, prices are likely to remain low. Only when enough producers realise that the crop is no longer profitable will the adjustment process commence.

2 *Increase production* This appears an extraordinary response to low prices, but frequently farmers react in such a way. The farmer reasons that since prices are low and profit margins narrow he will have to sell more to maintain his income. The decision may be strengthened by advice from agricultural experts that he will be able to reduce production costs if he increases production. This is a classic situation in which what may appear good for the individual works to his disadvantage if other farmers adopt the same course of action. The resulting increase in production will depress prices and further worsen the position.

3 *Reduce production or alter the product mix* This, as we have seen, is the response that will preserve the industry and enable some farmers to operate profitably. Switching to alternative products sounds an obvious solution but is not always suitable. The farmer may lack the necessary know-how, his farm or the climate may be unsuitable for alternative products and he may be unable to raise the necessary funds to change his operations. A reduction in output may not be feasible either, because a reduction in output on the individual property fails to produce a significant reduction in average costs. The third alternative is to leave farming entirely, but farmers will seldom react to a single season of low prices by leaving the industry. Once a farmer leaves the industry it is difficult to re-establish himself.

Many farmers regard their occupation as a way of life and believe that they can live more cheaply than city dwellers. On the farm they can make use of cheap or unpaid family labour, who would not be able to work for wages in the urban sector. Employment opportunities near the farm may be limited and the farmer's lack of training may prevent him from obtaining a well-paid city job, even if he can afford the costs of moving and re-establishing himself in the city.

All of these considerations explain why farmers are reluctant to reduce production. While they stay in the industry, living standards are depressed and the rural areas may suffer from an acute depression.

19.1

Figure 19.1 demonstrated the effect of an increase in supply when demand was inelastic.

1 What effect on the price of the product would an identical shift in supply have if the demand for the product was elastic?

2 How would the total sales revenue of the industry be affected:
(a) when demand was inelastic,
(b) when demand was elastic?

3 If total sales revenue increases after an increase in supply, is it possible that some producers may be worse off than before? Explain your conclusion.

4 If total sales revenue falls after an increase in supply, is it possible that some producers are better off, or must all be worse off? Once more, explain your answer.

19.2

To what extent is a rural industry that exports its products more likely to face fluctuating prices than one which produces solely for the domestic market. It may be a help to think about specific industries and the problems they encounter.

19.3

Figure 19.2 illustrated the effect on an industry of a fall in demand, when the industry responded by reducing production. Redraw the diagram to show what would happen:

1 if producers decided not to adjust production,

2 if they decided to increase production, having been convinced by the local agricultural advisers that they would be able to reduce costs of production by doing so.

In each case indicate clearly the new equilibrium price and quantity sold.

19.4

Price per case (£)	Quantity demanded at the stall ('000 cases)
2.00	nil
1.80	1
1.60	2
1.50	2.5
1.40	3
1.20	4
1.00	5
0.80	6

Class Discussion 'Is a roadside stall worthwhile?' A farmer produces 10 000 cases of apples. His production costs are £1 per case and the cost of transporting the apples to the local market is 50p per case. He can sell any amount at the local market at £2 per case. This year he considers the possibility of setting up a roadside stall, selling part of his crop at the stall and sending the remainder to market. The advantage of selling from the roadside is that he avoids paying 50p per case in transport costs. He estimates that the following demand schedule will apply for fruit he offers at his roadside stall.

1 Discuss why it will be in the producer's interests to establish such a stall. Show that he can increase his profits by selling some fruit at the stall and sending the balance to market.

2 What price should he charge at the stall if he is to maximise profits?

3 What will be his total profit from sales to the market and to the stall combined, if he charges this price?

To maximise profits from the combined operation (market and roadside stall) it is necessary to follow the rule that the *marginal* profit from the last case of apples sold at the stall is equal to the marginal profit from a case of apples sent to the local market. To determine this marginal profit calculate the *total and marginal revenue* gained from additional roadside sales. The marginal profit can then be derived and compared with the marginal profit from each additional sale at the market.

4 What effect on the farmer's operations would a 30p increase in freight costs have? Discuss the effect on the roadside stall, the policy that would maximise profits and determine the profit the farmer would make.

The Common Agricultural Policy (CAP)

The preceding discussion explains why, given the particular nature and problems of the rural industries, it was considered necessary to introduce policies to stabilise incomes in agriculture and introduce price controls, subsidies and incentives. These policies for the whole community are collectively referred to as the CAP.

In Chapter 7 (see Figure 7.9), the effect of the CAP in the market for agricultural products was discussed showing that one effect of a policy that fixed high prices to protect farmers' incomes may result in over-production and surpluses of products. This may be strongly criticised, as leading to a mis-allocation of resources and a distortion of the market signals to producers indicating what level of output would be reached in equilibrium conditions. To counter this argument, it must be remembered that the motive behind such action is to protect farmers' incomes, to guarantee the sector sufficient funds to provide for investment and the introduction of technology and to counteract the natural tendency for rural incomes to be highly unstable. It is also a consequence of particularly powerful agricultural lobbying and political pressure in some member EEC states where agriculture forms a greater proportion of employment and production in the economy. The overall effect of the CAP on the UK is generally agreed to be disadvantageous since the contributions that the UK makes to CAP funds from the levies on food imports are greater than the receipts from the Guidance and Guarantee Fund which benefit the agricultural sector. The Guarantee section of the Fund makes the payments that support the farmers' income by setting the EEC price and buying up surplus production.

The Guidance section provides funds to encourage modernisation, investment and capital development in agriculture. The agricultural sector in the UK is relatively small and therefore the receipts accruing from the Fund are similarly small. However, much of the discussion of the terms of entry for the UK into the EEC and subsequent agreements have rested heavily on the thorny issue of the amount of repayments to the UK in relation to the contributions made to the total EEC budget. There have been several negotiations on the terms and amount of the net contribution. As a result of these renegotiated terms the UK has received a higher level of refund and rebate from the Budget, substantially reducing the net contribution.

19.5

Table 19.1 gives an indication of how self-sufficient the EEC is in production of a number of basic foodstuffs. A figure of 100 per cent indicates that production is equal to requirements; over 100 per cent shows surplus production; less than 100 per cent then requires supplementation from outside the community.

More than 100%		Around 100%		Less than 100%	
Sugar	117	Wheat	105	Maize	52
Butter	111	Rye	106	Rice	67
Poultrymeat	105	Barley	106	Fresh vegetables	93
Cheese	103	Oats	96	Citrus fruit	42
Skim milk powder	110	Potatoes	99	Other fresh fruit	76
		Eggs	100	Mutton & lamb	65
Whole milk powder	310	Liquid milk	100	Vegetable oils & fats	25
		Beef	96		
		Pigmeat	100		

Table 19.1 Degrees of self sufficiency of the community for various basic foodstuffs (average 1976–79)

Source: Agricultural Situation in the Community: 1980 Report

1 Summarise in a short paragraph the position of the community, as a whole, in food supply.
2 Is it possible to explain using these figures that the CAP has achieved its other objectives, alongside self-sufficiency, of improving productivity and stabilising farm incomes?
3 Are there any instances in the table of self-sufficiency in related products?
4 On the basis of this information, what inferences can you draw as to the level and types of EEC food exports and imports?

19.6

	% of World Production traded	Proportion of world trade: Imported by EC	Exported by EC
Cereals	12½	16	5
Oilseeds	13½	45	neg
Sugar	23½	8½	10
Butter	7½	23½	36½
Cheese	5½	15½	36
Meat	3½	18	7½
All agriculture products (1978)	na	18	10

Table 19.2 Share of the EEC in world food trade (1977)

Source: FAO and Eurostat

1 In what products is the EEC a net importer and a net exporter?
2 In terms of all agricultural products (1978) the community imported 18 per cent and exported 10 per cent. Does this imply that the Community is not able to feed itself?
3 Compare the results of Table 19.1 with 19.2 and comment upon the position of community food trade revealed by the figures. Are the inferences drawn from Table 19.1 consistent with the data in Table 19.2?

19.7

Figure 19.3 shows that agricultural employment has fallen from 1968 and agricultural output has increased generally from 1968 to 1974 and from 1976 onwards. Explain how it is possible that output has increased while employment has fallen in agriculture.

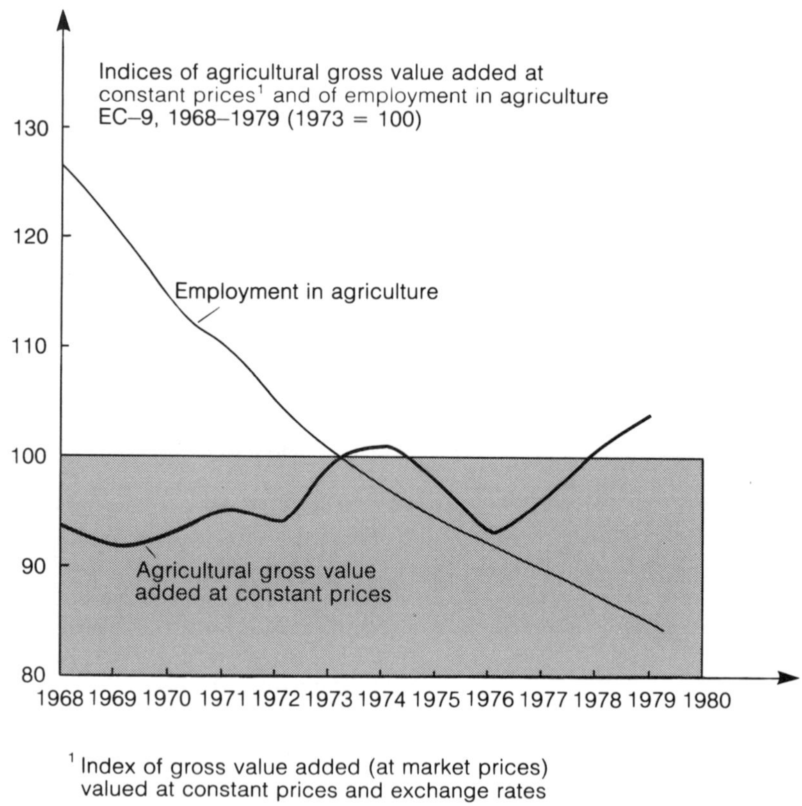

Figure 19.3 Employment in agriculture and agricultural output, 1968–79

Source: Eurostat and OECD

19.8

1 Account for the changes shown in Figure 19.4 in the level of real incomes per head in agriculture.
2 Compare Figure 19.4 with Figure 19.3 and, from the data in both figures, make an assessment of the prospects for the agricultural industry in the EEC.

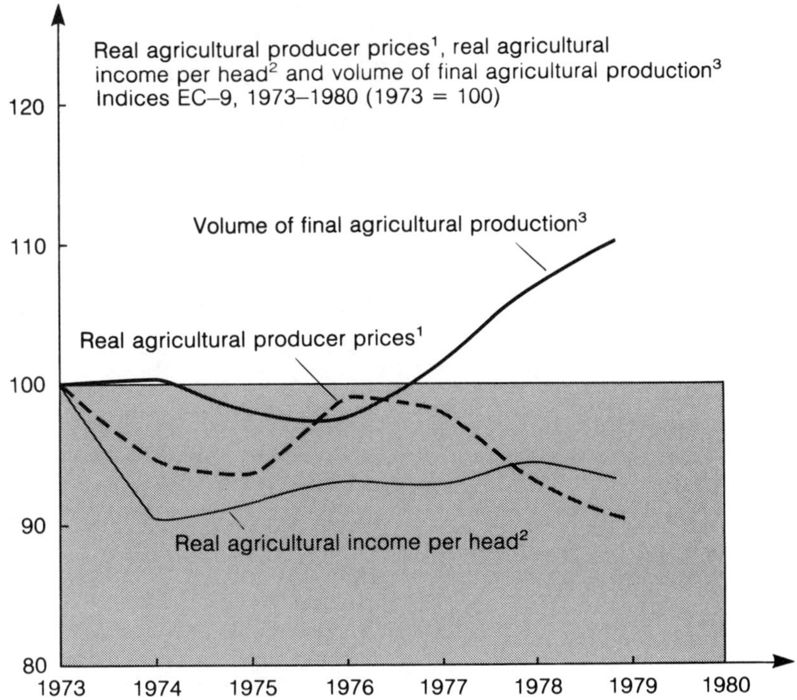

[1] Agricultural producer price index deflated by the implicit price of GDP
[2] Index of net value added at factor cost per capita in agriculture deflated by the implicit price of GDP
[3] Index of final agricultural production at constant prices and exchange rates

Figure 19.4 EEC agricultural prices, volume of production and real income per head, 1973–79

Source: Eurostat and OECD

19.9

	1979	1980	(F) 1981
Cereals	1 610	1 730	2 180
Milk products	4 530	4 750	4 190
Meat	930	1 620	2 000
Oils and fats	610	690	1 090
Sugar	940	580	700
Fruit and vegetables	440	690	750
Other (incl wine, tobacco, etc.)	1 390	1 270	1 430
Total	10 440	11 330	12 340
	£ m[(1)](6 800)	(6 800)	(6 600)

(1) Conversion rates: in 1979 £1 = 1.55 ECU, in 1980 £1 = 1.67 ECU and in 1981 £1 = 1.86 ECU
(F) = Forecast.

Table 19.3 Distribution of EEC budget spending on agriculture (million units of account)

Source: FAO and Eurostat

	Days
Butter	2.6
Skim milk powder	60.0
Beef	10.5
Lamb	–
Cereals	16.0
Sugar	–
Table wine (end June 1981)	97.0

Table 19.4 Estimated supply, in days, of intervention-type stocks held in the EEC, August 1981

Source: FAO and Eurostat

Tables 19.3 and 19.4 provide data on the level of Community spending on Agriculture and the level of intervention stocks of certain food products held in community stores.

1 Compare the information presented in Tables 19.3 and 19.4 with Table 19.1. What explanations can you offer for the proportion of the budget spent on milk products and the showing of these products in the other tables?

2 What objections could be advanced against the stock-piling and surplus production of certain agricultural products? How would the market mechanism react to such a situation in a free, unregulated market?

3 What alternative policies could be put forward for European agriculture other than those in the CAP?
How would they tackle problems of (a) falling real incomes (b) stability of prices (c) ensuring self-sufficiency in those products suitable for European climatic and geographical conditions?

4 How successful do you judge the CAP to be in the light of the data in the tables and figures?

Regional policy

The aim of the EEC's regional policy is to reduce the differential in incomes, employment and economic environment between the member states and provide remedies and solutions to the particular problems faced by the varying regions. Generally speaking, it is the peripheral areas of the EEC that have the lower levels of per capita incomes when compared with the more centrally placed areas. This fact has given rise to the idea of a so-called 'Golden triangle' in the Northern European States – an area including the cities of Paris, Bonn and the Hague and surrounding territory – where per capita incomes are the highest, levels of unemployment lowest and consequently standards of living are the highest in the EEC. There is a wide degree of differential in income levels there compared with the periphery where average incomes may be as low as one quarter or one third of those in the wealthy central regions.

The main mechanism in reducing these inequalities lies in the work of the European Regional Development Fund which redistributes EEC budget contributions in the form of aid to the poorer regions and states. Such aid and assistance from Europe supplements the individual nation's own regional spending. Much of the European funds are used to provide important infrastructure projects (such as roads, docks and community amenities) which help to encourage new development and also attract new firms to depressed areas. In the UK, the North East, Clydeside and Northern Ireland have been recipients of European assistance. The criteria for assistance given to projects is generally the same as those for national aid from member governments. Local authorities and planning departments have been able to make applications to the European Fund for additional finance and since the Regional Fund started in 1975 the UK has received about a quarter of the total aid distributed.

1973	23.9	1976	44.3
1974	25.9	1977	85.1
1975	45.9	1978	75.1

Table 19.5 EEC Social Fund, UK allocations 1973–78 (£ *million*)

The United Kingdom's £75.1 million share from the European Social Fund in 1978 went to schemes to assist the following:

Beneficiaries	Main type of aid	£m received
Unemployed people in Assisted areas	Training	£36.50
Young people under 25 (First job seekers)	Training	£25.38
Disabled people	Rehabilitation and training	£7.34
Former clothing/textile sector workers	Retraining and resettlement	£5.07
Migrant workers and their families	Resettlement and integration into social and working environment	£0.51
Workers needing retraining because of technical progress or sectoral changes in production or marketing processes	Retraining	£0.26
Women	Training	£0.01

Allocations from the European Social Fund in 1978 were as follows (£ million):

Italy	156.7	Denmark	9.5
United Kingdom	75.1	Belgium	7.5
France	57.9	Netherlands	6.6
West Germany	38.5	Luxembourg	0.1
Ireland	29.8	Total	381.7

Questions answered

Q Does the European Social Fund provide assistance for all types of 'social' scheme?

A No. Despite its name it is an employment fund, providing assistance for schemes of training, retraining and resettlement to help mainly the unemployed and under-employed.

Q Is it essential for all schemes seeking Fund assistance to have financial support from a public authority?

A Yes (apart from a small part of the Fund which provides support for studies and pilot schemes). It is a basic condition of eligibility for Social Fund assistance that schemes must have financial support from a public authority, and that a public authority should guarantee completion of the operations. Public authorities accepted for this purpose include Government departments and agencies, local authorities and industrial training boards.

Q Do all eligible schemes receive support?

A Not necessarily. The Fund's budget is not sufficient to allow the payment in full of all eligible applications. Degrees of priority are assigned to applications. Award of a high level of priority usually means that the application will receive a full allocation. Award of a lower priority may mean an allocation to part of an application only. In some instances where demands are particularly heavy, allocations may be made to the higher priority levels only.

Q Is Social Fund assistance allocated on the basis of fixed national shares in the same way as the European Regional Development Fund?

A No. Each individual application to the Social Fund is considered on its own merits.

Q What kind of expenditure is eligible for assistance from the Social Fund?

A Running costs (e.g. administrative costs, trainee income, overheads). Capital costs are *not* eligible for assistance.

Q How are applications made to the Fund?

Applications to the Social Fund from the United Kingdom are made through the Department of Employment who will advise on the eligibility of any particular scheme and assist with presentation of an application.

Figure 19.5 European Social Fund

Source: Department of Employment

Regional imbalance

Regional economic imbalance within the EEC results from a wide variety of causes as each member nation recognises in its own policies for assisted areas. European funds may help with some remedies and alleviate a few problems but the basic imbalances remain. Indeed with the expansion of the Community in future years and the different economic growth rates of the various states the degree of imbalance within the Community is likely to remain, if not increase.

The European Investment Bank is also involved with the problem of less developed regions by making available loans for projects on advantageous terms. The EIB also provides loan finance for projects involving common interests of member countries rather than benefiting a single country which are therefore not so easily funded. Similarly the EIB is able to help provide funds for very large projects which are beyond the capability of the individual country.

Social policy

Mobility of labour

One of the early objectives of the community was to provide a much freer labour market with greater opportunities for mobility of labour geographically and occupationally. This has, for example, lead to the possibility of large numbers of migrant workers taking up employment in other member countries with protection of their rights in respect of social security, trade unions, holidays and hours of work, conditions of work and so on. More important have been the policies aimed at reducing unemployment by training and retraining schemes, job creation programmes, schemes to implement new technology and new skills. There are also funds to help resettlement of workers and provide new opportunities following closures. An example of this is the special funds made available in the UK to help steel-workers after the closure of plants at Corby and Consett. These funds have been used to finance a large number of small projects where ex-steel workers have started up and developed their own firms and businesses. European funds have been available to supplement the assistance available from the government and the steel industry. With growing unemployment in Europe, the Social Fund has also grown and the UK has benefited accordingly, receiving 28 per cent of the total fund in 1975 for example. There is, however, considerable scope for extension of the Social Fund's activities in the EEC labour market.

Industrial policy

Certain aspects of industrial policy have a long history within the EEC, such as the European Coal and Steel Community which dates from 1952. The scope of such policy has extended into many areas now beyond the important basic industries. These policies are best considered as a package of measures which taken together can be seen to reinforce the basic aims and objectives of the community. They cover industrial structure, competition policy, trade, energy, technological changes, research and development.

A number of these can be highlighted as examples of community moves towards a more genuine European common market. Regulations regarding weights and measures, safety, contents, unit pricing, product descriptions, health and hygiene, production standards have been introduced into many different products (e.g. foodstuffs) which has enabled much freer and open trade in the commodities. Monopolies and large oligopolies have been made subject to EEC competition policy, which is also able to consider the operations of multi-national firms within the European market.

The industrial structure policies aim at the encouragement of technological development and specialisation in advanced technology as well as the growth of European–sized firms able to supply to a European market. The objective here is to benefit from economies of scale and increased specialisation and therefore lower consumer prices. This may be at odds with the aim of increased competition, however, if the process of growth and technology results in European monopoly firms.

It is in the area of nationalisation of declining industries in Europe that the greatest difficulties have arisen. Excess capacity in steel production in Europe has given rise to the need to cut back on those plants which have fallen behind in terms of technology and productivity. Where closures occur, this has caused particular regional and social difficulties at a time of already high unemployment. This has produced situations where conflicts have arisen with other policies and aims such as those of regional and social policy. Another UK industry to suffer has been the fishing industry, where repeated attempts to find a satisfactory European fisheries policy have failed. Meanwhile, UK fishing ports and fleets have been severely hit by competition and recession with important repercussions for the communities that depend on fishing as their livelihood.

Energy policy

Energy policy is a more recent area of concern for the EEC, particularly after the OPEC oil price increases and consequent oil crises. The UK is centrally placed in any consideration of future EEC energy supplies with the major contributions of oil and gas from the North Sea oilfields. However, the longer term prospects for energy supplies are of more immediate concern to other EEC states, and to the UK in the eventuality of a depletion of the North Sea oil supplies. The main worries have stemmed from two factors, the price of future energy supplies and the problem of security and stability of supply. EEC energy policy has concerned itself with these two issues and the members have been moving slowly towards generally agreed policies and projects. The European–Soviet Gas pipeline is an example of European nations' concern with the longer term energy problems but the EEC is far from a satisfactory common energy policy, and individual member countries continue with their own policies and national interests.

19.10

	Population (1979) (million)	GDP (1979) (US$ billion)
Total EEC of which:	270	2 432
Belgium	9.9	112.3
Denmark	5.1	64.9
France	53.5	569.4
Germany	61.4	758.0
Greece	9.5	37.8
Ireland	3.4	15.1
Italy	56.9	321.1
Luxembourg	0.4	4.1
Netherlands	14.0	150.9
United Kingdom	56.0	398.0

Table 19.6 European Economic Community population and GDP, 1979

Source: Abecor Report, Barclays Bank, February 1981

From the data in Table 19.6

1 Calculate the level of GDP per capita for each of the member states. Put the countries in rank order with highest GDP per capita first in the list.

2 Write out the rank order of the EEC members in terms of population and of GDP. Compare these two rankings with that of GDP per capita. Comment on the results obtained.

19.11

Table 19.7 gives data for the EEC, the USA, Japan and the USSR in 1979 for a number of major economic indicators.

1 Comment on the relative position of the EEC to the other three countries in the table.

2 What conclusions can you draw, if any, from the relationship of the figures for imports and exports to the level of GDP and GDP per capita in the table?

3 How do the figures for GDP per capita for each member EEC country, as calculated in question 19.10, compared with the data given in Table 19.7 for Japan, the USA and the USSR?

	EEC[1]	USA	Japan	USSR
Population (million)	270	221	116	264
GDP (US$ billion)	2 432	2 353	1 010	950[3]
Per capita GDP ($)	9 000	10 650	8 700	3 600[3]
Total imports of goods ($ cif billion)	302[2]	172	111	58[3]
Total export of goods ($ billion f.o.b.)	244[2]		104	65[3]

Notes:
(1) including Greece
(2) by including intra-EEC trade these figures would more than double
(3) estimate

Table 19.7 The EEC in the world economy in 1979

Source: *Abecor Report*, Barclays Bank, February 1981

Chapter 20

Government Policy

The role of the government in the formulation and implementation of economic policy has been discussed in part in earlier chapters. The position of fiscal policy in managing the level of demand in the economy was discussed in Chapter 14; the part that monetary policy plays in Chapter 16, which also includes discussion of prices and incomes policy. This chapter draws together the different strands of economic policy, looks at other areas of the economy where the government is active and considers the issue of the degree of mixing of the public and private sectors in the UK economy.

It was stated earlier that the main objectives of the policymakers in the UK are to ensure high levels of employment (the full employment objective), low levels of inflation, a satisfactory balance of payments and external balance, and increases in the standard of living through economic growth. Fiscal policy is concerned with the levels of government expenditure and revenue in the economy and the impact that budget deficits and surpluses have on aggregate demand. The distribution of income is also directly affected by measures involving the tax system, notably income tax, and in the government's expenditure plans. Monetary policy works on the level of consumer spending and behaviour, especially in relation to expectations of inflation, and also on the supply side of the economy through influences on the volume and price of investment, costs of production and efficiency and productivity. Changes in administration in the UK in the 1970s have involved major changes in direction and emphasis in the policy approach of governments to the major economic problems of unemployment and inflation.

The Conservative administration of Margaret Thatcher, elected in 1979, determined that a more rigorous market economy approach would be taken with increasing emphasis on market forces and the power of free competition in the economy. Inevitably this involves very different priorities for government spending and action within a changed environment of state control and responsibility. The Conservative election manifesto of 1979 promised sweeping changes in the areas of government control and 'interference' in the economy but not all of these reforms have been incorporated. However, there are significant areas where considerable modifications to existing policies have been made. In addition, there have been instances where the state has relinquished responsibility for control and ownership and has actively sought to restore the private sector. With the Conservative government being re-elected in 1983, the commitment to a reduced role for the government and a strengthening of market forces in the economy and the position of the private sector was reaffirmed.

20.1 The data in Table 20.1 and in Figure 20.1 shows how taxation, as a percentage of GDP, has varied from 1970 to 1981 in the UK. From 1979 the tax burden has increased from almost 35 per cent to 39 per cent but the share of personal income tax in the total has fallen from almost 33 per cent in 1978 to 29.3 per cent in 1981.

On the basis of this information would you argue that taxation has increased or decreased with the change of administration in 1979?

	Tax as percentage of GDP	Percentage annual change in: GDP	Taxation
1970	37.4	+2.2	+2.4
1971	35.3	+1.9	−3.0
1972	33.8	+3.3	−2.2
1973	33.0	+7.2	+5.0
1974	36.1	−1.9	+8.3
1975	36.7	−1.0	+1.1
1976	35.8	+2.6	+1.1
1977	35.3	+2.4	−0.2
1978	34.1	+3.8	+0.1
1979	34.9	+1.9	+4.1
1980	36.7	−2.1	+2.9
1981	39.0	−2.2	+4.3

Table 20.1 Taxation and GDP, UK, 1970–81

Source: National Income and Expenditure Blue Book 1982

20.2 Compare in Figure 20.1 the levels of government expenditure and tax, as percentages of GDP, and comment upon the trends identified. What are the implications of a fall in personal taxes from 1977 when the trend of expenditure and taxation is increasing?

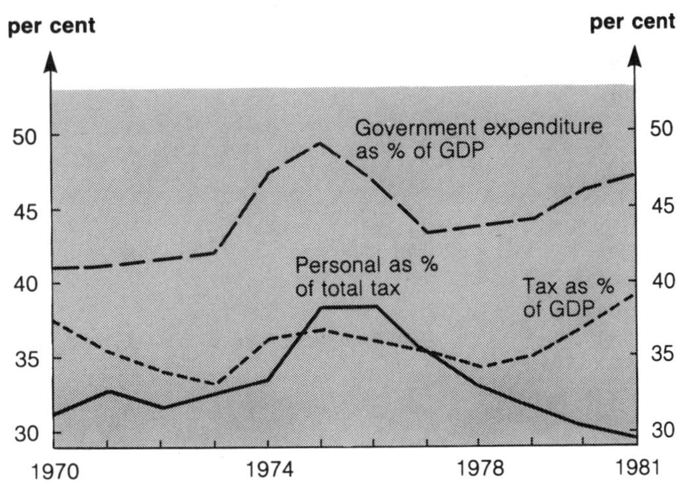

Figure 20.1 Tax and government spending burdens

Source: Blue Book 1982, Table 9.1 and OECD Revenue Statistics

20.3 Is it possible to identify in Table 20.1 any causal links between the annual change in GDP and in taxation? Is there any evidence for the view that cuts in taxation act as incentives for the economy and encourage growth in GDP?

20.4

Why should the level of taxation increase during a recession in the economy? If consideration of the level of government expenditure is introduced into the argument, is a more convincing explanation possible?

20.5

Table 20.2 reveals how the sources of taxes in total taxation have varied in proportion from 1970 to 1981.
1. Descibe briefly the major changes in taxes in the table. (It might help to consider the pattern up to 1976 and after that date)
2 Use the information to present an argument showing how the burden of taxation has altered.
3 Imagine you are a politician explaining the changes in taxation burdens to the electorate
(a) in favour of the changes and stressing the advantages;
(b) against the changes and outlining the disadvantages of such a policy.

Taxes on:	Personal income †	Corporate income †	Social security *	Property (rates, etc.)	Goods and services
1970	31.1	9.2	18.3	12.5	28.8
1971	32.7	8.1	16.8	13.3	28.7
1972	31.5	7.5	17.6	14.7	28.7
1973	32.3	8.6	17.0	13.6	28.2
1974	33.4	9.6	17.1	12.6	27.1
1975	38.2	6.2	17.4	12.6	25.4
1976	38.2	5.1	18.6	12.1	25.8
1977	35.1	6.5	20.1	12.0	26.2
1978	32.9	7.5	20.9	12.0	26.6
1979	31.4	7.6	21.8	12.1	27.0
1980	30.0	7.7	21.1	11.9	29.5
1981	29.3	8.4	19.8	13.4	28.3
OECD Average 1980	33.3	7.5	24.4	5.4	29.1

* Including national insurance surcharge.
† Including capital gains tax.

Table 20.2 Taxes as percentage of total taxation, UK

Source; Lloyds Bank Economic Bulletin No.46. October 1982

Industrial and regional policy

The state is responsible for a great deal of activity related to the position of firms and enterprises in the economy ranging from consumer protection, health and safety standards to competition policy and monopoly legislation. Earlier chapters provide more detailed information on these areas of government involvement. Reference was made in Chapter 19 to the role of the EEC in regional policy in the UK where forms of assistance are available to supplement domestic policy aids.

The state is involved in the location of industry through the assisted areas which make provision for various forms of aid to firms according to three defined categories of need. Development Areas, which cover a large area of the UK (e.g. Scotland, Wales, Northern and North-West regions) are entitled to regional development grants towards the cost of plant, machinery and buildings at a rate of 15 per cent (before 1979 the rate was 20 per cent of cost). Special Development Areas, where problems of decline and job loss are particularly severe, are entitled to 22 per cent grants, e.g. Tyneside, Clydeside and Merseyside. A third type of area where some assistance is available is the Intermediate Area, where aids such as low-cost loans, reliefs and subsidies, training facilities, purpose-built new factories and premises on government-run trading estates are available. These aids are also provided in the DAs and SDAs. Additional to all of these are various forms of regional selective assistance for employment creating projects.

The objective behind all of these policy measures is to counteract the problems of regional imbalance, especially those created by higher than average levels of unemployment. This is to protect jobs and to provide new opportunities where industries are declining. The various forms of assistance are intended to attract new firms to locate in the Assisted Areas and to enable new and existing firms to develop and grow. The effect of the assistance available is to influence the locational and investment decisions made by companies and, through the different subsidies offered, to alter the normal choices that would result from free market forces. Other measures have also been used in this context, notably the Industrial Development Certificate required for any new factory or industrial project above a stated minimum size - a form of planning permission. By refusing applications in some areas and making IDCs more easily available in others, a very direct form of control of industrial location could be exercised. In 1979 the minimum requirement for an IDC was increased to 50 000 sq. ft. from 5000 sq. ft. in the South East and 10 000 sq. ft. in the non-assisted areas. Office Development Certificates have been used in a similar fashion. With all of these forms of assistance, it is apparent that regional disparities have not increased by as much as would otherwise have been the case but the problem of regional imbalance remains.

Capitalist cells

To attract new industries to depressed areas, some 11 enterprise zones have now been opened or soon will be (see map). Firms starting up inside a zone do not have to pay rates for up to 10 years; nor are they required to supply the statistical information to government that other businesses are asked for. Planning controls are less rigid, so factories can be built more quickly.

Enterprise zones have come in for a lot of criticism. The rate-free 10-year period has the same effect on a business as a rent subsidy (rates are usually about half of the rent on a factory). That makes enterprise zones attractive relative to sites just outside the zone, pushing rents and land values up inside the zone, and down just outside it. Some critics allege the benefit of the rate concession goes straight to the landlords lucky enough to own sites in the zones.

The government is unmoved by these criticisms. It says it is encouraged by the speed at which firms are going into the zones, and claims that half the companies setting up in the Clydebank zone are entirely new firms.

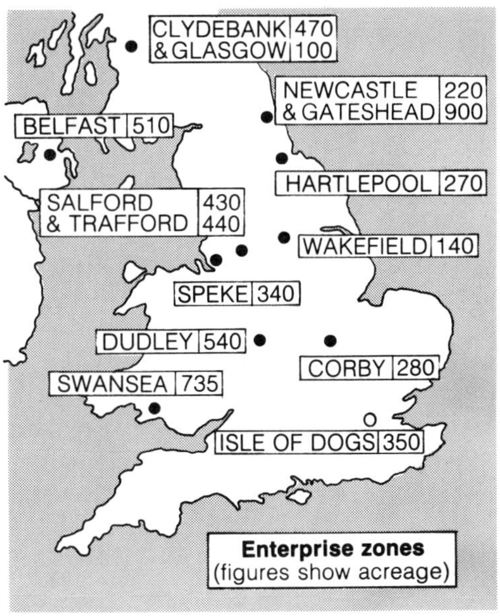

Figure 20.2 Enterprise Zones

Source: *The Economist*, 28 November 1981, page 103

Nature and purpose

The Government is setting up a number of Enterprise Zones (EZs). The idea is to see how far industrial and commercial activity can be encouraged by the removal of certain tax burdens, and by relaxing or speeding up the application of certain statutory or administrative controls. The Zones will last for 10 years and it is hoped that the first ones will come into effect this summer.

Eleven sites have been announced as prospective EZs. They vary widely, but all contain land ripe for development. In size they range from about 50 to over 400 hectares (about 125 to over 1000 acres). EZs are not part of regional policy, nor are they directly connected with other existing policies such as those for inner cities or derelict land. The sites chosen will continue to benefit from whatever aid is available under these policies.

Location and further information

The EZ sites are in Corby, Dudley, Hartlepool, the Isle of Dogs (in London's docklands), Newcastle/Gateshead, Salford/Trafford, Speke (Liverpool) and Wakefield in England; the lower Swansea Valley in Wales; Clydebank in Scotland; and Belfast, Northern Ireland.

Benefits

The following benefits are available, for a 10 year period from the date each Zone comes into effect, to both new and existing industrial and commercial enterprises in the Zones:

- i. Exemption from Development Land Tax.
- ii. Exemption from rates on industrial and commercial property.
- iii. 100% allowances for Corporation and Income Tax purposes for capital expenditure on industrial and commercial buildings.
- iv. Applications from firms in EZs for certain customs facilities will be processed as a matter of priority and certain criteria relaxed.
- v. Industrial Development Certificates are not needed.
- vi. Subject to the passage of the Employment and Training Bill, employers will be exempt from industrial training levies and from the requirement to supply information to Industrial Training Boards.
- vii. A greatly simplified planning regime; developments that conform with the published scheme for each Zone will not require individual planning permission.
- viii Those controls remaining in force will be administered more speedily.
- ix. Government requests for statistical information will be reduced.

Figure 20.3 Main Features of Enterprise Zones

Enterprise Zones

The Enterprise Zone (EZ) became part of industrial policy in 1981 and marked a distinct alteration from previous policy. The EZs were deliberately created to encourage industrial development in derelict areas which could not otherwise be expected to attract such development. The zones offer rate-free accomodation for ten years and a restriction of the planning and administrative regulations and requirements normally expected with industrial projects. Lack of interference by outside authorities and agencies and simplified procedures instead of complex bureaucratic administration is the keynote. This freedom from restriction is clearly a reflection of the Conservative government's philosophy of the role of state vis-a-vis the firm and market.

Eleven EZs were first established in 1981–82 and a further eleven were announced in July 1982. Whether the EZ has achieved its objective is not yet clear. They have been criticised for creating low-cost areas which are unfairly competitive with sites outside the zones. In some instances the zones simply encouraged local firms to move from outside into the zone for the free rates and other incentives. The implication being that after ten years when the financial incentive has gone that the firm may simply pack up and move to some other local EZ. Moreover, the EZ may not have been successful in the creation of new jobs in large numbers in that service and distribution centres have been attracted to the sites and not manufacturing firms and employment.

20.6

Study Figures 20.2 and 20.3 on Enterprise Zones.
1. How far is it reasonable to consider EZs as potential 'capitalist cells' as the *Economist* describes them?
2. Explain how the EZs provide subsidies to employers located inside them.
3. Use demand and supply analysis to show the effect on rents and land values within an EZ compared with locations outside them.
4. On what grounds have EZs been criticised and how reasonable do you consider these criticisms to be? What further data would you require about EZs in order to judge their degree of success or failure in meeting the government's objectives for EZs?

Employment policy

The government has a general responsibility for the level of employment as a result of its fiscal and monetary policies. However, there are additional areas where the state plays a more precise part in influencing employment and manpower in the economy. Responsibility for training and retraining, the mobility of labour, the information services for manpower, job creation and youth opportunities programmes are some of the areas where the government is active in the field of employment.

A distinction can be made between those policies which are aimed at making the labour market more efficient in some way and those which lead to direct employment through job creation or subsidisation. The labour market may prove unable to ensure an adequate supply of sufficiently skilled workers in the appropriate areas and thus frictional unemployment may result. Workers may be occupationally and

Immobility of labour

geographically immobile. To counteract this the government, through the Department of Employment and Job Centres, organises the transmission of information about vacancies and the availability of workers to meet the deficiencies of the market and reduce the amount of job searching. Since vacancies may occur outside the worker's home area, various schemes are available to assist re-location of workers through grants towards expenses and other benefits. Lack of particular skills may be a problem as also the workers whose skills are no longer required and are redundant due to improved technology or industrial decline. For these workers, a number of training and retraining schemes are organised through skill-centres and the work of the Manpower Services Commission. Another form of state involvement comes in the aid given to industrial training boards funded by employers' associations in conjunction with the state. The occupational mobility of workers can be increased by these means which thus help reduce unemployment and are also conducive towards economic growth through combating scarcity of particular skills. Re-training also provides a way of cushioning the social impact of industrial closures on the community, the redundant workers and their families.

Job creation schemes have become more important since the recession of the late 1970s. These publicly financed schemes, by the end of 1981, accounted for almost a quarter of a million young people on the Youth Opportunities Programme. There are other programmes available such as the Job Release Scheme (where workers may retire early and whose jobs are taken by an unemployed person); the Community Enterprise Programme (young unemployed workers engaged in socially beneficial projects); and a scheme for a subsidy to be paid to employers towards the cost of wages of young workers. Another scheme designed to try to keep workers off the unemployment register is the short-time working compensation scheme where employers are paid a subsidy to keep workers on the payroll rather than declare them redundant. The latest development is a new training scheme called the Youth Training Scheme (YTS) which is designed to give all unemployed school leavers work experience, further education or off-the-job training as well as pay them a weekly allowance for a year after leaving school.

Workings of the labour market

These schemes have been open to criticism on the grounds that they constitute direct subsidies to employers and, by reducing wages costs, create a situation of unfair competition between employers through lower prices. It can also be argued that they represent distortions of the normal market forces and prevent the market reaching an equilibrium quite so readily. There are other reasons why the labour market is not freely competitive such as the action of trade unions and restrictive practices so that the criticism of distortions is perhaps not so strong. The effect of the subsidy is to create more employment, by pricing young people into jobs, and also to ensure that some vocational training and development of skills takes place. The benefits from these are believed to be sufficient to outweigh any disadvantages that may ensue and are seen to be consistent with other longer term objectives of promoting growth and encouraging efficiency. The overall cost of these schemes is not small but against that could be set the savings made in terms of unemployment benefit that would otherwise be paid out and the increased tax revenue to the Exchequer from the incomes and expenditure of those involved. Moreover, in international terms the amount that the UK has set aside for youth employment and training remains comparatively small in relation to other European nations.

There are manpower implications involved in many of the government's measures (e.g. regional policy and industrial policy) and for technological development. In practice, these may also operate as labour subsidies or employment creation and can be examined and interpreted in this respect.

20.7

1. To what extent do you consider that job training and youth employment are the responsibility of central government?
2. It could be argued that forces in the labour market are sufficient to ensure that training is provided for new skills and occupations, that adequate compensation and rewards are paid for undergoing training and adequate opportunities and vacancies are available, if those market forces are free from external influence and modification. To what extent do you agree or disagree with this argument?

Nationalised industries

The nationalised industries, as a group, account for a major part of the UK economy in output, employment and investment. They provided some 11 per cent of the GNP and 18 per cent of employment, and accounted for a 22 per cent share of investment in 1977. They constitute some of the largest organisations and employers; the Post Office with over 400 000 employees being by far the largest individual concern in the UK economy, with all the problems concomitant with extensive size and level of operations. Nationalised industries were discussed earlier in Chapters 4 and 8 in general terms of ownership and operation. The reasons for nationalisation are many and varied but are mainly concerned with

1. controlling a monopoly situation to prevent possible abuse of market power,
2. basic industries in key sectors supplying other industries with such important elements as raw materials, fuel and power, transport and communications,
3. economies of scale and efficient operation on a national scale,
4. capital investment and technological development for a strategically important or vital industry or other instances where under-capitalisation results,
5. political arguments,
6. social reasons by providing a social service function.

A combination of these factors generally explains why a particular industry is in the public sector but this is very much open to the contemporary political opinions at the time of state takeover. Changing times and attitudes may result in an industry being re-considered and its status revised as happened to the road transport and steel industries with a change of administration from the post-war Labour government. Steel was subsequently renationalised by Labour in 1967.

The Conservative government elected in 1979 declared its intent to reduce the share of the public sector in the economy and reverse the trend towards greater state involvement. There are three major elements in this change of direction:

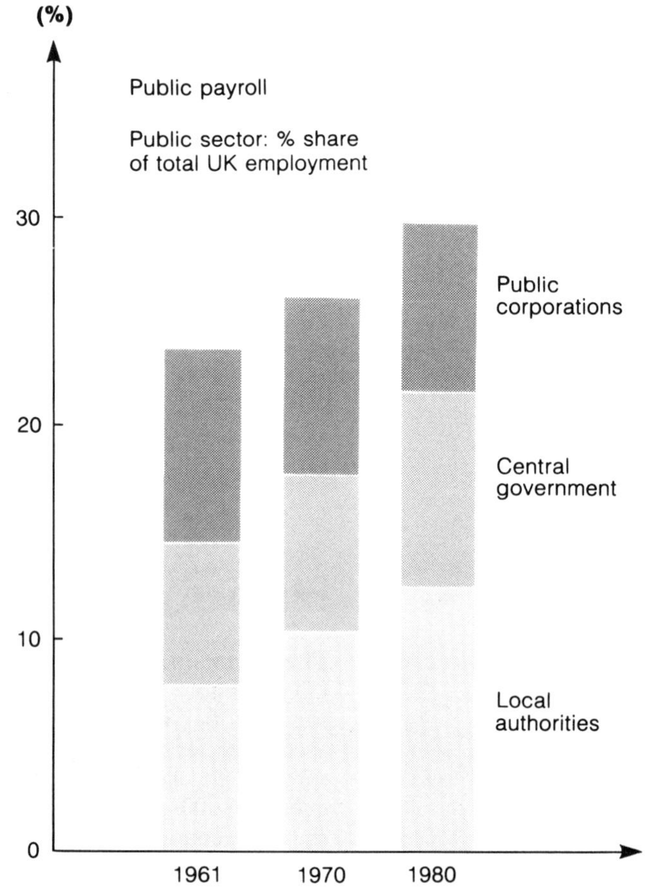

Figure 20.4 Public payroll

Source: *The Economist*, 28 November 1981, page 103

1 denationalisation or selling off parts of the public sector
2 reducing the element of monopoly enjoyed by the state concerns
3 encouraging the private sector to take over services previously considered to be the state's prerogative.

It is hoped that, by these measures, the private sector disciplines of profit maximisation and greater efficiency will be directed towards the state's monopolies and provide the competitive edge and stimulus said to be lacking. In addition, the burden of state financing can be reduced and, as well as raising funds from the sale of public assets, the PSBR is reduced. The grounds for shifting the balance from the private sector to the public sector are as much doctrinal as economic and the Conservative party in the election campaign and manifesto of 1979 had made the issue a central plank of its policy intentions.

The nationalised industries are only one part of the whole public sector activities in the UK economy. Taken in full, the public sector accounts for some 30 per cent of GDP and employment. The state services of education, health, welfare, government (central and local) administration and public corporations make up the rest of the total.

Privatisation

Privatisation is a term coined to refer to the selling off, or denationalisation, of the public sector. Returning such assets to the private sector is easier to describe than carry out in practice. There are several reasons for this. Firstly, only the profitable activities are likely to be saleable to the private sector of the economy. There is no sense, presumably, in which the 'deficit nationalised industries' can be returned to private control and ownership but the profit-making British Aerospace, the state's shares in British Petroleum, Cable and Wireless, BNOC (British National Oil Corporation) and parts of British Gas have been sold or are planned to be sold, in full or part, to private investors. Any further denationalisation is dependent on the industry's circumstances; for example losses made by British Rail, British Airways, British Shipbuilders, British Leyland and others, make it difficult to foresee any immediate sale.

Once an industry has been sold off, the possibility may arise with a change of government that the industry is renationalised. This introduces an element of insecurity into any privatisation attempt and may influence the success of any sale and the price that private investors would be prepared to pay. Financially, the government benefits from a sale but only initially, for future revenues from the operation are lost. If only the profitable sectors can be sold then this changes the nature of the public sector in that the growth industries and efficient producers migrate leaving only loss-making parts as a drain on government spending with no surplus-earning elements to counteract the deficits. It can be argued as being against the public interest to let such profitable elements go, especially where these are involved in high technology where rapid future expansion is expected. In all of this, the conflict can again be seen of the benefits of short-term expediency against longer term goals and objectives.

Since many state activities are by their nature monopolies, disposing of them may produce a situation where private monopolies are created. This creates a problem then of control if that monopoly is open to possible abuse. Monopoly policy, and its control on private companies, have already been seen to be difficult to enforce adequately and it has been the case that nationalisation has been used for this very purpose. Obviously a serious dilemma arises over this basic issue. The solution may lie in reducing the state's monopoly by allowing and encouraging the operations of the private sector. This has already happened in telecommunications, where the monopoly on the provision of telephone equipment has been relaxed allowing private firms to compete with British Telecom. The same principle has been extended to other state activities, for example, the tendering to private contractors of local government services of refuse disposal and building and maintenance work. The sale of council houses by local authorities provides further evidence of extending the private sector. Services such as education, security and health are partly catered for by private enterprise (e.g. security firms, independent schools, private health care and medical insurance) so that these are not the exclusive preserve of the state. The political arguments for the private sector have tended to follow party lines with the Labour party from time to time mounting attacks on the existence of a separate private provision outside the state.

20.8 In your opinion, is privatisation (selling off public sector assets to the private sector) a purely economic or political matter? Is it possible to separate the economic from the political arguments in such issues?

20.9 Select two nationalised industries and for each draw up a list of the advantages and disadvantages of privatisation and the arguments for and against nationalisation of that industry.

Energy policy

The UK has been self sufficient in oil production from 1980 and is now the world's sixth largest oil producer. How long the North Sea oil and gas boom will last is a matter for conjecture but most forecasts predict that at the end of the century Britain will again need to import oil. The effect of North Sea oil on the UK economy is considerable and influences other aspects of government policy. The reasons for this are a consequence of the rapid increase in oil prices since 1973 which has caused the value of oil production to rise far above the original forecasts. The oil has immediate impact on the balance of payments as a foreign currency earner and for its import-saving content. Moreover, North Sea oil offers a new source of government tax revenue, especially important at a time of recession and when expected growth is slow or even non-existent. This benefit is amply illustrated in Table 20.3.

	Percentage of total government revenue
1976–77	0.2
1977–78	0.4
1978–79	0.9
1979–80	2.9
1980–81	4.0
1981–82	5.3 (est.)
1982–83	6.3 (est.)

Table 20.3 Government revenue from North Sea oil and gas

These revenues in Table 20.3 arise from four sources: royalties, Corporation Tax, Petroleum Revenue Tax, and supplementary petroleum duty. Together these four taxes amounted to a hefty £6000 million in 1981–82 but this is still less than the revenues from VAT and excise duties on petrol and oil products. This important source of extra revenue from oil reduces the need to raise finance from borrowing, or increasing direct and indirect taxation, for any given level of government spending or new programmes of expenditure. Royalties accrue to the government at the rate of 12.5 per cent of the value of production. Supplementary petroleum duty was introduced in 1981–82 to raise an extra £2 billion and is to be replaced by an increase in the rate of petroleum revenue tax (PRT). PRT was levied at 70 per cent (till 1982) on the oil companies' profits after royalties. With the supplementary duty being incorporated into PRT the rate is 75 per cent from 1982 onwards.

Against PRT the companies are able to offset costs of investment and exploration, a minimum amount of oil produced from each field and a safeguard of exemption for the very small and marginally economic oil-fields. On top of all of these taxes, the normal rate of Corporation Tax at 52 per cent applies on taxable profits as for any other private company. Oil companies, not suprisingly, have complained that the tax regime they face is too severe and that taxes are not only too high but too complicated as well.

It is not surprising that any tax payer should complain that taxes are too high. It is easily seen why the government should take a share of the riches offered by the opportunities presented by the oil bonanza. The question of how big a share then remains. The objective is not only to raise revenue but to ensure that sufficient funds and rewards are available for continued development and operation in the fields that remain to be explored. These are likely to require greater capital investment and technology than the present producing areas. The rate of depletion is another open question for energy policy and is dependent on future oil prices and the size of reserves in present and future fields. Clearly the answers to these questions rest in the hands of the government's policy makers and what they see to be the greatest long-term benefit for the UK.

20.10

Discuss the view that the prime objective of the government in the economy should be to create an environment where market forces are dominant and state involvement should be limited to enabling such conditions to operate. If you disagree with this view then what, in your opinion, should be the role of the government in economic policy?

Chapter 21

Economic Growth

Economic growth is the fourth of the UK government's economic objectives. Others, discussed in earlier chapters, are price stability, full employment, and a satisfactory balance of payments position. In Chapter 6 it was explained that economic growth is the term normally used to express the rate of increase in the production of goods and services. Alternative concepts of economic growth are discussed later in the chapter. The most common way of measuring economic growth is by calculating the increase in gross domestic product at constant prices, either in the aggregate or in per capita terms.

In the UK, gross domestic product increased at an annual rate of 2.2 per cent on average between 1962 and 1972. Gross domestic product per capita increased at an average rate of 2.7 per cent over the same period. Gross domestic product at constant factor cost from 1968 to 1980 is given in Table 21.1. Variations in annual growth in GDP can clearly be seen.

For many years it was thought self-evident that economic growth was a desirable economic objective for a country. The case for economic growth was seldom explicitly discussed. The implicit assumption was that if the flow of goods and services produced each year continued to increase then living standards would rise and that welfare must increase also. Accordingly, it was held that government should provide the conditions under which gross domestic product would increase as rapidly as was consistent with the other economic objectives.

Acceptance of these assumptions and their implications led to detailed international comparisons of growth rates, and to investigations of variations in the country's growth rate. It sometimes led to the conclusion that a country's economy must be weak if its growth rate was lower than that of countries in a similar stage of economic development. A reduction in the country's growth rate was viewed with concern and the prospect of a negative rate of growth was seen as an indicator that the economy was about to collapse.

Since the mid 1960s the economic growth objective, particularly when expressed as a desire to achieve a high rate of increase of GDP, has been attacked on the grounds that its pursuit leads to a decline in welfare rather than an increase. Among the arguments that have been put forward are that people are not happier or more satisfied than they were years ago, and that economic growth wastes resources and pollutes

	1968	1969	1970	1971	1972	1973	1974	1975	1976	1977	1978	1979	1980
GDP at constant factor cost	88.3	90.4	92.1	93.4	95.9	102.8	101.1	100	102.8	105.0	108.3	110.2	107.9

(Average estimate of GDP based on expenditure, income and output data)

Table 21.1 Index number of GDP 1968–80

Source: *Annual Abstract of Statistics, 1982*, Table 14.9 p 351, HMSO and destroys the environment. At one extreme is the view that economic growth is doing irreversible damage to the environment and that zero economic growth is necessary to prevent disaster overtaking the planet. This chapter examines the objective of economic growth. It questions the role that the economist is taking in the debate. It examines some of the possible benefits of economic growth, some of the costs and investigates the possibility of controlling economic growth in a way that might satisfy conflicting interests.

The economist's role in the economic growth controversy

Before development of the controversy on whether economic growth was desirable, economists concerned themselves with the investigation of the ways in which a rapid rate of economic growth could be achieved. Also they investigated the potential conflict that exists between economic growth and two other economic objectives: price stability and external balance.

The main sources of economic growth have been identified as

1 the use of increased *quantities* of productive resources,

2 technological innovation that increases *productivity* of available resources,

3 specialisation and increased international trade,

4 favourable movements in the terms of trade.[1]

Relationship between capital formation and growth

As we saw in Chapter 4, particular attention has been paid to the relationship between capital formation and the growth of production, because it is easier to increase the quantity of the capital stock than the quantity of labour and land. Second, increases in population, often associated with increases in the labour force reduce the per capita level of production. Third, technical progress more commonly applies to capital equipment. There is more scope for technical progress to improve the performance of machines than to improve the performance of labour. As machines wear out so the opportunity and pressure exists for their replacement by superior, more productive machines, or for the introduction of a new production system.

Conflict between economic growth and price stability

The short-run conflict between economic growth and price stability was referred to in Chapters 15, 16 and 17. In the short run a country's productive capacity is limited by the size of its labour force as well as its capital stock and the state of its technology. The extent to which economic growth can occur as a result of capital formation is dependent on the availability of labour. If expenditure on capital formation produces excess demand, there may be some increase in production, but the excess demand will also generate inflationary pressures. Alternatively, if the demand is met by increases in imports, or by exporters switching to supplying the domestic market, there will be a tendency for a balance of payments deficit. The need to eliminate this deficit or to reduce excess demand may force the government to adopt policies that reduce the rate of growth. Between 1950 and 1966, the economy of the UK was subjected to 'stop-go' policies that reflected, on the one hand, the necessity of containing inflationary pressures and the recurring balance of payments deficits, and on the other, the attempts to raise the level of real production. The result was a short-term business cycle that was repeated about every two years.

Role of the economist

However, economists have paid little attention to the proposition that economic growth might be undesirable in the long term, nor to the associated claim that there is conflict between the welfare gains from growth and the welfare benefits from preserving the existing environment. Their apparent lack of concern has drawn the charge that economists are responsible for society's blind adoption of the economic growth objective and are therefore to be held responsible for any present and future deterioration of the environment. The question 'does economic growth make people happier?' is a philosophical question and as such cannot be determined by economists. It is a question that contains normative and positive elements and like all such questions cannot be settled by an appeal to the known facts. Hence the determination of whether economic growth is desirable must be decided by society as a whole, or its governments.

The economist cannot shelter entirely behind the statement that this is a normative question in which he has no special responsibilities. The general case for economists participating in matters involving value judgements was stated on page 27 in Chapter 2. It has been stated more specifically in relation to the economic growth objective by Beckerman.[2]

1 The economist knows that differences in opinions on growth versus environment are either the result of different value judgements or different explanations of how the economy works. He can identify and distinguish between the two sources of difference.

2 The economist's training has made him aware that such conflicts can seldom be resolved by giving absolute priority to one objective. He is familiar with the idea of a 'trade off'.

3 The economist possesses specialist knowledge about the working of the economic system that is relevant to the choice of objectives. He can demonstrate the costs that society will incur by foregoing economic growth. He is thus placed in a position of responsibility at least equal to that assumed by the biologist or chemist who urges a course of action as a result of his own technical investigations. For example, it might be said that economists have a responsibility to indicate the weaknesses in the gross domestic product measure as an economic welfare indicator.

In Chapter 2 it was admitted that in the past economists have been concerned rather narrowly with the economic problems of a materialistic society. But the point was also made that as society becomes less concerned with achieving material objectives so the attention of economists will shift also. The work of Galbraith[3] in criticising the materialistic society and of Mishan[4] in questioning the prominence given to the economic growth objective is an indication that economists as well as environmentalists are prepared to question society's objectives. The response to Mishan's *Costs of Economic Growth* revealed first a willingness by many economists to debate the issues, bringing to bear the special skills of the economist; and second that there was a wide measure of disagreement amongst economists on both the facts and what was desirable.

21.1

Four main sources of economic growth were mentioned in the text.

1 Explain how each of these sources might lead to a country enjoying a faster rate of growth.

2 In each case discuss whether UK government could adopt specific measures to increase the growth rate. What policies could it adopt?

3 To what extent might the adoption of any of these policies threaten the achievement of the government's other three macro-economic objectives?
4 Can you think of any other major sources of economic growth? If so what policies might be followed to utilise these sources.

21.2

The table below provides information on the UK's growth rate, the rate of inflation, unemployment and the balance of payments position in recent years. Do the figures provide any evidence of conflict between economic growth and the other economic objectives? Explain how you would analyse this information.

	Index of GDP at constant factor cost (1975 = 100)	Retail price index (15/1/74 = 100) monthly averages	Unemployment annual average per cent rate	Balance of payments current account (£ million)
1974	100.9	108.4	2.6	−3307
1975	100.0	134.8	4.1	−1621
1976	103.1	157.1	5.7	− 842
1977	105.1	182.0	6.2	+ 293
1978	107.9	197.1	6.1	+1032

Research more recent data for the UK economy for the economic indicators in the table. Is there any significant difference between the position of the UK economy from 1974 to 1978 and after 1978 shown by the data you have researched? Comment as to whether the conflict between economic growth and other economic objectives has changed since 1978.

The case for economic growth examined

Three closely related arguments are presented in support of the economic growth objective. These are:
1 People prefer more goods to less, other things being equal.
2 Growth offers the individual the opportunity of increasing his material possessions, without the welfare of others suffering.
3 Growth offers the possibility of removing poverty within the community, or in other counttries, without a reduction of living standards of the affluent.

People prefer more to less

The implication of this assumption is that, on obtaining more possessions, welfare is increased. The opponents of economic growth claim that although more may be preferred to less it does not follow that welfare will be increased when more possessions are obtained. It is argued that our desires, fostered assiduously by advertisers, are increasing constantly. We are wooed into wanting and possessing,

'It's astonishing how personal possessions accumulate!' Copyright London Punch, 14 October 1970

colour TV, hi-fi equipment, electronic organs, automatic dishwashers, stereo outfits for the car, video recorders and billiard tables. As we satisfy each desire, so a new status symbol is placed before us by the advertising industry, acting for producers. Because we are always striving for something else we are in a sense dissatisfied, or are at least no happier than we were before we knew about and possessed some of our more recent acquisitions.

It was stated earlier that the economist is not well equipped to meet this type of argument. He cannot demonstrate that people are happier and more contented with more possessions. All he can note is that there appears to be a universal desire for higher living standards measured in terms of more possessions and that it is difficult to persuade people that what they desire will not make them any happier.

21.3

Consider the following statements.

(a) People want more goods and services because they believe their use will increase their welfare.
(b) Wants are created by the advertising industry acting for producers who have a vested interest in economic growth.
(c) Additional possessions bring enjoyment and satisfaction.
(d) Wants are insatiable and people remain dissatisfied even though their possessions are increasing.

1 Do you agree with any of these statements? Is there any way in which each of the statements can be tested?
2 Suppose all four statements were tested and found to be valid. Would they, by implication, form the basis for abandoning the economic growth objective?

3 Suppose statements (a), (c) and (d) were found to be valid, and (b) was untrue. Would they then suggest that economic growth should be abandoned?

Growth offers the opportunity of increasing welfare without others suffering

Unless economic growth is taking place, an individual can only become better off, if others are becoming worse off. The only alternative to growth is a redistribution of income. The argument follows logically if it is accepted that more possessions can lead to an increase in welfare.

The opponents of economic growth have advanced the relative income hypothesis. This says that a person's welfare depends on his relative position in society rather than on his absolute wealth. This means that a person will feel that his welfare has increased if his real income rises relative to the real incomes of others in the society. It also suggests that if his absolute real income rises in such a way that his relative position is unchanged he may see himself as no better off. If the relative income hypothesis is accepted, another implication is that if one group in society benefits by an absolute increase in real income, and the absolute real incomes of members of a second group are unchanged, the welfare of the second group will be reduced. Consequently, the same effect could have been achieved by a redistribution of income with zero economic growth. Hence economic growth is incapable of increasing welfare of the community at large.

Growth and the removal of poverty

The third argument for economic growth is that it makes possible the reduction of poverty without reducing the living standards of the rich. Governments have, among their main economic objectives of price stability, full employment etc., more general goals relating to the level of welfare and living standards. There are those who would argue that considerations of welfare should replace the goal of economic growth in its own right as a government objective. However, it can be claimed that the economic growth argument should be retained as an objective because growth makes possible the removal of poverty by providing the additional goods and services needed to raise living standards of people in poverty.

Obviously the pursuit of economic growth for its own sake misses the point; the aim must be to improve the welfare of the community. Policies directed to this latter end are likely in fact to lead to increases in real output of the economic system per head of population and can thus fairly be described – without abuse of language – as policies for economic growth.[5] The above quotation comes from an Australian government paper and refers to the problem of welfare in Australia. A commission of inquiry into poverty in Australia reported that more than 10 per cent of Australian income units were living below the poverty line. Many were living in sub-standard accommodation, had insufficient food and clothing, and were unable to afford necessary medical treatment. The cost of removing this poverty was put at over A$ 800 million a year. It is certain that there would be great resistance within the community to any attempt to find such an amount solely by a redistribution of income through taxation. Economic growth opens up the prospect that such needs can be met, at least in part, without reducing the real incomes of those above the poverty line.

The case for economic growth to assist in the attack on world poverty is even stronger. If statements to the effect that over one third of the world's population are living in absolute poverty and facing starvation are accepted as authoritative, economic growth represents the only method of removing such misery. A massive redistribution of income would not solve the problem. Of course a planned reduction in the world's population would reduce absolute poverty but the commonly advocated population policy of birth control would take many years to have a significant effect.

The arguments against economic growth fail badly when placed against the need to remove poverty. When the rich tell a poor person that he is really better off because he lacks the worries that go with material possessions they are likely to be accused of insincerity. Likewise, poor countries seldom respond with enthusiasm to suggestions from the rich industrial countries that they should avoid policies that will develop their economies and reduce the threat of starvation and disease.

Similarly, the relative income hypothesis is less convincing when viewed within the context of absolute poverty. A family living in grinding poverty, with sick children to care for, will be more concerned with its absolute level of real income and of solving the immediate problem of survival, than of maintaining their relative position against others.

It is sometimes said that economic growth within a country does not lead to the reduction of poverty. Instead the economically powerful groups benefit from the growth. Similarly, it is argued that world economic growth is producing an ever widening a gap between rich and poor countries. These are not arguments against economic growth as such but arguments against an economic system that distributes production in an unequal way. The case for growth is that it provides more goods and services which can then be distributed in the way society determines.

21.4

On a number of occasions in recent years when pensioners have been given increases in their pensions, their representatives have commented to the media that they were worse off after the pension rise than at some previous time before the rise. Can such statements be taken as evidence that pensioners' welfare is dependent on the relative income hypothesis? What alternative explanation of their comments could be presented?

21.5

It has been said that economic growth is not an end in itself and therefore should not be one of the Government's economic objectives. Do you think that an economic objective should be an end in itself? Do you consider the other economic objectives, balance of payments equilibrium, price stability and full employment to be objectives that are ends in themselves? Do you think that the replacement of the economic growth objective by an 'elimination of poverty' objective would make any difference to Government policies?

21.6 One argument for the abandonment of economic growth as one of the Government's specific economic objectives is that policies that attempt to produce full employment are also the policies that produce economic growth. State whether you agree or disagree with such a conclusion and illustrate your answer by referring to specific policies that a government might adopt. You may find it necessary to distinguish between the short run and long run effects of such policies.

Arguments against economic growth

Unsatisfactory nature of the GDP measure

So far it has been assumed that the annual rate of increase of gross domestic product at constant prices is a good and reliable measure of economic growth, and that it can be expressed either in aggregate or per capita terms. There are several reasons why GDP should not be considered as either the perfect measure of economic growth or the sole measure.

1 The title 'gross domestic product' is a reminder that the measure makes no allowance for depreciation.

2 Increases in GDP at constant prices tend to underestimate increases in the value of production because new products did not exist in the base year.[6]

3 The annual percentage increase in GDP at constant prices measures, hopefully, the rate of increase of the flow of production. However, a person's standard of living and his welfare may depend on his wealth; his stock of assets. It is possible that an individual's real income may remain constant over many years but that his stock of assets may increase steadily as he acquires more possessions. Similarly, it is conceivable that living standards in a society may rise even though production at constant prices is unchanged. Undoubtedly the GDP growth measure is preferred to the changes in the stock of assets measure because the latter would be extremely difficult to measure. However, the difficulties in measurement do not mean that the concept has no economic significance. It raises the question: 'under what circumstances could economic growth and a steady increase in living standards be achieved without the need to increase production each year and hence without the need to increase the use of scarce resources?' The situation is one in which the existing steady flow of goods and services is greater than the rate at which those goods and services are being exhausted. It requires that goods be made to last rather than to wear out and be replaced. It therefore requires the abandonment of built-in obsolescence.

External consequences of economic growth

One of the principal arguments against economic growth is that it brings external disadvantages. External effects can be described as the conse-

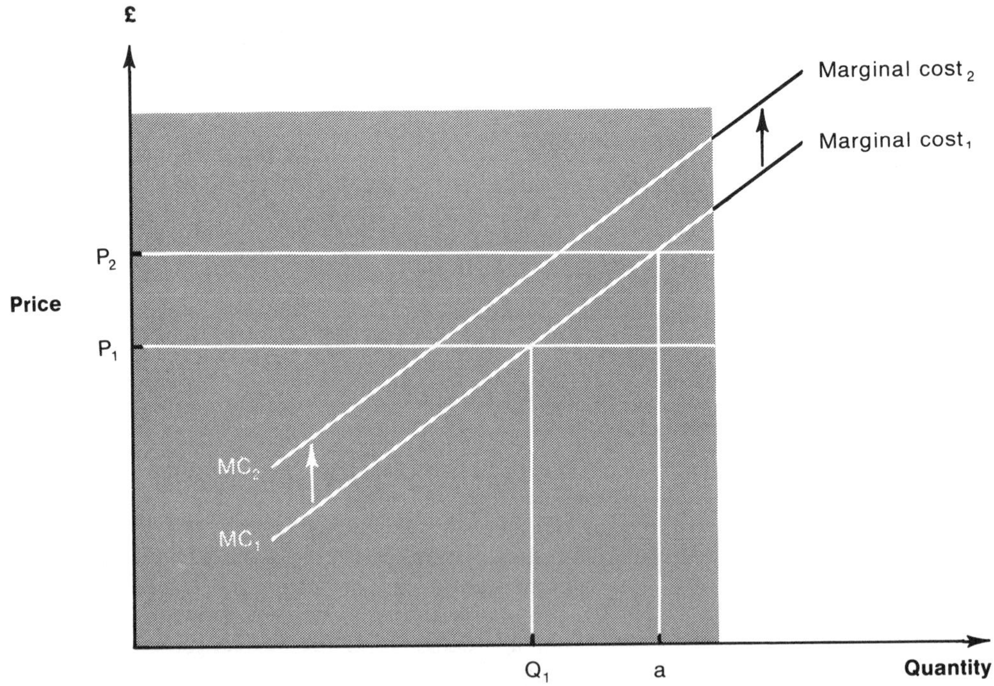

Figure 21.1 External diseconomies

quences experienced not as a result of direct conscious actions but as the result of actions of others, or society in general. The principle of external effects as it may apply to an individual business is illustrated in Figure 21.1

Figure 21.1 shows the situation facing a single firm in an industry made up of many firms producing similar or identical products. Initially the ruling market price is P_1 and the firm maximises profits by producing and selling Q_1 units. Suppose now that there is an increase in demand for the industry's product as a result of a successful advertising campaign. The market price may increase to P_2. In this situation the individual business will consider increasing its output to a, thereby equating marginal cost with price P_2 and maximising profits. However, as we saw in Chapter 8, the marginal cost curve is constructed on the assumption that all other factors such as the price of materials are constant – a reasonable assumption when the individual firm is too small to influence prices by itself. The conditions that prompt the individual firm to increase production may also prompt all other firms to increase their output and the effect may be to increase demand for essential resources within the industry. The single firm's marginal cost curve may shift up, not because it has increased output but because the other firms in the industry have decided to increase output. This may be an increase in the industry's demand for labour, or specialised transport services, that results in firms having to pay higher wage rates or having to meet higher freight charges. The external nature of these cost increases is demonstrated by the fact that if the individual business had decided not to increase its production, it would still have had to meet the higher charges because of the actions of other businesses.

Irreversible cost increases

A second type of external diseconomy is where the growth of the industry produces irreversible cost increases for all firms. Then, if the industry as a whole subsequently contracts to its original size, the disavantages of the temporary expansion remain.

Mishan's arguments against economic growth based on the external disadvantages have concentrated on the effects on society as a whole, rather than on the disadvantages to individual businesses.

As individual consumers strive to raise their personal living standards, economic growth produces external disadvantages that outweigh the direct benefits. The growth of private motor car transport is cited as one example of how the apparent benefits to the individual from car ownership must be offset against the disadvantages created by mass ownership of motor vehicles: traffic jams, parking problems, exhaust emissions, noise, road accidents, motorway developments that change the urban environment, the collapse of public transport services. The disadvantages of owning a car in the UK appear to be matched only by the disadvantages of not owning one. In addition many of these effects are either irreversible or can only be remedied in the long period and at great expense.

Distubance of natural beauty and ecology

Other external disadvantages of economic growth that are commonly referred to are the destruction of natural beauty and disturbance of ecology by the extraction of mineral resources and the growth of manufacturing plant. The creation of National Parks is said to be but a feeble attempt to rescue small pockets of the earth from the ravages of the developer. Pollution, the urban sprawl, the pulling down of buildings of architectural and historical importance and the rapid rate at which non-replaceable resources are being used by private businesses seeking profits are all given as examples of how economic growth brings with it undersirable consequences.

Mishan also argues that the development of mass tourism has been responsible for destruction of the opportunity for enjoyable leisure activity.

> As things are then the tourist industry, in a competitive scramble to uncover all places of once quiet repose, of wonder, beauty and historic interest to the money-flushed multitude is in effect literally destroying them. Once serene and lovely towns such as Andorra and Biarritz are smothered with new hotels and the dust and roar of motorised traffic . . . None the less the tourist agency continues to conjure up for the young and gullible visions of far away places, mysterious, romantic, primitive even, to be enjoyed with all 'mod cons' at a cheap package price.[7]

21.8

Recently, an economist opposed the argument that living standards increase with the stock of assets and that it is possible to increase welfare by holding production constant and making things last longer. He claimed that if products lasted longer there would be a reduction in demand for them and unemployment would be created. Discuss the validity of his argument.

21.9

Discuss the arguments presented in the text on the external disadvantages of (1) increasing car ownership and use and (2) the rapid increase in tourism. What steps would you advocate to deal with each problem?

An approach to the problem

Earlier sections of the chapter have examined some of the main arguments for and against economic growth. Plainly there is no simple solution, nor a solution that will persuade everyone. The following comments are very much by way of being a personal opinion.

The pressing need to remove or reduce poverty appears a sufficiently convincing argument to suggest that some types of economic growth can be used to raise living standards and to reduce misery and starvation.

Weakness of the market system

It must be apparent that certain types of growth generate considerable external disadvantages and that in many situations the private costs of a particular development understate the true social costs (the costs to society). Similarly a system based on obsolescence can be criticised for wasting scarce resources. Short-term costs understate the long-term social costs because they fail to reflect the costs to future generations. In short, the existing market system may be criticised because it reflects private and immediate costs rather than the social and long-term costs, and sanctions growth that would otherwise be rejected as too costly.

If it is accepted that economic growth can bring benefits and that the market system understates the true costs of many developments, the logical approach is to search for an appropriate way of measuring the true costs and benefits of each development; new industries, housing developments, power schemes, farming projects, transport systems, mining enterprises, fisheries, deforestation. Chapter 22 examines the evaluation technique known as cost benefit analysis and discusses the nature of the problems that are encountered in the attempt to measure these costs and benefits. There is little justification for a government to engage in, or sanction, new industrial developments without first attempting to assess not only the general social effects of the development, but also the effects of similar decisions, for our concept of justice places great store on precedence. If the problem of measuring relative costs and benefits is set aside for the moment, the conclusion must be that some industrial development should be rejected by government because of the high costs to society. But other projects should be approved even though they have undesirable features because it is considered that on balance they are beneficial.

Economic developments are already subject to many regulatory controls. Buildings require planning permission; factories often have to be located in industrial zones. Without such regulations the social costs of many developments would be much higher. There is a strong case for requiring that economic growth be controlled, because the additional private costs incurred in avoiding heavy social costs are often quite small. For example, the additional cost in laying electric cables and telephone wires underground rather than in erecting unsightly power poles is small. Nevertheless, it can be argued that the social costs measured in terms of their lack of aesthetic appeal and the costs of road accidents would more than make up the cost difference.

Economists with faith in the market system have suggested ways by which the market system could be used to help determine whether economic development should occur. They have suggested that businesses might be taxed in such a way that their private costs are made equal to the estimated social costs. Alternatively, it has been suggested that the businesses might be subsidised so that they can introduce pollution controls which reduce the social costs. The proposals are

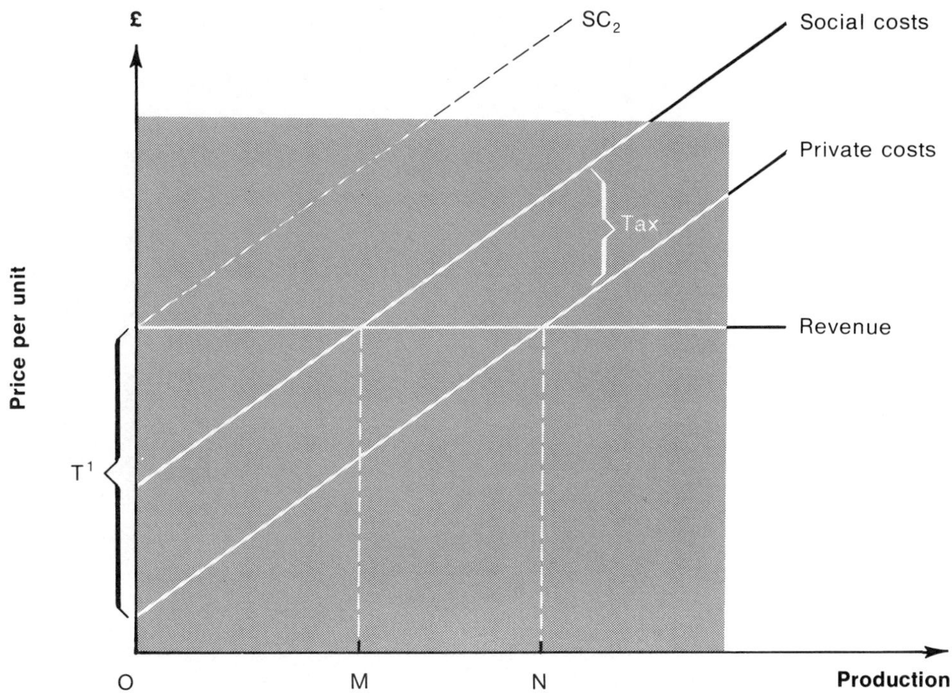

Figure 21.2 An environment tax

somewhat similar in effect but not identical. Figure 21.2 shows the effect of levying a special environment tax on a business.

In Figure 21.2 the profit maximising business would equate its (marginal) private costs with revenue and expand to a size at which it produced ON units. Suppose it can be calculated that the net social costs are greater than the private costs. These social costs can then be represented by the social costs line on the diagram. If an environment tax is levied on output this will have the effect of making the business' private costs increase to the same level as social costs and the business will react by reducing output to OM units. The tax has the effect of reducing output and of providing revenue with which the government is able to compensate the community for the welfare losses incurred by the development. It may be that the social costs are very great in which case (SC_2) a much higher tax (T^1) is required. In Figure 21.2 such a tax would be prohibitive and the business would cease production. It is said that taxation is superior to banning a development because it opens up the opportunity of a trade-off between the interested parties. By allowing compensation, it makes it possible for some to gain from the development without others being made worse off. In practice the problem that arises is in the calculation of the social costs and of devising a compensation system that would satisfy all.

A subsidy may be justified if it is judged that an alternative no pollution production system is available to the business at higher cost than a system that pollutes the environment. In Figure 21.3 the private costs of a no pollution production system are also well below the social costs of a system which pollutes the environment. A subsidy that enabled a business to introduce a pollution-free system, that is, one

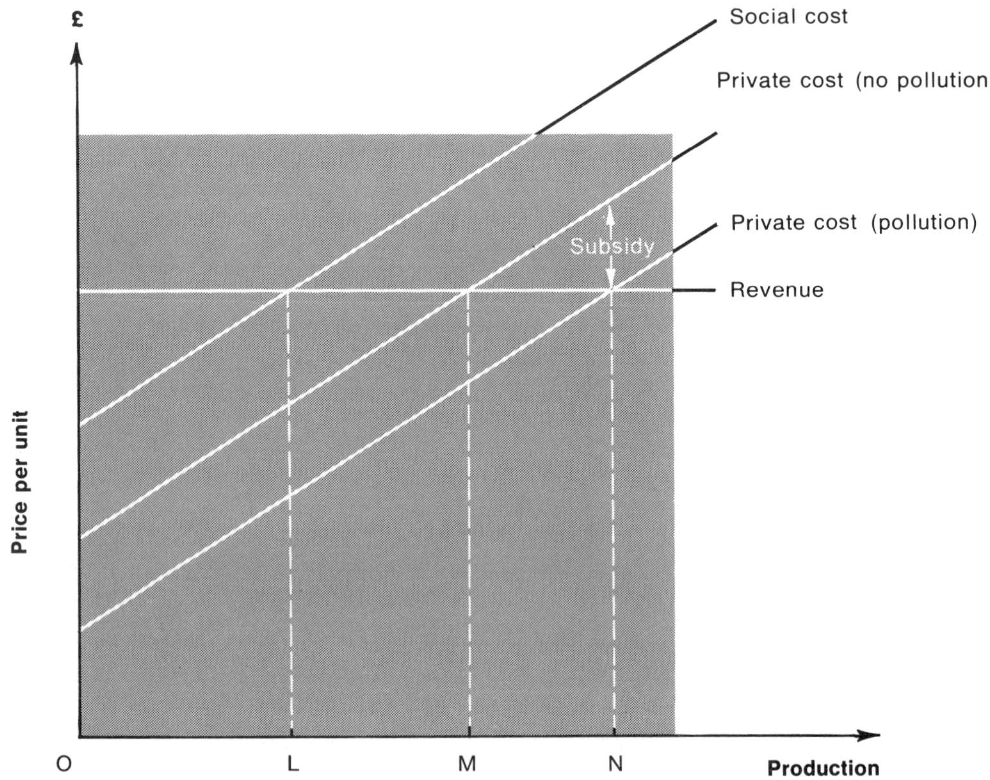

Figure 21.3 A subsidy

equal to the difference between the unit costs of the two systems, would enable a business to maintain output at ON. The alternative approach of compelling the business to introduce pollution controls at its own expense would result in a reduction of output to OM units. The question becomes one of whether the extra production brings benefits to society that outweigh the cost of the subsidy. Notice that the effect of a tax would have been to reduce output to OL and to leave the pollution problem unsolved.

21.10

Study Figure 21.2 carefully.

1 Two alternative government policies are to subsidise the business to remove pollution or to make planning permission conditional upon adopting pollution-free techniques. In what circumstances do you think that subsidy would be the appropriate policy? Try to suggest a specific situation in which you as an economic adviser would be prepared to recommend to the government a policy of subsidies.

2 Investigate the effect that the shape of the private business' cost curves will have on the different levels of output that would result from pollution-producing and pollution-free production techniques.

3 Suppose that the social costs of the pollution-producing system were lower than the private costs of the pollution-free system. What implications would this have for government policy? Might it mean that the government would give the business a free hand to produce as much as it wished?

21.11

It has been admitted that the market system is a poor device for ensuring that economic growth does not lead to external disadvantages and to losses in welfare. If this is so why should economists persist to trying to use the market system to solve growth versus environment problems?

21.12

It has been said that accurate measurement of social costs is extremely difficult. Investigate whether a taxation system or a subsidy system would be more difficult to implement in the light of this problem.

21.13

The benefits of North Sea oil to the economy of the UK are undoubtedly significant, in particular the contribution of petroleum tax revenue to the government budget, the import-saving effect on the balance of payments, and the earnings from oil exports. How these benefits are to be disposed of has generated much debate and alternative policies have also been put forward as to how the oil supplies should be depleted and the pricing of oil. Comment upon the effect that the alternative suggestions below would have on the economy:

1 that the oil be deliberately depleted slowly to extend the life of the energy resource until such time that world energy prices increase sufficiently to increase in real terms the value of the oil.
2 to use domestic oil supplies as a form of subsidising domestic manufacturing industry and increasing the level of international competitiveness through a deliberate cheap energy policy of low prices for North Sea oil.

Notes

1 For a discussion of these sources of economic growth and the measures a government can introduce to promote economic growth, see J McB Grant A J Hagger A Hocking 1969 *Economic Institutions and Policy*. Cheshire, Melbourne, pp 376–380.
2 W Beckerman 1970 Why we need economic growth. Paper presented to Section F of the British Association, Durham 1970, abridged and reprinted in *Lloyds Bank Review*, 102, pp 1–15.
3 J K Galbraith 1962 *The Affluent Society* Penguin and 1969 *The New Industrial State*, Penguin.
4 E J Mishan 1969 *Costs of Economic Growth* Penguin.
5 Economic Growth: Is it Worth Having? Treasury Economic Paper no 2 June 1973, Australian Government Publishing Service, Canberra, p 6.
6 Discussion of this technical point and of other problems in the measurement of GDP at constant prices are to be found in J McB Grant A J Hagger A Hocking 1969 *Economic Institutions and Policy* Cheshire, Melbourne, pp 372–373.
7 E J Mishan *The Costs of Economic Growth*, pp 140–141.

Chapter 22

Cost Benefit Analysis

The discussion on economic growth in the previous chapter led to the conclusion that a decision on whether to proceed with a development project is more likely to be made in a rational manner if the advantages and disadvantages are calculated and compared. It was said that many projects have external consequences in that they affect the welfare of people other than the decision maker; the business or the government directly concerned. Cost benefit analysis[1] is one technique that seeks to *identify* each of the important direct and indirect effects of a policy or project, and then attempts to *measure* the costs and benefits associated with it. Cost benefit analysis can therefore be used to assess the effects of a development on society as a whole rather than merely on a business or government department that is seeking to maximise some objective of its own. The technique places monetary values on each of the direct and indirect benefits and costs, so that the total costs can be compared with the total benefits.

Indirect or spill-over effects

Many of the indirect, or spill-over effects, are extremely difficult to measure and to express in money terms. For example, it is hard to measure the feeling of well-being that a community obtains from better recreational facilities, or to measure its sense of loss of amenity when pollution, or an unsightly building robs an area of its natural beauty and charm. But all these effects need to be taken into consideration if the cost benefit analysis is to be a valid exercise. Fortunately, some of the indirect effects are easily measurable. For example, when considering the construction of a motorway, the estimate of the effects on the railway system is most conveniently expressed in money terms.

If the benefits (expressed in money) exceed the costs (expressed in money) it is normal to say that the scheme has positive value. This does not mean that it should be adopted. It is essential that the true opportunity costs are considered. It may be possible to set up only one of a number of schemes in a locality, despite the fact that the benefits exceed the costs for each project. The decision maker will then have to determine which scheme is best; in which one do the benefits exceed the costs by the greatest amount? He will also need to determine whether those groups who suffer net loss from the project should be compensated. On the other hand it will be difficult to justify proceeding with a scheme for which the costs exceed the benefits to society for the gains of one group will be insufficient to compensate those who suffer. Under such circumstances, advocates would have to argue that the analysis had ignored some important elements or had employed faulty techniques.

This chapter examines the types of problems to which cost benefit analysis has been applied in recent years, the main difficulties associated with its use, and concludes with an example of cost benefit analysis.

The development of cost benefit analysis

The earliest use of cost benefit analysis on a significant scale was in the United States in the 1930s. It was used by government agencies as a basis for determining the use and development of water resources in the most efficient manner. The 1936 Flood Control Act carried the requirement that before an investment project using water resources was undertaken it had to be established that the benefits, 'to whomsoever they accrue' were in excess of the estimated costs. Public authorities in the United States developed and refined the techniques used to measure

Subject	Problem
1 Government research and development	Government research and development is said to be vital for national security. How much should be spent on research? When should a research project be supported?
2 Outdoor recreation	Money spent by the Government on outdoor recreation facilities leads to immediate enjoyment, long-term benefits to the individual and benefits to the nation as a whole. How much should be spent on outdoor recreation and what is the best way to spend it?
3 Education	In the United States the problem of school 'dropouts' was causing concern. What are the costs and benefits of programmes designed to cut down the number of dropouts in American schools?
4 Civil aviation expenditure	To what extent should civil aviation be subsidised and regulated by the Government? (Applicable to any complex and important transport system.)
5 Urban renewal	Amongst the objectives of slum clearance schemes are reduction of poverty, providing safe and sanitary housing and attracting middle income earners back to city centres. What are the benefits and costs of such urban renewal programmes?
6 Public health programmes	Measurement of benefits arising from prevention and control of diseases where benefits are: saving in production, reduction in treatment charges and reduction in pain and discomfort. The problem is comparing costs and benefits of alternative types of control and eradication programmes.

Table 22.1 Suggested areas for cost benefit analysis

Use of cost benefit analysis

these costs and benefits, but for many years cost benefit analysis continued to be applied primarily to water resource development.

By the early 1960s, it had been recognised that the techniques of cost benefit analysis had a much wider potential application. It was suggested that other areas of government expenditure such as public health, social welfare and education be investigated in the same way to find out whether the expenditure of funds could be justified. In 1963 a conference[2] between interested parties was held in Washington to discuss some of the areas in which cost benefit analysis might be applied, and to consider some of the more serious problems that would have to be tackled. The subject areas of some of the papers presented are listed in Table 22.1. It gives an idea of the range of topics for which cost benefit analysis is now used.

Since then, cost benefit analysis has been used in many countries to evaluate public investment programmes. In the UK it has been applied to transport studies, such as motorway development, and to select the site of the third London airport. Advertisements for positions with the British Department of the Environment indicate that much of the future work of research staff in that department will be in cost benefit analysis.

The technique developed as a means of assisting government departments in their evaluation of investment projects. Such techniques were considered helpful because governments were unwilling to use the normal estimates of private benefits and private costs that are the concern of the profit maximising business. The private business as we have seen already is not normally concerned with any spill-over effects on society. In deciding whether to provide a service, many governments now accept that they have an obligation to consider the broad social consequences of providing the service. Thus their decisions are based not on the narrow concept of private profitability but are taken in a more systematic way that has the objective of maximising social welfare.

Although cost benefit analysis has usually been applied to public authority projects, there are strong arguments for applying it to *private* investment projects. Increasingly, private developments are being subjected to public examination to see if they are in the general interest. Planning permission is required for industrial projects and urban development. But, by and large, there has been little attempt to use cost benefit techniques to decide whether such projects should be approved. However, in time, it is likely that all major private projects will be investigated in a more systematic way to determine their overall value to society.

Problems in the use of cost benefit analysis

Despite its rapid development in recent years the use of cost benefit analysis raises many problems and there has been considerable controversy about the circumstances in which it should be used.

The identification problem

Activities 1.5 and 1.6 in Chapter 1 were exercises in identifying the direct and indirect effects of projects. The identification and listing of such effects is essential before the task of measuring the costs and benefits can begin. In the early stages of the evaluation of a project it will be obvious that some effects are more important than others. The investigators have to decide which of the effects are sufficiently important to be included in the analysis and which should be left out. Seldom do researchers have the necessary time and money to consider every single effect, and hence every potential benefit and cost.

The measurement problem

A much more serious problem is that of finding a way of measuring benefits and costs of a project satisfactorily. It has been mentioned already that the aim is to measure these benefits and costs in money terms and this may mean attempting to put a money value on such intangibles as the loss of welfare brought about by the noise of aircraft landing at a nearby airport. The approach cost benefit analysts have used is to calculate the amounts people are prepared to accept in compensation for the inconvenience of a scheme. Thus in calculating the cost to a neighbourhood of extending an airport, or providing new runways which bring the flightpath over houses a cost benefit team might well include in its calculations:

1 Compensation to householders to permit them to install double glazing to reduce the noise nuisance.

2 Compensation, based on an assessment of the fall in the market prices of houses of the area, because of the unwillingness of outsiders to move into the area.

The technique, then, is to attempt to place a market value on the nuisance caused by the project. But sometimes it is impossible to find a suitable measure. For example, even though the Roskill Commission's study of the third London airport site calculated the costs of noise it abandoned attempts to measure other intangibles such as the loss of historic buildings, destruction of scenery and the removal of small village communities from site areas. Yet arguments on these points figured largely in public discussion of the relative merits of the four sites.[3] Critics of cost benefit analysis have argued that the most important social effects of government or private decisions will never be capable of measurement by cost benefit analysis.

> One of them likened the problem to appraising the quality of a horse and rabbit stew, the rabbit being the consequences which can be measured . . . and the horse as the amalgam of . . . social, emotional, and psychological impacts, and historical and aesthetic considerations that can be judged only roughly and subjectively. Since the horse was bound to dominate the flavor of the stew, meticulous evaluation of the rabbit was hardly worthwhile.[4]

Net benefits

Another problem lies in the measurement of benefits to society of a policy. Economists have tried to measure the benefit an individual gets from consuming a good or service by comparing the amount of money he would have been prepared to pay for the article and the amount he actually pays. This difference between what the consumer is willing to pay and what he pays has been called the *net benefit*, thus,

Willingness to pay – Amount paid = Net benefit

The difference between willingness to pay and the amount paid can be illustrated by considering the behaviour of a buyer at an auction. He will probably have determined in advance of the sale what is the maximum price he will be prepared to pay for the item and if he then succeeds in buying it more cheaply than his reserve he makes a benefit equal to the difference. The term *consumer surplus* is sometimes used to refer to this benefit.

Consumer surplus

In the nineteenth century the French engineer, Dupuit, linked the notions of consumer surplus with the demand curve. It is illustrated in Figure 22.1.

Suppose DD to be the demand curve of a single consumer for a particular product. The demand curve shows that this consumer is prepared to purchase 1 unit of the product even if the price is as high as £8.00 per unit. Should the price be £7.00, then the consumer will be prepared to purchase a second unit. If it falls to £6.00 a third will be purchased, and so on. In fact, the market price is only £4.00 per unit and the consumer finds it worthwhile to purchase a total of 5 units. 4 of those units yield a consumer surplus. The first unit carried a surplus of £4.00 (£8.00 – £4.00), the second £3.00 (£7.00 – £4.00), the third £2.00 (£6.00 – £4.00) and the fourth £1.00 (£5.00 – £4.00). In all the consumer had a net consumer surplus of £10.00 (£4.00 + £3.00 + £2.00 + £1.00). If the commodity was perfectly divisible, the shaded triangular area on Figure 22.1, bounded by the demand curve, the market price line and the price axis would be a measure of this consumer surplus. As it is, it provides an approximate measure of that surplus.

The argument has been presented in terms of a single consumer. A

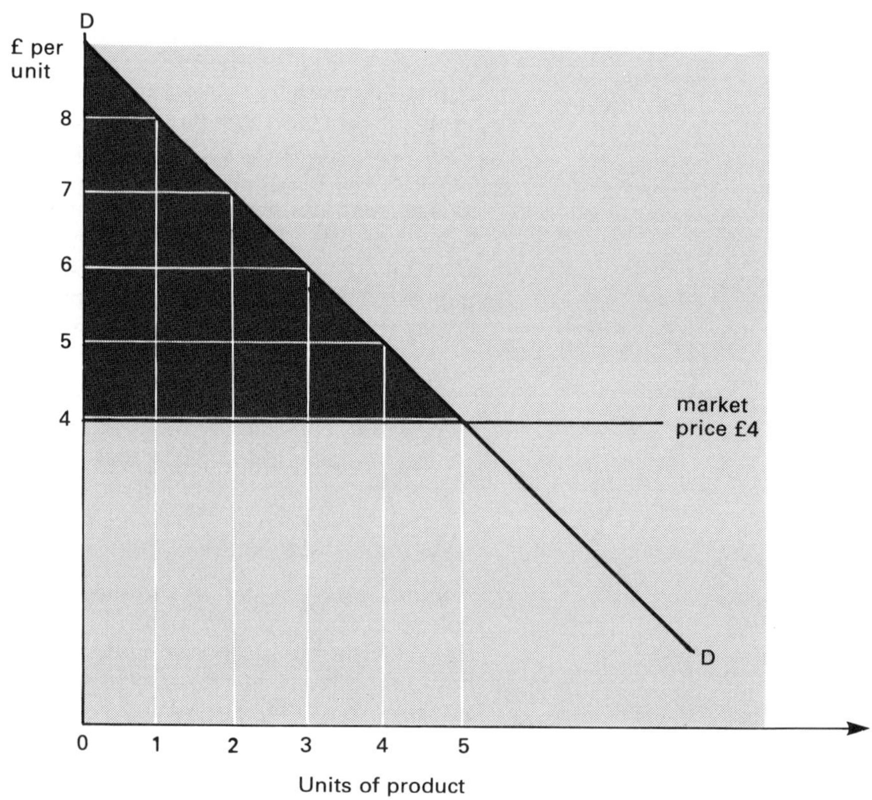

Figure 22.1 Consumer surplus

market demand curve can readily be used to obtain a measure of the consumer surplus accruing to a group of people.

This approach to the measurement of consumer surplus has caused controversy, particularly when applied as a general welfare measure. Nevertheless, it is widely used in cost benefit analysis, and has great value. It has the advantage that economists can often estimate the demand for a product or a service and the use of econometric techniques makes it possible to estimate the consumer surplus.

However, cost benefit analysts are on dangerous ground if they claim that they can measure benefits to consumers accurately. They do better to adopt the argument that the measures they do have are imperfect, but better than nothing, provided the imperfections are realised.

The time problem

So far it has been assumed that all costs and benefits can be added up and compared directly. But many projects take years to complete and the benefits and costs associated with them may last even longer. Cost benefit analysis requires an evaluation of these costs and benefits over time, and simply adding them up is not good enough. Why worry about the effects of a project on future generations? Obviously we do care about the unborn and the conditions in which they will have to live, but how *much* do we care about them? Is a £2 benefit for someone living in 20 years time worth the same as £1 benefit for a person today?

Discounting future benefits to compare with current benefits and costs

Using the maxim 'a bird in the hand is worth two in the bush' most people value a benefit of £100 at the moment more highly than the prospect of £100 in 5 years time. Similarly, few would consider £100 well spent today if it returned only £100 in five years time. The problem is tackled by *discounting* future benefits and costs. For example, if one considers that £120 in 5 years time is worth as much as £100 today to the investor then benefits estimated to accrue at that time have to be measured and revalued or discounted so that they can be compared with current benefits and costs. There are two problems:

1 Determining which of the various methods of discounting costs and benefits should be adopted. In periods of rising prices the additional problem of converting money values into real terms has to be faced.

2 Determining the discount rate to be used for any particular benefit or cost.

The time problem has been of great importance in the United States water resource studies where the benefits of projects accrue over many years. The choice of discount rates and discounting methods is arbitrary, but the selection can be of critical importance in determining whether a project has a benefit-cost ratio of more than one; that is whether the benefits exceed the costs.

The distribution problem

Another problem is that the benefits and costs of a project may be borne unequally by different sections of the community. Some gain whilst others lose. How do we weigh up the benefits and costs to each section of the community? In theory, the net benefits are positive if the benefits going to one group are sufficient for the other group to be *compensated* for its losses of amenity and still leave the first group better off. In practice assigning compensation values for the loss of such amenities has proved an intractable problem.

The usefulness of cost benefit analysis

As we have seen, there are a number of serious problems which most cost benefit studies have to meet, and seldom succeed in fully overcoming. This has led many people to dismiss cost benefit analysis. Nevertheless, its use is increasing and seems certain to continue as an aid to government decision making. Two points are worth making:
1 The larger the intangible component in a project the less useful cost benefit analysis is likely to be.
2 The measurement of any of the costs, or any of the benefits, may be valuable for the planners and may be preferable to taking decisions based on hunches or rules of thumb.

22.1

Some cost benefit studies have approached the distribution of income problem by giving some groups in the community a higher weighting than others. For example United States Indians have received a special weighting. Do you think that giving different weights to benefits received by different sections of the community is desirable? Which sections of the community do you think might be given special weightings? What problems could you foresee in attempting to carry out a cost benefit analysis in this way?

22.2

Screening systems have been developed which make the detection and treatment of some forms of cancer possible. Would government authorities be justified in refusing to finance such systems if
1 costs outweighed the benefits from such projects.
2 projects not connected with public health had higher benefit cost ratios?

Case study: the Cambrian Coast railway

The Cambrian Coast line runs along the shore of Cardigan Bay from the southern side of the Lleyn peninsula to the Dovey estuary and Machynlleth, where it connects with the line to Shrewsbury and the rest of the UK rail network. As a coastal route and one which connects a number of tourist resorts such as Barmouth and Harlech, it is much used by summer visitors. The rail bridge across the Mawddach estuary between Barmouth and Fairbourne provides the only direct link on the coastal route, the alternative being a lengthy journey by road to the nearest crossing point of the river several miles inland. The line provides the only rail service in the area where communications are generally difficult given the geography of the region.

British Rail in the 1960s, was faced with a growing problem of losses on its services and had responded to that with severe cutbacks after the Beeching Report. By 1967 the Ministry of Transport, the government department responsible for the general running of the rail system, introduced new methods of appraising and assessing railway services in the light of continuing losses. The aim was to establish the social desirability of loss-making routes so that they might be subsidised by direct grants from the government. The 1968 Transport Act made provision for such a social subsidy and over 200 railway services have received this form of support since then. Various studies of the Cambrian Coast line were undertaken including surveys and questionnaires into the costs and benefits of the line, investigating deeper than a conventional financial appraisal that compared costs of operation against revenue from fares. The Ministry of Transport published its findings to the effect that the line would cost approximately £750 000 to be retained indefinitely. (There were a number of alternative schemes suggested for the Cambrian Coast line and which had different cost implications if the line was to remain in use either completely or partially. The financial costs arrived at took different assumptions and estimates of cost into account.) How this figure of almost £750 000 was arrived at is shown in Table 22.2.

Costs		£'000
1	Rail costs	1821
2	Less cost of labour with no opportunity cost	534
	Total cost	1287
Benefits		
1	Cost of extra travelling if line closed	37
2	Loss of journeys	38
3	Extra road costs	50
4	Extra bus costs	413.5
	Total benefits	538.5
Net cost of retention i.e. costs less benefits		748.5

Table 22.2 Cambrian Coast railway – costs of retention

Source: P Barker, K Button *Case Studies in Cost Benefit Analysis*, © Economics Association 1975, by permission of Heinemann Educational Books

The results of this cost benefit analysis are interesting for the manner in which they were arrived at and the factors taken into account. The actual figures were challenged and criticised by a number of later studies which reworked the Ministry of Transport's analysis using different calculations for alternative sets of assumptions. The conclusions of these later studies suggested that there were positive benefits to be gained from the railway line rather than a net social cost as the official study concluded. Although the line was threatened with closure in 1971, there was a major review and later a change of policy which was announced in late 1973 as an acknowledgement that the railways were to be run as a social service and that lines such as the Cambrian Coast were to remain in service and receive an operating subsidy.

Costs of the line

The main costs of the line were those directly resulting from its operation plus the costs of maintenance and capital. However, the study offset against this cost of over £1.8 m, some £534 000 to represent the cost of labour employed. The study argued that since this amount represented the labour costs of railwaymen, who would be made redundant if the line were closed and would be in all probability unemployed with little chance of finding alternative jobs in the area, then this meant a very small 'opportunity cost' in terms of retaining man-power from employment in other industries locally. From the point of society, this calculation of costs goes further than the costs imposed by British Rail alone. In terms of the cost to society, the line was providing work where the alternative was unemployment. In a different locality where employment opportunities were wider than in this part of North Wales, then using labour inputs would impose a 'cost' in terms of the production foregone in other areas of employment. It is also worth remembering that, even if the alternative for labour is unemployment, then this imposes a cost in financial terms to society in the form of unemployment and social security benefits as well as a resource cost of lost production and output.

Benefits of the line

The calculation of benefits of the line was largely determined by the alternative costs that would be imposed by a bus service to replace the railway. These benefits are listed in Table 22.2 and in total were over £0.5m. The major item was the cost of providing an alternative bus service to take the passengers. Additional to this was the cost of extra travelling time since, for the middle section of the route in particular, the bus journey would be less direct than the rail. Time has a value to the individual and imposing longer journey times implies a cost to the passenger. It is, of course, very difficult to put a precise figure on the valuation of such time but it is possible to calculate an average figure to represent this based upon actual observations of trade-offs that people make when faced with choosing between routes that are direct but expensive and less direct but cheaper e.g. using toll-bridges, the extra fuel costs from longer journeys, and so on. This form of analysis, involving putting values on items that are not otherwise directly paid for, is known as *shadow-pricing* and forms an essential part of cost benefit analysis. For example, in the third London airport cost benefit analysis, the study calculated the cost to householders of additional noise from aircraft and the nuisance value that would be imposed.

Shadow-pricing

Extra road costs would be imposed if the line were closed, for example, the cost to local freight services. Moreover, the study also costed the loss of benefit that would accrue if some passengers decided not to travel at all if the rail service was withdrawn because the bus was not a suitable or practicable alternative. From this calculation of benefits the conclusion was reached that the retention of the line imposed a net cost to society since the costs far outweighed the benefits. The study therefore recommended closure of the line.

Criticisms and further considerations

The list of benefits did not include the fare revenue from rail passengers using the line, which is an omission that a number of further studies of the Cambrian Coast line pointed out. Moreover, apart from challenging basic assumptions and cost factors in the survey such as the valuation of travelling time, many other factors have been mentioned that were not included in the costs and benefits as calculated. Generally these fall into the category of 'spill-over' effects or externalities for the community at large. For example, the railway network in isolated areas is generally more reliable in adverse weather conditions than bus services. The effect of the railway in the community and the impact of its closure on local industry and employment is also highly relevant. The effect on tourism, since the line forms part of the rail network that connects North Wales with the rest of the UK, is especially important in the case of the Cambrian Coast line. The number of day-trippers coming into resorts by rail and general access for holiday makers has an important bearing on the local economy and its future development. If passengers feel that the rail journey is more convenient, pleasant and comfortable than a bus ride, then closure of the line would impose a loss of consumer surplus and sense of satisfaction to the passenger. Another consideration is the impact of increased road usage on the community that closure of the local rail service would involve. The number of road accidents would increase imposing a cost to the community for health services, emergency treatment and so on. Any road accident fatalities further involve a cost to society as a whole. It may be difficult to put a figure on such costs and benefits, but any serious attempt to include all relevant considerations to aid decision making must aim to include them.

22.3

1 How would you go about calculating the average cost of an accident on the roads in a cost benefit analysis of a road improvement scheme or a new motorway development?
2 In what ways would you wish to use such information as a policy-maker in local and central government?

22.4

'. . . despite the high degree of uncertainty in many projects and the difficulties involved in measuring intangibles, cost benefit analysis is nevertheless a valuable aid to decision making.' Examine this statement critically.

22.5

What would be the advantages and disadvantages of introducing cost benefit analysis into public works projects at local and central government level as a matter of course?

Results of cost benefit analysis

Generally if a project demonstrates a positive net benefit then this would indicate that the decision to go ahead should be taken. The result may be expressed as a benefit cost ratio; the higher the ratio the greater the benefit in relation to cost. But before the findings of any study are accepted, it is important to examine the results in more detail. In particular two questions need to be asked.
1 Are all the important costs and benefits included? (The identification question.)
2 How were the various costs and benefits arrived at? (The measurement question.)

The identified costs and benefits relate to tangible, and theoretically measurable items. Intangible effects may be important such as the costs of pollution or noise, but they pose many measurement problems. Figures included in studies for intangible costs or benefits are no more than estimates. They can therefore be challenged by economists or engineers who disagree with the assumptions adopted or the methods of calculation employed.

Notes

1 Cost benefit analysis was introduced in Chapter 1. See page 10 and Activities 1.6 and 1.7.
2 R Dorfman 1965 (ed) *Measuring Benefits of Government Investments* Brookings Institution, Washington DC.
3 For a critical assessment of the study on the third London airport see D W Pearce 1971 *Cost-Benefit Analysis*, Macmillan, Chapter 9. Also E J Mishan 1979 'What is Wrong with Roskill' in *Journal of Transport Economics & Policy*.
4 R Dorfman (ed) *Measuring Benefits of Government Investments* p 2.

Chapter 23

Other Economic Systems

This chapter compares some of the principal features of two socialist economies; the Soviet Union and Yugoslavia. First, it outlines some of the main ways in which the Soviet economy differs from a market economy. It then illustrates the point made in Chapter 3 – that there are considerable differences in the degree of planning in socialist economies – by discussing the Yugoslav system of decentralised socialism.

Naturally, the question to be asked is: What are the distinctive features of either system, and what are its advantages and disadvantages? Likewise, there is value in asking whether either system would bring benefits if adopted in the UK. Neither question can be answered without reference to the social and economic objectives in each country, because the system considered appropriate to achieve one set of goals may be quite inappropriate for the attainment of different goals.

The Soviet Union: a command economy

Economic and social objectives

When the Bolsheviks, under Lenin, came to power in 1917, the Russian economic system was in ruins. The disastrous war with Germany and Austria had decimated its population. Two million Russians had been killed in battle, double that number had been injured and unspecified numbers were the victims of epidemics and starvation. The economy itself was primitive by the Western European standards of the day. Its agriculture was backward and based on a land tenure system of large landowners and millions of peasants living at subsistence level. Secondary industry was little developed, and there, too, the workers lived in great poverty.

Pure communism

Lenin's long-term objective was to hasten the state of *pure communism* that Karl Marx has described. 'From each according to his ability, to each according to his need' is the guiding principle of pure communism. It would apply in a society in which each member worked without payment and drew whatever he needed or desired from the pool of goods the society produced. In addition to communism, Marx identified a number of other stages in the development of societies, including:

1 *Feudalism*, in which each social class acknowledged the authority of the class above it and enjoyed its protection, in return for the services it rendered:

2 *Capitalism*, characterised by the accumulation of private capital;

3 *Socialism*, where the means of production were owned by society as a whole.

Marx claimed that just as feudalism had given way to capitalism, so capitalism too was doomed. His argument was that capitalism contained within itself the seeds of its own destruction and that the proletariat would rise against the profit-orientated market society, in protest against their exploitation. Socialism was seen as the necessary intermediate step in the inevitable progress towards pure communism. In Russia, under Lenin, the government acquired ownership and control of non-human resources. Businesses, capital equipment (with minor exceptions) and land were appropriated by the new government in its early years. It then set about the task of designing a centrally-planned economic system to replace the market economy.

The short-term objective of Soviet leaders (the means by which the transition to pure communism is to be achieved), being a rapid rate of economic growth the Soviet Union has devoted a large part of its gross domestic product to investment, particularly in heavy industry. For many years the production of consumer goods was given a low priority so that the productive capacity of the economy could be developed more rapidly.

In the 65 or so years since the communists came to power in the Soviet Union there have been many modifications to the command system. In the early years, 1917–21, civil war raged and a system of 'war communism' prevailed. Money was little used as the production of goods, the procurement of foodstuffs and their release for consumption was determined by decisions of local committees. The 'system' was a response to crisis rather than a pre-determined way of achieving pure communism. Far from bringing plenty, it was accompanied by great poverty.

After the civil war, the requisitioning of agricultural produce was abandoned and a 'New Economic Policy' operated from 1921 to 1928. Small-scale industry was de-nationalised and a limited market system was reintroduced in an effort to raise the level of production.

In its turn the new economic policy was replaced by a system of state ownership. Comprehensive production planning was coupled with the use of incentives for managers and workers to help in the attainment of production targets. The system was based on strong central control exercised from the central government in Moscow. In 1957, sweeping reforms changed the system and greater autonomy was given to the regions. The Soviet Union is nominally a federation.

A further radical change in policy in 1965 led to a reversion to a centralised ministerial system. In recent years the strong emphasis on heavy industry has been reduced. More attention is now paid to the development of light industry, to raising the level of agricultural production and to increasing the production of consumer goods.

The Soviet Union's economic system cannot be regarded as rigid and unchanging. Nevertheless, it is possible to distinguish a number of characteristics that have applied to each of the variants of the command type of economic system since the abandonment of the new economic policy in 1928.

Features of the modern Soviet economy

Comprehensive planning of production and investment
Widespread use of incentives for managers and workers
Limited freedom of choice for consumers
Agricultural production largely undertaken by state farms and collectives

Comprehensive financial control exercised by the state bank
International trade restrained by rigorous controls

Comprehensive planning of production and investment

The main decision making institutions in the Soviet Union are shown in Figure 23.1. A parallel system operates in which the government and the Communist Party share in the determination of policies.

Major economic policy decisions are taken at the highest level by the top policy making bodies in the Communist Party and in the government. Responsibility for devising, implementing and supervising economic plans that give effect to these policies lies with the State Planning Commission, Gosplan. The State Planning Commission, which has existed in one form or another since 1921, is responsible to the Council of Ministers.

The task of planning production and investment for the economy necessitates the determination of target levels for each of the main economic aggregates. Gosplan has to perform the immense task of calculating production targets for each industry and for individual enterprises. It needs to estimate the needs of each for power, raw materials and semi-finished goods and to build all these requirements into a plan that will incorporate all the inter-industry and inter-enterprise flow of materials and products.

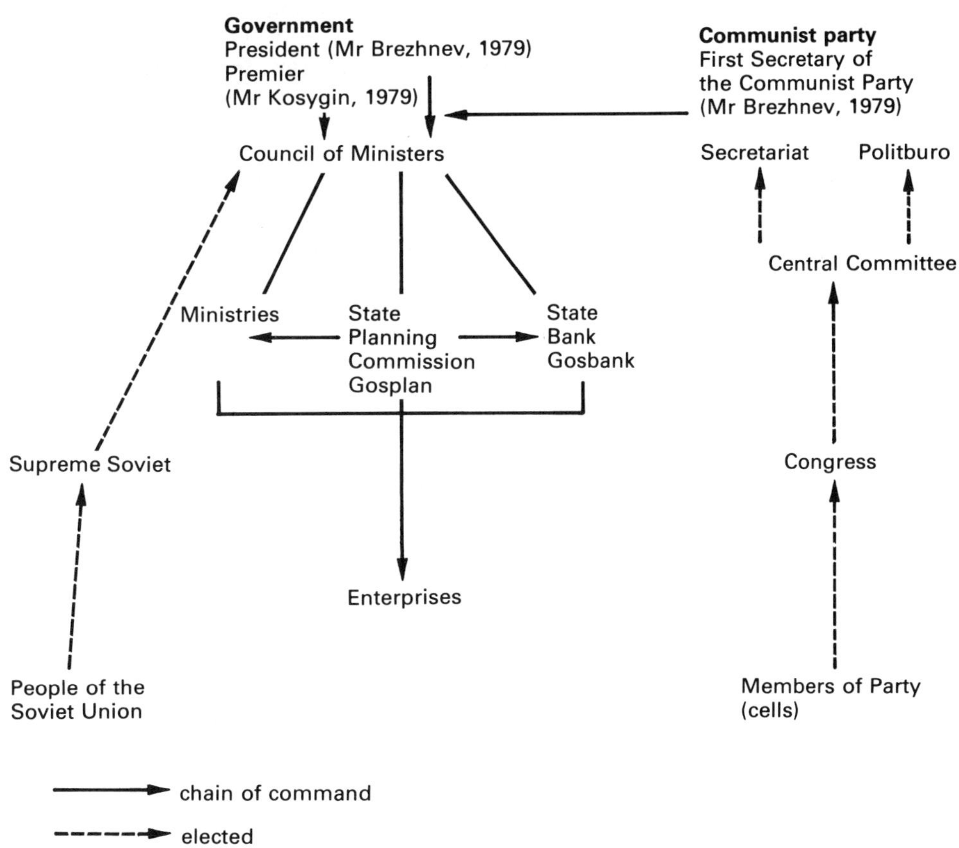

Figure 23.1 Institutions in the Soviet Command system

Types of planning

It is necessary to distinguish between *perspective* plans and *operational* plans. Perspective plans are the long-term (5 to 7 year) plans which relate to the major goals and policies emanating from the Politburo. Operational plans are the more detailed annual, quarterly and monthly plans that are prepared to assist in the achievement of the perspective plan. Gosplan receives these broad directives, discusses what is practicable with the ministers and enterprises, and then formulates the detailed plans.

An essential feature in the planning process is the establishment of productivity *norms*. Norms are production standards for processes and many thousands have been established by Gosplan. They provide the basis for calculating the physical production levels with specified amounts of resources. As the norms are then used to determine production goals, the ability of any enterprise to fulfil the target set by Gosplan depends on its workers achieving the norm. If their skills are below average, if the production processes operating in their factory are inefficient, or if the norm was incorrectly calculated in the first place, the enterprise may fail to reach target production.

Another reason why a factory may fail to achieve its production target is because it has not received the materials specified in the plan. A large part of total sales occurs between enterprises and the failure of one enterprise to fulfil its targets may then jeopardise plan fulfilment in other industries.

Widespread use of incentives

The use of incentives to assist in the fulfilment of production goals has been a feature of the Soviet system for many years. They provide the means of increasing production by encouraging productivity improvements.

Concentration on reaching production targets

Managers receive inducements in the forms of bonuses, and payments in kind such as superior housing and status in the community. The pressure on the Soviet managers is to produce to target level. However, there is little to be gained by the manager if he overfulfils his plans. Excessive profit is frowned upon as much as making unplanned losses.

The manager's task is easier than his counterpart in a market economy, because the state takes what the enterprise produces, and there are no *marketing* decisions to be taken. There is no need to determine the price of the product, and no threat from the competitive policies of rival enterprises. It is said that the system has the advantage that the manager can concentrate on achieving his production target. A disadvantage of the system is that because the enterprise has no marketing problems the emphasis on producing target quantities, and the lack of competition, mean that *quality* suffers. Also, the Soviet manager may adopt any 'mix' of products permitted under the plan that appears to give the best level of achievement.

Inducements are commonly offered to workers on a piece rate or payment-by-result system that relates payments to established norms. A system of wage differentials is used to reward skills and high productivity in certain occupations, and to induce labour to move to occupations where it is most needed.

Limited freedom of choice for consumers

The consumer may spend his income in whatever way he wishes but the choice is restricted by the limited range offered. In a market economy, shortages commonly result in higher prices and often businesses respond to the opportunity for making profits by increasing production of the article to meet demand. In the Soviet system there is no such mechanism to provide the required goods. A change in the economic plan is needed and it is far from certain that the planning authorities will sanction such a change in priorities.

Agricultural production largely through state and collective farms

State and collective farms

The organisation of agricultural production has presented the Soviet Union with a series of problems. The two forms of production unit developed by the system are the *state farms* (Sovkhozy) and *collective farms* (Kolkhozy). State farms are operated in a similar manner to manufacturing enterprises with a manager and workers who are paid on an incentive system. The first state farms were set up shortly after the revolution. Initially they developed slowly and today contribute only about 40 per cent of agricultural output. State farms might appear to be the logical type of institution for a socialist economy, but their introduction met with considerable opposition from the peasantry. After the revolution the Russian peasant aspired to own his land after years of control by feudal landowners. Instead, a system was established which substituted control by government for control by landowner. The subsequent history of agriculture in the Soviet Union was a continuing story of government attempts to control the agricultural sector by a mixture of pleading and threatening.

In 1928–1929 Stalin adopted a policy of forcing agricultural producers to form collective farms – a policy that was marked by brutal suppression of those who refused to conform. The collective farms are managed jointly by groups of farmers on land leased from the government. The members of the collective farms decide what to produce (within the restraints of the economic plan), and decide how to market their output. A given proportion must be sold to the government at a predetermined price, but the remainder may be sold at local markets where it commands premium prices. Another feature of the collective farms is that the individual is permitted to work a small area of land on the collective farm for his own benefit. He may sell any production that is surplus to his needs. It has been observed that output per hectare from these small plots is considerably higher than output from the collective proper and this had led critics to suggest that state control is not an efficient means of organising agriculture. It is said that the direct incentive provided by the private lots is an indication of how much more productive a 100 per cent private enterprise system would be. This may be so, but the high output levels on the small private areas almost certainly reflect the fact that they are usually used for horticulture and other highly intensive forms of agriculture. The collectives account for over 50 per cent of Soviet agricultural production.

Problems of agriculture

Agriculture has provided Soviet leaders with a series of problems. Collectivisation in the 1920s and 1930s produced great social bitterness. Catastrophic harvest failures and the slow rate of growth of agricultural production have subsequently produced further strains on the Soviet system. Agriculture was given low priority in some of the economic plans, and these planning mistakes resulted in production falling far short of required levels. Investment was neglected. Farmers received little inducement from the low fixed prices at which the government bought part of its output. The decision to scrap central machine tractor stations in 1958 and to provide each collective farm with its own machinery led to turmoil. The tractor station operatives had to be found jobs but their previous conditions of work and pay scales made it difficult to assimilate them in the collectives.

During the 1970s considerable emphasis was placed on the development of the agricultural sector. The 27 000 collectives have become much more like the 20 000 State farms in terms of capital, the use of large-scale farming techniques and specialisation. Despite the two bad harvests of 1972 and 1974 there has been a marked increase in agricultural production in the late 1970s, and wheat production averaged 250 million tonnes compared with 130 million tonnes in the 1960s.

The Soviet Union still has a far higher proportion of rural workers than western countries, 40 per cent of its population lives in the country and 25 per cent of the labour force is engaged in agriculture.

Comprehensive financial control exercised by the State Bank

The operation of the Soviet economy has often been likened to that of a large multinational corporation, in which many diverse activities are co-ordinated within the corporation's overall plan. The Soviet financial system is dominated by the State Bank (Gosbank). The functions of this bank are very similar to those of the accounting department of a large company. Although the requirements of each enterprise in the Soviet economy are determined in physical units, the system also requires money for transactions as a measure of account. However, a central

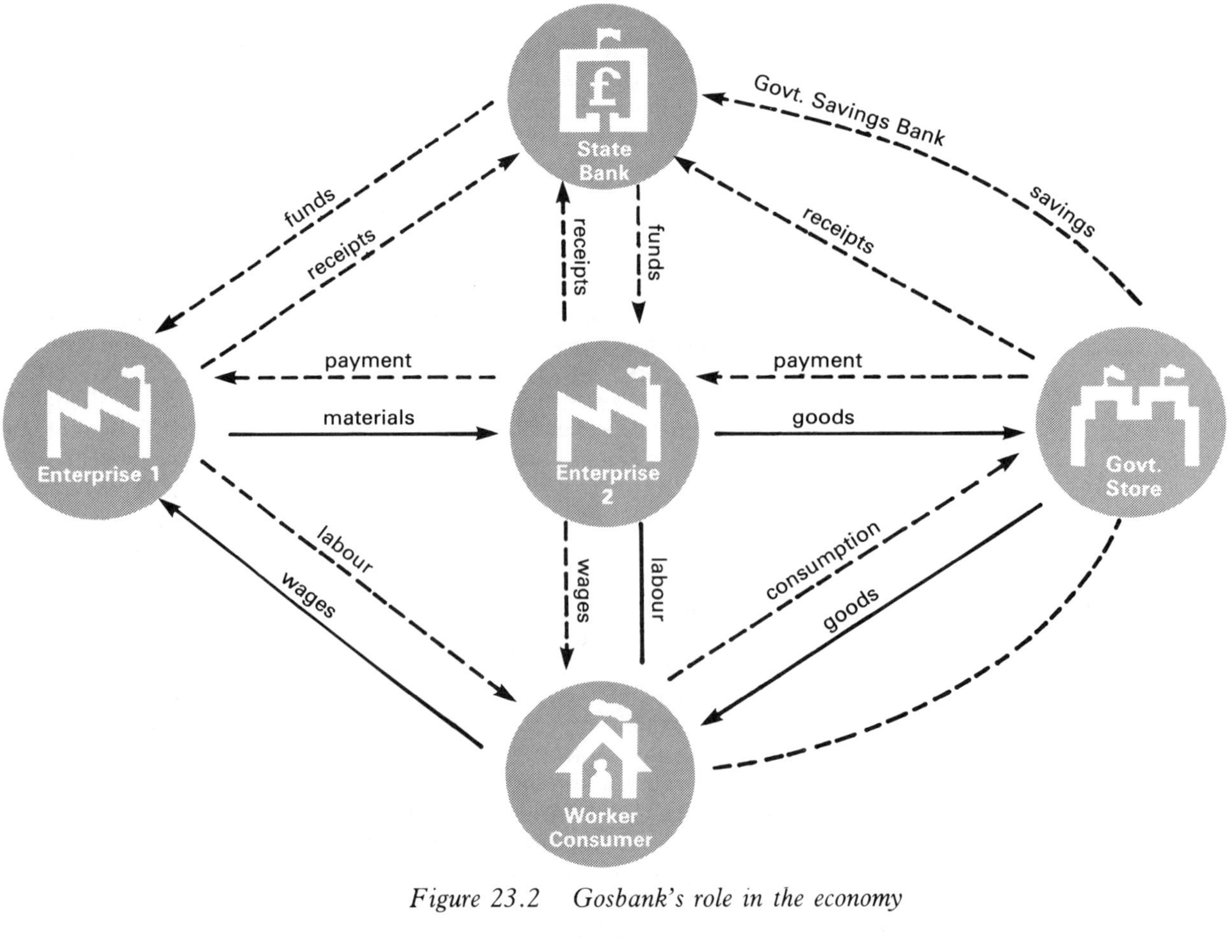

Figure 23.2 Gosbank's role in the economy

feature of economic policy has been that monetary and financial considerations should never be permitted to interfere with production. Gosbank issues money and investment credits, sanctions payments that are in conformity with the economic plan, and may withhold approval for any requests not consistent with the plan. It thus acts as a financial watchdog for the State Planning Commission. Its relationship with business enterprises and consumers is shown in Figure 23.2. In the figure, dotted lines represent money flow and solid lines the flow of goods and services. Each enterprise is required to deposit its funds with the State Bank and can only transact business by drawing a cheque on its funds at the bank. As the bank has powers of scrutiny, it has wide powers of control. Enterprise 2 in Figure 23.2 will have an allocation of funds from the bank through the plan for production purposes. These funds can be used to pay wages, to buy materials at fixed prices from other enterprises, and to carry on production. If the enterprise produces consumer goods, these are delivered (again at a fixed monetary price), to government stores and the receipts deposited with the bank. In one sense the efficiency of the enterprise can be judged by its financial transactions. With prices of materials and products fixed, the efficient firm may be able to show a book profit for its target production. An enterprise with low productivity may be forced to apply to the bank for additional funds to meet its production targets. However, goal fulfilment is the ultimate measure of success for the Soviet enterprise, unlike businesses in a market system where the profit obtained is the criterion.

Goal fulfilment, not profit, is the criterion of success

Economists in market economies have criticised Soviet pricing policies and have argued that they do not reflect the true values of products. In addition there are important differences between Soviet and market systems in the calculation of gross domestic product. Broadly, the Soviet Union leaves out all 'services' and its gross domestic product relates to transportable goods. Consequently, comparison between rates of production in Russia and other countries is not feasible.

International trade restrained by controls

Increasing Soviet trade with market economies

International trade is carried on by government trading agencies acquiring goods needed to meet economic objectives. Goods are exported to obtain foreign exchange and to further political objectives. Financial arrangements are handled by the Bank for Foreign Trade, a subsidiary of the State Bank. Much of the Soviet Union's trade is with other communist countries in Eastern Europe but there has been increasing trade with the market economies in recent years. The lack of convertibility of the Russian rouble and the rigid controls exercised by the Soviet government mean that Russia does not compete freely in trade; rather, it selects the products it wishes to export or import and either concludes a bilateral trade agreement in which goods are bartered, or determines a price which may have little relation to production costs.

If physical production is all important in the Soviet system it may be asked 'why use money and prices at all?' The answer is that it is virtually impossible to imagine a successful exchange system operating without a unit of account. Even in the Soviet system, prices are an attempt to fix relative values on products and are therefore useful in the assessment of the value to the economy of particular activities. They provide a basis for determining whether a given investment will be more or less productive in one industry than another, and a measure of the rate of economic growth.

During the 1970s there was a significant increase in Russia's trade with the western industrial countries. Long-term wheat contracts were signed during the years of crop failure. A wide range of imports were purchased. Soviet exports, including oil, increased substantially and by the end of the 1970s overseas trade was increasing faster than production. In 1978 it was estimated to amount to 7–8 per cent of GNP.

23.1

The Soviet Union is entering the most responsible and at the same time the most joyous stage of its development. We are building a Communist society. Figuratively speaking, this society might be compared to a bowl overflowing with food, clothing, footwear, apartments and books, which would be accessible to all. This is what we call communism. In that society every person will work according to his ability – for everyone and for himself – and people will receive things according to their needs. We have already started to fill up this tremendous bowl of communist abundance with the fruits of our labours. We have much work ahead of us but the beginning has been made. We are confidently advancing to this remarkable stage in the development of human society – to communism. (N. Kruschev, former 1st Secretary of the Communist Party of the Soviet Union[1])

1 Discuss in class whether you consider the achievement of pure communism inevitable throughout the world within the next 50 years.
2 If you consider it is not inevitable, do you nevertheless consider it to be a *practical possibility* within the Soviet Union during that period?
3 If it were achieved would there be an economic problem any longer?
4 If it is impossible to achieve pure communism does this mean that socialism is a failure as an economic system?
5 Could a market system also evolve to a communist state of plenty as described by Kruschev without the intermediate step of socialism?

23.2

The Soviet economic system makes use of incentives to encourage increases in productivity.
1 Can you think of any disadvantages of paying workers on an incentive scheme, such as piece rates?
2 If not can you suggest any reasons why trade unions in market economies are often lukewarm towards proposals of payment by piece rate, productivity agreement or profit sharing?

23.3

Class discussion topic
Consider the features of the Soviet economic system listed in the text. Discuss the extent to which each of these features is desirable or undesirable when considered from a *social* standpoint rather than from an economic viewpoint. To what extent would any of these features be politically acceptable if proposed for the UK?

The performance of the Soviet economy

The performance of the Soviet economy must be assessed in terms of its major objective – a rapid rate of economic growth. This can be done by examining its success in attaining the targets set in the perspective plans and by comparing its performance with the market economies.

The Soviet Union claims to have attained a rapid rate of economic growth (in excess of 10 per cent per annum during the 1950s and over 7 per cent during the 1960s). Economists from the advanced market economies, notably the United States, have variously treated these claims with deep suspicion and a degree of caution. However, the initial claims that the Soviet Union's performance was greatly exaggerated *for propaganda purposes* have moderated in recent years. It is appreciated that the Soviet equivalent of gross domestic product is calculated on a somewhat different basis from most market economies. As we saw in the previous section it excludes services. Nevertheless, after making allowance for the different approach, conservative United States estimates have placed the Soviet Union's growth rate at over 7 per cent in the 1950s and around 5 per cent in the 1960s. Their growth rates were considerably higher than those achieved by the United States, the United Kingdom and Australia in the same period. The faster growth rate of the Soviet Union can be attributed largely to its high rate of capital formation during these years (25 to 30 per cent of GDP compared with 17 or 18 per cent by the United States).

Growth rates of the Soviet Union

It is significant that the lower rate of growth in the 1960s corresponded with a switch in Soviet policies towards consumer goods and agriculture and away from capital formation in heavy engineering. Critics of the Soviet system have argued that it will be unable to maintain the previous high rate of economic growth and also raise consumption and hence living standards. Others have pointed to the high rates of economic growth achieved by some market economies, notably Japan, Israel and Taiwan. The debate on the question of which type of system, command or market, will produce faster sustained growth rate is not conclusive. But the preference for planning amongst developing countries seems to indicate that a command system is better able to provide for a high level of capital formation and to hold down consumption expenditure in the short term.

Not conclusive that planning produces faster growth

The Soviet Union also claims that all but two of its nine perspective plans have been successful. Targets for the 8th Plan (1966–70) included increasing industrial output by 50 per cent, agricultural output by 33 per cent and consumption goods by 20 per cent. Such targets are based on what appears possible to the planners rather than what is merely desirable. The 'success' of a plan does not entail the fulfilment of all targets. Success is judged on the overall achievement. Substantial modifications to a plan have been necessary on occasions. The agricultural crisis of 1963 led to a massive plan revision. There was also a change in priorities towards consumer goods. The result was the formulation of a new Two Year Plan to cover the balance of the period designated for the 7th Plan to operate.

The 1970s was a decade dominated by Mr Brezhnev as First Secretary of the Communist Party and later as executive President. During this period the following significant changes occurred:

1 the import of western technology,
2 increasing trade with industrialised countries,
3 increased investment in the rural sector,
4 greater emphasis on consumption goods and raising living standards.

An indication of the increase in living standards is shown in Table 23.1.

Even so, there has been a continuing fall in the rate of growth of the

Soviet economy. The 10th Plan (1976–80) aimed at an annual growth rate of 5 per cent. In 1977 the actual growth rate was less than 4 per cent; less than one third of the rate achieved consistently in the 1950s.

Supporters of the Soviet type of command system claim that in addition to its superiority over market systems in securing a rapid rate of economic growth, the Soviet system also overcomes the main problems faced by the market economies: unemployment, inflation and balance of payments difficulties. The Soviet objective of maximising the use of resources and maximising production tends to maintain full employment. Any unemployment is either frictional (as workers move from one job to another), or structural (as workers move from one industry to another; assisted by government retraining schemes). It is said that cyclical unemployment, the product of business recession in market economies, has been avoided.

	1965	1975
Radio	60	80
Television	25	75
Refrigerators	22	66
Vacuum cleaners	10	25

Table 23.1 Ownership of consumer durables in the Soviet Union 1965–75 (number per 100 households)

Source: The Economist, 4 March 1978

Despite claims to the contrary, inflation is possible under the Soviet system. For example, prices rose rapidly during the 1930s. When the government controls prices rigidly excess aggregate demand may exist, so in that sense inflation is present. It means that consumption goods are inadequate and queues appear. But by and large Soviet planners have managed to arrange for the production of consumer goods and the level of aggregate disposable income to be such as to avoid either serious shortages or the need to increase prices greatly in the post war period.

23.4

The four main economic objectives of many market economies (including the UK) are:
- full employment
- price stability
- a rapid rate of economic growth
- balance of payments equilibrium

It is claimed that the Soviet economy is able to achieve all of these simultaneously. Does this indicate that the Soviet command system is superior to a government-regulated market system? If so, does it imply that the UK should introduce a command system?

If the Soviet system is not superior, how would you demonstrate the superiority, or at least the advantages of maintaining a government-regulated market system?

23.5

Two non-communist countries that have achieved high rates of economic growth in recent years are Korea and Taiwan. In each case the rate of growth was greater than that of the Soviet Union during the 1970s. Can you think of any reasons why the growth rate in either of these countries was so rapid? Does their rapid growth rate indicate that it is possible for all market economies to achieve growth rates as high as that of the Soviet Union? If it does, then why have the growth rates of the United Kingdom and the United States been relatively low?

Yugoslavia: self-government socialism

Development of the system

The Yugoslav economic system presents a sharp contrast to that of the Soviet Union. In the years immediately after World War II Yugoslavia's communist government established a centrally planned command economy based on the Soviet model. Between 1946 and 1951, the state acquired all large land holdings and redistributed them. It also nationalised the mining and manufacturing industries, transport, banking, wholesaling and retailing. By 1949 it was attempting to run the economy as a single enormous enterprise, by planning the production of many groups of commodities. According to Horvat[2] the state budget amounted to two-thirds of national income and the annual economic plan weighed over 3300 pounds! Yugoslavia also followed the Soviet lead during this period in placing emphasis on industrialisation, socialisation and the rebuilding of its war-shattered economy. Consumption was given a low priority.

In 1948, Yugoslavia's political status changed suddenly. It was accused by Stalin of departing from communist orthodoxy, was expelled from the communist bloc and its economic ties with its communist neighbours were severed. The event was of great importance to Yugoslavia because, apart from the economic strain it imposed, it led to a rethinking by the Yugoslavs of the nature of communism and to a reshaping of the economic system. The Yugoslavs decided that state ownership and central planning were not the only alternative to private capitalism. They justified their position by claiming that Karl Marx had been aware that bureaucratic government control of production would lead to worker exploitation. A command economy was no advance on a capitalist economy because it replaced private capitalism by state capitalism.

Decentralised socialism as an alternative to state capitalism

The alternative the Yugoslav's was *decentralised socialism*. This is characterised by a minimum of central planning, and self-government by workers. Self-government entails direct ownership and control of enterprises by the workers. Within the system there are independent workers' communes and within each commune autonomous enterprises. Workers make the business decisions about what to produce, how much to produce and how much the enterprise should pay them. They benefit from profitable operations and suffer when losses are made.

The idea of self-management applies throughout all facets of Yugoslav society. For example, there is the opportunity for individual members of society to participate in the decision making on matters such as health, the arts, education and scientific research. It is even claimed that the political system aims to provide individual members of society with an effective political voice rather than subjecting them to the authoritarian control of a narrowly-based communist party, as in the Soviet Union. During President Tito's years of office, there was conflict between ethnic groups within Yugoslavia and the government and the Party have maintained fairly stringent controls.

A comparison with the Soviet Union

Some of the principal differences between the Soviet Union's state ownership system and the Yugoslav social ownership system are shown in Table 23.2.

Soviet Union State ownership	Yugoslavia Social ownership
1 A central planning system determining production and allocation	1 Decentralised system with social planning by individual units
2 Government determined wages and prices	2 Working collectives determine wages, and market forces influence prices
3 Collectivisation of agriculture	3 Agricultural producers in business co-operatives
4 Overall financial control by Gosbank	4 Commercial independent banking system, since 1965. Use of financial instruments to regulate the economy

Table 23.2 Principal differences between Soviet and Yugoslav economic systems

The features listed above are features of 'models' of the two systems which are not necessarily completely met in practice. For example, Yugoslavia's system does not completely rely on market forces; price and wage controls play a part in the system. Likewise, in the Soviet Union the command system's determination of wage differentials reflects the need to attract workers to particular jobs.

Essential feature is worker control

The essential feature of the Yugoslav system has been the principle that workers should be given control of their own productive units and that they should make the production and marketing decisions. It is believed that, if workers make decisions such as how much they should be paid and what proportion of funds should be reinvested, then this will remove the 'owners versus workers' conflict and retain the advantages of an incentive system in industry.

The *New Economic System*, introduced in 1952, established the workers collectives in which the businesses were run by elected workers councils and managing boards. Central planning was abolished, many price controls were removed, and membership of the existing agricultural collectives was made optional. In the 1960s further reforms included the development of a more independent monetary system, the liberalisation of foreign trade and the introduction of self-governing non-profit-making organisations dealing with education, culture, social welfare and health. The structure of the economy and the relationship

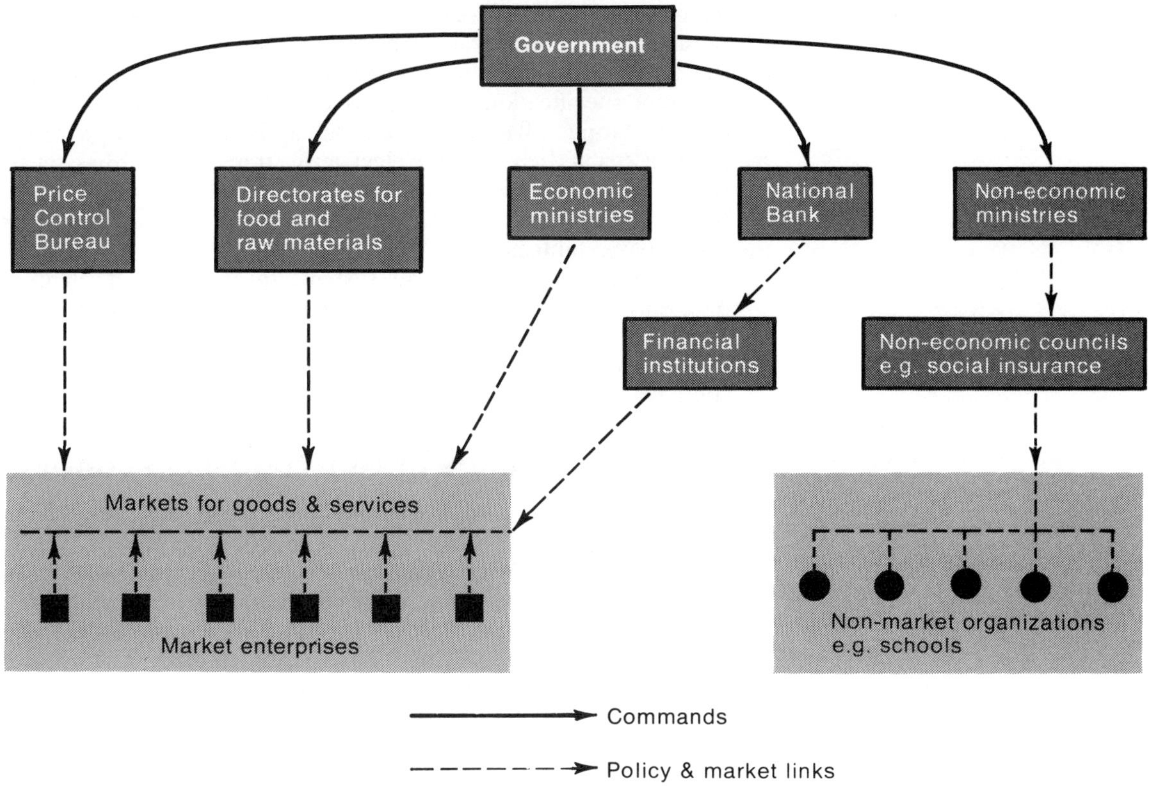

Figure 23.3 Structure of the Yugoslav economy

between government and the self-governing units can be seen in Figure 23.3.

The dotted lines represent either economic policy links (for example, between the economic ministries and the markets) or market links (for example, between the banking institutions and the enterprises). The enterprises in the market sector have an important role in determining what is produced.[3]

Figure 23.3 shows that the central government exercises a certain amount of control over the system. It also shows the chains of commands which affect the functioning of the individual enterprises. It does this in the following ways.

1 *The General Plan* This sets targets for capital formation, foreign trade and regional policies.

2 *The banking system* The National Bank regulates the money supply and finance available to industry.

3 *Directorate of Food Reserves* This administers agricultural support prices and is obliged to buy food production at guaranteed prices.

4 *Directorate of Industrial Products* This intervenes in the market to deal with excess demand or supply.

5 *Price Control Bureau* This controls about 40 per cent of industrial prices, though the percentage has been as high as 70 per cent at times, since 1952. It may seem strange that Yugoslavia claims to have a market system, yet also has a price control system. The commonest method of 'controlling' industrial prices is through a price registration system in

which enterprises have to obtain approval for price changes. This requirement of approval for *price changes* can sometimes be avoided by the introduction of *'new' products*, that is, products with slightly different specifications. These price controls are not an effective means of eliminating inflation in Yugoslavia. However, the government has fixed prices and charges for electricity, transport and has set maximum prices for a number of basic materials.

6 *Wages* The government does not fix wage rates in the private sector but it has established *minimum* wage rates.

In contrast to a command system, the purpose of planning in the Yugoslav system is to produce an economic environment in which the worker-controlled enterprises can function effectively. There is less control over the overall performance of the economy than in some of the advanced market economies of Western Europe.

The performance of the Yugoslav economy

By 1968 a number of important production indicators showed that production per head was still at the level of the more advanced industrial countries of Western Europe before the Second World War. Nevertheless, the increase in Yugoslavia's production between 1946 and 1968 was considerable. Electricity production increased ten fold, steel increased six fold and cement production trebled. The economy's rate of economic growth, first under central planning and then under self-government socialism, is shown in Table 23.3.

	Central planning 1947–52	Self-government 1952–60	Socialism 1960–68
Gross domestic product	2.3	9.8	6.8[b]
Industrial output	12.9[a]	13.4	7.9
Agricultural output	–3.1	11.7	7.0

Note:
(a) 1946–52
(b) 1960–67

Table 23.3 Yugoslav growth rates per annum 1947–68

Source: B Horvat 1971 Yugoslav Economic Policy, Problems, Ideas and Institutional Developments. *American Economic Review*

The gross domestic product rose rapidly under self-management socialism. The central planning period had been marked by a rapid increase in industrial output but a fall in agricultural production. Overall, GDP increased by 2 per cent per annum. Under self-management socialism, all sectors of the economy developed rapidly in the 1952–60 period, but less rapidly between 1960 and 1968.

During the 1970s, Yugoslavia had to face the same economic problems as the western industrial economies because of its reliance on the market system and its close economic links with those countries. It has been suggested that Yugoslavia's self-management socialism was less fitted to cope with stagflation than the other market economies. Critics have pointed to a high level of inflation and to rising unemployment during the period.

One way of assessing the Yugoslav performance during these years is to compare it, not with western countries in general, but with its near neighbours, Greece and Italy.

Table 23.4 shows the rate of increase of consumer prices for the three countries for the years 1972–78. The table shows that prices increased by about 160 per cent between 1972 and 1978. The overall increase in prices was somewhat lower in Greece and Italy (nearly 140 per cent). In the latter part of the period Yugoslavia had some success in reducing its rate of inflation and its performance was not so very different from that of its neighbours.

	(Annual percentage change in the consumer price index)		
	Yugoslavia	Italy	Greece
1973	19.2	10.8	15.6
1974	22.2	19.9	26.9
1975	23.5	17.0	13.4
1976	11.2	16.8	13.3
1977	14.6	17.0	12.2
1978	14.1	12.2	12.5
6 years 1972–78	161.5	136.4	137.9

Table 23.4 Rate of inflation in Yugoslavia, Italy and Greece, 1972–73 to 1977–78

Source: *International Financial Statistics*, International Monetary Fund, March 1979 (Washington D.C.)

	Yugoslavia	Italy	Greece
1973	7.5	9.7	15.9
1974	10.5	4.4	–1.9
1975	5.3	–9.1	4.4
1976	4.0	12.4	10.6
1977	8.7	1.1	1.4
1972–77	53.8	18.5	33.1

Table 23.5 Rate of increase of industrial production in Yugoslavia, Greece and Italy, 1972–78

Source: *International Financial Statistics*, International Monetary Fund, March 1979 (Washington D.C.)

Despite the poor inflation record, Yugoslavia was able to sustain economic growth during the period and its achievements compare favourably with its near neighbours and the OECD countries generally. Table 23.5 compares the rate of increase in industrial production for the three countries for the period 1972–78. Over this six year period, industrial production was increased by about 50 per cent in Yugoslavia, compared with a third in Greece and less than 20 per cent in Italy. Another indicator of rising living standards, gross national product per head at constant prices, shows an annual average growth rate in excess of 4 per cent. Nevertheless, the attempt to reduce inflation in the 1970s was not costless and unemployment rose steadily from 300 000 in 1972 to 700 000 in 1977.

Along with many of the OECD countries Yugoslavia faced balance of payments difficulties in the 1970s. For most of the period, it ran a deficit on its balance of trade. In 1972 exports earned enough foreign exchange to pay for 70 per cent of the country's imports. By 1977 they paid for scarcely more than half. A major problem was the increasing oil import bill. In 1972 oil imports cost 2 billion dinars but by 1977 their cost had increased to 21 billion dinars.

Despite the deteriorating trade position, Yugoslavia was able to maintain its international reserves, initially with the assistance of the special fund facilities provided by the IMF to help meet oil import payments. Substantial capital inflows and invisible earnings enabled it to convert the trade deficit into an overall balance of payments surplus for much of the time.

In conclusion, the Yugoslav economic performance can be considered a satisfactory one considering the pressures it was subjected to in the 1970s. It has probably been less successful in controlling inflation, but it may well be that the good growth record and rising living standards are an indication that control of inflation need not necessarily be the principal objective of a developing industrial country.

23.6

Compare the economic performances of the UK and Yugoslavia during the 1970s using material contained in this chapter and earlier chapters.

23.7

Study a recent edition of either *International Financial Statistics* published by the International Monetary Fund, or *Principal Economic Indicators* published monthly by OECD. Assess Yugoslavia's continuing economic performance relative to Greece and Italy. What problems are there in comparing some of the information presented for the three countries?

23.8

Suppose a country such as Yugoslavia decided it would do little to check the rate of inflation but would try to raise production as quickly as possible. In what ways might a rapid rate of inflation threaten the attempt to achieve a rapid rate of growth?

23.9

Imagine that the UK adopted a Yugoslav-type economic system. What effects might this have on:
1 industrial relations,
2 consumption and investment,
3 the mining industry,
4 health services,
5 living standards,
6 any other aspects of the economy?

23.10

The photograph on page 409 is of a group of workers discussing the running of Zagreb's railways.
1 What significant points does the photograph suggest about the operation of the managing board?
2 Imagine a similar scene in your city or town with the workers attempting to run the bus service. What problems would they face?

Notes

1 *Moscow News*, 9 July 1960 cited by W N Loucks, W G Whitney 1969 in *Comparative Economic Systems*. 8th edn, Harper and Row, New York, p 502.
2 Branko Horvat 1971 Yugoslav Economic Policy in the Post-War Period: Problems, Ideas, Institutional Developments. *American Economic Review*, **61** (3), part 2, supplement.
3 A discussion of the efficiency of self-government in economic decision-making is to be found in M Kamusic 1970 Economic efficiency and workers' self management and J Tinbergen 1970 Does self management approach the optimum order? in M J Broekmeyer (ed.), *Yugoslav Workers' Selfmanagement*, Reidel. Dordrecht-Holland.

Chapter 24

Economic Development

The meaning of 'economic development'

Chapter 21 discussed the economic growth controversy; whether economic growth is a desirable economic objective. Much of the argument related to the conflicts that face the advanced industrial countries as they seek to increase production and living standards. Many of the economists' economic growth theories relate to the rate of growth in advanced countries. This chapter is concerned with the special economic problems of the poor countries and the term 'economic development' is used to refer to the economic growth of poor countries. The term implies that some countries are more developed than others; that some are undeveloped, or underdeveloped, or developing.

Definitions of underdevelopment

The term 'underdeveloped' can be used in several ways. Professor Kuznets has suggested three definitions of underdevelopment:

> 1 It may mean failure to utilise fully the productive potential warranted by the existing state of technical knowledge . . . resulting from the failure of social institutions.
>
> It is in this sense that the UK can be considered underdeveloped, though the same can be said of all countries to a greater or lesser degree.
>
> 2 It may mean backwardness in economic performance compared with the few economically leading countries of the period. In this sense the vast majority of countries are underdeveloped at any given time . . .
> – though the UK is probably not one of them, by this definition.
>
> 3 It may mean economic poverty, in the sense of failure to assure adequate subsistence and material comfort to most of a country's population.
>
> The problem of underdeveloped countries in current discussion reflects elements of all three definitions; its acuteness arises largely out of the material misery stressed in the third definition, it is sharpened by realisation of a lag compared with economically more advanced countries, and it is generally viewed as a social problem originating in the failure of social institutions rather than in a lack of technical knowledge.[1]

Absolutely poor and relatively backward countries are vitally concerned with economic growth. The governments of most of them have the urgent objective of achieving rapid increases in their country's real domestic product and in achieving increases in real domestic product per head. But economic development means more than securing economic growth, more even than closing the gap between rich and poor countries. Sears[2] has pointed out that three important criteria exist for determining whether there has been any economic development. Has there been:

1 a reduction in poverty?
2 a reduction in unemployment?
3 a reduction in income inequalities?

The real gross domestic product of a country may be increasing (economic growth is occurring) without there being any reduction in poverty or unemployment. The benefits may go to one group in the community; to government officials, to the ruler, to one racial group or even to foreign residents. 'Is Kuwait more highly developed than the United Arab Republic because its GDP per head is higher?' asks Sears. Or is South Africa more developed than Ghana?

GDP per head as a measure of economic development

Nevertheless, there is often a close link between economic growth and the economic development of a country, and this has led economists to use GDP or GDP per head as a measure of economic development. It is at least possible that if GDP per head is increasing some of the benefits will spread to the poorest members of the community. Growth makes the reduction in absolute poverty possible as we agreed in Chapter 21. However, if there is no economic growth it is unlikely that there will be substantial economic development because the conditions do not exist for the reduction of poverty, or the redistribution of income. Another argument for using GDP per head as a measure of economic development is that it is often a matter of sheer necessity to

Country	GDP (US$ millions)	Population (millions)	GDP (US$ per head)
Sweden	78 187	8.2	9 535
United States	1 686 000	215.1	7 838
France	397 870	53.1	7 493
Australia	88 350	14.1	6 266
Japan	571 509	112.8	5 067
Saudi Arabia	45 103	9.2	4 903
United Kingdom	208 420	55.9	3 728
Italy	164 410	56.2	2 925
Greece	21 974	9.2	2 388
Iran	77 043	34.3	2 246
Yugoslavia	32 560	21.6	1 507
Turkey	39 461	41.1	960
Malaysia	10 986	12.3	893
Tunisia	3 795	6.0	633
Papua New Guinea	1 300	2.8	464
Philippines	17 896	43.8	409
Sudan	5 100	16.1	317
Indonesia	37 270	139.6	267
Pakistan	13 119	72.4	181
India	87 727	610.1	144
Bangladesh	6 993	78.7	89

Table 24.1 Gross domestic product, population and GDP per head for selected countries, 1976

Source: *International Financial Statistics*, International Monetary Fund, Washington D.C., March 1979 do so. Gross domestic product as the aggregate, which measures in money terms the value of goods and services produced in a given period, is estimated by many countries. For some it is the only statistical record of the aggregate changes that are taking place in their economies. Often, the statistical measurement is crude, but it is again a case of economists making what use they can of scanty information.

Table 24.1 sets out recent comparative figures of GDP per head for a number of countries, expressed in US dollars.

The third column of Table 24.1 shows that there are very considerable differences in GDP per head between the countries in the list. Compare the figures for the United States, France and Australia with those for India, Indonesia and Tunisia.

International comparisons of income figures present problems

There are weakness in comparing figures of various countries. Prices as well as incomes differ from country to country. The poorer countries often have a large non-market sector in which goods and services produced are not bought and sold. For example, there will be domestic laundry rather than dry cleaning, and generally a much smaller degree of specialisation and exchange in the market place. The values of these services are not recorded. Statisticians attempt to estimate some of them but generally understate the value of this production. Thus the very low figures for some of the countries over-emphasise poverty in these countries. But even after making allowances for understatement and for differences in the cost of living (perhaps even doubling the figures given) it is clear that there is a great disparity between the more affluent countries and the poor.

24.1

1 Some writers have attempted to make a threefold division between rich countries, partly-developed countries and poor countries. Try to classify the countries listed in Table 24.1 on this basis, indicating any problems you find, or misgivings you might have about such a procedure.

2 In Table 24.1, GDP per head in Tunisia in 1976 was US$633 per head. It was estimated that the lower-paid workers in the Tunisian community (farm workers, hotel staff and fishermen) were earning about US$1200 per head, per year. How might the difference between the two figures be explained?

Development gap

Statistics in Table 24.1 are supported by additional evidence that a vast gap exists between the small number of rich industrial countries and the remainder. Differences in per capita incomes are reflected in differences in material living standards; in health, housing conditions and personal possessions. It has become fashionable amongst the anti-growth school in affluent countries to claim that the benefits of economic growth are illusory; that poorer countries and their inhabitants would be better off without urbanisation, industrialisation and the destruction of the environment. Significantly, however, in the poor countries there is a general willingness to tolerate these disadvantages of western affluent society, in return for economic advancement.

Since the Second World War more and more attention has been paid to the development problems of the poor countries. To a large extent this has been because the colonies of the rich countries gained independence and because their representatives have obtained voting rights at meetings of world organisations such as the United Nations and the

Development gap is widening, even if poor countries have faster growth rates

signatories to the General Agreement on Tariffs and Trade. The United Nations Conference on Trade and Development (UNCTAD) was established specifically to develop international policies to aid the poor countries, at their instigation.

The demand in the newly independent countries has been not just for economic growth and the reduction in poverty, but that the gap between the rich and poor countries should be closed rapidly. It is claimed, frequently, that far from the gap between rich and poor getting narrower it is widening and the poor are becoming relatively poorer. This can happen, even when poor countries are achieving faster growth rates than rich countries.

	Gross domestic product, 1975 prices (US$ thousand million)	Population	US$ per head	Increase	Percentage increase
Australia					
1972	71.42	13.2	5410		
1977	83.93	14.1	5952		
				542	10.0
Tunisia					
1972	3.21	5.33	602		
1977	4.36	6.07	719		
				117	19.4

Table 24.2 Growth in real gross domestic product, Australia and Tunisia 1972–77

Source: *International Financial Statistics*, March, 1979 International Monetary Fund, Washington D.C.

Table 24.2 makes this point by comparing the real per capita growth of gross domestic product of Australia and Tunisia, between 1972 and 1977. Australia's rate of growth of GDP per head was small during this period; a 10 per cent increase in the five years. Tunisia did much better despite a more rapid rate of population increase. Real GDP per head rose by nearly 20 per cent in Tunisia over the period. Notwithstanding the faster rate of growth in Tunisia, the ***absolute*** gap between the average in the two countries widened considerably. Australia's GDP per head at constant 1975 prices rose by US$542 to US$5952, whilst the Tunisian increase carried its average from US$602 to US$719. The gap widened from US$4808 per head to US$5233.[3] The reason for this is that increases in income start from a very much lower base in Tunisia and the poor countries than they do in the rich such as Australia.

As we have already seen, by economic growth economists can mean either:

1 the increase in aggregate real gross domestic (or national) product, or

2 the increase in real gross domestic (or national) product per head.

(1) is the measure that is important if an indication is required of the increases in a country's production of goods and services – the growth of its economy. (2) is more important as an indicator of the reduction

in poverty in the country. In a country experiencing a rapid rate of population growth, the rate of increase in real gross domestic product and the rate of increase in real gross domestic product per head will vary considerably. In many developing countries, it is the rapid rate of population increase which acts as one of the principal checks on economic development.

24.2

	Real gross domestic product (1975 prices) millions of units of local currency		Population (mid-year estimate) (millions)	
	1972	1977	1972	1977
United States	1 489	1 695	209	217
France	1 331	1 554	51.7	53.1
Japan	79 736	167 068	107	114
Saudi Arabia	95	171	8.2	9.5
Iran	2 873	3 859	30.6	34.3
Papua New Guinea	0.88	1.04	2.6	2.9
Philippines	92.6	130.0	39.0	45.0
Indonesia	10 052	14 530	126	143
Pakistan	98	128	64.3	75.3
India	648	739[a]	563	610[a]
Chile	46.5	47.4	9.7	10.7

Note:
(a) 1976 data

Table 24.3 Real gross domestic product and population of selected countries, 1972 and 1977

Source: *International Financial Statistics*, International Monetary Fund, Washington D.C., March 1979

1 In some of the countries listed in the table the percentage increase in real GDP per head was far below the percentage increase in aggregate real GDP over the period 1972–77. In which countries was this difference particularly great? What interpretation do you place on this pattern of growth?
2 Increases in an underdeveloped country's population nearly always have an adverse effect on its rate of economic growth. Discuss this statement in the light of the table.
3 Is there any evidence to suggest that the more affluent countries (France, Japan, and the United States) have a less serious population problem than India, Pakistan or the Philippines?
3 The figures in Table 24.3 are given in the local currencies of the respective countries. This makes it impossible to make an international comparison of income per head and thus it is impossible to say whether the gap between the rich and poor countries widened or closed between 1972 and 1977. Such comparisons can sometimes be made by converting each figure for gross domestic product into United States dollars so that there is then a common unit as a basis for the comparison. What circumstances during the 1970s have made this procedure potentially misleading?

Non-monetary indicators of economic development

There are, as we have seen, considerable problems in making international comparisons of income levels and of rates of economic growth. An alternative approach is to use non-monetary indicators. As the term suggests, these indicators refer to the quantities of physical goods or services which a country produces in a given period, or to the total stock of goods it has at its disposal at a particular time. The advantage of using such non-monetary measures is that they avoid many of the problems caused by international differences in money prices and exchange rates. But they are only indicators; that is, they give, at best, a rough guide to relative living standards and growth rates.

Indicators of development

In 1966, Beckerman and Bacon[4] proposed the use of seven indicators to be used to produce an index of the absolute levels of real incomes in 80 countries. The seven indicators, which were tested against independent national income estimates were:

1 production of crude steel per head of population,
2 annual cement production per head of population,
3 annual number of domestic letters per head,
4 stock of radio receivers per head,
5 stock of road vehicles per head,
6 stock of telephones per head,
7 annual meat consumption per head.

Using these indicators Beckerman and Bacon obtained the results for 1960 which are given for selected countries in Table 24.4. It shows there was a very considerable difference in real consumption in 1960 between the rich countries (say the first five in the list) and the very poor coun-

	Index points	*Ranked position*
United States	140	1
Sweden	125	2
Australia	106	4
United Kingdom	100	5
France	75	11
Japan	46	19
Soviet Union	35	26
Spain	34	27
Singapore	24	34
Yugoslavia	22	39
Brazil	20	44
Malaya	18	48
Tunisia	13	54
United Arab Republic	10	60
Ghana	8	64
Congo	5	72
India	5	72
Pakistan	4	76
Sudan	2	78

Table 24.4 Estimated levels of real consumption in 1960 (UK = 100)

Source: Beckerman and Bacon, *Ibid.*, Table VI, p. 533

tries (those with less than 20 index points). Nearly half of the 80 countries had less than 20 index points and a quarter had less than 10 index points.

The indicator method has been developed further since Beckerman and Bacon's work. Others have selected different indicators. A common one is electricity production in kilowatts per head. The United Nations Research Institute of Social Development (UNRISD) produced a list of 18 indicators in 1970 including average number of persons per room, newspaper distribution and school enrolment. However, the more indicators used the more difficult the collection task and the less chance of getting comparable figures for all countries.

24.3

Use UK official statistics to collect figures for 1975 and 1980 for each of Beckerman and Bacon's seven indicators. Give each of the indicators equal weight and then calculate the percentage increase in real consumption in the UK between 1975 and 1980. Compare the result obtained with the percentage increase in gross domestic product per head over the same period.

The first part of this chapter has concentrated on examining the statistical material economists work with when studying the problems of developing countries. Despite the inadequacy of the material and the problems raised when making international comparisons, the following conclusions hold.

1 There are great differences between the rich countries and the poor countries no matter how their relative positions are measured.
2 Aggregate economic growth is taking place in many poor countries.
3 Population growth is a serious obstacle to the removal of poverty in many countries.

Problems and policies of the underdeveloped countries

Not all developing countries have the same problems

The rest of this chapter looks at some of the problems facing the poor countries – such problems as establishing the conditions for economic growth and development. In particular, it examines the development problems of Tunisia in the 1960s, because they are fairly typical ones. But the selection of one country for a case study should not lead to the conclusion that all developing countries face identical problems. One country may have a serious shortage of production resources, another may have a population problem, whilst a third may have difficulties in attracting foreign investment or aid, or of selling its exports on world markets. Tunisia has most of these problems, but it is neither the poorest of countries, nor without hope for the future.

In 1972 Tunisia had a population of over five million living in an area somewhat smaller than England with a gross domestic product per head of about US$280. The country gained its independence from France in 1956 and a Republic was established under President Bourguiba the following year. It was, and still is, essentially an agricultural economy but there is a small and developing manufacturing sector.

In 1959 the Food and Agricultural Organisation (FAO) reported:

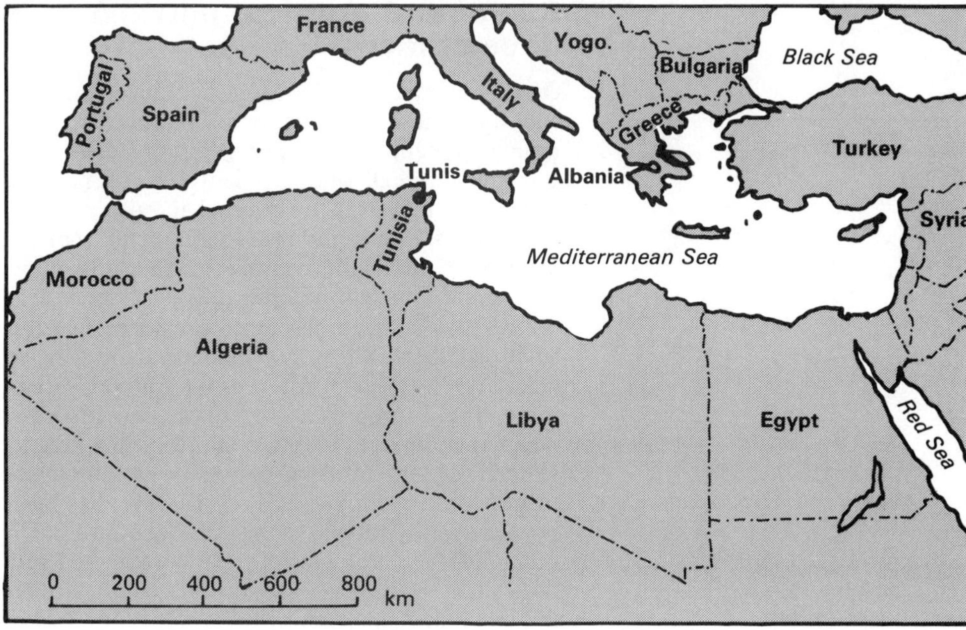

Figure 24.1 Tunisia

> Few signs of the upward surge in productivity and output which is essential if the Tunisian economy is to emerge from an era of stagnation and dependence on foreign aid into an era of progress and self sustained growth.[5]

Twenty years later the FAO conclusion appears somewhat pessimistic, for in fact the Tunisian economy has been able to record a modest rate of economic growth during the period. GDP at market prices increased from under 400 million dinars in 1960, to 661 million in 1970 and to 2122 million in 1977. Of course, inflation also played a part in this increase. Nevertheless, there has been a steady increase in real gross domestic product, as shown by Table 24.2. Over the twenty year period, Tunisia has achieved an annual rate of increase in real GDP of over 4 per cent. Thus, despite an annual rate of population increase of over 2 per cent, there has been an annual rate of increase in real GDP per head of around 2 to 2.5 per cent.

Problems facing developing countries

The problems facing Tunisia, and other developing countries, can be listed as follows:

1 How to remove social, religious and political barriers to development?
2 How best to use available natural resources? (Scarcity of natural resources is a major problem.)
3 How best to utilise human resources? (The population problem is an important factor.)
4 How to increase savings and investment?
5 How to develop international trade?
6 How to obtain foreign aid?
7 How to select the appropriate economic system and the best development strategy?

Social and political barriers to economic development

Often a poor country's economic development is held up by its social conditions and attitudes, or by political instability or bad government. Religious beliefs may prove an obstacle to what westerners would consider rational and efficient use of resources. Similarly, political conditions may lead to internal misallocation of resources (as in Indonesia in the 1960s) and also to a reluctance of foreign countries to invest in or give aid to the country in question. Likewise, extensive bribery and corruption will hamper development.

In Tunisia there has been considerable progress towards removing such problems. Since independence, social reforms have been considerable. Women have entered the public service and are forming an increasingly important part of the workforce, though their degree of emancipation still falls far short of the freedom achieved by British women. It is a Moslem country but religious attitudes do not appear to impede development. Tunisia, also, has been fortunate amongst the new countries in that it has enjoyed internal political stability. Bourguiba and the Neo-Destour Party remained in power during the 1960s with little visible opposition. The country's foreign policies have been moderate and apart from friction with France in the early 1960s it has retained good relations with both rich and poor, and communist and non-communist countries.

Lack of resources

This is often the fundamental reason for lack of development in a poor country. Tunisia is not particularly well endowed with natural resources, but the discovery of oil and its development in recent years has been an important aid to growth. Other resources include phosphates and superphosphates. Fertile soils make it possible to grow a variety of warm temperate and sub-tropical agricultural products and of these, cereals, olives and citrus fruits are important export earners. But they do not offer the potential for rapid economic development.

In recent years, Tunisia has developed a considerable tourist potential. The country's abundant natural resources of sand, scenery, local customs and ruins of Roman and Carthaginian civilisations are offered to British and European tourists on cheap package holidays made possible by modern jet travel, and the growth of charter tour companies. (Tunis, the capital, is now only 3 hours from London.) The rapid development of the tourist industry has also stimulated local craft industries such as pottery (using local clays), leatherwork and carpets. Much of this work is highly individualistic and the government is attempting to control the quality of some of the products offered for sale.

Human resources and the population problem

A country may have little in the way of natural resources, but its residents may still achieve high standards of living if they develop industries calling for skilled human resources, after educating the workforce to the required standard. The Swiss watch industry is based on local skills rather than local raw materials – labour costs are the main

Population and development

component in the value of the output. Along with most developing countries, Tunisia has an abundance of manpower. Unemployment and underemployment is high in the agricultural sector and a high birth rate results in an annual increase in the population of over 2 per cent.

One might react to this information by saying that Tunisia must be well endowed with human resources and should therefore develop industries which will use these resources. But first there is the problem of raising the skills of the workforce to the required quality; of developing those skills which enable them to compete with established industries in other countries. It is estimated that Tunisia's workforce has increased by about 30 per cent in the last ten years. If all these workers were highly skilled, the task of absorbing them into the developing, but still very small, manufacturing sector would be impossible. As it is, many are not skilled and agriculture, with its low productivity per head, has had to absorb still more workers. This has prevented the productivity gains that might be achieved by improvements in farming technology. The 'solution', in a country with a superabundance of labour, is to use labour instead of machines. Roadmaking and construction work, ploughing with camel rather than tractor are common sights. The labour is employed, but there is no prospect of a rapid escape from poverty.

Education is now compulsory in Tunisia for both sexes and the goal is primary and secondary education for all, followed by the opportunity to go to university. But with half of the population under 20 the financial cost is great. Thirty per cent of government revenue was devoted to education in 1972, but even so, a shift system operated in many schools. Some people question whether the attempt to provide a modern education system is not too ambitious and too costly; that it would be better to concentrate on primary education and limited vocational training.

Population control is an obvious policy to be pursued. If the birth rate can be cut and the size of families reduced, pressures on the education system and on industry to absorb more labour would be reduced. The government encourages family planning, but as in most other developing countries, these policies have had limited impact.

Savings and investment

The earlier chapter on economic growth explored the relationship between investment and the growth of gross national product (or gross domestic product). Provided a country has resources capable of development, a suitably trained and skilled workforce and has identified viable investment projects correctly (conditions that are by no means guaranteed in a poor country) then the ratio of capital to output[6] is about 3 or 4 to 1. In other words, an increase in investment (net capital formation) of 12 per cent of national income will produce a 3 or 4 per cent increase in production. Capital formation is of critical importance to a country that is attempting to increase its gross national product rapidly. The problem is to mobilise the necessary funds, from domestic savings or from foreign investment.

Capital formation is of critical importance

Attraction of foreign funds depends on the profitability of available projects and confidence that the investment is secure. It carries the usual problem of foreign ownership and control (see Chapter 13). The mobilisation of domestic savings is a problem in poor countries; the poor have a relatively high propensity to consume, a low propensity to save. In Tunisia there has been a successful campaign to encourage family saving and savings bank deposits have risen rapidly.

	Millions of dinars at market prices 1965	1969	1972	1977
Gross fixed capital formation	132	145	214	660
Gross domestic product	496	627	1078	2122

Table 24.5 Capital formation in Tunisia

Source: International Financial Statistics, various issues International Monetary Fund, Washington DC

24.4

1 Calculate the capital output ratio for Tunisia over the period 1965 to 1977 from the figures given in Table 24.5.
2 What interpretation would you place on the figures you have calculated?

24.5

Discuss the possible methods available to the government of a poor country wishing to increase the level of investment in the country.

24.6

One of the traditional features of the economy of many poor countries is that many of the economic transactions are completed after going through a ritual of bargaining or primitive haggling. A typical conversation in a Tunisian market would go something like this:

Vendor: 'You look at my shop, things very inexpensive.'
Buyer: 'How much is that leather belt?'
Vendor: 'Very nice, hand made, only 2 dinars 800 millimes.'
Buyer: 'I will give you 600 millimes.'

There follows protests on both sides about the unfairness of the other's offer; the vendor lowers his price, the buyer raises his. Eventually the buyer walks out of the shop to be called back by the vendor and the deal is completed at 1 dinar or about 35 per cent of the original asking price.

However, there is no set relationship between the vendor's original asking price and the final price. The latter may be 50 per cent, 75 per cent or an even higher percentage of the former.

Why is it that this market form is more or less restricted to underdeveloped countries? What advantages and disadvantages does it have over fixed price selling for buyer and/or seller? In particular, are there any reasons for believing that the abolition of primitive haggling would lead to a faster rate of economic development

24.7

Tunisia has a considerable unemployment problem. In this situation can the government's policies of universal education and female emancipation be justified?

24.8 Study the photograph of the Tunisian market scene. Suggest possible ways of measuring the gross domestic product of a country in which such conditions operate.

International trade

A major objective of most developing countries is to increase exports at a rapid rate. Exports are the main source of foreign exchange needed to buy the imports of raw materials and producer goods essential for the development of secondary manufacturing industries. Most of the poor countries with good growth records in recent years have derived stimulus from the export of petroleum or other mineral resources. Tunisia's export of crude petroleum totalled 161 million dinars, or 40 per cent of export income. The increase in oil income has been of critical importance to Tunisia. Other important exports have been phosphates (38 million dinars), and oil (25 million dinars). Other poor countries have not been so fortunate. Slow increases in world demand for agricultural products and policies of rich industrial countries to protect their own farmers are major obstacles. Tunisia has also benefited from its association with France which has enabled its products to gain access to the European Common Market on favourable terms. It has also gained foreign exchange from increased exports of phosphates and the development of its tourist industry.

Other countries have been less successful. Overall, world trade in manufactures has been increasing more rapidly than trade in agricultural products. But the developing countries are not equipped to share in the growth of trade in secondary products; their manufacturing industries are in their infancy, protected from foreign competition on home markets by high tariffs and quotas. On world markets they face the low cost, high quality industries of the United States, Western Europe and Japan. In the 1960s the United Nations Conference on Trade and Development (UNCTAD) was set up. The first meeting was held in Geneva. Attended by representatives of governments of most of the developed and underdeveloped countries it had as its purpose the consideration of ways by which the underdeveloped countries might obtain a larger share of world trade. The poor countries advocated that existing trade liberalisation measures be extended to agricultural products. They also advocated a system of tariff preferences applying on manufactured goods so that the exports from developing countries would be admitted into the rich countries more cheaply than products from the rich countries. The rich countries refused to accept the case put forward and the second meeting of UNCTAD broke up without making progress.

This pattern has continued. Subsequent meetings of UNCTAD have failed to make any significant progress and the representatives of the poorer countries have expressed bitter disappointment over the failure of the western industrial countries to make concessions.

24.9

Tunisia's balance of payments, 1972, 1976 and 1977 US $ million

Item	1972	1976	1977
Exports	313	779	949
Imports	–453	–1399	–1762
Net invisibles	136	231	278
Capital, etc.	76	372	452

1 Calculate (a) Tunisia's balance of trade, (b) its balance of payments on current account, and (c) the net monetary movement for each of the years.
2 Comment on the significance of any changes in the balance of payments during the period.

24.10

In common with many other developing countries Tunisia has imposed strict controls on the export and import of its currency. Why?

Foreign aid

Countries which overcome the major social and political barriers to economic development find that the principal obstacles to a rapid increase in aggregate national income are:
1 Lack of resources and human skills.
2 Lack of sufficient investment to build up the capital stock in the required way.
3 Inability to earn enough to buy essential imports for development.
Foreign aid is vital for developing countries because it can make up for deficiencies of the second and third types and can also be used to improve the quality of human resources. It was estimated by Chenery[7] that in the ten years, 1956–1966, the United States and Western Europe made capital transfers to the developing countries of US $8–9 billion, of which $6 billion was in the form of aid and the rest was autonomous investment. This aid took four main forms:
1 grants to ex-colonies and military allies – 40 per cent,
2 loans for specific capital projects – 25 per cent,
3 loans for general development programmes – 15 per cent,
4 transfer of agricultural surpluses against loans – 15 per cent.

A large part of total aid to the developing countries is given in the belief or hope that it will benefit the donor country in some way as well as the recipient. Frequently, aid is directed at political allies and often for military purposes rather than economic. Such aid may perhaps be defended on economic grounds if it adds to the political stability of the country and thus contributes to economic growth, but often, as in the case of Vietnam, such aid is necessary for short-term survival rather than for the prospects it holds of permanent economic development.

Transfers of surplus agricultural products may help to overcome a farm problem in the donor country, whilst capital transfers often take the form of loans which carry an obligation to buy necessary materials from the donor country. Such aid may have as its objective the development of a permanent export market for the donor in the developing country. Frequently, too, loans for capital projects yield the donor country reasonable rates of return on their investment, though there may remain an element of political uncertainty which is sufficient to deter private investment.

Self-interest in giving foreign aid

It is easy to understand why self-interest should play such a large part in international aid. A government can justify foreign aid to its electorate more easily if it can show that the domestic economy will benefit too. It is natural to restrict aid to one's allies rather than to hostile or non-aligned countries. The UK government's decision to cut foreign aid to Uganda following that country's expulsion of its Asians was welcomed by the British people. Likewise, France cut its aid to Tunisia following the sequestration of French assets in the 1960s. Only recently have Franco-Tunisian relations improved and a new aid programme implemented.

When aid is conditional on being spent in the donor country it is referred to as 'tied' aid. This aid still benefits the recipient country, but there are two main disadvantages:
1 The type of aid given may be determined by the benefits to the donor rather than the benefits to the recipient. It may, therefore, not be the best form of aid, and may even produce an undesirable development pattern with the wrong industries being established.

2 Tying the aid to the donor country may deprive the developing country of obtaining the materials it requires from the cheapest source. In addition this may reduce the amount of 'real' aid it is able to obtain.

There is no doubt aid without strings is preferable from the recipient's viewpoint because a given amount of aid can be used more effectively. As the total aid forthcoming is inadequate anyway the abolition of tied aid is an important objective of developing countries. Ideally, this could be accomplished by ending bilateral aid (agreements between donor country and recipient) and by channelling all aid through international bodies such as the United Nations and the World Bank and its affiliates, although these institutions are not without critics of their disbursement of aid in the past.

Distribution of aid

A second problem is deciding the best way to distribute aid. Chenery distinguished between *project* aid and *programme* aid. Project aid usually takes the form of a loan for a specific project, the viability of which is appraised by the government of the donor country or the international agency. In contrast, programme aid considers a country's overall needs and its development programme and then allocates the funds to the government for use within the framework of an agreed development strategy. Project aid has the advantage that it appeals to the donor country's direct interests (often it is tied aid as well). It is flexible because the donor can finance individual projects on an *ad hoc* basis. It can also terminate aid with a minimum of political repercussions simply by not supporting the next project. The disadvantage of project aid is that it does not consider the overall economic development of the country. Vital parts of a development programme such as the provision of social overhead capital (ports, roads, railways and power supplies) may be neglected because it appears less attractive from an investment standpoint in the short run.

A third problem is to determine which countries should receive aid. It has been suggested that if the rich countries were each to contribute the equivalent of 5 or 6 per cent of their respective gross national products then foreign aid would be adequate to supplement internal savings in the developing countries. During the period from 1960–1970 the United Nations set a goal of 1 per cent of GDP for rich countries. All failed to reach this level and it is now regarded as unrealistic.

As total aid is quite inadequate for the demands placed upon it, there is considerable disagreement about what criteria should be adopted for distributing it. Chenery advocates the use of 'incentive programming' which means that aid should be varied according to economic performance of the recipient. The better use a country makes of aid, the more it receives. Such incentive programming is only fair and effective as a stimulus to growth if it is given without strings and on a programme rather than a project basis. But there are other schools of thought including that which sees the primary task of the rich countries as relieving severe poverty.

Economic systems and economic planning

In Chapter 4, and again in Chapter 23 it was said that there is no evidence which points to the superiority of either a command system, or a market system, or of any mixture of the two. There is then no 'ideal' economic system for the developing country, though some people would say that a command system incorporating manpower direction is more likely to succeed in breaking down social attitudes that might act as barriers to growth. Whether this is desirable, even if true, is another matter.

The majority of developing countries have found it desirable to formulate development plans even when retaining a market system. The plan provides a framework within which the government can follow its fiscal and monetary policies and within which it allows prices and profits to influence the allocation of resources.

Tunisia has provided opportunities for foreign private investment, but at the same time it has prepared a series of national economic plans; the first, 1962–64, the second 1965–68 and the third from 1969–72. These plans set targets for public expenditure and private investment, for domestic savings, foreign capital investment and for investment programmes in the main sectors of the economy. The third plan proposed total investment of 1200 million dinars of which 250 million dinars was to go to agriculture. There was a target rate of growth of GNP of 6.5 per cent per year. Even when such plans are not achieved, they have the merit that a planning exercise has to be carried out. Desirable growth patterns have to be considered, problems explored and conflicts resolved.

Balanced and unbalanced growth

There has been considerable discussion about how development plans should be implemented. In the 1960s there was controversy between the advocates of two, apparently different, approaches; balanced and unbalanced growth. The feature of balanced growth is that the various sectors of an economy (agriculture, manufacturing and the export sector), need to grow in an orderly way in some given relationship to one another because they are interdependent. It calls for an investment programme which will develop them together, with the necessary support facilities.

The alternative of unbalanced growth is based on the notion that advancing all sectors of a country's economy will be a costly and hence slow procedure. It is claimed that by concentrating on specific projects instead, bottlenecks are created, but the very existence of the bottlenecks produces strains and tensions which stimulate the system to remove the bottleneck and thus accelerate the rate of development. Thus the construction of offices will soon create a demand for, and hence a supply of, office furniture.

The differences between the two approaches are probably more apparent than real. Bottlenecks occur even when governments are trying to develop different sectors harmoniously, and such bottlenecks are frequently relieved. Likewise, developing one sector at the expense of others (unbalanced growth) is only likely to be successful if pressures evertually produce the necessary developments in the other sectors. The suggestion then is that that two groups are really looking at the development process in different ways. One looks at the trend over a period of time and sees balanced growth as necessary. The other looks at month to month progress and sees the lack of balance as an important stimulus.

24.11

Investigate the UK's aid programme of recent years. How much aid has the UK given and which countries have been the principal beneficiaries? To what extent has this aid policy benefited the UK economy also?

24.12

The Cambridge Conference Report on the Criteria for Allocating Aid suggested five alternative methods.[8] These were:
1 Allocating aid on a per capita basis so that countries with large populations get proportionately more in aggregate. Using this approach aid to African countries would be reduced and aid to Asian and Latin American countries would increase.
2 Allocation on the basis of need, to raise all living standards to a minimum level – the poorest get more aid.
3 Allocation on the basis of economic performance – incentive programming.
4 Allocation on the basis of potential. This might mean confining aid to the 8 to 10 richest 'poor' countries, getting them to a position of self-sustaining economic growth quickly and then turning to the next group. A variant of this is selecting the group of countries closest to achieving economic growth. The two are not the same because a poorer country may be closer to achieving self-sustaining economic growth than one which is richer.
5 Determining a fixed sum to be allocated and then leaving it to the recipient countries to determine how it should be allocated between them – the method used by the Marshall Plan to distribute aid to Western Europe after World War II.

Discuss the merits of these alternatives and propose your own criterion or set of criteria for allocating aid to developing countries.

24.13

Occasionally, it is proposed that aid should be supplied in the form of consumer goods, such as food, to alleviate poverty. Discuss the problems such a course of action may produce and thus explain why such suggestions are seldom acted upon except in crises.

Notes

1 S Kuznets 1968 *Towards a Theory of Economic Growth*. Norton, New York, p 2.
2 D Sears 1972 What are we trying to measure? *Journal of Development Studies*, **8**, (3), 21–36.
3 If Tunisia continued to record a faster real rate of growth than Australia the gap between the two would eventually close, but only after many years.
4 W Beckerman, R Bacon 1966 International Comparisons of Income Levels; A Suggested New Measure. *Economic Journal*, **76** Cambridge University Press.
5 Reported by the International Labour Organisation in *Labour Survey of North Africa*, Geneva 1960, p 37.
6 The term 'output' is used synonomously with 'production' in this section because of the common use of the term 'capital output ratio' in writings on economic development.
7 H B Chenery 1972 Effectiveness of Foreign Assistance, in R Robinson, *Developing the Third World, the Experience of the Nineteen-Sixties*, Cambridge University Press.
8 *Ibid.*, Chapter 20, especially, p 227.

Index

absolute advantage 48, 208–9
advertising
  effect on demand 102–3
  false and misleading 336
agreements
  horizontal 330–2
  vertical 330
agriculture 114–16, 341–9
arbitration 181–2
  Advisory Conciliation and Arbitration Service (ACAS) 165
assets
  measure of economic growth 375
automatic stabilisers 257

Bacon, R. 415–16
balance for official financing 234, 237
balance of payments 231–4
  deficit 305, 308
  on current account 235
  policy objective 304–5
  principal relationships 232
  surplus 308
balance of trade 234–5
balancing item 232
Bank of England
  bank deposits 195
  competition and credit control 193
  control of money supply 201–3
  directives 202
  Exchange Equalisation Account (EEA) 196–7
  functions of 195–7
  funding 202
  interest rates 201–2, 205, 288
  lender of last resort 195–6
  minimum lending rate (MLR) 197, 202–3
  public sector borrowing requirement (PSBR) 289–90
  open-market operations 202, 288
  special deposits 193, 201
  structure of 194–5
  treasury bills 197–8, 201–2
banks
  asset structure 191–2
  deposits 190–1
banks, commercial 190–2
  advances 193–4
  assets 191
  overdraft system 194
  personal loans 194
barter 56–7
Beckerman, W. 370, 381, 415–16
Benedictine monasteries 19
black market 115
bonds 186–7
borrowing short, lending long 187
Boulding, K.E. 154, 164
budget
  balanced 290
  deficit 291
  surplus 291
built-in obsolescence 375

capital
  definition 55, 58
  man-made resources 58
capital expenditure
  government gross fixed 70
  gross domestic fixed 70–1
capital formation
  gross 70–1
capital stock 53
cartels 140, 330
certificates of deposit 197–8
cheque accounts 190
circular flow of incomes 273–4
collective bargaining 177–8
collective farms (Kolkhozy), Soviet Union 397
collusion 140, 330–1
collusive tendering 331
Communism 393–4, 403–4
  'war' system 394
comparative advantage 48, 208–9
competition 136–40, 320–6, 329
  foreign 320–6
complementary goods 145
conciliation 182
consumer
  lack of knowledge 328, 335
  weak position in market economy 328
consumer protection 328–36
consumer sovereignty 328–9
consumer surplus 386–7
consumerism 334–5
consumption
  aggregate 74–80
  defined 54, 67–74
  real 71–2
consumption expenditure
  affected by past production 69
  and level of economic activity 74–7
  and savings 77–8
  defined 54, 67–8
  determinants of 68–70
  measured at constant prices 71–2, 74
  measured at market prices 71, 74
  patterns 73, 82
  per capita 72
  principles used in classifying 67–8
convertibility 314
cost–benefit analysis 9–11, 378, 382–8
  application 383, 388
  Cambrian Coast railway 388–90
  externalities 379, 382
  identification 384–5
  measurement problems 385–7
  spill-over effects 382
cost of living 301
costs of production 121–31
  average 127–30
  fixed 125
  long run 122, 127–30
  marginal 127, 131, 133–4
  short run 122–3, 127–30
  social 377–8
  variable 125–6

credit creation 192–3
credit multiplier 192–3
cross-section analysis 82
currency
appreciation of 306–7
depreciation of 306–8
floating 315–16
realignment of 314–15
customs union 213, 339

decision-making 4
under uncertainty 12–13, 139–41
demand 98–104
aggregate 264
conditions 101–13
curves 99–100
defined 98
determinants of 98
excess 284–5
in international trade 211
market 99–100
schedule 9, 99
demand and supply 98–117
limitations 113–17
mechanism 108–9, 114–16
depreciation 53, 71
allowances 71
devaluation and terms of trade
effects of 227–8
development finance 200
diminishing returns 123–4
discount market 197–8
discount rates 198, 201–2
distribution
of income 79–80, 254–7, 283
of wealth 189
disutility 6–7
double-counting 69, 86
dumping 324

earnings 166
drift 166
economic development 410–26
defined 410
non-monetary indicators 415–16
planning 424–6
population problem 95, 418–19
savings and investment 55–6, 419–20
social and political barriers 418
trade and foreign aid 421–4
economic growth 23, 368–77
and economists 369–70
and the environment 370, 377
arguments against 368–9, 375–7
balanced 425
benefits of 371–4
conflict with price stability 369
measurement 92–3, 415–16
sources of 369
unbalanced 425
economic models 30–1, 46
economic objectives 279, 368
economic problems
and survival 27
defined 13, 19–22
of materialistic society 17–18
of spiritual communities 19–20
of the household 18
of the state 18
economic sanctions 214
economic systems 36–45
classification 38
command, planned 38–9, 60–3
market 39, 60, 62
modern 44–5, 59–60
traditional primitive 39, 45
economics
definitions by
Marshall 20
Robbins 20
Viner 20
scope of 27–8
economics, normative 26–8
economics, positive 26–7
economies of scale 129, 339
economists' methods 29–32
elasticity of demand 80–2, 143–7
effect on total revenue 146–7
income 80–2
price 143–5
employment, full
defined 23, 162–3
policies 361–3
employment, overfull 294
environmental costs 378–80
equilibrium 33–5, 108–9
between aggregate demand and supply 266
changes in equilibrium of production 269–72
defined 33
market 108–9
stable 34
unstable 35
Esso Petroleum Company 122–3
European Economic Community (EEC)
aims 338–9
budget 347
commission 340
Common Agricultural Policy (CAP) 114–16, 346–7
common external tariff 339
competition policy 353–4
Court of Justice 340–1
energy policy 354
Euratom 338
European Coal and Steel Community (ECSC) 338
European Investment Bank (EIB) 200, 353
European Monetary System 315
European Parliament 340
Regional Development Fund 200, 350
share in world food trade 347
Social Fund 351–2
statistics 347–50, 354–5
structure and organisation 340
Treaty of Rome 338
European Free Trade Association (EFTA) 213, 339
exchange 56–7
exchange rates 211–12, 236–7, 306–7
fixed 313
floating 315–18
excise duties 84, 248
export subsidies 306
exports 217–23
commodity classification 217–18
fluctuations 224
major products 218
principal destinations 219–20, 222
external balance 309
external disadvantages 375–7

family allowances and benefits 245–6
finance companies 199
financial institutions 58, 184–200
Bank of England 194–7
building societies 199–200
commercial banks 190–4
discount houses 197–8
life assurance companies 198–9
financial system, principal features 184–9, 206

fiscal policy 290–2
  and external balance 309
flows
  defined 53
free goods 17

General Agreement on Tariffs and Trade (GATT) 325
gold
  demonetisation 318
  two-tier price 314
golden triangle 350
Gosbank 398–9
Gosplan 395–6
government
  arguments for command economies 60–3
  arguments for uncontrolled economy 60
  business undertakings 120–1
  control over financial institutions 201
  expenditure 244–7, 293
  sources of revenue 247–8
government spending
  component of aggregate demand 272
gross domestic fixed capital formation 68, 70
gross domestic product (GDP) 83, 85–90, 92–5, 368
  and development 411–12
  at constant prices 93–4
  at factor cost 88–90, 368
  at market prices 83, 93
  compared with GNP 262
  defined 83
  measure of economic growth 92–5, 411
  real 94
gross national product (GNP) 71, 262

health services 246
Hirschman, A.O. 40, 45
horizontal agreements 330–1
Horvat, Branko 405–6

immigration 150–3
import duty 213, 322
import penetration 225
imports 216–20
  commodity classification 216–17
  economic classes 216
  principal suppliers 220
income
  demands for increases 285
  taxable 251
income, disposable 75
  and consumption 8, 76–7
  and market demand 161
  real 77–8
income controls 302
income redistribution
  in favour of consumer 329
  through income tax 254–7
incomes policies 298–302
indexation 301
Index of Retail Prices 167, 172, 280–2
industry, sectors of 89–90, 158
industrial disputes 178–80
infant industries 303–4
inferior goods 81
inflation 279–96
  and aggregate demand 285, 293–4, 296
  and money supply 290
  and wage demands 285
  causes 284–5
  control 286–7, 298–302
  cost–push theory 284
  defined 279
  demand–pull theory 284
  expectations 178, 285
  processes 284–6
  redistribution effect 283
  undesirability 283–4
  world wide 284
interest rates
  defined 184–6
  determinants 184–5, 188, 202
  effective 194, 207
  MLR 197, 202–3
  structure 205
intermediate goods 86–7
International Air Transport Association (IATA) 332
International Monetary Fund (IMF) 313–15
international monetary problems 317–18
international trade
  obstacles to 213–14
  reasons for 208–13
investment
  defined 23–4
  spending 68, 267–8
investment, foreign 238–9
  and capital flows 237–9
  and government policy 239
invisible trade 235–6

Jamaica Conference 317–18
job creation schemes 362

Keynes, J.M. 36, 45
kinked demand curves 140
Kruschev, Nikita 400
Kuznets, S. 63, 410, 426

labour force 149–57
  definition 149
  determinants of 150–7
  participation rate 149, 155
  structure 157–9
  supply 154–7
Lenin, V.I. 394
life assurance companies 198–9
liquidity crises 312–13
local government finance 258–9
long-run 122
Lorenz curves 255–6, 259
lotus-eaters 20

Malthus, T.R. 148
margin 5
market-sharing 331–2
marketing schemes 332–3
market socialism 39, 403
Marshall, Alfred 20
Marx, Karl 393
mass production 49
materialism 16
merit goods 242–3
Mishan, E.J. 370, 377, 381, 392
monetarism 288–90
monetary movements 234–7
monetary policy 193, 203
  to produce external balance 309
money
  aid to borrowing and lending 58–9
  control of money supply 193, 201, 203, 290
  means of exchange 56–7
  quantity theory 187, 288
  store of value 57–8
money market 197–8
monopolistic competition 138–9
monopolisation defined 136–7
monopoly 135–8, 330
monopoly policy
  collusion 330–1
  concentration ratio 137

Fair Trading Act 137
Monopolies Commission 136–7
public interest 137, 330
multinational corporations 239
multiplier 272–3, 275

National Debt 195–6
national income aggregates 71, 260–2
nationalised industries 120–1, 363–4
privatisation 365
reasons for 59–60, 120, 363
net benefit 385
normative statements 26
norms 396
North Sea oil and gas 24
Sullom Voe Oil Terminal 11
note issue
government control 193, 195

Office of Fair Trading 334
oil crises 317
oil industry 10–11, 122–3, 332, 366–7
oligopoly 139–41
opportunity cost
and international trade 208–9
and specialisation 48
defined 4, 208
Organisation for Economic Cooperation and Development (OECD) 338
Organisation for European Economic Cooperation (OEEC) 338
ownership and control 118–19

pensions 245
perfect competition 134–5
plans
operational 396
perspective 396
pollution 379
population
activity rates 149–50, 155–7
age distribution 155
and living standards 148
birth rates 150–1
death rates 150–1
government policy 152
labour force 149–59
migration 150, 152–3
natural increase 150
optimum theory 148–9
pyramids 155
working 154, 158
pressure groups 37
price
determination
in market 108–17
under monopoly 135–6
under oligopoly 139–40
price controls 298–302
effect on inflation 299
effect on market mechanism 115–16
price followers 139–40
price index
consumer 280–1
GDP implicit deflator 282–3
Tax and Prices 282
weighting 280
wholesale 282
price leaders 139–40
price-makers 135–41
price system 39
price-takers 132–5
price wage freeze 299
prices and incomes policy 298–302
product
average 124–5
marginal 123, 125
production
components, of value 87
defined 54
measurement 85–90
per capita 95, 411
technology 121–2
value of 87–9
production, aggregate 263–8
production frontier 22
productivity 124, 168, 173
and demand for labour 168–71
profit maximisation 8, 118–21, 132–3
of monopolists 135–6
of price-takers 132–4
profits 118–19
of financial institutions 186
propensity to consume
average 75, 84
marginal 75–6
propensity to import
marginal 275
propensity to tax
marginal 251, 275
propensity to save
average 76, 84
marginal 76
public ownership 120–1, 363–4
public sector 120–1, 299
public sector borrowing requirement (PSBR) 289–90

quantitative controls (quotas) 213
and balance of payments 305
and market mechanism 114–16

rates 258–9
rationing 17
referenda 243
regional imbalance 161–2, 353
regional policy 358–61
Assisted Areas 358–9
Development Areas 358
Enterprise Zones 359–61
Industrial Development Certificate (IDC) 359
Intermediate Areas 359
Office Development Certificate (ODC) 359
Special Development Areas 359
relative income hypothesis 373–4
resale price maintenance 331
reserve assets ratio 191–3
resource allocation 21–2
full employment 23
resources
differences between countries 210–11
exhaustion of 24
human 13
natural 13
restrictive trade practices 330
Retail Prices Index 167, 172, 280–2
revenue
average 8, 132–5
marginal 8, 132–5
maximisation 133, 135
Ricardo, David 63
risk 12
Robbins, L. 20
Robinson, J. 45
Roskill Commission 9–10, 385

satisfaction 3
maximising 6
saving 77–8
savings ratio 77
scarcity 13
and the economic problem 13–14, 17
evidence of 17–18

short-run 122
Smith, Adam
on consumer interests 328
on production 91, 97
on taxation 248–9
social security 244
benefits 244–6
socialism 393
self-government 403–4
solo marketing 332–3
Soviet Union 393–403
agriculture 394, 397–8
consumer choice 394, 396–7, 402
economic and social objectives 393–4
features of economy 394–400
institutions 395
'new economic policy' 394
performance 400–2
use of incentives 396
special drawing rights (SDRs) 314–15
specialisation 46–52
benefits 46–8
cooperative 49
dynamic advantages 49
on overseas trade 51–2
problems 51–2
stagflation 295
standard of living 16–17
defined 16
difficulties in measuring 94–5
state farms (Sovkhozy), Soviet Union 397
statistics
official sources 29
stocks
changes in 86–7
defined 53
subsidies
and GDP 89–90
to control pollution 379–80
substitutes 145
supply 104–8
conditions 106–8
curves 105–6
defined 104
determinants of 105
system
defined 33
ecological 33–5
economic, defined 35–7

tariff 319–26
and balance of payments 326
arguments in favour 322–6
effects of imposition 319–21
tariff negotiations, Kennedy Round MTN (Tokyo) 325
tastes
effects on demand 102–3
tax direct 84, 251, 292
incidence of 251–2
rates 250–1
tax, environment 379
tax, income 250–6
tax indexation 301–2
tax, indirect 84, 251, 292–3
in fiscal policy 292–3
measurement of GDP 89
tax, value-added (VAT) 251–3, 292
taxation
and allocation of resources 254, 292–3
automatic stabilisers 257
canons 248–9
corporation 250
percentage of GDP 357
personal income tax 250–2, 254–6
Petroleum Revenue Tax (PRT) 366–7
progressive 249–50
proportional 249
regressive 251, 253
terms of trade 226–7
Japan 229
UK 227–8
USA 227, 229
textile industry 22
tied aid 423
total currency flow 232, 237
trade
arguments for free trade 208–9, 212–13
liberalisation 339
pattern and structure 214–23
protectionism 213–14
statistics 215–22
trade unions 176–80
transfer pricing 239
transport costs 214
treasury bills 197–8, 201–2
Tunisia 413–22
gross domestic product 413
population 413, 418–19
problems and policies 416–20

uncertainty
and decision making 12–13
unemployment 159–63
alternative views 176
and industrial disputes 179–80
benefit 149, 245
cyclical 161
duration of 160
frictional 160
hard-core 160–1
international comparisons 163
measurement 149, 159–60
policies to combat 293–6
reasons for 160–2
regional 161–2
registered 245
structural 161
United Nations Conference on Trade and Development (UNCTAD) 412–13, 422
unproductive activity 90–1
utility
diminishing marginal 5–6
marginal 4–7

value added 85–7, 252–3
value judgements 25–8
vertical trade practices and agreements 330–1
Viner, J. 20

wage determination 176–82
ACAS 165, 181–2
role of government in 166
wage drift 166
wage indexation 301
wage rates
basic 165
incentive payments 165
margins for skill 165–6
minimum 166
piece rate 165
total 165–7
wages
and prices 166–8, 298–302
and unemployment 171, 173–4
real earnings 167, 171–3
wages share 174–5
welfare (well being)
general 16
material 16

Yugoslavia, economic system 403–8

comparison with Soviet system 404
comparison with Greece and Italy 407
development 403–8
evaluation 406–8
institutions 405–6
'new economic system' 404–5

zero population growth (ZPG) 153